GOOD HOME COOKING

across the U. S. A.

Nell Nichols reports . . .

Illustrator: **RAY IRWIN**

Publisher: **The Iowa State College Press, Ames**

GOOD

HOME

COOKING

across the U.S.A.

A Source Book of American Foods

NELL B. NICHOLS

Field Reporter
Woman's Home Companion

Library of Congress Catalog Number: 53-5323

This book is for

Betsy McCracken

Foreword

Greens Farms,
Connecticut

DEAR READER,

I wish I could fix it up so I could drop in at your home for dinner a couple of weeks from now. I'd like to meet you, but frankly I'd also like to go to work on that meal you'll be serving. No matter how accomplished you are in the kitchen now, you can't have Nell Nichols' book around for long without picking up a lot of wonderful new ideas.

You'd like Nell, and she'd like you. Let me tell you about her. She is a Kansan, a wife and mother and a genuine food enthusiast. She's also the food field reporter for the *Woman's Home Companion.* For the last three years she has traveled thousands of miles for us, crisscrossing the country, to dig out homey secrets of cooking successes and failures. Her reports have been of tremendous value to the editors of the *Woman's Home Companion* and to influential people in the food field.

These travels, plus her long experience, qualify her distinctively as an authority on Good Home Cooking Across the U.S.A. Her "Food Calendar" in the *Companion* is one of the oldest and most widely imitated features in any magazine.

Nell Nichols likes people. When she arrives in a town, she discusses local dishes with many good cooks. Warm-hearted, friendly, she gets to know homemakers. She sits with them in their kitchens, and out of lengthy, informal conversations come the ideas and recipes that make up this delightful book.

Funny thing, but Nell has noticed that many women believe the dishes they prepare and serve in their homes are exactly the same as cooks in other sections of the country prepare and serve. For instance, when she visited the Pennsylvania Dutch country, where the dishes are highly distinctive, the natives looked her straight in the eyes and said, "We cook exactly the same as you do in Kansas." They never dreamed that few people in the Sunflower State have ever tasted shoofly pie.

My bet is that as this book makes the rounds the delights of shoofly pie will become familiar to plenty of Kansans, and New Yorkers and Californians, too.

Nell's book has an importance beyond widening your culinary horizons. Today's cooks are nationalizing the more popular sectional dishes. Many of tomorrow's favorites will have their origins in the blue ribbon numbers described in this source book. Do you realize that when the western cowboy — who was to be away from ranch headquarters for a few days — first added baking powder and salt to flour and tied the muslin bag containing them to his saddle he originated the forerunner of the many modern quick and easy packaged mixes? So it goes. *Good Home Cooking* primarily is an idea book. Anyone who works with foods will pick up innumerable helpful new hints. It won't be long before you'll wonder how you ever got along without this book.

But don't let me waste any more of your time. I know you're itching to start whipping up that Virginia batter bread. Or is it persimmon pudding and raspberry salad?

Good luck to you, and good eating.

Sincerely,

WILLIAM A. H. BIRNIE
Editor and Publisher
Woman's Home Companion

Preface

I suppose everyone who reaches for *Good Home Cooking Across the U.S.A.* will turn first to the chapter in which the foods of his native state appear. This is a frightening thought. Perhaps some of the delicacies are left out! It may be an oversight. Certainly no one individual in a lifetime can cover all the communities in this broad land. Nor does everyone in a family or town agree on what tastes good. Next door neighbors, mothers and daughters, and fathers and sons frequently dispute about which dishes qualify for honors. I have tried to spotlight the ones most praised by hundreds of men and women from Coast to Coast. Indeed, a descriptive title for this report is *What People Said*.

Yet it is more than a record of what people told me. As I browsed around the countryside off the beaten paths I weighed the statements of local epicures and the impressions of what I saw and tasted. Hospitality was generously and graciously extended to me, and gratefully accepted. It introduced the culinary masterpieces in their native habitats. I visited markets, filled my luggage with exotic foods, and later duplicated the treats of many areas in my Kansas kitchen. From these experiences I made my own interpretations. And as I compiled the facts and wrote about them the realization gradually emerged that this source book is the story of good home cooking.

My assignment from the Editor of *Woman's Home Companion*, when we launched this food scouting expedition, was to find, for background material, the best-tasting, most distinctive dishes in the U.S.A. It was necessary, as a convenience, to divide the country into several parts. That injected the regional theme. Soon I became alert to the variations in the food preferences of the dozen geographical sections into which I partitioned the nation. They provided a challenge, for the differences are not obvious like the similarities. You have to search for them. Regional dishes always are the offspring of isolation. Those enjoyed today are like the last of the Mohicans. And in many instances they are disappearing. New techniques frequently take their place. After someone creates a food combination, modern methods of communication, transportation, processing, and merchandising carry it quickly across America. The tasty cookies containing small pieces of semi-sweet chocolate that a Massachusetts home economist invented offer a splendid example.

On the other hand, as home economists know so well, food preferences change slowly. A realistic observer doubts if South Carolina soon will forsake its Hopping John, Virginia its batter bread, New Orleans its gumbo filé, and Middle Tennessee its spiced round of beef. And who believes the Hoosiers will forget their persimmon pudding and raspberry salad, Minnesota its wild rice, New Mexico its chili and pinto beans, the Pacific Coast its Crab Louis, and New England its Boston baked beans? Milwaukee remains true to tortes, Georgia to Lane cake, the Pennsylvania Dutch counties to shoofly pie, and the Dakotas to pheasant dinners. Does anyone think Texas will give up barbecued beef, or that pork chops, fluffs of mashed potatoes, and brown milk gravy will disappear from Iowa tables?

As I traveled across the country I relied confidently on members of my profession, the home economists. Everywhere they offered suggestions and inspiration. All the chapters in this source book have been read by them. But please do not cast blame in their direction if some of your favorites are omitted and if others you do not treasure win the bouquets. I have endeavored to report what I heard, saw, and tasted. Now I am tempted to display a sign like the one used by an old-time cowpuncher pianist in my former home town, Dodge City, Kansas, the Cowboy Capital. When the cattle drives northward from Texas were at their height my husband's father took a thrilling trip along the Santa Fe Trail. While eating dinner in a frontier restaurant in Dodge City he observed this crudely lettered message on the piano above the musician: Don't Shoot the Professor — He's Doing the Best He Can.

Good Home Cooking is not a recipe book, although you will find in it directions for making a few of the five-star specialties. For the increasing band of collectors a bibliography of some of the colorful regional cookbooks is included.

The taste triumphs described do not represent a cross section of what people eat. Business surveys and sales figures provide accurate pictures of that. I searched only for the prize winners, and then jotted down notes about how they looked and tasted. I did not waste the lead of my pencils on inferior food. Unfortunately it exists. Anyone who travels the byways knows no one area has to bear all the shame of it.

I did not consider the cost of the treats or the time and labor involved in their preparation. How do they taste? And how do the natives regard them? That was what I wished to know. Many of the dishes now come to the tables only on glamorous occasions. Others are daily fare. All of them are what Americans like to eat in their homes when they have a chance. The index quickly will introduce them to you regardless of where you live.

When I was covering the nation in hot pursuit of the most delicious and most favored foods I had no idea of writing a book about them. That came later over a dinner table in Denver. My companion was an old-time friend, Katherine Goeppinger, home economics editor of The Iowa State College Press. She had read my travel reports which the *Woman's Home Companion* sent as a service to a group of business home economists. This may explain why we chatted about the more luscious jewels of regional cooking. Or perhaps the conversation mirrored my single-track mind. In those days food exploring filled my thoughts.

I remember mentioning a desire to collect in organized form many details that could not be crowded into the reports. It was my belief, that if properly indexed they would be of practical value to my daughter, a young home economist and writer. Kay then asked, "Wouldn't many other people find the information useful?" I presume *Good Home Cooking Across the U.S.A.* was conceived there in the shadow of the Rockies.

I shall be delighted if you feel a few tantalizing hunger pains as you read. Dare I hope you will catch something of the spirit of adventure I felt on my Grand Food Tour? It was like eating around the world in a comfortable atmosphere of home-town friendliness.

NELL B. NICHOLS

Topeka, Kansas

Acknowledgments

A book like *Good Home Cooking Across the U.S.A.* represents the generosity of many persons who enjoy delicious food. I regret that it is impracticable to print the names of everyone who shared with me her intimate acquaintance with regional taste triumphs.

I wish to thank *Woman's Home Companion* for permission to present the information collected for reports that were the forerunners of this volume. Also I am grateful for encouragement by two of my magazine associates, Helen C. Otis and Ada Bessie Swann.

Sixty-one home economists read the chapters in which the culinary masterpieces of their individual areas are described. Their assistance was priceless. Without it I would not have attempted to write this story of America's great dishes.

Among the women who advised me about the delicacies of their respective communities are Eleanor Ahern, Cleo M. Arnett, Mabel Ashenfelter, Marjorie H. Black, Clarice Bloom, Elsie Boatman, Rena Bowles, Gertrude Brammer, Kathryn Briwa, Rita Calhoun, Genevieve Callahan, Janet Cameron, Dorothy Canet, Barbara Clendinen, Hortense Clifford, Jessie Alice Cline, Harriet Cooke, Helen L. Corbitt, Eloise Davison, Iris Davenport, Lorna J. Desha, Elizabeth Dyar, and Dorothy Ebbott.

Essie L. Elliott, Roxana Elliott, Vera Ellwood, Jewell G. Fessenden, Esther Foley, Florence Forbes, Estelle Fournet, M. Mabel Fraser, Regina G. Frisbie, Pauline Girard, Helen E. Goodrich, Evelyn Gose, Eunice Grady, Cissy Gregg, Dorothy Hacker, Roberta Hershey, Dorothy J. Hill, Sallie Hill, Verna J. Hitchcock, Margaret O. Holloway, Fleeta Hoke, Maude Pye Hood, Marjorie C. Husted, Elizabeth Huey, Winnifred Cannon Jardine, Lillian Keller, Janet Kelley, Ruth D. Kruger, and Ella Liner Lambert.

Cathrine C. Laughton, Emily Chase Leistner, Virginia Leslie, Edna Mae McIntosh, Marian McCoughan, Gladys Mason, Erma

C. Meeks, Elizabeth Mellor, Elna Miller, Verna Miller, Arra Sutton Mixter, Veronica Morrissey, Nell Morris, Eleanor Morrison, Luella Mortenson, Marie Mount, Grace K. Nadig, Juanita H. Neely, Phyllis Owen, Verna Payson, and Ada Peers.

Catherine J. Personius, Judson Purvis, Margaret E. Reigel, Ruth Rhode, See Rice, Evelyn Rietze, Mary K. Rissinger, Helen Robertson, Jeanne Roy, Ann Satter, Naomi Shank, Ruth Sheldon, Margaret C. Shepard, Josephene Simpson, Elizabeth Simpson, Katherine R. Smith, Anna Smrha, Clara G. Snyder, Marjorie Standish, Mary Stanfill, and Emma States.

Wilma Phillips Stewart, Ellen Stillman, Celeste Sullivan, Margaret Swanson, Maida D. Tabor, Janet Crawford Taylor, Joellene Vannoy, Sibyl Watts, Mary P. Wilson, S. Virginia Wilson, and Norma V. Young.

NELL B. NICHOLS

Table of Contents

GOOD HOME COOKING

across the U.S.A.

New England

IT WAS the Fourth of July. Our hostess, at her country home near Boston, served the traditional dinner. Boiled salmon with tender peas and tiny new potatoes came to the table, followed by warm, crisp-crusted biscuit shortcake with sugared, red-ripe strawberries on top. We poured cream over the glorious dessert.

The conversation was as satisfying as the food. Eventually it turned to the Kansas wheat harvest. For a few minutes home and wind-tossed waves of grain monopolized the friendly talk.

I saw in memory the moving black dots, men and machinery at work in fields of gold. I visioned big platters heaped with fried chicken and enormous bowls of new potatoes and peas. My arms ached sympathetically as I remembered the little boys and girls who at that moment were turning the cranks of ice cream freezers. This was Uncle Sam's birthday there in the Heart of America, too — a star-spangled occasion that called for homemade ice cream flavored with a blend of vanilla and lemon.

These nostalgic recollections of my Kansas home pointed up differences in the traditional meal patterns of the two places. It was a great moment. A curiosity about regional foods was born. From that day on, every trip became something of a gastronomical adventure. I looked for, asked about, and tasted distinctive dishes in many states and countries. And almost before I knew it, the food scouting I rode as a hobby grew into a career.

That memorable Fourth of July occasion influenced years later the choice of New England as the springboard for my Grand Food Tour of the nation. There my interest in sectional cookery came to light. And there, I subsequently discovered, many of the Western Hemisphere's food masterpieces were developed.

The names of northeastern taste triumphs carry a familiar ring to all Americans. That speaks for their acceptance on a national scale. It testifies, too, for the genius of our foremothers who borrowed a few tricks from their Indian neighbors, stirred in experience gained in European kitchens, and came up with culinary creations delicious enough to stand the test of time.

Food and Calendars Co-operate

New England always has associated certain foods with definite days of the week. Baked beans and brown bread simplify Saturday's supper plans. Chicken fricassee stars in countless Sunday dinners. "Cape Cod turkey" (all cooked fish now answers to that name) rates as a favorite on Friday.

If a boiled dinner is scheduled, it frequently belongs to Thursday or Monday, as in olden times, with red flannel hash the next day. Open-face bean sandwiches, with ribbons of crisp bacon on top, are common for Sunday's brunch or supper. And hundreds of homes in the Boston area remain true to the tradition of serving light, puffy, and browned codfish balls for breakfast on the Sabbath.

Famous Firsts Travel Far

People to the west copy the boiled dinner and Boston baked beans with brown bread more than other New England foods. Sometimes their versions vary enough from the originals to defy first-sight recognition. The real McCoy in both instances possesses definite characteristics. Corned beef is the meat for the boiled dinner. Potatoes, carrots, onions, beets, white turnips, and cabbage are the vegetables included in it. The beans come from the oven whole; they are deep brown in color and are surrounded by rich juices. The salt pork baked in them wears a golden, crusty top. Although pea beans lead other varieties in popularity, kidney, yellow-eyes, and horticultural beans have ardent followers. Yankees declare the cook's technique is largely responsible for the fame of this New England specialty.

How To Bake Beans

When women describe their methods of baking beans they say:

On Friday evening wash 1 quart of beans and put them to soak in cold water to cover. Next morning drain and pour them with fresh water into a kettle and parboil them until the skins, but not the beans themselves, start to break. To determine when this stage is reached, take a few beans in a spoon and blow on them. If the skins ruffle, it is time to reach for the earthen pot.

Add the parboiled beans with 2 teaspoons of salt, ½ teaspoon of dry mustard, ¼ cup of molasses, and 1½ to 2 tablespoons of brown sugar, dissolved in a little hot water, and ½ pound of fat salt pork streaked with lean to the pot. First score the rind of the meat and press the pork into the beans even with their top or

preferably to protrude a quarter of an inch. Only the rind shows.
Then add hot water not quite to cover.

Set the pot in a slow oven, 300°. When the beans start to simmer, adjust the lid. Keep them leisurely bubbling for 8 hours,
but add boiling water occasionally to replenish that which
evaporates. Remove the lid for the last hour of baking. This
encourages the juices to boil down and the meat to brown.
Stirring at any time is undesirable, for spoons crush the beans.

Almost every kitchen prizes pet seasoning tricks. Connecticut cooks especially like to hide a peeled onion among
the beans to steam tender and provide its flavor. Some women
stick a few whole cloves into the onion. Cape Cod people
occasionally pour a half cup of cream over the beans during
the last hour of baking. Vermonters consider maple sirup
essential for sweetening and substitute it for the molasses and
brown sugar. Residents of Maine quite often choose horticultural beans for baking.

A few bits of broken bay leaves scattered hit and miss in
the pot contribute flavor. So does ginger — a teaspoon more
or less — blended and added with the dry mustard. Many
households prefer that the baked beans of autumn show the
yellow of corn kernels. The cook cuts the corn from the cobs
and simmers it briefly in a little water. Then with a delicate,
light hand she folds it into the beans for the last 25 minutes
of baking. Most experts remove the salt pork before adding
the corn. Canned whole kernel corn substitutes for the fresh
kernels when they are unseasonable.

The end product, despite the variations, sends out a smell
so intriguing that everyone within its range listens for a call
to come and eat.

A 24-Hour Cooking Ban Was Enforced

Food historians point out that brown bread and baked
beans, produced by cooking skills learned from the Indians,
for Saturday supper survive as the last of Puritan food customs with almost no alterations. The religious connection
has gone, but an affectionate appreciation of the food team
lingers. (The Puritans in the Boston area observed how

nearby Indians cooked their earthen pots of beans in glowing coals mixed with ashes. These early English settlers enforced a 24-hour cooking ban that started with the beginning of their Sabbath at sundown on Saturday. Filled bean pots set in brick ovens at the sides of fireplaces, they learned, were kept warm, and the flavor of their contents actually improved.)

As evidence that the popularity of the old-time dish never dies, a food scout observes the characteristic earthen pots of many sizes offered for sale at crossroads stores, in villages, and cities. Many home kitchens, as well as those for school dining rooms and public eating places, take pride in the large quantities of beans their cooks bake at a time. (They freeze the surplus for later use.) Some families depend primarily on commercially canned beans, New England style. Usually they doctor them up with seasonings as they heat. Why baked beans and brown bread retain their prestige through the centuries is no mystery. Natives, if asked about it, say, "Tradition lives long and dies hard in New England," or they merely retort, "We like them."

Hostesses Like Bean Suppers

One beautiful autumn morning down Cape Cod way, when colored leaves twirled in the air like confetti and big orange pumpkins stood as sentinels by white doorways, I chatted with a retired home demonstration agent. She confessed that she serves on most of the local refreshment committees for community suppers. Her procedure is to plan and present a different menu every time. Her co-workers invariably welcome her suggestions wholeheartedly.

But just before the session adjourns, someone pipes up with, "Why don't we serve what we always have? Nothing could be better." Everyone agrees that the idea is wonderful.

A bean supper is what they always have. "Nothing could be better."

Smart hostesses throughout the Northeast capitalize on the popularity of the historic meal in their informal entertaining. Often they set the food out buffet style. Highlighted

on the board, the genial, warm pot invites guests to help themselves. After one whiff of the steaming food, few people
hold off. They ladle it to their plates and pitch in. The ice
is broken!

BEAN SUPPER

Boston Baked Beans

Brown Bread   Hot Rolls

Pepper Relish   Mustard Pickles

Chili Sauce

Cole Slaw

Apple Pie   Coffee

An infinite variety of relishes appear at these supper
parties. Piccalilli, green tomato and mustard pickles, chutney,
and pepper relish qualify as top numbers. Almost always
chili sauce lends its color to the buffet, but never does the
true Yankee add it or ketchup to the beans as they cook. A
tossed green salad frequently replaces cole slaw. Nevertheless,
cabbage salad — garnished with the crinkly leaves of Savoy
cabbage or the deep color of red cabbage — has not completely
surrendered to newcomers.

Meat provides an acceptable addition to the menu when
a hearty note is desired. Sliced baked or boiled ham, browned
little pig sausages, or heated frankfurts fill the bill, although
a surprising number of New England men vote for beefsteak
with beans. Pumpkin, squash, maple-custard, and apple pie
vie for the dessert role in the scrumptious feast. Lemon
sponge pudding also competes for the limelight in the last
inning.

Now the Brown Bread Is Steamed

Originally Boston brown bread was baked in brick ovens.
Around the turn of the Eighteenth Century, historians record,
people began to steam it in the manner of today. The hot
molasses-flavored loaves, commonly made with corn-meal, rye,
white, and graham flours — and frequently containing raisins
— hold an immortal place on Saturday's bread tray. "Cut the
hot slices rather thick, and lather them with butter," the
men advise, as they speak of the region's greatest taste treats.
Some families steam a rather large supply of the bread at one

time. The loaves not eaten immediately are cooled, wrapped, and frozen for the weeks to follow. Other households buy the bread at bake shops or in cans for quick reheating. Hot rolls challenge the supremacy of brown bread. Hostesses from one end of New England to the other recognize the trend. When they give a bean supper for friends they provide both. Most guests help themselves to each kind.

Corned Beef Is Brown

While a boiled dinner no longer makes weekly appearances in all households, many people nominate it as topnotch fare for company dinners. Especially do they favor it during those mellow late summer and early autumn days when vegetables are succulent and plentiful, and frost is in the offing.

A Yankee cook chooses lean corned beef for the boiled dinner. The brisket is her favorite cut. She covers it with cold water and simmers it gently until almost tender, or from 3 to 4 hours. Then she adds the vegetables. Strangers in New England observe with astonishment that the beef appears brown rather than having the reddish hue familiar to them. Absence of saltpeter in the cure accounts for the more somber color and the different and regionally preferred flavor.

Some women find it convenient to simmer the meat tender a day early and to reheat it just before mealtime as the vegetables cook in the broth. They add the vegetables at different intervals in order not to overcook any of them. As mentioned, onions, cabbage, carrots, beets, white turnips, and potatoes commonly are selected. Most women boil the beets separately to avoid tinting the other vegetables. Well cookers of modern ranges, pressure saucepans, and electric roasters now aid in preparing the famed dinner.

Although improved equipment simplifies getting the meal, grandmother's old-fashioned and charming style of service remains unchanged. Slices of piping hot, fork-tender meat occupy the center of the platter. A bouquet of vegetables forms a border around it. Orange-hued carrots and white turnips show up at opposite ends. Wedges of green cabbage and shiny red beets hold down opposite sides. Potatoes and onions snuggle in between.

Freshly grated horse-radish, hot-to-the-touch yellow johnnycake or corn bread, butter, and coffee or tea complete the menu for many New Englanders, although some people with sturdy appetites insist on apple pie for the climax.

Almost as soon as the natives, well fed and happy, leave the table they start dreaming of the red flannel hash due the next day. Gourmets laud the Yankee creation as the noblest of beet dishes, and there are many in the regional cuisine. In some households the cooks hold that chopping rather than grinding the leftover potatoes, beets, and beef from the boiled dinner makes the superlative hash. The proportions of ingredients vary, but 3 cups of the cooked and chopped potatoes to 1 or 2 cups of beets and 1 cup of beef yield good results. Most people like to include one small uncooked onion, chopped.

Experts Use a Wooden Bowl

Culinary experts champion the use of a wooden bowl and a chopping knife. Most of them handle the beets separately to reduce the spread of their color, although some families prefer the hash a vivid red. The stunt is to slowly brown the mixture in butter to form a crust on the bottom. Experienced hands then fold it in the manner of an omelet. Perfectionists swear by the supremacy of a heavy frying pan as an aid in turning out perfect hash. Green tomato pickles "belong" with the entree in the way of brown bread with baked beans.

Beet hash differs from its cousin, red flannel hash, in that it is meatless. The cooking method is the same. Equal parts of chopped, cooked potatoes and beets with one or two chopped raw onions are browned in a small quantity of butter or other fat. Favorite accompaniments include pickles, horseradish folded into whipped cream, and johnnycake.

New Hampshire women steadfastly follow an old and tried way with corned beef hash:

They combine equal parts of cooked beef and potatoes, add

chopped raw onion to season, and moisten the mixture with a little thin cream. They slowly brown it on one side, and then turn it with a spatula and brown it on the other side. They list four rules that insure good results.

Chop the meat and potatoes instead of grinding them.

Pan-fry the hash lazily to brown it and give the potatoes time to absorb the meat's flavors.

Never stir the mixture as it cooks.

Serve the dish with hot biscuits or johnnycake.

Fish Take Meal Honors, Too

Throughout the nation people generally believe fish and cod are synonymous in the Northeast. Perhaps the misconception arises mainly from the oft-quoted ditty, "So this is Boston, the home of the bean and the cod." Many kinds of fish are important enough to give beef a run for the money, a situation unheard of on the Plains. Fish loaves reap compliments equal to those of meat loaves in this center of the commercial fishing industry, where wealth comes from the water just as it stems from the pastures on western ranches. Yankee eyes sparkle at the suggestion of a shore dinner, a reaction identical to that of Kansas Citians when steak talk starts.

Centuries ago Indians started periodical treks to the seashore to feast on sea food. Yankees recognize a good thing when they taste it! They quickly adopted the practice of their Red Skin neighbors, and cling to it to this day. Cars stream toward the ocean, especially on week-ends, with people bound for shore dinners. Menus vary. Indeed, they range from the simple to highly elaborate in restaurants and homes from the coast of Maine to the southern end of Connecticut's shoreline.

SHORE DINNER
Portsmouth, New Hampshire
Lobster Stew   Crackers
Celery
Steamed Clams   Fried Clams
Boiled Lobster
French Fried Potatoes
French Fried Onion Rings
Hot Rolls
Coffee

SHORE DINNER
Massachusetts
Clam or Fish Chowder
Crackers   Sour Pickles   Celery
Steamed Clams   Clam Bouillon
Boiled Lobster   Potato Chips
Corn on the Cob
Tomato-Cucumber Salad
Coffee

To experience such feasts is to be truly well fed. In these dinners which I sampled, as in all of them, individual dishes of melted butter appear for use in dunking the luscious sea foods.

Clam chowder contributes to the region's reputation for marvelous food. The invigorating climate helps to stimulate the appetite-arousing appeal of steaming chowder. Topflight recipes flood the countryside, with practically everyone positive *her* inherited directions are the most rewarding ones.

The famed controversy about tomatoes in clam chowder never loses its fire. Many Rhode Island and Connecticut cooks uphold the merits of the tomato. The other four states present a united front against what to them is a culinary crime. Rhode Island prefers quahogs, the Indian name for hard-shell clams, or at least half-and-half hard-shell and soft-shell varieties, while Massachusetts chooses the soft-shell kind.

All chowders call for salt pork, onions, potatoes, and clams. Most of them include milk, although some Connecticut homes use water instead. The dish originated when families had backyard gardens to yield potatoes and onions, a cow to furnish milk, a hog destined to supply salt pork, and clams to be had by digging.

Almost all native cooks ladle the hot chowder over split common crackers. These thick, flaky crackers with a characteristic nutty flavor also are known as *Boston* and *pilot* crackers.

As I browsed around the green and white countryside, I concluded that New Englanders seated around a table with napkins tucked under their chins are a happy lot. Anticipation of steamed clams and cups of hot clam broth make them eager and responsive. When the hot clams arrive, heaped on soup plates, everyone gets busy. Guests from mid-America observe with a tinge of envy the deft way natives handle them. And Westerners appreciate the universal Yankee courtesy of modestly showing how it is done.

How To Eat Clams

"Just hold to the neck while you take the clam from the shell, remove the veil from the snout, and then dunk the clam in melted butter, and eat all of it. That's all there is to it." However, some persons leave the necks untouched; there are Yankees who enjoy them, but not the "bellies."

Fried clams and clam fritters, pies, and cakes temptingly punctuate food conversations. Sometimes their names intrigue a visitor, like *Fanny Daddies,* Cape Cod's designation for the fried ones, and *Boat Steerers,* as the fritters frequently are called. On the Cape the vent or hole in the center of a deep clam pie shows a decorative build-up of twisted pastry. Pickled beets and brown bread often escort the entree.

The clambake registers with countless Americans as the Northeast's most glamorous seaside rite. It is the political and fraternal gathering point. Indeed, many tourists approach the region with a secret, fervent hope they will be invited to one. This festive occasion is to New England what a beef barbecue is to Texas, a fish fry to the South, a salmon barbecue to the Pacific Northwest, and a luau to Hawaii. Properly defined, it is a native feast.

Indians take the salute for this colorful affair. They originated and enjoyed it, and passed their techniques on to the early settlers. There has been little improvement in the cooking, although the menu has been elaborated and refined. The Red Men prepared only fish, corn, and clams.

Bakemasters Are in Demand

Every bake has its bakemaster, and if the guest list is long he has assistants. Most communities near the seashore produce men with natural aptitudes for developing superior flavors in these outdoor meals. Socially they are popular fellows. Some of them wind up as professional bakemasters.

Opinions on how to prepare for and put on a bake vary, but the general plans are similar. A Cape Cod clambake given for three hundred visiting home economists at Carver, Massachusetts, by the National Cranberry Association serves admirably as a striking example. The directions followed on this occasion show how the job can be done successfully.

THE PIT. For a bake with a guest list of three hundred people, dig a pit 4 by 6 feet, about 9 inches deep. Fill with stones the size of a cabbage until even with the ground. Stack two layers of firewood on top, then a layer of stones, and two more layers of firewood, and more stones. Repeat until the pile is 3 or 4 feet high. Let the kindled fire burn at least 2 hours. As the wood burns the stones settle.

Rake away the charred wood and embers, leaving the heated stones. Cover them with a thick layer, 6 to 8 inches, of rockweed or seaweed.

FOOD ARRANGEMENT. From bottom to top: clams, sweet potatoes and onions, fish, sausage and frankfurts, corn, lobsters.

LOBSTERS. Buy them of uniform size, for uniform baking. Take large squares of cheesecloth and lay the lobsters in them side by side. Tie and knot the four corners of the cheesecloth together.

CORN. Strip to the last two layers of husks. Tie in cheesecloth like the lobsters.

SAUSAGE AND FISH. Place in individual paper bags or wrap in paper.

CLAMS. Wash thoroughly in sea water to remove all sand and mud. Do not tie the clams in cheesecloth.

Now cover all the food with 4 to 6 inches of seaweed. Finally comes a piece of canvas large enough to extend over the ground and fasten down tightly around the edges with rocks, to prevent the escape of steam.

TIME OF BAKE. Allow 1 hour.

For large crowds, wire baskets rather than cheesecloth frequently hold the foods, except the lobsters. They must be enclosed in cheesecloth; otherwise the moisture oozes out and the meat turns to an uninviting gray. Sausages are wrapped in paper to contain the fat and prevent it from running over other food. Fish wears a paper covering to aid in retaining its shape and flavor.

There's Showmanship, Too

Yankee showmanship impresses hungry guests as the big moment arrives, when the bake is "undone." The canvas and seaweed are removed. Everyone takes a glance at the picturesque foods, such as clusters of pinky lobsters that alternate with bundles of pale green corn. The tantalizing aroma drifts about the scene. It is time to eat.

While seated on a seawall or around tables nearby — often in a pine grove — guests reach for the taste teasers spread before them, like crisp cucumbers and luscious ripe tomato slices, buttered Boston brown and white breads, and sip the hot clam broth that makes the rounds. Then the steamed clams are carried on, about 2 quarts for each guest, piled high on a paper or tin plate. Everyone moves his little cup of melted butter nearer. Some epicures drop in a touch of peppersauce or vinegar.

Cups of hot clam broth are forever showing up. Desserts hold little interest after the guests do justice to the clams, fish, sausage, lobsters, sweet potatoes, and corn. Coffee will suffice, although watermelon usually appeals. First you eat the cool red heart of the melon. Then you press your fingers into the rind for the favorite finger bowl of the bake. The juices remove the grit from under the nails. Of course paper napkins are standard equipment, although some Yankees consider them inadequate and show up carrying dish towels or other large ones made of cloth.

In clambakes just for a family or a small group of people, a wash boiler or galvanized garbage pail reserved for this purpose substitutes for the pit.

You need to fit it with a metal or wooden rack. A lid is essential. You put the rack in the container, pour in about an inch of cold water, and add the layers of food. First come onions in their jackets or skins with both ends cut off, then scrubbed, unpeeled sweet potatoes, cut in halves. Next come sausages wrapped in oiled paper or placed in small paper bags, and then fish wrapped in paper. Above the fish is bread dressing, the kind used to stuff chicken, held in cheesecloth, and lastly come lobsters, also tied in cheesecloth.

You adjust the lid and simmer the contents over a beach or other fire about 45 minutes. In a separate dish you steam 1 peck of washed clams without water 10 minutes. You start them half an hour before the remainder of the food will be ready. When the clams are cooked, you pour half the juice surrounding them into the big kettle to add flavor to its contents.

Song and conversation serve as the final course. Usually they are gay, mellow, and sentimental. Bakes have that effect, especially on the beach in moonlight.

Lofty Eloquence in Lobster Talk

Visitors in the Northeast quickly observe that the people there, although friendly, hospitable, and patient in answering questions, normally are not loquacious about their foods. No doubt this reticence contributes weight to their talk about lobster. As a preface to their remarks they state frankly that they refer to the two-claw kind. Then want nothing to do, in conversation or otherwise, with the crustacean that consists mostly of tail — the crayfish.

Lobster dishes glorify the area. The stew is particularly popular in New Hampshire, and boiled live lobster in Maine. For a summer party on a leaf-shaded porch a platter of lobster salad personifies New England. The white meat is mixed with dressing, heaped in lettuce cups crisp enough to snap under a fork's pressure, and garnished with the pinkish claws of young lobsters. Served with hot buttered rolls and a beverage, the meal is certain to win bouquets.

A small lobster or half of a large one, boiled or broiled, commonly is allowed for each person. A crustacean that weighs 3 pounds or less rates with Yankees as a better selection than a heavier one, which they say is more likely to be tough. When natives talk about *chicken lobsters* they refer to the young of the species that weigh 1 pound or less. Corn pudding, French fried potatoes, and cole slaw head the list of favorite accompaniments.

Everyone stresses the importance of buying the lobster green or alive, and of cooking it pronto. Fishermen frequently give their customers seaweed to cover it when plunged into unsalted boiling water. Without the seaweed, from 2 to 3 tablespoons of salt are required for every 2 to 3 quarts of water. Generally they need to boil about 15 to 20 minutes. Then they are drained and split into lengthwise halves.

Newcomers to New England sometimes wonder how much of the lobster to eat. The answer is all of it except the shell that turns the lovely color in cooking, the stomach or lady (a small hard sac just back of the head), the lungs (the white spongy tissue inside and outside the shell), and the wide black intestinal vein that runs the length of the tail. The coral or roe — recognized by its scarlet color — and the greenish liver, or tomalley, are edible. Many connoisseurs consider the tomalley the choicest part.

Fried soft-shell crabs are an example of another sea food delicacy. Of the many marvelous crab dishes, perhaps deviled crab and crab à la king reecive as much praise as any others.

Fondness for oysters stems from early colonial days when the abundant sea food was carried inland as far as western Vermont. Women of all six states talk of their pet ideas about how to handle the bivalves. On Rule 1 they all agree. It bans the thickening of the stew. Whole milk, cream, or half-and-half milk and cream supply the liquid. Cotuit oysters are highly praised. Many New Englanders place them at the head of the class.

Scalloped Oysters Are Tasty

The stew appears on Christmas Eve in a smaller proportion of homes than formerly, but many community Watch Party services on New Year's Eve continue to feature it as the pièce de résistance.

Native cooks achieve special recognition for superb scalloped oysters. Commonly bread or cracker crumbs, or the two mixed, are alternated with the oysters in a shallow buttered baking dish, with the crumbs in the top and bottom positions. Dabs of butter dot the alternate layers, as do sprinklings of salt and pepper. Rich milk or cream is poured over, and some women add a touch of sherry or white wine. Cooks say the cardinal rule to success is to use a shallow casserole and never to bake more than two layers of oysters in it. They run the dish in a hot oven, 400°, for 20 minutes.

A mention of oyster-corn soup or of creamed oysters gives many Yankees hunger pains regardless of where they are. Creamed oysters atop crunchy buttered toast, over split biscuits, or in crisp pastry shells are an unforgettable delight. When one friend became my hostess on the spur of the moment and presented creamed oysters over rice, with cranberry sauce and buttered broccoli on the side, I rejoiced in the fruits of what she called "pot luck."

Rhode Island turns out fabulous deep oyster pies crowned with biscuits. Then there are oyster-celery and oyster-chicken pies that spell meal success, as do various chicken-oyster casserole combinations to which the bivalves are added near the end of the cooking. Men vote for broiled steak rare, topped with oysters and slipped under the heat just long enough to curl the oysters' edges. Melted butter and lemon juice, mixed and doused over, enhance the regal fare.

Cod, haddock, mackerel, sea bass, salmon, shad, brook trout, and halibut ably represent the more popular fish. Because mackerel is fat, most good cooks broil or bake it without adding fat. On the platter it challenges codfish for approval. Cod, like haddock, is the mainstay of many dishes. Baked fish stuffed with bread-oyster dressing holds many ardent admirers.

Connecticut River shad, one of the regional delicacies, signify the arrival of spring. In the state of the same name the silver harvest comes off in March or early April. Farther north, natives start somewhat later to watch for the creamy white blossoms on the shad bushes along the streams. Their flowering suggests that the shad are running.

Any doubt about the best relish to serve with this choice fish is quickly dispelled in food talk. Butternut pickles win the blue ribbons.

Big eel runs were ruled out years ago by dams in many

rivers, beyond which the eels, salmon, and shad cannot pass. The occasional eels now caught never go begging. Cooks cut them, when dressed, into 3-inch pieces, roll them in corn meal, and pan-fry them. Eel stifle made with the eels, onions, potatoes, and salt pork enjoys popularity at Martha's Vineyard. *Stifle* is a New England name for a stew made with either meat or fish.

Make My Order Scrod

Broiled scrod intrigues almost every visitor to Boston, an attitude natives understand and appreciate. They know from experience that it can be a first-rate treat. The fish industry refers to a small young haddock or cod that weighs 2½ pounds or less as *scrod*. The original definition was any young fish prepared for planking.

Good cooks take pains to explain exactly how they broil the whole fish, split, or cut in fillets, without removing the skin. They warn against breaking it when scraping off the scales and broiling the flesh side up.

They season the fish with salt and pepper, sprinkle it with melted butter or dip it in salad oil and roll it in fresh bread crumbs. Then they broil it flesh side up until tender. Next they turn it and broil the skin side up until it becomes a light brown. New England kitchens allow from ½ to ¾ pound of scrod for a serving. Just before the fish is carried to the table the cooks drench it with melted butter laced with lemon juice.

Tongues and sounds belong to the region. They are cod cheeks and tongues, and often come to the kitchens in the salted form. The cook soaks them overnight in cold water to remove the surplus salt. Then she pan-fries them to brown delicately. At this stage she frequently pours on a white sauce and scatters on a coverlet of buttered bread crumbs. A quick reheating in a hot oven, 400°, to brown the topping completes their preparation.

Cod tongues, pan-fried, are a Boston specialty. After being dipped in milk, rolled in flour, and pan-fried in butter, the tongues are pronounced by many people an elegant dish.

Melted butter, pointed up with lemon juice, and minced parsley provide the garnish.

Brook trout bring out the adjectives when people engage in food talk and also at the table after the first bite. Men thrill over the delicacy of the fish — fresh from the cold streams — which they cook by dangling them on birch saplings over campfires. Ladies beam with pride when presenting them, browned handsomely in the fat of salt pork, on their polished silver platters. They invite their most fastidious friends to dinner!

Salt Fish Keeps Its Friends

While tangy salt fish no longer plays a leading role in menus as it did before refrigeration, frozen food, and transportation facilities became what they are today, it is no stranger. When salt cod and other fish were the backbone of the diet a liking for them developed. The fondness lingers. In many homes codfish potato balls — light as a puff of air and browned in fat — take the spotlight in the Sunday breakfast. In weekday luncheons and suppers these same fish balls call for scalloped or stewed tomatoes as their first choice escort.

Salt Fish Dinner or "Picked Fish" illustrates one of the many classical hearty menus born of frugality. The salt fish, simmered in a little water until tender, is lifted to the center of a warm platter or chop plate. A wreath of diced and buttered beets surrounds it. Boiled or baked potatoes and milk gravy prepared with salt pork drippings are additional accompaniments. To complete the main course of this old-time dinner, cottage cheese and corn bread are required. It is an unwritten kitchen law, Yankee cooks say, never to cut salt fish with a knife when preparing it. They tear it apart with the fingers.

"Cape Cod Turkey" first designated salt codfish, cooked in water, on a warm serving plate encircled by boiled potatoes and beets and with drawn butter and egg sauce on the side. Today it is the common nickname for any cooked fish.

Red fish hash and fish hash emphasize a bred-in-the-bone respect for leftovers. Both are highly esteemed. The first one contains chopped cooked beets as well as potatoes and fish.

Small, sweet bay scallops from off Cape Cod, and the larger sea scallops both give variety to meals. The liking for them inspired many of the dishes that now wear the prefix, *scalloped*. The first New England foods cooked and served in the large scallop shells are believed to have been the forerunners of the many scalloped dishes Americans eat with enjoyment.

Fish chowder probably surpasses clam chowder in regional popularity. Thousands of families cherish special recipes for it handed down by seafaring ancestors. Haddock or cod universally are basic in this savory dish. The other ingredients include milk, onions, potatoes, salt pork, seasonings, and common crackers.

How To Pack a Chowder

One of my hostess-guides offered to demonstrate how she packs a chowder by the directions she inherited from her great-grandmother, who lived in Gloucester, Massachusetts.

She first cooked the heads and bones of the filleted fish in a little water. In the meantime she thinly sliced the pared onion and salt pork, and cut the pared potatoes in ⅛-inch slices and the haddock fillets into 3-inch pieces.

Then she pan-fried the salt pork slowly until it turned a light brown. She removed the rashers to a paper towel that lined a hot dish. Then she strained the water from the fish bones, added enough milk to make 2 quarts, and warmed it. After that she started the packing, and talked as she worked.

"I use a heavy kettle for cooking the salt pork, and for packing the chowder," she said. "I add half the potatoes to the hot salt pork drippings, then a layer of fish, and next half of the onions. Then I sprinkle on a little salt, pepper, and flour. I repeat the process and then I gradually pour in the hot milk. Using heated milk is very important. It helps to prevent curdling. I cover the kettle and place it over low heat to simmer slowly for 25 minutes. About 5 minutes before the chowder is to be removed from the range and served, I add two common crackers that have been soaked in cold water 10 minutes and then squeezed dry in the hand."

As I looked on that snowy evening my mouth watered in contemplation of the fish chowder my friend transferred to an heirloom tureen she had warmed. The pieces of fish and the potato slices were unbroken, a sign of perfection. A few minutes later at the table she dished individual servings into soup plates. Everyone ate the rashers of salt pork from the fingers, made away with his portions of green salad and chowder, and later smiled over a chilled fruit compote and molasses cookies.

Scalloped Fish From a Plymouth Home

The following spring I sat one balmy afternoon with another fascinating hostess and her sister, plus a friend and two of my favorite business associates, in a Plymouth hilltop home overlooking the immortal bay. While almost spellbound with the setting, familiar to every school child who has studied history, I listened to the description of a favorite fish medley modestly called *scalloped fish*.

My hostess said she separately cooks and then mixes at least four kinds of fish and sea food. Haddock makes the foundation for the dish. Cape Cod scallops, lobster, and shrimp team with it. Usually a bit of bay leaf is added to the cooking water to contribute its subtle flavor.

As the fish and sea foods simmer, mushrooms pan-fry in butter and the cook makes a velvety cream sauce. She alternates layers of it — the fish, sea food, and mushrooms in a shallow baking dish, with the sauce, sprinkled with bread crumbs, on top. After heating the entree in a moderate oven, 350°, she proudly carries it to the table. Cranberries from nearby bogs, sweetened and cooked, supply a jellied piquancy and a rewarding splash of color. Chilled celery hearts and buttered hot rolls complete the course.

Happy Holidays Establish Traditions

Traditional foods help celebrate the holidays. Citizens of Plymouth eat a quaint succotash on December 21, Forefathers' Day. A three-piece meal—the succotash, hot johnnycake, and Indian pudding — compose the dinner that commemorates the landing of the Pilgrims.

The succotash classifies as a stew. This is how one gracious resident of Plymouth prepares it.

She gently simmers lean corned beef and a whole chicken in water until tender. Her preference in beef is the second cut of the rattleran, a section of the plate above the brisket. Often this part of the cooking process takes place on December 20. That night she puts large white beans, usually of the Great Northern variety, to soak in water. Next day she boils them until they are tender enough to mash, and adds hulled corn and enough fat and broth from the beef and chicken to season and to keep the vegetables from sticking during 2 hours of simmering.

She stirs the mixture frequently to prevent scorching, but warns that the vegetable blend should be about the consistency of thick soup. One hour before mealtime she drops one turnip pared and cut into 1-inch slices into the broth. Half an hour later she adds cut-up potatoes. For the historic dinner she serves the sliced meat and the carved chicken heaped on a large platter, the vegetable soup mixture in a tureen.

Residents of this community where the famed visitors bravely stepped ashore into a New World insist that the leftover stew improves in flavor every time they reheat it. Some of the younger people fail to share this enthusiasm for the distinctive dish of their ancestors. One young lady, whose forefathers arrived on the Mayflower, admits she has christened it "supper trash," but quickly adds, "Daddy really likes it."

Hulled corn never has relinquished the important spot it holds in the cuisine. It is similar to hominy, save that it is made with yellow instead of white corn, and the kernels require longer cooking. Most households buy cooked hulled corn, or the canned type.

As all true Americans know, New England celebrated the first Thanksgiving Day. Here the holiday carries a certain significance rarely observed in other places. Perhaps the atmosphere is best defined as one of universal planning and anticipation. An air of expectancy permeates the countryside. And the kitchens! The region's food customs for the November holiday have been accepted throughout the nation, along with the back-home or to-grandmother's movements.

Roast turkey with dressing, cranberry sauce, and pumpkin

or mince pie highlight the menu. Sage, according to Westerners, frequently predominates the seasoning of many dressings. Those containing oysters and butternuts also boast of friends. Traditional vegetables include mashed winter squash of some kind, onions in cream, and white turnips.

Baked cracker pudding, reminiscent of cracker barrel days, occasionally ends the feast. Studded with soft, seeded raisins, this dessert makes a gala entry with foamy sauce as its accompaniment. But pumpkin pie on the last November Thursday refuses to forfeit its recognized position of honor.

Sugaring Off Stays in Style

When you are in Vermont and New Hampshire you are in the heart of the maple sugar country. There late in February or early in March, when the days are warm enough to thaw and the nights cold enough to freeze, people begin to discuss the probable size of the year's first crop. Alternate cold and warm weather encourages the sap in the sugar bush or orchards to run. Talk of parties to celebrate the end of winter's grip buzzes around the countryside.

Maple sugar and sirup command widespread fame across the United States similar to that of the wild rice of Minnesota and Wisconsin. These indigenous foods were plentiful before the white men came. Today they are so much in demand that their costs have skyrocketed beyond the reach of many pocketbooks. Even so, countless New England cooks use maple products, as did their ancestors, to elevate an otherwise ordinary dish high above the commonplace.

Who can forget the ham basted with maple sirup as it bakes, or baked apples sweetened with it? Or, for that matter, candied sweet potatoes with the maple flavor? Maple cakes, cookies, candies, frostings, puddings, gingerbread, sauces, muffins, custards, mousses, pie fillings, and ice cream also register near the top on the roster of matchless regional delicacies.

For special occasions like a tea, maple sugar instead of granulated sugar converts cinnamon toast into a delectable offering. The sirup glorifies pancakes, waffles, biscuits, French toast, corn and other fritters, fried hasty pudding (corn-meal mush), and numerous members of the bread family.

Maple sirup and butternuts have an affinity for each other, and they pair off in many out-of-this-world dishes.

For a mouth watering confection you cook 2 cups of maple sirup, a tablespoon of light corn sirup, and ¾ cup thin cream over low heat to the soft ball stage, 238° to 240°. After the mixture cools until lukewarm, beat the candy until it thickens, and then fold in ¾ cup of chopped butternuts. Pour the tantalizing treat into a buttered pan, and when cool cut in into squares or bars.

Cakes and cup cakes sweetened with maple sugar or sirup and spread with butternut frosting illustrate a perfect union of flavors. When my daughter at the age of 15 years returned from school in New England, her conversation was embroidered with eulogies of the tasty combination. And tucked in a duffle bag, where in youthful fashion she had packed her ice skates and a fragile pink evening dress side by side, was a slip of paper on which was hopefully written:

Mrs. H's Butternut Frosting

Cook 2 cups of heavy sour cream and 4 cups of maple sugar to the softball stage, 238° to 240°. Remove the saucepan from the heat, add 1 cup of chopped butternuts, and beat the frosting until it is of the spreading consistency.

Sugaring off parties suggest the North Country. I enjoyed a unique one on a July evening in Boston. The snow had been frozen the previous winter and shipped from the Green Mountain State along with a bountiful supply of the sirup. (Natives of Vermont and New Hampshire who were present mentioned confidentially that only a sugar house, when the sirup and sugar are being made, provides the proper setting for such an occasion.)

The parties run more smoothly if advance preparations are made. Many hostesses partly boil down the sirup before the guests arrive. This shortens the cooking time. They often pack snow firmly in tin pans or soup plates, stack and cover them and store them in a very cold place. Then they can be mobilized quickly. Most people consider pans or plates about 10 inches in diameter the ideal size.

One quart of maple sirup serves 6 persons. Cook it until it reaches a temperature of 236°, or until it spins a fine, short thread. Then test it. The easiest way is to drop a little of the hot sirup on the snow. When a waxy mass, called a leather apron, forms and stays on top of the snow, it is time to eat.

Everyone takes a snow-filled plate, a fork, and a pitcher of hot sirup. Guests pour the sirup on the snow as fancy dictates. Some make a steady stream that falls in one spot. Others dribble it on in delicate lines to form intricate patterns. Regardless of the shape, everyone rolls the chilled waxy sweet around the tines of a fork, or a skewer, and eats to his heart's content. My daughter insists that for unsurpassable eating the leather aprons need to be rolled around butternuts as well as the fork. Some people like to stir the leftover cooked sirup until it becomes a creamy candy to eat from the fingers.

Guests eat leather aprons — also called frogs and sheepskins — until they reach the saturation point. Then they feast on sour cucumber pickles, hard-cooked eggs, doughnuts, and coffee. Sometimes cheese is on the menu. These foods counteract the sweetness of "sugar snow," and promote a revived interest in starting all over again. No whistle blows to announce a new round, but everyone pitches in with eagerness.

Yankees Are Fond of Lamb

"Lamb Fores," written with chalk on village store windows, announce you are in the Northeast. These words, replaced by "lamb shoulders" in the vocabulary of people living in most other regions, remind visitors that the area has a genuine fondness for lamb. Boned fores and breasts are stuffed with dressing and roasted. Roasted lamb legs, stews, and broiled chops never lack for enthusiastic support. Often the stews carry a faint taste of bay leaf, and fluffy dumplings steam on their tops.

Yankee pot roasts set the pace for chefs elsewhere. Why the beef tastes extra delicious may be anyone's guess, although long, slow, deep preliminary browning in melted fat from salt pork may be the reason. The addition of a small quantity of water at a time, and slow simmering in a tightly covered heavy utensil contribute to flavor and tenderness. Cooks emphasize how desirable it is to keep a scant cup of water under a large pot roast all the time, except for a brief period when they let the meat "catch on." My New England grandmother always permitted the beef to stick to the pan briefly. She said that guaranteed brown gravy and enhanced flavors, a statement she backed up with convincing table exhibits. In a surprising number of households old iron pots continue in service for braising this platter favorite.

Family whims determine the vegetables to cook around the pot roast. Carrots, onions, and potatoes almost always are included. The different vegetables are tucked around the meat just in time to become tender. It is something of a tradition in many families to add one white turnip, sliced, to contribute a flavor New Englanders like.

The popularity of sliced or cubed salt pork with milk gravy gives evidence of how old-fashioned, homely dishes are respected. A Yankee cook cuts the meat into cubes or slices and soaks them in cold water to remove some of the salt. Then she dredges the pork in flour and pan-fries it slowly until crusty and brown, or until "crackly and brittle," as my grandmother used to say. She lifts it to a hot platter and makes a milk gravy with the drippings. Some women stir the crispy cubes into the gravy just before pouring it into the service dish.

For many natives the salty tang of meat and milk gravy, with baked or boiled potatoes and hot biscuits, stimulates memories of the big, black, wood-burning range. It heated the country kitchen, helped produce food masterpieces, and gave off a cheerful warmth that drew the family together for talk and a shared anticipation of the next meal coming up.

Scraps of pan-fried salt pork, women say, have no worthy substitute as a garnish for the fish platter, and especially the Salt Fish Dinner. Lemon quarters associate with them in an amiable fashion.

Among the other regional meat specialties are ham baked in cider, meat balls and loaves vaguely seasoned with allspice, stews and pot roasts faintly flavored with bay leaf, frizzled smoked beef or creamed dried beef (often called red flannel stew), upside-down meat and vegetable pies with johnnycake or biscuit crusts, meat shortcakes and pies that display sage flavored biscuits, and ham teamed with raisin sauce.

Tripe Stars in Many Meals

Fresh and pickled honeycomb tripe qualifies throughout the region as fine eating. The fresh product, cut in pieces about 4 by 6 inches, is pan-fried, broiled, or stewed. In many households mustard sauce accompanies the platter's offering.

The rule is to parboil pickled tripe about 3 minutes and then drain it before cooking. One of my hostesses I observed dried the pieces thoroughly, dipped them in beaten egg, and quickly browned them on both sides in fat. Some women prefer to drain the parboiled tripe and roll it in corn meal before pan-frying. Experts say the ideal plan is to cook it just long enough to brown the pieces attractively on both sides. The epicures pair tripe off with oysters in dishes that delight Yankee palates.

New Englanders praise a whole flock of concoctions that feature beef liver, tongue, and kidneys. And no wonder! They know how to prepare these sundries skillfully. Boiled tongue with a well-seasoned vegetable sauce — usually containing onions, tomatoes, celery, and carrots — hits the jackpot of compliments. Traditional accompaniments are buttered spinach and pan-broiled mushrooms.

Of the bacon dishes that intrigue and satisfy people gathered around luncheon and supper tables, nothing surpasses bacon and scallops en brochette. The Cape Cod scallops are first choice for the entree.

To make it, a cook alternates pieces of bacon, inch cubes of bread, and scallops on skewers — starting with the bacon. She broils the tempting combination about 3 minutes on each side 4 or 5 inches from the heat. For the sake of variety and more good eating she sometimes substitutes sweetbreads for the scallops.

It's Chicken, Not a Fruit, Pie

Chicken fricassee and dumplings answer many a Yankee's dream of the right Sunday dinner. State of Mainers like to hide little potatoes and onions under the cooking chicken just in time to become tender. Their practice typifies a regional habit of preparing a dinner in one pot. Even the gravy is stirred in the same kettle. Disjointed chicken frequently is baked, with a little water added, in a tightly covered bean pot set in a slow oven, 325°. It goes to the table in the homely earthen utensil.

Many Yankees drain the fricasseed chicken pieces, roll them in flour, and brown them slowly in butter for what they frequently call fried chicken. In the meantime they convert the broth into gravy, pale in color, but remarkably rich in flavor. One of the unique and original customs of kitchens in the Connecticut River Valley is to stir a wee bit of sugar into the chicken gravy.

Chicken pies forever go into and come out of the region's ovens. Some first-time visitors to Cape Cod have mistaken thin chicken pies for apple filled ones. Between two pastry crusts is well-seasoned, boned chicken, cut in small pieces. At Grange suppers and other community meals — traditional gatherings of the New England countryside — guests from afar often hesitate, to the polite amusement of the natives, to spoon gravy over what they diagnose as a fruit pie.

Some chicken pies wear crisscross pastry tops. I encountered several magnificent exhibits of this type in New Hampshire. Perhaps more commonly, biscuits are baked on the hot cooked and boned chicken.

Whole cranberry sauce goes with chicken and turkey. New Englanders generally prefer it to the chopped raw cranberry relishes most of America adores. Some hostesses serve jellied cranberry sauce in a ring with the uncooked orange-cranberry relish in the center. They say their guests usually take second helpings of both.

They Call It Garden Sass

According to food lore, vegetables first acquired the name of *garden sass* in the Northeast, possibly in Maine. While there may be some disagreement about the origin of the colloquial term, no one questions the supremacy of the regional dishes containing the sass. The cooks have a special knack of handling root vegetables. (Another expression heard in the area is "cranberry sass.")

Beets lend their flavor and brightness to a variety of dishes. There is no need to search for the geographical homes of Harvard and Yale beets. About the only difference in the two other than the nomenclature is that orange juice in the Yale version substitutes for the vinegar in the Harvard one.

Parsnips walk away with the early spring vegetable honors. When time for the first thaw approaches, many a countryman looks to his spade with thoughts of digging a mess of the winter mellowed roots for a parsnip stew or chowder or any of the many other dishes featuring this vegetable. Fritters containing parsnips testify of the regional cooks' artistry with common foods. They mix the boiled and mashed parsnips with seasonings of salt and melted butter, add rich milk and a bit of flour, shape the mixture into flat cakes, and pan-fry them to brown.

Sweet corn tops the summer garden group. Women speak tenderly of sweet kernels to specify the milk stage, and somewhat sadly about the "corn that has gone by being sweet." They cherish two sets of recipes, one for the ears in their

prime and the other for ears a little too mature. Corn puddings, oysters, fritters, and relishes enjoy prestige. Roasted
corn with slices of baked ham — the meat is carried from
home — and potatoes cooked like the corn in the embers and
ashes, whet the logiest of appetites for supper in the outdoors.

Aroostook County, Maine, pours many fabulous soups
into bowls and tureens. Among them are famed potato compositions. Peas and potatoes join forces in one. Home chefs
rub cooked fresh garden peas through a sieve into a potato-
milk soup that carries the taste and scent of onion. They
strew minced parsley on top. Succotash soup fulfills many
a man's wish for something good to eat. Into it go green
or canned whole kernel corn and cooked horticultural beans
to blend with salt pork, milk, and seasonings to tastiness.

Squaws Told of M'Sickquatash

Frequently succotash (not the Plymouth type) is composed of cooked fresh or canned red and white striped horticultural beans or cooked fresh kidney beans (an autumn
delight) with cooked fresh, frozen, or canned whole kernel
corn. In some homes lima beans and green beans join the
corn in the classic dish. It was borrowed in the early days
from friendly squaws, and derives its name from *m'sickqua-
tash,* a Narragansett Indian name for corn boiled whole.

Natives relish squash of all kinds, in sharp contrast to
the relative disinterest for the vegetable in mid-America. As a
student in New England my Kansas-bred daughter acquired
a fondness for it that continues to astonish her home town
friends. The Butternut variety stays on the northeastern
cooking scenes during September, October, November, and
December. Early in November it reaches its peak of perfection. After Thanksgiving Day it rapidly loses quality. Before
then, many women cook and freeze a supply of it.

After the first of the year Buttercups and Blue Hubbards
have their inning. When baked and mashed they frequently
spring a bit of magic — the maple taste. July and August
bring the summer types. Here the mature, larger squash are

more acceptable than in the South and along the Pacific Coast, where the tiny baby ones are in demand.

Peas retain their position of honor in the Fourth of July dinner, along with boiled salmon. For this vegetable, as with sweet corn, many kitchens keep two groups of recipes. One is for the tender, young seeds in green pods, and the other for end-of-the-season peas. The more nearly mature ones deserve credit for popular soup hits and for that noble Maine entree, peas with egg dumplings. For it Yankees steam the dumplings atop the cooked and seasoned vegetable. The high regard for the tastiness of this garden gift and regret that its season ends no doubt were responsible for the old saying, "The last of pea time." My grandmother used it to designate what Kansans mean when they remark that someone is hard up, as, "It's the last of pea time for them with the wheat crop a total failure."

Turnips score highly in numerous dishes. Women speak of them by color, as white or yellow turnips, a practice uncommon elsewhere across the U.S.A., where the white ones are called *turnips* and the yellow ones *rutabagas*. Natives of Cape Cod say this root vegetable is one of their best.

Exotic Dishes From Faraway Ports

In Indian summer, New England's exquisite golden season, pan-fried green tomato slices frequently are served with cold cuts and other meats. Some women season them with a trace of curry powder, a taste which often is noticeable in the regional cuisine. It no doubt was introduced long ago by native seamen who visited faraway ports, sampled the foods there, and brought spices and recipes for exotic dishes home along with Paisley shawls, brass pieces, carved ivory, and Chinese vases.

Cooked onions — notably the boiled ones of Connecticut that are seasoned with salt, pepper, and cream and the onion-cheese dish known as Milton onions — personify the area.

Fiddleheads — delicate, uncoiled fronds of ostrich ferns, cooked and buttered — top the selection of greens for State of Mainers. The season for them is short, scarcely more than a week, usually early in May. Perhaps that explains in part why most of the year the people there either remember with pleasure or look forward with eagerness to fiddleheads, a delicacy the Indians prized. Other greens the natives like to cook in the spring when they are available are marigolds, or cowslips, gathered when the plants are in the bud; sorrel; and dock leaves.

Gardeners who sell vegetables and berries from roadside stands advertise them as "native products;" in the Middle West farmers advertise them as "home grown."

Please Pass the Store Cheese

People speak of *store cheese, mousetrap cheese,* and *rat cheese* to designate their aged cheddar. Vermont cheese makers sometimes add chopped fresh sage to the cheddar before it ripens. This results in the production of their beloved marbleized specialty. Women frequently refer to cottage cheese as *Dutch* or *sour milk cheese;* in the Connecticut River Valley some people call it *pot cheese.*

Vermont used to have more cows than people. That was when the state's cooks began to gather in the medals for their sour cream and milk triumphs. Sour cream date and raisin pies especially rate the superlatives, as do many of the cakes, waffles, griddlecakes, doughnuts, biscuits, muffins, cookies, corn bread, and other dishes that are indebted to sour cream or milk for their superior flavor.

Of course the Green Mountain State has no corner on these taste teasers. Before refrigeration became almost universal, much milk and cream soured in homes throughout the region. Yankee women — resourceful and pennywise — evolved dishes which salvaged them. And most delightfully!

Boston Is the Home of Folded Rolls

No man remembers or knows when the chef first made and baked pocketbooks of bread dough at the Parker House in Boston. Yet the folded bread to this day carries the hostel's name. These rolls are newcomers in comparison to the corn-meal bread that colonists called *journey cake,* later simplified to *johnnycake.* The first name originated from trips into the wilderness on which corn bread was cooked by campfires along the way. Rhode Island people spell it without an *h,* or jonnycake, and fashion it with white meal, which they first scald. Cooks in the other five states use yellow meal. They include the *h* in the spelling.

New England corn bread commonly is made with equal quantities of yellow meal and flour; usually it is sweetened with about ¼ cup of sugar to 1 cup each of meal and flour. Many of the breads are so rewarding when spread with freshly churned butter that no explanations need be given for their continued high standing through the centuries in the region's meals. Some women sweeten the corn bread with maple sirup. In the summer many cooks like to add whole blueberries and a whiff of nutmeg to the batter, and in the winter grated apples.

I suppose Rhode Island jonnycakes most frequently are singled out by connoisseurs for citations. They literally are one of the good things of life when, hot off the griddle, they are buttered and perhaps served with meat or fish.

To make them the cook uses stone-ground, fine, ivory-colored meal made from flint corn. She mixes 2 cups of it with 2 tablespoons of sugar and ½ teaspoon of salt. Then she pours on boiling water to make a batter that will drop from the spoon. She bakes little cakes of it on a lightly greased skillet, and browns them on both sides.

Another specialty of Rhode Island cooks is huckleberry jonnycake. It is made from a mixture of corn meal and flour, sour milk, molasses, and soda. Fresh huckleberries are added, and the batter is baked in a buttered dish instead of on a griddle.

Maine Guides Are Griddlecake Tossers

Griddlecakes command esteem in all six states. Almost always they team with butter and maple sirup. Frequently blueberries, corn, chopped cranberries, diced apples, or other additions are stirred into the batter. Occasionally women in food talks discuss the difference between pancakes and griddlecakes. Usually they settle for size as the determining factor, with pancakes smaller in diameter and thinner than griddlecakes. Maine guides, lumber camp chefs, and other outdoor cooks flip the cakes high in the air in turning them, and let the unbrowned side fall on the griddle. This showy fete at social gatherings draws an admiring group of spectators. New England men often demonstrate the achievement to visitors from other regions.

In Vermont large thin hot cakes just off the griddle frequently are spread with butter, sprinkled with maple sugar, and stacked 6 or 7 cakes high. Before serving they are cut in wedge-shaped pieces. Blobs of whipped cream sometimes crown them.

Throughout New England the biscuits are quite tall — that is, thick, and they are well browned. If a dash of sugar and some blueberries are added to the dough, a Maine edition comes from the oven. Dumplings usually stem from biscuit dough, as do many prized desserts. *Pandowdy* certainly is one of the best known and appreciated ones. For it the cook fills the baking dish with sliced, sweetened, and spiced apples and covers them with a rich baking powder biscuit dough. She previously has cut a decorative design in the center of the dough to permit the steam to escape. Then she crimps the edges around the outside of the dish. After that the dessert is baked in a slow oven, 300°, for 2 or 3 hours. It is served hot with pour cream sweetened with sugar and flavored with nutmeg or with a maple sugar sauce. In many homes pandowdy has lost out to the more quickly made *apple betty,* although I have met Yankee gentlemen who declared that pandowdy is worth a trip across the continent. For *roly poly,* biscuit dough is rolled around sweetened and spiced fruit and baked. The best berry shortcakes still demand a biscuit crust.

I found doughnuts available for breakfast practically

everywhere in New England. They go with coffee at breakfast in the best of society! Maine continues to turn out
molasses doughnuts spiced just right. At least one memorable
cook — my grandmother, who was reared in Maine — in-
trigued her grandchildren by cutting the rolled dough in
strips about an inch wide by 4 inches long. She twisted these
pieces of dough, pinched the edges together, and fried them
in deep fat. Other times she made them in the conventional
shape with a hole in the center. The payoff came as a hand-
out — a warm doughnut and a glass of cold milk.

An astonishing array of the sugared golden rings is made
with sour milk and buttermilk. Then there are potato doughnuts and those rolled and cut from a light yeast-leavened
dough. For informal refreshments on a frosty winter evening,
doughnuts often are assigned to a leading role.

WINTER EVENING REFRESHMENTS
Doughnuts
Hot Popped Corn   Cheese
Sweet Cider

The cheese-doughnut team might startle a Westerner,
but it is pretty much at home on Yankee soil. Names of the
brown rings with holes in the center amuse many people
from other areas. *Holy pokes* and *Baptist bread* or *Baptist
vanities* are typical. The balls from the centers of the doughnuts when fried become *jolly boys* or *huff puffs*.

A Lazy Wife Made Food History

Anadama bread is so typically New England (it almost
never appears elsewhere) that a food scout hears much about
its merits and origin. The inventor of this yeast-leavened,
corn-meal loaf is said to have been a Massachusetts fisherman.
Exasperated by his lazy wife's habit of serving corn-meal mush
every day, he added yeast to the mush and baked a loaf. He
unwittingly christened his successful creation in honor of
his wife by exclaiming, "Anna, damn her." Polite society
slightly altered his words.

Take a Peep Into the Fruit Closets

Anyone who looks into the fruit closets about the countryside quickly concludes that relishes spark up many a meal. Beach plum jelly, tulip-red cranberry sauce, and spicy, thick chili sauce belong to the region as truly as do the white houses and tall church steeples. On the shelves with them are other glasses, bottles, and jars filled with such tastiness as tomato and grape ketchups, a stupendous variety of cucumber pickles — like those in mustard sauce and piccalilli — chow chow, pepper relish, and chutney sauce. On the sweeter side are apple and tomato marmalades, blueberry jam, grape conserve, and a wide selection of jellies.

Because few outlanders, as the Bostonians say, are acquainted with beach plums, visitors to the area always wish to taste the jelly made from the fruit. As you drive near the ocean, glasses of it shimmer like jewels at roadside stands. A taste reveals that the tart, refreshing jelly is more like that of wild cherries than plums. One curious characteristic of the bushes is that while they bloom every spring they bear fruit only once every three years.

To a Kansan, harvest means rivers of wheat flowing from trucks into the dumps of tall elevators by railroad tracks. In the Northeast it conjures, at least to many people, a bustling kitchen with tangy scents of pickling spices, sugar, and vinegar heating in saucepans, and bountiful baskets filled with vegetables and fruits.

Winter Picnics Flourish in the Area

Skiing has developed a comparatively new regional food institution, the winter picnic. People of almost all ages enjoy dining among the snowdrifts, just as their grandparents liked ice skating and sleighing in the moonlight.

The winter picnics feature hot, hearty food. Steaming soup or chowder starts the feed, coffee ends it. What you eat in between varies, but popular dishes are broiled steaks and hamburgers, frankfurts cooked in wire corn poppers (hamburger cakes shaped at home frequently are cooked the same way), baked beans, flapjacks with maple sirup, and stews. Vacuum jugs or well-wrapped kettles deliver the soups, chowders, and stews to the picnic spot. If the roads are closed by drifts or the place selected for the meal is not near a road, the supplies are divided among the skiers for delivery. Then the commissary consists of compact items, like canned soups, beans, and stews.

As an aid in catching the spirit of a winter picnic, a letter from a young girl in Vermont to her mother at home in Kansas describes her first experience with one, and pictures briefly the happy scene.

DEAR MOTHER:

Saturday we went on a picnc. That's why I didn't write. Hold on to your chair, it was 3 below zero. No one seemed to mind. We came off the ski trails at noon to eat because the sun makes it warmer then.

Most everyone in the school had a rucksack and carried his own plate, mug, knife, fork, and spoon. We tucked in some snacks, too, like candy bars and nuts.

The snowplows had cleared the road up the hill. Much of the food and the firewood were hauled to the picnic spot by a school truck. We started the fire in a jiffy at the side of a big boulder.

Soon we were eating the first course, hot vegetable soup, sent from the school kitchen. A kettle of it had been wrapped in newspapers and blankets to hold the heat, but it was so thick we thinned it with snow and had to reheat it by the fire.

We used snow to make coffee, too, but we made it pretty weak. Then we poured some hot milk into our mugs with the coffee. We just heated everything. The mugs were thick pottery. They keep coffee warmer than metal cups.

The cook sent a big pot of baked beans from the kitchen, too, and they stayed warm on the trip, but they were fiery hot to start with and were well wrapped. We had long-handled frying pans and we baked griddlecakes on them from batter brought from the kitchen in jars. Some of the fellows really flipped the cakes high in the air as they turned them with long-handled spatulas. They landed back on the griddles on the right side. It was fun watching them. I kept thinking: There goes my flapjack into the snow. We heated maple sirup until it boiled, added butter and melted it, and poured the mix over the stacks of hot griddlecakes. Daddy and I will have to practice flipping hot cakes next summer in Colorado.

Mother, if you'd been with us you could have had your tea. Lots of skiers say it's the most refreshing thing to drink when you come back to the warming huts.

Maybe you shouldn't tell the gang about my going on a picnic when everything is covered by deep snow and it's below zero. They might think I'd gone crazy. Maybe I have, but it was real fun. We sang on the way back to school. Yes, I was glad to get in my warm room again, but I felt just fine. And I slept like a log last night.

Please write me all the news.

Love from
BETSY

Here Come the Desserts

New England opens a treasure chest of desserts to a food explorer. Many of the most luscious ones have been tested and approved on the local scene through the years at church and Grange suppers and at family tables. Among the galaxy of famous names are many that are at home all across the U.S.A. They have been good travelers.

Puddings keep their well-established foothold in northeastern meals, a reminder of the English heritage of the early settlers. The area remains a great pie-eating country. And many of the desserts are double — like ice cream with cake, simple puddings with cookies, pie with cheese or ice cream, fruit sauce with cookies, and Indian pudding with ice cream. Many flavors of ice creams are distributed throughout the six states. Some of the eating places along the highways offer thirty to forty kinds.

Naturally there are cakes of all descriptions. As in the South, some of the New England ones bear the names of national or state heroes. *Harrison cake* made its bow when everyone knew the meaning of Tippecanoe. *Wellesley fudge* cake enjoys a wide acceptance in the six states. It is a brown sugar chocolate layer cake and wears a creamy fudge frosting. Sour cream spice cakes are legion. Then there are those seed cakes, flavorful with caraway seeds and thinly sliced candied orange peel. What could hit the right spot more successfully on a blustery, raw afternoon than a generous slice of one of them and a cup of tea? New Hampshire women tipped me off on this one.

Maple butternut and maple sponge cakes also deserve honorable mention. Then there are marble and marbleized ones. My Yankee grandmother specialized in both kinds. In the former one she dropped alternate spoonfuls of the dark and white batters into the pan. For the other kind she poured all the white batter into the pan and dropped spoonfuls of the dark chocolate portion on it. She swirled these big dusky polka dots with her spoon through the light batter to produce the marbleized effect.

Cakes and Politics Were Mixed

Political bigwigs no longer provide Hartford election cake, named in honor of its natal city. Once in Connecticut such a gift repaid people who voted a straight ticket. Nowadays the cake is made for special occasions, as for refreshment at election day parties. It is simplified from the onetime elaborate loaves, although the modern versions show all the earmarks of their ancestors. The soft yeast dough, rich with butter, sugar, eggs, and spices, and studded with fat raisins and thin slices of citron, is baked in round pans. The loaves commonly are lightly frosted.

Pies in New England include all the great American ones. Here and in the Pennsylvania Dutch country most of them originated. Squash pie, a near relative of the pumpkin-filled pastry crust, wins greater renown in the Northeast than farther west. The custard filling generally is spiced, but some splendid cooks in Concord, Massachusetts, use rose water in it. They consider spices lusty enough to conceal rather than enhance the delicate squash flavor.

Pumpkin pies usually are made with brown sugar rather than white sugar. Always they are seasoned with ginger, and commonly with nutmeg or cinnamon. Some cooks add a smidgen of ground coriander seeds. It is something of a tradition in many old families to top cold pumpkin or squash pie with 1 cup of heavy cream whipped until stiff, after ¼ cup of maple sirup has been poured on it in a fine stream, and carefully folded into it.

Maple custard, maple-butternut custard, Concord grape, crabapple, cranberry, and blueberry pies de luxe frequently are encountered in New England. Other examples of pies at their best are Yankee apple, cherry, mincemeat, rhubarb, strawberry, cranberries mixed with apples, and cranberry-mince. In the latter number cranberry sauce is combined with mincemeat.

Concord grapes originated in Massachusetts, in the historic town whose name they bear. Naturally they are associated with their birthplace. And cranberries, which are cultivated so successfully on Cape Cod, connected long ago with pastry. On the Cape — and in New England that means Cape Cod — cooks heed tradition and give this pie a latticed top. No doubt centuries ago women were aware that the bright color of the native berries peeping through crisp, browned pastry strips made for eye and appetite appeal.

Down East in Maine, and indeed in all six states, natives burn incense before blueberry pies. Rules to heed in making the dessert are few, but strictly observed. They call for freshly harvested berries when available, and for eating the pie while still faintly warm, or in less than an hour after baking.

Spices have figured prominently in pies, cakes, cookies, and other regional dishes since the merchants first engaged in trade with the East Indies. Friendly debates, informal and jolly, wage about them whenever women talk of food. One school of cooks holds that apple pie calls for a predominating taste of cinnamon, while another equally positive one votes for nutmeg.

An Inning for Slumps and Grunts

A native trick with apple pie is to lay the top crust loosely over the sliced fruit in the pastry-lined pan. When it is baked the crust is lifted off and sugar and spices as desired are added to the fruit. Then the cook sets the pastry hat back on top. Natives rave about this dessert. They say the fruit carries a fresh-from-the-orchard flavor so heavenly that everyone who takes a bite later dreams of May's apple blossoms.

Peach pies respond favorably to similar treatment. After the baked top crust is removed the cook pours a soft custard over the hot peaches and puts the pastry lid back on the pie.

Slumps and *grunts,* mysterious desserts to many persons who live to the west, warrant gold medals for their ease of preparation. A Yankee hostess drops dabs of soft biscuit dough into a frying pan partly filled with bubbling hot, sweetened fruit or berries. She forgets about it for 10 minutes. Then she adjusts the lid and cooks it 10 minutes longer. Everyone gives three rousing cheers for the light-as-a-feather dumplings bathed in the fruit or berry sauce when they reach the table. A pitcher of cream supplies extra richness and flavor.

Among the slumps that make meals red letter occasions are blueberry, cherry, apple, apricot, peach, and plum. On Cape Cod blueberry slump is known as *blueberry grunt.* Steamed berry puddings also are called grunts.

Without question steamers work more hours in New England home kitchens than they do in other regions. The steamed desserts, like the puddings and dumplings, offer proof of that. However, blueberry and apple dumplings, filled with sugared berries or fruit, commonly are baked. Many people rave about steamed strawberry dumplings. The lush ripe berries are mashed until they resemble jam. Natives blend a half cup of butter, whipped until light and fluffy, into 1 quart of the crushed berries. The amount of sugar they add depends on the natural sweetness of the berries. When the airy, hot dumplings with their dry hearts are crowned with the crimson sauce, many a Yankee forgets his reticence to praise. Cooks say they steam the dumplings about 15 minutes or until when one broken apart with a fork is dry.

Baked strawberry dumplings also win applause. When

making them women roll the rich biscuit dough about ½ inch thick and cut it in 4-inch squares. On the center of each one they place about 2 tablespoons of strawberries cut in pieces and sprinkled with a couple of teaspoons of sugar and a dash of salt. Then they fold the squares over to cover the fruit and to make the dumplings. They brush them with milk, arrange them in a shallow pan, and bake them in a hot oven, 400°. If served hot with the same strawberry sauce as for steamed dumplings, the dish is something to brag about.

Among the cherished originals, New England suet pudding stands apart for its excellence. It is thriftier and less substantial than English plum pudding, but becomes quite hearty when eaten warm, as it commonly is, with a fluffy hard sauce or whipped cream on top.

Indian Pudding Is a Traditional Treat

Indian pudding, of the characteristic reddish brown hue and "wheyey" texture, captures many honors in the dessert class. This pedigreed delicacy calls for pour cream, hard sauce, tart jelly, or vanilla ice cream just starting to melt. Milk, molasses, and corn meal are three of its components. The major rule for success in making it is to bake it slowly in a heavy dish. Indeed, some recipes specify that it takes from 5 to 7 hours to make a good pudding. As a short-cut some cooks use canned pudding. They dump it into a dish, pour on a little milk, and bake it slowly as they make the rest of the dinner and eat the main course.

Boston cream pie starts out as a two-layer, one-egg cake. A smooth, sweet custard filling is spread between these layers. Often confectioners' sugar is dusted on top — sometimes through a fancy paper doily to produce an intricate pattern. Chocolate cream pie also resembles a cake more than a pie. The difference between it and Boston cream pie is in the topping. Chocolate frosting supplants the confectioners' sugar.

Other classics of the region include Irish or sea moss blanc mange, chilled chocolate pudding with cream, delicate tapioca puddings, maple flavored and other baked custards, coffee jelly with and without nuts, an infinite variety of gingerbreads, snow balls or white cake batter steamed in custard cups and served with sugared fresh berries or peaches, and bird's nest pudding.

Bird's nest pudding appears in enough different versions to baffle visitors who wish to know how to make the dessert. Apples are the common denominator of them all. In New Hampshire and Connecticut the puddings I sampled had traveled the same preparation route. Whole, peeled and cored apples tenderly simmer in sugar sirup until soft. Care is exercised to keep them intact. A custard mixture is poured over them, then baked until it sets. In Vermont women said their rule is to slice the apples, sweeten them with maple sugar, and to top with a biscuit crust. They bake the dessert and serve a sweet-sour pudding sauce with it; the sharp note usually is supplied by vinegar. Massachusetts likes shaved maple sugar on her editions of bird's nest puddings. Other names for this dessert are crow's nest, apple cobbler, and apple shortcake.

A widespread belief that New England stands for hearty desserts is only partly true. Many of the favorites fall into this group, but there are lighter delicacies. Cranberry granite always wins a welcome. In its frozen depths cranberries, sugar, and lemon juice mingle. The fruit whips, snows, and syllabubs also represent the less substantial side. Then, of course, there are the cooky-fruit sauce duets.

The Cooky Jars Bulge

Here is an area where cooky jars are standard kitchen equipment. Many of them are big. And often they hold irresistible nuggets. You might as well try to count the daisies in a New England meadow in June as to attempt to name all the varieties. I met and enjoyed the recent addition to the nation's stars, *Toll House cookies,* born in Whitman,

Massachusetts, and all kinds of molasses cookies, big and little, thin and crisp, plump and soft, and sugary. Biting into any of them is rewarding.

New Hampshire's seed cookies cannot be surpassed. Hermits, butternut, spice, date, and raisin ones, serve as noteworthy examples of something satisfactory to munch on between and in meals. Two old-fashioned cookies tickle the children as of old. Both contain molasses. *Gingerbread men* and *monkey faces* are their names. Sometimes the little men are miniatures. Most cooks mold the dough with their hands into the proper shapes. The monkey faces are drop cookies with three raisins, two for the eyes and one for the mouth. During the baking these faces take on different, droll appearances. Of course the children clap their hands over them.

Yankee Dishes Moved West

On my numerous trips across the country I have collected a wide assortment of menu cards from many public eating places. On them I find the names of such dishes as Boston baked beans with Boston brown bread, New England clam chowder, Harvard beets, Connecticut creamed onions, Maine lobster, New England boiled dinner, red flannel hash, Yankee pot roast, Boston cream pie, New England chicken fricassee, Parker House rolls, and other culinary triumphs born in the Northeast. Imagine ordering Yankee pot roast in Houston, Texas. That was my privilege and pleasure. Red flannel hash I found in Minneapolis. Boiled live Maine lobster is something of an institution in South Bend, Indiana, and other spots far removed from the Atlantic Coast.

A traveler across the U.S.A. constantly is aware of the widespread Yankee influence on the meals. No doubt the New Englanders who moved westward carried their best recipes with them. A fondness for the dishes made from these blueprints took root on the prairies and on the mountainsides, and many of them have entered the all-American cuisine that slowly and steadily is emerging from diverse regional ones.

Pennsylvania Dutch Country

Upcountry from Philadelphia the Pennsylvania Dutch region spreads like an open fan. There fertile soil and farming skill met before the Revolutionary War. The combination thrived from the start; it continues to prosper. Out of the congenial union gradually emerged one of the remarkable cuisines of the nation. Women in no other area appreciate more the charm of color. At mealtime, tables frequently appear gay in the manner of an old-fashioned flower garden in full bloom. Guests feast first with their eyes.

But quickly you discover that the dishes also are designed for good eating, and not merely as pictures to admire. You understand why the culinary fame of the Pennsylvania Dutch reaches far. What you wonder about is that the cooks in a handful of southeastern counties in the Keystone State, scarcely a dozen at most, created so many original dishes!

Food Masterpieces Are Hearty

The early immigrants, mainly experienced farmers of German stock, lost no time in producing magnificent crops and livestock. Their womenfolk, trained to practice thrift and to cook, busied themselves in spic and span kitchens. They came up with miraculous, gigantic meals — earthy and rib-sticking. Practically all the masterpieces classify as hearty. *Ponhaus,* generally known in other localities as *scrapple, shoofly pie, pepper pot soups,* and a brilliant array of fruit-custards exemplify the taste treats.

Color in foods is evident everywhere throughout the region:

Relish plates flash like rubies with red beet or pickled eggs.

Autumn's cabbage salad shows the gaiety of chopped red, yellow, and green sweet peppers.

Sugar cakes, light as a feather, fragrant, and fresh from the oven, blush with sugary cinnamon.

Dusky molasses cookies, cut in a myriad of fancy shapes, frosted white, and splashed with pink sugar, hang on Christmas trees.

Fruit pies wear puffed up, browned strips of sweet dough as if to display their fillings of red cherries, golden apricots, lemon-yellow custards, or purple plums.

Soon Farm Markets Were Opened

The mush made from the meal of roasted corn carries a rich brown hue, intensified when thinly sliced, pan-fried until crisp-edged, and stacked on breakfast plates with molasses or apple butter at its side.

When towns and cities came to the countryside, some

frugal rural cooks visualized in them profitable outlets for the surplus food of their kitchens. They established farm markets, a system of merchandising that attracts huge numbers of today's shoppers. Visits to them give you a bird's-eye view of current food favorites, or of dishes sweet-faced country women make to sell to their city and town sisters.

What does a visitor see in a farm market on a Friday morning early in autumn? Take a fleeting over-all glance for first impressions. Neatness prevails. There are no pin-feathers on the plump, dressed poultry. The fruits and vegetables, scrubbed to perfection, literally shine with cleanliness. You behold a rainbow on the earth — bunches of seasonal garden flowers; red, yellow, and green apples; pickled eggs and red beets (many natives refer to the vegetable as red beets); orange-hued pumpkin pulp cooked for easy pie making; deep yellow-amber dried corn; green endive; purple grapes; creamy white schmier kase or cottage cheese; and snowy drifts of shredded coconut.

The air is fragrant with pungent and spicy scents of grated horse-radish, fruit vinegars, apple butter, spiced crab-apples, potato salad, sauerkraut, Lebanon sausage, country cured ham and bacon, cinnamon, and loose or bulk molasses. The baked foods are exhibits of genius.

All Aboard for a Food Tour

It is a delight to walk up and down the aisles and loiter here and there to talk with the saleswomen-cooks, who greet everyone in a neighborly manner. You hear from the women in the food stalls, "We make and like the same dishes you do in Kansas." In a sense their supposition is correct, for some of the Pennsylvania Dutch have migrated and settled in other areas. Kansas has splendid communities of them. I also have met them in western Maryland, Delaware, the Shenandoah Valley of Virginia, North Carolina, South Carolina, New York, New Jersey, Ohio, Indiana, Illinois, and Iowa.

Without doubt many of the region's great dishes are

widely enjoyed. Yet millions of Americans never have heard of Montgomery pie, or thrilled at the lusciousness of its rich lemon-molasses custard alternated with sips of hot coffee. Nor has the hostess west of the Mississippi River carried vanilla ice cream to her guests with crunchy, salt-besprinkled Reading pretzels as its escort.

Locally manufactured in a variety of shapes, the pretzels appear in all the area's markets, and on the streets of some towns in stands that are suggestive of the popcorn vendors in the heart of America.

When Is Bread a Cake?

As you motor along southeastern Pennsylvania's smooth highways, flanked by well-kept, intensively cultivated fields, and large houses and larger barns, you occasionally see old outdoor bake ovens adjacent to kitchen doors. No longer used, they mutely stand to remind a food explorer that the splendid baked foods of today descend from the triumphs that once came from them. Do they hold the answer to the riddle, when is bread a cake? The line that divides the two is so hazy that strangers become confused about it. Eventually, a visitor discovers that *kuchen* or cake ranks as a favorite designation for bread, pie, and cookies, as well as cake.

Sugar cake, also known as Moravian cake, belongs to the bread family. Yeast leavened, it is sweet with sugar, tender with eggs. It invites dunking in coffee — an enjoyable, permissible custom.

To make sugar cake, Pennsylvanians shape the light dough, which contains mashed potatoes, to fit into layer pans to a depth of about ¾ inch. When doubled in bulk, they spread sugar-water, as natives call sugar dissolved in water, over it, and dust on cinnamon. Then with a thumb they punch holes in it at 2-inch intervals and fill the miniature wells with dabs of butter, other shortening, or thick cream, and brown sugar. Sugar cake fresh from the oven has that come-hither aroma that only hot bread imparts.

Sugar cake is not the only good coffee cake. Many women

scatter sweetened crumbs on their baked foods as if by second nature. They brush the dough, just before baking, with melted butter or shortening, and sprinkle on the crumbs, a mixture of flour, sugar, cinnamon, and shortening worked into a crumbly mass. Some expert cooks prefer brown sugar to the white, but everyone agrees on cinnamon for the spice. Frequently they also mix in a few trickles of molasses as an aid to further tastiness.

Light cake with buttons or dollars, as the natives call it, deserves honorable mention. Composed of a yeast-potato dough, it rises tall and handsome, and wears its decorations with an aristocratic air. When the loaves are ready to bake the cook rubs them with milk or melted fat and places the buttons or dollars — the difference is one of size — on top.

She makes the buttons from a mixture similar to hard sauce with flour added. Into 1 cup of sugar she blends ½ cup of flour and ⅓ cup of butter, or other shortening. The trick is to use just enough shortening to hold the flour and sugar together.

The modern way is to shape the mixture into a slender roll, frequently about the circumference of a silver dollar. During chilling it becomes firm enough to slice thin with a sharp knife. The buttons were formed in old-time kitchens with nimble forefingers and thumbs.

Fortunate you are to ring the door bell just in time to watch your hostess put the finishing touches on *butter sem-mel,* or butter rolls. She pats out the light yeast leavened dough about ¼-inch thick on a floured board, brushes on melted butter, and cuts it in 2-inch squares. Then she laps each of the four corners to the center of the square, and repeats the process until all the dough is used. When the tempters are risen, she bakes them in a hot oven, 400°. She again brushes them with melted butter and scatters on a little sugar. By this time your appetite is whipped up to a high pitch, but one the rolls satisfy most delightfully. They melt in your mouth!

Strickle Sheets Are Popular

You are not likely to talk with many people in the area until someone asks, "Have you tasted strickle sheets?" One new friend demonstrated to me how to make them. She rolls the risen dough, and cuts it in small rounds. Then she pushes these circles together in a greased shallow pan and lets them rise still more. When it is time to bake them, she spreads their tops with a mixture made by cooking a small quantity of sugar, water, and butter, thickened slightly with cornstarch. In the heat of the oven the buns run together, and the bubbling sirup holds them in that position.

Sometime during the first visit to southeastern Pennsylvania, a mid-American learns that rolls commonly are known as buns. Your hostess at the morning coffee serves hot cinnamon buns, and the hotel's coffee shop lists them on the breakfast menu card. Sticky cinnamon buns represent the nearby neighbor, Philadelphia, as authentically as the Liberty Bell in Independence Hall. The stickiness commonly stems from the custom of dribbling a little dark or light corn sirup on the thin sheet of yeast dough spread with butter and sprinkled with brown or granulated sugar, raisins or currants, and cinnamon. The cook then rolls the dough like a jelly roll, cuts off $1\frac{1}{2}$-inch slices and puts them in a fairly deep greased pan that contains $\frac{1}{4}$ inch of the sirup; after they raise she bakes them.

Many Pennsylvania Dutch women omit the sirup. They spread the sheet of dough with butter, and sprinkle on raisins, cinnamon, and brown sugar, which they say adheres better than white sugar. After rolling and slicing, they arrange the pinwheels in a greased pan sprinkled with a little brown sugar, scatter more brown sugar quite lavishly and cinnamon lightly on top, and often press in nuts.

Who Is the Fastnacht?

Fastnachts, or yeast leavened doughnuts, sell in generous abundance at farm markets and bakeries throughout the year.

In addition, some households fry their own supplies. The gala day for this famous bread comes on Shrove Tuesday, when these festival doughnuts universally are eaten. Many women set the sponge on Monday evening and fry the fastnachts on Tuesday morning. Tradition calls for the dough to be rolled and cut in squares or rectangles with slits made in them, but they also are cut the customary doughnut shape, the circle with a hole in the center.

Some of the natives in describing their fastnacht recipes say, "Frequently I divide the dough in two parts. From one I make fastnachts. With the other I make cinnamon buns."

Thousands and thousands of doughnuts come from kettles on the morning of the last day before Lent. The member of the family who arises latest or the one who comes to the breakfast table last on Shrove Tuesday receives the title of fastnacht, or the lazy fastnacht. He is given the final scraps of the dough, fried like the other cakes, but shapeless.

The celebration has its roots in South Germany. There the day that ushers in Lent is called the Fastnacht. Housewives in the German Palatinate fry doughnuts on Tuesday afternoon and the festivities continue until midnight.

Funnel cakes gradually are fading from the region's culinary accomplishments because not too many women can make them successfully. Anyone who has the skill at her fingertip willingly puts on a kitchen show — and that is exactly what it is — to appease a food scout's curiosity. She pours batter into a good-sized funnel, which she closes and opens with a finger. Then she holds it over hot fat, as in frying fastnachts, and permits the flow of batter at the speed she desires. The stunt is to produce a variety of interesting shapes by turns and twists of the funnel. One of the favorites resembles a snail. She swirls the batter into the deep fat in gradually enlarging circles, without letting them touch. After she takes the cake from the kettle she sifts on confectioners' sugar, and then serves it hot with tart jelly and coffee. Eating it is something to remember.

Sweet Cakes Wear Crumbs

Sweet cakes, or the quick coffee-cakes leavened with baking powder, receive fewer compliments than their yeast leavened cousins, but when crumb topped they never go begging. The crumbs are quickly prepared by rubbing a portion of the dry ingredients, before adding the leavening, with shortening to produce a coarse meal.

As in most communities north of the Mason and Dixon line, the hot biscuits are thick, at least by southern standards. Yellow corn meal lends corn bread its characteristic hue, but it shares honors with wheat flour. Proportions commonly consist of 1 cupful of flour to ¾ or 1 cupful of corn meal. In most kitchens at least 2 tablespoons of sugar go into the batter.

If the people in any section of the United States enjoy fried mush more or consume larger quantities per capita, I have yet to make their acquaintance. Men never stint their eulogies of the golden brown slices served at breakfast with liver sausage or bacon, apple butter or molasses, and coffee.

You need skill in your own kitchen to follow the regional technique for preparing fried mush. You cut the mold of chilled mush into ¼-inch slices and pan-fry them without rolling in flour or in egg and crumbs until their exteriors become a crispy brown. In some communities, notably in Lancaster County, people commonly prefer meal made by grinding roasted corn. It is brown, and dishes including it carry that somewhat nutty taste of parched corn.

Practically all muffins known to man appear in the meals. Perhaps their most distinctive common likeness shows on their tops, for the cooks instinctively scatter a little sugar and cinnamon over the batter before they bake it.

As indicated previously, Pennsylvania Dutch women possess talent with any dish made from batter or dough. Certainly *pfannkuchen* and *griddlecakes* offer no exception. Pfannkuchen, or pancakes, designate large cakes, baked singly in traditional German style; griddlecakes are smaller. They bake several of them at a time on a griddle, and refer to them as cakes, like buckwheat cakes, corn cakes, bread crumb cakes, and flannel or wheat cakes. Both yeast and baking powder leavened buckwheat cakes have a following. Their popularity extends to northern West Virginia, where some communties have buckwheat cake festivals.

Quite commonly griddlecakes are served with butter and sirup or molasses. Milk gravy also is a popular companion for them. The cook makes it from the drippings after pan-broiling bacon, sausage, or perhaps fresh pork. Bacon gravy sometimes contains bits of crisp bacon, stirred in at the last minute before serving.

Grandmother and I Talked of Food

In many households, waffles provide a perfect background for what the Pennsylvania Dutch speak of as chicken gravy. It is the broth thickened with egg, no milk added. You forever wish to pin medals on the region's good cooks, as you travel among them, for their art and skill in incorporating eggs in many dishes to enhance flavor.

Fresh corn waffles, or those with kernels grated or scraped from the cobs stirred into the batter, are a summer feature. In winter the dried corn, soaked overnight in lukewarm water and pulped, stars in this dish. Out-of-this-world fritters are favorites about the countryside. For a supper worth writing home about I agree with the natives when they choose corn fritters or waffles, butter, bacon, plenty of sirup, and coffee.

Pennsylvania Dutch fritters! What memories they awaken, not directly of the Keystone State but of a gracious little lady in her seventies when we met at her Kansas home, Oak Hills. My husband's maternal grandmother and I sat in the warm spring sunshine, with the perfume of her orchard's blossoms on the air, and talked of food. I, a graduate in home economics fresh from college, literally sat at her feet and lapped up every word she spoke, for her prestige as a wonder cook was great.

"Spring," said grandmother reminiscing, "takes me back

to my home in eastern Pennsylvania, and to the grapeleaf fritters mother used to make." I asked how she made them, for they sounded like a romantic fairy tale. Grandmother continued, "We gathered the first green leaves from the vines. Mother lovingly washed them, patted them dry, and then carefully spread the choicest sweet from her bulging fruit closet on them. We liked thick strawberry or red raspberry jam, although we also were happy if red currant jelly was selected. She rolled the leaves, dipped the tender green packages in fritter batter, fried them to a golden brown, drained them, and sprinkled on powdered sugar. We ate them hot, and thought nothing could be better. And I don't think anything could be.

"Mother was not satisfied to make fritters only of the fruits, like apples and peaches, and the vegetables, such as corn and onions, but she also used blossoms, including those of elderberries and the black locust that grew by the garden wall. Delicate and sweet they were, too. The onion rings, nicely browned, she sprinkled lightly with cinnamon. Like all the Dutch women she liked to use cinnamon often."

From there our talk branched out to the Pennsylvania Dutch pies. We settled down to a long visit; it was my first contact with one of the famous American cuisines. Years later, on my food tours of the area, Grandmother's shadow was with me.

There's Magic in the Pies

You view Pennsylvania Dutch pies with admiration and respect when you confront a collection of them. A touch of the fork cuts through their luscious fillings and tender crusts. The women who made them deserve the crown they wear. The variety and quality of their pastry rate as a marvel. In the homey colonial kitchens of the area, which contained among other foods an abundance of carefully rendered lard, evolved much of the progress in developing the delicate, flaky, thin American pastry from old-time European favorite types.

Give almost any cook of the region a fork, a knife, and an hour in her tidy kitchen and miracles occur. Pies fragrant with fruits, custards, vegetables, molasses, and spices appear — pies resplendent with fancy tops. Her techniques come from a bag of heirloom culinary tricks that have been accumulating over the countryside for the last two centuries.

For instance, she draws the point of a knife vertically and then horizontally over the pastry rolled on the board for the top crust. The plaid thus made assumes different shades of brown in baking and lends the charm of an individual touch.

Although the art of knife decoration is not applied generally, some of the women still use it. They outline a design on the rolled pastry with a knife's point. Some of it they cut entirely through, to form vents for the escape of steam. In other parts they cut deep, but not through the pastry. They gently lift the cut edge up; it ripples slightly and browns more than the remainder of the pattern, forming an intriguing contrast. Or as one culinary artist explained, "It is our way of shading the picture on the pie."

Before two-crust pies reach the oven the cook often brushes their faces lightly with softened butter or shortening and dusts on granulated or confectioners' sugar. She also pricks hearts, bow-knots, apples, flowers, or other designs in the top crust. Occasionally she cuts them from pastry and bakes these decorations on the pie.

A Weave of Pastry Ribbons

By tradition certain pies wear crisscross tops. Among them are the dried fruit treats, such as prunes spiced with cinnamon, apricots, peaches, schnitz, and raisin. Sour cherry and rhubarb filled ones also frequently display a lattice. Some cooks cut the strips with a pastry wheel to obtain scalloped edges, but more of them prefer the older and fancier effect they obtain by twisting the pastry ribbons as they weave them.

Sweet dough pies take the dessert role in meals in other localities, but hardly with the regularity you meet them in Pennsylvania Dutch communities. No doubt they are an offshoot of *muerbe teig,* a German type of crust for fruit pies, a favorite in many West Virginia homes.

The Pennsylvania way is to blend 1 cup of flour sifted with ½ cup of sugar with ¼ cup of butter and lard, mixed, and 1 egg. You chill the mixture. After that you reserve a third of it, and roll out the larger portion to fit the pan. Then you chill it again. Into the remainder of the mixture you blend 1 teaspoon of baking powder and 3 tablespoons of milk. You roll it into 1-inch strips, and place them on the filled pie in one direction. Because the pastry puffs up in baking, a lattice interferes with the rising. Instead of strips some women cut the rolled dough in tiny circles and arrange the "dollars," as they call them, over the filling.

Strip pie is a memorable meal ending — be it red raspberry, green gage plum, elderberry, lemon, currant or apricot strip pie. It is served while still faintly warm, with the fruit fillings showing between the puffed, browned pastry strips or "dollars."

You meet crumb pies wherever you go in the country, and also in the cities of York, Reading, Allentown, Bethlehem, and Harrisburg. The crumbs are riveled up, as the natives say. They rub the flour, sugar, shortening, and a dash of salt between their fingers until the mixture becomes a mass that resembles coarse meal. They scatter it on instead of a top crust, and usually dust on a whisper of cinnamon. As the dessert bakes, the crumbs become crunchy and brown.

Although most women have their pet ways of preparing the crowning glory for pie, some of the super cooks mix ¾ cup of flour, from ½ to ¾ cup of sugar, and ⅓ cup of butter.

Here Comes the Pie Parade

Wherever you travel in rural neighborhoods you hear much *boi* talk (the colloquial name for pie). From these conversations I have tabulated the desserts consistently described as regional favorites. Here are a few of the almost endless array on which many of the women maintain their culinary reputations.

APPLE BUTTER PIE. The spicy filling is made with apple butter, a beaten egg, and a touch of flour. Many families choose sweet dough and bake strips of it on top.

APPLE CRUMB PIE. The sliced, sugared fruit, perked up with a suspicion of cinnamon, carries a top crust of crumbs.

CONCORD GRAPE PIE. Along with green gage and other plum pies it frequently teams with sweet dough and wears strips or dollars, although some women make two-crust pastry numbers of them. They also draw crumb toppings.

CRUMB PIE. Its unique tastiness is unforgettable. The cook mixes flour, sugar, and soda, sifted together, works in some butter, and adds a little sour cream. Then she rubs the mixture until it forms coarse crumbs, pours them loosely into a pastry-lined pan, and bakes the dessert. Its original name, *gravel pie*, explains its appearance.

CURRANT PIE. Either green or ripe currants appear in this one. The green fruit goes into two-crust pies, and the ripe one universally ends up with strips of sweet dough. An old school of excellent culinary artists adds a little currant jelly with the sugar to sweeten the currants if they are unripe.

ELDERBERRY PIE. Usually the berries team with apples for a two-crust or crumb crowned pie. Of course, elderberry-custard pie ranks with the immortals.

FRUIT CUSTARD PIES. Custard pies made by the Pennsylvania Dutch frequently hold pleasant surprises, like black walnuts, coconut, the taste of lemon, or pieces of fruit. Cottage cheese-custard pie, for instance, carries the taste of lemon. Among the fruit custard pies are those that contain rhubarb, apples, apple butter, apple-lemon, coconut, peaches, elderberries, lemon, or sour cherries. A few custard pies wear a top crust. Raspberry-custard pie, described later, is in this class. On others baked in one crust, meringues are spread and lightly browned. Pennsylvania Dutch women have no competition on a national scale for their glamorous fruit-custard pies. They have a knack of baking smooth, velvety custards that emphasize the deliciousness of fruits, the flakiness of pastry.

GOOSEBERRY PIE. As with currants, you use either ripe or green berries. Tradition seasons them with a suggestion of cinnamon. The green berries take a top pastry crust, ripe berries take strips or "dollars" of sweet dough.

LEMON CUSTARD PIE. Frequently it is a lemon sponge with the beaten egg whites folded into the filling and baked in a pastry-lined pan. Many lemon custards appear cloudy.

Native cooks account for the phenomenon as due to the milk they use instead of water, which they believe yields a superior flavor. A few of the pies wear meringues, tall and appealing; lemon strip pies, as indicated, rate as one of the region's foremost dessert successes.

What's in the Name?

MONTGOMERY PIE. Or is it a cake? It has a two-layer filling. The first one in the pastry-lined pan contains molasses, sugar, water, beaten egg, lemon juice, shredded lemon peel, and sufficient flour to thicken the custard that ensues. The second is cake-like. Half pie and half cake, the dessert answers to both names. In Montgomery County, its orginal home, most people call it pie.

RAISIN PIE. Some gourmets consider it the tastiest of all. Traditionally a lattice tops it, but today's versions often are two-crust or crumb-crested affairs. The filling has the subtle taste of lemon juice, and yellow flecks of peel, although a trace of vinegar instead of lemon frequently supplies the tart note. This is the famed funeral pie. Through the generations it has solaced the bereaved family after a burial. Especially in the older days funerals usually took place in the mornings and were followed by tremendous feasts. The clan gathered from far and near and the visitors prepared the dinner. Since raisins keep well, they are available many months of the year, and pies filled with them usually appeared in those Gargantuan meals. The custom explains the dismal saying still heard occasionally about the region in reference to an illness, "There will be a raisin pie soon."

A Feast for the Gods

RED RASPBERRY PIE. In the simpler version sugared berries bake between two pastry crusts. The more sumptuous one has a creamy cornstarch custard sauce poured over the sugared berries after they are in the pastry-lined pan; then the top crust goes on and the pie is baked. Both kinds make feasts for the gods.

RHUBARB PIE. In this pastry delight of spring, the sweet-tart pink of rhubarb shows through a pastry lattice. Commonly both cinnamon and nutmeg help step up the flavor. Rhubarb-custard pies, previously mentioned, also are among the famous triumphs.

SCHNITZ PIE. Dried apples are soaked overnight, then simmered until they resemble sauce, and sweetened. Pared, tart varieties of fruit are dried for pies. Some cooks put the cooked schnitz through a sieve. The addition of a few shakes of cinnamon, drops of lemon or orange juice, and shreds of either fruit's peel are among the traditions heeded.

AMISH HALF MOON PIES. They resemble turnovers. Spoonfuls of schnitz pie filling are dropped on half of 8-inch pastry circles, and then folded over. The edges are pressed together to seal them. These dripless pies have quieted many children during lengthy church services.

SHOOFLY PIE. It probably is the most famous nationally of all the regional pies. Its heart of molasses, with hot water and soda added, bakes between layers of crumbs, like those for pie tops, in a pastry-lined pan. Natives advise that you pick this one for breakfast, if you like to start the day with pie, as they do. If you try to find out how this dessert was given its unusual name, you learn it also is called *molasses crumb cake*. A home economics student said she heard in class that it stems from the French word for cauliflower, *choufleur*. The connection seems to be that the crumbs on top of the baked pie resemble in texture, at least to the eyes, the head of a cauliflower. Such an explanation amuses many practical cooks, who obviously consider it a fable.

SLICED GREEN TOMATO PIE. A two-crust marvel, this pie stands for the region in autumn, if the Pennsylvania Dutch in faraway places are the judges. Green tomatoes, thinly sliced, scalded with hot water, and drained, unite with brown sugar, molasses, butter, and cinnamon. The creation is enjoyed a few weeks in late summer, and early autumn before Jack Frost arrives.

SOUR CREAM APPLE PIE. It illustrates perfectly the

lusciousness of sour cream in fruit pies. The cook whips, sweetens, and spices the cream and folds in chopped apples along with a proverbial pinch of salt and a bit of flour. Most hands dust on cinnamon for good measure.

Sour cream peach pies have a spicy touch. Halves of peeled and pitted peaches crowded close together in a pastry-lined pan, are spread with whipped sour cream, sweetened and spiced.

WALNUT PIE. This has been mentioned as a member of the custard family. It is made of equal parts of brown sugar and either molasses or corn sirup, and eggs beaten separately, with the whites folded in at the last. Water supplements the sirup for the liquid role. A full cup of chopped black walnuts is allowed to a pie.

No truer confession ever was made than that any exhibit or description of Pennsylvania Dutch pies falls far short of doing them justice. In a large book written about these treats perhaps the author might introduce all of the gems. But even an incomplete parade makes you realize that while the good cooks may not pull rabbits from their hats, they pull magic from their ovens. You can readily conjure up the generously filled old-fashioned pie safe or cupboard made of pierced tin to provide ventilation. And true to form, the Dutch cabinet maker worked out decorative patterns with the holes in the tin, designs that were qualified artistically to house the pies with their fancy tops. Nowadays some of these cupboards are valued antiques in parlors.

Cakes Challenge the Pies

Cakes challenge pies for the coveted top position among the desserts. Usually, though, the Pennsylvania Dutch relegate them to second place. Not that the women do not bake handsome, delicious cakes, but rather that they assign them to play supporting roles. Pie stands alone. Cakes almost always escort ice cream, fruits, light puddings, delicate custards, and other culinary triumphs.

Perhaps some of the many layers and loaves are regional

originals, but it is difficult to sift them out. In the area are all the kinds currently popular on the national stage. The natives have a glint in their eyes when certain cakes enter food conversations or meals. Descriptions of them put you in a mood to pull up your chair and have a few slices.

APPLE BUTTER CAKE. Women say the spicy loaf is a "good keeper." The men speak about its tastiness.

CIDER CAKE. The juices of apples perform as the liquid in this spice cake studded with raisins.

CINNAMON FLOP CAKE. This one is sold in the Lancaster and other farm markets. The hostess who shares it explains it is a one-egg cake with brown sugar and cinnamon on top. Women refer to it as a breakfast or luncheon speciality, and thereby illustrate a regional habit of labeling a cake by the meal in which it appears. The richer, fancier ones classify as dinner cakes. For breakfast, cinnamon flop is sliced and toasted, then dunked in coffee.

CHOCOLATE CAKE. If you collected and lined up a year's supply of chocolate cakes you could cover the highways in any one of the counties! One of the favorites contains brown sugar, and comes to the table with fudge frosting swirled on top.

CLOVE CAKE. You have no question about the spice that dominates this loaf after you take a bite. With coffee it is excellent.

CREAM-ALMOND CAKE. This almond-flavored white cake has coconut spread on the batter and baked atop it. For summer refreshments or dessert it is served with Philadelphia fresh peach ice cream. Whoever originated the combination deserves an award.

"Colorful as Wedding Ring Quilts"

CRUMB CAKES. They indicate the people's Germanic background. To make them cooks first blend flour, baking powder, sugar, a dash of salt, and shortening, and save out 1 cupful to scatter on top of the batter made with the other portion of the crumb mixture, eggs, and milk. The crumbs substitute for frosting. This crown is spicy at times, for the natives generously dust cinnamon on breads, cakes, pies, puddings, and countless other dishes, like applesauce.

DAFFODIL CAKE. On special occasions, like a children's birthday party, you never go wrong on this selection. Daffodil cake looks good, tastes good, is not too costly, is easy to make, and presents a gala showing.

As made in New England it is a marble cake. A Yankee ladles alternate spoonfuls of the white and yellow batters into a tube pan for baking. Many Pennsylvania Dutch cooks pour all the vanilla-flavored batter, or the white portion into the tube pan and spread the orange-flavored yellow batter on top. Thus they achieve a layered effect. Some of them believe their way springs from the festive rainbow-hued, old-fashioned ribbon cake. It consists of different colored layers, produced by baking pink, white, yellow, and chocolate batters in layer pans. To glorify the special occasion dessert the layers are stacked with bright red jelly between them and confectioners' sugar is sifted over the top.

FLOWER CAKE. Known also as the *pansy cake,* the old-time favorite blooms less frequently every year in the area's kitchens. Like ribbon cake it depends on colored batters for its charms. The cook drops the batters into layer pans and spreads them in bands or rings, the white on the outside, then pink, yellow, and chocolate. "As gay as the wedding ring quilts," is the way it is described. Although the personal dress of the region's women may be somber, especially among some of the religious sects, you cannot accuse the Pennsylvania Dutch of preparing and serving colorless foods.

NUT CAKES. Commonly they are loaves containing either black walnuts or shellbarks (hickory nuts), although a traditional one boasts of three layers with chopped shellbarks in one of them. A cooked white frosting is assigned to complete this favorite.

Far From Lebanon County

PEACH CAKE. Born in Lebanon County, it has traveled far from the kitchen where it first saw the light of day. The cook spoons one-egg batter into the pan. Then the fun begins, for she scatters on firm, ripe, sliced red-hearted peaches, sprinkles them with sugar, and shakes on a little cinnamon. Often coffee brews as the cake bakes. Presently from the kitchen come wafts of its spicy, sugary fruitiness, and soon the loaf is delivered from the oven. After it has cooled just enough to handle, the hostess breaks off the first piece for a visitor and serves a two-piece banquet, peach cake and coffee.

PINEAPPLE CAKE. Such a taste and fragrance of crushed pineapple and a blend of vanilla and almond flavorings in the white layers! When "companies," as some of the natives say, are expected they dress up this favorite with billows of fluffy white coconut frosting.

POTATO CAKE. Economical and tasty enough to travel westward with the pioneers, the loaf contains mashed potatoes, spices, cocoa, and sometimes nuts. Women highly regard its ability to remain moist and fresh for a long time. It is an exhibit of how clever the Dutch are in using potatoes in unique ways.

PRUNE CAKE. Another spiced loaf, this one is chock-full of chopped cooked prunes. Cinnamon plays the stellar role among the spices. Certainly it demonstrates, as do many other dishes, that the people in southeastern Pennsylvania vote for well-spiced and full-seasoned foods.

ROCHESTER CAKE. Popular for many generations, this cake fills you with nostgalia for the cozy farm kitchens where it was at home so long. This two-egg, sour milk cake is especially distinguished by the cooked buttery filling with raisins between its layers and frequently on its top.

SCHNITZ CAKE. The batter is prepared with sour cream as the liquid and expertly spiced; then the cooked and chopped dried apples are folded in.

SOUR CREAM CAKES. The members of this dessert family are numerous, tender, and delicious. They are as distinctive to the region as the geometrical motifs, or hex marks, that decorate the big barns.

SPONGE CAKE. High, light as a feather, and tasty, too, these cakes bake lazily in earthen molds with a tube in the center.

WALNUT GINGERBREAD. Rich in brown sugar, molasses, and the spices, gingerbread becomes a new eating experience when you find black walnuts in it.

Cooky Baking on a Grand Scale

For the Christmas city, the Pennsylvania Dutch will settle for Bethlehem, Pennsylvania. Anyone who likes to make or eat wonderful cookies finds the Dutch kitchens of the community an inspiration. You want to shower the women with handfuls of blue ribbons when you gaze on their cookies with embellished tops and bite into the brittle, soft, or chewy sweetness. The Moravians, who founded Bethlehem on Christmas Eve, 1741, did not conceal their handwritten or memorized recipes in their kitchens. They shared them with other women in the region. With them added to the favorites of many other neighborhoods, the households in the southeastern section of the Keystone State early acquired a brilliant cooky repertoire.

While on a summer visit to Kutztown, in the heart of the Pennsylvania Dutch country, I stopped at the housewares' counter in a hardware store to look over the cooky cutters available. The salesman viewed me with an air of amazement, and then, recognizing me as a stranger, he explained, "Cooky cutters are seasonal. We bring them out in the autumn. If they do not sell by spring, we store them until fall." His statement added proof to the conclusion I previously had reached that cooky baking on the grand scale starts with thoughts of Christmas.

For the holidays, and to a lesser degree at other seasons, fancy-shaped cookies speak for the region. Some homes have treasured collections of old tin cutters, hand-me-downs from one generation to another. The cutters move into action on special occasions. They represent dolls, houses, eagles, sitting cats, dogs, fish, horses, men on horseback, birds, chickens, camels, stars, angels, bells, sheep, shepherds, Palm Sunday asses, St. Nicholas, and Christmas trees.

MORAVIAN WHITE COOKIES. For this treat, praised in most food conversations, Pennsylvania Dutch women make the dough extremely soft with powdered sugar, butter, eggs, and a little flour, and add nutmeg and sherry or brandy to flavor it. They chill the dough in the refrigerator; their grandmothers, if they had attempted to make the cooky in midsummer, would have placed it in the springhouse. The trick is to roll the dough as thin as paper, and to cut it in a variety of shapes. Among the traditional ones are angels, bells, stars, hearts, and diamonds. A fragile creation, guests handle it with care, and marvel that anyone can create such thin deliciousness.

MORAVIAN SCOTCH COOKIES. Tradition rules that the dough should be rolled very thin, and that they be cut in diamond shapes, and then baked. After they are cool their tops are covered with white frosting and sprinkled with pink sugar. This cooky has a taste of caraway seeds.

Slapjacks Deserve Wider Acceptance

LEMON FLAVORED COOKIES. A faint reminder of anise seed is detected in these treats. Almond and lemon-flavored cookies are dear to the hearts of many people.

SLAPJACKS. When these brown sugar-molasses cookies with black walnuts, and frequently with coconut, too, were described to me in Philadelphia by a home economics teacher of Pennsylvania Dutch descent, I resolved to make them. I never regretted keeping such a resolution. The wonder is that other sections of the nation know so little about this gem.

MOLASSES COOKIES. These faithful standbys are flavored by ginger and molasses. The thick, chewy ones with shiny tops are popular. The glaze, natives explain, comes from brushing on beaten egg before baking.

GINGERSNAPS. When dressed traditionally for special meals or occasions, they are frosted in white.

SUGAR COOKIES. The most distinguishing characteristic of these cookies shows in their thickness. Granulated sugar and cinnamon are sprinkled on them before baking.

APIES. With the Pennsylvania Dutch debating the correct way to spell its name, a food scout does not attempt to decide whether it should be *eepies, apeas, apees, A P's, apies,* or some other combination of letters. A Pennsylvania Dutch home economist who introduced them to me said she uses the *apies* spelling, and explained that some people thought the cooky originated in Philadelphia in the home of an Ann Page who impressed her initials on them. Regardless of its past or where it came from, this unspiced, vanilla-flavored sugar cooky almost always is included in the Christmas bakings. The dough is cut with some of the simpler cutters, like those that turn out stars, leaves, circles, and circles with scalloped edges. Natives pronounce the cooky's name with a strong accent on the first syllable.

SPICED TONGUES. These are shaped like small tongues, with the dough rolled in sugar and cinnamon before baking.

KISSES. Miniature meringues or kisses, crisp and satisfying, show up at parties. Chocolate, vanilla, and almond kisses are among the most tasty. Sometimes shellbarks or black walnuts are added. Some people call the hickory nut kisses *touch-me-nots,* a name which the guests, to their good fortune, are not obliged to take seriously.

Native black walnuts and hickory nuts (shellbarks) figure prominently in many delightful dishes. History records that the early immigrants made a special effort to select land on which walnut trees were growing, for to them these trees (like white stones with blue streaks) were a definite indication of a fertile soil.

SNICKER DOODLES. When hot from the oven these are highly delicious. Even the most impartial judge surrenders to them. Characteristically, you roll the balls of dough in sugar and cinnamon to coat them. In the oven they puff up and then flatten out somewhat, a process that gives them their crinkly tops.

CHOCOLATE COOKIES. They are as plentiful as the daffodils and lilacs of spring. Perhaps the most distinctive ones are the thin kind. Many of them are so delicate you wonder how they hold together. Most of them contain brown sugar.

Custards Are Dessert Giants, Too

Pies and cakes qualify as dessert giants, but they do not eclipse the region's smooth, luscious custards, which have an affinity for fruit out of pastry shells as well as in them. Many of them carry the taste of lemon juice and shredded orange or lemon peel. Have you ever tried fresh peach halves baked in lemon custard? And have you topped this favored Pennsylvania Dutch dish with almond-flavored whipped cream? Or have you tasted dried figs, softened by soaking in cold water, cut with scissors into slender strips, and baked in custard? Coffee, orange, and coconut custards, and tapioca puddings of the custard type, are so delicate and tasty that you forever associate them at their best with the region. One festive tapioca dessert contains apples first tinted red and flavored with cinnamon.

Plump apple dumplings appeal on a wide scale. Any doubt about their popularity disappears as you watch trays of them sell in a farm market. They are the large ones with flaky pastry jackets wrapped around whole apples cored and filled with sugar and spices and baked. In many households sweetened top milk is the favored sauce for the dessert.

Dumplings and more dumplings! They write a glowing chapter in the region's dessert story. Apple dumplings are both baked and steamed. Sweetened cherries or peaches, ripe and juicy, with dumplings steamed on top, and pitted, sugared cherries added to dumplings made with dry bread crumbs and steamed, typify other gastronomic specialties.

A Pennsylvania Dutchman has a sweet tooth. Statistics on the sales of ice cream and candy in the area show that both are consumed in immense quantities. Mid-Americans generally observe that the ice creams taste sweeter than those made in their home region.

Bethlehem, a Center for Sweets

Moravian candy mints qualify as the most historic confection. They continue to bloom, as they have for generations, in Bethlehem kitchens and on candy counters at the Christmas and Easter seasons, with the regularity that poinsettias and lilies blossom in greenhouses. Gay with color and refreshing with flavor, the candies have won their way across the country. White ones taste of peppermint, the yellow of lemon, the pink of wintergreen, and the green like gently bruised mint leaves from the garden.

Another Christmas treat with an almond flavor that lends a riot of color to candy trays is *marzipan,* an old-world confection introduced to the Keystone State in colonial days, possibly by settlers from Switzerland. For years this confection was turned out in home kitchens, and it was a painstaking chore. The candy is molded into the shapes of fruits and vegetables — like strawberries, apples, peaches, and potatoes — and tinted with vegetable colors until they become lifelike. It pleases both youngsters and oldsters. Nowadays commercial candy kitchens prepare almost all of the marzipan.

Molasses candies cause no surprise for the top cooks depend on molasses to flavor many of their finest dishes. Taffy is pulled in all of the counties; the kind that wins the widest acclaim contains black walnuts. Among the other holiday sweets are many nut brittles.

Popcorn cake appears in different versions, but most of them start out as a mixture of popped corn and nuts, with hot molasses or other sirup poured over them, as in making popcorn balls. Some cooks pour the sirup over the popped corn and nuts, mixed, and pound the mixture with a wooden mallet until it becomes hard. Then they break it in pieces. Others pour a layer of the popped corn and nuts mixed with hot sirup into a buttered pan and press it in firmly. Next they add a second layer, and force it down, too. They repeat the process until the pan is full. Then they slice the confection.

Those "7 Sweets and 7 Sours"

Once upon a time, so the true food story unwinds, all etiquette-conscious housewives endeavored to provide their dinner tables with exactly 7 sweet and 7 sour dishes. In these modern times that ambition has vanished, but the liking for appetizers lingers. Evidence of their popularity shows in the numerous jellies, jams, marmalades, and pickles that appear in meals, farm markets, and county fairs.

When you are a guest in some homes you sense a ripple of anticipation moving around the table ahead of the relish tray as it approaches, and a settling back to satisfaction after it has made the rounds. Name any jelly, jam, or marmalade you ever heard of and the chances are your hostess makes or knows it.

Among today's foremost sweets are apple butter, spiced cantaloupe, kimmel cherries, ginger pears, various spiced fruits, tomato preserves, and jams, jellies, and butters of many kinds and combinations of fruits.

To make the famed kimmel cherries, cover 8 cups of stoned fruit with 3 cups of vinegar and let them stand overnight. The next day drain them and add 8 cups of sugar. Place them in a deep bowl, cover them, and stir once a day for 9 days. Then seal them in sterilized jars.

Apple butter appears daily at mealtime in a high proportion of homes, as it has for generations. Most rural households prefer sweet apples to make it, although they also use the more tart varieties with additional sugar to counteract the acid. Natives pour the fruit, sugar, and spices into the cider and simmer the purple-black deliciousness slowly until it is thick, while stirring it almost constantly. Around this cookery rite developed one of the old-time social gatherings of the harvest season. The neighbors visited one another and took turns stirring the apple butter in the big kettles to keep it from scorching. Some farmers say they throw a piece of sassafras root into the boiling apple butter to provide a faint, exotic flavor touch.

The sours whet the appetite, give meals a lift. Cabbage-filled peppers, grape ketchup, pickled cabbage, chow chow, pepper hash or the Christmas relish of red and green peppers, corn salad, pickled beets, red beet eggs, mustard beans, pickled mushrooms, tomato ketchup, chili sauce, green tomato pickles, spiced pears, and pickled artichokes are near the head of the parade. Jerusalem artichokes thrive in the area, and when pickled the crunchy appetizer helps many women retain their cooking spurs.

Pickled Red Beets Lend a Special Appeal

Applesauce, cinnamon flavored, and pickled red beets lend their special appeal to relish trays. With schmier kase they compose a trio the years cannot dethrone. Most cooks prefer brown sugar for pickling beets, and some of them use spices. Among the countless additions to them you note uncooked onion rings, fresh grated horse-radish, chopped sweet peppers, and prepared mustard. Of the spices, perhaps mace with a touch of ginger commands the most enthusiastic following.

Red beet or pickled eggs capture regional relish honors. A cooked, sliced beet, or possibly two, is added to equal parts of beet juice and vinegar, delicately spiced, and heated to the boiling point. The shelled, hard-cooked eggs are dropped into the hot mixture; after cooling they are chilled a couple of days. By that time they are beautifully red with a sharp, zesty flavor.

The red eggs appear at the table — lengthwise chilled quarters of them — nestled among crisp celery hearts. A Dutch cook tucks rings of them in salads of lettuce and other greens as a tasty garnish, and inserts them in sandwiches. At informal buffet suppers you set out a pottery, wooden, or crystal bowl of gala eggs for your guests. The younger set proclaims them a perfect accompaniment to hamburger sandwiches. For the picnic they are a *must,* for who can imagine one in the Pennsylvania Dutch country without the pretty pickled eggs as part of the feast?

Salads Reflect a Seasonal Rhythm

The Pennsylvania Dutch salad drama has two acts. In the first the dressings perform. There are two classes of them, those made with sweet or sour cream, and the hot bacon-egg-vinegar ones. More characters come on the stage in the second act, the vegetables for the salad bowl. Dandelion leaves, lettuce, cabbage, endive, spinach, cucumbers, onions, and potatoes complete the cast.

If you are in southeastern Pennsylvania early in the spring or late in winter, you see men, women, and children carrying baskets and stooping over as if looking for something. That is exactly what they are doing. They are searching for and gathering the very young, tender dandelion greens before the plants bloom. These leaves are something of a tradition. On Maundy Thursday the Pennsylvania Dutch heed the ancient superstition of eating something green to insure good health for the remainder of the year. Dandelion salad answers as their favorite green for the Thursday of Holy Week, and indeed throughout its short season that follows.

Some visitors to the region are startled as the hot dressing goes over the crisp leaves, but that culinary custom is entrenched firmly, and is not likely to be abandoned. And why should it be? These salads are delightful. They surprise strangers to the area, for the hot dressing doused on the snappy leaves does not completely destroy their crispness. The seasonal salad consists of dandelions in early spring, followed in summer by lettuce, and later autumn's endive; spinach and cabbage bring cheer to winter's meals. Only in a few rural homes do turnip sprouts now put in a late winter appearance. In a manner suggestive of the bean sprouts of the Chinese, the first white sprouts on turnips stored during the winter formerly were served as a regional salad on a wide scale. Some older men speak of it in glowing terms.

Almost every kitchen considers its recipe for the hot salad dressing the superlative one. While they vary in detail, the end products are similar.

If you want to make the hot sauce, you usually start out by pan-frying 3 or 4 slices of bacon, diced, and then removing the little squares to a hot plate. Mix about ⅓ cup each of vinegar and water into the drippings. Then beat 2 eggs, after which you add ⅓ cup of water, 3 tablespoons of sugar, and a dash of salt to them. Pour the mixture into the frying pan containing the drippings, vinegar, and water, and cook the combination over low heat, while stirring constantly, until it thickens. Experienced hands turn out a sauce smooth as satin.

Pour it at once over the washed and drained leaves and "work them," as the natives say, to coat the leaves thoroughly. Then sprinkle on the bacon and usually a chopped hard-cooked egg. For dandelion greens, lettuce, endive, and spinach, this dressing generally rates tops in the region, and it also fares well on cabbage. A touch of prepared mustard frequently is added.

Holland Dutch Say It's Cole Slaw

Because some women insist the best hot dressing for dandelion greens contains cream or rich milk, this kind also warrants a mention. This is the way one of my hostesses, an outstanding cook, made it.

She slowly pan-fried 4 strips of bacon until they were crisp, removed them to a hot plate, and crushed them. Then to the drippings she added a mixture of ½ cup of cream, ¼ cup of vinegar, ¼ cup of sugar, 1 tablespoon of flour, and salt to season. While stirring constantly she brought the dressing to a boil. Then she poured it over the dandelion greens; they were garnished with the bacon crumbs and a chopped hard-cooked egg.

While sour cream dressing is regarded highly for serving with lettuce and cabbage, cucumbers accept no other.

In its simplest form, the Dutch mix 2 tablespoons each of sugar and white vinegar into ½ cup of sour cream (or sweet cream if no sour cream is available), and season it with salt and white pepper. Cooks often enhance it by folding in chopped green onions or chives. They also like to whip a beaten, uncooked egg into it when used on cabbage.

Cabbage salads are almost without end. The finely shredded vegetable wins both the hot and cream dressings. You find that most people use the Holland Dutch name, *cole slaw*. Celery is a distinctive feature of the cabbage salads and it shows up repeatedly as you travel about the area. Small amounts of finely cut celery are added. Noticeable, too, in discriminating households is the habit of salting the salad at the last minute to head off undue wilting.

Autumn Paints With Vivid Colors

Pepper cabbage, as the Pennsylvanians make it, requires no introduction to American epicures. They consider it a perfect companion for meat. Shreds of green pepper, or chopped bits of it, supply flavor and color. When autumn paints the countryside with her vivid colors, cooks meet the challenge and toss red, yellow, and green sweet peppers, chopped, into the cabbage salad. Frequently the only dressing they add consists of vinegar and sugar, mixed, in the amounts they desire. Other occasional additions to cabbage salads consist of celery seed, minced onion, sliced or chopped hard-cooked eggs, and cubes of well-drained canned pineapple.

Potato salads hold their own through the years. While they are of all descriptions, the German type, or the heated one with bacon dressing, captures the spotlight in menus. Cartons of it in farm markets seem to melt away as the customers file down the aisles. As one career girl explained her purchase, "It is easy to dump the salad into the top of a double boiler to heat while you set the table and assemble the remainder of the supper. It's no trouble to fix potato salad this way!"

Fish Are Not Farm Food

With no outlet to the ocean, except through Philadelphia, settlers in colonial days found sea food not readily available. That largely explains why the cuisine of the Pennsylvania Dutch, in contrast to those of New England and the Colonial States of the South, developed without an extensive utilization of fish or sea food. Shad and oysters from the Delaware River were in favor from the start in the eastern counties, but no great original dishes evolved from them. Oyster stew registers as a favorite soup.

Schmeir Kase Sells Readily

Like other people of German, Swiss, and Alsatian origins, these Pennsylvanians like cheese. Rural kitchens continue to manufacture the native types, all of which are composed of the curd of skimmed milk. Practically all stalls in the farm markets offer *schmier kase,* or cottage cheese. Some bowls contain the fluffy dry kind to which the customer adds cream. Other containers hold mounds of cheese with cream added and beaten in an electric mixer until they resemble shortening whipped until light for cake making. Before the schmier kase goes to the table in some households the cooks pour on enough cream to float a film of richness.

The perfect snack of the region consists of bread slices — like homemade rye bread — spread with schmier kase, and then lathered with apple butter. Instead of the apple butter some people prefer molasses or thick red raspberry, strawberry, or cherry preserves. Occasionally caraway seeds are added to cottage cheese. There also are other combinations. One woman in Kutztown remarked, "We like cranberry sauce with schmier kase."

Cup cheese journeys to market from farm kitchens in large amounts, as it has been doing for more than a century. It is transported in white cups without handles but the cups are emptied when the cheese is purchased. Farmers carry them home to use again. Cup cheese is made of sour milk curd, salted, and stored in a crock about 7 days. Then it is melted over heat and butter, cream, egg, and soda are incorporated. When the mixture comes to a boil it is poured into the cups. Some persons call this product *pot cheese*.

Naturally the quality varies from kitchen to kitchen. To some natives Berks County cup cheese denotes a superior product, but there are excellent examples of it in every county. At its best, it is free of lumps and soft. To Americans who have traveled in Europe it at least suggests the gruyere cheese of France. When paired off with Reading pretzels it is a memorable snack.

Ball cheese is not so soft. After it has dried about a week, $2\frac{1}{2}$- to 3-inch spheres of it are wrapped in cheesecloth or paper and stored several weeks in earthen jars to ripen. Sometimes it is called summer cheese, and you may encounter it in June, but later it becomes too aggressive for universal enjoyment.

Except in pies and cakes, cheese almost never serves as an ingredient in dishes. People consume large quantities of it with their beloved pretzels. Schmier kase makes almost standard supper fare, with applesauce dusted heavily with cinnamon at its side.

Soups Are "Rich or Poor"

Pennsylvania Dutch soups may not bask in fame's spotlight as do the contents of French kettles, but they deserve special recognition. Of a sturdy nature, they almost always make a meal, and especially supper. The garnishes that decorate them intrigue visitors from other areas. Minced parsley and chopped hard-cooked eggs furnish their colors, and countless women possess a gift in making rivels, noodles, dumplings, and soup balls.

Rivels designate the region. To make them, the cook rubs flour and beaten egg, salted, between her fingers, or cuts it with two forks, to mix. She commonly drops these flakes of dough about the size of a cherry stone from her fingers or knife into the soup, although some experts rub the dough through a colander. The secret to success is to simmer rivels just long enough to cook the flour in them, from 3 to 5 minutes. Their texture should be like that of boiled rice. If overcooked they lose their shape and spread through the soup.

Noodles are extremely popular. They are not always the thin, slender kind, or the Hungarian variety; sometimes they are somewhat thicker and broader.

Butter balls, as their name implies, contain butter. Butter is mixed with flour and seasoned with salt. The wee spheres are shaped with floured fingers and then steamed about 5 minutes in soups, especially the beef-vegetable soups.

Soup dumplings also are tiny. The soft dough contains an egg.

Almond balls enhance soups, too. They are placed in the tureen or bowl and the hot liquid poured over them. The balls are made by mixing chopped blanched almonds with bread crumbs, and beaten egg white binds them. The small balls are browned quickly in a frying pan and served hot. They are at the summit of perfection, natives explain, with clear soups, and especially those made of chicken.

Soups are divided into two great families, the rich and the poor (or poverty). Historically the poor ones came first. Most of them have a milk base that could be provided easily at almost any time in a farm kitchen. Doubtless they functioned in colonial days as a great mainstay against hunger. The liking for them lingers.

Rivel Soup Has Friends and Foes!

BROWN POTATO SOUP. Almost everyone tosses word bouquets when this soup is mentioned. The pleasing flavor derives from the careful browning of flour in butter or shortening without scorching the fat. You cook the diced potatoes in a little salted water until tender, add milk, and heat the mixture. Then you stir in the flour browned in fat. Either minced parsley or chopped hard-cooked egg supplies the garnish.

FRESH CORN SOUP. This full-fledged sister of brown potato soup starts out as corn scraped from the cob into hot milk. The rule is to simmer the mixture briefly and to add flour, mixed with milk, to thicken it. Butter and salt provide the seasoning. Rivels may be included. Especially does this soup answer as a first-class treat when accompanied by sliced tomatoes fresh from the garden.

RIVEL SOUP. This is a poor soup with a host of ardent friends. To make it you heat milk and cook rivels in it. The reactions of people to this creation rarely are mild. Those who do not like it insist that those who do base their affections for it on nostalgic memories. In some kitchens chicken stock substitutes for the milk.

PRETZEL SOUP. This can be made in a jiffy, which may explain some of its popularity and general use, especially as a refreshment on cold winter evenings. Hot milk with plenty of butter added is poured over Reading pretzels broken into bowls.

POPCORN SOUP. In this number popped corn substitutes for the pretzels in pretzel soup.

YELLOW TOMATO SOUP. This delicacy resembles the more familiar cream of tomato soup of other regions. Yellow rather than red tomatoes are used.

At Picnics on Summer Evenings

Rich soups started to bubble and sing in the region's kettles when they could be afforded, or after the land was cleared and the soil gave generously of its bounty. Some of the favorites of today belong to this family.

CHICKEN-CORN SOUP. This number is associated with Sunday School picnics on long summer evenings in the corn season, and it spells deliciousness. You simmer the chicken softly in water until you can take the meat from the bones, which are discarded. Then you cut the meat in small pieces, return it to the broth, and add minced onion, celery, and celery leaves. About 10 minutes before you wish to serve the soup you add minced parsley and corn cut from the cobs. Noodles or rivels frequently are incorporated in this one. Chopped hard-cooked eggs furnish the traditional decoration.

PEPPER POT SOUP. Many epicures select this potpourri as the greatest soup of the region. Especially does it score success with the men. Most women enjoy it, too, although some of them find it too peppery. There are several varieties of pepper pots. One of the great regional favorites includes the knuckle of veal, tripe, potatoes, and onions along with various herbs, and black, red, and cayenne peppers for seasoning. This kind can be bought in cans; many homemakers use it as a seasoning ingredient in their cooking campaigns. Some pepper pots are made with beef. One of them contains bits of green pepper. And all of them frequently wear dumplings no larger than walnuts. Occasionally noodles take the dumplings' role for a pleasing change.

DUTCH BEAN SOUP. Here is another rich soup, and one to awaken memories, say the natives, who long for it when they are far from the region. To them it brings thoughts of home and childhood and meals mother used to cook. In making it, they simmer a ham bone and navy beans with chopped onion, celery, and celery tops. Wisps of parsley commonly float in it. In the springtime they serve succulent small green onions, recently pulled from the moist earth and washed, as an accompaniment.

This is the classic Amish preaching soup, so named because it frequently is served by the House Amish, who meet for religious services in their homes rather than in churches. With the traditional 7 sweets and 7 sours, homemade bread, and freshly churned butter, Dutch bean soup for generations has constituted a favored Sunday dinner between preachings. Noodles and rivels frequently cook in it, and occasionally the sly flavor of cloves can be detected.

The Pennsylvania Dutch cordially welcome meat three times daily. This in itself does not set them apart from other Americans, but some of their unique dishes clearly distinguish the cuisine from those in other regions. At least four of them qualify for the honor role. *Ponhaus, potpies, Dutch goose,* and *schnitz un knepp* represent the area as faithfully as the mammoth barns that dot the landscape.

Ponhaus Has Traveled Far

Scrapple, or *ponhaus* in colloquial language, perhaps has traveled away from home with greater success than the others. Many of the natives applaud it as their superlative creation. Originally it was a product of winter butchering on farms. Now you see it in local meat markets, and in cans on the shelves of grocery stores. Many women make it in their kitchens. Today's versions differ somewhat from those of a century ago.

Properly defined, the foundation of scrapple consists of the pork scraps available when animals are slaughtered on a farm or in a packing plant. The scraps are simmered until tender in water in which liver pudding has been cooked and to which the liver is returned after being ground. Then corn-meal and buckwheat flour, (usually 1 part of meal to 2 parts of flour) are dribbled into the kettle to make a thick mush. Constant stirring is important at first, and then only occasionally, until the mixture is ready to pour into loaf bread pans. Seasonings are added during cooking. Salt and pepper generally suffice, although some splendid cooks add a bit of sage — possibly only one or two crushed leaves.

The scrapple is chilled, unmolded, sliced in ¼-inch slices, and pan-fried to brown.

Naturally there are many variations of the dish. Some natives make the mush entirely of corn meal or oatmeal. Others use corn-meal and whole-wheat flour, but the favorite combination is the corn meal-buckwheat one. Many women say scrapple splatters less if it contains buckwheat.

In city kitchens where meat must be purchased, cooks commonly simmer pork or beef liver in water a few minutes; then they chop, and return it to the broth with bits of pork. They simmer the mixture until the meat is very tender and then gradually stir in the corn meal and buckwheat flour. Some persons do not relish the flavor of liver. They make scrapple, or a reasonable facsimile of it, with pork.

Often strangers confuse ponhaus with pot pudding, another distinctive dish favored by various famous sons of the area.

For pot pudding you cook the cleaned hearts, tongues, heads, and scraps of pork (beef, too, if available) in water until the meat separates from the bones. Then you skim off the fat, discard the bones, put the meat through the coarse blade of a food chopper, and add it to the broth with seasonings of salt, pepper, and thyme or sage. You continue to cook it until the mixture has the consistency of scrapple. Then you pack it in jars, pour fat over the top, and set it in a cold place until you wish to use it.

"Hog's Maw" Commands Prestige

Potpies cook on the range — literally they are pies in a pot.

You first simmer the meat or chicken in water with seasonings until tender. Then you cut it fine and discard the bones. Next you alternate ¼-inch slices of raw potatoes and onions, 1½-inch squares or tiny dumplings of potpie dough, and the cut-up meat or chicken in a fairly small kettle, while adding seasonings of salt, pepper, and often minced parsley between the layers. Noodle squares or wee dumplings cover the top. You pour on the piping hot chicken or meat broth, at least 2 cups of it. Then you cover the kettle and cook its contents about 20 minutes. The dough, a cross between that for noodles and biscuits, usually is rolled thin like noodles, cut in squares, and dried slightly before use. Some women prefer to make a dough of soft dumpling consistency and to drop bits of it from the tip of a small spoon.

Speck (ham) and beans also are a regional meat and potato favorite.

To make the dish, natives cook 2 or 3 pounds of speck in water to cover until almost tender. They add 2 pounds of green beans cut as desired, and more water if needed. After simmering 20 minutes they add 6 medium potatoes, quartered. When they are tender the hearty dish is ready to serve.

Carried high on the platter, Dutch goose, or stuffed "hog's maw," commands the prestige it has enjoyed for generations.

To prepare the winter favorite you thoroughly clean a pig's stomach and soak it in salted water. Then you stuff it with your choice of various mixtures: one composed of diced potatoes, onions, and sausage or spareribs, and seasoned with salt, pepper, and parsley maintains a wide acceptance. Sew up the opening in the stomach and cook it gently in water to cover about 2 hours. Many women first wrap it tightly in cheesecloth as an aid in retaining its shape. When it is tender, they lift the heartiness from the kettle, and put it in a roaster to brown in butter, with frequent bastings.

Sweet Apples, a Regional Treat

Schnitz un knepp (dried apples and dumplings) challenges *ponhaus* for top ranking. The combination classifies as a meat dish because the fruit and dumplings commonly team with ham. The apples are of the sweet varieties that contain little acid. To aid in reducing disintegration in cooking, the Pennsylvania Dutch do not pare the fruit before drying it. Usually they cut the cored apple in eighths.

They soak the fruit overnight in cold water to cover. In the morning they simmer a ham bone in water about 2 hours. Then they add the apples and the water in which they soaked and 2 tablespoons of brown sugar. After gently cooking the mixture another hour, they drop in the soft dumplings, cover the kettle, and continue the simmering about 25 minutes. They serve the ham in the center of the platter and arrange the schnitz un knepp around it.

Now that hams do not hang in smokehouses in every backyard, modified editions of the classic evolve. One of my hostesses used a slice of country ham. First she cooked the schnitz in water and added the brown sugar. Then she pan-fried the meat and spread the apples on it. She dropped the soft dumplings on top, covered the frying pan, and simmered the contents until the dumplings were steamed. Smoked pork sausages occasionally substitute for ham.

No consideration of the region's meaty fare can afford to omit a tribute to a native beef sausage named for Lebanon County, its birthplace. This sausage is seasoned highly, and is about 5 inches in diameter. It generally is available in the markets throughout the area.

Mummix and *hexel* are words in the food vocabularies of the Pennsylvania Dutch women. When asked what they mean, some of them say, "Hash." Others think a second or two and respond, "Leftovers." Two characteristics of their hash are distinctive. Frequently they bake the chopped meat and onions blended with mashed potatoes with milk added. The slightly sharp taste noted at some tables is due to the addition of a dash of vinegar.

The goodness of roast pork impresses a visitor. The cooks have a habit of rubbing the surface with salt, pepper, and a trace of ginger. They put it in the refrigerator for a few hours before roasting it. Just before they tuck it in the oven, some women pat on a tablespoon of brown sugar. Potatoes frequently bake in the pan around the pork, and applesauce, dusted with cinnamon, comes on as a favored accompaniment.

Ham on a Frosty Evening

The Dutch prepare and like the meat dishes familiar to all Americans, but they are especially proficient in giving pork a different twist. You marvel that the ham they cook is totally unlike that served next door in Virginia.

One frosty evening my hostess gave a slice of ham the position of honor in the supper she prepared quickly and easily. She attractively browned it by pan-broiling, and then lifted it to a hot platter. In the drippings she pan-fried sliced onions. When they were tender and delicately browned, she stirred in a cup of sour cream. And presto! She had a delightful gravy for the cooked noodles yellow with egg. I well recall every dish in the menu, which certainly suggests how delicious and memorable it was.

PENNSYLVANIA DUTCH DINNER
Ham with Onion Gravy
Noodles   Buttered Corn
Endive Salad
Apple Crumb Pie
Coffee

Chicken, geese, and duck share honors most of the time, but turkey becomes king on Thanksgiving Day.

Please Pass the Potato Filling

The Pennsylvania Dutch refer to the dressings they stuff into turkey, chicken, and other poultry as fillings. For the most part they feature bread or potatoes, and rarely, if ever, corn bread or rice. Potato filling leads in popularity in most households. You taste it wherever you travel in the area. It fills meat pockets, as well as poultry, and also bakes in casseroles to accompany meat.

Every kitchen cherishes a special recipe for this unique dressing. Crumbs or cubes of bread and chopped onions are lightly browned in a little fat and stirred into mashed potatoes along with minced celery and parsley, salt, and pepper. In many households a pinch of poultry seasoning goes into the filling.

A quite different and less used potato filling omits the bread. Beaten eggs, melted butter or meat drippings, minced parsley, and finely chopped celery and onions are folded into the fluffy spuds.

Among other popular stuffings are chestnut and oyster with bread for the base. The Pennsylvania Dutch consume more chestnuts than any other nationality group in the United States. The chestnut has been important in their meals since these people settled in the Keystone State. The use of this nut has been reduced by the blight that has destroyed many trees. For instance, chestnut soup is now rare; but if you ever do bend over it you face a sublime feast. It is so rich and satisfying that it makes a meal unforgettable.

Other food observations of the region call attention to spiced pot roasts, souse or pickled pigs' feet, gravy with a sharp flavor due to the addition of bread crumbs moistened with vinegar, and stewed chicken on a platter bordered by halves of hot biscuits with gravy doused over all. *Hasenpfeffer* comes into its own here.

The Garden Patch Thrives

Take off your hats to the region's gardeners! They have green thumbs, and they exercise them. So long as the vegetable patches spread like bright patterned handkerchiefs about the countryside the farm markets will gleam with their freshly gathered and thoroughly washed products. A characteristic of many gardens is the way flowers and vegetables mingle side by side.

These Americans once segregated vegetables into two groups, the Sunday and everyday kinds, and they still favor the Sunday or elite ones, although the classification no longer holds. Actually the Sunday vegetables never were served only on the first day of the week, but the name complimented them.

Among the Sunday garden gifts are asparagus, corn, dried corn, endive, celery, lettuce, peas, sweet and white potatoes, onions, and lima beans. Everyday vegetables include turnips, beets, green and yellow beans, carrots, eggplant, and tomatoes.

Dried corn continues to maintain a top place in the scale of regional favor. In summer, when corn is in season, a rural housewife dries a supply of it for the winter use of her family, and often to sell in the local markets. Its superior flavor depends primarily on cooking the ears quickly after pulling them from the stalks, and then drying the cut off kernels in sunshine or artificial heat.

A keen demand for the dried cereal springs up in late autumn, and no adequate substitute for it in the Thanksgiving dinner has been discovered. Most people soak it overnight in lukewarm water and then simmer it slowly about an hour, with pot watching to see that it does not scorch. Their aim is to evaporate all of the water as the corn simmers. Salt, butter, cream, and pepper qualify for seasonings.

Considerable commercially dried corn appears in southeastern Pennsylvania. The packages carry directions for preparing it. As to flavor, if you are obliged to describe it to the unlucky uninitiated, perhaps stressing how the taste resembles that of parched corn is the best way out. Many natives believe a chicken or turkey dinner is incomplete without it.

Fresh corn pies command esteem, as do chicken-corn pies. In the former, milk supplies the moisture for the corn baked between two pastry crusts. Chicken stock assumes the liquid role in the fresh corn-chicken ones.

Have a Piece of Onion Pie

I doubt if any other vegetable pie receives the current honors given onion pie. Many women prefer to make it with thinly sliced green onions. They season the vegetable rings with salt and pepper, put them in a pastry-lined pan, strip the top with bacon, and then bake their favorite. There also are other versions, including onion-custard pie. Vegetable pies and dumplings steamed atop vegetables greet you at mealtime in many homes.

While pan-fried eggplant slices are no different from those in other areas, the Pennsylvanians frequently serve them with ketchup or chili sauce, or with applesauce.

Jerusalem artichokes and English pod peas, which many natives refer to as sugar peas, are eaten in larger per capita amounts in the region than in any other section of America. Pickled artichokes, previously mentioned, and peas simmered in their pods with water barely to cover win countless ovations in food talk. Culinary artists cook only the young, succulent peas, without shelling them. Some drain and dress them when tender with butter and salt, while others prefer sour cream to butter. When tiny new potatoes are half cooked, the Pennsylvania Dutch like to add shelled sugar peas to them. Most women dress the early summer garden medley with butter and cream. My husband's grandmother (and at least one of her granddaughters follows in her footsteps) went to the garden with a fork to rob potato hills of a few tubers, the size of marbles, to team with the first mess of sugar peas.

Parsnip fritters never go out of style. The cook takes this humble root, and cooks, peels, and mashes it. Then she stirs in eggs, milk, flour, salt, and a trace of sugar. She drops spoonfuls of the mixture into a frying pan that contains hot fat and browns them on both sides.

Creamed cabbage on the menu designates the fine shreds boiled briefly in salted water, drained, and dressed with cream and butter. When women say they *cream* vegetables they refer to their way of adding cream or top milk, butter, and seasonings, but no flour.

Panned red cabbage responds to a roll call of favorites. Almost always the colorful vegetable carries a faint taste of vinegar, and frequently a more subtle one of cloves.

A favorite seasoning for vegetables consists of flour browned in butter, with care not to let the butter scorch.

Sauerkraut eaten on New Year's Day brings prosperity throughout the months ahead, according to an old superstition many Pennsylvania Dutch people heed. Perhaps they like to have an extra excuse for eating their great favorite, which was introduced by them to this continent. Dumplings frequently steam on the sauerkraut; caraway seeds and potatoes are often cooked in it. For special occasions pork simmered until tender in a small amount of water, drained, and browned in a little fat, goes into the shallow pan. Then it is sprinkled with a dash of brown sugar, covered with sauerkraut, and the dish baked to heat thoroughly. This recipe I inveigled from my hostess, who served the pork in the center of an oven-proof platter, wreathed first with sauerkraut, and then with a circle of mashed potatoes. She ran it under the broiler to delicately brown the tips of the fluffy spuds.

Westward in Conestoga Wagons

Snitzel beans, or green beans cut fine, suggest a traditional triumph. You leisurely cook the vegetable with a little ham or bacon, tomatoes, and onions. Vinegar is the favorite accompaniment.

Potatoes stand in a class by themselves. The Pennsylvania Dutch cook deserves a brilliant place in the history of great

American dishes for her successes with the humble tuber. She uses it in dumplings, breads, fillings (stuffings), soups, cakes, pies, griddlecakes, doughnuts, and salads. Leftover boiled potatoes she elevates to a high plane of deliciousness. She slices them carefully, browns them in a little fat, and then adds either sweet or sour cream. In the slow cookery that ensues the vegetable absorbs the cream.

Mashed potatoes occasionally reflect the green of parsley; some cooks whip beaten egg into them to enrich the color and flavor, and then bake the dish. They also sometimes mix mashed carrots with them.

People who adore raw potatoes fried, and that means almost all Westerners, owe gratitude to the Pennsylvania Dutch for their way of preparing the dish. They slice the peeled spuds so thinly you can see the blade of a knife through them, and then pan-fry them to cook and brown them. Favorite seasonings include salt, pepper, celery seed, and minced parsley. When bacon drippings supply the cooking fat, many women fold in crisp cubes of bacon just before serving.

Southeastern Pennsylvanians introduced their fried potatoes to every state. I have no doubt the fondness for them traveled westward in those sturdy Conestoga covered wagons the Dutch designed and built in what is now Lancaster County, near the Conestoga River.

Like the cuisines of New England and the South, that of the Pennsylvania Dutch country influences the meals of the entire nation. The first two had their roots in the British Isles, while the Pennsylvania Dutch one evolved mainly from the Valley of the Rhine.

The South

T HE ROYAL ROAD to food adventure leads to southern
kitchens. On gastronomical tours of the South you
walk through the corridors of history and salute the past as
you observe and enjoy the present. This American pageant
started before Columbus sailed across the Atlantic Ocean.
When the first European explorers arrived they journeyed
wide-eyed through a supremely beautiful and astonishingly
productive region. Among the Indians they met competent
cooks, proud to share their food treats and culinary secrets.

Settlers followed from England and Scotland, and in

lesser numbers from other European nations. Through the years they prospered. Plantations with fertile acres and spacious homes spread over the countryside. Their reputation for fine food, gracious living, and unstinted hospitality extended in all directions. It kindled competition in the mixing bowls around open fireplaces. The cooks in one kitchen vied with others in the neighborhood, county, state, and all the Southland to create something superlative.

Before the War Between the States the art of southern cooking flowered. With abundant farm products — like poultry, eggs, pork, milk, cream, sugar, molasses, wheat, corn, hominy, rice, fruits, berries, and vegetables — provisions gave no concern. Game and fish provided a sportsmen's paradise, and southern gentlemen liked to hunt and fish. Plentiful labor with no outlet for industrial employment contributed brawn and talent to the kitchen scene.

How Southern Cooking Was Born

An unlimited supply of food and labor linked with prosperity explains how the fabulous cuisine was born, and offers a clue to its survival in the lean years during and following the war. The people, poverty stricken, valued their ability to set a marvelous table. They combined this skill with a spirit to uphold their standards. In catering to a forlorn budget, inexpensive dishes from humble pioneer and slave homes moved into mansions. Some of them, lovingly prepared by faithful cooks, tasted so wonderful they became classics to extol the virtues of simple fare and multiply the epicurean glories of the region. Among these are greens with "pot likker" and corn pone, black-eye peas along with tomatoes, and a whole garden of vegetables in the soup kettle, with corn bread in the oven timed to come out when the ladle reaches the steaming broth.

From luxury to poverty and on up again the southern food drama unwinds, as an agricultural area gradually merges into an industrial empire. Time and kitchen help now are at a premium. Food supplies reach many market channels and command high prices. Yet you need not put on rose-colored glasses to find excellent meals or to view the luster which the past sheds over home tables.

In this afterglow you are reminded that the early cooks who set the pace were trained largely by women of Anglo-Saxon descent. They took treasured European recipes and adapted them to the remarkably different locally grown foods. They served their meals, planned for leisurely eating, in magnificent style.

A Galaxy of Great Dishes

Some of the more fabled masterpieces which once appeared in daily meals, now come forth on special occasions, as for discriminating guests, weddings, and holidays. Hospitality, excellent food, and attractive service continue. Many families possess exquisite heirloom silver. This they use as their ancestors did.

As a magazine reporter who attempted to explore the best home cooking in the South, I felt helpless, like a child whose parents ask her to count the stars on a clear summer night. Added to the magnitude of the task I faced complications due to unfamiliarity with many of the delicacies. From my first pilgrimage in the region throughout the many that followed, I adored the tasty meals, and the friendliness, helpfulness, and charm of countless natives interested in my gastronomic tours.

I make no claim that my descriptions include all or half of the noble culinary creations. In one chapter I can merely skim the cream of the delicacies I sampled.

The South is an expansive country. It includes four Colonial States — Virginia, North Carolina, South Carolina, and Georgia — along wth seven neighbors who joined them in the Confederacy: Florida, Alabama, Tennessee, Mississippi, Arkansas, Louisiana, and Texas. It embraces the border states of Maryland, possibly Delaware (with foods), Kentucky, Missouri, and youthful Oklahoma. Southern ways with cooking reach into some kitchens of that onetime part of the Old Dominion, West Virginia. (Taste treats of the South also appear in two subsequent chapters. One deals with those of the Atlantic Coast, or seaboard cooking. Another presents the gems of kitchens along the Gulf Coast, or creole cooking.)

Old southern food customs become collector's items to a roving reporter. Here are just a few of the treasures.

It's an Old Southern Custom

Christmas and New Year's with their "at homes" or open houses call for exotic food and drink. At Yuletide, punch bowls offer eggnog splashed with nutmeg. Silver trays display sliced fruit and pound cakes; bowls of nuts and candy flank them. At wedding parties are zephyr-like layer cakes, almost too pretty to eat, but too inviting to forego.

Some kitchens cherish two sets of recipes for a dish — one for company, usually richer and tastier, and the other for everyday use. Families prize the well-thumbed pages of old ledgers with "receipts" written in fine Spencerian, handed down from one generation to the next.

Beaten biscuits team with thin slices of old country ham for immortal sandwiches.

Thin horseshoe slices of country ham, the dark red lean meat laced with flecks of white, and framed with amber-hued fat, grace the holiday buffet, often accompanied by the sliced breast of roast turkey.

Steaming hot oyster stew comes to many breakfast tables on December 25th with golden dabs of butter melting in its depths.

Oyster pie frequently supports roast turkey.

Ambrosia, the golden dessert of peeled orange segments tossed with grated fresh coconut, appears at Christmas as regularly as decorations of pine boughs and candles, and carol singers at the door. Occasionally it glistens in all its splendor on the buffet table, heaped in one of those great and gorgeous old glass bowls designed for it, a family heirloom or a lucky find in an antique shop.

Platters in Kentucky piled high with crisp coated, golden brown pieces of fried chicken sometimes make room for chicken biscuits. Cream gravy, piping hot, tags along in their wake.

Fried cream, a few people whisper, ranks as a perfect accompaniment to broiled chicken.

Batter or spoon breads, high, handsome, and hot, hurry from the oven to connect with butter and to escort platters of chicken to dinner.

All Dixie boasts of corn pudding, the young tender white kernels of field corn cut very thin and then scraped from the cobs and suspended during baking in a fragile custard like a dream on the tip of a cloud.

Black Walnuts From the Great Smokies

Shimmering molds of cranberry salad in the Great Smoky Mountains of North Carolina carry the taste of black walnuts. In the farm market at Knoxville, Tennessee, little paper bags of shelled hickory nuts change hands readily, and later they find their way into old-fashioned pound cakes.

Sweet potato dishes come from ovens, candied or creamed (mashed), scented with the fragrance of oranges, lemons, spices, and bourbon or wine. You meet sweet potato biscuits, waffles, pies, and puddings.

The array of southern puddings suggests an English setting; some of the leaders are tipsy squire, plum, Bishop Whipple's, and Woodford puddings, and President Tyler's pudding pie.

Chess pies and tarts, rich and tasty, rival the most luscious French pastries in both delicacy and flavor.

Transparent pies are popular, as are their cousins, jelly and sugar pies. There is a whole family of cream (custard) pies, among them the Jeff Davis.

Nashville celebrates Christmas holidays with thin triangles of spiced beef round on her platters; it is as traditional in this Tennessee city as the iris that bloom or the steeplechase that comes up in the spring.

In the Kentucky bluegrass region cream pull candy originated. If it touches the tongue it melts into unforgettable deliciousness. Throughout the horse country, a visitor to home kitchens occasionally sees hooks on which to pull the candy.

Syllabub froths in churns, and then in tall glasses. And chilled "boiled" custard, or soft custard, is smooth as velvet. With pound, coconut, or fruit cake at its side, it suggests that it's time to listen for Santa Claus in the chimney.

Peach pickle maintains a certain supremacy among the relish clan; watermelon rind pickles also have excellent popularity ratings.

Layer cakes are out of this world. On the buffet their light-hearted slices decorate silver waiters; their fillings are lush with nuts, coconut, raisins, figs, candied pineapple and cherries, crystallized lemon and orange peels, or other goodies. Jam cakes, slyly spiced, flaunt thick, creamy caramel frosting.

Salt Roe Herring Is a Breakfast Dish

Fried apples give breakfast a boost, especially with country ham or sausage alongside. And in Virginia and North Carolina many people enthuse over pan-fried salt roe herring and herring roe in the day's first meal.

Arkansas champions the taste and pink blush of hot and iced sassafras tea, persimmon cake, a score of apple puddings, and huckleberry cobblers, the kind to which mountain women give their touch of genius.

Lacy edged batter cakes (corn meal), hot off the griddle, meet butter and cane sirup at the altar, the dining room table.

That country special turkey hash is the kind swanky New York restaurants strive so painstakingly and unsuccessfully to copy.

A procession of vegetable dishes wins bouquets. Included are those made with eggplant, corn in tomato cases, fried corn, boiled corn, gumbo or okra-tomato combinations, snap beans, butter beans, black-eye peas, English peas, cymblings, collards, and turnip tops.

Mint juleps frost the glasses.

The picnic frequently is a fish fry with hush puppies.

Drive-ins serve a barbecued pork or chicken sandwich with cole slaw, a wee paper cup of fiery sauce, and a cola or a cup of coffee.

Kentucky prizes its picnic stew, Burgoo, and Maytime Derby breakfasts at 10:30 a.m. Georgia, Virginia, and the Carolinas express a fondness for Brunswick stew, but Alabama prefers her camp meeting special.

Hostesses pass small, brown coated biscuits or corn muffins, hot enough to burn your fingers, but oh! so good with butter melting on them.

Such are a few nominations for representatives of southern foods in the Hall of Fame. They testify for country cooking, or the goodness of the fat of the land when it falls into the hands of culinary artists. Among the entries you will recognize many old-time delights of which countless adaptations and versions appear repeatedly in the nation's commercial test kitchens, in home ovens and saucepans, and in the packages and cans of jiffy-quick products that fill the up-to-date supermarkets.

Hot Breads — A Southern Wonder

If your southern hostess offers you cold bread, you may wish to pack your suitcase soon and bid her a fond farewell. An old custom in many households is to serve only the hot breads to guests. Indeed, many a wife and mother believes she "neglects" her family if she provides slices of cold "light bread" for dinner.

Beaten biscuits make an exception to the rule. They are served cold. An invitation to share these favorites is a compliment. Gone from home kitchens is the thump, thump, thump of mammy beating the dough. Factories now turn out and package the historic bread. Some few women, usually in the grandmother group, treasure their skill in making the classic. They display it on special occasions. I prize memories of the delightful beaten biscuits a lady in Sardis, Mississippi, made for me and brought to the scrumptious "Befo' the Wah" breakfast given in my honor.

You Beat or Grind the Biscuits

Because beaten biscuits rate as an unsurpassable American original, they deserve more than a passing salute. Recipes varied from kitchen to kitchen, but all of them had common characteristics. Here is the way my Mississippi friend describes how to make them.

Place the very stiff dough, composed of flour, a trace of sugar, salt, shortening, and sweet milk or icy water, on a wooden meat block and beat it with a rolling pin. The trick is to beat the dough with something until it blisters and becomes smooth as satin. Then roll it a little less than ½ inch thick, cut it in tiny rounds, and prick every circle with the tines of a fork. Old-time kitchens valued cutters with stickers in the center.

For the hand beaten method, Mammy allowed 100 strokes to beat everyday biscuits, and from 150 to 200 when guests were expected. Hammers, axes, heels of sad irons, and other tools have been substituted successfully for the rolling pin.

Bake the biscuits on a cooky sheet in a medium oven, about 350°, 25 to 40 minutes. This slow cooking, in comparison to that for other biscuits, gives them their characteristic texture and light brown color. They never are a deep or golden brown. As previously mentioned, beaten biscuits and ham pair off for memorable sandwiches. They also excel as an accompaniment to cream soups. And at parties they frequently show up with chicken salad.

A few homes still have beaten biscuit machines. The device consists of a marble slab or a wooden box with a double roller and a handle to turn. The dough is put through the rollers many times, or until it blisters and becomes smooth.

Take Two and Butter Them

Southern biscuits and northern biscuits are quite different. The authentic southern one, small in circumference, and thin, has a somewhat flaky brown crust that conceals the light, smooth interior. The tradition is to help yourself to two at the first passing. The biscuits are almost too hot to handle. Southerners immediately break them open, tuck butter into their hearts, and put them together again.

In many households self-rising flour (soft wheat flour with leavening and salt added) is used. Other good cooks use soft wheat flours, milled by southern companies, or those especially prepared for the area's kitchens by organizations that distribute their brands nationally. They add the salt and leavening agent. Milk, sweet or sour, or buttermilk answers for the liquid, with buttermilk the A-1 selection. Throughout the South people like the taste buttermilk gives baked foods. They say it makes for flakier, more tender products. They prefer churned buttermilk, and many homes have standing orders with nearby farmers for the delivery of a gallon of it weekly. Cultured buttermilk is more generally available. If too thick, it is diluted with a little water; if too sweet, a trace of vinegar is stirred in.

Southern biscuit dough is soft, but an experienced cook can handle it. She rolls it about ½ inch thick, or possibly a little thinner, and cuts it in small rounds, about 1½ inches in diameter. She lines them up on a baking sheet so they do not touch, and bakes them in a very hot oven, 450°.

Raisin biscuits retain a sizable following, and cheese biscuits are served at both luncheon and breakfast. I remember my astonishment in Chattanooga, Tennessee, at having open cheese sandwiches for breakfast. *Cheese toast,* my hostess called the offering, which she made by placing toast, stripped with cheese, under the broiler for a minute or two.

Chicken Biscuits Come From Kentucky

As already noted, chicken biscuits, sometimes called *chix crullers,* share space with fried chicken on platters in the bluegrass country of Kentucky, and elsewhere. When Mammy served chicken biscuits to me and my Ohio and Kentucky home economist friends at a fabulous dinner in Lexington, she stacked them with the fried chicken and passed cream gravy separately. At some tables the gravy is doused over the hot bread on the platter. To make chicken biscuits, Mammy cuts the rolled dough in small squares or fancy shapes with a pastry wheel. She drops them into the fat in which the chicken is fried until they, too, become golden on all sides and are cooked within.

Perfect party food, or an accompaniment to salads, are tiny hot biscuits, often only an inch in diameter, pulled apart with a fork or "cracked open." Shavings of cooked country ham, thin sausage patties, or cheese are inserted.

Please Pass the Sally Lunn

Sally Lunn is another favorite southern bread. There are two types, that leavened with baking powder, or the quick one, and Risen Sally Lunn, of English descent; it is leavened with yeast. Women commonly bake the kind containing an egg, a touch of sugar, flour, milk, shortening, and baking powder in round cake or pie pans. They usually cut it in wedges, and serve it hot. In some Alabama kitchens the rule is to bake this one in an oblong pan and then cut it in 2-inch squares. And in Virginia the yeast-leavened hot bread commonly comes from the oven in a tube mold, called a Sally Lunn mold. Leftover Risen Sally Lunn, split, buttered, and toasted on the buttered side, brings universal praise. A custom in making the toast, as observed in Missouri and some kitchens in other southern states, is to toast the bread on one side, and then to butter the other side and toast it.

Sweet potato waffles and biscuits, both leavened with baking powder and yeast, provide other good reasons for visiting the South when it is time to eat.

Muffins (sometimes called flour muffins or baking powder muffins) appear in countless menus. Two tempters favored in the Ozarks, are the summer editions, blue with native huckleberries, and the winter ones, rich with black walnuts. When hot and buttered they bring out the best flavors in crunchy apple-celery salads. Graham biscuits, big but thin, and fried sirup in both North Carolina and Georgia spell perfection. Fried sirup is made by gradually mixing cane sirup into ham drippings — heating and stirring the blend until it boils. Thoughts of this fried sirup on hot biscuits remind me of a childhood treat of one of my friends, a fifth generation Floridian. She confesses that when her mother was not observing, she and her sister liked to punch holes in the tops of hot biscuits, insert butter, and pour in cane sirup. She preferred the butter-and-sirup-filled biscuits to candy, and still does!

Sweet Additions for Breads

Southerners serve sweet sirups of many kinds over hot breads, but generally they do not care for the sweet, sticky yeast rolls of the North. They like simple sugar sirup made with pineapple juice for all or part of the water, and brown sugar and caramelized sugar sirups. Excellent cooks practice a bit of magic and convert many a plain-Jane dish into something special by carefully browning or caramelizing the sugar called for in the recipe. Orange-flavored sirup dresses up waffles and pancakes, and down in the heart of Texas the sirup drained from canned figs is heated, and lends distinction to pecan waffles.

Southern waffles traditionally come from the grids so light you can hold one on the tip of a pin. I never have made the test, but I know the satisfaction of eating crisp-coated waffles with amazingly light centers. In Virginia waffles containing green corn and accompanied by creamed chicken are not to be passed up. Neither are those tagged around the table by strawberry hard sauce. At Windy Hill, a plantation home in the Mississippi Delta, my hostess brought the fluff of pink to the table in a glass bowl. Later, as an encore to the compliments, she confided her recipe.

She creams ½ cup of butter with 3 cups of xxxx confectioners' sugar, adds 1 cup of crushed frozen or fresh strawberries, and chills the sauce until time to pass it with the waffles.

Perhaps the most delightful and delicate griddlecakes (most Southerners call them pancakes) contain bread crumbs. They are soaked in milk or buttermilk overnight or at least several minutes before the batter is made.

Light Rolls Resemble Puff Balls

Equally as famed as hot biscuits are the South's light rolls, which also are served piping hot. These yeast-leavened puff balls literally melt in your mouth when you take a bite. Like biscuits, they wear a brown, somewhat flaky crust, and their centers are so delicate you decide their texture is not unlike that of angel food cake. Sometimes they are miniatures, according to northern standards, and often are shaped like pocketbooks. In some kitchens the custom is to roll and cut the yeast dough like biscuits. Frozen rolls for busy households enjoy a ready sale in various communities. Occasionally the dough is shaped, wrapped, and frozen for future use. Some women prefer to bake the rolls, then cool and freeze them to reheat later.

Virginia has a lemon-flavored raisin bun that awakens the appetite. In it, as in some other "light breads," buttermilk supplies the liquid, and yields its characteristic flavor. (Light breads in the South designate those made with yeast and white flour.)

Although golden pats of butter on hot biscuits and rolls fill the bill for eating satisfaction, little balls of butter mixed with brown sugar lift the menu above the commonplace. Cane sirup whipped into butter and then chilled connotes fond memories of a wonderful supper al fresco in the garden of a home in the Mississippi Delta (a region of large cotton plantations and topnotch cooking). The mixture, beaten light as whipped cream and chilled, came from the refrigerator as the wee hot, feathery pocketbook rolls arrived from the oven. They met at the moon-drenched table built around a large tree near the kitchen door. I still remember the heavenly taste of these rolls with the spread, the talk, the jolly laughter, and the heavy perfume of petunias, moonflowers, nicotina, and four o'clocks on the evening air.

Scotch scones know their way about in the South, and salt-rising bread is at home in the region. Some bakeries carry a version of this pioneer bread, which many people regard as tops for toast. Today's interpretation properly defined is *mock salt-rising bread,* for it contains yeast, something that would have shocked old-time cooks. Bakers explain they add leavening because they can buy only bolted corn meal, which does not ferment so readily as the unbolted kind.

People Search for Rural Mills

One descriptive definition of the South is: The country of tasty, hot corn breads. The farther toward the equator you travel the more frequently you meet corn breads. To a major extent they depend on water-ground white corn meal for their excellence. In some communities people scour the countryside in a search for rural mills that grind the coarser white meal. When they find a supply they tote it home and store it in a home freezer or freezer locker. It is somewhat perishable if kept at a room temperature. (Imagine my surprise and thrill to receive by parcel post from generous friends in Blacksburg, Virginia, a bag of the precious meal! Imagine also what a conversation piece batter bread fashioned with it was at a Kansas table!)

No flour enters the mixing bowl, and rarely is more than a teaspoonful of sugar incorporated. I remember how I formulated a plan to determine whether my next door neighbor, Missouri, belongs to the South. On a local train to Columbia, I decided to ask the women passengers certain questions. Among them were the following: Do you use yellow or white meal for corn bread? Do you add flour? How about sugar? (The other question was about what kind of ham they prefer. To this the one retort was, "Country ham, a year old.") Every reply was true to Dixie, with white corn meal the favorite, no flour added, and not more than a teaspoonful of sugar to 2 cups of meal, if any.

Buttermilk, sour milk, and water, interchangeably, play the liquid role, with sweet milk taking over on a few occasions. One of the differences between Maryland and Virginia which food scouts observe is that while Marylanders frequently serve corn bread with fish, sometimes they pass hot light rolls. In Virginia corn bread of some kind is served with fish, and there is no debate about it.

Here Comes the Batter Bread Express

Spoon and batter breads are eloquently significant of the South. These breads often resemble soufflés in their lightness. So soft they cannot be sliced with a knife, they are served with a spoon from the casseroles or deep dishes in which they bake. If the utensil needs to be disguised a snowy white napkin is twisted around it. The steaming, fluffy bread, topped with brown, is ladled to your plate and you add butter. For a few minutes, at least, nothing in life seems more important than the task at hand, partaking of the food for the gods that is before you. It is as rewarding today as when the relay of little darkies — sometimes called the batter bread express — on Virginia plantations ran from the kitchen houses to dining rooms to deliver the triumph, browned, airy, and hot.

Spoon breads commonly are rich with eggs. Almost every Dixie family prizes its recipe for the delicacy as the most wonderful one.

Many excellent cooks use 4 eggs, separated and beaten light. They pour 1 cup of boiling water over 1 cup of corn meal, with salt and shortening added, and before the mixture cools they start adding milk. Then they fold in the eggs, the lemon-colored yolks first, and lastly the whites whipped until stiff. This fluffiness goes into a heated, greased casserole and bakes in a moderate oven, 350° to 375°, 30 to 40 minutes, or until a knife inserted in the center comes out clean.

Many recipes call for fewer eggs and for leavening, as soda or baking powder. These batter breads bake in a hotter oven, 400° to 425°. The eggs frequently are beaten without being separated. Some directions specify the addition of sour milk or buttermilk. Regardless of how made, you hurry spoon or batter bread to the table, where it glorifies the meal. Virginians and Carolinians say it especially complements chicken and pork, while Georgians insist that with "fried" (pan-broiled) country ham and red-eye gravy it answers their prayers.

In Tallahassee, Florida, a choice spoon bread contains equal parts of cooked grits and corn meal. Grits and hominy, as well as rice, are daily foods in many southern homes, especially in areas well to the south. They will have their innings in later chapters.

BRUNCH IN THE BLUE RIDGE MOUNTAINS
Orange Juice
Country Sausage   Fried Apples
Batter Bread
Coffee

Anyone who lives north of the Mason and Dixon line is likely to become confused about the different kinds of corn bread served in the South. Their development followed a definite pattern. *Ash cakes,* composed of corn meal and boiling water, were covered by and baked in ashes of open fires. First a favorite of the Indians, they were adopted by the negroes for cooking in their cabin fireplaces.

Joney cake, as Southerners call journey cake, formerly was enjoyed by pioneers while traveling in the wilderness. Made like ash cakes save that it was patted into one flat cake, it was cooked on a white oak or other board in front of a hot fire, usually a campfire. *Hoe cakes* are like ash cakes, little croquettes of batter originally baked on a helveless hoe in an open fireplace. They also were onetime favorites of the Negroes.

The first *corn dodgers* were made like ash cakes, but were oven baked. Some of them were so hard that if an angry cook threw one, everyone nearby dodged to avoid being hit. Today's dodgers and corn pones are lighter. Leavening is added and usually buttermilk plays the liquid role. The pones or small cakes are shaped with the hands, leaving the imprint of four fingers across the top, and baked in a hot oven, 425°, or fried until light brown. Dodgers may be baked or fried in the form of pones, or baked in a square pan and sliced. Pones are eaten hot or cold, often without butter, and especially with meals featuring such vegetables as the greens, like turnip tops, collards, and cabbage; snap beans; and vegetable soups. The coastal areas consider corn pones a natural with fish.

Egg bread, skillet corn bread, corn muffins, and corn sticks stem from the same batter, or one that contains one or more eggs. Egg bread is baked in a heated, greased shallow pan, and cut in squares to serve. Skillet bread, as its name implies, is baked in a skillet, the muffins in muffin pans, and the sticks in corn-stick pans.

Southern cooks vote for heavy utensils heated sizzling hot before adding the batter for corn breads. For corn-meal waffles they prefer a baker with heavy grids. The waffles, like other corn breads, are crisp crusted, and feathery light within. Served with creamed chicken, they are truly delectable, and even better, some gourmets say, with chicken or turkey hash.

Batter cakes (griddlecakes) with lacy edges appear especially in Virginia and Kentucky. To make them you drop the thin buttermilk-cornmeal-egg batter by spoonfuls into a hot greased skillet. The batter, when it strikes the heat, spews out and forms the lace. You serve these thin hot cakes in stacks of four with butter and cane or other sirup. Some cooks make larger ones as a base for browned patties of turkey hash, and occasionally they design sandwiches of them and hash. How many of these pancakes appear annually in Kentucky's Derby Day breakfasts is anyone's guess, but they are as much a part of the bluegrass country as colonels, mint juleps, and long-legged colts.

Hush Puppies at St. Marks, Florida

A Virginia custom of serving tiny, thin corn-meal batter cakes on the platter with fried chicken reaches Texas, where little griddlecakes made with flour with cream style corn added also appear with chicken and pork. There they often are eaten like Mexican tortillas from the fingers.

Crackling bread starts out like the batter for corn

pones (no eggs). To the batter is added the cracklings left after rendering lard. Many cooks crush them with a rolling pin or dice them. In some mountain homes this product is known as *fatty bread*. It is shaped into pones with the hands or baked in a shallow pan and cut in squares to serve.

Hush puppies, while now accepted with enthusiasm throughout the South, hailed originally from the northern Florida and southern Alabama and Georgia areas, where they have been appreciated for many years. Fishermen, while eating around campfires, tossed little corn cakes to hungry, whining dogs with the command, "Hush puppies." The corn bread that carries the colorful name contains chopped green or dry onion, and is fried in the fat in which the fish is cooked. You eat hush puppies in homes as a fish accompaniment, and a fish fry without them is beyond imagination. I observed a chef in St. Marks, Florida, prepare them. The description from my notebook follows:

"He pours the rather thick batter composed of white corn meal, buttermilk, egg, and minced onion into a large shallow pan. After he fries the fish in deep fat, he dips his spoon into the hot fat and then into the batter and cuts a crescent out of it. He drops it into the kettle, and repeats the process. He fries the hush puppies like doughnuts, drains them on absorbent paper, and serves them with the fish."

Tiny home fried hush puppies, highly seasoned with onion and black pepper, frequently appear at cocktail parties, where they win applause.

My introduction to the classic picnic of the region, a fish fry, came off in northern Mississippi. Here is the meal everyone enjoyed.

MISSISSIPPI FISH FRY
Fish   Hush Puppies
Potato Salad
Sliced Tomatoes
Watermelon
Coffee   Colas

Women in many kitchens bake hominy breads in a shallow pan and serve them cut in pie-shaped pieces. Made with grits, these first are cooked like corn meal to make a mush, with egg, salt, and butter added. They often pinch-hit in a meal for a starchy vegetable. Rice and hominy breads, and rice griddlecakes and waffles enjoy popularity throughout the South, but especially in the Southeast. Curiously, they do not show up so frequently in Virginia and Kentucky, and almost not at all in Missouri. But it's a Dixie coffee shop if it serves country ham and red-eye gravy with hot biscuits and snowy mounds of grits for breakfast.

How To Fry Chicken, Southern Style

All America likes fried chicken, but thoughts of it frequently suggest a southern platter stacked high with the golden pieces. Menu cards in almost every state carry the line, "Southern Fried Chicken." Sometimes when delivered it carries little resemblance to the kind you eat in Dixieland's homes.

For the fried chicken that Southerners and their guests from afar rave about, select young birds, usually weighing from 1½ to 2 pounds, live weight, although some Virginians prefer heavier ones up to 3 pounds, live weight. Disjointing rates as a kitchen art. Use a sharp knife that has a respect for joints no cleaver possesses. Cut the breast in two parts.

Some cooks like to soak the chicken pieces in buttermilk or sweet milk while they refrigerate. The sweet milk, after being drained off, later appears in the gravy. They dredge the chicken in flour seasoned with salt, and white pepper by shaking the chicken pieces in a paper bag containing the seasoned flour. (As a home demonstration agent in Mississippi in giving a cooking demonstration explained, "If you add black pepper to fried chicken, shake it on just before serving so it will not discolor the white meat.") One chicken requires about 1 cupful of flour and 1½ teaspoons of salt. For an exceptionally crisp crust the floured pieces are dipped in cream, then in flour again, and pan-fried.

While many households prize pet tricks in chicken frying, almost everyone agrees on the following points, as described to me by home economics students in a home management house at the University of Georgia. Proof of the success of their methods had been shown at the Sunday dinner table.

Use a heavy cooking utensil with a snugly fitting lid.

Use enough fat to cover the lower half of the chicken pieces and deep enough practically to cover them when it bubbles up. About 2 inches in depth is right.

Have the fat hot when the floured chicken is placed in it. Lay the pieces flesh side down, the thicker ones first, and see that they do not touch.

Reduce the temperature so the chicken will not cook too fast. For moist chicken, cover the utensil after browning.

During the last quarter hour of the pan-frying remove the lid and increase the temperature to encourage browning and crustiness.

Some star chefs hold that chicken should be turned only once. Others believe it makes no difference. The cooking time naturally depends upon the bird's size and age, but from ½ to ¾ hour after the initial browning and covering is about right. They spread the browned pieces out in a shallow pan so they do not touch and keep them warm in a hot oven. With the oven door open they watch the chicken while they make the gravy and finish the other meal preparations.

Most gravy recipes call for 2 tablespoons of the drippings and the crunchy crumbs in the fryer to every cup of sweet milk, or half and half cream and milk. The gravy is passed separately. Many Southerners abhor the thought of anyone pouring it over chicken.

At a country table in the Ozarks, I tasted the most fabulous chicken gravy. My hostess gave the credit for it to the Indians. She uses an old seasoning trick her grandmother learned from them. She stirs a tablespoon or more of toasted native pecans, rubbed to a powder with a wooden potato masher in a wooden salad bowl, into the gravy.

As previously mentioned, many Southerners like biscuits fried after chicken.

How Maryland Cooks Fried Chicken

Chicken Maryland differs from southern fried chicken. To prepare it you roll the pieces in seasoned flour and fry them in deep fat. Traditionally you serve them sizzling hot on slices of pan-fried corn-meal mush with gravy made from the drippings, flour, and cream poured over the mush but not over the chicken. Corn bread sometimes substitutes for the mush.

Batter Chicken Maryland, a variation of fried chicken, enjoys considerable popularity. The pieces are dipped in a batter composed of egg, milk, flour, baking powder, and salt, and fried in deep fat. In many Maryland homes the southern style rates tops, but this border state early developed a distinctive cuisine, especially on the Eastern Shore, and many unique and marvelous dishes originated on her plantations. The state's hostesses, as do those in Virginia, serve fried chicken, cream gravy, and waffles together.

Broiled Chicken Is a Favorite, Too

Southerners have more than a speaking acquaintance with broiled chicken, although the treat appears less frequently than the fried kind. Delaware, with a cuisine similar to that of Maryland, has a fondness for the broiled birds. Chickens weighing from 1½ to 1¾ pounds, live weight, are dressed and split down the back, but not disjointed. Melted butter is brushed on and they are broiled from 45 minutes to an hour, being turned once. Mississipi Delta cooks like to use sherry-butter for basting.

On a horse farm in Kentucky, my hostess, at what she called a simple supper, elevated country food to a high pinnacle of deliciousness. With broiled chicken she served baked potatoes, plenty of carefully browned butter, hot biscuits, spiced fig preserves, a tossed salad, containing some Bibb lettuce, with a tart French dressing, banana soufflé, and black coffee.

Larger chickens — those that dress out around 2 to 2½ pounds — instead of going into the broiler, frequently are smothered. This way of cooking comes as a happy surprise. Definitely it yields a blue ribbon creation that has not been publicized adequately, and one that challenges fried chicken in eating quality. Most families have their own private techniques for preparing it.

In Virginia one accepted procedure is to rub the birds, after they are split as for broiling, with butter and then to place them breast side down in a roasting pan. You add a little water — about a cupful — adjust the cover, and bake in a moderate oven, 350°. When half done, you remove the lid to insure browning. During the last few minutes, some imaginative hostesses brush on the tart, spicy juices of peach or watermelon rind pickles. Added at this stage, the vinegar does not have time to evaporate. This is an easy but pleasing variation of barbecued chicken.

At least some of the Kentucky women like to broil split chickens, after they are rubbed with soft butter, just long enough to brown them. Then they put them in a roaster and pour in about a cup of hot water that first rinsed out the broiling pan, to salvage the drippings. They bake the chickens in a moderate oven, 350°, until tender — usually about 45 minutes.

Smothered Chicken à la North Carolina

Here is the way a leader of home economics extension in North Carolina prepares smothered chicken for Sunday dinner, as jotted down while she graciously described the procedure.

You dress a bird that weighs from 1½ to 2 pounds and split it down the back. Then you place it breast side down in a pan, add 1½ cups of water, and spread the top of it with butter, with conscience your guide on the amount to use. You cover the pan and cook its contents 1½ hours in a slow oven, 325°. You perhaps start it in the oven as you leave for church. Then after you return home, or when the 1½ hours are up, you turn it. If there is less than 1½ cupfuls of liquid in the pan, add more water to make that amount. You sprinkle on salt and pepper, dust on a little flour, and continue the baking another ½ to 1 hour in an uncovered pan, to brown delicately and to tenderize. Serve it with fluffy boiled rice, and spoon over some of the pan-made gravy.

A friend on the home economics staff at the University of Georgia prepares a slightly different version.

She flours the chicken a little less than for frying and browns it in butter lightly and carefully, which means slowly to prevent burning. Then she adds 1½ cups of water, adjusts the cover, and puts it in a slow oven, 325°. When the liquid cooks low, or in about 1½ hours, she adds milk instead of water, and prefers top milk. If more flour is required to yield a gravy the consistency of thin cream soup, she mixes it into the milk before she pours it on. After baking uncovered 20 minutes to a half hour longer to dry off the top of the chicken and to develop brownness, her pièce de résistance is ready, to the delight of everyone on hand to partake of the treat.

Not the least of the charms of the dish is the self-made gravy that develops. It is guaranteed to prod all slumbering appetites.

How To Barbecue Chicken

Many Southerners like to broil chickens, brushed with butter, long enough to brown before barbecuing them. They place them in a roaster and pour on barbecue sauce. The lid goes on the pan and the birds simmer in the sauce in a moderate oven, 350°, about 45 minutes.

A Mississippi home demonstration agent of rare cooking talent introduced me to barbecued chicken, planters' style.

You soak the bird overnight in the barbecue sauce, and then place it in a paper bag, which you set in another paper bag, slightly larger, to strengthen the package. Slip a third paper bag over the open ends to provide a cover and additional strength. Bake it 15 minutes in a very hot oven, 500°, then 45 to 50 minutes in a slow oven, 325°. This method eliminates basting. The chicken so prepared is not browned, but it is juicy, tender, and exceptionally tasty. Planters enthuse over it.

Both barbecued chicken and turkey conjure up social gaiety in the South. Commonly the turkey, unstuffed, is roasted whole for 2 or 3 hours, or until browned. Cooks then drain off the surplus fat, add the barbecue sauce, cover the roaster, and cook the bird until, as southern women say, "it sticks tender." Many people baste it with the pungent sauce every 20 to 30 minutes. If it becomes too low in the pan they pour in a little hot water. Texas people, and especially those in the Houston area, sing the praises of barbecued turkey.

Southern Missouri and northern Arkansas put on jumbo-sized chicken barbecues. Occasionally they reach an extraordinary magnitude. One staged at Fayetteville, Arkansas, indicates how such affairs sometimes come off.

The barbecue pits were constructed of two rows of cement blocks, three blocks high, that extended for 300 feet. The grill consisted of a roll of welded fencing 300 feet long stretched between the two rows. White oak was used for fuel. After it had burned until only coals remained (the grill was 20 inches above the embers), the chickens, weighing from 1½ to 2½ pounds dressed, were split in halves and arranged on the grill. They were brushed with barbecue sauce before and during the cooking, and were turned every 5 minutes; the sauce was applied at every turn. It was a picturesque sight to see the chefs lined up on one side of the grill with their white bristled brushes (the kind used for spreading whitewash). The broiling time ran from 45 minutes to an hour.

Barbecue sauces vary, but a simple favorite of the Ozarks consists of 1 pint of 50-grain pickling vinegar, ½ cup of table salt, 1 teaspoon of black pepper, ½ ounce of garlic salt, and hot water enough to make 3 pints of sauce, or enough for 5 chickens.

SUMMER CHICKEN DINNER
Georgia

Fried Chicken
Stewed Fresh Corn   Snap Beans
Sliced Tomatoes
Hot Wilted Garden Lettuce
Hot Biscuits   Blackberry Jelly
Ice Cream or Peach Cobbler
Tea   Coffee

Roast turkey reigns on many holiday dinner tables, both at Thanksgiving and Christmas. In the Ozarks, the Carolinas, south Georgia, and other southern locales, wild turkey sometimes makes the feast. For supper parties during the Yuletide, the sliced white meat of the barnyard bird frequently alternates on silver platters with uniform slices of country ham. And in Virginia homes the tradition of a roast turkey on one end of the table and a whole baked ham on the other at Christmas still holds.

The way the fowl is stuffed depends on personal preferences, and there are many of them. In some kitchens it carries two kinds of dressing, one in the body and another in the neck cavity. Many families especially like a peanut-corn bread or a pecan-corn bread variety for the front one. Also I have talked with several exceptionally clever cooks (one of them is director of home economics in a well-known Texas university) who never have stuffed the countless turkeys they have roasted. They bake the dressing separately, usually in a pan, although sometimes in the roaster around the bird. A common practice is to shape it in balls and bake them during the last hour of cooking, or long enough to heat and brown. After they are on the platter the spheres make waiting to taste an effort.

Countless dressings are favorites, like oyster, sausage, chestnut, pecan, rice and pecan, peanut, and egg bread. In Virginia and Carolina kitchens the dressing may be fashioned of biscuit crumbs, with minced celery, cooked giblets, eggs, seasonings, and frequently oysters added. It is not uncommon to shape a part of it in round, flat cakes, which make, when browned, an attractive garnish for the platter.

Without question the favorite dressing on a wide scale contains cubes of light bread, toasted, mixed with crumbled egg bread (corn bread), with minced onion, celery, salt, pepper, and beaten eggs stirred in. For moisture the stock made by simmering the turkey's feet, giblets, and neck in water often is used. While sage gets involved in some dressings it fails to achieve the prominence it enjoys in New England.

An Arkansas home economist showed me her system of roasting turkey. She stuffs and trusses the bird, and then slips it into a heavy paper bag, the kind food markets pile little packages in, that first has been scalded with boiling water. She folds the open end of the bag to close it, and then pins it with a large safety pin, sets the sack on a cooky sheet, and puts it in the oven. When the fowl is cooked she opens the package and pours the juices for gravy-making into a frying pan. Then she arranges the beautiful turkey on a platter, and rejoices that she has no roaster to wash.

Turkey in a fence, as one of my Tennessee friends describes her platter treat, is something to behold. After the fowl is roasted to a turn, its tantalizing aroma permeates the house. Around the regal bird are pastry strips arranged like a rail fence. The pastry contains some baking powder; it is cut in desired lengths, and baked. Perhaps the garnish stems from that old southern habit of arranging a lattice of puff pastry strips, crisp and lightly browned, over fried chicken heaped on a platter.

The gravy that escorts this glamour on a platter is quite tasty. Like most of the gravies made to accompany roast turkey or chicken, the liquid is water. To the Tennessee number, cooks add a few sautéed button mushrooms and sweetbreads, cooked and cut-up.

In western Maryland sauerkraut ranks as a favorite accompaniment to roast turkey.

A Daisy Chain Around the Hash

From roast turkey or chicken (fat chickens are called "hens"), comes glorious hash, another star in the southern cook's crown. It is a magnificent dish, and one without a recipe, like a song without words. Everyone agrees that you cut the cooked meat with kitchen scissors into small pieces, "about the size of hazel nuts," and that you never grind it. To it you add gravy, if it is available, turkey broth, or consommé. For additional moisture you may pour in a little cream, but never does the hash resemble a creamed dish. If you wish, you stir in a little minced onion and celery, salt, and pepper. You may simmer the mixture gently in a heavy utensil, covered, to blend the flavors. Only of dire necessity do you add potato cubes, and that is when you must stretch the turkey. Instead of potatoes many households prefer tiny toasted and buttered biscuit halves.

What a fascinating color picture it makes as it arrives heaped on a platter, surrounded with a daisy chain of sliced hard-cooked eggs, and crowned with a pimento poinsettia! Either hot biscuits, waffles, or corn breads make excellent escorts. Here is what a Tennessee hostess served me one spring evening when the mountain side was a tapestry of white stars, dogwood in bloom.

TENNESSEE SUPPER
Tomato Juice
Turkey Hash　　　Corn Muffins
Celery Hearts
Pineapple and Cranberry Sherbets
Tea

The two kinds of sherbets shared space in the dessert glasses, and complemented each other. The tea was hot, and just right. Perhaps due to the many early Anglo-Saxon settlers, tea drinking flourishes as quite an art throughout the South.

Introducing Other Native Americans

Both chicken and turkey salads, native Americans, are entrenched in the affections of Southerners. Perhaps the way they taste when served with hot biscuits or light rolls explains their favor. In Texas big balls of them are rolled in chopped parsley and snuggled in lettuce hearts. Some Virginians like to add crunchy unpared apple cubes that have been dipped in lemon juice. Almonds, cut in strips, sliced pimento stuffed olives, and chow chow also mix occasionally into these treats, the ones rich with turkey or chicken and celery, and with just enough salad dressing to moisten them.

Traditionally you cut the fowl in inch pieces, the celery in $\frac{1}{3}$-inch lengths, mix half as much celery as chicken or turkey with the dressing, and add sliced or chopped hard-cooked eggs, 1 dozen to a large chicken. If you cook a hen especially for salad, you simmer it in water until tender, and cool it in the broth.

Country Captain Hails From Georgia

Country captain, an exotic Georgia interpretation of chicken curry, won its way about the nation as an extraordinary dish. It starts out as fried chicken. After the disjointed birds are fried, usually about 3-pound ones, they are kept warm while the sauce is made. The cook lightly browns finely cut green pepper, onion, and a bit of garlic in bacon fat, and then adds tomatoes and seasonings of salt, pepper, minced parsley, and curry powder. The chicken simmers in the sauce about 45 minutes. Then it is lifted to the hot platter and encircled with a ring of fluffy boiled rice. To the sauce are added a few blanched and toasted almonds and dried currants. It is passed in a gravy boat for ladling over the rice.

One of my hostesses varied the style of service. The rice was snowy white in a dish of its own. Buttered asparagus accompanied it. The tossed green salad in a spacious glass bowl was set on a large glass plate. Around its rim were elegant peach pickles gleaming like a gold bracelet. She said that frequently she omits the green salad and substitutes for it a grapefruit-lettuce combination mixed with chutney dressing.

Fried Cream Appears in Nostalgic Talk

Fried cream, an old-time delicacy, and a companion to broiled chicken, now appears mostly in nostalgic table talk about fine foods. It awakened my curiosity. On observing my interest, a Louisiana hostess offered to demonstrate how to make it. Here is her procedure step by step.

She drops a stick of cinnamon into 2 cups of sweet milk and heats it. When it is just below the boiling point she stirs in a generous ½ cupful (measured it is ½ cupful plus 1 tablespoonful) of sugar. Then she adds 2 tablespoonfuls of cornstarch mixed with 1 tablespoonful of flour, dissolved in 3 tablespoonfuls of cold milk. She stirs and cooks the mixture about 2 minutes, removes it from the range, and whips in 3 beaten egg yolks. She returns the mixture to low heat and cooks it slowly, while stirring constantly, only until it thickens.

After that she removes the cinnamon stick, adds 1 tablespoon of butter and ½ teaspoon of vanilla, and pours the pudding into a buttered shallow pan or deep platter to a depth of ⅓ inch. When the pudding is chilled, she cuts it in fine strips, about 1 by 3 inches, and carefully rolls the strips in cracker meal, then in slightly sweetened egg, and in cracker meal again. She dips them in deep fat hot enough to brown quickly, after which she places them in a hot oven for 4 or 5 minutes, or until they soften. Then she lights the dining room candles, and hurries the broiled chicken and fried cream to the table to join other southern delicacies in a great Louisiana feast.

Cook and Host Know Their Chicken Pie

No observing food reporter travels about the South without acquiring great respect and admiration for the chicken pies. They do not feature scraps or leftovers in cream sauce; the crusts conceal big pieces, usually bones and all, although sometimes the bones are removed. Generally a crust is on top, a rolled rich biscuit or pastry one, crisp and beautifully browned. It carries a pattern of vents to permit the escape of steam. Little biscuits occasionally substitute for it.

Sometimes when I dream of sublime native American dishes my mind drifts to the cotton country, and blossom-filled Greenville, Mississippi, in May, where I met the supreme chicken pie. My host, with the pie before him, inquired, "Do you prefer light or dark meat?" Wondering how he could see through the pastry crust, for the vents were tiny and filled with spouting steam, I replied, "Light." In went the lovely silver spoon, and out came a chicken breast surrounded with flavorful broth and topped with a flaky crust. Only by watching him did I learn that the cook had placed the light meat on the left side of the pie, and the dark meat on the right. The host had a perfect understanding with her.

Southern People Like Their Hams

Remembrance of hot breads, fried chicken, and country ham awakens nostalgia in Southerners away from Dixie, and anticipation in those who live in the region. For more than two centuries the three foods have distinguished the area's cuisine.

Most kitchens vouch for special ways of preparing country ham. All of them appear to give wonderful results, although success leans heavily on the condition of the meat. You have to know your hams in the South. Virginia, for example, enjoys three kinds, Smithfield, country, and western.

Smithfield hams follow epicures to every state, but they get the cure in Smithfield, Virginia, in the southeastern section. Fortunately most of them are packaged with directions for cooking and carving. The hogs which produce them are raised almost entirely in Virginia and Georgia. They have a razorback ancestry, so are of the lean type. During the early months of their existence the animals feed on the fat of the forests where they roam. They eat hickory nuts, acorns, grass nuts, and whatever else they find. Then they go into freshly harvested peanut fields to root among the lush plants and rich nuts left behind.

Peanut-fed pork has a characteristic soft fat that lends itself to long smoking and the Smithfield cure. Corn feeding follows the peanut eating stage. Naturally knowledge of the cure never is broadcast over the country, for the recipes are trade secrets. Natives explain that it consists partly of salting, spicing with black pepper, and heavy smoking with hickory, apple, and oak woods. Then the hams hang for months, or indeed years, to age, a process that concentrates the natural flavors of the meat, smoke, and spices.

You find country hams on farms in all southern states. Most of them are sugar cured and hickory smoked. Georgians especially like them from peanut-fed hogs. Of course the quality and flavors of the meat vary, for individual farmers have their onw ideas and standards for feeding the animals, and curing the pork. Many of them rub on salt and pepper and turn it daily. Sugar usually teams with salt in the cure. Most farmers smoke them, although a few do not.

As a general rule good country hams are heavy, with a weight of 16 to 20 pounds, or more. Many splendid cooks say, "I'm afraid of the small ones. Usually they are too salty."

A Kansan, when hungry for southern country ham, dreams of those on Boone County and other Missouri farms in that area of the state known as Little Dixie. She believes with all her heart that they cannot be surpassed. When she visits Kentucky, the mother of Missouri, she also is thrilled over the marvelous productions of the land where the blue-grass grows. Then when she dines in Virginia, Kentucky's mother, she decides those her hostesses serve there also deserve silver cups. Later in Tennessee, Georgia, Arkansas, and Alabama she continues to praise similar platter treats. You can find them throughout the region.

The Ham Has a Birthday

The age of a country ham figures in food talk. When it celebrates its first birthday it steps into the coveted class known as *old* country hams. Natives speak of them in a different tone of voice, for they declare they taste better. Opinions vary about when they reach the peak of perfection, but most connoisseurs believe the flavor does not improve beyond the 2-year mark. Between 1 and 2 years seems to be the golden age.

Basically there are two ways to handle them. One is to "boil" or simmer them gently in water, and the other is to pan-broil slices. After you cook the ham in water, you frequently bake it about an hour to brown and glaze its exterior. And although almost everyone talks of fried ham, the slices universally are pan-broiled.

Both the country and Smithfield types need to soak in water to cover for from 12 to 36 hours before cooking. The length of time depends on the dryness of the meat. First the surface must be scrubbed, using a brush, elbow grease, and warm water. Some cooks choose soapy water for the chore. When thoroughly cleaned they rinse it several times and then immerse it in cold water.

After the soaking you commonly cook ham without draining off the water. Gentle simmering is the A-1 rule for success. When you pierce the flesh side with the sharp tines of a fork and they easily reach the central bones, when you feel that the exposed bones are loose from the flesh, or when the ham turns over of its own accord if simmered in a boiler, it is cooked. As a general rule, from 15 to 20 minutes a pound are required, although the age and hardness of the meat have much to do with it. Unless you wish to serve the ham immediately you cool it in the broth.

Occasionally, you add seasonings to the water in which the whole ham simmers. Many of Missouri's epicures vote for 1 cup each of molasses and brown sugar, ½ cup of vinegar, and a few handfuls of apple peelings.

Utensils with a cover and large enough for the cookery occupy a position of prominence in many households. Only a few of the old cast iron ham boilers remain in Virginia. Copper clothes boilers often fill the bill, and in some rural households a covered lard can works out satisfactorily. Electric roasters also have moved into the culinary scene. Usually the hock is removed, and the meat is turned a few times as it cooks. In cities some families purchase hams and pay to have them boiled and baked by individuals engaged in the business.

Some women sew a thin cloth, like cheesecloth or a sugar sack that fits snugly around the ham, to hold it in shape while cooking. The wrapper also helps keep the meat firm when the carver is at work. It is sliced very thin. Experts with the knife always command a special respect from the hostess.

Only extravagant cooks discard the broth. Many of them salvage it by storage in home freezers or compartments in freezer lockers. For seasoning vegetables, like greens and beans, the juices recognize no worthy competitors. Women use them by cupfuls and tablespoonfuls to impart the coveted taste.

"Best Ham This Side of Cumberland Gap"

One mellow afternoon, after we had been eating magnificent country ham in an eastern Kentucky mountain home, the home demonstration agent encouraged me to ask for the recipe. Here is the procedure as dictated by our hostess.

"I scrub the ham and soak it overnight in cold water. We cure our own. In the morning I trim and scrape it, and put it on to cook in a lard can with cold water to cover. I adjust the tightly fitting lid and bring the water to a gentle boil. I know when that stage arrives, as I listen for the sound of the bubbling water. Then I look at the clock. The constant, soft simmering continues for an hour or two longer.

"After that I line a tub with many layers of newspapers, and set the lard can in it. At no time do I remove the lid. Immediately I wrap the can with lots of newspapers, carefully covering its top and sides to insulate it thoroughly. Then I heap on old blankets, coats, rugs, and whatever else I have to help retain the heat so the cooking will continue. The insulation must be good, for on it hinges success. I forget about it for 24 hours, and then I open the package to remove what my family and friends call the best tasting ham this side of the Cumberland Gap."

Once a ham is "boiled," or cooked tender in water, it frequently goes into the oven to brown. Usually it is simmered a little less time if baking is to follow. The skin is removed and then the meat is roasted until the fatty side is a golden color and crisp. For buffet suppers and other special occasions, Virginians sometimes "dress the ham," as they call it, although a surprising number of them are partial to a "boiled" one.

Occasionally they coat it before baking with brown sugar, cracker meal, and celery seed, and stick it with whole cloves. As it roasts they baste it with cider, other fruit juices, or Madeira or sherry wine. In some Mississippi kitchens cooks rub on peanut butter mixed with brown sugar and a little spice, and baste with a cola. A much praised Kentucky treatment features dots of black pepper and brown sugar over the surface. You can moisten a forefinger in the broth and work the sugar and pepper into the fat. I have watched home chefs spread a thin layer of prepared mustard and then pat in a bit of brown sugar, with a suggestion of water-ground corn meal added.

The glaze obtained in these and other ways is optional. Some households consider it contributes glamour as frosting trims a cake. Others do not approve, or at least are lukewarm to the practice.

It Seems That Company Is Coming

One of the popular routines consists of basting during baking with mixed equal parts of a tart jelly and broth, the juice from peach pickles, or ½ cup each of corn sirup and brown sugar blended with 1 cup of orange juice. Frequently ham is rubbed with mustard and brown sugar, with the fat scored in diamond designs (with care not to cut into the lean meat). Then stuck with cloves, it goes into the oven to bake as watchful cooks baste it with champagne. Regardless of what the barometer indicates, when such kitchen campaigns flourish a prudent forecast is: Company is coming.

Country ham appeals when served hot or cold, and "boiled" or baked. (Slices of it sometimes are reheated gently in sherry wine.) Thin horseshoe slices of the dark red meat with neat borders of fat displayed on a polished silver platter are enough to whet anyone's appetite. To taste is to touch your tongue to and set your teeth into one of the South's prime taste treats. If it is at its local best you can travel around the world and not find its equal.

Whole cooked country hams answer the call for special occasion food. Their supply is small, their cost high. Every year fewer farmers cure meat. When they do, it frequently is for their own use. Flaunting dollars in their faces does not always lure them to part with their prized smoked pork.

In the place of country hams commercial ones come to the front. They are spoken of as the *city, western,* or *packing house* variety. Every company follows its own recipes in curing. The product is standardized, and thus brand names become guides of what to buy. These hams require no soaking, and thus are streamlined to meet today's requirements for easier preparation. Usually, Southerners bake them, fat side up, in a slow oven, 325°, from 3 to 4½ hours, or until tender. Then they remove the rind, score the fat, and brown the surface in a hot oven, 400°, about 15 to 30 minutes.

Fried Country Ham Produces Red Gravy

One of the epicurean experiences south of the Mason and Dixon line is to face fried country ham and red-eye gravy at the table. As previously noted, the meat commonly is pan-broiled. The cook rubs the heavy frying pan with a piece of the amber-hued fat, and, when the pan is fairly hot, she adds the ham slices, cut ¼ inch thick. She turns them frequently as they cook, to keep them flat with their lovely fat edges rippling evenly from the red center they frame. As the fat cooks, it becomes a transparent, deep golden color.

When the meat is ready she makes the gravy. She adds about a cup of hot water to the drippings, or enough to loosen the brown particles that adhere to the pan. Then she stirs and cooks it until most of the water evaporates. She may season it with pepper but the cure provides ample salt.

One school of cooks prefers coffee to water for the gravy. Another group does not remove the ham from the pan, adds the water or coffee, and lets it boil up around the meat. After that they reduce the heat and simmer it gently for 15 or 20 minutes, or until the meat sticks tender. Most of the famed red or red-eye gravy disappears, although there remains enough to moisten the meat.

If thicker country ham steaks are desired, such as those ½ inch in depth, the cook parboils them before pan-frying. She simmers them until tender in a heavy utensil, covered, with 1 cup of water poured over, or else steams them in a pressure cooker about 10 minutes under 15 pounds pressure. Then she browns them in a frying pan, but in either case the superlative gravy is lost.

To Maryland go the honors for one of the most unique compositions, Maryland Easter ham, an old-time delicacy of the Eastern Shore. Traditionally it comes to the Easter table as spring colors the roadsides. Here is the recipe for it.

Soak the country ham overnight or longer, and then parboil it in water until it softens. Then remove it and with a sharp knife make deep gashes to the bone, about ½ inch apart. Twist the knife to form pockets. There should be at least 20 of them on a ham. Stuff them as full of the greens of spring as possible. First wilt the greens — chives, spinach, green or wild onions, kale, parsley, mint or whatever mixture is available — in the highly seasoned, boiling hot ham broth. Pile and spread the remainder of the greens on top.

Then tightly wrap the ham in a firm cloth and sew it on. Continue the slow, gentle simmering until the meat is tender.

Some families like it hot; more of them prefer it cold. The tradition is to slice it thin and to pass the vinegar cruet with it. Hot biscuits are the favorite accompaniment — the tiny, crusty Maryland kind. The lovely pink meat with the veining of variegated shades of green is handsome on the platter. Maryland Easter ham is appropriate both for breakfast and for dinner on the greatest of the spring holidays.

Stuffed ham has a religious background. Many colonial settlers of Maryland deemed it imprudent after observing Lent to eat too much meat at Easter. They introduced the early greens to their favorite and much prized cured pork, and thus created an American spring original that represents Maryland as faithfully as the fabulous sea foods from Chesapeake Bay.

Country Sausage Is Popular, Too

Although chicken and country ham commonly steal the show of distinctive platter treats, not even unobserving visitors in the area overlook the savory country sausage. A surprising number of households treasure their personal tried and true directions for making a champion product from fairly lean pork with a blend of such seasonings as salt, black pepper, crumbled sage, red pepper, and occasionally crushed coriander seeds. Home refrigerators often hold rolls of the ground pork that resemble those of dough for refrigerator cookies. For breakfast pieces about 1½ inches thick are sliced off and pan-fried.

Southerners like sausage with fried apples at the start of the day. They also team the zesty meat with griddlecakes and waffles of numerous descriptions. For brunch they have a habit of breaking open tiny hot biscuits with a fork and inserting thin piping hot sausage cakes to fit.

All pork cuts are at home in the region's meals. For a special dinner, the loin roast rises to the occasion. Thin chops, floured, browned, then covered and cooked until tender, pair off with rich, meaty gravy to achieve meal success. Pork with fragrant sweet potato accompaniments is another regional food.

North Carolina Barbecues Are Tasty.

As already suggested, à la king dishes fall into the aristocratic class. Among these compositions of turkey and chicken, visitors discover a gamut of appetite teasers that include one made with chicken livers and served on melba toast. Sherry-flavored chipped beef à la king frequently crowns rice.

Old southern favorites are barbecued meats, including Tennessee's leg of lamb — tasty both hot and cold — beef tenderloin, meat loaves, and spareribs. Barbecued pork and chicken command large and most enthusiastic followings. North Carolina enjoys fame for her chopped or minced barbecued pork and chicken. Two gracious members of the extension foods staff at the North Carolina State College introduced the delicacy to me at a luncheon in Raleigh. They explained the directions this way:

Roast the pig or chicken over oak coals, and brush occasionally with barbecue sauce. Sometimes vinegar with red pepper pods suffices. When the cooking is completed, cool the meat enough to handle and then cut it into small pieces. Never put it through a food chopper. Only outsiders commit such a crime! When the meat is cut up, dump it into a bowl or other dish and season to taste with salt and the sauce used for the basting. The trick is to work the seasonings into the meat.

North Carolinians remain faithful to their tradition of

serving a crisp cole slaw and hot corn bread with their barbecues.

Texas barbecues all kinds of meat on a jumbo-sized scale, with beef the top selection.

Nashville Claims Spiced Beef Round

Certain communities cherish platter traditions. Spiced round of beef at Nashville, Tennessee, is an example. Its popularity scarcely extends throughout middle Tennessee, but it reaches to all spots over the world where former residents of the Nashville-Gallatin area now live. Packages of the meat fly by air parcel post to faraway places when it is time to hang tiny bells and silver glitters on the tree. A century ago this Christmas meat was cured in homes, but nowadays meat dealers prepare it for home cooking or cook it in advance, whichever the customer prefers.

As the name suggests, the specialty consists of the upper round of beef. The meat man lards it with pork fat and cures it in a pickling solution that contains, among other things, saltpeter, brown sugar, vinegar, spices, black pepper, and salt. It is ready to cook when needed. Then it is soaked in cold water to cover at least an hour, and drained. After that more water and a cup of brown sugar are added, and it is simmered gently until tender. Natives cool the beef in the broth, and then drain and refrigerate it.

Citizens of Nashville carve spiced round in a certain way. First they cut the circle in five or six pieces, as for pie. Then with a very sharp knife they slice each wedge across the grain of the meat as thinly as possible. They lay the reddish brown triangles with the white checks of fat on their most handsome platter. Garnished with greenery, the dish says "Merry Christmas" to everyone who helps himself.

In North Carolina I first sampled pineapple-mint soufflé as an accompaniment to roast leg of lamb. My hostess explained that she makes it with canned crushed pineapple, mint jelly, and egg whites, with a little flour for thickening.

Shortly before removing it from the oven, she spreads on additional egg whites tinted a delicate green and browns them lightly. She serves the tasty and hot, yet cooling dish immediately, for like most soufflés it will not hold up long.

Here's Baked Steak, Kentucky Style

Kentucky people, as almost all visitors to the bluegrass country agree, have a right to boast of many wonderful, native foods. Among them is baked steak.

For it they use a 2-inch sirloin. They line the baking pan with sliced onions, add pieces of butter, and plenty of tomato ketchup mixed with a little Worcestershire sauce. On this they bed the steak and then broil it, browning on both sides. After that they cover the pan and bake the steak in a hot oven, about 400°, until tender. Then they serve it with the pan sauce poured over.

From roast beef, an All-American favorite, Southerners take the leftovers and convert them into magnificent hash. They *cut* the remnants into small pieces instead of grinding them, and add chopped onions, peeled and diced Irish potatoes, and gravy or consommé, along with seasonings that include two favorites, Worcestershire sauce and kitchen bouquet. Slow simmering blends the flavors.

A northern food explorer observers certain characteristics of meat cookery in the South. Almost always the beef and lamb, as well as pork and veal, are liked well done. The nearer the Gulf of Mexico and Texas one stops, the more Tabasco sauce is used to spark up the flavor.

Southern gravies generally are brown. Many an expert cook relies on skill in browning flour and butter, as well as sugar without scorching for superb seasoning. A few women, especially in the Lexington, Kentucky, district, add what locally are called *charred onions* to the gravies and meat dishes for a subtle touch. They bake the unpeeled but washed and thoroughly dried onions until dark in color, but not burned. They drop the onions into many gravies, especially lamb or veal, and into the sauce for barbecued lamb. In simmering the onions impart a distinctive flavor.

Boiled beef tongue commands a higher regard than in most other regions. After it has been simmered tender in water with seasonings added (including an onion stuck with whole cloves) the tongue is skinned and served sliced, with or without tomato sauce.

Stews From "Befo' the Wah"

Among the legacies left by hospitable families of "Befo' the Wah" days, you meet the stews at picnics and other large social gatherings. Kentucky has her *Burgo*. Although it commonly is prepared outdoors for a crowd, as on Derby Day, some cooks reduce the recipe to make smaller amounts for backyard and in-the-house guest meals. Like many other such dishes, Burgo improves if it is refrigerated and reheated. A multiplicity of ingredients supply flavor: lamb, beef shank, and representatives of the vegetable kingdom, such as Irish potatoes, butter beans, carrots, green peppers, onions, okra, tomatoes, and corn cut from the cob. Seasonings include red and black pepper, salt, and garlic.

Kentuckians first slowly cook the meats in water, and when tender add the vegetables at intervals depending on how long they need to simmer for doneness. The corn goes into the kettle last. The trick of the chef is to watch and stir the food to prevent scorching. From 4 to 7 hours is allowed for the cooking. Just before serving the tempting Burgo, minced parsley is added. Corn pones and plenty of butter are passed with Burgo, and the strains of "My Old Kentucky Home" fill the heart of a guest.

Brunswick stew attains still wider popularity in Virginia, Maryland, the Carolinas, and Georgia, and certain communities in all other southern states. An old recipe used in Brunswick County, Virginia, starts with this advice, "First catch your rabbit." Formerly game of various kinds, including rabbit, was used much more extensively than now in its preparation.

Brunswick stew commonly appears as a refreshment at picnics and other celebrations outdoors, where the chefs often stir it in big iron kettles with new hoes. While scores of recipes for the masterpiece circulate about the region, most of today's versions contain chicken, pork, tomatoes, butter beans, and corn. Home adaptations make a satisfactory one-dish meal. One I sampled with enjoyment on a Mississippi plantation contained squirrel, beef, pork, and chicken, steamed in a pressure cooker until the meat fell from the bones. As with Burgo, the corn — cut from the cob — simmers for only a few minutes at the end.

There's a Use for Leftover Stew

Frequently Brunswick stew is prepared in advance and frozen for quick reheating when needed. Frozen corn and butter beans and canned tomatoes make it an around-the-year dish. Leftovers that follow a community celebration do not waste in these modern days! They are readily salvaged by freezing. For a meal in which Brunswick stew takes the lead role, corn bread of some kind, cole slaw, and iced tea or hot coffee generally complete the menu.

Camp meeting stew speaks for Alabama. It resembles the Burgo and Brunswick varieties in that its original popularity came from splendid service in picnic meals.

To prepare it you first pan-fry bacon, then remove it and pan-fry the other meat to brown in the drippings. It may be veal or chicken, or a combination of 1 part veal, 1 part pork, 2 parts lamb, and 2 parts beef. Add the meats and crumbled bacon to the kettle and simmer softly. Then lightly brown chopped onions and diced green pepper in the drippings, and add flour and water to make a smooth gravy. Stir it into the mixture that bubbles leisurely in the kettle. After that add tomatoes, cut-up celery, and your choice of seasonings: black pepper, Worcestershire sauce, ketchup, bay leaves, a trace of sugar, salt if needed, cloves, allspice, and a dash of Tabasco sauce.

This stew simmers 4 to 5 hours. Before the meat disintegrates, as it is supposed to do, remove all bones and skin, especially if chicken is in the pot. After you drop in cubed Irish potatoes and corn kernels cut from the cob, stir the thick, smooth, velvety stew, to keep it from sticking and scorching, until the vegetables are done. Serve camp meeting stew with a corn bread, coffee, and iced tea.

Poor John's stew belongs to east Texas, where it is at home on the ranges in kitchens as *son-of-a-gun stew* is in west Texas. For it, Texans simmer bite-sized pieces of Texas beef until tender with vegetables. While the selection of vegetables depends to some extent on personal whims, four kinds are considered essential: Irish potatoes, carrots, onions, and green peppers. With Poor John's stew, like with other traditional stews, corn bread wins the role as queen of accompaniments.

Squirrel stew wins compliments in the Ozark country. Crusty hot biscuits commonly are the escort, although dumplings sometimes are steamed in it.

Those Snap Beans and Ham Hock

No discussion of southern meats begins to do justice to their succulence without a description of that universal regional habit of cooking vegetables — especially beans — with side meat, hog jowls, or country bacon. Perhaps it rates as a vegetable dish, although on many tables it occupies the platter. And most culinary experts warn, "You can't skimp on the meat and have good beans."

They allow 1 pound of meat to 2 pounds of snap beans. First they simmer the meat slowly in water, a pod of red pepper added, in a covered kettle about 1½ hours. Then they dump in the beans, snapped into 2-inch lengths, and 1 teaspoon of salt if required. Eastern Virginia likes young beans that snap and with no or very tiny seeds, while southwestern Virginia, Kentucky, Tennessee, Missouri, and many communities in other states vote for a more mature bean. There in late summer when shell-outs are available, women like to add them (the seeds) to cook with green beans.

Some excellent cooks simmer the vegetable with the meat until just tender, a half hour or a little more, although the old-fashioned timing of perhaps 1½ hours has ardent champions. The juices should be decreased greatly. A true kitchen artist never stirs the beans with a spoon, which breaks them. She merely shakes the kettle. To serve the delicacy, she heaps the beans on a hot platter and tops them with slices of the meat. Over all she pours the reduced juices or "pot likker," and then sees that everyone has plates, hot corn bread, and little saucers or bowls to hold some of the broth. Sliced tomatoes receive nominations as the top accompaniment, although many Ozark women advise, "Make a big bowl of crisp, cool cole slaw, and bring in some tender, juicy radishes and green onions from the garden to serve with the beans."

Ham hock frequently substitutes for the side meat, jowls, or bacon in the kettle of snap beans.

Laboratory tests made with beans cooked with pork in comparison to those cooked in salted water, drained, and dressed with melted butter indicate the latter frequently contain more fat! This is true despite the appearance of those teamed with the meat. They seem more greasy due to their wilted condition.

On top of snap beans Southerners steam various succulent vegetables, like tender ears of corn, potatoes so youthful the skins can be scrubbed off, and tiny summer squash, both the green-white patty pans and the yellow goosenecks, or crook-necks. Wee okra pods also cook atop the beans. The idea is for these foods to absorb some of the meat's flavor. Such additions to the bean and pork fare, as popular in the region as Boston baked beans in New England's earthen pots, illustrate perfectly a trait of the southern cook. She likes to catch the garden vegetables when they are young. Her people prefer them that way.

Vegetables Glorify Summer Meals

The field fills with candidates when someone announces a popularity contest among the vegetables. Corn, snap beans (green beans), potatoes (sweet potatoes), greens, butter beans (small lima beans), and okra usually win pennants. Tomatoes, eggplant, and black-eye peas also frequently cross the line with the winners.

A liking for field corn persists even though sugar corn (sweet corn) definitely gains prestige every year. Like other garden products, it enjoys a long season, which increases as you journey southward. In Florida vegetables fresh from the garden are served every day of the year.

If you visit Maryland and Virginia in corn eating time,

you will observe that while Marylanders delight in corn-on-the-cob, as well as dishes composed of cut-off kernels, the Virginian tosses his hat in the air for the cook who discards the cobs in the kitchen. A mention of boiled corn, called *stewed corn* in some communities, brings a gleam of anticipation into most eyes. This old-time dish is made by cutting the kernels from cobs and cooking them in a little water for a few minutes, or until tender. By then the liquid practically disappears. Butter, cream, salt, and black pepper are added to season. (Southerners speak of *black* pepper to distinguish it from other regional ones, like red, white, and chili peppers.)

Fried corn likewise awakens enthusiasm across the countryside. The kernels are pan-fried in bacon drippings or butter until tender, or for about 10 minutes. If they start to brown, a suggestion of cream is stirred in. Most natives warn that corn burns readily. They keep an eagle eye on it during the pan-frying, and stir the kernels frequently.

Some people refer to corn cakes as *fritters* or *fried corn*.

To make them they mix the kernels from 6 tender ears with 2 eggs, beaten very light, and add a little corn meal, plus salt to season. Then they drop small spoonfuls of the mix into a fairly hot frying pan containing a little fat, and brown them on both sides. Almost everyone thoughtfully reminds a Yankee, "You need add no flour."

Corn Pudding, a Native American

Few native American vegetable dishes can touch southern corn pudding for delicacy and taste. It graces discriminating tables throughout the region, and too rarely away from the South. While directions for preparing corn pudding vary from one home to another, they are similar.

CORN PUDDING

6 large ears of corn	2 tablespoons corn meal
3 eggs, well beaten	1 teaspoon salt
2 cups sweet milk	½ teaspoon black pepper
2 tablespoons sugar	2 tablespoons melted butter

For rewarding results use young field corn. After the ears are shucked and the silks removed, wash and dry them. Then cut off the tips of the kernels, and next hold the ears, one at a time, above a bowl. With the back of the blade of a dull knife scrape out the insides of the kernels with care not in include any of the outside covering.

Beat the eggs until very light, add the milk, and beat to mix. Then fold in the other ingredients and pour the combination into a greased, heavy casserole. Bake it in a moderately hot oven, 375°, from 35 to 40 minutes, or until the pudding does not shake when the casserole is moved. (Some women like to set the dish in a shallow pan of warm water during the baking.) When the mixture starts to stiffen on the sides while cooking, lightly fold or pull it toward the center. Or gently lift the corn up through the pudding with a spatula three times while it bakes. The trick is to keep it suspended in the custard rather than to allow it to settle, and not to overcook.

For another popular pudding, the following ingredients are used:

Four ears of corn, 2 eggs, 1 cup of sweet milk, 2 tablespoons of sugar, 3 tablespoons of melted butter, ½ teaspoon of salt, and ¼ teaspoon of black pepper. In these, as in other southern recipes, milk is specified as sweet, sour, or buttermilk. In the North, milk denotes the sweet fluid, with the less frequently used sour or buttermilk so designated.

Some kitchen artists grate corn from cobs, although most of them prefer the scraping technique. For an off-season pudding in winter months, some cooks use frozen corn-on-the-cob.

In the Nation's Okra Belt

Other famed corn dishes include baked tomatoes and parboiled green peppers stuffed with "boiled" or pan-fried and seasoned kernels, and the combinations with okra, onions, and tomatoes. Often, two or more vegetables are cooked together. These medleys are regional favorites.

Bacon frequently is at the bottom of okra dishes. Southern women pan-fry it, lift out the crispy slices and slowly cook a sliced onion, ¼-inch rounds of tender okra pods, and the corn kernels for 10 minutes, while stirring constantly. Then they add peeled and diced tomatoes, and chopped green pepper. They cook the mixture very gently for about 20 more minutes, or until it is quite dry. When they pour it into the serving dish they sprinkle the top with crumbled bacon and buttered, toasted bread crumbs. One hostess has a smart stunt for company. She adds cooked shrimp or cut-up cooked ham to okra and serves it over fluffy boiled rice for an entree.

Both in Georgia and northern Florida corn dishes have a charming habit of blending with pimento. Not only does the flavor recommend the dish, but the splash of color also lends eye appeal.

Perhaps one reason why okra maintains so many loyal friends in the region stems from the habit of selecting the young, delicate pods rather than larger and more mature, but less tender ones. Commonly cooks simmer them in a little salted water, and add seasonings of butter, salt, and black pepper. Sometimes they pan-fry them in bacon drippings. Okra, corn, and chicken, gourmets specify, complement one another. Tomatoes and okra also get along famously, and the dish they compose answers to gumbo, its favorite name.

Since the discovery that okra freezes successfully, quantities of it are stored in food lockers and home freezers.

A Dallas home economist who is famed as a wonderful cook explained to me her favorite way of preparing okra to avoid the slippery or slick texture obnoxious to some people. She said:

"You take two kettles of rapidly boiling salted water. Into one you drop succulent okra pods and cook them briskly until the water becomes slightly discolored and thickens a little. Then you lift them out with a slotted spoon and drop them into the other kettle of boiling water. When barely tender you drain and season them. Under the Lone Star we settle for salt, pepper, butter, and lemon juice."

Potatoes Mean Sweet Potatoes

Descriptions of sweet potato dishes Southerners rave about could fill a book. Their popularity increases as you travel south. The word potato throughout the region connotes the *sweet* potato. The white tubers are designated as *Irish* potatoes. In the South *creamed* potatoes are what Northerners call *mashed* potatoes. When a southern cook mashes the cooked potatoes she follows the mashing with a thorough whipping which she calls *creaming*.

For most of the *sweet potato* dishes the potatoes are cooked first, often in water, although in some kitchens the rule is to rub them sparingly with fat and then bake them in a Dutch oven, or some other heavy utensil with a snugly fitting lid.

Southern types of candied sweet potatoes circulate generally over the country, in every state. The creamed or mashed potatoes commonly have beaten eggs incorporated to increase their lightness. They carry an infinite variety of seasonings, like those from citrus fruits, nuts, coconut, spices, marshmallows, raisins, brown sugar, sherry wine, bourbon whiskey, rum, and pineapple, both the juice and the crushed fruit. Usually a Southerner bakes and serves them in heavy casseroles.

Sweet potato balls definitely belong to the region's winter holiday and special occasion meals. The trick is to shape the seasoned and mashed vegetable in spheres the size of golf balls, usually around luscious hearts of nuts, raisins, soft prunes stuffed with nuts, or pineapple chunks. Then they are rolled in cornflakes or nuts and chilled. Just before mealtime they are run into the oven or immersed in hot fat just long enough to heat and brown.

Certainly one of the taste thrills at Christmas time comes from Tennessee and North Carolina kitchens. The creamed sweet potatoes, seasoned, with chopped black walnuts and raisins folded in, surround marshmallows. These orange-hued balls are rolled in crushed cornflakes. When baked the marshmallows disappear for an elusive taste that complements the flavorful potato.

Here Come Greens and "Pot Likker"

Greens and "pot likker" typify the simple dishes that stud the cuisine and enhance it. Many a nutritionist, aware of the food value of "pot likker," has shed tears because people in other sections rarely appreciate its virtues. Countless Southerners do not care that their pet rates as a gold mine of vitamins and food minerals; to them the taste is so pleasing that nothing else matters.

When asked to define "pot likker," a native son or daughter replies, "It is that delicious liquid in which greens cook with pork — the broth carries the flavor of both. Most frequently it contains the juices of young turnip tops or collards, although other leaves also are good." The fat pork answers to several names — salt pork, side meat, middlin' meat, and sowbelly.

All lists of favorite greens include turnips, collards, kale, spinach, mustard, and plants that grow wild, colloquially known as *Fence Corner greens.* Tennessee people name as a few of their favorites from the roadsides (in the spring the highways sometimes are lined with brightly clad, stooping, singing Negroes, out in the sunshine, and taking their time to gather the delicate plants) mustard, poke, wild cabbage, narrow leaf dock, dandelion, lamb's quarter, plantain, and *careless weed.* Virginia likes land cress, commonly called *creasy greens.* Florida beams over a cultivated kind, called *tender greens,* a cross between turnip tops and mustard greens.

Regardless of what greens are chosen, the fat pork is first simmered in water for about 1½ hours, or until it sticks tender. Then the washed greens are added and cooked until they, too, are tender. In many homes the tradition is to simmer them a long time, perhaps 1 to 1½ hours. People who are fond of them cheerfully explain to questioning Yankees, "They taste good that way."

In serving, a sauce dish or small bowl is supplied for some of the juices. Also provided are hot corn bread, a cruet of cider vinegar, and, if available, chopped green onions for a garnish. There is no competition for a menu of greens with "pot likker," green onions, and corn bread almost hot enough to burn the fingers.

Black-eye Peas Bring Good Luck?

That vegetable known as green or garden peas in the North becomes *English peas* in the South. The name distinguishes them from the field varieties rarely cooked above the Mason and Dixon line. *Black-eye peas* are historic fare to which many Southerners are devoted. Texans off the home base and unable to buy them become unhappy. They freeze large quantities of the vegetable when it is in season, and also can it on a commercial scale. Black-eye peas with hog's jowls, if eaten on New Year's Day, are said to bring peace and plenty throughout the year to come.

Virginians are especially enthusiastic about black-eye peas when served with tomatoes. A favorite treatment is to simmer the beans until tender in salted water and then to drain, mash, and brown them in bacon fat. The beans are topped with tomatoes "cooked down" until quite thick and seasoned with salt, pepper, a little sugar, and butter or bacon fat. Ribbons of crisp bacon garnish the homespun dish. Some southern cooks simmer the peas until tender in water and season them with ham drippings.

Two kinds of field peas are praised in north Florida, the area north of an imaginary line drawn from east to west through Gainesville, and where customs of the South prevail. Both *Lady Finger* and *Acre* peas retain their light color during cooking. A Florida habit is to shake a little "liquid fire" from a bottle of tiny, hot bird's-eye peppers, covered with vinegar, over them at the table. (An old Savannah custom is to mash one of these freshly picked green peppers in the bowls before adding soup. Then the condiment is removed, for it is extremely hot — too hot to eat. Its flavor quickly permeates the soup.) These peppers, bottled, sell well at Christmas bazaars in north Florida. Texans like to sprinkle an aggressive pepper sauce on greens. Indeed, a cruet filled with it is as much standard equipment on many southern rural tables as are salt and pepper shakers.

Both green and ripe tomato slices, dipped in corn meal and pan-fried, create a cheerful mood at mealtime. These appear to be more popular in Kentucky, Virginia, Maryland, and Delaware than farther south. The accepted technique is to slice green tomatoes ¼ inch thick and ripe ones ½ inch thick, and to discard the stem end pieces. Bacon drippings or butter is the favorite fat for pan-frying; salt and black pepper are the seasonings. The stunt is to brown the vegetable slices on both sides, and then to reduce the heat and simmer gently until tender. Green tomatoes accompany sausage, chicken, and pork, and ripe ones accent the flavor of broiled steaks and chops, as well as chicken.

Maryland Cooks Are Tomato Experts

Maryland and Delaware cooks, after lifting the warm tomato circles to a hot platter and arranging them atop buttered toast, make a cream gravy with the drippings and pour it over the vegetable. Then there are the unique Maryland creamed tomatoes. They start out as a fried treat, and are seasoned with salt, pepper, and a bit of sugar. After they are lightly browned and tender, the cook stirs them, and continues the gentle cooking to evaporate the juices. When they are quite dry she folds in a little cream, either sweet or sour. This simple, superdelicious dish goes to breakfast, brunch, and luncheon tables as an escort for bacon and toast.

Delaware tomatoes enjoy a remarkable reputation for their superior flavor, and the diminutive state also assumes prestige for its celery dishes, especially the celery-tomato concoctions. Celery grows in many backyard gardens, and gets involved in various food combinations to lend a crunchy note, as in macaroni and cheese, creamed dried beef, and English peas, as well as in salads.

Opinions about creamed vegetables vary in different sections of the South. Virginians use no flour. They season the cooked vegetable with a little butter, salt, and black pepper. Then they pour in barely enough cream to keep the food from sticking to the pan, or about 2 tablespoonfuls to a family serving.

Creamed cymblings caper in and out of food conversations in the Old Dominion, where they command much favor. Cymblings are succulent little squash, the crooknecks and patty pans. Cooks simmer the whole, wee squash in a little water, just enough to provide steam. Frequently they add a few onion slices. When the vegetables become tender and the liquid evaporates, they mash them and season with butter, salt, pepper, and a small amount of cream. Sometimes the cymbling-onion combination, after it is mashed, is browned in a little bacon drippings; then cream is omitted. Young white turnips, cooked like cymblings without the onions, and butter beans (lima beans) also score highly when creamed the Virginia way.

Eggplant Commands a Broad Acceptance

Eggplant reaches a high plane of deliciousness in the southern cuisine. There are dozens of glamorous, taste-tantalizing dishes in which it appears. I met one of the memorable ones in the Mississippi Delta when the gracious wife of a prominent planter invited me to her idea (mine, too!) of a good southern dinner. It is called eggplant soufflé.

To make it you drop slices of eggplant and white bread in hot fat to brown. Then you drain and alternate the slices with cheese slices in a baking dish. You start with eggplant and end with the cheese on top. Over this you pour 1 cup of sweet milk folded into 4 eggs beaten very light and seasoned with salt and pepper. You bake the dish at 350° about 20 minutes.

PLANTATION DINNER
Frosted Mint Julep
Shrimp Cocktail
Southern Fried Chicken   Cream Gravy
Rice   Eggplant Soufflé
Tender Greens with Ham Hock
Sweet Potatoes en Casserole
Corn Pones   Hot Rolls
Eggnog Pie
After Dinner Coffee

Following the dinner, which was served in the early afternoon, plantation style, I walked in the bright spring sunshine to watch the planting of cotton in fields as level and unending as those of western Kansas wheat. And when late that night without supper I tumbled drowsily and happily into bed, I still was dreaming of the magnificent dinner and the picture dessert. The delicate eggnog pudding, molded in a spring form pan lined with lady fingers, came to the dining room on a large round silver plate. A hat of whipped cream, trimmed with red cherries, graced its top, and wreathed on the plate's rim were trailing vines of red honeysuckle in full bloom.

Potatoes Bake in Resin

One unusual picnic triumph of north Florida goes by the name of potatoes baked in resin. It in no way does justice to their wonderful taste. Here is how the picnic chef prepares them.

He drops scrubbed spuds of baking size into kettles of boiling resin (undistilled turpentine). The molten mass almost instantly seals them. The juices, unable to escape, provide vapor with a magnificent tenderizing effect. No flavors are lost. The coating of resin insulates the tubers and keeps them hot for several hours.

When cooked they rise to the top of the boiling resin. The chef lifts them out with a long-handled spoon, and places each one in the center of a 1-foot square of heavy paper. He wraps it around the potato, to provide more insulation, and twists both ends. Thus you have a hot potato that resembles a giant candy kiss.

At the picnic you make no attempt to remove the paper. You cut through it to eat the vegetable's steaming heart as it melts the butter you lavish on it.

A Galaxy of Delightful Salads

If you see salad listed on a menu card in Virginia or North Carolina and order it, you need not be surprised if the waiter delivers piping hot greens. In various communities cooked and seasoned plant leaves carry the salad name.

Cole slaw appears everywhere throughout the region; many editions show the gay color of pimento, and are mixed with homemade "boiled dressing."

Wilted lettuce, a colonial favorite, continues in favor. North Carolinians first called it *Mountain Salad*. In the early westward trek of people from this state to southern Indiana and other places in the West, they carried the knack of making the spring delicacy beyond the Great Smokies and across the Ohio River.

Bright red tomato slices, without benefit of dressing, also assume the salad position. Sometimes they alternate with circles of sweet onions. Cucumbers and onions, sliced, and dressed with vinegar, salt, pepper, and a trace of sugar, serve as salad, although they go to the table in a relish dish. For summer guests, tomatoes and cucumbers on lettuce frequently win the honors, while in winter grapefruit and avocado take over in grand style.

Stuffed tomato salads, cheerful in appearance, refresh your spirits in warm weather meals. What the red vegetable cups contain cannot be lost sight of, but at least some of their goodness stems from the shivery cold temperatures; they are partly frozen. Often they encase cottage or cream cheese with nuts, like pecans or peanuts, and ample seasonings folded in. Summer ushers a myriad of frozen fruit salads to chilled plates. If they are served with hot, buttered rolls, thin slices of ham, and tall glasses of iced tea or chilly buttermilk, no supper complaints are forthcoming.

For supper in the country, ham-cheese balls enter the champion class. The chopped cooked ham is mixed into cottage cheese, along with minced chives and a few drops of onion juice. Half as much meat as cheese is used. The mixture is shaped in balls, rolled in toasted, chopped nuts, and fringed with lettuce. Hot biscuits and something to drink, such as iced or hot tea, accompany it.

Bibb lettuce, a sport (bud variation) discovered in a Kentucky garden, shows up in countless salad bowls. The ruffle-edged leaves are more tender and fragile than leaf lettuce, have a sweet, flavorful taste, and no bitter under-tone. The plants grow in small, loose heads. Not the least of their good points is the brilliant yellow-green coloring that contrasts so handsomely with the darker green edges of the leaves.

For Christmas, Georgia people like strips of pimento, chopped celery, and broken pecans molded in lemon flavored gelatin on greens. North Florida favors grapefruit, avocado, and strips of pimento on lettuce for the great Yuletide dinner. Farther south on the peninsula, where sunshine streams through open kitchen windows in mid-winter, trans-planted Northerners on December 25th like to fashion a salad of lettuce, sliced radishes, and green onions, fresh from the garden.

Relishes Help Make the Meal

In many kitchens the relishes to serve with meals receive considerable thought. Good cooks know these aids can almost insure the success of a menu, or at least give it more than ordinary status. They select the one that complements the meat, fish, or poultry. Sometimes it substitutes for the salad.

Peach and watermelon rind pickles, veteran contributors of zest, maintain their places. In Georgia and the Carolinas, artichoke (the ground or Jerusalem kind) pickles and relishes enjoy considerable prestige. Pickled tiny onions also have a wide circle of friends. In the mountain homes of North Carolina some hostesses present grape leaf pickles. Every cucumber is wrapped in a leaf from the vine before it takes the cure. It comes out extra delicious.

Spiced pears and crabapples enhance a number of menus. In northern Florida many women prepare a tasty relish from their rather hard native pears. They run the fruit through a food chopper with green and red sweet peppers and onions, then cook them with sugar, vinegar, celery seed, and spices. Tiny okra pods, dilled like cucumbers in other areas, and guava jelly provide delight on the flowery peninsula, while corn-pimento relishes in Georgia give promise of a chicken dinner.

Fig preserves and pickles also contribute flavor to meals. For generations they have been as dear to Southerners as cranberries are to residents of Cape Cod. Frozen figs from lockers or freezers denote a newer delicacy of the region.

BREAKFAST IN SARDIS
Mississippi
Frozen Figs
Cream   Lemon Juice
Pan-broiled Country Ham
Red-eye Gravy
Hominy Grits
Hot Biscuits
Coffee

Maryland cheers for pickled and spiced cherries, yellow tomato preserves, sweet pickled figs, and homemade chili sauce so brimful of flavor that it answers as a sandwich filling. On Kentucky tables the homemade sauce often accompanies fried green tomatoes.

Some Blackberries Are White

Blackberry jelly and jam speak with a southern accent. So do jellies made from the white and fragrant scuppernongs and the purple muscadines, native grapes that grow singly on the vines rather than in bunches. Tennessee has white blackberries, but in the kettle during jelly making they turn red. Wild blackberries command high esteem; natives describe the cultivated ones as lacking in flavor.

The tartness of Mayhaw jelly, made from a fruit named for the month of May, points up meat flavors. Missouri kitchens turn out gooseberry jam, jelly, and preserves by the quarts to serve with chicken, turkey, and pork. Damson plum preserves especially occupy a prominent place in dressing up desserts. Pepper sauce, green tomato pickles, and a hundred and more other relishes lend distinction to the regional cuisine.

Virginians hold that their uncooked cucumber relish

improves the taste of the pork or sausage it accompanies. To make it they peel cucumbers and grate them. Large cucumbers or those with well-developed seeds are avoided.

Then they squeeze the pulp in cheesecloth to remove the juice. To it they add a little grated onion, salt, and black pepper. After that they pour on cider vinegar to cover. This simple recipe proves to any doubting Thomas that not all topnotch southern recipes are elaborate and labor consuming.

When Is a Pie a Cake?

A first-time visitor browsing around the South gets confused with the pie talk. Not until he discovers that some persons refer to all pies as *cakes* if they are not fruit filled does he understand the conversations. After that he feels as if he were walking with Uncle Sam in a wonderland of desserts.

Chess pie, of English descent, possibly typifies the outstanding southern pie. Uncle Sam bows and tips his hat to this jewel. Beautifully crimped, flaky, tender, and crisp pastry shells hold the rich filling. The farm's best gifts go into this filling: butter, eggs, cream, and sugar (brown or white or both), usually with vanilla or lemon flavoring. Puffy and rich yellow when delivered from the oven, the filling falls as it cools and becomes jelly-like in consistency. Some cooks bake the filling in tiny pastry shells and to store them when cool they stack the very thin tarts in one another like sauce dishes on the cupboard shelf. Other cooks spread the top with Damson preserves, and cover it with a meringue to brown delicately in a slow oven.

Transparent pie I first met north of the Ohio River in Cincinnati as a gentle, gracious Kentucky lady of some 80 years described the delicacies of her native state. She said, "In Kentucky we make transparent pies, so good tasting that once sampled you never forget them. For our picnics we like the pie or tarts as dessert."

After I crossed the Ohio River and jaunted around in the bluegrass country I encountered the famous dessert. Indeed, I shall always remember it. This treat is so rich and satisfying that to many of its friends a dream picnic has merely the two-piece menu, transparent pie and black coffee. One of my hostesses demonstrated step by step how to make it.

First you line the pie or tart pans with a rich pastry. Then you spread on a layer of tart, homemade jelly. An 8-ounce glassful is the correct amount for a 9-inch pie. Then you add the filling, of 1 cup of butter, 3 eggs well beaten, and 1 cup of sifted sugar, beaten with an electric mixer until light and spongy. You spread it over the jelly and run the pie in a very hot oven, 450°, for 5 minutes. Then reduce the heat to 375° to complete the baking, which requires about 20 minutes more. When the center of the pie is *almost* firm, as you gently shake the pan, the time has arrived to remove it from the oven.

As I learned that evening in Cincinnati, and later in Virginia and the Carolinas, the transparent pie is served faintly warm or cold. Never, even in the greatest time of hurry, does it come to the table hot. The filling resembles what the English used to call "a cheese." Perhaps all chess pies in America descended from it.

That same glorious evening the delightful lady from Kentucky gave me my first description of old-time *stack pie,* which is a treat I never have seen. Before the War Between the States, she said, people in her community came to all-day picnics with from four to six transparent pies stacked on top of one another and held together with a cooked white frosting. This simplified transporting several pies in a picnic basket. The bottom pie was of regulation size, but the ones layered above carried a thin filling about ¼ inch thick. While freshly baked and before the pastry became cool and brittle the cook trimmed it off above the filling.

Sugar pies belong to the transparent pie clan. They do not have a layer of jelly, are vanilla flavored, and wear a fluffy meringue. Possibly they are first cousins!

Cream Pies Are Custard Pies

Desserts the Southerners refer to as *cream pies* classify in some other areas as *custard pies*. They contain egg-thickened cream fillings.

Also among the desserts appears buttermilk pie. The custard filling is composed of buttermilk as the liquid; it is flavored with lemon juice and the grated peel, and is dusted with cinnamon. In some kitchens the lemon is replaced by bourbon, and the cinnamon by nutmeg.

My eyes first saw the recipe for this pie years ago in a *Woman's Home Companion* contest, in which a distinctive dish of every state was chosen from entries submitted by readers. Buttermilk pie won the trophy for Georgia. After it was made for photographing in a New York test kitchen, its deliciousness created a flurry of excitement that rippled along Park Avenue. It boasted orange pastry, which contained 1/4 teaspoon of grated peel and 1 tablespoon of sugar. In this same memorable contest I discovered the unique black cake of Kentucky, which presently is described with other fabulous southern cakes.

Jeff Davis pie carries a nutmeg flavored cream filling, of cream, sugar, eggs, and shortening. *Burnt sugar pie* depends on caramelized brown sugar for its claim to distinction. This cream pie dresses up with a meringue. Jelly pie contains jelly whipped into creamed butter and sugar in its custard filling. And *burnt butter pie* owes its superior quality to the skillful browning of butter and flour in making the custard.

President Tyler's pudding pie reminds you of transparent pie. The filling contains both white and brown sugars, cream, butter, eggs, and vanilla, with nutmeg grated over the top. When the pies come from the oven they are dusted with powdered sugar, and then removed from the pans. Because the individual pies can be picked up and eaten from the fingers, they appear at many backyard picnics. That is exactly where I met this pudding pie, and on a similar occasion orange pudding pie, flavored with the juices and grated peel of the citrus fruit.

Pecan Pies Have Traveled Extensively

Coconut cream pies cross all state boundries in the South. They are of the kind a Kansan calls *coconut custard pies*. *Sweet potato custard pies* suggest those filled with pumpkin; in them the taste of bourbon whiskey or sherry wine sometimes may be detected. *Pecan pies*, once a regional dessert, have traveled to every part of the nation. Almost all Americans consider them among the best of our native dishes. In northern Florida my hostesses advised that their idea of the best pecan pie is one containing no more than ½ cup of sugar, with cane sirup furnishing the remainder of the sweetening.

Virginia people enjoy a rather unusual sweet potato pie in that slices of the vegetable, arranged like apples in a pastry-lined pan, provide the filling. They cook the potatoes first, but not long enough for them to become mushy. Even, unbroken slices are desired. After that they peel the cooled vegetable and slice it into the pastry-lined pan. Then they scatter on dots of butter, add sugar and spices, usually cinnamon and cloves, and 2 tablespoons of bourbon whiskey with a little water, just enough to create steam. A well-vented or latticed pastry top covers the pie.

Damson plum pies, with their latticed tops and dainty spicing of cinnamon, climb into the gourmet group. No wonder many home freezers and locker compartments contain the frozen, pitted fruit for off-season baking.

Any American who has not sampled lemon jelly pie needs no other incentive to make friends in the South. My husband's paternal grandmother, a native Virginian of high spirits and beauty, was an artist with the crisp, delicately browned pastry holding the sublime jellied filling composed of butter, eggs, sugar, and the juice and grated peel of lemons. Her great-granddaughter holds that the dessert with a scoop of vanilla ice cream on top makes one of the South's most luscious of all pies à la mode. The same lemon jelly without pastry is encountered in Delaware and Maryland and on southward as a sandwich spread and cake filling. Lemons play an important role in many of the region's taste treats.

A Signal From the Wild Turkey Contests

Cobblers substitute for pies, especially when a crowd is to be fed. In the Ozarks huckleberry cobblers testify to the bounty of summer. Peach cobblers also usher goodness to tables throughout the hill country. When cranberry cobblers with their tops of pastry strips come to the dinner tables and accounts of wild turkey calling contests appear in the county papers, Thanksgiving Day is just around the corner.

Some cobblers have a pastry crust on top. In others the pastry and fruit alternate in the deep dish, with butter and sugar added to the fruit, and a layer of pastry on top. Women say they are easier to make than pies.

Berry rolls deserve pretty words. Perhaps the coverlet of pastry spreads over more blackberries than other berries and fruits. However, sour cherries, apples, and many other offerings of berry patches and orchards get mixed into this superb concoction. The rich pastry is rolled into an oblong shape about 15 inches wide and the sugared and spiced berries or fruit are spread on it. Although spices are not always included, Southerners do like to add the proverbial pinch of cinnamon, especially to blackberries. They wind the pastry around the berries or fruit like a jelly roll, and press the ends and edges together to seal them. After that they brush it lightly with milk. They may or may not baste it during baking with a little sugar and butter dissolved and melted in hot water.

For ethereal fragrance and flavor, the kind remembered as a mountain top in gastronomical journeys, try Virginia's berry rolls. Cut the rolled, rich pastry in circles, heap on the season's choice ripe berries, sugared, and gather the pastry to form little bags. Place them side by side in the baking pan, tuck it in a hot oven, and if you peep within a few minutes later you see the luscious sugary juices bubbling up in the openings of the pastry tops.

When I left the fanciful blue haze of the hills, and the other thrilling charms of the Old Dominion behind, I recorded in my notebook, "Wonderful berry rolls that look so good, smell so good, and taste even better."

Tipsy Squire Reigns at Christmas

Evidence of the South's Anglo-Saxon heritage appears in puddings that climax many meals. For the Yuletide and other festive occasions, *tipsy pudding* or *tipsy squire* often crowns the feasts. To make it, most cooks thickly stud with blanched almonds a sponge cake about an inch in thickness. The almonds are split in lengthwise halves, with the pointed ends up. Then they place the cake in a glass bowl with a larger circumference than the cake and pour on about a cup of scuppernong or sherry wine to saturate it. Next they blanket the cake generously with a velvety soft custard and spread it lightly with faintly sweetened cream — the cream is not beaten stiff, but has about the same consistency as syllabub. Frequently the cream is flavored with a little of the wine. The masterpiece is chilled thoroughly. To serve the dessert the hostess brings the sparkling bowl to the table and cuts down through the custard and cake with a spoon, while everyone who witnesses the rite holds his ravenous appetite in check.

Grated sweet potato puddings rate as an authentic regional gem. Although they vary in minor ways, they carry certain earmarks. Standard ingredients are grated raw potato, eggs, sugar, butter, leavening, and vanilla, and often sour cream as the liquid. Georgians prefer cane sirup as a part of the sweetening. Many women like to bake the dessert in an iron skillet, which they say gives it the desired dark color similar to that of plum pudding. Traditionally Damson preserves accompany it, although plain cream is permissible. The southern gods frown on whipped cream for this dish.

It appears only as the choice of a misguided stranger or new-comer.

Puddings composed of cooked and mashed sweet potatoes commonly boast the flavor of spices and grated lemon peel, and sometimes of brandy or bourbon.

Woodford pudding — a spiced, baked number, that Kentuckians rave about — contains jam, usually blackberry jam. It is served with a sweet pudding sauce. Without question it is an offspring of English jam pudding.

Bishop Whipple's Pudding Connotes Alabama

Bishop Whipple's pudding seems to belong to Alabama, although you meet it elsewhere. Briefly defined, it is a delicious date dessert rich in pecans. For some unexplained reason, the pudding is baked and cooled, and then broken up at serving time and mixed with whipped cream.

Ozark apple puddings of many styles appear from the friendly kitchens of the hill country, an area where many cooks of rare talent live. These crisp crusted desserts often bristle with spices. Whipped cream glorifies them. Persimmon pudding fares well in Arkansas, North Carolina, and Kentucky, but it creates little fanfare in comparison with that generated by Hoosiers in southern Indiana over this native dessert.

Confederate pudding illustrates the unending possibilities in new twists with bread pudding. Of coure this one is not new; it is a wartime creation (War Between the States). For it, cooks spread slices of white bread with butter and jam or jelly and stack them in a greased baking dish. Then they pour on milk, with beaten eggs added, almost to cover. After the bread absorbs the milk they bake the old-fashioned dessert.

Ambrosia and Christmas Arrive Together

Ambrosia associates with Christmas like turkey and Thanksgiving. Sections of peeled and seeded oranges are alternated with a sprinkling of sugar and grated fresh coconut. (Coconut graters are a favorite kitchen gadget.) Always the coconut spreads its snowy white splendor over the golden fruit. Many hostesses emphasize that you should prepare the dessert a day early, to chill, and blend the flavors. Everyone warns, "Do not add too much sugar. The sweetness of the fruit determines how much, but ambrosia on the tart side tastes best."

Various additions to ambrosia are favored nationally, such as sherbets, grapefruit sections, pineapple, dates, bananas, cherries, and frozen berries. Mostly they displease Southerners, who consider them rank intruders.

Soft custard challenges ambrosia for the title of champion Christmas dessert. Custard — flavored with almond, vanilla, or sherry, and chilled — frequently is served with fresh coconut layer cake or pound cake.

All during the year, especially throughout the Colonial States of the South, berry and fruit floats climax meals. Floats consist of chilled custard in dessert dishes with berries or fruits. In winter, applesauce and sliced bananas unite with custard for the treats. You meet them in southern Indiana and Illinois, too, where so many people from the South once established homes.

Syllabubs Feature Nature's Airiness

Syllabub churns on gala occasions put a foam on cream to skim into tall glasses. The cream commonly is sweetened and sherry flavored. People who live in Tennessee generally drop a long, slender spike of ice into each glass. Today's syllabubs descend from an English recipe brought to Virginia long ago. At that time, so historians record, cream, sugar and flavoring in a bowl were taken to the dairy. As the worker squirted a stream of milk into it, a froth rose to the top. It is this type of airiness that the churns are supposed to duplicate.

Eggnog for Christmas in Maryland, Virginia, Kentucky, and in many homes in all other southern states fills the bowls as regularly as mistletoe hangs over doorways. The bowl may hide in idleness the remainder of the year, but many families consider it essential for the one annual appearance during the Yuletide. Salted pecans and almonds, and slices of traditional pound and fruit cakes accompany it. Mulled wine and wassail parties also blossom around the region during the holidays, where open houses are legion.

Christmas tea parties bring out glamorous food, china, and silver on a wide regional scale. I well recall one in northern Alabama. At both ends of the beautifully appointed table were gleaming silver tea pots. From one, steaming amber tea was poured, and from the other, hot spiced cranberry juice. Dainty slices of delicious cakes, nuts, and candies completed the refreshments. Christmas cookies were not represented, although they are served frequently in social gatherings. The South, which is famed for gorgeous layer cakes, may not have numerous cookies to compare with those of Milwaukee and Minneapolis, but Southerners, too, know the art of saying "Merry Christmas" with the food they serve.

Kentuckians Pull Cream Candy!

Southern candies vie with other delicacies for their rightful place in the Christmas food scene. At Greenville, Mississippi, my gracious hostess tempted and delighted her guests with white squares of divinity studded with red and green candied cherries; plump pieces of chocolate fudge splashed with green sugar; and dusky homemade chocolate creams decorated with silver dragees that glittered in the candlelight.

Molasses, coconut, and peanut candies are southern, as are other specialties mentioned in the Coastal and Gulf regions. And then, as everyone who has tasted the confection remarks enthusiastically, "We have Kentucky cream pull candy."

I learned of this prize confection from the charming Kentucky lady who also introduced transparent pie to me. She gave a step-by-step account of how she made it. My mouth watered as she talked, as it did later in Kentucky, where many more natives told me of their gold medal candy. They showed me hooks in kitchens over which hundreds of ribbons of the candy have been pulled to perfection for many years.

That was the inspiration for my experiments in making Kentucky creams, some days with enviable success, and on others with disappointing results. The candy has a tricky way of turning to sugar prematurely, but when it behaves properly it is a confection second to no other. That is why it is worth working and striving for.

Aunt Phoebe's Kentucky Creams

For maximum chances of success use a heavy utensil and first cook in it ½ cup of water, 2 cups of sugar, ¼ teaspoon of salt, and a scant ⅛ teaspoon of soda. Don't stir until the mixture spins a fine thread 3 to 5 inches long when a little of the sirup is dropped from a spoon, about 250°. The sirup also signals when the cream-adding stage has arrived. Large, clear bubbles arise. That means it is time to introduce ½ cup of cream. Add it almost drop by drop so as not to stop the bubbling or boiling. It is important to keep the sirup boiling all the time. After the cream is in the sirup, lower the heat and simmer the mixture until it turns a very light butterscotch brown, and again will spin a thread 3 to 5 inches long, 250°. The entire cooking process takes no longer than 20 minutes, and often less.

Pour little rivers of the hot sirup, about 6 inches long, on buttered baking sheets or in shallow pans that have been chilled until *very cold* in the refrigerator or freezer. After the last sirup streamlet leaves the kettle, pick up the first one and start pulling. Add other pieces of candy just as soon as they are cool enough to handle.

When the candy turns a very pale ivory color, twist it in a rope about 1 inch wide and lay it on buttered plates or platters. It hardens quickly.

Hurry to cut it in 1½-inch lengths with the kitchen scissors. After that, lightly cover the candy with waxed paper and let it stand 3 or 4 hours at room temperature on the table top until, like magic, it creams. At this stage it dissolves into supreme sweetness and sheer delight when it touches the tongue. Before that it is chewy. Then, if you wish to save the candy for a special occasion, layer the pieces, so they do not touch, between waxed paper or aluminum foil in a tightly closed can.

That evening in Cincinnati my amiable informant confessed that she occasionally liked to flavor the candy with a few drops of peppermint and to tint it a pale pink as she pulled it; and then, after it creamed, to dip it in melted semi-sweet chocolate. Because the hours we spent discussing Kentucky food shine brightly in memories of my tours, and also because the gracious lady has gone to her final reward, I christen this candy *Aunt Phoebe's Kentucky Creams*. As an aristocrat of native American confections it carries the name with distinction and grace.

Here Come the Cakes

The fame of southern cooking stands steadfastly on cakes. Repeatedly they win dessert sweepstakes. Many old-time favorites greet you only on extra-special occasions like Christmas, wedding parties, or the arrival of a dear friend not seen for years. To a certain extent the elegant layer cakes represent a waning art, but one that still displays considerable vigor in some home kitchens.

Fruit cakes associate with other traditional foods during the Yuletide season. Kitchens time their making by the calendar. The Virginia rhythm starts in late September when the dark fruit cakes are baked, cooled, wrapped, and put away to ripen. Between Thanksgiving and December first the white fruit cakes claim attention. And around December 15th, pound cakes, an English heritage, dominate the Old Dominion's food preparations for the holidays.

A pound cake recipe serves as the foundation for fruit cakes in Virginia, Maryland, and southern communities elsewhere. Many women add 9 pounds of candied and dried fruits to it, although a few use 10 pounds or more. In some households the fruits are soaked overnight in brandy or lemon and orange juices to plump them and to make them easier to separate. Molasses is not added.

Often chefs douse about ½ cupful brandy over the warm cake as it comes from the oven. They dribble on some 2 tablespoonfuls of it every week during the aging. In Virginia and

Maryland, and to some extent in the other states, fruit cakes bake in heavy tube pans. Occasionally a kitchen has, as a prized and useful legacy, the old-time octagonal tube pans with the characteristic ridges in the bottoms.

Turk's Heads Appear in Maryland

For black walnut cake, cooks reduce the shortening in pound cake recipes by a fourth and add ¾ cup of chopped black walnut meats. Tennessee people like walnuts, but they also dote on pound cakes rich with native hickory nuts. Usually these nut cakes are baked in fluted pans with tubes, sometimes referred to in Maryland and Delaware as "flue pans," or Turk's Heads. (A real Turk's Head is a heavy copper tube pan, normally lined with tin.) Powdered sugar dusted over the warm nut cakes renders frosting superfluous.

Virginians and Carolinians, and some of their neighbors, reduce the shortening in white fruit cake and add freshly grated coconut. Neither the nut or coconut loaves keep so well as fruit cakes. Unless freezer space is available for them they are likely to be small. Sally White cake, a traditional favorite of eastern Virginia and the Carolinas, is said to have been named long ago for a beautiful belle. Among its contents are fresh grated coconut, citron, almonds, spices, and sherry.

South Carolinians serve slices of pound cake with soft custard, sometimes with fresh or frozen berries and fruits. If toasted, there is a crown of vanilla ice cream. A leader in home economics extension at Rock Hill explained, "Our men like pound cake best of all."

Black cake, a Kentucky original, belongs to the fruit cake family. The recipe uses browned flour, an unusual feature to people in most areas, but not uncommon in the South. To prepare it, spread the required measurement of flour in a heavy frying pan or other shallow utensil and run it in a moderately hot oven, 375°. Stir it occasionally from the sides and bottom to prevent it from sticking and burning. When it becomes an even tan color, the flour with the different taste is ready for the mixing bowl. This cake also contains blackberry jam, raisins, dates, figs, spices, nuts, sour cream, and bourbon for flavoring. It is baked in a tube pan, like other fruit cakes.

While fruit and pound cakes especially offer tribute to Christmas, other holiday treats perform brilliantly during the Yuletide season. Some enter the traditional group. One such layer cake goes by the name of *Japanese fruit cake* in Georgia, Florida, the Carolinas, and Alabama; *Chinese fruit cake* in Tennessee, and *Oriental fruit cake* in Virginia.

A Trend Toward Smaller Cakes

Although it now frequently has only two layers, the traditional cake boasted of four. The trend in the South, as elsewhere, is to smaller cakes. Yet most Southerners, if they speak from the heart, admit they prefer four-layer cakes. They do not object to thin layers if the fillings and frosting meet taste specifications.

Half the batter for a two- or four-layer Oriental cake is plain, and the other half is dolled up with chopped nuts, raisins, and spices. When the cake is baked, the plain and fruited layers are alternated with the tasty filling in between. The filling is a cooked concoction of grated coconut, the grated peel and juice of lemons, and sugar. The top and sides draw a cooked white frosting of the fluffy type with a coconut trim.

In the Carolina Low Country and the Shenandoah Valley — the Valley of Virginia — my curiosity was piqued as the virtues of Rocky Mountain cake were extolled. Later I decided that to see is to believe in its beauty, and to taste is to revel in its lusciousness. Here is a white layer creation containing a frosting-filling as festive as a Christmas tree.

You make the frosting like a boiled one, by cooking 3 cups of sugar with 1 cup of water from a coconut and 3 tablespoons of light corn sirup. Then you pour a thin stream of the hot sirup over the whipped-until-light whites of 3 eggs, beating constantly. While still warm you add all the colorful goodies used in white fruit cake. The selection includes candied fruits cut fine, pineapple, red and green cherries, and lemon and orange peels, along with chopped white raisins, dates, figs, and nuts. In some kitchens only the candied fruits are folded into the frosting. The color-dotted frosting looks like confetti when it is spread between and over the white layers; then you scatter shreds of coconut on top.

Lane Cake Comes Out for Christmas

Lane cake tops the Christmas cakes in Georgia and Alabama. Many women get out their Lane cake recipes when they hang Christmas wreaths on the door. The place where the cake was born is debated; members of the Camellia Garden Club in Tallahassee, Florida, believe Georgia wins the distinction, but that Alabama also had a star in the culinary show. The story appears in the *Camellia Cook Book,* published by the club. (The first time I was in Tallahassee this book was presented to me with a beautiful pink camellia taped to the cover, as if it grew from the volume.) Here is the history it records of the layer cake.

The first Lane cake was made by Emma Rylander Lane of Americus, Georgia. Alabama enters the picture in the person of a friend. In a cook book edited by Mrs. Lane in 1880 she refers to her accomplishments in a few words: "My prize cake is named Lane cake not from conceit of my own but through the courtesy of Mrs. Janie Pruett of Eufaula, Alabama."

Regardless of who thrilled over the first one, today's versions are spectacular to behold and delightful to eat. This white butter cake, composed of four layers made with 8 egg whites, has an exotic filling. For it women cook the egg yolks, sugar, and butter in a double boiler, and add chopped raisins, pecans, and coconut, with flavorings of bourbon and vanilla. A cooked, white frosting spreads in fluffs over the cake, and coconut decorates it. It differs from Rocky Mountain cake in its filling made with egg yolks. As mentioned previously, the filling for Rocky Mountain cake is a white icing with bright hued additions.

For parties and weddings, there are adaptations of Lane

cake — individual cakelets baked in muffin pans. After the cakelets are split in crosswise halves, with the filling spread between them and on the top, the frosting and coconut cover the miniature cakes. Or the centers of the wee cakes are removed with a grapefruit knife and the filling added, with more of it spread on top. In this case the frosting is omitted.

No conscientious consideration of southern cakes slights the spicy jam numbers. Old-timers treasure them with a fervor frequently matched by the younger generation. Not so rich as fruit cake, but truly delectable, they show up at Christmas time in thousands of homes. Most of them contain blackberry jam — the kind with seeds — although red raspberry jam also is liked when available. Jam cakes by tradition are baked in square layer pans.

In Middle Tennessee, and possibly in other areas, the preference for a square cake over a round one goes back to a prejudice born after the War Between the States when the humbler homes possessed no layer pans. They baked their batters in pie pans with slanting sides, and the unattractive cakes subtracted from the prestige of all round layers, at least in some households.

Jam cakes wear caramel or brown sugar frosting between the layers and on their sides and tops. To catch the spirit of the holidays, all you need to do is to step into a kitchen and sniff the fragrance of one as it bakes. It reminds you that a significant season lies ahead.

In this great pecan producing area, pecan cakes of limitless varieties are favorites. Some of them, away from the Southern Colonial States, win preference over fruit cakes. Women frequently bake them in heavy tube pans after their tops have been decorated with nut halves and candied cherries. Bourbon often flavors them.

Cakes Stimulate Food Talk

Two lovelies, *Dolly Varden* and *marble* cakes, occasionally tempt you at a party. Both of them are made by dividing the batter into two parts.

For Dolly Varden's *fancy* layers, Virginians add chopped cherries, nuts, citron, currants, raisins, and cinnamon. Mississippi's interpretation calls for molasses and spices. The fancy and plain baked layers are alternated with a fluffy white cooked frosting between them and spread over the top and sides.

For marble cake cooks generally stir melted chocolate into half of the 1-2-3-4 cake, pour a thin layer of the light batter into the tube pan first, and then alternately add big spoonfuls of the dark and light batters. Before baking they carefully stir through the batter in a zigzag fashion with the handle of a spoon to blend the batters for a marbleized effect.

Contacts with these fascinating cakes lend an atmosphere of pleasure to a food reporter's work. They stimulate mellow talk, which rightly associates with fine food, about other great cakes like the *ante-bellum Merry Christmas cake* of Kentucky: white cake with a generous drifting of boiled frosting between the layers and on top, and bedecked with an extravagant crown of fresh coconut. I sampled an almond flavored cake with home economists at the University of Alabama. Flecks of pineapple dappled the white cooked frosting that coconut shreds decorated. It came with peach ice cream at its side. That makes a dessert duet that tempts the gods. All that is needed in addition for perfection is black coffee, and we had that, too — along with conversation worthy of the refreshments and a heavenly spring evening.

Not all the South's cake masterpieces are elaborate. Take the Virginia servings of squares of plain cake with what the natives call white sauce, for example. The sauce is a surprise. To a Yankee it suggests milk thickened with flour and seasoned with butter and salt. It is a delightful sweet composition commonly touched up with spices or lemon.

As a homely delicacy, Kentucky hostesses occasionally present you squares of warm plain cake just out of the oven, as a companion to ice cream. And sometimes it is served elsewhere. I first tasted the dessert in Natchez, Mississippi, at a memorable early afternoon dinner in one of the elegant mansions. I remember exactly the superdelicious taste of the homemade burnt sugar ice cream and the warm cake fresh from the oven.

There's a Robert E. Lee Cake

Another regional delicacy, chocolate angel food cake, occasionally contains crunchy pecans. The tastiness of one of these tempters, and the hospitality of an enjoyable friend, once made my departure from Athens, Georgia, a deep regret. The cake was spread with mocha flavored butter-confectioners' sugar frosting.

The South classifies as a region of light, fluffy, and moist angel food cakes with brown exteriors, and a subtle taste of vanilla supplemented with almond and orange flavorings. I especially remember an angel cake in Knoxville, Tennessee. It was split, spread with a lemon flavored custard pie filling, and dressed with lightly sweetened whipped cream. Flowers of spring made with thin pieces of yellow and green gumdrops provided the trim. There was a candy blossom for every serving. The hostess cut the cake before us, breaking the old custom of displaying only the slices.

Signs of tradition linger, though. In Nashville, Tennessee, I observed pieces of unfrosted, light-as-a-feather angel food cake arranged in a wreath on a round silver plate. With the frosting in a pastry tube tinted a pale green tinged with yellow, the hostess piped a delicate trailing vine with dainty leaves over the cake. Later the picture created a sensation at a stunning buffet supper. The custom of serving cake slices is said to have originated because the southern hostess did not wish to reveal kitchen secrets, or show the size of her cake. "Your guests are not to know how much you have," mothers taught their daughters. "Let them think your supplies are unlimited."

Sponge cakes of the region often carry the taste of orange or lemon with vanilla. Indeed, in some kitchens the combination of citrus flavoring almost always blends with that of vanilla to hide the taste of egg yolks.

No northern food scout leaves southern kitchens without venturing to ask about the Robert E. Lee cake. She inquires, "How about the historic cake? Is it a myth? If not, what is it?"

You get a lively answer right off the tip of the tongue, like this, "Our General's favorite was a four-layer sponge cake, put together with a lemon jelly or filling. The cake was covered with an orange-lemon flavored frosting of confectioners' sugar and butter. We consider it one of our best cakes."

Still other food treats of the South appear in the two following chapters. They supply additional proof that in countless home kitchens cooking rates as a creative art, and eating one of our planet's major joys.

The Atlantic Coast

THREE stalwart branches of coastal cooking appear on Uncle Sam's food family tree. Geography christens them with descriptive names — eastern, western, and southern. Two oceans, the Atlantic and Pacific, contribute their riches. Another imposing body of water, the Gulf of Mexico, yields its treasures. Bays, sounds, rivers, and lakes also provide splendid gifts.

For more than two centuries the popularity of the eastern style of preparing sea food has snowballed along the curved shoreline of the Atlantic Ocean. Its glittering lights reflect a radiance like that of bright moonlight off water over the American food scene. Who has not heard of the triumphant dishes in the homes of Maryland's Eastern Shore, Tidewater Virginia, and the Carolina Low Country? There even a casual observer finds enough differences in the family and guest meals from those of the Mountain West and Farm Belt to silence the chatter about the disappearance of sectional foods across the U.S.A.

What an adventure for any American who enjoys good food to meander the first time from the Coast of Maine to the Florida Keys! Curious thoughts haunt anyone who comes from the inland when he sits down at the table to eat. Three times a day I wondered: Where has the magic carpet taken me? Am I on a new planet? Or did we stop off on the moon?

Kind hostesses volunteered as guides in my food explorations. When time permitted they ably demonstrated in their kitchens how to make the famous dishes. As I listened to their free and easy talk about lobsters, clams, crabs, oysters, scallops, and terrapin masterpieces, the conversation took on a fairy tale quality. Their obvious familiarity with the shore fish that abound in such miraculous variety flabbergasted me even more.

Beautifully cooked marine offerings came to dinner to tempt and to please — pompano, mackerel, shad, spot, rockfish, weakfish, bluefish, croaker, haddock, cod, and swordfish. The adults explained that impressive as the lineup was, it fell pitifully short of including half the species. School boys described how many of the fish live mainly in the open ocean and told how they migrate from season to season like the birds — often shoreward and to the north in the spring and summer, and out to sea and in a southerly direction when autumn reflects a promise of colder weather.

What? More Clam Chowders?

New England's fish and sea food specialties have appeared in a preceding chapter. The spotlight turns on those of the Gulf of Mexico and the Pacific Coast on subsequent pages.

Favorites of the Middle and South Atlantic differ from all of them. People who travel southward from New England note that the clambake gives way to crab feasts and oyster roasts. They encounter New York's version of clam chowder named *Manhattan* for the island on which it originated.

It is mainly a heart-warming vegetable soup without milk. Potatoes, onions, celery, green pepper, and tomatoes or tomato juice cook with the clam juices and water. Minced clams and seasonings complete the list of ingredients. When an uninitiated visitor takes the first sip he almost always remarks about the taste of thyme.

Farther south in New Jersey, Cape May clam chowder crowds the other types out of most bowls. It is thick and tasty. Natives say it improves every time the cook reheats it. No doubt that explains why many households with adequate refrigerator space prepare a quantity for more than one meal at a time. The South Jersey favorite contains onions, potatoes, salt pork, chopped clams, and water.

Cape Hatteras Forms a Marine Line

Anyone who wishes to investigate eastern coastal foods and have fun eating along the Atlantic Seaboard will never regret first getting acquainted with the more important fish and shellfish. Then mealtime is more rewarding. I not only visited and dined with men and women recognized in their respective communities as exceptional cooks. I also badgered the people who staff the fish markets for nuggets of their wisdom. That is how I filled many notebooks. These jottings reveal something of the fish story even if they do start off like a short course in geography.

Cape Hatteras, the farthest easterly point of North Carolina, where the gulf stream leaves the shore, is the Mason and Dixon line in the marine world. North of it to Cape Cod the Middle Atlantic species live. Southward the warm water types hold forth. Cape Cod divides the North and Middle Atlantic varieties. With approximately one-third of North Carolina's shoreline north of Cape Hatteras and the other two-thirds south of it, the fish of both regions mingle off the Old North State's shores. The marine separation is not absolute at any place. Travelers among the fish stray far from the areas where their respective families live in abundance.

Chesapeake Bay provides a splendid nursery for young stock. It offers an environment favorable for the spawning and growth of immature fish, many of which migrate when they become adults. The area, like that of other bays, the sounds, and the mouths of rivers attracts members of marine society which like water less salty than that the open ocean affords.

Introducing the Shellfish

CLAMS. The two Atlantic varieties of clams most prized are the soft-shell or long necks that thrive mostly north of Cape Cod, and the hard-shells or little necks, also called *quahogs,* that extend from Cape Cod to Texas. When the little necks come to the table on the half shell, people speak of them as *cherrystone clams.*

CRABS. Rock crabs inhabit coastal waters from Labrador to South Carolina. More of them abound off New England shores than elsewhere. Blue crabs are found from Massachusetts to northern South America, with Chesapeake Bay the principal commercial source of the delicacy. For their homes crabs choose shallow bays, sounds, and river channels instead of more salty ocean waters. The so-called *sweet* or *fresh water crabs* dwell in various places, as in the Atchafalaya River of Louisiana and North Carolina's Newport River.

Crabs moult many times before they finally reach maturity during their second summer. When they have discarded their shells and before new ones harden, they are soft-shell crabs. These young crabs are especially abundant in the upper Chesapeake Bay. They are recognized as a matchless delicacy.

LOBSTERS. Truly American, these crustaceans live only on the eastern shore of North America. They have been found as far north as Labrador, and as far south as North Carolina. Larger numbers of them wander in the waters north of Cape Cod than elsewhere, and especially from Maine northward along the shores of Canada.

Oysters Come From Underwater Farms

OYSTERS. Eastern oysters live in shallow waters from Cape Cod to Texas in large quantities, and sparingly north of Massachusetts to the Gulf of St. Lawrence. These mollusks grow most satisfactorily in enclosed bays, sounds, and river mouths where the influx of fresh water reduces the salinity. Great underwater oyster farms, cultivated as scientifically as the citrus groves of California and Florida and the corn fields of Iowa, produce the finest specimens.

SCALLOPS. The smaller bay scallops are considered the most tasty. The larger and more abundant sea scallops come from the ocean. Both kinds swim by rapidly opening and closing their two shells. The only part eaten in the United States, in contrast to Europe where all the scallop is enjoyed, is the rather large muscle called the eye. It controls the shell movements. Bay scallops normally live along the entire shore, or from New England to Florida. In recent years the mysterious disappearance of much of the eel grass, a plant that shelters them in their early stages, has greatly reduced the supply as far south as Bogue Island, North Carolina. South of this point eel grass does not grow.

SHRIMP. This crustacean, which resembles a miniature lobster, dwells along the shore from Maine to Texas. The commercial fisheries in the Gulf of Mexico are the most important. Small young shrimp winter along the beaches. The mature, larger ones move out into the ocean to escape the cold. Fishermen follow the jumbo or adult shrimp from March onward. The heaviest production comes in late summer and early autumn, usually in August and September, with a dwindling catch up through December.

SPINY LOBSTER. This species is not closely related to the American lobster and does not have giant claws. The meat comes from the flexible abdomens, called tails. The ones you see in the markets commonly range from 9 to 10 inches long. From the Florida Keys northward to Beaufort, North Carolina, they dwell on the rocky bottoms and coral reefs. Some people call them Florida lobsters.

Here Are a Few Shorefish

Strangers to the Atlantic coastal section frequently are confused by the way natives refer to the same fish by different names. This is noticeable in the following review of the pride of the eastern seaboard.

Butterfish. Strictly a commercial fish, it is sold throughout the year. The markets of Boston, New York, Philadelphia, Baltimore, and Norfolk offer it in sizes from 1/4 to 1½ pounds. This fat fish has a delicate flavor, and is ideal for pan-frying. Natives laud the way it cooks to a delightful brown and literally melts in the mouth.

Bluefish. Primarily a warm water species, it migrates up and down the Atlantic Coast from Florida to Massachusetts. Bluefish is a relative of the pompano, and rates as good eating when baked, broiled, or pan-fried. It is not the blue fish of Boston. That is the *pollock*.

Cod. This is a New England favorite that is found from Greenland to New Jersey, and irregularly southward from there to Cape Hatteras. Spring and summer bring the big catches. Market sizes normally weigh from 2½ to 10 pounds.

Flounder. About a half dozen species of flounders are native to the coastal waters from Maine to North Carolina. Three kinds are taken along the South Atlantic and Gulf Coasts. One of the favorites is the summer flounder or fluke; it is most abundant from Long Island to North Carolina. Although flounders on menus and in conversations are referred to as "fillet of sole," which they resemble in texture and flavor, they are not related to the renowned English sole.

Haddock. Most of the haddock of the western Atlantic Ocean live east of Massachusetts, Maine, and Nova Scotia. In winter some of them are found along the coasts of New

York and New Jersey, and a few reach deep water off Cape Hatteras. Cod and haddock are closely related, although haddock is smaller. New England's average size is 20 inches long, with a weight of from 2½ to 3 pounds. An average size cod weighs about 10 pounds. Frequently cod weighing from 50 to 60 pounds are taken from the deep sea.

Herring Is a Breakfast Favorite

HERRING. River herring, called *alewives* in New England, command a loyal following. They enter coastal waters in the spring, often in company with shad, and after spawning return to the ocean. These fish swim up the rivers of North Carolina and Virginia in tremendous numbers. The roe is much enjoyed. Small quantities of river herring are eaten fresh; when salted it ranks as a top breakfast favorite in coastal areas, and especially in North Carolina and Virginia. The traditional Sunday breakfast in North Carolina's Low Country features broiled salt roe herring and hot biscuits. Both the roe and herrings are canned commercially.

Sea herrings are another story. The young are canned, especially in Maine, for sardines. The smoked herring on Boston's markets is of this type — but in New York and southward smoked river herring is preferred.

KINGFISHES. This member of the croaker family also is known as the *king whiting*. It is popular in all Middle Atlantic States. This is a summer fish, and it occurs in greatest supply from New York to North Carolina. It is not the kingfish.

KINGFISH. Talk flourishes in North Carolina and Florida about this game fish. It is found from Brazil to Cape Cod. Its flesh contains few bones; its flavor is excellent.

MACKEREL. They are unpredictable fish that dwell much of the time in the deep ocean. In the spring they separate into southern and northern groups. The former division arrives in the Chesapeake and Delaware Bays in April. It summers off the Maine Coast. The northern group reaches southern New England in May and spends the warm weather in the Gulf of St. Lawrence. Usually mackerel are caught from March to December. They are appraised as fine eating when baked or broiled.

MULLET. This is a southern fish that frequently strays as far north as Cape Cod. It is found in abundance from North Carolina to Texas, and in many other parts of the world. Its roe also is eaten. A firm-textured fish, it commonly is broiled or baked, and it also is salted. There is a dividing line at the edge of the Piedmont in North Carolina where the marketing of salt mackerel ceases and the sale of salted mullet begins.

PORGY. In New England this fish is known as the *scup*. It lives along the entire Atlantic Coast. Markets in Norfolk, Philadelphia, New York, and other coastal cities offer it for sale. The porgy also classifies as a favorite of salt water anglers, especially off the southern shore of Long Island and around Camp May, New Jersey. The market sizes range from ¾ to 1½ pounds. Most people like porgies broiled or pan-fried.

Fish Connoisseurs Prefer Pompano

POMPANO. Many fish connoisseurs select it as the most delectable of the Atlantic Coast fishes. The pompano is rich, yet delicate in flavor. Unfortunately the supply is not large and its cost is relatively high. This situation prompts some persons to refer to it as, "a rich fish and a fish for the rich." The pompano thrives from Virginia to Brazil, and the young of the species have been known to travel as far north as Cape Cod. Most of the fishing for this aquatic jewel, which usually weighs from 1 to 1½ pounds, is off the east Florida Coast, with the top season from January to April. When split down the back and broiled it requires only the blessings of salt, pepper, butter, and lemon juice.

REDFISH or RED DRUM. This silver fish with a diffused red gleam over its scales loses its characteristic color soon after being taken from the water. Its range extends from New Jersey to Texas; it is most abundant in the Gulf of

Mexico, where it is known as the *redfish*. Along the Atlantic Coast it is called either the *red drum* or *spot bass*. Surf anglers like to struggle with this gamy fish. They refer to it as *channel bass*. It grows rapidly into a large fish, but only the young ones are selected for table use. They are sold whole or in steaks or fillets.

A relative, the *black drum,* is a lean heavyweight, which commonly is baked or broiled with fat added. Its main claim to fame lies in its musical ability. All drums make plaintive sounds by the vibration of band-like muscles against their taut air bladders. The black drum, according to fishermen, is responsible for the mysterious music issuing from some southern waters on summer evenings. Many Indian legends had their origins in it.

Shad Come From the Deep Ocean

SEA BASS. These fish move inshore and north in the spring, and south and offshore in autumn. A popular sports fish, bass also is marketed, usually in ½- to 4-pound sizes. While they generally are sold whole, sometimes steaks and fillets are available.

SEA TROUT. These fish with a delicate white flesh of good flavor extend from Cape Cod to Texas. The spotted trout are most common in the South.

SHAD. Easily a winner in the champion class is the shad. It is an inhabitant of the deep ocean, but runs up the coastal waters to spawn, from northern Florida to Nova Scotia. Normally the runs start in Florida's St. John's River in December, reach North Carolina's streams the last of February or early in March, the Chesapeake Bay by March, and New Jersey streams and the Hudson River by April. Market sizes range from 1½ to 8 pounds. The fish commonly is sold whole for stuffing and baking, and in fillets. It has a multiplicity of bones. Three kinds are marketed: the roe shad, or the female with eggs, which is the choicest; cut shad, a female with the roe removed and sold separately; and buck shad, or the male. Shad is pan-fried and broiled, as well as baked.

SHEEPSHEAD. This fish, which is not to be confused with a fresh water species of the same name, dwells from the Bay of Fundy to Texas. It is most prevalent in the South, where it enjoys prestige for table use.

SPANISH MACKEREL. Also called *king mackerel,* this predominately southern species is caught from Maine to Brazil. It is a beautiful deep blue fish with iridescent tones of gold and purple. Coastal people rate it most delicious when broiled or baked.

SPOT. This small pan fish is found along the Middle Atlantic Coast, and especially in Chesapeake Bay. It boasts of many admirers. The fisheries for it center along the North Carolina and Virginia shores. Markets of Norfolk, Richmond, and Baltimore carry it in the spring and autumn.

STRIPED BASS or ROCKFISH. The rockfish requires no introduction to sportsmen in the Chesapeake Bay area, to whom surf casting and trolling for it constitute a major pastime. Much of the commercial catch sells in the fresh fish markets, although some of it is frozen. People living along the Middle Atlantic Coast like this number prepared in countless dishes.

SWORDFISH. Of all New England's commercial fisheries, that for the swordfish is the most picturesque. The fishermen who cruise from off Block Island to the Nova Scotia Banks capture their prey with harpoons. Certainly it qualifies as one of the top foods of the sea. Steaks free of bones are cut from the large fish for broiling and planking. The flesh somewhat resembles halibut, but it is richer, and has a flavor different from all other fish.

WEAKFISH. This is the gray sea trout of the Middle Atlantic Coast. It also classifies as a favorite sport fish from Long Island to North Carolina. The central base for it is Chesapeake Bay. Weakfish are available in fresh fish markets throughout the year. They are taken inshore in summer and offshore in winter.

Geography Makes Some Foods Regional

Every year improved transportation shortens distance; methods of processing and refrigeration are improved so more city, town, and farm homes of the inland areas revel in the tastes of eastern fish and shellfish. Even so, a challenge remains. Perhaps many of the finest sea food dishes of the Atlantic shores, which have been enjoyed by battalions of coastal people for generations, eventually will enter the repertoires of Middle Western and Mountain West cooks. Today thousands of them have no idea of how to select a crab or clean a soft-shell one. They never have participated in an oyster roast or stuffed a shad and baked it. Neither has fish roe appeared on their tables. Thus at the midcentury, geography designates some of the choicest eastern food compositions as regional rather than national.

Riches Come From the Countryside, Too

While sea food contributes bountifully to the glory of coastal cooking, an able supporting cast lends prestige to the production. Kitchens prize their ways of handling migratory waterfowl and a variety of game. Even the orchards and gardens cooperate by providing highly succulent foods. Anyone who has not thrilled at the tastes of New Jersey, Carolina, and Georgia peaches, Virginia apples, and Maryland and Delaware tomatoes has missed some of the good things of life.

For more than three centuries ships have brought people, food, and recipes from foreign lands to the coastal areas. They have left their cosmopolitan imprint. What better example can be cited than that of a vessel sailing from Madagascar in 1685 that put into the port of Charleston (then Charles Town), South Carolina, when in distress?

The captain, grateful for the aid he received, presented a small bag of rice to a leading citizen. This seed produced the first rice grown in America. From it sprouted a major industry in the Low Country that prospered for many generations. And a regional dish, *pilau,* which may have been borrowed from Turkey and adapted to the Western Hemisphere, developed in the kitchens to keep pace with the expanding agriculture of the marshes. There also was the magic touch of southern cooks, for from Delaware and Maryland on south you meet food triumphs relished in all of Dixieland.

An International Cuisine Is Reflected

The cuisines of the great seaports and their environs are international. Long Island, like its neighbor, Manhattan Island, serves as an example. It is so highly industrialized and its people so diverse that a visitor can locate the superb food specialties of most of the nations around the world and of other parts of the United States easier than purely local ones. Even so, Long Island duckling still enjoys considerable prestige. Most of the old families like it best stuffed with bread or fruit dressing and baked. Long Island people also praise many of their oyster dishes, like the baked ones.

New Jersey's long coastline exposes her citizenry to a great and wonderful variety of fish and sea food. Her fresh water lakes in the northern sections also provide elements for good eating. The area fully earns its name, the Garden State. Most of the natives make full use of the vegetables that are grown on a wide commercial scale to aid in feeding the people in the nearby metropolitan communities. There are large orchards and berry patches, too. If more delicious peaches grow elsewhere they must be out-of-this-world fruit.

From New Jersey through Delaware, Maryland, and on down the coast, lemon butter belongs to the picnics. People talk enthusiastically about its taste as far south as Georgia. They make this spread with beaten eggs, sugar, and lemon juice cooked over water until the mixture thickens. Then they remove it from the heat, add butter and grated lemon peel, and beat it until smooth. When cooled they store it in the refrigerator. At a picnic, and at home for that matter, they spread it on bread for sandwiches, and on crisp crackers.

Sometimes it answers as a cake filling. Here, too, almost everyone speaks of broiled chicken with affectionate respect. They eat it with gusto, and with no disappointment that it was not fried.

Coastal cooks of Maryland, the Old Line State, pay homage to Chesapeake Bay and its tributaries for their offerings, from which stem many of the native sublime dishes. Nevertheless, Maryland's early culinary supremacy evolved on her plantations. The masterpieces were distinctively southern in flavor. While the comparative scarcity of labor and time and the high costs of food have greatly altered the meals, in some homes you still find mouth-watering signs of a former greatness. Food habits change slowly. Scattered along the coastal areas are families that have inherited a respect and liking for epicurean dishes — the classics in the cuisine. Like precious jewels and silver, the appreciation for them passes from one generation to the next.

Crab Dishes Are Legion

Crab cakes are at home in the region. Almost every Maryland cook makes them as frequently and easily as Kansas City women prepare hamburgers. Every household champions its own special recipes. Those calling for seasoned crab meat held together with slightly beaten egg are popular. In others the steamed crab meat and seasonings are mixed with cream sauce containing an egg, or with bread soaked in milk with egg added. Experienced hands shape the soft mixture into cakes, dip them in egg and crumbs, and pan-fry them in butter or deep fat to a golden brown.

People in Baltimore food markets sometimes pause a few minutes to buy crab cakes. They top them with minced onion and cooked bacon, tuck them between crackers, and eat a favored regional snack with relish. Crab cakes appear at picnics, in home meals, and indeed every place along the Chesapeake, and to some extent along the entire Middle and South Atlantic Coast.

Deviled or imperial crabs are of endless variety, but they

all bear common characteristics. The soft crab mixture is similar to that used in making crab cakes. It is more highly seasoned, as with dry mustard, Worcestershire sauce, and often with minced onion and green pepper, or sometimes with a grating of nutmeg. Cooks pat it into crab shells. Then they crown it with buttered crumbs. They bake it in a hot oven, 400°, about a half hour, or long enough to heat and brown the tops.

Only the shell backs are stuffed. To prepare them natives wash and scrub the shells, removing all traces of meat. Some women immerse them in water with a teaspoon of baking soda dumped in; then they boil them about 20 minutes. After that they drain, rinse, and dry them. Others find that a thorough scrubbing, rinsing, drying, and refrigerating suffice.

Crab flakes au gratin, crab soups, salads, soufflés, croquettes, and innumerable other compositions appear in coastal meals. *Crab Norfolk* is one of them. Cooks mix the choice lump meat with a touch of lemon juice, season it with salt, and pan-fry it in butter over medium heat until it is piping hot. Also there is the crab feast, a traditional and informal social gathering. Many households commonly allow 2½ dozen large shell crabs for 6 people. Six crabs usually yield around a pound of meat.

How To Give a Crab Feast

In giving a crab feast the rule is to first heat at least 2½ inches of water, with vinegar, salt, dry mustard, celery seeds, black pepper, and red pepper added, to the boiling point in a large container, like a lard can. A rack or netting fits into the bottom. Then natives add the live and kicking crabs that have been washed off with a hose if they need a bath. After that they place the cover on the container and steam them until the shells turn a bright pink-red or from 20 to 25 minutes. Then they drain and cool them enough to handle.

To boil crabs — only live crabs are cooked — plunge them into boiling water, with vinegar, salt, and red pepper added. Cook them rapidly for 5 minutes. Then allow them to simmer for 10 minutes longer. The vinegar facilitates the removal of the meat from the shell.

For an informal feast in the kitchen some people cover the table with newspapers. Then when everyone has eaten his fill the cleanup job is simple: just gather the newspapers and fill the garbage can. With the crabs heaped in the center of the table and everyone provided with a bowl of melted butter, a paring knife, and a nutcracker or hammer for use in cracking the claws (a heavy knife will do), everyone is on his own.

First break off the claws, remove the shell, and take out the gray fingers, or deadmen, and the intestines. The yellow substance surrounding the intestines is edible fat. Break the main body in two and pick out the meat with care to discard all the membrane.

What else is needed? Almost everyone will settle for plenty of paper towels, crackers, pickles, celery, and time — time in which to pick out white meat from the body and the somewhat darker meat from the claws, and to enthuse over their taste. Crab feasts also are defined as wonderful beach suppers, especially in the light of the moon.

The meat steamed in this manner is the foundation for the superlative coastal crab dishes. Most of the crabs are cooked on the shore where they are caught, and then hand picked, iced, and transported to market. However, many natives of the region like to steam and pick their own. They say the commercial product is washed, which removes flavor, and that it lacks some of the delicious fat, especially that at the tips of the shells. On the markets some of the finest steamed crab is the choice back-fin meat, or big *lump* crab. Only two of these pieces come from a crab. They are luscious, and the most costly. The middle quality is the white meat, and the third one, a trifle darker, is claw meat.

Soft-shell crabs are so tender, Maryland and other coastal people warn, that they need to be cooked only briefly. "Just long enough to brown lightly," they say, is the correct system. Some women prefer to dredge them in flour and fry them like chicken, for only a few minutes. Others like to brown them delicately in deep fat. One of the large schools of coastal culinary artists dips them first in melted butter laced with lemon juice, and then in flour. It broils them to brown delicately on both sides, and serves them with lemon quarters or tartar sauce.

Sea food and fish dishes find a ready and enthusiastic acceptance in Washington, D.C., that city where cosmopolitan food is the rule, rather than the exception, in many homes. The community is admirably situated so far as regional foods are concerned, in the coastal section between two brilliant states, Maryland and Virginia, and with a third noteworthy regional cuisine, that of the Pennsylvania Dutch country, almost in its lap. The treats of all three of them and other areas appear in the meals. Sometimes it is difficult to place them.

In Washington and in western Maryland around Frederick many people told me how they enjoy a Pennsylvania Dutch custom, that of serving roast turkey with sauerkraut on Christmas and Thanksgiving days. But I found that in the heart of the Dutch counties in the Keystone State the natives disown the practice. Or as one home economist of Pennsylvania Dutch extraction, born and bred in the area but who now works in Washington, said, "I had to come to this capital city on the Potomac to learn that in Pennsylvania sauerkraut associates with turkey. I can't imagine where this idea originated. We never use them together at home."

That Broiled Steak à la Maryland

To millions of Americans, plump and succulent oysters connote the Atlantic Coast, where they classify as a major treat. You greet them on the half shell, in stews, scalloped, in pies, in fritters, curried, and in an almost never ending array of other dishes. Some Maryland cooks like to dip them in batter for frying rather than in egg and crumbs. Fried oysters, great platters of them, bloom in the church and community suppers about the countryside. In both Virginia and Maryland, and indeed in other states, country ham and oysters have an affinity for each other. Then there is a type of Maryland broiled steak that makes a Kansan sit up and take notice.

A thick sirloin, one at least 2 inches thick is the first requirement. The cook slits it on each side and then completely around almost in the center. She fills these pockets with chopped oysters, cooked and chopped mushrooms, and bacon, and sews the edges together to close the opening. Then she broils the steak in the usual manner. (Maryland cooks have a free hand with mushrooms.)

Oyster Pickle for Christmas

Pickled or spiced oysters come to southern Maryland tables at Christmas time with the regularity that slices of fruit cake cover silver trays and eggnog froths in bowls. As for all traditional dishes, the recipes vary.

In most of them the chef heats the liquor drained from the oysters to the boiling point, skims off the scum, and adds vinegar, salt, pepper, and spices — usually a little mace and a few shakes of allspice. When the mixture reaches a boil she drops in the oysters and cooks them until their edges curl. After being cooled they go into the refrigerator. Exposure to light tends to darken them.

Some people wait to add the vinegar, and an equal quantity of white wine, until after the oysters are removed from the heat. In Savannah, Georgia, where pickled oysters rate as a favored hors d'oeuvres, neither mace nor allspice commonly is used; a touch of cloves is preferred.

How To Stage an Oyster Roast

The oyster roast flourishes during the *r* months along the coast. In the southern regions it ranks as a popular type of alfresco entertaining in winter.

Reduced to simple terms, the unshucked oysters are cooked over an open fire until their shells start to open. The equipment employed graduates from the simple to elaborate. Along the beach the trick is to stretch wire netting, with a 1- or 1½-inch mesh, over a hardwood fire, and to fasten it securely at both ends. On it the cooks spread the oysters. They shake the netting to turn them. Such a shore supper in North Carolina is known as a "brush roast." An outdoor fireplace that will accommodate a grill also may be used. Oysters are spread on the heated grill and turned with a shovel. Some establishments have troughs for holding the coals and oysters.

When the shells start to open someone lifts the oysters to the table. They are opened with oyster knives. If any of the guests are not proficient in the art — and few strangers are — a kindly native comes to the rescue. He gallantly indicates in helping that the pleasure is his. In the Low Country where Spanish moss festoons the trees, people take bundles of it as an aid in protecting the hand while holding hot oysters. Farther north a pot holder fills the bill.

Accompaniments vary. At all roasts every guest has an individual bowl of melted butter, usually with Worcestershire sauce added, or a favorite cocktail or barbecue sauce for dunking. In Maryland, Delaware, and New Jersey, pickles, cole slaw, and hot coffee commonly complete the menu. Citizens of the Old North State for their brush roasts choose chow chow (a green tomato relish), corn bread, and coffee — coastal corn breads in North Carolina, and in some other areas, frequently contain no salt. In the Savannah and Charleston environs, the oysters dunked in butter or sauce, are regarded as appetizers, to be followed by a dish of piping hot Hopping John, perhaps hot biscuits, and coffee. Sandwiches enter the menus at some of these gay gatherings.

If the night is stormy or chilly, the oysters are roasted in the kitchen. Natives arrange them on the oven shelves with a pan below to catch the drippings, or on the racks of broiler pans.

Packing Oysters Is a Fine Art

Until he has watched a coastal Virginian pack oysters, anyone who hails from the heart of America has missed a fascinating drama. The cook explains her technique in this way as she demonstrates it:

"I either fry oysters singly or I pack them first. If singly, I select big, fat ones, drain them from their liquor, and dry them on a towel. Then I dip each oyster separately in beaten egg seasoned with salt — the amount is dependent on the oysters — roll it in cracker meal, and repeat the dipping and rolling. I pat the oyster to shape it.

"If I pack them I dip two oysters at the same time in the egg and crumbs, and stack them one on top of the other with the thin muscles together. Then I press them. The wet crumbs help to bind them to each other. After that I carefully dip the packed oysters as if they were one in the egg and roll them in crumbs. They appear like one big oyster.

"I dry all oysters prepared for frying at least an hour. Usually I get them ready after dinner and run them in the refrigerator to chill until time for supper."

Oyster packing is practiced commonly near the shore from Maryland southward, and frequently with more than two oysters pressed together. Along the Georgia Coast some cooks put two oysters together with mayonnaise. They egg, crumb, and fry them.

Diamondbacks Speak of Elegance

To at least the older generation of Marylanders a mention of diamondback terrapins brings nostalgia for the golden age, when the amphibians were plentiful and not expensive. Eulogies of this delicacy just about require the past tense. The onetime plentiful creatures are almost extinct. Attempts to grow them in captivity have failed, and the natural supply is pitifully small. In a pond at Crisfield on the Eastern Shore visitors usually still can see hundreds of diamondbacks; there the turtles await shipment to ultra exclusive clubs of the East.

The preparation of terrapin stew classifies as a ritual, with no recipes forthcoming. Try to pry them from good cooks and they advise a food reporter they trust to judgment and taste as they go along.

After washing and cooking the counts — terrapins that measure not less than 5 inches from end to end under the shell — they simmer them in water until their toenails may be pulled out easily. They then drain them, and lay them on their backs to cool so the juices will collect in the shells when the meat, eggs, and liver are removed. They heat the terrapin meat, eggs, and cut-up liver in the juices with a lavish addition of butter — often in chafing dishes. An epicure practices austerity with seasonings. He uses only salt, pepper, and a dash of cayenne — nothing to cover the subtle deliciousness. In case the quantity of juices is small, natives simmer down the liquid in which the terrapin is stewed to evaporate some of it and to make a jelly.

Marylanders are horrified if a stranger asks about adding

sherry or Madeira wine. They say that either, and preferably dry Maderia, may be served in small glasses as an accompaniment, but never in the dish proper. On this point some epicures in other states disagree.

Other Turtles Are Popular, Too

Both sea and land varieties of turtles other than the coveted diamondbacks also command enthusiastic followings along the coast. *Red snapper soup* qualifies as one of the favorite dishes in and around Philadelphia. Although it and *red snapper stew* appear less frequently than in the past on the well-set tables of the City of Brotherly Love, a fondness for them still lingers. Some public eating establishments also serve them. An old-time relish made with sweet red and green peppers, cabbage, and celery with sugar, vinegar, and seasonings is not forgotten. Philadelphia pepper relish, many families believe, has no substitute as an accompaniment to fried oysters. Some people also serve it with crab. When properly made the zest retains a delightful fresh vegetable crispness and flavor.

Other famous, distinctive dishes of the city, which was settled in colonial times by the English and Dutch, include sticky cinnamon buns — their tops ooze delicious sweet, buttery sirup — and pepper pot soups. All the natives speak with pride about the splendid mushrooms that grow in nearby Chester and elsewhere. Also they praise the cider apple butter that smells so spicy and good as it bubbles on the kitchen range. It tastes good, too, they say, when obtained in glasses from a grocer and spread on hot bread to blend with melting butter.

Philadelphia people know good ice cream when they taste it. Originally they made it by freezing thin cream, sweetened and flavored. (New Yorkers then preferred one with a custard base.) And these Pennsylvanians continue to root for rich ice creams. Just one reason a visit with them is inviting! One hostess gave a roving food reporter something to remember — a piping hot chocolate waffle topped with chocolate ice cream and warm fudge sauce!

And Then There Are Fish

No visitor with observing eyes and an interest in food fails to note how clever Maryland cooks are with fish dishes. It is easy to detect a preference toward a native of Chesapeake Bay, rockfish or striped bass, especially when baked and garnished with bacon. The natives also enthuse over a spring visitor, the roe shad. Shad commonly is broiled or baked. It is when stuffed with dressing, planked, and baked to a golden brown that people really become eloquent over it. The cook opens the fish, cleans it, stuffs the cavity with a well-seasoned and rich-with-butter dressing, sews up the opening, and lays the fish on a plank. What locally rates as a proper plank is one of white oak that contains an indentation the shape of a fish. Nowadays many a shad cooks in a pan, with a little water added, instead of on a plank. After it is on the platter some women add butter or margarine, milk, and tomato juice to the drippings to make the accompanying sauce. The roe are both simmered in water, or poached, and broiled for the supreme coastal delicacy. Bacon escorts them. Water cress trims the platter.

Along the Carolina and Georgia shores a considerable amount of fish, after being dipped in corn meal, is fried in deep fat until it turns itself. Corn bread of some kind accompanies it. In northeastern South Carolina, the bread, called *red horse bread,* is said to have been named for a fish.

Maryland boosters for the *maninose* point out that the shellfish, similar to clams, has softer shells. They say it is easier to clean. Natives dig for it in the sand on wintry days. Usually the piping hot broth and steamed maninose are served together — there are individual dishes of melted butter on the side for dunking. Fritters made with it resemble little pancakes; they actually are baked on a griddle.

Ducks Win High-Flung Praise

You hear more high-flung praise for ducks around the Maryland countryside than for other waterfowl. The three kinds that appear most in conversations and festive meals are the *canvas back, red head,* and *black* varieties. The state's chefs follow precise rules in cooking them.

The main idea is not to lose any more blood than necessary, for it contains the flavor. They wipe the birds clean or wash them quickly in a little water and dry them. Then they rub the breasts with butter, place them unstuffed in a shallow pan, run them in a hot oven, 400°, and bake them 20 to 25 minutes. The flesh should be red, not blue. Dressings of all kinds are eliminated; cooks say they interfere with the quick penetration of the heat.

To shock a native Marylander all anyone has to do is to say he prefers well done to rare duck!

Frog legs constitute another Maryland favorite, as do rabbit dishes, especially brown rabbit stews. Marsh rabbits, or muskrats, have been eaten for centuries, first by the Indians and then by early explorers and colonists. Some church groups and gun clubs occasionally stage marsh rabbit suppers not only in Maryland, but also in Delaware and New Jersey. The meat often appears in the markets of Baltimore, Washington, Wilmington, and Philadelphia during the open trapping season. The dates vary in different localities, but they all fall between November and April. Most people soak the marsh rabbits in salty water before cooking them. Or they soak the cut-up pieces for several hours in a highly seasoned red wine marinade; then they drain, flour, and fry them to a crusty brown.

Throughout the coastal areas from Maryland southward many of the marshlands attract hunters. Natives qualify as experts not only in handling sea food but also in game cookery.

An Inning for Boiled Peanuts

Both peanuts and benne seed grow in the coastal areas.

In the summertime little boys hawk their wares along shady southern streets. "Dee-licious boiled peanuts," they cry. These are green peanuts cooked in salted water, shells and all. Before you eat them you slip the nuts out of the shells.

While every kitchen cherishes its favorite method of producing peanut brittle, this Virginia technique has a host of followers.

COASTAL PEANUT BRITTLE

2 cups sugar	1 cup roasted peanuts

Melt the granulated sugar in a heavy frying pan, stirring constantly to prevent scorching and to remove lumps. Chop the peanuts fine, or roll them to crush in tiny pieces, and stir them into the sirup to mix thoroughly. Pour the mixture onto a marble slab and roll it in a thin sheet with a rolling pin. The nuts will be uniformly distributed.

Sugar coated peanuts also please many nibblers.

SUGARED PEANUTS

½ cup water 1 cup sugar	2 cups raw peanuts

Cook the water and sugar in a heavy frying pan until the sirup spins a thread. Add the raw shelled peanuts, and stir constantly until every nut is browned and coated with a glaze. Remove from the heat and turn onto a marble slab or waxed paper to cool. Then separate the nuts.

Benne Stands for Good Luck

No other coastal candy is more distinctive than *benne seed brittle* and the other benne candies so characteristic of Charleston, Savannah, and adjacent spots. Benne seeds always are roasted, or *parched,* as the natives say, before use. To make the brittle they substitute 2 cups of them for the 1 cup of peanuts in the coastal peanut brittle recipe. Some cooks add 1 teaspoon of vanilla to the melted sugar before stirring in the seed, while others prefer ½ teaspoon of both vanilla and lemon extracts. Cooks pour the mixture to a depth of ¼ inch into a buttered pan, and immediately mark it in squares with a knife. When cold they break or cut the candy along the lines.

Benne, or sesame, is an East Indian herb which was brought to the Low Country from Africa by slaves. Some Negroes grow the plant in their gardens to this day, and use the seed in cooking — and to scatter on their doorsteps to bring good luck. Nearby coastal people like its nutty flavor in both hard and soft candies and other dishes.

Peach, apple, and apricot *leathers,* suggestive of old-time plantation kitchens, have not completely slipped into history. Even tourists can sample them occasionally in the eastern sections of Virginia, the Carolinas, and Georgia. Traditionally, a purée of fresh fruit, sweetened with granulated or brown sugar, is spread in thin layers in shallow pans or plates to dry in the sunshine. The fruity mixture, covered with mosquito netting, spends the daytime outdoors and moves indoors in the evening to avoid the dew. When dry it will pull away from the pan; then the cook rolls it in powdered sugar like a jelly roll and cuts it in slices that resemble miniature logs. If she stores the delicious leather logs under lock and key and in an airtight container they will remain in excellent condition almost indefinitely. In today's versions dried peaches and apricots commonly comprise the purée; the leather is dried in a very slow oven.

The Middle Atlantic region, and more precisely Atlantic City, New Jersey, wins distinction as the taffy capital of the nation. Everyone who walks along the famous boardwalk sees "Salt Water Taffy" signs. While the name appeals, salt water actually has no connection with the sweet other than its origin near the ocean. The taffy has reached a high plane of deliciousness; it carries many flavors. Some of it is chocolate coated, and almost none of it sticks to the teeth, as do many members of this confection family. From the convention city on the Atlantic Coast parcel post packages of the treat travel to every part of the United States. To thousands of people a mention of Atlantic City not only conjures a boardwalk on the beach but also remembrance of this old-fashioned candy.

There Are Superb Foods in Charleston

No other city on the Atlantic Coast consistently has enjoyed a higher prestige for wonderful regional foods than Charleston. It is a gastronomic shrine with an exotic type of cookery that extends along the shores in the Low Country, with Savannah, Georgia, another center for the colorful cuisine. Traditions, modified by time, dominate this enchanting South Carolina city. Great pride in recipes prevails, and directions for treasured family dishes pass from one generation to the next. Substantial breakfasts are the rule. Dinner in all its glory comes off at 2 o'clock in the afternoon. The evening meal is supper. Around 11 o'clock in the morning, business and professional men have coffee; this also is the hour for coffee or colas in many households.

Social life centers around the stately old houses, and entertaining at home is the rule. Perhaps wonderful Negro cooks, who still dominate the kitchens although their number diminishes every year, have much to do with keeping the custom alive.

When a curious food explorer visits the city she tries to figure out how this glamorous cookery came about. She wonders what its distinctive characteristics are. She discovers first and foremost that it is southern. Here you find many of the supreme delicacies of the South — hot breads, fried chicken, elegant layer cakes, and baked ham. Second, geography makes it *coastal cooking.*

In various dishes a pronounced French influence can be detected. It stems especially from the early Huguenots who settled in Charleston and its environs in considerable numbers after Louis XIV revoked the Edict of Nantes. And the West Indies have had a finger in the magnificent dishes. Settlers from the Barbados Islands brought their ways with foods and supplied the first coconuts; Charlestonians have delighted in coconut candies and desserts for more than 200 years. In addition, who can deny the original African touches of genius in the city's cuisine? Negro cooks have done something to the English and French recipes, and the results are good.

(While South Carolina's cookery is predominately southern, there naturally are distinctive variations in the topmost dishes of the different communities. Charleston and its environs personify southern coastal cookery. In the middle section, where the Welsh, Germans, and Dutch settled generations ago, some of the most treasured recipes had their origins in Europe. They are similar to those found in other spots across the United States where these nationalities have established homes. The Carolinas and Virginia, too, have enough citizens of Pennsylvania Dutch extraction to know, prize, and enjoy the fruits of their kitchens, which are described elsewhere in this book.)

Consider, too, the food production advantages of the Low Country. The waters abound in splendid sea food, and fresh water fish. The marsh lands are a hunter's dream come true. Succulent vegetables grow the year around. And kitchens profit from a world-wide exchange of food ideas, as they have since from before the Revolutionary War, when Charleston was an important seaport. It is no accident that the home cookery reaches a high plateau of achievement.

"Swimp" Appears at Breakfast

Situated on a narrow peninsula and almost surrounded by water, the city early won laurels for its sea food compositions. Shrimp continues as a favorite. After hearing hucksters call "Yeh Swimp" a few days, visitors start referring to the delicacy as *swimp,* as do many Charlestonians. Small native shrimp from the inlets and creeks of the Low Country rate as the region's first choice. Its flavor is truly delicious. You rarely can buy it in stores, but Negro vendors go from door to door to market their catch. They sell shrimp by the plate rather than by weight. One plate of the sea food weighs slightly more than a pound.

When it is in season practically all homes in the city have shrimp for breakfast. Usually it is pan-fried briefly in butter or margarine, or made into a paste, which is chilled and sliced. Hominy serves as the universal accompaniment.

Recipes for the paste are legion. Perhaps the simpler kind is the most popular. The cooked, peeled shrimp is ground in a food chopper and mixed with butter and deft seasonings of mustard, onion juice, mace, and sherry wine. Slices of it also visit the cold meat platters. They appear at parties for canapé making, and provide a marvelous stuffing for celery stalks. Another variety of shrimp paste is baked briefly, about 15 minutes. Crumbled biscuits are an additional ingredient. The loaf also is cooled, chilled, and sliced as needed.

The colossal assortment of Charleston's shrimp treats staggers the imagination of a mid-American. Among them are cocktails, salads, croquettes, curries, stews, hot and cold soups, casserole dishes, pies, and vegetable combinations. All of them warrant description — but no visitor ever forgets the surprising variety of the shrimp pies. Usually cooks mix the shellfish with bread crumbs and milk or tomato juice, and seasonings, like tomato ketchup, Worcestershire sauce, chopped celery and parsley, sherry, a suspicion of mace, and onion juice. These pies have no crusts, and are what people in other regions refer to as casserole dishes.

Shrimp teams with green corn — cut from the cobs — in pies. These also would classify elsewhere as baked dishes, because they are crustless. The pink sea food shows up, too, as the stuffing for green peppers, and in baked guinea squash, a local name for eggplant.

She-Crab Soup Is Tops

Crab dishes answer as another glorious Charleston specialty. *She-crab soup* leads these treats. It is available only in the laying season. She-crabs are considered more delicate than he-crabs. The hucksters who have them for sale always cry "she-crabs" with a louder voice, and they charge more for them. The cooked eggs and crab meat with seasonings of salt, mace, onion juice, pepper, and Worcestershire sauce mingle in the soup. The eggs enhance the flavor, and provide an almost indescribable glutinous quality that delights. When she-crabs with eggs are not available, some cooks crumble a little hard-cooked egg yolk into the soup plates when they serve the soup. The showing of yellow works magic — most people react kindly to the suggestion of the she-crab delicacy. Puffs of whipped cream, topped with minced parsley and paprika, garnish the delicate, rich dish that so fluently speaks the language of gourmets.

Oysters share honors with shrimp in hucksters' baskets and in meals. When scalloped and in stews they usually carry a faint tinge of mace. If creamed they almost always are subtly flavored with onion. Brown oyster stew classifies as one of the famed dishes that contains benne seeds. To make it the cook pan-fries bacon, and removes it. Then she pan-fries onions, which also are taken from the pan. Next she browns flour in the drippings and stirs in oyster liquor to make a smooth sauce, and adds the crushed or pounded roasted benne seed and the oysters, about 1 tablespoon of the seed to 1 cup of oysters. This stew, with the bacon and onion added, is served on rice or hominy.

Oysters rolled in corn meal make a favorite stuffing for quails for roasting. And oyster roasts, previously mentioned, qualify as fashionable winter social events.

Among the clam dishes, the combination of cooked, mashed, and seasoned guinea squash (eggplant) and clams in alternate layers, with dots of butter, salt, pepper, and cracker crumbs added, enjoys wide popularity. Natives add milk for the liquid and bake the dish to blend the flavors and heat thoroughly, as well as to brown the cracker crumbs on top.

Charleston Votes for Pine Bark Stew

Among the famed, historic dishes still prepared and relished at outdoor social gatherings in the Low Country, pine bark stew reigns supreme. Favorite fish used in it include bream, red breast, and big mouth bass, although any combination of firm fleshed ones is acceptable. The culinary ritual had its beginnings in colonial days. The trick is to serve the whole fish unbroken.

First, natives pan-fry bacon in an iron kettle, lift it out, and alternate layers of sliced Irish potatoes and onions. They barely cover them with water. After the mixture simmers about 10 minutes they arrange the dressed fish on top and sprinkle with a little curry powder. They alternate other layers of potatoes, onion, and fish in the desired quantity, and pour on more salted water, barely enough to cover. Then the stew simmers constantly, and very gently, from 45 minutes to several hours, depending on the amount.

Meanwhile the cooks put the sauce together with melted butter, Worcestershire sauce, tomato ketchup, curry powder, red and black pepper, and some of the broth from the fish stew. This mixture takes on a chocolate-like color similar to that of pine bark. Perhaps that explains the derivation of the name, although some people in the Low Country believe it came from the original use of pine bark for starting the fires over which these stews were cooked.

When it is time to serve the famous treat the cooks dump the hot sauce over it and arrange the bacon on top. Everyone eats this great American dish with relish, and with rice.

Another fish stew — or *muddle* as a fish stew often is called — enjoyed at picnics along the coast is somewhat simpler to make. The outdoor chef also starts its preparation by pan-frying bacon, lifting it from the Dutch oven or heavy kettle, and adding a layer of sliced Irish potatoes, one of onions, and another of whole dressed fish. Over this combination he douses well-seasoned tomato sauce or canned tomato paste. After simmering it from 30 to 40 minutes, he serves the stew containing the whole fish on rice. The regional fish stews or muddles commonly contain more than one kind of whole fish.

Shad and sheepshead constitute Charleston favorites. Cooters, or fresh water terrapin, are highly regarded. Cooter stew, containing turtle eggs, and flavored with sherry, a few whole cloves, onions, and Worcestershire sauce, ranks with the topnotchers. As a garnish, thin lemon slices yield to no substitute.

Many of the tasty meat dishes of the South come from

Charleston kitchens, but it is with sea food, chicken, and game that native cooks concoct their immortal dishes.

Hogshead cheese definitely is a blue ribbon number. It is a best seller at church bazaars, which especially display it at the Christmas season. Most families consider the cheese and hominy a *must* for breakfast at Christmas and on New Year's Day. For supper, thin slices of it never go begging.

A Countless Array of Chicken Dishes

Charleston people, in the true southern manner, like fried chicken. Perhaps the distinctive feature of their poultry cooking is reflected in the variety of tasty dishes that grace their tables. In some kitchens the floured pieces are pan-fried with onion added. The gravy, made with thin cream, is touched up with a shake or two of curry powder, and occasionally with brandy. Other cooks team fried chicken and green corn. They lift the fried chicken to a casserole and top it with succulent milk-filled kernels cut from the cobs, dot its top with butter, and season it with salt and pepper. They bake the deliciousness just long enough to cook the corn, but not dry it out.

Tomato sauce that contains chopped stewed giblets and their broth makes a tasty gravy to pass with fried chicken. Broilers usually are soaked overnight in equal parts of lemon juice and salad oil, with grated onion and sherry wine added. Cooks specify that to a quarter cup of lemon juice and salad oil, mixed, about 1½ cups of sherry are required.

White chicken fricassee maintains prestige. Cooks add a little native bayleaf and an onion to the kettle to cook with the chicken. The fowl goes to the table accompanied by egg sauce. To make it they thicken some of the broth with mashed hard-cooked egg yolks and a trace of flour. Just before serving, the cooked egg whites — after being mashed with a fork — are stirred in, and the sauce is poured into a bowl or gravy boat. On the platter, for color and flavor, every piece of chicken wears a daisy-like slice of hard-cooked egg.

Hunters Call It Paradise

Many kinds of fowl and game range in the marsh lands near Charleston. Local ways of handling these foods in the kitchens are inspiring, and to taste the dishes classifies as an epicurean experience. Call the roll of some of the favorites and the responses include wild turkey with chestnut dressing, wild duck with potato or orange stuffing, quails stuffed with oysters, all roasted; fried and smothered marsh hens, roast venison basted with port wine mixed with crabapple jelly, broiled squirrel, rabbit pie, and stewed rabbit and squirrel seasoned with a bit of native bayleaf.

Charlestonians consider young squirrel delicious. It has, they point out, little or no gamy flavor. They like to broil it, basting it frequently with fat, and serve it in the drippings, touched up with lemon juice poured over. Pressed venison answers as a regional treat. And wild duck reaches new taste heights when accompanied by a sausage pilau. While rice wins out as the A-1 game accompaniment, hominy also is acceptable.

Meet the Cereal Queens

One of the distinguishing features of the cooking in the coastal regions that sets it apart from the remainder of the South is the wider use of both rice and hominy. As already mentioned, hominy is the great breakfast dish, the perfect companion for shrimp, while rice is taboo with fish, except fish stews. Hominy — the *grist,* as grits are properly known — appears almost daily on supper tables.

Both grist, which in Charleston becomes hominy when cooked, and rice appear in dozens of characteristic dishes of the Low Country. Many of the breads memorialize one-time great plantations. For instance, consider *Awendaw,* a hominy-corn-meal number that is something of a cross between a custard and a spoon bread. Then there is, for another of the luscious examples, *Ashley bread,* an excellent spoon bread with the taste of rice from the rice flour it contains. Both call for prompt delivery from the hot oven and plenty of butter. A taste of either whets the appetite for more.

Beginning with the early development of rice growing on the marsh lands more than 200 years ago, the cereal became firmly established in the cuisine. Today it is served at least once a day in most households. *Pilaus,* commonly pronounced "pèlos" and often as "perleaus," personify the region. They had an early start. Probably they were imported from Asia, where in Turkey pilaf consists of rice cooked with butter and tomato juice. In Liberia perleau rice, containing chicken, ham, tomato paste, cabbage, onion, and seasonings, pleases discriminating palates. At Charleston local Negro cooks give old recipes new interpretations.

Reduced to simple equivalents, a pilau starts out with cubes or tiny squares of salt pork or bacon — usually bacon. It is pan-fried, lifted from the drippings; then the seasonings, the rice, and the ingredients for whatever kind of pilau is being made — such as fish, chicken, or vegetables — are stirred in. The mixture steams until it is tender. Just before serving the bacon is mixed into it.

The variations in pilaus are tremendous. Some are elegant. Others, such as okra pilau, which is known as *Limping Susan,* are simple and thrifty, but also tasty. Among the favorites are tomato, tomato-okra, chicken, chicken-okra, and shrimp pilaus. In the Pee Dee region (the eastern portion of South Carolina drained by the Great and Little Pedee Rivers), *chicken bog,* at least a relative of the pilau, rates as a favorite for mid-day and moonlight picnics.

In North Carolina chicken stews are something of a tradition. They are held in homes, churches, schools, and in tobacco barns when the men folks work at night. Most people in the southern coastal regions prefer pork, chicken, fish, or sea food on their platters — less frequently beef and lamb.

Red rice, christened for its color, answers as another traditional and much appreciated dish. For it you stir a

sauce containing canned tomato paste and onions into uncooked rice, and then steam the mixture until it is light,
tender, and fluffy.

Rice *shepherd's pie* salvages leftover meats and poultry.
Natives bake the diced cooked meat or chicken, mixed with
gravy, between two layers of the cooked cereal. Other favorites include curried, baked, and fried rice, rice baked with
cheese and olives, rice croquettes, and rice omelets. Then
there is the concoction designed as a companion for cold cuts,
which is most acceptable on picnics. When the grains are
about half cooked, or when the water in which bouillon cubes
are dissolved is absorbed, they add a small amount of bacon
drippings, and stir in peanuts, mashed with a rolling pin, and
diced celery. The combination steams until the rice becomes
tender and fluffy.

Introducing Hopping John

A foremost citizen of this food world is *Hopping John*.
This is the dish for which many natives who happen to be
on faraway shores long the most. It is as popular in the South
Battery district of Charleston as in the more modest sections
of the city. Composed of field peas (canned peas frequently
are used to shorten the cooking process), rice, bacon, and
onions, the dish steams and turns out as one of those humble
creations considered food for the gods. In Charleston you
always have Hopping John — with accent on the last word —
on New Year's Day, for if eaten then it is supposed to bring
good luck throughout the year. Hopping John is to the Low
Country what baked beans are to New England.

Cheese concoctions are especially featured in menus for
supper. Puddings, soufflés, croquettes, and open-face toasted
sandwiches called cheese toast, are specialties. Macaroni
pie — really macaroni and cheese — offers another example
of how in Charleston pies do not always wear crusts.

Here Comes the Vegetable Woman

The city is separated from the Atlantic Ocean by the

Cooper and Ashley Rivers that join forces to make the gorgeous blue bay, with long, slender islands. On some of these slivers of land surrounded by water, truck gardening comprises the major industry. With a climate that encourages vegetable growing around the calendar the bounty of garden stuff is amazing.

People pride themselves on their vegetable dishes. Homemakers buy their supplies mainly from Negro women, who push carts heaped with beautiful specimens of the gardens' offerings from door to door and announce their coming with "poetry" they compose as they chant.

Okra, an African importation, tops the list of choice, favored vegetables. Only the tiny, delicate pods are chosen. Low Country gumbo — gumbo means okra — specifies cooked okra, tomatoes, onions, and bacon, seasoned with Worcestershire sauce, thyme, salt, and pepper.

Jerusalem artichokes appear in a variety of esteemed dishes. Burr artichokes, as the natives refer to the other kind — the globe — win a place in special occasion or guest meals.

Cabbage, beets, green beans, sieva or butter beans, guinea squash or eggplant, onions, spinach, corn, tomatoes, yams, sweet potatoes, green or English peas, Irish potatoes, cymblings or summer squash, and broccoli receive a cordial welcome on the area's tables.

Potatoes speak either for yams or sweet potatoes, with yams much preferred. And certainly no city has more delightful ways of candying yams than Charleston. Most of the recipes feature the addition of brown sugar, butter or margarine, and orange or lemon juice and their peels, or both. Sherry wine is a frequent ingredient.

The best liked corn dishes are those in which the kernels are cut from the cobs. The traditional baked custard type of southern corn pudding never goes begging. It is known not as a pudding but as *corn pie.*

Black bean soup is at home in the tureens of the coastal

region. Slices of lemon and hard-cooked eggs keep their century-old places as favored garnishes.

White potatoes answer to two names, *Irish potatoes* and *buckra yams*. Buckra is the Negroes' name for white. Some of them call sieva or butter beans *see-wees*. Bell pepper-tomato dishes are without end.

The green salad has gained quite a toe-hold in the Low Country, but grapefruit, tomato, and other aspics appear frequently, and they often draw curry-seasoned dressings. For a substantial salad, the fish types do not know the meaning of competition, with shrimp the queen of the group. Summer ushers many frozen fruit tempters to the food scene.

Artichoke Pickles Stay in Style

Among the eternal finalists in the relish contests are chopped Jerusalem or root artichoke pickles, red pepper jam, green tomato pickles of many kinds, preserved and pickled figs, sweet pickled watermelon rind, chutneys, and peach pickles.

The coastal breads are southern types, with more rice and hominy in their make-up than in most other spots in Dixie. Light as a feather and crisp-crusted rice and hominy waffles, muffins, and pancakes, and the southern biscuits and corn breads win many compliments. For a change, roasted benne seeds sometimes are added to biscuits before baking.

Last and Sweetest, the Desserts

Charleston people praise the traditional puddings and whipped cream desserts. At Christmas time many households give "a lighted plum pudding" the spotlight. In others, if a less substantial dessert is relished, wine soufflé closes the feast happily. It contains walnuts and raisins.

Some of the prime puddings are the sweet potato, coconut, and lemon ones, charlotte russe made with angel food or sponge cakes, custards, coffee jelly, and wine jelly. Gingerbreads, especially those featuring coconut, score highly.

Usually they flaunt crowns of whipped cream, or welcome lemon or lemon-orange sauce. Pineapple fritters and upside-down cake occupy important positions on menus. Orange-lemon, wine, and pineapple sauces and hard sauce dress up many desserts.

Ice creams of many descriptions continue to win fame for Charleston hostesses. Leaders consist of fig-custard and fig-peach, from home-grown figs and peaches, coconut, frozen eggnog, lemon, orange, pistachio, and pineapple with rum flavoring.

Valedictorians in the dessert pie class, not too prominent in the Charleston cuisine, display fluffy, high meringues. Among the meringue wearers are such favorites as peach, lemon, chocolate, caramel-cream, and coconut-cream creations. Mincemeat-filled ones speak for Christmas, and mincemeat made with boiled tongue rates the superlatives. Pies filled with it contain both sherry wine and whiskey.

It's the Layer Cakes That Count

Delicate layer cakes are at home in the fascinating city's meals. *Lady Baltimore* takes the top honors without difficulty. In these days it shows mainly on special occasions, but parties come along frequently. Countless versions of it exist. One point of agreement about how to make it is that everyone selects white cake, and usually there are three layers. Practically everyone chooses a "boiled" frosting flavored with a medley of vanilla, lemon, and almond extracts. After the hot sirup is poured over the beaten egg whites and the frosting is almost ready to spread, most cooks fold in chopped raisins, pecans or walnuts, and dried figs. Frequently the raisins and figs are soaked overnight in brandy before being used.

In the cake almost everyone detects an elusive flavor few people can place. It comes from a filling distributed over the hot layers when they are taken from the oven. In reality this is a sirup made by cooking 1 cup of sugar and ½ cup of water until it spins a thread, or to a very soft "soft ball" stage, at about 234°. When the sirup is lukewarm, cooks flavor the sweetness with from ¾ to 1 teaspoon each of vanilla and almond. They beat it until the mixture thickens slightly. Then they cover the hot layers with it. After the cake cools, they spread the traditional frosting between the layers and on the sides and top. Some families prefer lemon fillings for their Lady Baltimore cakes.

Orange cake definitely belongs to the city and nearby areas. Every cook boasts of her variation of the treat. On some occasions the batter contains chopped figs or ground dates, and always shredded orange peel. Some women tuck the pulp of oranges between the layers, while others pour orange juice over them. These delicacies are served with whipped cream, often with shredded fresh coconut folded in. Quick modern versions start with sponge cake purchased at a bake shop, with orange juice, pineapple juice, or rum poured on. After chilling until the juice penetrates the cake, natives serve the pineapple and orange flavored ones with whipped cream and shredded fresh coconut. Usually rum cake proudly shows off puffs of sweetened whipped cream.

Stickies originated in Charleston. Today's hostesses serve them with confidence they will please in the manner they delighted the guests of their foremothers. This is the way a leader in home economics extension describes how to make them:

Roll a rich biscuit dough very thin and spread it with butter. Sprinkle on brown or white sugar and a dash of cinnamon. Roll this up like a jelly roll and cut it in ½-inch slices. Place them cut-side down in a well-greased pan, and dot them with more butter and sugar. Bake them until well done and brown.

"We serve them," she says, "at picnics, parties, and for dinner and supper."

The Fruit Cakes Have Almond Crowns

Charlestonians evidence pride in their superb mocha, coconut, angel food, chocolate with mocha frosting, and lemon flavored sponge cakes. They consider their famous fruit cakes, both light and dark, as blue ribbon numbers. Possibly the white ones enjoy a popularity edge over the dark cakes. They are rich in fresh coconut, which means their keeping qualities are not equal to those possessed by the darker or sun-tan numbers.

There is a way to determine the authenticity of Charleston fruit cakes. The genuine loaf commonly wears a crown of almond paste, normally from 1 to 1½ inches deep. Then a white frosting — either a "boiled" or an uncooked confectioners' sugar one — covers the top and sides of the cake. Clever cooks flavor these white frostings with orange and lemon, and frequently with a trace of almond extract. To make the paste, natives grind or pound almonds very fine and mix them with beaten egg whites and confectioners' sugar. They flavor it with 1 part of rose water to 2 parts of almond extract. These almond-topped fruit cakes also appear elsewhere in the South, especially at weddings, but scarcely with the frequency that they come to Charleston's tables.

Christmas is the cooky season, although many of the dainty varieties are baked throughout the year. Date and nut, and coconut kisses, benne seed wafers and drop cookies, coconut brownies, and lemon and orange cookies capture many compliments.

As a mid-American travels southward from Georgia into Florida he begins to encounter piquant touches of Cuba, Spain, and New Orleans at mealtime. He waves a fond good-by to the shoreline of the Atlantic Ocean with the thought that many of the neighbors back home would like to lead their children to some hallowed spot in the eastern coastal region and say, "This is where your people came from."

The Gulf Coast

NEW ORLEANS stands for exotic food and Creole cooking at its best. It is a shrine for gourmets, a source of pride to all Americans. Unique taste thrills come forth from the old and famed restaurants of the Vieux Carré. Homes throughout the Crescent City and southern Louisiana enjoy many of the same dishes. A traveler encounters them along almost the entire shoreline of the Gulf of Mexico. To the west they gradually merge in Texas with predominating Mexican and southwestern accents. Eastward they reach Florida, but by the time he sits down to dine on a flower scented patio at Key West they have vanished like a dream in the night. Cuban influences take over.

Who are the Creoles? How did their cookery genius come about? Why in New Orleans? The search for answers to such questions launches a food exploration without waste motion. They suggest what to look for in browsing around in the area.

The Creoles are of French or Spanish descent or mixtures of the two — people from nationalities famed for their table delicacies. They guided the destinies of Louisiana for a century and more before the Stars and Stripes waved above the colony. In those years they launched Creole cooking, reminiscent of their homelands, and mainly entrusted the interpretation of European dishes to African cooks. Give these picturesque culinary artists, who sang spirituals as they worked, a few curtain calls! Somewhere they may arise and bow to well-earned applause. Their rivalry with one another spurred kitchen achievement, inspired new twists to familiar dishes, and motivated them with spoon in hand to reach for the stars.

Especially does their knowledge of herbs show in the masterpieces they helped create. Perhaps the inherited taste of Creole gourmets held in check the exaggerated seasonings common in the tropics and semitropics. It makes no difference now who possessed the restraint and genius. Epicures agree that subtle, vague blends of condiments set New Orleans cookery apart from that used by Creoles elsewhere, as a diamond from other jewels.

The Women Staged a Food Strike

To comprehend how the Crescent City and the surrounding country became the focal point for a cuisine that spreads its sparkle over a wide radius, just turn a few pages of history. Also consider for a moment the blessings bestowed by geography.

New Orleans cookery got away to a colorful start. The

unique culinary fame of the Creoles began with a protest strike of less than a hundred women, the wives of French soldiers. That was early in the Eighteenth Century. They marched on the colonial governor to explain forcefully that they were tired of eating corn, and to demand wheat. Although the governor had no wheat, his store of diplomacy was large. He invited the women — whom he believed were homesick as well as hungry for familiar dishes — to talk with his housekeeper, a French Canadian.

Madame Langlois, an accomplished culinary artist, knew the meaning of loneliness in a wilderness and knew the limitations of the Louisiana larder. Fortunately she had been enterprising enough to ask friendly Indian squaws, especially the excellent cooks of the Choctaw tribe, to teach her how to prepare the native foods. Thus she was equipped technically to appease the strikers. She, also, was of a diplomatic turn of mind.

Spontaneously she invited the discontented women to meet with her every week for a social afternoon and a lesson on how to handle local foodstuffs. The informal gatherings that followed blossomed into the first cooking school conducted in what is now the United States of America. It soothed and steadied nerves, turned out some tasty dishes. Madame Langlois taught her guests how to grind the detested corn between stones to make meal, and how to prepare corn bread to serve piping hot with wild honey obtained from the woods. She displayed the art of making hominy and grits. Next she introduced the mystery of filé, young sassafras leaves dried on stones, pounded, and rubbed through hair sieves. It was a seasoning trick of the Choctaws.

Butter beans and corn she paired in succotash. Then she demonstrated how to broil young squirrels, and how to stuff and roast them; how to fill fish with savory herb stuffings for baking, how to make vinegar from citrus fruits, and how to crystallize wild fruits. In memory of this service she now is recognized as the Mother of Creole Cooking à la New

Orleans. For a half century reverence for French delicacies stimulated kitchen procedures — and then around 1760 Spain acquired Louisiana and the culinary art underwent a change.

Spaniards Brought Caribbean Condiments

The Spaniards came mainly by the way of their king's colonies in Mexico and other Latin American areas. They brought their favorite recipes, the condiments of the Caribbean islands, and the secrets of Indian civilizations — especially those built by the Aztecs and the Incas. To accepted and revered French dishes they imparted pungent seasonings. A synthesis of the theories of French and Spanish cooking gave birth to the Creole style. In Louisiana the French influence predominates.

At approximately the same time the Acadians were fleeing from Canada to Louisiana. These French speaking people knew how to wrestle food from the soil; the women were competent in preparing thrifty, substantial meals. Near the end of the century the guillotines of France swung into a terrible campaign. Many aristocrats who lost their heads left behind without employment some of the world's most imaginative and skillful chefs and a large corps of trained assistants. That was the end of an era when the noblemen hired food experts who vied with one another to create exquisite and elaborate dishes to win outstanding recognition for the tables of their chateaus. Some of the supercooks and their helpers, and a few of their employers lucky enough to escape, migrated to the French flavored region of New Orleans and adjacent territory.

Uncle Sam Runs Up the Flag

Uncle Sam purchased the Louisiana territory in 1803 from Napoleon Bonaparte, who in the meantime had taken it away from Spain. In the next half century the South enjoyed prosperity on a major scale. Presently the Mississippi River from Natchez southward was lined by magnificent plantation homes. Cotton was gold. New Orleans became a wealthy market for it, and a noteworthy cultural center. Negro mammies reigned over the kitchens, and in them turned out some of the most delectable meals America has known. They brought their imagination to Creole dishes, and stirred it into the specialties of the French-Spanish-Indian-Latin American cuisine. To them, as noted, goes much credit for the secretive, mystifying blends of seasonings.

At the end of the War Between the States poverty spread its depressing mantle over the region, and cooks were obliged to stretch slender purses. Their culinary skill and art, along with an intimate knowledge of local foodstuffs and the influence of inherited French thrift, gave the simpler meals both deliciousness and acclaim. In these modern days, changing conditions continue to influence the cuisine, and borrowings and adaptations never cease. But wherever you dine, as in New Orleans, the Teche country — the area bordering on the Bayou Teche — or along the Gulf of Mexico's wave-caressed shores, you observe that the patina of the Creoles has not worn off. Intermarriage has left few of them of pure French or Spanish blood, but the descendants of the early families swell with pride over their heritage. And they cling to the food traditions.

Geography Is Kind to the Gourmets

Nature is generous with superb food, in this land of bright sunshine. Almost at the kitchen doors are sea foods and fish from the Gulf of Mexico, lakes, and rivers. Vegetables of superior quality grow most of the year. Citrus fruits, rice, pecans, strawberries, sugar cane (with molasses and sugar), and many other crops flourish.

Why do Creole dishes win the honors? You might as well ask what makes the nightingale's song sweet. As I sauntered along the quaint narrow streets in the old French Quarter of New Orleans, I pondered the reason. Quickly I came up with one answer — the heavenly way they taste! Eventually other solutions to the riddle appear, such as the harmonious and mysterious blending of the seasonings, the universal use of carefully made brown roux, and the something undefinable, the quality or spirit that makes a noted painting a work of art. Creole cooking is an art, and is so labeled by the men and women who practice it and delight over its fruits.

After a wanderer's cup of gustatory joy has overflown around New Orleans for a few days his thoughts automatically turn to a bay leaf and sprigs of parsley and thyme, at the mention of fish or meat. That is because the trio bestows its charms on so many platter treats. Among other seasonings employed almost universally are onions, green onion tops, garlic, shallots, chives, celery, basil, cloves, allspice, chervil, burnet, savory, tarragon, Creole mustard, and red and green peppers. Some kitchens have little boxes of salt and black and red pepper (powdered) mixed for quick sprinkling on foods. The expert cooks combine selections of seasonings so skillfully that scarcely can the gourmets determine by tasting and sniffing what the magic is. Men and women (men are not only acutely interested in fine cookery but often excel at it) insist the A-1 rule is to go easy on the condiments and herbs but not omit them from a dish. "Just see to it," one of my hosts explained, "that no one of them predominates. Keep everyone guessing."

Bottled Liquid Fire Intrigues the Natives

Two kinds of parsley are favorites — the plants with ruffle-edged leaves, so attractive for garnishing, and those with plain-edged leaves. The latter figure prominently in kettles because they are more flavorful. A visitor sees both kinds in the markets, along with other favorite herbs, often mixed and tied in bouquets. There you also observe the dried and blended ones in packages. Out in the country, herb gardens thrive in dooryards, and frequently quite simply in window boxes attached to garages.

Creole mustard yields an elusive taste to countless dishes. It commonly contains mustard seeds imported from Holland or Austria. Natives grind them, add salt, and a locally distilled vinegar for a product believed to have been introduced by early German settlers. Nowadays most of the supply is commercially prepared. The taste faintly suggests horse-radish in the way wisteria smacks of spring.

Hot stuff, as the natives designate their characteristic peppery sauces, occupies a position of honor on seasoning shelves. One of the topnotchers of bottled liquid fire is Tabasco sauce. A home chef's hand without it becomes ill at ease, for she intuitively shakes a few drops on meat, fish, soup, and many sauces before serving them. Cooks also use the little cherry or bird's-eye peppers, bottled in dry sherry. A splash of their heat on boiled eggs, other egg dishes, soups, fish, and meats redeems many an otherwise ordinary number, local people say.

Flavored vinegars classify as a habit with good cooks. They especially prize the ones that taste of tarragon, basil, peppers (made with both the tiny red and green bird's-eye peppers) , and mixed herbs, usually with a chive base. For supplying zip to vegetables and fish, and to most vegetable juices as well, tarragon vinegar scores top success. Basil vinegar sometimes substitutes in the role; it has more fra-grance than the tarragon one, and almost no competition for flavoring tomatoes and tomato juice. Mixed herb vinegars glorify egg salads, deviled eggs, and other egg dishes, and meat and fish. A few drops of pepper vinegar splashed on cooked fish such as mackerel, lend the perfect touch, as they also do to soups, raw oysters, red beans with rice, cabbage, and a host of other favorites.

First the Cook Builds a Roux

Brown roux, pronounced *roo,* is at the heart of countless Creole dishes, especially the ones that contain meat, fish, and sea food. Take the fabled tomato sauce or red gravy for an example.

To make it the cook commonly melts half as much butter, lard, or other shortening as flour. She stirs the flour into the fat to brown lightly, using care not to scorch the mixture. (In some homes salad oil, ½ cup to ¾ cup of flour, composes the roux, which is prepared in advance and stored in the refrigerator for instant use.) For many dishes she adds chopped onion when the roux is a light brown. She continues the soft cooking and stirring until the flour gradually reaches the desired golden brown hue.

When the fat shows signs of separating from the flour, it is a signal to add the liquid to make the sauce or gravy. Then she stirs constantly as it cooks until the onion disappears. Creoles consider it a *faux pas* if pieces of onion, onion tops, or other vegetables float in a sauce, gumbo, or soup. The seasonings they stir into the sauce and simmer in it also blend for the subtle overtones for which the regional dishes are famed.

A visitor from the North never dreams it is possible to make so many different sauces for fish until he has eaten Creole food for a few weeks.

Creole gravy is red or brown. Both have a brown roux as a base, but in one water is the liquid, and in the other tomatoes. Rice also associates with gravy — cooked kernels snowy white, tender, fluffy, and separate from one another. "How do you cook rice so wonderfully?" I asked my delightful hostess-guide, a New Orleans business home economist, as we dined in the French Quarter. "It's easy," she replied. "You add salt and half again as much water as rice and bring it to a boil in a rice pan, and then simmer it half an hour. At this point you take off the lid and lift the rice lightly with a fork to fluff it. Then you cover it and let it stand a few minutes to re-absorb its own steam. The pan is one used only for cooking rice. It is heavy, fits the unit or burner of the range, and has a close fitting lid.

"As you talk next week with people in southern Louisiana you will find they eat rice daily. They will repeatedly toss bouquets for the mild, white kernels that complement their seasoned foods. Rice and Creole dishes have been happily married since New Orleans was young. That was a long time ago, when everyone on the narrow street outside the window there spoke either French or Spanish."

Sea foods personify Creole cooking in a sublime mood. Fresh shrimp from inside Louisiana waters, the rivers and lakes, and the Gulf; salt-flavored and river-fattened oysters from Barataria Bay, soft-shell crabs from Lake Salvador, soft-shell turtles, crayfish from the marshes when the rice fields are drained, and the Gulf's red snapper, redfish, trout, pompano, sheepshead, flounder, and other species of fish cooperate to elevate the cuisine to a place of international honor.

Thoughts of Gumbo Call the Natives Home

Visitors do not search in vain for celebrated dishes when in New Orleans or the Teche country. Local epicures lament that hundreds of old-time masterpieces have surrendered to the pressures of modern living, but rejoice that some of them have withstood the tests of time. Almost everyone agrees on a few of them that classify for the immortal group. *Gumbos* come first, and rank as the Creoles' finest gift to gastronomy. A gumbo is a soup among soups, a tongue teaser and appeaser, something to anticipate and remember. Or as one gentleman remarked, "A thrill to return to at the end of the day." It utilizes the treasures of the Gulf of Mexico.

Gumbos, unique in the region, divide into two noble families, *gumbo févi* and *gumbo filé*. Févi is the Creole name for okra, which also is called gumbo. Thick soups made from févi or gumbo give the name to the entire troupe of these treats in the cuisine. When filé entered the kettle as a substitute for okra, the gumbo name stuck. Filé — pronounced *fee-lay* — is powdered sassafras leaves. In favor since the Indian days, it is a staple item in most kitchens. People in Louisiana add it to the soup just before serving, for if cooked it makes the gumbo stringy. Many families add 1 teaspoon of filé to each bowl of gumbo, and of course stir it in.

Rice accompanies gumbo — plain boiled rice. The accepted custom is to serve several tablespoons of it in every soup plate with the hot, thick, steaming goodness ladled over. Naturally a visitor who takes his pick of the many kinds will not wish to overlook gumbo filé. It has chicken, ham, and oysters in its depths as well as seasonings. But what gumbos could anyone taste without using superlatives? Oyster, shrimp, crab, veal, giblet, turkey, chicken and green gumbo all delight the connoisseurs. *Gumbo Z'Herbes,* which I sampled at St. Martinville, contains 7 varieties of spring greens cooked with ham or salt pork, or chicken and the pork. The natives assure you that if served on Holy Thursday it brings good luck throughout the year. It is no hardship to try to win happiness by such a pleasant route.

Then You'll Know Why New Orleans Is Famous

POMPANO EN PAPILOTTES. Almost anyone who approaches New Orleans by car, plane, train, or boat carries in his heart a wish to set his teeth into this noble creation. Most people say the elusive pompano is the perfect foil for a velvety sauce that contains sautéed crab meat, shrimp, and mushrooms, and white wine. The tastiness is spread on the fish fillets, which first are simmered or poached in salted water about 5 minutes. Individual servings are wrapped in buttered or oiled paper or placed in paper bags with their ends folded to close, and fastened with paper clips. After baking briefly the hot packages are served. Everyone has his own portion. The proper technique is to slit the paper to meet the aroma of its contents, fold back both sides of the opening, and touch the fork and tongue to supreme delight. "Then," people in Creole land say, "you'll know why New Orleans is famous around the world for its food."

JAMBALAYA. In jambalaya, rice probably attains its greatest regional renown. Indeed, it is a dependable mainstay in everyday meals. Possibly of Spanish descent, it somewhat resembles *Paella,* save that here fish and meat do not mix. It is a meal in a dish, thriftiness in a delectable dress. Natives make it with chicken, a variety of meats, and fish and sea food. Oyster jambalaya rates as a giant among entrees. A characteristic that helps the tasty creation sustain popularity through the centuries is its remarkable ability in salvaging scraps of leftover roast pork, chicken, turkey, baked ham, and fish. Chaurice, a highly seasoned Creole pork sausage, vienna sausages, oysters, crayfish, and shrimps at one time or another glorify the dish.

A local legend about the origin of jambalaya, as told to me by a lady of Creole descent, centers around a little French cafe near the river front in New Orleans during the French reign in the Eighteenth Century. Late one night a distinguished visitor came in to eat. The proprietor, having nothing fine to offer him, said to Jean, his cook, "Balayez" (blend together everything that's good). The visitor was so pleased with the resultant dish, so the story goes, that he suggested naming it "Jean Balayez," which eventually came to be jambalaya.

Recipes for it are almost endless, largely because in the old days Negro cooks competed with one another as to who could evolve the most tasty one. Basically all feature meat, fish, poultry, or sea food; and tomatoes, onions, rice, and seasonings. The art is to prepare the cereal so it will be tender, dry, and fluffy — in direct contrast to moist and gummy offerings. Shrimp, fish, and oysters are tossed in, usually with a fork, just in time to cook. Meats and poultry commonly enter the kettle with the rice at the beginning. Jambalaya carries seasonings of salt, pepper, a red pepper pod, and cayenne, and other additions, like thyme, parsley, and bay leaf, depending on the chef's whims.

Chicken Fricassee of the Lafayette Blend

GRILLADES. In France *grillade* means grilled food, but in New Orleans *les grillades* have nothing to do with a broiler. They are 4-inch squares of sliced round of beef or veal, browned in a little fat and removed from the frying pan while the roux with onions is made in it. Frequently tomatoes are included. Chopped bell pepper, garlic, a sprig of thyme, parsley, and a bay leaf often are added to the frying pan with the meat and about a half cup of water. Some women pour in a tablespoon of vinegar. They cover the pan and simmer the contents over low heat until the grillades are tender. Then they serve them with boiled rice or hominy. Anyone present thanks his lucky stars he is on hand to enjoy the princely fare.

CHAURICE. This hot or peppery sausage, a relative of Spain's chorizo, comes to the breakfast table. Usually its pungent flavor appears in pan-fried slices, although it also peps up many dressings for poultry. Among the seasonings in it are thyme, parsley, bay leaf, garlic, chili pepper, cayenne, and a touch of allspice.

CHICKEN FRICASSEE. "It's brown!" most visitors to the area exclaim when first they meet this dish. In Lafayette, Louisiana, I watched my hospitable hostess, a French teacher and an excellent cook, prepare the entree. As she worked she described her procedure.

"First you brown the chicken pieces carefully in fat. Many women then remove the boney ones for simmering on a later day with butter beans. Next you make a brown roux in the kettle with onion, add about a quart of hot water and the browned chicken, and simmer it until tender, replenishing the water as needed. Favorite seasonings include salt, celery, pepper, cayenne, chopped parsley, thyme, bay leaf, and green onion tops. The experts stir the stew as it thickens to prevent scorching."

Poultry so prepared sometimes winds up as filling for chicken pie.

Rice is the traditional and favored accompaniment for chicken fricassee.

Beans and Rice for Wash Day

POULTRY STUFFING. Sage steps down and allows thyme to play the lead role in dressings. Many of them are made with rice and corn bread, and contain touches of minced onion — cooked first in a little fat to brown lightly — pecans, oysters, celery, onion tops, parsley, salt, and pepper.

FRIED CHICKEN. While the southern style, often garnished with fried onion rings, commands a loyal following in Creole country, another version also wins much praise. After the disjointed birds are browned in a little fat, cooks add sliced onions and brown them lightly, and sift on flour and brown it; next they add sliced tomatoes, chopped garlic, sliced pimento, seasonings of salt, pepper, and herbs, and hot water.

Simmering continues about 45 minutes. Then the chicken and its delightful sauce over boiled rice goes to the table.

RED BEANS AND RICE. As traditional on Monday as baked beans and brown bread on Saturday in New England are red beans and rice. The custom of serving this food team started when Monday was the universal wash day. Natives soak the beans overnight in cold water, and then cook them in the same liquid with pickled or smoked pork, the shoulder preferred, a minced onion, a clove of garlic, a chopped carrot, and herbs. To serve the meal-in-a-dish they heap the vegetable on a platter and top it with the meat; the rice forms a snowy border. It was eaten by slaves preceding the War Between the States. Following the conflict, necessity and poverty introduced the dish to epicures. It was a winner from the first mouthful.

COURTBOUILLON. This creation, pronounced *coo-bouillon,* is true to its name; it is regal. It classifies as the most typically Creole of all the New Orleans fish entrees. Slices of redfish, red snapper or other fish, after being browned lightly in fat, are introduced tenderly to a prepared full-bodied sauce that contains an array of seasonings. In simmering about a half hour the fish absorbs the exotic blend of onion, onion tops, allspice, thyme, bay leaf, parsley, tomatoes (or tomato paste or sauce), celery, garlic, sweet pepper, Worcestershire sauce, butter, lemon juice, claret, salt, pepper, cayenne, and Tabasco sauce. Many families serve the classic with golden, piping hot French fried potatoes, which often are cut in cubes. (The French say Louisiana Creoles do not use the name *courtbouillon* correctly; in France it designates the water, usually containing vinegar or wine, vegetables, and seasonings, in which the fish cooks. The Creole custom is to refer to the fish when ready to serve as *courtbouillon*; it is delicious regardless of name.)

Jellied Meats Have a Loyal Following

DAUBE GLACÉ. Creoles simmer beef, veal shanks, and pigs' feet in water spiked with allspice, black pepper, cayenne, cloves, onions, a leek, 2 carrots, a stalk of celery, and a bay leaf until tender enough to fall from the bones. After that they remove the meat and reduce the stock about a third by cooking, and strain it through a cloth until perfectly clear. They mince the meat, or leave it uncut but boned, place it in a bowl or mold, and pour on the stock. In some households the tradition is to line the mold, before adding the meat, with cooked carrots cut in fancy shapes. In other households the orange-hued vegetable pieces are added to the stock after straining. When thoroughly chilled, the jellied platter delicacy is sliced with a sharp knife and garnished with lemon slices and chili peppers. Salad — crisp, brittle green leaves with French dressing — frequently accompanies it.

Several kinds of jellied meats are popular in the region. One favorite contains the brisket of beef cooked with calves' feet in water; there are seasonings of peppercorns, thyme, bay leaf, celery leaves, parsley, and thin lemon slices. For some of these, women add a little gelatin softened in water to the strained stock before pouring it over the meat. Chicken glacé is made the same way.

Cold jellied meats and chicken, so much a part of the Creole cuisine, in general differ little from those of France, although there is one noticeable variation. They are more highly seasoned. Usually chili peppers are served with them. The normal practice is to garnish the glacé with sprigs of lacy-edged parsley leaves and the little hot, pointed pods.

DAUBE. The brown pot roast varies from those in most other areas of the United States primarily in its more pronounced seasoning. Slits are cut over the surface of the meat, or a pocket is made near the bone, if there is one. These cavities are filled with chopped garlic, bits of fat meat, salt, pepper, and cayenne. Among the common additions after browning and while braising are chopped or canned tomatoes, sliced green pepper, onion tops, parsley, thyme, bay leaf, Tabasco sauce, and cayenne.

A Gift From Truant Husbands

TONGUE. The Creoles like tongue boiled in water until tender, with pickling spices, a bay leaf, and chopped celery added. Then they skin it, remove the fat, and dress it in many styles. In some kitchens the cooked tongue is placed on a baking sheet and heated in the oven with bastings of guava jelly. Almonds are scattered over the top. Sometimes an ambrosia made of melted blackberry jelly or cranberry jelly or sauce plus raisins that have been cooked in water until soft is spread on the tongue; then it is run in the oven to heat. It is the custom to squeeze on lemon juice just before serving.

Anyone who lives in Creole country occasionally browns the cooked tongue lightly in a little fat, removes it from the pan, and makes a brown roux with onion. Tomato paste mixed with some of the water in which the tongue cooked is added. The meat is heated and served in the sauce.

TRIPE A LA CREOLE. Men praise this dish. After it first has been simmered until tender in water with traces of vinegar and salt added, cooks drain and slice the tripe in strips about ½ by 2 inches in size. They brown them lightly in fat, with chopped onion, green onion tops, finely cut celery, parsley, bell pepper, tomatoes, and bay leaf added. They simmer the mixture about 20 minutes. Before serving with grits they shake on a few drops of Tabasco sauce.

OYSTER LOAF. In New Orleans it is called the peacemaker, because truant husbands in the old days were said to have carried it home late at night to appease their waiting wives. The oysters, preferably from Bayou Cook or Barataria Bay, are dipped in flour, brushed with beaten egg yolk seasoned with salt, fried in deep fat, and drained on absorbent paper. The chef cuts the top off a loaf of bread, scoops out the inside to form a case, rubs the inside with melted butter, and heats it in the oven. She places the oysters in the bread, garnishes them with slices of gherkins, and replaces the loaf's top for a cover. The treat is sliced or broken apart for serving. It is at its best when piping hot.

At picnics individual oyster loaves with French rolls substituting for the bread loaves are popular.

Some motorists fill a large hollowed out loaf of bread — buttered — with fried chicken, add gherkins, and put on its top. Tucked in a paper bag, they have a quick luncheon — buttered bread, chicken, and gherkins. They break off the bread and eat it, the chicken, and gherkins from the hand. Louisiana bread is French style, with long loaves and a crunchy crust, but southern type corn bread also has an ardent following.

Creole Coffee Is Something Special!

POOR BOY SANDWICHES. They contain slices of ham and American cheese; the bread is spread with Creole mustard instead of butter.

BRIOCHE. The favorite coffeecake of the Creole territory is *brioche*. Small, individual brioches also are made. The traditional shape is a ring with a ball in the center. Sometimes the tops are glazed or frosted white and sprinkled with bits of candied fruits or nuts, or both.

According to an old Spanish custom adopted by early Creoles in New Orleans, a bean or some trinket was hidden in the large brioche, called King's cake. It appeared first in the year at parties on January 6, or Twelfth Night. The guest who cut the slice for himself or herself that contained the talisman became the king or queen for the evening. The honor obligated the gentleman or lady to become host or hostess at the next week's party! This plan kept social gaiety flowing through the carnival season that ends with the advent of Lent. During the Mardi Gras, one of the modern customs is to keep doughnuts and coffee on hand for informal guests who call.

CREOLE COFFEE. Visitors think it is as black as sin, but the natives prefer their brew to any other. Indeed, they have been known to carry a supply of the finely ground berries and the paraphernalia required for dripping it on their travels. The beans are roasted a very dark brown. In New Orleans, but usually not in the Baton Rouge and Teche areas, from 10 to 15 per cent of chicory is incorporated to provide the body that people in the Crescent City like.

In some kitchens from ½ to 1 hour is required to drip the coffee properly. An earthen pot is set in a pan of hot water, often over heat, during the process. Business women who do not have time to make the beverage in the morning frequently get it ready the night before. One of my most gracious hostesses, a member of the home economics extension staff at the University of Louisiana, demonstrated her procedure. She lets the coffee drop into a small glass fruit jar. When the process is completed and the jar is filled she puts on a self-seal lid. In the morning she pries open the jar, pours the coffee into an earthen pot, and sets it in a pan of water for heating.

An old-time breakfast still respected consists of orange juice, hard rolls, butter, and café au lait — or equal parts of coffee and of milk heated but not allowed to boil. In the food market of New Orleans the steaming coffee and milk are poured into the cup simultaneously. A pitcher of hot cream goes to the table for people who like the extra richness in café au lait. If cereals are included in the meal they are the ready-to-serve varieties, which are popular throughout the South.

While Hissing Green Flames Play

CAFE BRULOT. Sometimes this after-dinner beverage answers to the name of *Café Diabolique*. It specifies the union of flaming brandy, spices, and citrus fruit peels with strong coffee — "black as the water in a bayou," one of my hostesses said. The Creoles and many of their friends make quite a ceremony of the serving, both in restaurants and homes. A Brûlot bowl is part of the equipment in many

well-appointed households. It is a spun silver-plated bowl
with a tray beneath to protect the table against heat. Where
one is not available a large silver-plated bowl — without
soldering to melt under the alcohol's heat — substitutes satisfactorily if some provision is made to safeguard the table's
finish.

The shredded yellow parts of orange and lemon peels are
placed in a bowl along with broken cinnamon sticks and
allspice. At the proper moment, 3 lumps of sugar for each
person to be served are dropped in, along with cognac or
100 per cent proof bourbon whiskey, 1 cup to 12 persons.
The mixture is set on fire and the electric lights are turned
off. As the hissing green flames play, the liquid fire is dipped
with a long handled ladle over the sugar to burn and melt
it. Not all the alcohol is permitted to burn. The hot coffee
is poured into the bowl, and as the fire goes out in it the lights
are turned on in the dining room.

The fragrant, steaming beverage is strained into tiny
after-dinner cups; many ladles have strainers built into
their bowls to remove the peels. The drink, natives say, must
be sweet and piping hot to be delicious. They liken its flavor
to that of their rich dark fruit cakes. Recipes for it vary in
details. In one type the brandy burns in half an orange
shell turned outside in to aid in extracting the flavor of the
fruity yellow peel. Then it unites with black coffee.

Many natives are great sugar addicts. Perhaps their
proximity to sugar cane fields and sugar houses (factories)
has something to do with it. (Apples on sticks dunked by
children in cane sirup when it is boiling down are known as
Louisiana stickies.) A high proportion of the people prefer
their black coffee very sweet. The two best liked fruit preserves in the Teche country are those composed of figs and
pears; both of them contain much sugar. Either one and
French bread serves as an ample dessert in many simple
evening meals. Rice waffles spread with butter and sprinkled
with sugar and cinnamon make a pleasing dessert, too. Some

families enthuse over hot corn bread served with peanut butter and cane sirup.

Rich Pralines Connote New Orleans

PRALINES. Anyone who has missed this confection has been cheated out of a taste delight. The thin, sweet wafers of brown or white sugar, cooked with water or cream and nuts or coconut, are as unique in the confection world as they are delectable. In France *pralin* signifies almonds cooked in sugar for addition to desserts, like cakes, ices, and soufflés. They were named for a famed French Marshall, the Duc de Choiseul-Praslin, for history records that in his home almonds first were coated with sugar over heat.

Almost everyone in New Orleans regrets the disappearance of the Negro mammies who carried trays of this candy, covered with immaculate white cloths, through the Vieux Carré. In the olden days their voices filled the air with musical and vivid descriptions of the sweets they were offering for sale.

In Creole pralines either nuts or shreds of coconut are cooked with sugar and liquid, which usually is water. Those made with white sugar contain coconut; natives say they boil the mixture until it may be drawn in a thread between the finger and thumb. Then they drop spoonfuls of it on a marble slab or a chilled buttered platter or baking sheet. The cakes are supposed to be 1/4 inch thick and from 4 to 5 inches in diameter. They are light, crisp, and *delicious*.

Pecans figure in brown sugar pralines. (They do in Texas, too, but there the sugar often is the white kind, caramelized.) Part of the nut meats are chopped fine, others are left in halves. Simmering them in the candy gives it the enticing flavor of cooked pecans. A few people also make the brown confection with coarsely chopped peanuts. Another praline is known as LA COLLE; it contains New Orleans molasses, no water, and peanuts. The traditional Creole rule is to pour this one from the kettle into paper cases.

Then there are the Creole crescents which are so delicious with coffee.

CRESCENTS

¼ pound butter or margarine	1 cup sifted flour
1 cup pecans, cut fine	¼ teaspoon salt
2 tablespoons powdered sugar	½ teaspoon vanilla

Add all the ingredients to the butter or margarine (at room temperature). Roll on a lightly floured board very thin, or about ¼ inch thick. Cut in crescent shape. Arrange on a baking sheet and bake in a very slow oven, 250°, until a light brown color, or about an hour. Roll in powdered sugar.

Crayfish Bisque — a Tureen Treat

CALAS. Comparatively few of these wonderful piping hot rice fritters appear at breakfast to keep company with coffee, but on very special occasions some homes still serve them. They are those fabulous tempters Negro women formerly made and sold mornings in the French Quarter of New Orleans from big wooden bowls carried on their heads. Yeast-leavened, the soft dough contains rice, cooked until soft and mushy, a little flour, eggs, and sugar. Mixing spoons add big drops of it to hot fat, as for doughnuts, which are fried until a golden hue appears on all sides. After being drained and sprinkled with sugar, the fritters are the ultimate in deliciousness, especially if served with café au lait on a balmy morning in a New Orleans courtyard.

CRAYFISH BISQUE. Who would dare dispute the high regard in which the natives hold this supreme treat? To taste it fresh from the kettle in a home near the banks of the Bayou Teche or elsewhere in the region makes an unforgettable experience. Women who prepare the tureen favorite confess the chore is a laborious ritual, and that they devote parts of two days to it. There is a growing tendency to buy it frozen, when available, or to prepare a large supply at a time and to freeze the surplus. During the crayfish season, in April and May, many people purchase large gunny sacks filled with crayfish along the highways leading into New Orleans.

In many other lands they are rare and costly; epicures consider the Louisiana profusion a great regional blessing.

"How do you make crayfish bisque?" I asked the home demonstration agent in New Orleans. "It's this way," she replied. "I've done it many times and hope to continue making it every year so long as my family and I enjoy the blessings of this world."

"The live crayfish must be 'purged,' or 'purified,' before being scalded. This is done by placing them in large tubs of salted tap water, and stirring them occasionally with a long stick. After about 15 minutes of purging, the live crayfish are added to boiling water. They are not boiled, but merely killed.

"Picking the meat then becomes the order of the day. That from the tail is placed in one bowl, and the fat from the head is shaken into another. The head shells are cleaned and saved so the dressing may be stuffed into them later.

"The tail meats then are put through a food chopper, and mixed with dry bread crumbs and seasonings of onion, garlic, parsley, red pepper, and traces af allspice and cinnamon. Egg binds the ingredients together, which are heated through in a heavy skillet or other utensil. After cooling for handling this dressing is stuffed firmly and painstakingly into the clean head shells. You roll them lightly in flour and chill overnight, as the dressing stays in place better when so handled. Later these stuffed heads are added to the bisque gravy for final cooking. In serving you allow from 4 to 6 colorful and delicious filled heads to each soup bowl.

"The bisque gravy starts cut as a brown roux with lots of minced onion, possibly a pint. After these are cooked until they are no longer distinguishable — with the addition of hot water occasionally — other seasonings of shallots, parsley, thyme, bay leaf, garlic, salt, and cayenne or Tabasco sauce are added. Finally the stuffed heads are introduced to this thickened gravy and the mixture is allowed to simmer about 20 minutes longer. Then comes the addition of the refrigerated fat, and only a few minutes more of heat are required to complete one of the most delectable of dishes."

MAYTIME SUPPER
Teche Country
Crayfish Bisque
French Bread
Tossed Green Salad
Black Coffee

For festivity of the picnic kind the crayfish boil surrenders to no other meal when the gift of the marshes is in season.

Sea Foods — and More Sea Foods

BOUILLABAISSE. The Creole version is a near relative of the French masterpiece, with local redfish and red snapper substituting for the sturgeon and perch of Marseilles. Crabs, crayfish, shrimp, wine, and Creole seasonings enter the New Orleans dish, which is served over toast.

REMOULADE OF SHRIMP. The New Orleans interpretation of the sauce varies from the more bland ones of France. Instead of mayonnaise the base is French dressing, which usually is made with a tarragon or basil vinegar. Some of the lusty seasonings included are prepared Creole mustard, horse-radish, the tender tops and young leaves of celery, shallots, or chives cut fine, garlic, salt, and paprika to add its color. Recipes vary from one household to another, as they do for all Creole food works of art, but here is one I begged from a brilliant hostess. It makes good eating.

REMOULADE OF SHRIMP

4 tablespoons salad oil	1 teaspoon horse-radish
2 tablespoons tarragon vinegar	1 stalk celery
1 teaspoon salt	2 green onions
2 tablespoons Creole mustard	1 tablespoon parsley
2 teaspoons paprika	1 pound shrimp, cooked

Make a dressing of the oil, vinegar, and salt. Add the mustard, paprika (more of it if a deeper color is desired), horse-radish, finely chopped celery, small (young) onions chopped fine, and the minced parsley. Pour this mixture over the seasoned, cooked shrimp and refrigerate it at least 24 hours. When the hors d'ouevre is served arrange nests of crisp lettuce on each chilled plate, and in each one place at least 9 of the shrimp.

FISH. Redfish, flounder, sheepshead, and other fish weighing around 4 pounds, poached or simmered in water, are enjoyed cold as well as hot. The fish, after being simmered in water containing salt, a bay leaf, and pieces of lemon peel, is skinned and boned with care to keep it whole. At serving time the home chefs place it on a cold platter and cover it with mayonnaise thinned with a little white vinegar, and with finely chopped green onion tops, minced celery tops, and mustard folded in. They garnish it until emerald with minced parsley, and then add the yellow and white of minced hard-cooked eggs and grated lemon peel. After that they stick in capers to make a decorative design, the cook's trademark.

Baked sheepshead stuffed with a bread-oyster dressing seasoned with a medley of herbs, scores another mealtime triumph.

FROG LEGS. Frequently they are pan-fried and served with tartar sauce. Another favored treatment is to boil the legs, remove the skin, roll them in cream, and broil them. In some kitchens white wine is added to the pan-fried number after the initial browning.

CREOLE SHRIMP. This specialty on the menu means New Orleans pan-fried shrimp simmered in a sauce made with a brown roux containing onions. Tomatoes, celery, and bell peppers also cook in it. Among the seasonings are old favorites, thyme, parsley, bay leaf, and cayenne or Tabasco sauce.

Flounder frequently reaches the dining table baked with a bread crumb-crab meat dressing in its center. The early Creoles called flounder *sole* because to them it resembled the Mediterranean fish of that name both in flavor and texture.

Tossed Green Salads Are Tops

SALADS. Crisp tossed leaves with French dressing reign supreme. People like them so much they have little desire to try other kinds. There is an unwritten law that a bowl of mixed greens that contains water cress should have a French dressing made with tarragon vinegar.

POTATO SALAD. The dish differs somewhat from that served in other localities. While hot, the cooked and diced potatoes are mixed with French dressing. When cool, boiled and chilled shrimp and chopped celery, parsley, onion, and green pepper are folded in. Slices of hard-cooked eggs and small, fiery chili peppers provide the garnish.

STUFFED VEGETABLES. In kitchens where Creole cooking is practiced, stuffed vegetables are no newcomers. The custom is to first simmer such garden gifts as eggplant, summer squash, and mirlitons or vegetable pears in salted water. Then cooks scoop out a part of their interiors, chop the pulp fine, and mix it with steamed crab meat, shrimp, sausage, or ham plus bread crumbs and seasonings. They simmer the stuffing thus made about 5 minutes and then pile it into the vegetable shells. After that they scatter cracker crumbs and dots of butter on top and bake to heat and brown.

Cushaws — neck pumpkins — are favorites in Creole areas as they are in north Florida, where the people commonly speak of them in food conversations without realizing that some visitors from the North have no idea to what vegetable they refer.

Natives say that often they parboil the cushaw an hour, and then cut it in 6-inch squares. They arrange the pieces in a pan, add just enough water to prevent scorching, and sprinkle the vegetable with brown sugar, a trace of cinnamon, and dabs of butter. Then they bake it in a moderate oven, 350°, to glaze the tops, while basting frequently with butter melted in a little hot water.

Boiled vegetables are not tolerated in many homes. The universal and traditional methods are to bake them in a casserole or their skins, or to cook them to a creamy consistency in a covered saucepan. The Creoles refer to this dish as *etouffe,* or they use the word *smothered.* Frequently they smother two vegetables together, with squash and eggplant one selection gourmets rave about. Also they often add cooked fish, meats, game, or chicken to the vegetables.

For example, the squash and eggplant union is teamed with chicken giblets, ham, ground beef or pork, shrimps, crabs, or oysters. So far as Uncle Sam's domain goes, eggplant dishes probably attain their greatest glory in the Creole cuisine. As already noted, okra ascends to fame in gumbo, the soup that carries the vegetable's name. It also makes a great reputation for itself when sliced and simmered with corn cut from the cob, tomatoes, and chopped green peppers, along with seasonings of salt, pepper, and butter.

Cottage Cheese Teams With Other Foods

CREAM CHEESE. A Yankee who orders the cream cheese listed on the breakfast menu card of a New Orleans coffee shop discovers that what the waiter delivers to him is an old and unexpected friend, cottage cheese. In many households it is served with berries, or cooked or fresh fruit, and sugar and cream at breakfast. My introduction to the custom came in a home management house at the Southwestern Louisiana Institute in Lafayette, where a home economics student said to me, "We like cream cheese, especially with strawberries or prunes, and sugar and cream. And its valuable protein at a reasonable price recommends its use." Frozen cream cheese rates as an acceptable dessert. For it the cook adds sugar, vanilla, and usually both milk and cream before freezing.

PIES. With Creole territory a part of the United States, naturally pies are not strangers! Four kinds that win plaudits are dewberry, pecan, cream of banana, and cream of coconut. Along with talk of pastry treats there is praise for cherry, banana, and strawberry jubilees, the fruit and ice cream duet that glows with flaming brandy. This is not surprising, for fruit and brandy a-blaze in chafing dishes classify as a Creole heritage. (For a quick substitute for pie, some cooks roll peeled whole bananas in sugar and cinnamon, wrap them individually in pastry, and bake them quickly. They serve them with whipped cream. Bananas possess the dignity that springs from many years of high standing. Perhaps natives like best to bake them, often combined with orange juice.)

Books with many chapters have been written about Southern Louisiana's Creole cookery. Obviously any attempt to condense a description of the nation's most unique cuisine into a few pages eliminates many Olympian dishes. But even a brief mention indicates something of the brilliance it imparts to home cooking in the United States. A food reporter who spends some time in the territory and travels on to other scenes notes that dazzling taste triumphs of Creole origins, like the sunlight, follow her into Texas, where they share honors with beef, and to Florida, where they frequently are interpreted with Cuban slants. Wherever they show up they are a delightful breath of the South, of which they fully are a part. They associate with the warm hospitality for which Dixieland is so justly famed.

All Aboard for Florida

There is no such thing as an authentic all-Florida cuisine. Certainly the people on the flowery peninsula follow the South's meal patterns more closely then those of any other region. This is especially true in the northern sections — those counties north of a line drawn from east to west through Gainsville. But it takes more than an imaginary line to shut out the fondness for tiny hot biscuits, corn breads turning brown in the oven, fried chicken, peach pickles, ham, coconut layer cake, and other Dixie favorites. And what observer fails to note how the flavor of New Orleans permeates the cookery? Creole seasonings pep up many a dish, and Louisiana ways with fish and sea food enhance the meals.

You note Yankee touches on the home tables along the East Coast. No doubt the recipes were imported by Northerners who moved to the area to enjoy mild winters. On the state's prospering cattle ranches both the food and cowboy jargon carry a southern accent. Jacksonville enjoys a kinship with other cities along the southern half of the Atlantic Seaboard. Her finger is in coastal cooking, eastern style. Tampa boasts of Cuban, Spanish, and Italian culinary triumphs as fine as can be found any place across the United States.

At Tarpon Springs, near St. Petersburg, Greek treats warm the cockles of the hearts of many people. There a green salad that resembles a Christmas tree comes from the kitchens. And down Miami way in subtropical country some of the fruits that grow and contribute to good eating include the avocado, coconut, banana, pineapple, papaya, litchi, carambola, cashews, sugar apples or sopadillas, guavas, persimmons, pomegranates, tamarinds, and Haden mangoes.

Carambolas cut crosswise give star-shaped slices that decorate marmalades. The juices are refreshing in iced ades. Northern visitors who ask about cashews learn they are a combination fruit and nut.

Key West, the black dot on the map, is the southernmost city in the United States. A small place — for the island in miles measures merely two by four — it makes up in color what it lacks in size. It suggests a luscious dish slipping from Creole control under the spell of Cuba and the tropics, with a dash of England for contrast. It spells candles flickering under hurricane shades on the table in the evening, trade winds and tides, grits and fish, the perfume of bananas, pineapples, and Haden mangoes in desserts, jelly coconuts converted into ice cream, very black coffee five times a day, delicious stone crabs, and the sharp accent of lime juice.

Both Persian and Spanish Limes Are Grown

Certainly the wide use of local fruits characterizes Florida's meals. Limes are as popular as lemons in California. Two varieties grow, the Spanish type of Key West and the Persian lime. The *key limes,* as the natives call the former, are small and yellow when ripe — often about the size of a walnut or a little larger. The skin of the *Persian lime* is green. It is much bigger. The trees bear two crops a year. For use when the fruit is not available, Key Westers and some other Floridians make Old Sour. They extract the juice from ripe Spanish limes and add salt to it. They let the mixture stand awhile before straining it through several layers of cheesecloth. Then they pour it into bottles. After the liquid ferments it is ready for use. Some families like to include a couple of bird's-eye peppers in every bottle before adding the juice. Everyone testifies that the results are authoritative. Most natives add only a few drops at a time.

The Cuban procedure is to drop the lime juice or Old Sour into a dish during cooking, while the Conch way is to shake it on precisely at the dining table, with care not to get too much out of the bottle. The Conchs are Caucasian residents of the Keys who are descendants of Cockney or Tory English that arrived mainly by way of the Bahama Islands — and some people also say by way of the South (U.S.A.). They are named for the conch, pronounced *konk,* a small shellfish that inhabits local waters. This backdrop helps explain why Key West cookery is a blend of Cuban, Spanish, and English dishes. To England goes the credit for some of the heavier desserts, like the duffs, which many households consider peerless.

In Florida almost everyone squeezes the juice of limes into iced tea, over fruits, melons, and fish, and into such dishes as Harvard beets, French and other salad dressings, and sweet sauces for gingerbread and puddings. It plays the role assigned to vinegar and lemon juice in many regions. Thin slices of limes float on black bean and chilled turtle soup. Then there is Key West lime pie, the pride and joy of home folks and their guests from far and near.

To make the pie the cook mixes egg yolks, lime juice, and sugar and heats them over water in a double boiler until the custard coats the back of a metal spoon. Then she removes it from the heat and stirs in unflavored gelatin softened in cold water, and a bit of shredded lime peel. As the mixture starts to thicken when chilled, she folds in egg whites, beaten stiff and sweetened. Then she pours it into a crisp, baked pastry shell. Many families like a thin layer of whipped cream spread on top just before serving.

Recipes for the dessert are legion. Everyone naturally prefers her own version. Some chiffon pies have graham cracker crusts. Others feature a custard filling composed of sweetened condensed milk, egg yolks, and lime juice. But in all of them — even the most fabulous editions — the filling is a yellowish color, a hue derived largely from the egg yolks. To the annoyance of some hostesses, the visiting firemen — the people who follow the birds south in autumn and stop off in the state — often are disappointed that it is not green. Many of them vow they will tint it when they make the dessert. No doubt they make good on the assertion when they arrive home!

Tart Oranges Come From Mother Stock

Important as limes are in the kitchens, they do not over-shadow oranges. When a party with fruit punch comes up — and that is often — many sparkling bowls fill with 1 gallon of fresh orange juice mixed with 1 quart each of ginger ale and lime, orange, or cranberry sherbet.

When natives speak of orange meringue pie made with the juice of sour oranges, they smack their lips and say, "What a dessert!" Old-timers, and newcomers, too — there are many of them on the sunlit peninsula — agree on the delicacy of it. The *sour orange* or tart fruit is produced by the mother stock of the commercial groves, the kind that grew first in the area. It yields a sharp flavored marmalade, suggestive of the kind English people like.

Pleasing ways to use the marmalades from the sour and the sweet oranges intrigue visitors. The sweet version is made from the oranges grown commercially. Cooks spread them on the cut surface of wonderful grapefruit halves to be eaten en natural or broiled. A teatime hostess adores serving tiny orange biscuits. To make them she rolls rich biscuit dough thin, spreads it with marmalade, winds it like a jelly roll, cuts off slices, and bakes them with a cut side down in small muffin pans. After baking them a few minutes she brushes their tops with sugar dissolved in a little orange juice. She repeats this process several times. That is how she obtains a shiny, appealing glaze on them.

Both the tiny hot southern biscuits, a universal favorite, and grapefruit halves spread with *tupelo honey* are worth writing home about. Light amber in color, this exquisite honey is a gift of west Florida, where tupelo gum trees grow along streams. It is heavy bodied, mild flavored, and does not granulate. Natives praise it as people of east Tennessee eulogize sourwood honey, and residents of Arizona laud that produced by bees which feed on the mesquite.

Orange ice commands a broad following in the south-eastern section and Key West, a good sized one elsewhere. In the simplest form it consists of 1 cup each of orange juice and sugar to ½ cup of lime juice. Women freeze the mixture in the refrigerator tray. Another dessert friend that smacks of the tropics is prepared by freezing the juices of 2 oranges and 3 limes with the mashed pulp of 2 bananas and ¼ cup each of sugar and water.

One Christmas salad popular in the southern half of the state displays the red of sliced radishes and the green of sliced young onions on lettuce. Some people gather the vegetables from their gardens on December 25th. Often the French dressing for it is made with the juice of sour oranges assuming the customary vinegar role. Then there is that Grecian salad which I had the good fortune to meet in Tarpon Springs. It comes to the table on a platter throughout the year, heaped high. It starts out with lettuce. Then celery, cucumbers, tomatoes, onions, green peppers, and avocado — all sliced — are arranged on top. The "Christmas tree" is decorated with anchovies, Grecian cheese, and green olives. A dressing of olive oil and lemon juice or vinegar, seasoned with salt, pepper, and oregano, is poured over.

Key Westers especially refer to "stranger" recipes. These are the ones recent citizens like. Many of them are for salads. Two such favorites are made with grapefruit. In one the juicy segments are permitted to stand in a bowl rubbed with a plug of garlic — there a clove of garlic is a *plug* — before the French dressing is poured on. In the other the fat fruit sections encircle a mound of steamed and chilled crabmeat seasoned with mayonnaise.

Tall fruit drinks are dear to Floridians the year around. Some of them are made with electric blenders, which get a real workout in the state.

A Fruit Plate Makes a Meal

A characteristic, regional fruit plate fills the bill for luncheon or supper any day of the year. Natives and visitors alike cheer — at least inwardly — when such loveliness and tastiness comes their way. In the center of the plate is a mound of seasoned cream or cottage cheese, topped with a soft, cooked, and nut-stuffed prune. From this hub radiate leaves of crisp, brittle lettuce. Each one displays a different local gem, such as sweet orange sections, grapefruit segments, slices of cultivated persimmon (Japanese), papaya (called pawpaws in Key West), avocado, fresh pineapple, or whatever other fruits are in season, and if available melon balls. Frequently just lime juice serves as the dressing.

Grapefruit and tomato aspics are not without honor in the area, and neither are shrimp, lobster (crayfish), and crab salads. The favorite tossed treat of the salad bowl contains cucumbers, tomatoes, and avocados in addition to the green leaves. The gala color and piquant flavor of kumquat slices molded in lemon flavored gelatin made with ginger ale as part of the liquid spark up many dinners.

When it comes to dessert, hundreds of families settle for wine colored guava jelly with cream cheese and salty, crisp crackers. Guava paste often substitutes for the jelly in the combination; it tastes good and costs less. The paste — guava marmalade cooked very thick — is imported from Cuba in small oblong wooden boxes. One of my hostesses served guava shells instead of the jelly. They are prepared in home kitchens and canned, although some of the supply now comes in cans processed in Cuba, where the red-fleshed guava grows in abundance. To make the shells cooks peel the fruit, scoop out the seeds, and simmer it in a heavy sirup. My hostess served two of them in a sauce dish with a finger of cream cheese; she placed them and three crackers on a dessert plate. Guava shells on vanilla ice cream compose a favored sundae.

Instead of guava jelly, some households prefer fig preserves with cream cheese and crackers. Among the choice relishes are peach and fig pickles, and pickled grapefruit and sour orange rinds. *Carissa jelly, tamarind preserves,* and *mango chutney* also receive many bouquets.

Fresh coconut cake appears on Christmas and other special occasions, and frequently wears a white cooked marshmallow frosting. A simple but delectable cake some

citizens of Spanish or Cuban descent vouch for and sometimes choose for gala affairs consists of two plain layers put
together with apple jelly, covered with a 7-minute frosting,
and sprinkled generously with shredded fresh coconut.
Sponge cake often contains not only lime juice but also a
whisper of the fruit's grated rind.

The wives and daughters of orange growers specialize in
luscious orange cakes that tempt even the people most conscious of calories. Some of them are in layer form and are
made with sour milk as the liquid, with an orange — seeded
but not peeled — and dates or raisins, all ground, stirred into
the batter. A confectioners' sugar frosting, moistened with
the citrus fruit's juice and rich with butter, contributes to
the dessert's glory. Either shredded coconut or pecans supply
the decorative note. Spanish bun cakes are enjoyed. They
are cinnamon flavored. Commonly women bake them in a
square pan. On the loaf they frequently bake a frosting composed of egg whites beaten stiff and sweetened with plenty
of brown sugar, and with nuts folded in .

Ice Cream Calls for Jelly Nuts

Fresh coconut cream pie enjoys considerable prestige.
Mango pie, containing either the ripe or green fruit, with
coconut ice cream wins the championship; it is the favorite
pie à la mode. The ice cream at its best — and much of it
so qualifies — is made with what Key West and some other
people call *jelly nuts.* In its early stages the palm's fruit is
filled with a liquid, and they refer to it as a *drinking nut.*
Later some of this liquid forms a soft jelly, and at that stage
the coconut becomes a *jelly nut.* As maturing continues the
jelly devolps into the white meat that is so tempting when
shredded and drifted over desserts. Good cooks have a habit
of teaming coconut with oranges. Occasionally they add the
white shreds to whipped cream to dress a dish displaying the
taste and fragrance of the citrus fruit.

Some women crystallize fruits for cakes, cookies, and other
desserts. Sweet orange, lemon, and lime peels and green

papayas commonly are candied. The papaya substitutes for citron in recipes. Hostesses tempt their guests with long, narrow strips of sugared grapefruit and orange peels, moist and tender. At parties they show them off. *Sweetmeats,* women label them, and then add, "We make them quickly and like to have them go quickly before they dry out. Our ideal is a candied peel that in texture resembles soft candy jelly beans." This recipe shows how the job is done.

Candied Grapefruit Peel

Wash and peel a medium-sized grapefruit. Cut the peel with sharp scissors or a knife into strips about ½ by 3 inches. Pour about 3 or 3½ cups of cold water with 1 teaspoon of salt added over the peel and let it stand overnight, or from 8 to 10 hours. Boil in the same water about 10 minutes. Drain. Boil 1 cup of sugar with the same quantity of water until the sirup spins a thread, 232° to 234°. Add the peel and simmer slowly a quarter of an hour. Remove the strips from the sirup and spread them on waxed paper to dry about an hour. Then roll them in sugar.

100 Varieties of Edible Fish!

Florida people boast of about 100 varieties of edible fish. Some of the species, including the illustrious pompano, made their bows in the preceding chapter. *Pompano al papilla,* in Spanish, the fish baked with the rich sauce containing sea food in parchment, enjoys the prestige *pompano en papilottes,* in French, is accorded in New Orleans. Since few Americans who have not dined in Key West have tasted the conch, tourists ask endless questions about it also.

Only the heavy muscle is edible, but it inspires many excellent dishes. The shells are so beautiful that almost all visitors who see them wish to send a supply home for friends to use as flower holders. When cooked, the conch somewhat resembles California's abalone, although it is a trifle more salty. It is inclined to be tough and needs to be handled just right. Culinary experts add lime juice to it, and they grind, pound, or score it. They feature it in soups, fritters, and combined with onions and green pepper, and often avocado, in appetizer salads.

Conch steaks frequently ring the bell for good eating. Women have the tough outer skin removed at the market. Then to flatten the steak they pound it on both sides with the edge of a small plate. They sprinkle on lime juice and let the steak stand a few minutes — about 15 — before they dip it in beaten egg and cracker crumbs. They brown it quickly on both sides in a little fat. Overcooking, they caution, develops toughness.

Floridians toast their spiny lobster, the *langosta* or *crayfish,* with the same enthusiasm State of Mainers speak of their kind. Many natives prefer their type to the sweeter, more delicate, and finer textured New England variety. They feature it in all the same dishes as the Yankee one. Food conversations especially sound the merits of crayfish *à la Newburgh,* crayfish *thermidor, curried and deviled* crayfish, and the *boiled* and *broiled* ones. Only the flexible abdomen tails are eaten. They have no claws.

Small or medium sized ones to boil or broil are the first choice. Most households serve them with melted butter and lime juice. Some cooks broil them with minced garlic, lime juice, Worcestershire sauce, and dabs of butter scattered on top. Often they stuff the head portions of the shells with whipped or mashed potatoes, well seasoned with butter and mayonnaise, dot them with butter, and broil or bake them. On some occasions they substitute a sea food sauce for the potatoes. Crayfish salads frequently appease the appetite most satisfactorily.

The Natives Like Their Shrimp

Like other people along the Gulf of Mexico, those who live on and visit the flowery peninsula consume huge quantities of shrimp. Methods of preparing it are countless. No *one* is named as the favorite way. But everyone agrees that it is essential to avoid overcooking. Soak the raw shucked shrimp in salted lime juice before frying it, women advise. Then at the last minute dip it in cracker meal, egg, and more meal. Immerse it in hot fat to cook and brown quickly.

Or cut the big Key West shrimp in pieces and fry them in deep fat for those wonderful puffy morsels. Almost everyone considers it a sacrilege to precede the frying by cooking in water.

To boil shrimp, natives cook it 5 minutes and then remove the kettle from the heat. They permit the rosy sea food to remain in the hot but not boiling water 5 minutes longer. By that time it is tender and at its best. Most women add a clove of garlic and a few lime slices to the cooking water.

Creole style shrimp dishes with their peppery seasonings are at home in the state. And so are various types of shrimp pies. One of the more famous ones starts out with shrimp pan-fried with chopped sweet green pepper and onion; tomato and a bit of bay leaf also are added. This delicious mixture then bakes in tart pans lined and topped with rich pastry. Beautiful yellow rice answers in many meals as a favorite accompaniment of shrimp cooked in water. Saffron supplies the color and pungency that so pleasantly complement the vivid red-pink, mild flavored sea food.

Large oysters, like those from Apalachicola Bay and other waters, and the jumbo shrimp from Key West are marinated in lime juice with salt and minced onion before broiling. Most cooks wrap the marinated oysters in slices of bacon and fasten them with half toothpicks before running them in the broiler. Shrimps take the same treatment only the cook dips them in chili sauce before she fastens on the bacon.

Scallops and hard- and soft-shell crabs are available many months of the year. They come to the table in versions similar to those relished along the entire Atlantic Coast. When Floridians speak of their stone crabs the tone and inflection of their voices denotes something hallowed and very special. In the Gulf of Mexico the habitat of this delicacy extends as far north as the Pinella Keys, and terminates at the Anclote Light. At no place is it abundant. Natives eat only the large, brilliant orange claws, which are tipped with shiny black. They cook this matchless gift in sea or salted water and eat it pronto because its elusive flavors disappear quickly when it is refrigerated. They serve it with melted butter and lime juice. On some ultra special occasions they combine the steamed meat with olives for what they rate as one of the greatest of all sea food salads.

Key Westers say they welcome kingfish and Spanish mackerel when their cool weather starts. (Sometimes the mercury in their thermometers dips to 60°!) Occasionally they bake these fish stuffed with pitted green olives. They like red snapper, as do other natives of the state, for baking and pan-frying at any time. They laud the *grouper* for chowder, *jewfish* for broiling, and *yellowtails* and *grunts* for quick pan-frying.

Fried and boiled fish commonly team with grits. On the Keys the union is especially commended. There another accompaniment is avocado, mashed and seasoned with a whisper of lime juice, vinegar, salt, pepper, and olive oil.

Some of the fish from warm southern waters have rather soft flesh, but the meat of jewfish and of the grouper is quite firm. Kingfish on the platter quite closely resembles New England's swordfish.

Tourists Marvel at Turtle Kraals

The people of Key West, an important marine turtle market, say tourists always show a keen interest in the *crawls* or *kraals*. In the city there are many favored turtle dishes, such as turtleburgers, turtle meat loaves, soup — hot and cold — and steaks that substitute for the more highly priced beef. They appear in other markets, too. Shoppers in Tampa, for example, usually can buy them. A Kansan confronting a breaded turtle steak thinks it is similar to breaded veal or a chicken-fried beefsteak. Most cooks dip the scored meat in beaten egg and cracker crumbs before pan-frying it quickly to brown on both sides. A food reporter also observes that Floridians commonly substitute cracker crumbs or cracker meal for bread crumbs or flour when pan-frying fish. In Key West this use of crackers is just about universal.

Some households buy canned turtle soup. Women say, "It is no trick to heat it in a jiffy." They add that the local brands satisfy. When the turtle boats arrive in Key West from Honduras some epicures look forward to what they regard as rare, pleasing delicacies — yellow turtle eggs and turtle livers. To prepare the eggs, cooks carefully remove the membrane and then place them in a sieve or colander. They sprinkle on salt and pepper and set them aside for a quarter of an hour. Then they deftly turn them into a warm frying pan containing melted butter. They simmer the eggs very gently for about 20 minutes. Too hot a pan, the experts warn, will break the eggs every time. They serve them like an omelet, but without folding, and the local tradition calls for grits, cheddar cheese, and black coffee in the menu.

Mullet always is available. When fried until golden along with hush puppies — a corn bread — the fish served at supper indicates the state belongs to the South. On the West Coast near St. Petersburg the smoking of mullet flourishes as a growing industry. People in Tampa and elsewhere like to feature it in Dutch luncheons. And in some homes the fish, after being warmed in the oven, pleases at breakfast.

A FLORIDA BREAKFAST

Orange Juice
Smoked Mullet
Hominy Grits
Coffee

Florida, especially in winter, bulges with visitors from colder climates who seek the cheer and warmth of its sunshine. Many families forever are entertaining relatives and social and business friends from the North. Some hostesses adopt a definite type of menu for their guest meals. The specialty of one charming lady in Tampa, who frequently welcomes her husband's business friends from the skyscrapers of New York, Chicago, and other northern cities, is the shrimp supper. She says she allows 2 pounds of shrimp per person. If there are leftovers she pickles them or salvages them in soup made with milk. Often there are none. This is her menu which so admirably fills the bill.

BOILED SHRIMP SUPPER
Tampa Style
Crab Cocktail
Boiled Shrimp
Melted Butter   Cocktail Sauce
Crackers
Oregano Flavored Green Salad
Coffee

As an example of a company sit-down dinner, the favorite menu of a Tampa newspaper woman makes everyone's mouth water. Guests call an opportunity to face it an unforgettable experience.

CHICKEN DINNER
Shrimp or Crab Cocktail
Chicken en Casserole
Hot Cuban Bread
Tossed Green Salad
Black Bottom Pie
Coffee

The dishes offered on this occasion typify good cooking in the area. This is how the writer-culinary artist gets dinner.

She sprinkles the disjointed young chickens with lime juice, salt, and minced garlic. Then she refrigerates them at least 2 hours, often longer. In cooking them she first carefully browns the pieces in a little olive oil — or other salad oil — or fat and transfers them to a casserole. To the drippings she adds 1 to 2 tablespoons of sugar and browns potato balls in them. She arranges the potatoes on the chicken. Next she browns a little flour and small onions in the frying pan and adds sauterne, paprika, Tabasco sauce, and canned mushrooms. This mixture she pours over the chicken and potatoes in the casserole, and adjusts the lid. She bakes the entree in a slow oven, 325°, about an hour, or until the chicken is tender.

To her happy guests she presents the chicken in an adaptation of the Spanish Arroz con Pollo. First she spreads boiled rice, with the kernels tender, dry, and separated from one another, on the hot platter. (In Key West some women refer to the cereal so cooked as *one-one* rice to indicate that every grain stands apart from its neighbors.) Then she arranges the chicken and other contents of the casserole on top. She garnishes the entree with bright strips of pimento and tiny hot peas, buttered.

The true Spanish style of service differs in that the rice is cooked with saffron and thus is yellow. Many hostesses commonly serve chicken, fried or baked, on the rice. Pimento strips and green peas generally are selected as garnishes.

The affections of a Tampa meal planner are torn between heated Cuban style bread and wee piping hot biscuits. She likes the region's favorite tossed green salad — one that contains tomato, cucumber, and avocado slices.

The layer of vanilla custard in black bottom pie, a dessert favorite along the entire Gulf Coast, is flavored with rum from the West Indies. Many home chefs say they add rum to food for its aroma. Some of them like it in whipped cream for topping pumpkin pie.

Let's Try a Cuban Sandwich

Anyone who drives along Florida's highways is likely to see the signs "Cuban Sandwiches." They introduce visitors to that wonderful crackling-crusted bread. Less than an hour after I reached Tampa I sat in the sunshine, as if to defy the snows I had left behind in Kansas, and ate my first one. And after first squeezing lime juice into it, I sipped iced tea, an around the year beverage in the state.

Cuban bread comes in loaves about 3 feet long, 3 inches wide, and 2½ inches high. Often it is baked in banana leaves. The baker slashes the shaped dough on top, not very deep, and inserts a pencil of dough or the rib of a palmetto leaf. No one knows why. Or at least the only explanation forthcoming is tradition. The pointed rolls made of the same dough are known as *copers*. Within, the bread is extremely white and fine textured, outside it is crisp and brown. Key West bakeries keep it coming hot from the ovens at various hours of the day. Families sometimes buy a hot loaf for dinner and another for supper.

For the sandwiches that make a meal the cook cuts the bread into 8-inch lengths, splits it lengthwise, and spreads on mustard — and frequently mayonnaise as well. She inserts paper-thin slices of meats, cheese, pickles, and vegetables. My first one contained ham, salami, roast pork, tomatoes, pickles, and lettuce. Later that day I chatted with a handsome hostess of Spanish descent who said she had served that noon Cuban sandwiches, peach pickles, a small vegetable salad, and coffee at an impromptu bridge luncheon. She took the sandwiches, made without vegetables, from her freezer and quickly reheated them in the oven.

A home demonstration agent explains some of the kitchen tricks borrowed from the Cubans like this, "Many cooks prefer cinnamon bark to the ground spice, add bay leaf to soup, meat, and fish dishes, and use lime juice widely, or Old Sour when the fresh fruit is not in season. They substitute cracker crumbs for bread crumbs in recipes, and give rice and soups the cheerful yellow glow of saffron."

Saffron is available at many grocery stores as short, dark orange threads. A cook holds them in a spoon over low heat and crushes them. She adds them to rice, soups, and other foods to impart the characteristic yellow color, flavor, and aroma so many people like. An imitation of imported saffron is sold in the stores. The powder comes in folds of yellow paper and also contains some oregano and cumin.

Cellophane bags of rice with the seasonings and the yellow coloring included appear in many markets. When cooked the yellow kernels make picture-book dishes. A yellow and green one I encountered in St. Petersburg consisted of sweet green peppers parboiled, stuffed with yellow rice, and baked. Some households add cut-up cooked ham to rice cooked with saffron. They garnish it with diced pimento.

Oregano — a wild marjoram — which thrives locally rates as a favored seasoning. So does the *sweet basil* that grows in many dooryards. Garlic lends its liveliness to countless dishes.

Peppers Grow Near the Kitchens

Old-time Floridians like bird's-eye peppers. Bushes of

them, about 4 feet high, grow near many kitchen doors. They are quite ornamental when covered with tiny green or bright red spikes about a half inch long, the pepper pods. How innocent and mild they appear! If tasted they are "deadly" — in the opinion of one visitor with whom I talked. The green ones, she declared, are especially hot. Natives hold that the flavor from these small, pointed pods is matchless when correctly incorporated in dishes. Tarragon, chives, mint, and capers also have the good cook's blessing, as does the paprika imported from Spain.

In my wanderings across the United States I have found *plantains* in New Orleans, New York, Tampa, and Key West markets. The fruit grows in bunches like bananas, and usually it resembles giant green bananas. Perhaps this explains why the first taste is disappointing. It does not have the banana taste. Many households prepare plantains in a variety of ways. The crunchy *Marquitas of Key West,* called *plantain chips* in Tampa, intrigue and delight visitors and home folks alike. They are a great favorite at cocktail parties. To make them a cook first removes the skin with a knife. One's unaided fingers cannot peel it off. Then she cuts the plantain diagonally in very thin slices and fries it like potato chips in deep fat. Salt and pepper are sprinkled on before serving.

Ripe plantains, sliced lengthwise, are gently pan-fried in fat and sprinkled with sugar for a favorite vegetable. Natives vouch for it as a perfect teammate for ham.

Florida has fresh vegetables throughout the year. They come to her tables, as do the strawberries and home-grown fruits, in an abundance that Americans everywhere would like to duplicate.

Let's Get Acquainted With Key West

Key West, the finger that projects into the Gulf of Mexico and the Straits of Florida, is famed for deep sea fishing and for generations of people who lived primarily on food from the water and from cans. One of the curious likings of the

Conch that lingers, although they no longer are separated from the mainland, is their fondness for salt fish, especially salt cod. This hearkens back to the era when sailing vessels from New England brought supplies. It indicates how slowly food habits change.

For years, too, the meats available in this southerly community have been mainly lean cuts, Cuban style. People still like them. They supply fat either by larding or threading the lean with strips of fat meat or bacon. Or they pan-fry them in fat or oil. Pork and beef reach the Keys, but not much veal or lamb. Two favored cuts of beef are the *Bolichi* or *tenderloin,* and *Palomilla.* The first one is stuffed, dusted with paprika, and baked. For the latter dish cooks pound the beef slices on both sides with the edge of a small plate. Usually they pan-fry them quickly in oil or garlic. Or they cut the beef into cubes and add cut-up vegetables to make a steam. A *steam* on the Keys is known as a *stew* elsewhere. There are chicken steams, turtle steams, beef steams, and other kinds.

Then there is *Piccadillo,* a ground beef mixture that contains onions, tomatoes, garlic, green pepper, stuffed olives, raisins, and capers, all mixed. Women pan-fry it slowly in a little oil. They like to cool and refrigerate it for use when needed. They say its taste improves with every reheating.

One of the favorite ways of serving Piccadillo is in *Moyettes.* The cook breaks off one side of a bun near the edge and carefully scoops out the interior. Then she stuffs the meat mixture into the cavity. She pins the edges back on the bun with toothpicks, dips the bun in beaten eggs and pan-fries it like a doughnut in deep fat until browned. Hot Moyettes, two to the person, make a meal if topped off with a green salad or fruit.

Soups are the hearty, meal-in-a-dish and thick kinds, like the black bean, conch chowder, black-eye pea, and saffron-tinted garbanzo numbers. Usually Cuban bread accompanies them. A fruity dessert winds up the feast.

'Oppin' John Appears on the Keys

Hopping John — South Carolina's famous dish of rice and field peas — is just about as popular on the Keys as in the area where is originated. The Conchs refer to it as *'Oppin' John*. Their English ancestry crops out in their universal habit of not sounding the *h* in a word that starts with that letter and of omitting the final *g* in an ending. Grits, at least in many homes, qualify as the staff of life.

Sweet potatoes are a delight in a variety of dishes. Indeed, the bakers turn out bread made with them, usually at least one day a week. Sweet potatoes are cooked in water, pared, and sliced for use as a vegetable. Generally they are served with butter and salt, but like women elsewhere in the United States those of the Florida Keys also mash them. They add crushed pineapple and salt, and bake them to heat. Orange-sweet potato dishes also are relished.

Ask a native cook about her favorite vegetables and she promptly lists them in the order of their importance to her family. Rice heads the list (even if it is a cereal!), and then come plantains, sweet potatoes, dried black beans, black-eye peas, garbanzos or chick peas, lima beans, navy beans, grits, and okra. In the next breath she lauds canned or frozen corn, peas, green beans, canned pimentos, and canned tomatoes.

Some women include avocados on their honor roll. When in season, they serve the fruit as a vegetable with meats as well as fish. They remove the deep green skin, and slice and season the chartreuse pulp. Also they fill halves of seeded avocados — splashed with garlic vinegar — with hot creamed fish, chicken, ham, or crabmeat, top it off with shredded cheese, and bake the entree in a moderate oven, 350° to 375° just long enough to melt the cheese.

Coffee Is Served Five Times a Day

The Cuban influence is noticeable in many homes. Coffee berries are roasted until extremely dark, and usually there is a fresh supply every day. Frequently it is delivered to the homes while still warm. Some natives drink about a half cupful of the strong, hot beverage five times a day.

All kinds of drip coffee makers win acclaim, but some families follow the old, traditional method. They place the finely ground coffee in white cotton flannel bags, pour on boiling water, and permit the liquid to filter slowly into a vessel of some kind. Frequently they suspend the bag from an iron tripod. A visitor observes these cotton bags, which are washed daily, hanging in the sunshine by the kitchen doors to dry.

Newcomers and tourists marvel at the references of these natives to evaporated milk as *cream,* and to sweetened condensed milk as *milk.* Both canned products are used extensively. This is another custom that was established before a highway was built to the mainland, which of course brought in welcome refrigerator trucks. Nevertheless, the Conchs continue to prefer evaporated milk, or cream, as they call it, in their coffee. The Cuban coffee drinkers in the city remain faithful to their favorite, sweetened condensed milk — and continue to call it milk.

A few homes cherish favorite plum pudding recipes. They are English heirlooms. These families also vouch for the tastiness of *duffs. Spanish flans* have equally ardent champions. Then there are the delightfully cool treats, ice creams and ices made with semitropical fruits. Favorites include those containing flavors from the soursop, guava, jelly nuts — or immature coconuts — mangoes, and sugar apples.

Anyone who visits a home in enchanting Key West finds that dinner often comes at noon. A siesta follows. Supper is light, and served around 6 o'clock. At about 8 o'clock in the evening many natives and their guests seek ice cream parlors for refreshment and sociability. The night, scented with a million flowers and cooled by trade winds, contributes to the enjoyment. How could a food reporter better end a firsthand experience in exploring the picturesque food customs that with distinction rim the Gulf of Mexico from Florida through Texas?

The Southwest

A RIZONA AND NEW MEXICO lie at the heart of it, but
the Southwest also embraces parts of Texas, Oklahoma, California, and the southern third of Colorado. Deserts
and mountains meet in the area; the sky spreads out like an
open turquoise umbrella, and saffron sunsets tint the clouds.
Beef is king of the table. Along with the meat from local
corrals, menus spotlight lush fruits and vegetables that grow
in green irrigated valleys on the deserts and between mountains. Sometimes, when you taste a dish, ghosts of former
years walk before you — the Chinese cooks of pioneer mining

and cow camp kitchens. To them go the thanks and credit
for the pleasant, surprising Oriental touches you occasionally
encounter at mealtime. The main influence is Spanish.

Although it is an old country, the Southwest also is new.
Spanish colonists settled under its lofty peaks long before
Captain John Smith sailed up the James River, or the Pil-
grims stepped ashore on Plymouth Rock. Yet Arizona, the
Valentine State, was not represented by a star on the field of
blue until February 14, 1912, when statehood was attained.
A native who arrived within its borders before or during
1890 qualifies as a pioneer.

Geography contributes contrasts that affect the life and
food habits of the Southwesterners. To the south, deserts
bustle in winter with people from all states who come to
seek the sun. There in hot weather the natives remain relatively comfortable in their old thick-walled adobe houses, or
in modern air-conditioned ones. To the north some of the
mountain tops dress in snow most of the year. The beautiful
country around remote Durango, Colorado; colorful Taos,
New Mexico, and its internationally known art colony; historic Santa Fe, and hundreds of other places draw summer
tourists from afar to keep cool and to motor along splendid
and scenic highways.

Thick Steaks Broil Over Mesquite Coals

When I try to sum up my vivid impressions of the region's
cuisine, I reflect on its Spanish background as a glamorous
panorama spreads out before me.

The ranch country gives you beef and big biscuits. There
cowbelles and cowboys often wear plaid shirts, tight-fitting
breeches, and 10-gallon hats.

Spanish-Americans eat hot, ethereal *sopaipillas* fresh from
the frying kettle, and sip coffee.

Indians squat by small fires on which they do their cooking,
and their hands, bedecked with handsome silver and turquoise
rings, pat out blue corn-meal cakes.

Thick steaks sizzle while they broil over coals of mesquite
wood on guest ranches, as the hostess sets out a large bowl of

garlic-scented green salad. Hungry Easterners, in their expensive western style garb, glance at their watches to learn how much longer they must wait before eating.

Crunchy, crisp corn chips, dunked in mashed and seasoned avocado, relegate potato chips to the background.

Tourists step from their cars, buy piñon nut candy, take a bite, and then mail boxes of the sweet to friends back home.

Chilies (peppers) lend an aggressive flavor to daily meals.

Pinto and pink beans have no contenders for the throne they occupy in the vegetable kingdom.

After the sun goes down, Phoenecians in Arizona's Salt River Valley and people in other southwestern cities gather in gardens and on patios for parties, large and small. Hostesses frequently serve barbecued short ribs of beef from electric roasters plugged into outdoor outlets. Ice cream on sticks occasionally answers for dessert.

Thousands of holiday-minded citizens — in their Sunday best — rally at traditional barbecues.

High seasonings startle and please the palate, with chili, oregano, garlic, mocha, aniseed, cinnamon, chocolate, and olive the ones most readily recognized.

If you are lucky while in the Southwest you will have an opportunity to taste roasted olive-fed turkey, son-of-a-gun stew, licorice ice cream, *panocha* for dessert on Ash Wednesday, and vinegar pie, with its subtle, tantalizing smell of apples from the cider vinegar. Turkey is the regal dish in some Thanksgiving Day picnics on the desert.

A Food Scout Has Tricks

In every area I visit I meet intelligent, modest women who believe their locality has no distinctive dishes. To help tide myself through these perilous interviews I keep some questions in mind, such as:

"Do you have children away at school in other parts of the country? Do you have relatives who have moved from this area to other states?"

If either of these inquiries brings an affirmative answer I am in clover. The follow-up starts.

"Do you ever send food gifts to them?" And, "What do the packages contain?"

Like a magic key, words unlock the door.

In Albuquerque a mother said, "Chilies. We ship the slender, pointed, hot green pods quite regularly by air to our daughter and her family who now live in Springfield, Massachusetts. Just imagine, they are not available in the markets there!"

Chilies (peppers) speak for the cuisine of the Southwest in an authentic and often in a fiery manner. Many varieties grow in the region. At off seasons for local crops, importations from Mexico gain a ready acceptance. They have a somewhat different flavor, as do those produced in Spain.

Peppers may be divided into two major families that stick to the Christmas colors, red and green. Uncooked, the green pods put zip and authority into a hundred and more dishes, such as scrambled eggs, salads, corned beef and other meats, beans, macaroni and cheese, spaghetti, and sandwiches. Like sweet bell peppers they also sometimes are stuffed with meat, cheese, and other foods, and then dipped in pancake batter and pan-fried.

How To Peel Chilies

A cardinal rule, heeded throughout the region, is to harvest the green pods before they start to turn red. The chilies are peeled before they are used. In old-time kitchens, with plenty of workers on hand from early morning until late at night, cooks ran the pods into hot ovens or held them over heat to blister the skins until they puffed up. Then they wrapped them in wet towels to provide and retain steam to make peeling easier.

In the newer method they snip the ends from the pods and drop them into boiling hot paraffin for 3 or 4 minutes. Then they plunge them into cold water. The skins slip off readily.

Wise cooks coat their hands with melted fat before they start to peel chilies. Othewise the skin may be burned. The seeds of green ones are so hot they almost always cause irritation unless protective measures are taken.

In the Southwest you cook with chili (pepper) sauce. The kind you use depends on the dish you are preparing, and taste preferences. Grocery stores stock canned ones, but many women prefer to make their own. From July until late autumn you sniff the pungent sauces that lazily bubble in home kitchens about the countryside.

Cooks simmer the peeled, seeded green chilies in water until tender, run them through a food mill or press them through a sieve. Then they stir in enough water, if the mixture is dry, to make a sauce of the desired consistency, or about as thick as tomato paste. For seasonings, salt, garlic, oregano, and a little fat fill the bill. When the sauce boils it is ready for use.

Red Pods Dry in Golden Sunshine

Red chilies never are eaten without cooking; sauce is prepared as with the green ones. Large quantities of them are dried. They are the brilliant red pods natives string and hang to dry in the golden autumn sunshine by the sides of their adobe homes with the clean-swept yards.

From these dried pods chili powder is ground. There is nothing dainty about the sizes of the packages of powder most families buy if they do not make their own supply. Commonly 1, 2, 3, or more cupfuls are purchased at a time in cellophane bags, in striking contrast to the tiny tins of the seasoning you see on grocery shelves elsewhere.

When cooked, chili powder, mixed with water, salt, and a little fat, turns out as a sauce. Often tomato juice substitutes for the water; despite the improvement it makes, fine cooks state positively that such a composition lacks the superb, delicate flavor of one produced from fresh pods.

Visitors to the Southwest find that chili sauces are quite awakening! Hospitable natives explain their pet methods of softening the heat. Perhaps the favorite stunt is to boil for 2 or 3 minutes 1 cup of water mixed with an equal amount of sauce, thickened with 2 tablespoons of flour. The magic ingredient — for its cooling effect — is flour, but some women prefer to add corn meal or milk.

Famous Spanish-American dishes often are hot, and yet again they may be comparatively mild. They are an amalgamation of Indian, Spanish, Mexican, and American treasures. Some of the famed compositions are likely to start a stream of tears down your cheeks! It all depends on how much chili they contain.

500 Pounds of Chilies for a Family

When you bite into food too peppery for your palate, it is polite to take a bit of butter or margarine on the tip of your tongue and roll it around in your mouth. Such treatment is guaranteed to mitigate the heat — pronto!

While welcome any time, hot chili dishes spring into high popularity with persons who are coming down with colds. They are prized as preventives just as a Kansan, under similar circumstances, pins her faith on hot lemonade.

The Government's estimate of the quantity of chilies consumed in New Mexico speaks for their importance in that state. The average rural family every autumn puts up about 500 pounds of this vegetable by canning, freezing, and drying.

How frequently the traditional regional dishes appear in meals is determined primarily by individual tastes and ancestry. Spanish-Americans eat them daily. Anglo-Americans, or people not of Spanish or Mexican descent, commonly enjoy them once or twice a week, or oftener. The first Caucasian cooks in the area were Spanish, but the supply road to Mexico and the sea lanes to Europe were hopelessly long. Like English colonists in New England, Spanish residents of the Southwest borrowed techniques from the Indians, used their own European skills, and invented new dishes made from locally produced foodstuffs. Thus the cookery is neither Spanish nor Mexican, but Southwestern.

Most women interested in good food have at their finger tips a repertoire of the area's classics. They spring them on their families and on visitors from other regions, who frequently regard what they call a *Mexican dinner* as something of a gastronomic adventure. The list of dishes varies from one kitchen to another, but there are certain items that figure so prominently in menus that almost everyone knows how to make them. Here are the backbone dishes on the list.

Cooks Favor Meal From Calico Corn

BREAD. *Tortillas,* the staff of life to many of the people, resemble very thin corn pancakes, which is exactly what they almost always are. (Tortillas sometimes are made with wheat flour.) Several types of corn meal are used, but many expert cooks insist that corn meal ground from the native *blue* (or calico) corn, and *concho* (a white flint variety) rate as top selections. This bread has changed very little from what it was during the centuries the Indians made it before white men arrived on the western continent.

The meal for the *masa,* or dough, comes from *nixtamal,* or lime hominy. You dissolve lime in water, stir in the corn, and cook it in a granite pan until the hulls loosen. After draining you wash the kernels in cold water, while rubbing the kernels between your hands to remove the hulls. You grind the hominy with the medium knife of a food chopper several times, and then you have *harinilla,* the meal for making tortillas and tamales. To it you add water, if necessary, to mix a dough that will hold together. You can buy harinilla at food shops. With the commercial product you add boiling water to make the masa, which local cooks describe as medium hard.

You shape the dough into balls about the size of a hen's egg. Old-time cooks, and some modern ones who possess the skill, moisten their hands with water and pat the balls out to make circles about ⅛ inch thick. An easier way, at least for some women, is to place the ball of dough on one end of a bread board that is covered with the end of a wet towel. The other end is spread on top of the dough. With another bread board you press the ball into a thin round shape.

Most commonly the tortilla is baked on both sides without adding fat, on a soapstone or heavy griddle. When cooked the corn cake is speckled with brown spots. At the table, the family spreads on butter, rolls or folds it, and revels in superb eating.

An increasing number of households buy tortillas from factories that have mushroomed over the region. Or you may purchase them at your grocer's, in tin cans or frozen, for speedy baking or frying in deep fat. If canned tortillas are removed from the tin, wrapped in a damp cloth and re-frigerated for several hours, they are less likely to crack when heated. Leftover ones also need refrigeration, for they sour quickly at ordinary room temperatures.

During Lent Tuna Appears in Tacos

SANDWICHES or TACOS. These sandwiches, built on recipes originally imported from Mexico, carry the south-western cooks' own interpretations. Cooks fry tortillas in deep fat, folding them in the centers to make pockets. Then they fill them with chopped meat, or mixtures thick enough to stay put, such as equal parts of chopped cooked potatoes and beef, moistened with chili sauce. During Lent tuna appears in the fillings, but at other seasons chicken or turkey are often used. Space is left in the folded tortilla for top-pings — almost anything the family likes. Among the common favorites are finely shredded lettuce, chopped green and dry onions, diced ripe tomatoes, shredded cheese, and chopped green chili.

One of my hostesses gave tacos the spot of honor in a buffet supper. She carried to the table a hot pottery platter of tortillas containing a beef-vegetable combination. The relishes were lined up on the side, in the manner of those that accompany a curry. Everyone helped himself to what-ever he enjoys most in a sandwich; many of the guests took two or three of the offerings. Crisp shreds of lettuce seemed to appeal to everyone. All the natives added an extra touch of chili sauce.

MAIN DISH SHORTCAKES or ENCHILIDAS. This entree represents the Southwest as truly as the women who slip quietly in and out of the adobe churches, and the Indian maidens you see on the streets, with their full, gaily colored calico skirts and snug black velvet bodices.

I watched a hostess prepare enchilidas — which are almost

a complete meal — in her modern kitchen. She described every act as she worked.

"You dip the cooked tortilla in heated chili sauce and place it on a baking sheet. Next you sprinkle on grated cheese and finely chopped onion. You repeat this, stacking them as you go along. The number of layers you use depends on the appetites of the people who are to eat at your table."

As a Titian-haired home economics teacher in an Albuquerque junior high school later explained, "The general rule is three tortillas for a lady and five for a gentleman."

As you build the enchilidas you arrange them on a baking sheet in a warm oven. To give the entree a characteristic heartier note, it is a regional custom to top every serving at the last minute with a fried egg, sunny side up. Tortillas also are rolled around a meat or other filling, in true Mexican style, but the shortcake type rates first in New Mexico and in some other southwestern spots.

Here Comes Chili Con Carne

CHILI CON CARNE. This stew — meat with chili — requires no introduction to the thousands of Americans who regard it as a topflight national dish. Versions about the country vary, and many of them are but distant relatives of the southwestern triumph. In most places hamburger is selected for it, but two home economists at the University of Texas emphasized repeatedly that you should have it coarsely ground. Indeed, they insist that some discriminating cooks choose small cubes of meat. In New Mexico several women expressed a preference for tiny pieces of "boiled beef," because the pre-cooking contributes extra deliciousness.

Brown the meat with a half onion, slightly chopped, in a small amount of fat. Then you add seasonings like chili sauce or powder, salt, garlic, and oregano. Water is stirred in, or broth, if the beef has been cooked first in water. Simmer the mixture gently a half hour. Pinto or pink beans are a favorite accompaniment. They are served on the same plate at the side of the chili con carne.

Talented cooks stress that chili con carne is not a standard product if it is greasy. They will not tolerate even a thin film of fat on its surface. Almost all grocery stores carry acceptable canned and frozen editions of the dish for hurried households.

TAMALES. This ancient Mexican original travels far afield and yet maintains unlimited popularity in the Southwest, and South of the Border. Tiny tamales, no bigger than your little finger, tempt at cocktail parties, while larger versions satisfy in meals. A flood of tamales comes from factories located throughout the region, and the canned ones enjoy an appreciative following. Especially in rural areas, they also are homemade.

After washing corn husks, you soak them in warm water at least an hour. On each husk you place a layer ¼ inch thick of corn-meal mush made from nixtamal. Over this you spread about 2 teaspoons of chili con carne. Fold the husks to enclose the filling, and tie every bundle with strips of husks. Then you steam the tamales 25 minutes, or cook them 10 minutes in a pressure cooker under 15 pounds of pressure. If they are not eaten immediately you reheat them in a double boiler.

While beef tamales are favorites, many other kinds are liked, such as those containing chicken, beans, pork, cheese, and green corn fillings.

How To Make Tamale Pie

Tamales, with their jackets of husks removed, get involved in many delightful dishes. Cooks break them in pieces and combine them with corn and cheese in interesting casserole combinations. And tamale pie, a hostess specialty, is at least an offshoot. I refer to it with genuine pleasure, for it served as the entree in one of the most memorable supper parties I experienced in the Southwest.

When making tamale pie the hostess first lines a baking dish with corn-meal mush, like that used for tamales, and fills it with chili con carne, chopped tomatoes, onions, and green chili. Then she scatters in a few whole ripe olives and grated cheese, and spreads on the remainder of the mush. Or for a topping on the fancy side she may drop it on in strips to form a lattice, or in little pointed dabs or peaks. The dish is heated in the oven until piping hot. About a quarter of an hour before it comes from the oven shreds of cheese are sprinkled on top.

As we sat on the patio enjoying supper, soft, delightful breezes dropped down from the mountains. A full moon, bright as a new silver dollar, watched over us. Everyone described his or her favorite tamale pie variation. Alternate layers of mush and chili con carne, with the bottom and top ones of mush, compose a praised version. Every addition of meat is sprinkled with chopped ripe olives and raisins.

PATIO SUPPER
Latticed Tamale Pie
Tossed Green Salad
Garlic Dressing
Melon
Coffee　　Buttermilk

GUACAMOLE. This famed salad reigns supreme when the ingredients are available: avocados, tomatoes, onions, and chilies. A Spanish-American food demonstrator of unusual ability gave her directions for its preparation to a large group of women in a cooking school at San Antonio at which I occupied one of the front seats. Her story ran like this:

"You use 2 ripe tomatoes and 2 ripe avocados, both peeled, and 'smash' them to make a very smooth mixture. Then you fold in seasoning of salt, pepper, minced onion, and green chili, and minced celery if you wish.

"Most Texans and Sooners — natives of Oklahoma — add a drop or two of Tabasco sauce. When pomegranates are in season their bright colored seeds either are scattered on top or are folded in for a gay touch. You heap the avocado mixture on thick slices of ripe tomatoes and serve them on lettuce lined plates, or ring them around the edge of a bowl of green salad."

In some households guacamole is served with corn chips, as a luncheon entree.

SOPAIPILLAS. The brown, crispy, and hot "sofa pillows" are fried like doughnuts, but have hollow centers similar to popovers. They are much in demand in Mexican restaurants, where you frequently have your choice of them or tortillas for bread. Natives rarely spread on butter or margarine when they break open the puffs, and in conversation they point out that Yankees do not so embellish doughnuts. Tourists generally add not only butter, but jelly or honey as well. If they are lucky it is mesquite honey, for the sweet has an exotic flavor.

The unsweetened dough, made with wheat flour, is rolled like biscuits, cut in squares, and fried. Some women prefer to buy canned dough, which is ready for rolling.

There is some controversy about the derivation of true sopaipillas (pronounced *soap-ah-pee-yeh*). One home economist, a member of a famous colonial Spanish family, says the historic "sofa pillows" are sweet hot cakes rolled in sugar, the kind served at 4 o'clock in the afternoon with coffee or hot chocolate. Both kinds are fried and enjoyed.

When the Pink Beans Arrived in Omaha

BEANS. In many communities beans are called *frijoles* (pronounced *free-ho-les,* with accent on the second syllable). Although there are several kinds, in the main they consist of two favorites, the pink bean and the pinto. If you label the central part of the nation as the *meat-and-potato section* you will classify the Southwest as a *bean-and-chili area.* The light buff colored bean with brown spots, the pinto, is consumed in larger quantities than all other varieties put together, but pink beans have ardent champions. One of them is my youngest brother, who for many years lived near Flagstaff, Arizona. After he moved to Omaha he pined for his pink beans. When a bag of them arrived from the Southwest at Christmas time, as something of a practical joke, he was elated; after declaring the household was in a festive mood he put the beans and bacon on to cook.

Southwestern people have as decided ideas about how to prepare beans as New England housewives have. On at least two points they agree, the use of an earthen pot, and long, slow simmering.

Although soaking the beans overnight in water shortens the cooking time, many women confess they do not bother to do it. They stress the importance of starting the legumes to cook in lukewarm water. When the water bubbles the chef drops in a little diced salt pork or a few bacon rinds and scraps. She lets them simmer lazily for 2 hours and then stirs in a minced clove of garlic, a large dried red chili, and salt to taste. Within 3 to 6 hours for pinto beans, and in somewhat less time for pink ones, the dish is ready to serve. Pressure saucepans tenderize them quickly; this is a godsend in high altitudes or where the water is quite hard. These beans are eaten daily or twice daily throughout the area.

To test for doneness, the cook determines whether the skins and the insides of the seeds are equally tender. Then, if fried beans are on the menu, the potato masher is brought out. For satisfactory results, the beans need to simmer until the liquid evaporates; a watery dish is inferior. A Southwesterner mashes the legumes with the skill of a Hoosier housewife at work on potatoes! Then she melts bacon drippings or other fat, just about a tablespoonful, adds a little flour, and the beans, and if required, salt for seasoning. She pan-fries them from 5 to 10 minutes, with some stirring, because the thick mixture scorches easily.

Some people say that leftover fried beans surpass or at least equal the first showing. They stir melted fat through them for seasoning, and quite commonly add shredded cheese. The cooking is brief, just enough to heat the beans and melt the cheese. For *tostadas* they spread tortillas with butter or margarine, and toast them in a very hot oven, 450°; then they top them with the hot re-fried beans, sprinkle on grated cheese, and add shredded lettuce.

Panocha Appears on Ash Wednesday

PANOCHA. This occupies the same position in Spanish-American homes on Ash Wednesday that Indian pudding enjoys in some of New England's traditional meals. Native women put the dessert together with sprouted wheat flour, obtainable in many food stores, and whole-wheat flour. They cook the pudding mixture gently atop the range for about 2 hours, and then add butter; after that they run it into the oven to bake slowly, uncovered, until thick and rich brown in color; usually this takes about an hour. If the pudding is sweetened; caramelized sugar does the trick, but many families think it is unnecessary because sprouted wheat flour has a characteristic sweetness of its own.

In a few communities where the sprouted flour is unavailable housewives turn miller and make it. They wash wheat but do not dry it; then they hang the grain in a cloth bag in some warm spot. When sprouts appear they spread the kernels in the sun to dry; later they grind them.

BOILED CUSTARD. Although it is as popular as the dessert of the same name in the South, the southwestern delicacy is somewhat different.

The cook beats the egg whites until light and pours them into heated milk to cook. Then she skims them into a serving bowl, and makes the custard with the egg yolks, sugar, and milk. When the mixture coats the back of a metal spoon she pours it into the egg whites, dusts on cinnamon, and chills the natillas (custard) thoroughly.

Shrimp Is Praised in Spanish and English

FISH. The treasures of the sea are greatly enjoyed, with an ardor that almost equals their acceptance by neighbors to the south. Dried shrimp and oysters have been imported for centuries from Mexico, especially during Lent. Today you see the fresh, frozen, and canned shellfish in the markets, and meet countless dishes in which they play a leading part. Fried shrimp heated in chili sauce brings compliments in two languages, Spanish and English. Oysters in ramekins, topped with bits of butter and green chili, and heated in a hot oven until they puff up and their edges curl, also win bilingual praise. Trout stands highest in favor among the native fish.

It would be folly to imply that fish is more popular than beef, but a high regard for it exists in many homes. After all, some of these citizens are descended from a nation in which one of the Aztec emperors kept a staff of several hundred runners busy delivering fresh fish from Veracruz over steep slopes to Mexico City more than 450 kilometers away. This was a force that, in size, makes almost insignificant the crews of little Negro boys who ran between outdoor kitchens to the gracious dining rooms of Virginia plantations with hot spoon or batter bread.

Tidbits. Among favored tidbits are the corn chips and tiny tamales previously mentioned. *Pepitas,* or squash seed, frequently appear throughout the region. The tiny green seeds soak in water containing charcoal ash for half a day; then their husks are removed, and they are toasted with a little fat or oil.

While this recording of Spanish-American food delights falls far short of a complete representation of the regional treats that come from Spanish and Mexican kitchens, it indicates a few of the dishes that are made extensively. You sample them wherever you go, in cities like San Antonio, Amarillo, Dallas, Fort Worth, Santa Fe, Taos, Tucson, Phoenix, Albuquerque, and El Paso, deep in the ranch country, throughout the Indian land, and wherever the fiesta spirit reaches.

Gentlemen Tip Their Enormous Stetsons

The Southwest is cow country, and it takes pride in its rancho dishes. It is sheep country, too. The vast livestock empire extends over mountains, plateaus, and plains, and recognizes no regional boundaries. Cookery in the isolated kitchens throughout the West carries distinctive earmarks. Many of the famous food creations are presented in the chapter on the Mountain West.

Barbecues assume such important social leadership in Texas, and indeed in the entire Southwest, that no food reporter in her right mind would slight them. Nor would she fail to observe that no cooks under the Stars and Stripes respond more gallantly to her questions than these gentlemen who tip their enormous hats, which they call Stetsons, and lead you step by step through the barbecue preparations they know so well.

You discover quickly that to these glamorous chefs *food* means *beef!* Consequently there is no surprise in learning it is the favorite selection for outdoor meals. Other meats

rarely substitute for it, although pork, kid, and poultry sometimes are barbecued at the same time, and especially in Texas.
Occasionally lamb also is cooked in this manner.

Two Types of Barbecues Are Favored

There are two kinds of barbecues, one with open pit
cooking and the other with a closed pit. Both styles command
loyal followings. Ordinarily the true Texan likes to cook
meat directly over coals, the open pit method. While rumors
prevail that the people of New Mexico and Arizona prefer
the closed pit, it depends somewhat on to whom you are
talking. Cattlemen in all southwestern states, or at least
many of them, go along with the Texans in this culinary
matter.

As residents near New England shores delight in a clambake, Southwesterners enthuse over a barbecue. The barbecue may be for a small group of family friends, for a political
or fraternal gathering, for a business or church organization
outing, or for the colorful pioneer celebrations, which often
are stupendous affairs. Many of the area's homes have fancy
fireplaces on their patios or in their gardens. However, guest
lists for southwestern barbecues commonly are long — three
to five hundred, up to a thousand, and indeed a few thousands!

One afternoon after I had enjoyed a Texas barbecue I
cornered the chief cook and asked him to explain just why
the beef tasted so wonderful. I told him the memory of it
would tantalize me in my hungry moments. To him and
a Dallas home economist I am indebted for information on
how to barbecue in the open pit way. This is what they told
me.

How to Barbecue With an Open Pit

"We usually dig the pit about 20 inches deep, 24 inches wide,
and 8 to 10 feet long, although the width and length depend
on the amount of meat to be cooked. Then we build the fire
with hickory or other hard wood. It gives a steady heat for a

long period. We try to select sticks of the same size so they will burn to the ember stage at the same time.

"In this type of barbecuing we get some of the flavor of the smoke into the beef. Hickory is rated first for the taste it imparts except in areas where the mesquite grows; its flavor is lighter and even more subtle. Desert sage, some people say, also provides a superb touch. Other popular southwestern fuels are oak, pinon, juniper, and cedar (to keep the fire burning). Some dudes like to cover the coals with bark, sawdust, or shavings (to yield smoke) just before they lay the meat over the coals to cook. But rarely do ranchers relish a heavy smoky flavor — they like to taste the beef!

"We spread the coals over a larger area than the space required for the meat. When the embers glow and there is no blaze, we arrange it over them on railroad rails or iron rods, on metal grates, mesh chicken wire, welded fencing, or whatever other arrangement we have. The shoulders of the pit hold the rods or grates; its sides protect from the wind, and help keep ashes out of the food. Usually we cook the meat about 12 inches above the coals.

"Nearby we have an auxiliary or feeder pit in which we keep a fire burning to obtain coals to replenish the supply in the main pit. For even cooking, which is essential to success, we always keep the coals under the meat at the same level.

"As the chunks of fat-coated meat broil, we occasionally baste them by brushing on our favorite barbecue sauce. At large gatherings we keep the sauce in a tub at the side of the pit, dip a new broom into it, and brush the beef. How long we cook the meat depends on the quantity; for several hundred people we barbecue it a day and a night, with frequent turnings."

Designing a Barbecue Sauce Is an Art

It would be difficult to select the most popular character-istic, nostril-rousing sauce. Every household has its own, and many men and women almost constantly experiment in hopes of improving their favorites. Most of them contain tomato ketchup, a staple in the ranch country, although in a few combinations tomato paste substitutes for ketchup. Fre-quently additional ketchup is stirred into the sauce during the last hour of cooking to encourage the meat to take on a deeper brown.

Some of the specialties contain bottled condiments, like ketchup; beefsteak, Worcestershire, and chili sauces; mustard, and horse-radish, along with grated or chopped onion or garlic, lemon juice, paprika, salt, red and black pepper, and sugar. Another I sampled was composed of coffee, ketchup, butter, sugar, salt, and garlic. The farther west you travel the more pronounced is the garlic flavor, and the nearer you journey to the Louisiana line the more frequently you meet the sharp taste of red hot peppers.

The food is presented buffet style, regardless of whether it is served on a patio, in a garden, or out in the open spaces. At a large gathering two people handle the meat. They place it atop split buns, and spoon on additional tingling sauce if desired. One person serves pinto beans, and two others pour coffee.

TEXAS BARBECUE
Beef, Kid, and Pork
Cowboy Beans
Cole Slaw   Potato Salad
Sliced Tomatoes and Onions
Buns   Pickles
Apple or Pecan Pie
Coffee

Stewed apricots and peaches occasionally substitute for the pie. This is a custom that carries over from chuck wagon days, when no ovens were available on the range. Throughout Texas and other ranch country of the Southwest, people venerate and respect canned and dried apricots and peaches, for which a liking developed before modern transportation shortened distances. (For the same reason, salmon croquettes, made from the canned fish, command a big and vigorous following.)

Although barbecuing with a spit over an open pit is less popular than the usual Texas method, ardent fans vouch for its merits. Especially do some persons esteem it for kid or suckling lamb. No doubt the most important reason the system is not used more frequently is that it demands much of one person's time to keep the meat rotating, or else it requires a mechanical device. In some Arizona communities Basque barbecues have considerable appeal; they are so-called because many sheepmen are of Basque descent.

For a Basque barbecue, the whole dressed carcass of a suckling lamb, usually weighing from 30 to 40 pounds, is attached to a spit of green wood about 6 feet long. Mesquite is a favorite for the spit. This spit is supported on two forked sticks so the meat is 12 inches from the coals. Then the lamb is roasted slowly for about 3 hours. It is given a quarter turn every 15 minutes, while the upper side is basted with a stinging sauce. Most of the sauces for lamb and kid contain garlic, onion, green chili, and tomato paste. These sauces are set on a gentle fire to simmer very slowly.

Closed Pit Barbecuing at Phoenix

Advocates of the closed pit system talk much about its advantages. No watching is required. All cuts of beef are rendered almost equally tender, which is a great economy. The slow, lengthy cookery of the meat in its own juices results in a splendid flavor which they believe more than compensates for the lack of a tangy smoke taste, and the inability of the chef to baste it.

People in Arizona, New Mexico, and Colorado generally favor the closed pit for large groups of guests. They employ two methods, the tub and the wrapping styles. The pit usually is about 4 feet deep and 6 feet wide. Its length depends on the amount of meat to be served. I saw one pit 30 feet long.

A Phoenix home economist described to me the tub barbecue her company gives annually for its employees. She stresses that the success that can be achieved with the food depends primarily on a hot pit.

If the pit is lined with black malapi rocks, or some other good heat holder available in the community, and the fire kindled 10 or 12 hours in advance, chances of excellent results are promising. It is a good idea to place railroad rails or iron rods of some kind in the bottom of the trench on which to set the tubs, so they will be level.

A No. 2 tub holds 200 pounds of beef, and that is about the amount required in feeding 200 Southwesterners. An expert cuts the meat in pieces of uniform size, using both the tender and less tender parts, seasons them with salt and pepper, and puts them in the tub. Neither water nor fat is added, for the beef makes its own, delectable sauce. The chef covers the tub with another tub inverted over it, lowers it into the hot pit, and rakes coals around it almost to the top. Then he shovels on from 4 to 6 inches of dirt to prevent the escape of steam and smoke. To make an even better seal he pours water on the dirt and starts a fire on top to bake it and thus close the tiny openings.

He cooks the meat from 12 to 15 hours. To insure brownness he may build a fire over the pit during the last hour of cooking.

After the pit is uncovered, two men, one on each side, fasten ganch hooks to the tub handles, and lift out the fragrant, tempting food. At large barbecues some kind of a bridge usually is built across the trench on which the men stand while removing the tubs. Logs, planks, or railroad rails are used for this purpose.

The spirited barbecue sauce, which has been slowly cooked separately, awaits nearby in another tub to be ladled over the meat. Every chef champions his own version. Usually he stirs some of the beef juices developed during the cookery into the sauce for superlative goodness.

Wrap the Beef in Burlap

In the wrapping method of barbecuing the chef divides the beef into the sizes of big roasts, using all the cuts. He rubs each piece with olive oil or salad oil, salts and peppers it, and holds slices of onion, tomatoes, and celery around it with several layers of cheesecloth tied securely with a string. Next he covers every piece with three layers of burlap, fastens on the covering with baling wire, and soaks the bundles in water. He removes the coals from the pit, places the packages on the hot rocks, and lays metal sheets over them to prevent the burlap from touching embers and burning. Then he shovels the coals, and next the soil over the food, and waters it down to retain the steam.

Some men like to top the packages of beef with a few similarly wrapped chunks of pork, although this is a variation of the usual procedure. After cooking from 10 to 12 hours it is time to open the pit, fasten the hooks into the wire bindings that secure the packages, and lift them out. The careful chef keeps a pail of cold water on hand to help extinguish fire in case an ember happens to touch the burlap.

A few devotés of the tub method of barbecuing hold that wrapping makes the meat dry, because some of the juices escape. But if the meat is fat, which always is desirable, the taste is unforgettable.

ARIZONA BARBECUE
Barbecued Beef
Cowboy Beans
Tossed Green Salad
Garlic French Dressing
Buns
Olives   **Green Onions**   Radishes
Ice Cream
Coffee

Cowboy beans are *pinto beans,* and the men who ride the ranges like to eat them once or twice a day. Originally the dish was prepared in a closed pit, and it still is on some occasions, as at barbecues. While away from ranch headquarters a cowpoke builds a fire over a small pit. He adds water and salt pork to the beans in a bucket, covers it, and heats the contents to the boiling point. When the wood turns to embers he rakes some of them into the bottom of the pit; he lowers the bucket into it and heaps on the remaining embers, and then earth. He builds another fire on top. By morning, if the beans are buried in the evening, or by late afternoon, if they started to cook in the morning, the dish is ready to refresh the hungry and often lonely cowboy.

Recipes for preparing cowboy beans present different versions. Almost always they are simmered slowly in water with salt pork, bacon, or ham hock; or bacon or ham drippings; an aji (green chili) cut in two, chili powder, a grated onion, a clove of garlic, Worcestershire sauce, and salt. Sometimes the chef adds a drop or two of red hot pepper sauce.

How To Make Son-of-a-Gun Stew

West Texas ranchers admit they brag about their most famed meat dish, *son-of-a-gun stew,* a popular treat on cattle spreads (ranches) throughout the Southwest. It rarely appears in city or town areas, for the makings are not procurable. Only where animals are slaughtered young do you find this southwestern original. Marrow gut is the most unusual ingredient. This is the long, slender tube that connects the two stomachs of cud-chewing animals, like cattle, deer, sheep, and elk.

Usually the stew is made with the marrow gut from calves, always in the nursing stage when the tube is filled with partly digested milk, a delicate, flavorful substance resembling marrow. When ranch chefs give their recipes — and there are a hundred and one versions — they specify the amount of marrow gut by its length, such as 20 inches, 2 feet, or 3 feet. In the stew, almost always, are sweetbreads, brains, and liver, and often tongue, onions, and suet, with seasonings. But no substitute for marrow gut ever has been discovered for this pièce de résistance of the cowboy's dinner.

Vinegar Pie Rates as a Ranch Treat

A generation ago vinegar pie was synonymous with dessert perfection on many ranches of west Texas. The taste for it has not entirely disappeared even though apples now commonly are available even in remote spots. Many cattlemen have described it to me as one of their favorite foods. All of them stressed how the faint but wonderful smell of apples from the cider vinegar fills the ranch house while the pie bakes.

VINEGAR PIE

2 egg yolks	¼ cup flour
2 cups water	1½ cups sugar
½ cup cider vinegar	½ teaspoon lemon extract
1 tablespoon butter	

Line an 8-inch pan with pastry. Combine the egg yolks, water, vinegar, and melted butter. Mix the flour and sugar and stir them into the vinegar mixture. Add lemon extract and pour into the pastry-lined pan. Bake in a very hot oven, 450°, 10 minutes, then reduce the heat to moderate, 350°, and bake 20 to 30 minutes longer. Cool.

Favorite Dishes in the Sun Country

Many square miles of the Southwest bask in a blaze of sunshine from late autumn through early spring. It is hot and dry the remainder of the year. The climate naturally affects the food. Patio and garden suppers under a canopy studded by twinkling stars end summer days pleasantly. Frequently one hot dish, hearty and heartening, carries the honors, like barbecued short ribs, or a spaghetti-meat mixture. In some households the hot dish is cooked on the patio in electric roasters plugged into outdoor outlets. In other quarters women do the bulk of the cooking in the morning before the blistering heat rays from the sun penetrate the kitchens. Quick reheating at mealtime makes little bother.

Home economists and old-timers in the area stress the wisdom of the almost universal practice of eating at least one hot meal, generally in the evening, regardless of how high the mercury climbs in thermometers. Experience has taught the people that some warm food every summer day provides comfort and promotes good health. Desserts definitely are light and simple. Melons and fruits have no substitutes. Sharing dessert glories with gifts from California's orchards and vineyards are Texas watermelons; honeydew and casaba melons and cantaloupes from the Salt River Valley and other fertile spots; and peaches from New Mexico's Farmington area and Arizona's Oak Creek Canyon.

Meals appear gay with vivid-hued pottery set on the tables. Nests of Mexican earthen casseroles, used in both cooking and serving foods, contribute to that typically southwestern look, and decrease dishwashing. When topped with aluminum foil the Mexican utensils, which usually are without covers, become doubly useful.

Church Groups Picnic on the Desert

When late autumn comes, the tempo of life gains momentum. Picnic meals on the desert, cooked on the spot or else at home and carried to the meeting place in cars, become of increasing importance on the social scene. Some Arizona churches have them on Sunday following the morning services, with plans well-laid in advance by committees. In the Phoenix area many families traditionally take the New England type of Thanksgiving dinner to the desert, where they eat roast turkey, cranberry sauce, pumpkin pie, and all the trimmings under a blue-green sky and the soothing, cheering rays of a beneficent sun. Water, fruit drinks, and coffee are carried from home kitchens, usually in vacuum jugs or bottles, for except in unusual spots there are no wells or springs on the deserts.

In the sun country Citizenship Days dot the calendar with festivity. People who hail from neighboring Mexico make an occasion of the anniversary of the day they became citizens of the United States. They may choose to relax on the desert, with eating and sunlazing on the program, or a trip to view the mountains with snow on their peaks and wild flowers on their sides.

If you sit on the comfortable patios, or indoors in front of lively, crackling fires on the hearths — depending on where you are and the season — with the region's superb cooks at your side, your mouth waters over food talk. You read a choice recipe, while the author or collector describes its merits and peculiarities. Before you know it you have an exemplar of some of the southwestern food treats. Many of them you later are privileged to eat.

A list of choice dishes follows. It includes various favorites women prepare as an expression of affection for their loved ones. I hope their descriptions reveal something of the friendliness and enthusiasm with which they were given to me.

Some Foods Well Liked in Texas

Grapefruit brightens salad plates in Texas from November to May. At Christmas time gay poinsettia salad has sections of red grapefruit for petals and grated carrots for the center. Grapefruit shells are lined with lettuce and hold intriguing fruit salads. Gelatins of different hues and flavors are chilled in them, and then the shells are sliced in quarters and served on greens. That's a salad as colorful as a fiesta with its processions and banners. The grapefruit shells are as shining yellow as if polished for teacher. That southwestern Yuletide specialty, alternate sections of grape-fruit and avocado slices on greens, goes merry with chopped maraschino cherries stirred into the French dressing at the last minute. Avocado halves heaped full of cranberry sherbet sometimes substitute for salad on Christmas.

Alternate sections of white, pink, and red grapefruit on a backdrop of greens, and doused with poppy seed dressing, are Texas personified. If the red citrus fruit is not available you can soak white segments overnight in frozen red raspberry or strawberry juice. This tasty tinting stunt was the dream of a New Yorker who has adopted Texas and lives in Austin. It spread like wildfire to Lone Star hostess tables.

Salads compete with the sun in brilliance. Shredded purple cabbage is tossed with shredded carrots, sweet green peppers, and a snappy French dressing, and heaped in cups of purple cabbage leaves. The color lends charm to a table like the brilliance which a bougainvillaea covered village imparts to the landscape.

Stetson salad contributes regional atmosphere, and tastes wonderfully good. With pineapple rings for brims of the hats, cones of well-seasoned cream cheese represent the crowns. The crowns are creased in the center with a silver knife handle. All you require to complete the delectable picture are strips of pimento and sweet green pepper for the hat bands and bows, greens to line the plate, someone to pass the dressing, a fork, and a signal from the hostess that it is time to taste. *Sombrero salad,* the New Mexican interpretation, differs in that the hat crowns are peaks or cones of seasoned cream cheese with no creases. Strips of pimento and sweet pepper simulate hat bands and streamers, and dots of them here and there suggest the beads on the brim of a Mexican hat.

Lemon flavored gelatin, studded with crushed pineapple, chopped sweet pickle, and broken pecans, fills the salad bill in many famous game dinners.

Creamed hominy soup and beef-vegetable soup with a starchy base, either barley or macaroni, earmark the big state's cuisine with the finality that a brand specifies cattle ownership — and designate my son-in-law as a true Texan, for that is the way he likes soup!

For a step-up in color and flavor, yellow whole kernel corn often is stirred into chili con carne shortly before it is served.

Pralines Along San Antonio's Historic Streets

Among the confections, pralines capture the gold medal. Spanish-Americans make them, stack them on trays, and sell them along the picturesque and historic streets of old San Antonio. Take a bite of the candy and you know it did not originate in New Orleans, for instead of being brittle and sugary it is chewy, on the order of a soft caramel. These candy disks, rich with crunchy pecans, have no opposition for the dessert in Mexican style dinners, which a southwestern hostess sometimes puts on for her family and friends, and especially guests from the North. Some pralines are rum flavored.

Cooks generously brush the barbecue sauces over steaks, chops, hamburgers, chicken, and other meats as they cook in their home kitchens. Busy women frequently reach for commercially bottled peppery sauces, but many households cherish their own versions. A friend of mine at the University of Texas parted with the recipe for her No. 1 sauce. It calls for a mixture of 2 parts each of butter or margarine and lemon juice, 3 parts of Worchestershire sauce, and salt and pepper to season.

Fried steaks are Texas, too. Natives treat the piece of beef as if it were chicken — they roll it in flour and pan-fry it.

Candied sweet potatoes carry a subtle suggestion of cinnamon.

Pinto beans respond to a seasoning stunt, the addition of a little brown sugar as they simmer.

Green beans slip away from the southern influence in some quarters. They are cooked until just barely tender, and then mixed with chopped onion and green pepper that have been pan-fried in a little oil. Texans take pride in their gorgeous sweet onions.

Both lamb and pork when roasted suggest a vague taste of sage.

In the ham loaf you may detect sliced pimento-stuffed olives.

Many hostesses offer their guests dilled carrots and tiny pickled onions. The gay orange carrot sticks are pickled like cucumbers.

Pecan pies and waffles appear regularly on the food scene throughout the Southwest. The Christmas salad of cherry flavored gelatin contains pecans, too. Part of the liquid is the juice of two oranges and sweetened cherry sirup drained from canned pie cherries. The drained cherries and pecans are molded in the gelatin. Most cooks add a little shredded orange peel.

Slender strips of ripe olives and minced onions, pan-fried gently in butter until heated, and then thickened with a little flour, top broiled steaks delightfully — especially in Houston.

Corrals for the Strawberries

A Dallas hostess, a member of the home economics staff of Southern Methodist University, nominates her mother's shortcake for a Lone Star specialty. She rolls the dough, almost as rich as pastry, cuts it into strips, and bakes it. For every serving she arranges 8 lengths, log cabin style, on a plate. She fills these corrals with sugared strawberries, and tops their red-ripe juiciness with blobs of whipped cream.

Corn chips sprinkled lightly with chili powder and dunked in garlic and lemon flavored mashed avocado please party guests.

One of my friends in Dallas makes delightful cookies, quick as a wink, with a bag of corn chips.

With a roller she crushes the chips into small pieces right in the cellophane bag in which they are purchased. She melts a

6-ounce package of semi-sweet chocolate over hot water, adds 1½ cups of the corn chips, and drops the mixture by spoonfuls onto waxed paper.

Just as the Pennsylvania Dutch serve pretzels with ice cream, the Texas hostess scatters bits of crisp, salty corn chips on the frozen dessert. She also tosses them into green salads at the last minute.

Angel food cakes are the traditional birthday cakes for Texans.

Treats From New Mexico's Kitchens

Yellow rice contributes character and flavor to numerous dishes in New Mexico. Cooks heat the rice along with a chopped onion in a little fat until it becomes the color of ripe yellow corn. Then they add cold water and cook it about 30 minutes longer, or until tender. For seasonings they stir in salt, pepper, and asafran. While the *asafran*, or wild saffron, gives the desired color it lacks the flavor of Spanish saffron.

New Mexicans bake thin pork chops between layers of the yellow rice with either canned tomatoes or canned tomato soup poured over. Sometimes they substitute partly cooked sausages or weinies for the chops.

Macaroni and cheese tastes quite different from the dish of the same name in Wisconsin. Women stir an onion, chopped and pan-fried, but not browned, into the cooked macaroni, and add salt, red or green chili sauce, and tomatoes. Then they scatter shredded cheese on top and bake it in a moderate oven, 350°, 20 minutes.

Southwestern stews tempt the appetite. Usually they feature beef, although New Mexicans also like both lamb and mutton. It is the combination of vegetables cooked tender in the kettle with the meat that is extraordinary. One favored selection includes carrots, green beans, green onions, corn-on-the-cob, and tiny patty pan squash. The corn is cut in 2-inch lengths, or rosettes, and eaten from the fingers. When some of the stew is left over the day is considered lucky. Women who know their *p's* and *q's* cut the kernels from the cobs and add them to the meat and vegetable remnants that have been put through a food chopper. They heat the mixture in a little fat — that is, they gently pan-fry it.

Hostesses in Santa Fe Like Blue Corn Meal

As a trump card, hostesses in Santa Fe and some other places use blue corn meal from calico corn with the white meal or with wheat flour for a conversation piece. It imparts color and flavor to waffles, biscuits, crusts for meat pies, and other treats. Tiny meat balls containing blue meal, meat, and seasonings also typify New Mexico. So do meat balls or strips of meat cooked in a chili sauce or with vegetables.

Before the leg of lamb is run into the oven to roast, knowing hands stick it with garlic cloves and brush it with vinegar in which dried mint has been soaked. To accompany the roast, they coat new potatoes with bacon drippings, roll them in dried mint leaves and then in flour, and nestle them around the lamb to bake with it.

Avocado, shrimp, and tomato juice comprise the favorite meal starters. Peeled quarters or cut-up squares of avocado wear a sauce of tomato ketchup mixed with finely diced celery, laced with lemon juice, vinegar, salt, a trace of sugar, and a shake of Tabasco sauce. Cooked and chilled shrimp, heaped in glasses, draw a sauce of tomato ketchup and minced celery, spiked with lemon juice, powdered chili, and Worcestershire sauce. A pimento stuffed olive supplies the top decoration. In chilled tomato juice, with sprigs of mint for a garnish, you find such seasonings as salt, celery salt, onion juice, red chili pepper, and lemon juice.

Aniseeds come into their own in many kitchens. Taffy is sprinkled with the seeds. The taffy is made with brown sugar and molasses. When cooked, the sirup is poured into a shallow buttered pan, and given the local treatment, a sprinkling of aniseeds. After it is cool the taffy is pulled in the usual way. Yeast rolls, made sweeter and richer than they ordinarily are, contain the aromatic seeds, as do sugar cookies that are lemon flavored.

Gumdrop cookies follow the customary recipes except that the cook is somewhat choosy. She selects only orange flavored candy for the cooky dough that she also sweetens with brown sugar.

Pineapple makes the valedictory appearance for desserts in Mexican style suppers. Slices of the fruit, or a sherbet containing it, satisfy the guests. In various discriminating households pineapple sherbet accompanies the entree, in menus otherwise patterned to some extent on those served South of the Border.

Those New Mexico Meals Have Zip

Bacon and eggs for breakfast give the day a proper send-off. After the strips of bacon have been cooked and lifted to a warm platter cooks frequently stir a little chili powder into the drippings before breaking in the eggs to fry. They also poach eggs in chili sauce. For something tasty as the main dish they fold chopped hard-cooked eggs into well-seasoned white sauce along with chopped pimento stuffed olives and shredded cheese. They serve the heated mixture on top of corn bread. Dishes of this nature justified my young daughter's comment, after we returned to Kansas from ten days of food and fun in Santa Fe, that "our meals at home have no taste." She was right. Our customary fare in contrast to New Mexico's highly seasoned treats seemed mild and insipid.

Rancho sauce for fried eggs commands considerable respect throughout the state. Diced sweet onion, a minced garlic clove, and two cut-up ripe tomatoes are pan-fried in a little fat. Red or green chili sauce is added and the mixture is simmered half an hour.

As in Texas, New Mexicans never lose an opportunity to serve corn chips and avocados together.

Prunes, cooked soft and tender, with a bit of stick cinnamon added, are chilled, pitted, and stuffed with cheese or nuts. They are attractive shiny black touches among the greens on salad plates. Frequently prunes match flavors and share space with a yellow fruit — such as oranges, peaches, or apricots — on one of those black and gold southwestern salad specialties.

Cabbage salad shows thin slices of pimento stuffed olives, and its dressing is French, often made with lemon juice instead of vinegar.

Chocolate and cocoa, hot and frothy, impart a faint taste of cinnamon, and sometimes nutmeg, too. Often they contain coffee. Almost always beating or whipping provides the bubbling top that appears so intriguing when the filled cup is set before you.

Lemon flavored gelatin, made with half water and half chili sauce, has a fire that makes you sit up and take notice! Most cooks season it with grated onion, a smidgeon of vinegar, and sliced pimento stuffed olives.

Pinon Nuts Get Along Well With Tomatoes

Tomato aspic also puts glamour into menus. As a crowning touch it is served with avocado dressing, and often with corn chips or hot tortillas. The avocado for the dressing is mashed with a fork, and cottage cheese is added with seasonings of salt, garlic, chili powder, and mayonnaise.

Pinon nuts, the rich delicacies the Indians have gathered for centuries from some of the pinon pine trees, have an affinity for tomatoes. Proof comes to the table as a salad, scooped out ripe tomatoes stuffed with the chopped pulp mixed with wee bits of celery and pinon nuts. If you want dressing you can ladle it on.

Pinto bean salad threatens the position potato salad elsewhere maintains. It is made the same way, only New Mexicans add lots and lots of minced onion and crisp celery to the cooked beans.

For unusual hamburger sandwiches, so far as taste goes, cooks mix the meat with chopped onion and green chili, add a little mayonnaise, spread the mixture on the bun halves to cover, and broil to cook. As the final touch they lay on thin cheese strips and run the buns in the oven long enough to melt the cheese.

Spareribs soak overnight in hot chili sauce before roasting.

Barbecued short ribs come to New Mexico tables on a bed of cooked noodles.

Chicken and noodles contrast with the composition of this dish in other regions. Cooks often stir the sliced or diced cooked chicken into a cream sauce along with pitted ripe olives and chopped pimentos, and add a little sherry wine. Then they heat the mixture and pour it over cooked noodles. After that they scatter shreds of cheese on top and bake the dish long enough to melt the cheese.

To redeem hash from indifferent treatment it is seasoned with chopped pan-fried mushrooms and bits of green chili.

Even those gentlemen who usually refer to spinach as *fodder* show respect for it when you spread the vegetable, cooked, in a buttered casserole and crown it with canned mushrooms and a cheese sauce pepped up with minced onion and mustard. You bake the dish just long enough to heat it.

Vegetable scallop starts out with different kinds of frozen vegetables, like corn, lima beans, and chopped green chili. New Mexicans alternate them in a baking dish with cheese, seasonings, and cracker crumbs, and then pour on enough milk to reach almost to the top of the combination. After that they put on a top layer of buttered cracker crumbs and bake the tempting food to heat and to brown. With fish or beef it never fails to please.

Sweet potatoes, cooked, mashed, and whipped light with a beaten egg, and with seasonings and a little whipped cream folded in, are spread in a buttered dish. The distinctive southwestern touch is to top them with diced salt pork and a little chopped garlic mixed with a small amount of flour, to brown in the baking.

If you taste scalloped tomatoes, you sense the undertone

of brown sugar and minced green chili. Scalloped tomatoes often are served with fish.

In New Mexico, cake frostings made with both brown and caramelized sugar win merit badges, along with chocolate frosting containing brown sugar, and that never-failing sign of the area, the mocha taste.

Among the Arizona Food Souvenirs

Roast beef, rare, heads the list of food favorites in Arizona. Polite as the cattlemen of the state are, they simply cannot understand why anyone would eat beef medium well or well-done or with sauces! In contrast, many Texans prefer well-cooked beef.

Barbecued short ribs, as has been indicated, also register success whenever served. Arizonans brown ribs which have been cut in 2- or 3-inch lengths, in a little suet, along with a chopped onion. Then they add their finest barbecue sauce and cook the ribs slowly at a moderate temperature, 350°, in a covered pan or electric roaster, from 1½ to 2 hours.

Mulligan stew, Arizona style, was brought up on the ranch, but now is well acquainted in towns and cities. Traditionally it wears light, fluffy dumplings. Among the vegetables cooked with the beef you find onions, bell peppers, tomatoes, carrots, potatoes, and whole kernel corn. You frequently note among the seasonings, as you also do with scrambled eggs, a reminder of the Chinese cooks in the cow and mining camps, in the soy sauce.

You also recall these same old-time Orientals when you taste spaghetti chop suey, for it, too, gives you the touch of soy. To make it cooks use cooked spaghetti, strips of beef, veal, and pork — or just beef — and diced celery, onion, and bell peppers.

ARIZONA DINNER
Spaghetti Chop Suey
Tossed Green Salad
Green Grape Pie
Coffee

Most of the sauces for spaghetti start in the frying pan,

with chopped onion, celery, garlic, and bell pepper pan-fried until soft, but not brown, in salad oil. Canned tomato juice or tomato paste is added, and ripe olives with the desired seasonings. In some kitchens both ripe and green olives go into the sauce.

Spaghetti, like noodles, shows up in many patio meals. Natives generally cook these starchy foods in the cool of the morning, then refrigerate them for quick reheating at mealtime in the sauce, often in an electric roaster on the patio. In the arid country many ranch housewives make, cut, and partly dry noodles. Then they hang muslin bags of them on the back porch or at the side of the house, along with strings of red chilies, to dry and await use.

Corned beef hash illustrates how the taste of the Southwest enters familiar dishes. To either the canned or home-made hash, cooks add fresh or frozen green chili, chopped. Frequently they bake alternate layers of this mixture and slices of hard-cooked eggs in cheese sauce.

ARIZONA SUPPER
Corned Beef Hash
Sweet Pickles   Hot Biscuits
Iced Watermelon
Coffee

Arizona BISCUITS you spell with capital letters. They are neither dainty nor small. Cowboy biscuits are thick, light as a feather, and somewhat bready in texture. When hot from the oven, and spread with butter, one taste convinces you they are manna from above. Whatever questions one has about the creativeness of the state's cooks are melted like snow in the sunshine after you get acquainted with what they do with biscuits.

How Calico Biscuits Were Born

For one of the sleight-of-hand performances Arizonans add finely minced onion to the milk, and chopped bell pepper and pimento to the flour and shortening mixture. That is how calico biscuits were born. Along with a shrimp-grapefruit salad they completely captivated me at my first luncheon in Phoenix. Wonderful shrimp, flown from Mexico, teamed with fat grapefruit sections. The cook tossed them together without a dressing, for the fruit juice serves adequately for this purpose. Like many other salads made with citrus fruit, it came to the table in lettuce lined halves of hollowed-out grapefruit.

SUMMER LUNCHEON
Grapefruit-Shrimp Salad
Hot Calico Biscuits
Hot Coffee

Grapefruit juice assumes the liquid role in another biscuit. A home economist at Tempe, Arizona, in the State Teachers College, commonly adds raisins with the dry ingredients in making it.

Fruited drop biscuits contain chopped apples, shredded orange peel, and raisins.

You taste some truly memorable cheese sandwiches. One of them is simply made. You insert thin cheese slices between split buns and then wrap each one with two strips of bacon that cross on top and fasten on the underside. You toast them over the coals of a desert or mountain campfire, or bake them in the oven at home.

Green salads, as in California, are made and served in spacious wooden bowls, first rubbed with garlic. Some excellent cooks toss grapefruit sections with the greens. Arizona, like Texas, grows beautiful grapefruit.

Among the molded salads no number holds a dearer place on the menu than the orange flavored gelatin salad with grapefruit segments and canned or chopped fresh cranberries. All gelatin salads for patio or desert meals commonly are made stiffer so the heat will not melt them too much. Grapefruit and avocados meet on salad plates as they do in Texas and California. Some green salads show the orange of raw carrots and orange peel cut as fine as native pine needles.

No one can be certain sunshine salads were Arizona born,

but if not they were adopted in their infancy and brought up in the state. They first skyrocketed to fame as an escort for rare roast beef. In their simplest form the slices of orange and sweet onion overlap alternately on lettuce and are drenched with a piquant French dressing. Some cooks fill crisp lettuce cups with orange sections and top them with chopped onion, and vice versa. Another unforgettable sunshine salad has alternate rings of oranges, onions, and avocados on greens. A universal practice is to soak the orange and onion slices in French dressing, and to pour this same dressing, orange and onion flavored, over the salad.

This sun region, like California, is salad conscious. When in season, melons play on the culinary stage. Slices of casaba melon and grapefruit sections maintain prestige from one season to another. Outstripping all other vegetable combinations in popularity is the one made with lettuce, tomatoes, cucumbers, bell peppers, and onions, tossed with French dressing.

With local grapefruit available much of the time in Arizona, great dishes have evolved from it. *Grapefruit pie,* similar to lemon meringue pie, is one of them. The custard for it is made with the fruit juice and a little of the shredded peel. Wreaths of the plump sections top some of these pies; they encircle the edge, with the meringue piled in the center.

Mesquite Honey Is Something Special

Other grapefruit delicacies you write home about and then wish for when you are far away include the sherbet, the velvety ice cream, and cake. In building the white cake, the citrus juice serves as the liquid, and the frosting of confectioners' powdered sugar contains it and a whisper of the shredded peel. When unfrosted, this cake wins the purse in the race for the best shortcake; with strawberries it ends up as sublime eating.

Grapefruit marmalade, made with the aid of commercial pectin, spreads over buttered toast quite frequently, and the broiled fruit is no stranger at tables. Arizonans baste the leg of lamb with grapefruit juice but have to watch the oven closely because at certain seasons the fruit has sufficient sugar to scorch easily.

The lamb stew's claim to distinction, other than its good taste, lies in the rather unusual vegetables in it. One of the well-accepted groups contains peas, carrots, onions, kidney beans, and coarsely cut green beans.

Arizona people waste no words telling you they consider mesquite honey a gift from heaven. They praise its flavor as light and mild, and above all exquisite. Local orange honey and alfalfa honey also have followings, but natives admit that orange honey may be rather flowery, and alfalfa honey occasionally somewhat strong in taste.

As has been indicated, gourmets select mesquite wood to burn to coals for cooking meats. One favored system is to broil the steak on one side, turn it, and spread on garlic flavored butter. As the undersize sizzles the butter joins the smoke for a tasty mingling of flavors.

These Turkeys Are Fed on Olives

Some turkeys in the Salt River Valley taste so good they rate superlatives; they are olive fed. They run under olive trees and eat the fruit that falls to the ground. Commonly turkey is roasted, although fried turkey is at home in menus, too. Roast turkey is the regal bird for special occasion desert picnics. It usually is stuffed with a bread dressing, oregano flavored, with no sage added. Citrus dressings also go into turkeys as well as into game birds and pork. The base is a bread dressing with the addition of chopped cooked bacon, shredded orange and lemon peels (more of the orange), poultry seasoning, chopped onion, diced apple, and eggs.

Cooks stew chicken frequently in the Southwest, but rarely roast it. On some ranches cowboys go in for cock fighting. These birds run with the poultry, and chickens bred of the union are strange in appearance, with their wide breasts and unusually long legs. Ranchers like to fry these chickens, especially if they are fond of drumsticks.

Vegetables are important commercial crops in the irrigated valleys. People nearby take pride in selecting succulent vegetables for home kitchen use. They cook tiny, delicate squash in these areas, not the large, less tender, mature ones. Usually they steam them, and serve them hot with melted butter and minced onion, salt, and pepper. Or they top the little cooked squash with small pieces of bacon and shredded cheese and bake them in a slow oven, 325°, just long enough to cook the meat and melt the cheese. For a dish on the fancy side they scoop out enough of the steamed squash so they can stuff them with a well-seasoned onion-bread dressing, which they top with bacon and cheese, and then slowly bake them.

Zucchini Has a Big Following

Zucchini grows extensively in the irrigated districts of Arizona. Women pan-fry cubes of bacon, pour out some of the drippings, and add about a tablespoon of water, and then the thinly sliced zucchini. They put the cover on the pan and cook the vegetable slowly until tender. Lastly they sprinkle on shredded cheese, or add whole kernel corn and tomatoes before scattering on cheese.

Green stalks of broccoli boiled until just tender and served with Hollandaise sauce are much appreciated. In some households the remnants of the cooked vegetable stand in high regard, because of their delicacy when scalloped with alternate layers of white sauce, minced onion, and cheese. This casserole qualifies as just right for a desert picnic. It is made at home and wrapped in several layers of newspapers for transporting to the festive spot.

After steaming about an hour in the top of a double boiler, shredded carrots with butter added come to dinner tables frequently. Some grated onion is mixed and cooked with the carrots. The carrot sticks that most eloquently speak for the Valentine State are the crisp, slender pieces strung with black pitted ripe olives.

Cookies outrank cake in popularity; they are on the

sturdy side. Arizona is date country, and perhaps the favored way of cooking with the rich fresh fruit is to bake date-oatmeal bars. When you peep in a home freezer you are likely to find a chocolate cake, which women like to serve with little defrosting. If there is a special occasion in the offing there may be a grapefruit cake.

Mincemeat Often Contains Venison

Although the state by no stretch of the imagination qualifies as cake country, it is important pie-eating territory. Apple pie wins the silver spurs for popularity, with cherry and berry filled pies — such as blueberry, loganberry, and blackberry — pushing up for recognition. For the most part canned cherries and berries make the pies. Mincemeat has an inning in the winter; often it is made with venison, and some cooks add grapefruit juice to moisten it. Pecan pie never goes begging any more than it does farther east, as in Oklahoma, Texas, and Louisiana; homegrown pecans long have been appreciated.

A distinctive regional pie hides green grapes, Thompson seedless, or malaga (seeded), between its pastry crusts. Arizonans gather and use the fruit about 10 days before it will be ripe. This pie filling in flavor somewhat resembles one containing cherries. That explains why some women can the under-ripe green grapes and cherries together, or the grapes separately, for future pie making.

When fully ripened, green grapes make excellent Bavarian pies. Add them to a gelatin mixture that contains pineapple or apple juice for all or part of the liquid, flavored with a touch of shredded lemon peel. When it jells, fold in whipped cream. Serve the Bavarian in a baked pastry shell.

Spiced green grapes occupy the most important spot among the relishes in regional game dinners. This zesty fruit frequently is molded in orange or lemon flavored gelatin.

As a confection, strips of candied orange peel, with one end dipped in semi-sweet chocolate, share space on the coffee tables with candied grapefruit peel cut in fancy shapes.

Usually divinity is rich with pecans and strips of fresh dates, cut with scissors dipped in cold water. Fresh dates stuffed with California walnuts and rolled in sugar also have friends.

Because in all my food wanderings I never encountered it before, I turn the spotlight on the licorice ice cream I met in Phoenix. It is a commercial product, and the recipe is a secret.

That Delightful Dinner at the Tall House

Arizona gave me an unforgettable eating experience. The custodian of the Wupatki National Monument and his wife, who were friends of my brother, invited him to bring our family to dinner in their home. It was in a few rooms of an incredibly ancient red stone apartment building — the Tall House — on the Painted Desert northeast of Flagstaff.

We entered their quarters through an opening in the roof, and backed down a ladder into a room that held us spellbound. The stone walls and floor were hung and spread with Indian rugs. Through an aperture we looked out for miles across the brilliantly colored desert in the noonday sunshine. I well recall the jovial conversation and the thrilling pattern of bright flowers on the black sand, beautiful enough to put any Oriental rug to shame.

We ate a delightful dinner of tomato juice, chili con carne, corn chips, fried pinto beans, and frosty watermelon from a refrigerator in the oldest house inhabited by Caucasians in the United States. As we laughed, drank coffee, and talked to our hearts' content I occasionally wondered silently and thoughtfully about the people who ate in that room nearly a thousand years ago.

Along the Great Lakes

MANY AMERICANS moved west. That is the abbreviated story of how the four scenic lake states that touch Canada, New York (up-state), Michigan, Wisconsin, and Minnesota, were settled. On these hopeful journeys, mainly by water, women carried along their cherished recipes and the determination to reproduce them in the promised lands they approached. Later waves of immigration from northern Europe and then smaller ones from the Mediterranean area flowed into the North Country. There today as an aftermath you can eat the characteristic and distinctive home cooked meals of all European nations and the British Isles — without crossing the Atlantic Ocean. I recommend the experience. You also will meet welcome New England and distinctly local accents in many dinners.

Up-state New York to me suggests what mother used to cook. (Down-state communities of the Empire State feature many of the Atlantic Coast specialties. Traditional food in Pennsylvania — especially in the northern counties and to a certain extent in northern Ohio — is similar to that of up-state New York.)

When my mother departed from the beautiful Finger Lakes region, where her people had lived since their westward trek from Connecticut in 1800, she changed her culinary habits only as the food supplies of the prairies dictated. Unavailable products came to our home in kitchen chatter as I watched and worked at her side, and unconsciously acquired an interest in foods — and what is still more miraculous almost without effort I learned how to cook from her daily practical demonstrations. My father and brothers promptly called all super delicious dishes *Tompkins County Specials* as a compliment to the woman who prepared them.

With such a background, I, as a food reporter, approached scouting trips in the Empire State with a unique brand of enthusiasm and anticipation. Were the memorable childhood meals of my Kansas home western renditions of eastern originals? Are the old-time favorites served today? As I crisscrossed the area in the hunt I repeatedly met familiar and delicious food friends.

Among them was baked beans.

Not Candy, Merely Baked Beans

While many New Yorkers prefer Boston baked beans, thousands of homes remain loyal to the more blonde ones, New York style. Important differences from the Puritans' version include the absence of molasses, a slow simmering in water until tender before reaching the oven, and the use of a shallow baking dish or a wide-mouthed old-fashioned crock instead of the standard New England pot. The beans, hot or cold — and genuine New Yorkers like them both ways — call for vinegar as the accompaniment. Tradition decrees the following method of preparation.

Wash a pint of navy beans, cover them with lukewarm water, and soak overnight. Drain and put them on to cook the next morning with warm water to cover. Bring to a boil, reduce the heat, and simmer from 1½ to 2 hours, or until the beans are partly tender. Then add slices of salt pork, about ½ pound, and two medium-sized onions, minced. Simmer about an hour longer, or until the pork and beans are tender; drain, but save the liquid. Place the pork in the bottom of a shallow baking dish, pour the beans on top, sprinkle on ¼ to ½ cup of white or brown sugar, dust lightly with pepper, and add the hot bean liquid to cover. Bake without a lid for about 2½ hours in a slow oven, 300°, adding hot water if needed, or until the top and sides around the edges display that delightful brown crust that to New Yorkers signifies perfection. Serve hot the first time, and either reheat or use cold on the second and third appearances. Always pass a well-filled cruet of vinegar with the beans.

In Ithaca I talked with a home economist from the western plains who several years ago signed with an eastern New York county as the home demonstration agent. She told a joke on herself. The first eastern social function she participated in was a supper given by a group of rural women in honor of their husbands. She helped members of the refreshment committee plan the meal, as an applied lesson in menu making.

Soon came the festive evening. The first course went off according to Hoyle. When the main one came on an unidentified, unexpected large plate appeared; it was covered with what seemed to be generous squares of brown sugar candy. The surprised home demonstration agent could scarcely believe her eyes, but she helped herself to a portion of it. What a strange accompaniment to meat and vegetables, she thought. She tasted, and lo! her tongue met baked beans, New York style, for the first time. Everyone was dashing vinegar on them. She followed suit.

Several days later she inquired of the hostesses why they

added beans to the menu. In amazement at her failure to understand a food custom more than a century and a half old, one woman sympathetically replied, "Our men would not have liked our dinner without the beans!"

Spuds From the Big, Black Stove

Another unique, homely vegetable dish of the up-state communities is a type of creamed potatoes referred to by some families as *stewed potatoes*. They prospered as an early version of spuds for supper and enjoyed their heyday when almost every kitchen had a big, black coal- or wood-burning stove and a woodshed nearby. The technique of fixing them, simple but exacting, was as follows.

Melt butter in a heavy frying pan. (Some women stirred in a little minced onion and simmered it in the butter, but not until browned. My mother omitted the onion.) Add finely cubed boiled potatoes and pour on enough rich top milk to cover. Season with salt and pepper. Put on the lid and simmer gently on the back of the range, lifting the potatoes off the bottom of the pan a few times with the spatula, until the milk is almost absorbed. Some families liked to brown the spuds on the bottom and then just before serving to moisten them with a little thick cream, but the browning was the exception rather than the rule.

The popularity of the vegetable so prepared declined with the coming and acceptance of the convenient electric and gas ranges and the trend to speedy cookery. Some households now substitute a heavy baking dish for the frying pan and in winter cook the creamed potatoes in a very slow oven instead of on the back of the range. Others pin their faith on a double boiler. Thus in some homes this dish continues to be a pride and joy. No doubt it inspired the unusual creamed potatoes that appear on many Michigan, northern Ohio, and up-state hostess tables.

New Creamed Potatoes

Pare and finely dice 8 medium size potatoes. Put in a double boiler, add salt to taste and 1 tablespoon of butter, and pour on enough cream to cover. Cook about 2 hours. The potatoes will absorb most of the cream.

Splendid fruits and berries contribute distinctive dishes to the regional meals that men say give them an incentive to hurry home. The pie eaters, of which there are legions, are quite snooty about the dessert. It must be plump with filling, they insist. Nothing else cramps a native cook's way with pie more than to have to skimp on the fruit. *A* in most places designates the first letter of the alphabet, but in New York it also stands for the first fruit, the apple, to thousands of its citizens. In up-state hotel lobbies, apple vending machines tempt travelers to reach into their pockets for coins to translate into fruit. In autumn the roadside markets turn red and yellow with the orchards' bounty piled in baskets.

At this mellow season, when the smoke from bonfires of fallen leaves in the towns becomes incense on the spicy air, the Greenings, Northern Spies, McIntosh, and other varieties of apples live their finest hours. Then it is an unwritten kitchen law not to spice the pies. In the spring — after time may have dulled the fruit's flavor — cinnamon or nutmeg, or a cautious blend of the two, have their chance. The traditional companion to triangles of pastry puffed with apples is aged cheddar cheese, the New York kind.

Many native cooks now and then muster some of the noble pie tricks their foremothers cherished and practiced. One stunt is to cut up a little cheese and layer it in the pie filling between the thinly sliced apples. Another is to pour 2 or 3 teaspoons of maple sirup or molasses on the fruit in the center of the pie, or to scatter on a smidgeon of maple sugar before adjusting the top crust in position. Above all, New York pies are fat and portly, with a super abundance of thinly sliced sugared and butter dotted fruit. This mouth watering filling bakes between as tender a pastry as women can create. Dollops of ice cream frequently decorate the wedges at mealtime, and thus give cheese a brief respite from its accompanying duties.

Apple dumplings, many kinds of apple puddings, and apple sauce also frequently wear vanilla ice cream. Another dessert relished about the countryside goes by the name of *quick apple fritters.* These consist of generous slices of the fruit dipped in quite thick batter, such as that used for griddlecakes, to which egg has been added. Often a packaged mix is employed. They are pan-fried to brown in bacon drippings, and crisp, fragrant bacon rashers and maple sirup enhance the service. New York ranks as the second state in the production of maple sugar and sirup, and for generations its citizens have counted these sweetenings among their blessings.

When autumn comes to this fabulous apple country, the children beg for the candied fruit on sticks, a famed confection of the region. Mothers of young fry select beautiful whole apples and insert wooden skewers into the blossom ends. They dunk them into a cooked mixture made with corn sirup and sugar, flavored with cinnamon, and tinted red. After an apple is coated with the sweet, the skewer is inserted in a candy board to hold it upright until the sirup cools and becomes a smooth jacket. In western New York a candy board is what its name implies, a board with holes drilled half way through to hold skewers with their prizes as they come from the hot kettle. Leftover sirup dropped into a buttered pan forms candy patties.

New Yorkers eat and relish almost all kinds of pies. The cherry, Concord grape, red raspberry, blueberry, pumpkin, and squash numbers always hover near apple pie on the honor roll. All of them please when served plain, with cheese, or with vanilla ice cream. And by the thickness of their filling anyone with observing eyes recognizes the typical regional dessert.

Concord Grapes Register Delightful Flavors

Western New York reaps widespread acclaim for the quality of its Concord grapes, a top-ranking crop, although many kinds grow with great success in the state's vineyards. One of the highly eulogized beauties of the jelly glasses is made with equal quantities of Concord and Catawba grape juices. As the home demonstration agent who had me in tow explained, when she held a glass of this jelly to the light, "Isn't it beautiful? You can see through this clear grape jelly that tastes so delicious."

It is an accepted kitchen custom as ham bakes to baste it with either grape juice or apple cider. Many women bottle or freeze the purple juice for winter jelly making. One natural born cook remarked, "A kettle of jelly bubbling merrily on a snowy wintry day provides the perfume we like best in our kitchen." Then there is that fetching lavender and yellow dessert, as much a part of the ladies' spring luncheons as the violets and jonquils that bloom then. It is a whip composed of Concord grape juice sweetened with sugar, pointed up with lemon juice, and gelatinized. When it cools and thickens, the cook whips it with a rotary beater until the treat is converted into lavender clouds. It is as delicate in taste as it is pretty to look at. Especially is it handsome when heaped in sparkling crystal dessert dishes with ribbons of soft, yellow custard sauce poured over, and slices of cheery sponge cake alongside.

A spoonful of quivering grape jelly on a leaf of garden lettuce connotes a regional plate garnish, and it is pronounced the perfect running mate for breaded veal chops. Jellies from the east to west in up-state New York satisfy as quick, last minute cake frostings. They make most natives wish to revive the old-fashioned custom of serving from three to six thin layers hot from the oven and spread with jelly and stacked — with the top dusted with powdered sugar. Few cakes, regardless of how elaborate they are, can surpass this quick treat of warm layers somewhat rough around the edges.

Today young women often copy this dessert with packaged mixes to the extent that they spread the fresh layers with jelly and serve them without cooling. The region's jams, jellies, preserves, and marmalades traditionally star as cooky fillings, but the superb New York cooky is the rather thick, molasses-ginger one, besprinkled with sugar. When hungry, reach into a jar and pull out one or two. Then pour a glass of cold milk. Even the gods could ask for no more!

Fruit butters and spiced fruits, like crabapple pickles, are legion. Then there is the rosy red crabapple jelly, frequently with a leaf or two of fresh sage in the bottoms of some of the glasses to aid in providing the relish that goes best with pork or poultry. More universal, and ultra delicious, are the glasses of apple and crabapple jelly with a single rose geranium leaf on top of each one. It is just under the layer of *wax,* as many New Yorkers refer to the paraffin that provides a seal. In some of the top-bracket food shops of the metropolitan centers these jellies command prices that flabbergast anyone who is budget conscious. A sight of them starts anyone who swears by the supremacy of up-state New York cookery at its best to bring out the fondest sugar-coated food memories of childhood. Gooseberry preserves also rate among the favorites.

New York Cheese Is Sharp

New York cheese means something to most Americans, no matter where they live. It speaks for a sharp flavored, pale yellow or honey colored product. Natives of the up-state areas, regardless of where they are, almost always prefer the cheese made in their home neighborhoods — a nippy, aged cheddar that literally melts in the mouth. Cottage cheese also holds its own in meals throughout the generations. When melted butter is mixed into it, the local people like to spread it on toast or crisp crackers and also to smear on a layer of thick whole strawberry or red raspberry preserves, blue grape marmalade, blueberry jam, or jelly. Cottage cheese with cream, minced onion, and parsley mixed into it answers as a favored dunking mixture for crackers and potato chips, and also as an ideal stuffing for tomato salad. Cottage cheese-lemon pies and cottage cheese-fruit salads, sometimes frozen, ably represent the many dishes to which this dairy food lends taste appeal as well as high nutritive value.

Good cooks stir bits of snappy cheese into dried beef gravy, as creamed or frizzled dried beef is called, just before they ladle it over toast. They also add them to yellow corn-meal mush immediately before they remove it from the heat. They pour it into a loaf pan to cool and chill for subsequent slicing and pan-frying. Countless cooked vegetables wear fluffy shreds of cheese or streamers of rich, velvety cheese sauce. Individual servings of asparagus often appear to be held together by bands of it. Many a household knows potato salad most favorably when it dons a mask of shredded cheese. Frequently the salad contains cubes of crunchy, unpared red apples along with the celery, onion, and potatoes, and the dressing that binds them together.

A whiff of cheese zips up the scalloped vegetable, fish, and chicken dishes. And one of the treats that successfully plays second fiddle to potatoes in dinners contains separately cooked and seasoned tomatoes and cut-up celery, mixed, topped with cheese sauce, sprinkled with bread crumbs, and run under a broiler long enough to brown here and there.

Ice Cream Calls for a Sauce

No observing visitor doubts that ice cream maintains an enviable spot in the area's dessert picture. Dollops of it enliven all kinds of desserts, some of which have been mentioned. Puddings, cakes, pies, canned and frozen fruits, baked apples, gingerbread, and brownies illustrate a few of the treats that respond to its magic. Ice cream with a fruit sauce poured over it — be the fruit fresh, canned, or frozen — comes forth as a typical sundae. Indeed, sweet sauces for serving with ice cream characterize up-state New York. As I talked meals, recipes, weather, babies, and local politics with many women they spoke repeatedly of how wonderful frozen or fresh berries and peaches, berry preserves, grape marmalade, maple sirup, and chocolate and butterscotch sauces taste when served on ice cream. Busy cooks depend on their grocers for prepared sauces, and others make their own, such as a thick sirup composed of brown sugar and thin cream cooked together and served faintly warm with nuts added. Ice cream socials with the loveliest of homemade cakes and the ice cream prepared in home kitchens — someone turns the crank — still are summer institutions in many small towns.

New York, like New England, qualifies as an important pudding area. Certainly few peoples of the world are better acquainted with and fonder of custards and custard type puddings. Tapioca custards frequently contain apples, peaches, or other fruit. And where, outside of the Netherlands, can you find more melt-in-the-mouth chocolate puddings, often resplendent with drifts of whipped cream and sometimes with fudge sauce as well? Coffee jelly, or gelatinized coffee, chilled, broken up with a fork and with whipped cream folded in and nuts sprinkled on, never loses its grip on the meal's last course. Luscious remembrances of it forever tantalize the menu planners.

One of the traditional desserts encountered today is the soft custard-rice pudding — generally containing raisins — which some families serve with cinnamon sauce, a reminder of the early Dutch kitchens. (Of course the Dutch were early colonizers of the state, with headquarters on Manhattan Island and nearby Long Island, and a society that was confined mainly although not entirely to the Hudson River Valley north to Albany. Dishes of Dutch origin now appear less frequently in New York than in west Michigan, and they are described in the story of Michigan's cuisine.) In preference to the cinnamon one inherited from Dutch forebears, in these modern days most New Yorkers prefer a sauce containing canned or frozen cherries, cooked until slightly thickened and faintly flavored with almond extract.

Among the homespun desserts that taste wonderful and never go out of style are the fruit sauces with cookies, and occasionally with cake. These are the cooked or canned fruits served in small dessert saucers. Rhubarb rates as a favorite when spring arrives. The pinkest stalks make the sauce. Others end up in pies. Some people speak of *rhubarb* sauce and *pieplant* pie, as did my grandmother. Many a household follows the old custom of placing a big tempting bowl of the pink or strawberry-red rhubarb on the dining room table. How it whets the appetite!

Wilted Lettuce de Luxe

Most regions of the United States boast of their interpretations of wilted lettuce. New York is no exception to the rule. Her people have relished wilted lettuce, spinach, and dandelion greens for more than two centuries. The methods of handling the crisp leaves are reminiscent of the Dutch. With them are tossed slices of hard-cooked eggs and bits of crisp bacon. The home chef stirs flour into the bacon drippings, adds water, and cooks the mixture to make a rather thick sauce. Then she stirs in vinegar and a bit of sugar, with salt to season. After the mixture is heated very hot she pours the bubbly dressing on the greens and tosses them to distribute it. The leaves wilt slightly.

One of the more unusual food habits of dyed-in-the-wool New Yorkers is to sprinkle a little granulated sugar on wilted lettuce, on lettuce served with sour cream-vinegar dressing, and on sliced ripe tomatoes first splashed with traces of vinegar. It provides only a touch of sweetness. What seems to count more is the grainy texture of the sugar, which a New York City food editor, reared up-state, described as, "Very delightful on the tongue." She added that, "Sliced cucumbers and scallions floating in vinegar compose a favorite summer relish — coarsely ground black pepper and salt season them."

As in all North Country across the United States, turnips and winter squash ably fill vegetable roles in many meals. Like their New England neighbors, eastern New Yorkers refer to rutabagas as *yellow turnips;* they excel in serving them in many ways. Shoestring turnips, or match-like strips of the yellow vegetable, are cooked until barely tender in a little salted water. They are drained and then heated with small amounts of sugar and butter to glaze and season.

Candied turnips, the right ticket for a menu featuring pork, are prepared like candied sweet potatoes. Thick slices of the cooked and pared vegetable are spread in a shallow baking dish, topped with dabs of butter and brown sugar, and then baked to glaze.

New York, like New Jersey, is famed for its gardens. All the vegetables in their prime play their delicious roles in family meals. Late in summer pickle-making starts. Is there any place where from August into October the kitchens send out more of that come-hither aroma?

Summer squash takes over when the winter vegetables are out of season or the frozen supply is exhausted. People favor a larger, more mature squash than those revered in the South and West. Both squash and pumpkin are frozen, and especially do the pie makers laud their convenience. *Onions au gratin* make a splendid and much appreciated companion for steak, and the creamed, fried, and scalloped ones also score success at mealtime.

Grandmother Traveled on the Erie Canal

Green peas, fresh from pods hurried from the garden, and baby new potatoes — after their thin, tender skins are rubbed off under a cold water faucet — separately cooked in a little salted water and drained, combine forces for the most triumphant vegetable dish of early summer. The union of these two succulent foods, heated in thin cream, with only salt and pepper for seasonings, constitutes one of the happiest marriages of New York garden products. It wins the same unstinted praise as it did in the days when my grandmother and her sister traveled between Auburn or Owasco and New York City on the Erie Canal and the Hudson River. These journeys were romance to me more than a half century later and nearly two thousand miles westward as I sat on their knees and listened to tales of their boat trips filled with adventure. And the same early summer dinner menu, simplified a little, delights one as it did in the faraway past, both in New

York communities and in neighborhoods scattered between the Atlantic and Pacific Oceans where people of New York ancestry live.

EARLY SUMMER DINNER
Fried Chicken, New York Style
New Potatoes and Peas in Cream
Buttered Carrots
Wilted Lettuce
Strawberry Shortcake
or
Cherry Pie

Frozen peas stand by for a traditional meal, a guest and Sunday country feast known as the *New York Chicken Dinner*. A description of it appears later in this chapter. Many culinary artists insist they achieve the best results when cooking peas by first partly defrosting them and then simmering them in their own juices, or at least with very little water added. Other frozen vegetables sometimes receive similar treatment.

A favorite evening snack of up-state New York men, which their Wisconsin brothers also vouch for, consists of buttered rye bread made into sandwiches with slices of sweet onions and aged cheddar cheese. As a nightcap to follow, a big glass of milk fills the bill. But then both states are fabulous dairylands!

Baked bean sandwiches are not strangers. Neither are ones made of peanut butter. In the Mohawk River Valley, where perhaps they are the most popular, cups of steaming cocoa often associate with them. And for the summer picnics, an institution of major importance in up-state New York, cucumber sandwiches are traditional.

Lemonade with egg beaten into it — a cool and refreshing drink — is another old-timer that reappears year after year in these outdoor meals. Someone also usually brings a big bowl of macaroni and cheese. There is no objection if it is cold. People who are accustomed to it that way prefer it to all the more modern and fancy chilled macaroni salads. Those who are not find it more than palatable — just downright delicious.

The trick is all in the way it is made. Cooked and seasoned macaroni and cut-up aged New York cheddar cheese make alternate layers in the heavy dish, starting with macaroni on the bottom and ending up with the cheese on top. Every one is dotted with butter. Then egg beaten into whole milk, 1 egg to ½ cup, is poured over. During the baking that ensues in a moderate oven, 350°, the egg and milk evolve into a custard, cheese flavored, that holds the macaroni in all its glory.

New York style baked beans already have appeared on these pages. Baked lima beans, the dry ones, also maintain a wide regional appeal. Women soak them overnight in water to cover, and alternate them in a baking dish with thick pared apple slices, onion circles, and pork chops. They first pan-broil the chops to brown them on both sides, but do not cook them. The accepted rule is to include at least two layers of each food, and to bake the dish in a slow oven, 300°, about 8 hours, with water to cover. The water is replenished as needed, or instead of it some families use tomato juice or canned tomato soup.

Red kidney beans commonly are baked with onion and salt pork, and often with a slight sweetening of maple sirup. The New York tradition is to serve baked beans of all descriptions with what the natives call *johnny cake* — a yellow corn bread, not with Boston brown bread.

NEW YORK BEAN SUPPER
Baked Beans
Ripe Cucumber Pickles
Cabbage Salad
Johnny Cake   Currant Jelly
Apple Pie
or
Apple Turnovers

Some women first cook the yellow meal for corn bread with the sweet or sour milk, the salt, and sugar in a double boiler to make a mush. When it is cool they add the leavenings, beaten eggs, baking powder or soda, and the melted shortening. The quantity of sugar varies from one household to another, but from 2 to 4 tablespoons to a standard recipe meets with approval in most quarters. The bread usually comes from the oven in a rather thick layer. Good cooks cut it into squares for serving. Sometimes they bake johnny cake without sugar in comparatively thin sheets and cut it in squares to team with milk gravy for a main dish shortcake. They make the gravy from the drippings after strips of bacon or salt pork, rolled in flour, are pan-broiled. The meat garnishes the shortcake.

Fabulous Strawberry Shortcakes Appeared

Almost everyone thinks of New York biscuits as on the thick side, like those of the Middle West. In the early years flour from the locally grown soft wheat supplied the area's kitchens. This pastry flour contributed to the delicacy and tenderness of the cakes, pastry, and hot breads. The biscuits were cut from a soft dough patted out on a board with no kneading and as little handling as possible. When baked in a hot oven they often came forth medium in height, or on the thin side, with a golden brown flush on their tops.

From this soft biscuit dough evolved the New York strawberry shortcake, famous in a state equally noted for its superb berries. Natives pour on cream to complete the dessert. The same dough with egg added was patted onto sweetened berries, cherries, peaches, and other fruits that almost filled a baking dish for extraordinary cobblers, much noted for their deliciousness. This is the backdrop for the state's biscuits, and as every home economist knows, food habits change slowly, and often merely from necessity.

Doughnuts appear as widely and they are as highly favored in the region as in New England. In Buffalo there are bake shops that specialize in them. Two kinds of rolls are popular in this city where the meals often have a pronounced German accent. One is the *Kimmel Weck,* an oblong roll with a cross in the center, which facilitates breaking it into fourths. Caraway seeds and coarse salt show on the surface, obviously held in position by a glaze. *Alligator rolls* carry a crust with markings on their exterior that suggest those of the animal by the same name. Many delightful yeast breads also are available in the environs of Albany.

Rusks represent Dutch breads utilized in different kinds of dishes. Some New Yorkers cut them in bite-sized pieces, arrange lettuce cups filled with chopped lettuce and hard-cooked eggs, quarters of small tomatoes and other selected vegetables on top, and pour a highly seasoned French dressing over all. The pieces of rusks absorb some of it — enough to season them — but they retain their crunchiness, and add a surprisingly pleasing note to the salad plate.

By tradition New Yorkers rally around buckwheat cakes hot off the griddle, as do the Pennsylvanians. They frequently stack several large wheat griddlecakes, each buttered and sprinkled with maple sugar, or with a little maple sirup poured over; then they crown this "cake" with whipped cream before cutting it into wedges. This is a custom shared with Vermont.

One old-fashioned humble number consists of slices of dry bread steamed atop the stew to pinch-hit for dumplings. Some of the area's dumplings contain no shortening; eggs, separated, beaten, and then combined with flour, baking powder, salt, and a little water make the soft dough. These light-as-a-feather puffs, with dry hearts, suggest that most famous of all meals in up-state New York, known by the modest name of *Chicken Dinner*. It connotes Sunday and company arriving at spacious farmhouses with nearby large barns which generally have silos at their sides.

CHICKEN DINNER
Chicken Fricassee
Dumplings   Gravy
Mashed Potatoes   Peas
Waldorf Salad
Pumpkin Pie   Cheese

Fried chicken, the New York version, starts out in a kettle, and is cooked like chicken fricassee. When dressed, the chicken often weighs from 3 to 6 pounds. The disjointed poultry simmers until tender in water. For frying it is drained, rolled in flour, and browned to a turn — preferably and traditionally in butter or chicken fat. The broth is thickened for gravy. Perhaps the custom had its roots in thrift — the belief that a large chicken is an economy — but its fine flavor perpetuates continual use. Today much of the fried chicken is southern style, but when the longing for the old-time kind develops, the New York type graces the platter with distinction.

Only one of my seven Kansas cousins returned to his ancestral home in up-state New York for college and a permanent abode. Not too long after his arrival, and not many years ago, he and his Kansas bred wife were talking with an elderly rural woman who inquired, "Is it true that in Kansas you fry raw chicken?"

The Chicken Dinner continues as a favorite at church suppers — the kind staged for fund raising. Generations of up-state New Yorkers have found that it does the job successfully. That speaks much for its merits. On such occasions there almost always are big bowls, frequently of glass, filled with flavored red gelatin. It is of the delicate, dainty type which tenderly holds white dice — cut-up bananas.

Turkey for Thanksgiving is a mandate, and chestnut or oyster bread dressing often fills the regal bird. For Christmas the choice falls between roast goose or turkey. Ducklings, a Long Island favorite, make their bows in the chapter on the Atlantic Coast.

Beef is the top ranking meat, although lamb is highly appreciated. Indeed, I belive my mother pined more for lamb and mutton than other classic New York foods, for Kansas is deep in the non-eating lamb belt. Cold cuts are much esteemed. The pot roasts are sublime, and equal to those of New England. There is but one noticeable prejudice and that is against veal. It no doubt stems from the slaughtering of young dairy calves.

Of course pork occupies many a platter during the winter. Which wins the most laurels — the loin roast or pork steaks — is a toss up. A home economist fully entitled to be called a gourmet now lives in Texas but came from that section of New York between the St. Lawrence River and the Lakes in the Adirondacks. She speaks with deep affection and perhaps a tinge of nostalgia about the pork roasts of the home community. Her mother's way was to rub the meat with dry mustard, brown sugar, salt, and pepper, and let it bake uncovered in a slow oven while the family was at church. The vegetables that accompanied it — as they often do today — were mashed potatoes with hunks of butter on top and creamed onions. Sometimes baked Hubbard squash forced its way into the menu to the gratification of everyone. It still does. Then as now applesauce came on to complement the meat.

Whitefish Is the Gem of the Catch

New Yorkers staunchly support their fresh water fish. They also vote for salt cod and mackerel, and oysters, which have been available to them from colonial times. *Cod fish gravy,* as they refer to the creamed fish, is elected as a wonderful accompaniment to baked potatoes. Along with other people near the Great Lakes they laud the *whitefish,* and consider it the cream of the catch. One of my college roommates, a native of Dunkirk, New York, when hungry entertained me with eloquence based on baked whitefish, which came to her home almost every Friday — the fish were fresh from Lake Erie. (Her other flowery bouquets were for Concord grape pies made with fruit from the Fredonia vineyards.) Pike, pickerel, and perch also rate as favorites from the lakes.

Across the United States pitch-ins and covered dish suppers gather people together for many happy social hours, with everyone bringing her Sunday-best contributions to the refreshments. Lift off the covers and some of the region's taste triumphs come into view. Western New York women speak of *tureen suppers,* for their covered dishes often are tureens, and many of them lovely old ones.

What do they contain? Among the treats almost certain to appear are macaroni and cheese with red-ripe slices of tomatoes baked on top; a southwestern importation, or Spanish rice; scalloped potatoes and onions, fruited cole slaw, apple salads, and if it is winter, ambrosia (sliced oranges and coconut). Then there are rolls, cakes — often sponge, angel, and chocolate layer — and fat pies, apple, cherry, and pumpkin, and sometimes sour cream numbers. There is plenty of hot coffee, too, several cups for everyone, to increase the enjoyment of the party, in a state where good food is abundant and old traditions colorfully mingle with the new.

Michigan Is Akin to New York

In the silence of the wilderness the fur traders' canoe paddles produced soft music as they dipped into and arose from the waters of many lakes and rivers. Soon the rhythm of axes and the crash of great trees joined the chorus. Then homes were built and seeds planted in what now is southern Michigan. Because many of the settlers hailed from up-state New York the smell of food on a frosty evening suggested suppers similar to those of the Empire State. Faint but telling signs in today's meals mark Michigan as a close relative of New York, as a visit to Missouri reminds one of its kinship to Kentucky.

The people of New York and Michigan thrill equally over fruit dishes, bake beans the same way, and believe whitefish cannot be surpassed among the fresh lake fish. They cook potatoes with cream or rich milk, team cottage cheese and fruits together, beam over fruit gelatinized with purple grape juice or apple cider as the liquid, and know a good cherry pie when they taste it.

Of course such a picture of Michigan's food scene is one-sided to the extent that it primarily represents the older families. This highly developed industrial state provides a home for many foreign born citizens and even greater numbers of people one or two generations removed from foreign shores. Naturally the cuisine is as cosmopolitan as the residents, not only in cities like Detroit and Grand Rapids but also in many communities elsewhere.

Wherever I sat at a table my hostess spoke of foreign dishes and in many instances she served them, or their Americanized versions. In Grand Rapids, for instance, the lady at my left said her favorite supper dish for guests is Peruvian shrimp stew. By the time she completed her description everyone within earshot wished to try making it. And the slender, blue-eyed, flaxon-haired young mother of Dutch descent — a picture in a simply cut scarlet dress — lamented that the wilted lettuce she fixes does not taste so good as that her grandmother made.

Cherries Lend Color Appeal

If one food were to be selected to stand for Michigan, as an emblem like a flower, motto, or flag, cherries might win. As an A-1 producer of the fruit, Michigan proudly points out that its cherry color and characteristic flavor are not without honor in the meals of the area. A home economist at the Michigan State College says it is rare for as much as a teaspoon of cherries or a dish containing them to come back to the college kitchens after a meal.

The trade refers to the crop as *pie cherries*. Native cooks make two-crust pies with them in the best American tradition, but the name proves to be no handicap, for they also feature the fruit in many other ways. They pit and then can or freeze quantities of it for out-of-season use. Also they spice and pickle a supply to complement meats and poultry. And cherry sauce turns the dessert cook into a magician. She tops many a dish with its crimson beauty for eye and appetite appeal.

For example, there is cherry glaze pie almost all women in the area mention as insurance for meal success. Serve it, they say, and you send everyone away from the table happy. They make this number a few hours in advance and chill it in the refrigerator. Defined, it is a cream pie spread with the colorful glaze. But here is the recipe a dozen women offered me the first day of my food scouting in the region.

CHERRY GLAZE

2 tablespoons cornstarch
½ cup sugar
½ cup water or juice from cherries

2 cups fresh pitted cherries, drained
1 tablespoon butter

Mix the cornstarch, sugar, and water or juice from cherries to make a smooth paste. Add it to the cherries and slowly cook about 20 minutes or until the sauce becomes thick and clear. Add butter, and if desired, a little red food coloring, mix, cool, and pour over the cream pie. Chill.

MICHIGAN CREAM PIE

½ cup sugar
⅓ teaspoon salt
2 tablespoons cornstarch
1 tablespoon flour

2¼ cups milk
2 egg yolks
1 tablespoon butter
1 teaspoon vanilla

Mix the sugar, salt, cornstarch, and flour, gradually add the milk, and cook over low heat, stirring constantly, until the mixture thickens and comes to a boil. Let it boil a minute, remove from the heat, and whip a little of the mixture into slightly beaten egg yolks. Then stir the eggs into the cream filling and heat, while stirring constantly, until the combination has boiled 1 minute. Remove from the range, add the butter and vanilla, and cool. Pour into a 9-inch baked pastry shell.

Cherry sauce, composed of the fruit cooked with sugar and cornstarch to sweeten and thicken it, and frequently with a few drops of almond flavoring added at the last minute, tops a layer of cake. Whipped cream trims it. Most hostesses serve the favorite at the table. The sauce also spreads its red mantle over lemon snow pudding. It decorates that dessert of desserts, adapted from Russian Cream. Some women have given it the name of their favorite state.

MICHIGAN CREAM

2 cups sweet cream
1½ cups sugar
1 tablespoon gelatin

1 cup cold water
2 cups sour cream
1 teaspoon vanilla

Add sugar to the sweet cream, heat until lukewarm, and add the unflavored gelatin after it has been softened in the cold water. When the gelatin and sugar are dissolved, remove from the heat and cool. As the mixture begins to thicken, fold in the sour cream, beaten until smooth, and the vanilla. Pour into a large mold or individual small ones and serve with cherry, strawberry, or red raspberry sauce.

How many gelatin salads hold cherries with combinations of other fruits no one professes to know. Muffins with drained cooked or canned cherries in them, baked cherry puddings with cherry sauce, and cherry tortes are uncontested Michigan favorites. Cherry juice starts many a meal in good form, as also does a combination of the juices of two of the state's important fruits, cherries and apples. A much praised vanilla ice cream is flecked and flavored with cooked and sweetened cherries.

Raspberries Contain Thrilling Flavors

Few discussions of good food progress very far before someone refers to the wonderful local red raspberries and strawberries. One of the premium dishes spotlighted in conversations and in meals starts out as a long, narrow, and shallow dish, or a bowl, often of wood, lined with grape leaves. On them the hostess spreads a layer of creamy cottage cheese. Over this snow she scatters a generous amount of red raspberries. Then she sprinkles the berries with brown sugar. At the table everyone helps himself to the dessert; most people pour cream over it. Berries with brown sugar mixed with a trace of cinnamon also qualify for dessert. And many a bowl of ready-to-eat cereal calls for berries when they are in season — and banana slices when berries are not — in the breakfast menu.

Natives actually rave about raspberry sponge cake. In a favored form the cake, split in crosswise halves, is put together with crushed, sweetened raspberries, or if they are unavailable with raspberry jam. It is crowned with whipped cream. Just after it comes from the oven, some hostesses divide the hot cake into crosswise halves with forks, and pour a quarter cup of rum or sherry wine over the lower half.

At serving time they add the berries and whipped cream to the cooled cake.

People talk with enthusiasm about raspberry rum sauce. To make it the cook heats the berries with sugar, just enough to dissolve the sweetening. Then she adds a few whole choice raspberries and stirs in a touch of rum or sherry wine for flavoring. During the summer, berry sauce takes a role similar to the one made from cherries. To complete the strawberry or peach sundaes — those made with the fresh or frozen berries or fruit — women heat canned red raspberries, sieved, with sugar and cornstarch. They mix them with red currant jelly, and continue the simmering until the sauce becomes thick and clear. This melba sauce is cooled before use.

No one doubts the excellence of the strawberries — not after tasting them. And glazed strawberry pies take second place to no other dessert. Blueberries are successfully cultivated and kitchen tested, and wild huckleberries bask in fame. "Give me an old-fashioned huckleberry pie," a gentleman said to me. "That always convinces me our Michigan cookery is expert. My wife's special occasion blueberry tarts are wonderful, too. And for another food that has attained stardom on our stage I nominate the whole strawberry preserves made in home kitchens. It also would be an unpardonable sin to overlook our spiced crabapples, cucumber pickles, and celery relishes. And has anyone mentioned our summer apple pies, winter apple turnovers, and coconut-cream pie? Any of these fit-for-a-king dishes are ably qualified to represent Michigan."

Kent County Displays 50 Apple Dishes

Apple growing is a major industry in Michigan. All of the favorite apple dishes of the United States are firmly established in the cuisine. One of the many gala food celebrations of the state comes off in Kent County. When autumn arrives, the wives of local growers set up an original type of smörgasbord. They arrange tables on a shady lawn, spread apple-green covers over them, and center a decorative basket of choice fruit on each one. On these tables they display 50 or more appetite-whetting apple dishes. Baked ham and coffee share honors in the feast.

One of the old-time salads I have not met elsewhere features chilled baked apples. Medium-sized, tart apples, with brown sugar in their centers, are baked until just tender, with care to keep their shapes intact. After chilling them the cook stuffs their cavities with chopped marshmallows and nuts — sometimes peanuts — moistened with mayonnaise. She serves them on lettuce with blobs of mayonnaise on top, and with a pretty jewel, a dab of bright jelly, on each fluff of the mayonnaise.

As a meal starter, the light-colored pasteurized apple juice, chilled, delights almost everyone. It is a child of the Michigan State College. There it was developed.

Dutch apple cake, with a name that infers its origin, has a wide acceptance. It consists of apple slices sprinkled with sugar and cinnamon, in the bottom of the pan, and the batter of a one-egg cake baked on top. Some families traditionally serve a brown sugar sauce with pieces of the cake, while others prefer whipped cream.

Along with the cherries and apples, luscious peaches also are produced commercially, and the state's kitchens excel in tasty dishes that feature the juicy, red-cheeked fruit. One of the more unique customs is to bake in a simple sugar sirup the whole, pared peaches until just tender. First the cook dots them with butter. She turns them two or three times while they are in the oven. These fruity balls of gold frequently are heaped on a platter holding overlapping broiled ham slices on one side. Corn muffins made with yellow meal, or southern spoon bread, often comes along as an accompaniment. Peaches also are baked in sugar sirup with a wisp of mace and grated lemon peel added. Some women pour in perhaps 2 tablespoons of white wine or brandy for additional flavoring. Canned peaches, prepared in the same manner with mace and lemon peel, usually are flavored with a little Muscatel wine, if any is used. Natives think it helps yield the taste imparted by the fruit pits.

For a cheerful salad mothers like to team shredded or grated raw carrots with canned yellow peach halves. They season 2 cups of the fluffy vegetable with salt, 2 tablespoons of sugar, and the juice and grated peel of 1 lemon. After the mixture stands a few minutes they heap generous spoonfuls of it in the centers of the peach halves — or in canned pears, too, for that matter. They serve the fruit on lettuce lined plates. And sometimes they pile the carrots in a salad bowl and decorate the top with big soft prunes, pitted and stuffed with peanut butter.

People like their peaches and cream almost any way. Sometimes they mix the fruit and sweetened whipped cream, gelatinize it, and mold it in a dish lined with ladyfingers or slices of sponge cake. After chilling the treat they serve it garnished with fresh peaches, pared, sliced, and sugared.

Concord grapes grow extensively. They remind a visitor — as do other of Michigan's fruits — of kinship with New York. The delectable juice flavors many dishes, especially salads and desserts. One of the popular dessert beverages consists of about a cupful of the chilled juice beaten with a large serving of vanilla ice cream, with a tablespoon of sugar and a few grains of salt to blend. It is served in a glass, and often with sugar cookies.

Big Crops of Navy Beans Travel Far

Michigan is recognized from one end of the United States to the other for her beans, of the navy, Great Northern, and other dry varieties. (Important truck crops include celery, onions, and potatoes. In fact, most of the familiar vegetables grow in the gardens of the area.) Beans are baked by both the New York and New England methods, with the former style traditional. Some families follow the Ohio-Indiana-

Illinois system of adding tomatoes, tomato soup, or tomato ketchup to them as they bake. For bread to serve with them most people settle for bran muffins studded with raisins, and sometimes with nuts. Here is the Michigan way to bake beans still used in many households, as dictated to me over a luncheon table by a native daughter.

"Soak a pint of home grown dried navy beans overnight in water to cover. Drain, cover with water, and add a medium-sized onion, a ¼-pound piece of salt pork, 1 teaspoon of salt, and 2 tablespoons each of brown and white sugar. Cook gently over low heat until the beans are tender, adding water as required. Then pour the vegetable into a baking dish. Discard the onion if you wish. Score the rind side of the salt pork about ½ inch deep. Press it into the beans so that only the rind shows. If necessary add hot water. The ideal is to have the liquid reach just to the top of the beans. Sprinkle on a little granulated sugar. Bake uncovered in a slow to moderate oven, 325° to 350°, until much of the juice is absorbed and the top of the beans is a golden brown. Serve them with tomato ketchup."

MICHIGAN BEAN SUPPER
Tomato Juice
Baked Beans
Bran Muffins   Jelly
Iced Celery Hearts
Cherry Glaze Pie
Coffee

At some seasons a cole slaw made with a sweet-sour or sugar-vinegar dressing replaces the celery. Ham frequently is included in the menu. Some households select a caramel cereal ring filled with ice cream as the dessert. Certainly these crisp, delectable circles with ice cream, and usually with a warm or cold caramel sauce poured over them, speak for Michigan. I encountered them every place I went. From my home economics hostess in Grand Rapids I begged the recipe just after we had dined well and happily at the Woman's City Club. A caramel corn flake ring ended the meal.

CARAMEL CORN FLAKE RING

5 cups corn flakes	2 tablespoons corn sirup
½ cup brown sugar	½ cup water
½ cup granulated sugar	2 tablespoons butter

Pour the corn flakes into a buttered mixing bowl. Mix the sugars, corn sirup, and water. Cook to the soft ball stage, 234°. Add the butter and mix. Pour the hot sirup over the corn flakes, stirring them constantly to coat the flakes evenly. Press lightly into 10 buttered individual ring molds and cool. Unmold on dessert plates and fill with ice cream. Top with a fresh fruit or a hot or cold caramel sauce.

I doubt if anyone has counted the kinds of bean soups that fill the bowls of the state with distinction. Surely few of them could equal the one a hospitable farm woman asked me to sample. The sour cream in it supplied a wonderful flavor.

To make it she said she soaked a cup of dried navy beans overnight in cold water to cover, drained them, poured on fresh water to cover, and cooked them until tender. Then she added 3 strips of bacon, cubed and pan-fried until crisp, a small onion, grated, 1 teaspoon of salt, and a little pepper. She heated the mixture to the boiling point and stirred in 1 cup of heavy sour cream. She thinned the soup with hot water to obtain the proper consistency.

Both lima and green beans, cooked and buttered, frequently draw sautéed mushrooms as a garnish. A farm way of preparing about a pound of green beans is to cook with them in a little water a medium-sized onion and potato, chopped fine. The water evaporates by the time the vegetables are tender. Salt, pepper, and a little cream provide adequate seasoning, and the potato slightly thickens the cream. Many expert cooks recommend Syrian green beans. They pan-fry a minced onion and a touch of garlic in olive oil until slightly soft but not browned. Then they add the cut-up beans and canned tomatoes and cook the dish very slowly almost an hour.

Potatoes have an affinity for cream. One woman said that she enjoys a certain pleasing prestige among her friends for her style of hashed potatoes. She boils the spuds in their jackets, then pares and dices them very fine. Next she heats cream and adds enough to cover the potatoes; the mixture

cooks in a double boiler at least an hour. By that time the
cream is absorbed.

She scallops potatoes by first slicing the raw spuds very
thin, seasoning them with salt and pepper and often with
minced onion, and adds cream almost to cover. After that
she bakes them in a slow oven, 325°, for 1 hour with the lid
adjusted, and 1/4 hour or longer without the lid to encourage browning.

Wilted greens, especially lettuce and spinach, achieve
acclaim. Many natives prepare them this way.

Chop or shred the tender leaves and add to them crisp
pieces of pan-broiled bacon. Add vinegar to the drippings, plus
a little salt, sugar, and pepper, and pour it over the leaves.
Mix and serve at once.

While there may be nothing especially distinctive in the
preparation of this foundation dish, Michigan cooks have
a few stunts of their own. They like to add not only chopped
green onions but also a few thinly sliced small red radishes.
And they serve fluffs of this salad on the hot vegetable plate.
In one home I encountered the warm salad in the center
of a cheese-potato mixture baked in a ring mold. (A universal fondness for cheddar cheese blankets the southern areas
of Michigan.)

More Pasties Are Baked Than in England!

Perhaps wilted lettuce and spinach attain their greatest
fame in west Michigan, near Grand Rapids in the Dutch
area — the well-known tulip territory. These thrifty Americans enjoy an enviable reputation for their cookery of red
cabbage with a sweet-sour or sugar-vinegar taste and a richness imparted by butter seasoning. Sauerkraut with potatoes
pleases many people, especially those of Dutch, German,
and Polish extractions. Indeed, the favorites of almost all
nationalities are at home in the state. On the Upper Peninsula many Finns and Cornish people live. Members of
the latter group enthuse over their *pasties* (the *a* sounds like
the one in hash). A food extension specialist at the Michi-

gan State College says it is believed that more of them now come from the ovens there than in England. This is one way to make them.

PASTIES

2 cups flour	½ cup onions, sliced
1 teaspoon salt	½ pound round steak, sliced
½ cup shortening	and diced
Cold water	Salt and pepper
2 cups raw potatoes, sliced	2 tablespoons butter

Cut the shortening into the sifted flour and salt until the mixture resembles coarse corn meal. Add enough cold water to make a stiff dough. Roll out into eight 5-inch squares. Arrange the vegetables and beef on half of each one. First add the potatoes, then the onions, and lastly the thinly sliced and then cut-up meat (½-inch pieces). Sprinkle with salt and pepper, dot with butter, and fold the other halves of the squares of pastry over over the fillings to form triangles. Moisten the edges with water and pinch to seal them. The trick is to close it tightly in order to retain the steam that develops during the cooking. That makes a juicy filling. Bake on a cooky sheet in a moderate oven, 350°, about 40 minutes. Some families bake one large pasty for a meal, and frequently use a chop plate as the pattern for cutting it.

The Big Lake People Like Perch

Many gourmets insist that buttered Fordhook lima beans, either the fresh or frozen ones, make the perfect companion for baked or broiled whitefish. In Michigan this fish lives up to its reputation as the finest of the fresh water species. People also have a high regard for lake trout, perch, and smelt. When the perch come in during the spring, especially to the shores of the Big Lake, as Lake Michigan is called, almost everyone within driving distance begins talking about how fine they will be for dinner tomorrow or the next day.

The beginning of the smelt run is greeted with something like the same enthusiasm. All the smelt in the Great Lakes came from the East, mainly New England. They were brought in primarily as food for landlocked salmon when this species was introduced. The salmon project failed, but the smelt multiplied so successfully that they now form the basis of an important industry.

A home cook snips off the heads of the fresh-from-the-water smelt with scissors and slits and washes them thoroughly. They are without scales. Then she rolls them in seasoned corn meal or in a batter and in cracker crumbs. After that she pan-fries or fries them. Many home chefs hold that a bit of brown sugar mixed with the corn meal is desirable in pan-frying. Others believe the use of two kettles of hot fat provides the best system, and the idea is to immerse the fish briefly in both — a trick borrowed from successful public eating places. That way, they point out, a fish always is in very hot fat, save for the instant when it is being transferred from one kettle to the other. The idea is to fry the smelt in about 3 minutes or less. The crust must be very crisp. People eat the bones and all. The spawning runs are made up of smelt from 7 to 9 inches long, while those in the Big Lake sometimes are 14 inches in length.

Beef and pork win compliments for the meal planners and cooks. Some women who rate as the culinary artists of their neighborhoods possess real talent with ham loaves. Most of these meaty dishes contain both ground ham and pork as well as soft bread crumbs, milk, and eggs. When the loaf is in the pan they pour over cooked or canned tomatoes, seasoned with salt and a little sugar. They first bake it covered. Then they remove the lid for the last half hour. Often it is sent to the table with mustard sauce as the escort. Many roasts, pot roasts, and meat loaves are covered with celery leaves during the cooking. A business home economist living in Battle Creek, who was reared on a southern Michigan farm, lists the popular platter treats of her community as fried chicken, country style, beef pot roasts with whole onions and carrots, veal birds, baked steak, pork loin roasts with cinnamon apples, and sauerkraut with pig hocks.

One of the favored meat combinations today, especially with the teen-agers, answers to the informal name *Sloppy Joe's*. It is a ground beef-onion mixture, browned and seasoned, and with canned tomato sauce stirred in. The custom is to serve it between the split halves of hot or toasted hamburger buns. It is the simplest of a whole flock of barbecued sandwiches that are much used and appreciated.

People throng to the Dutch communities every spring to *ah!* and *oh!* over the many varieties of exotic tulips. Some women visitors stop at the local bakeries, too. The macaroons — almond, coconut, and chocolate — always intrigue, as do the kitten tongues, ladyfingers, and figure 8's. Many family kitchens, as well as the bakeries, at Christmas time turn out almond rolls to mail and carry to friends and enjoy at home. This treat is called *Bankette.*

BANKETTE

1 cup butter	1 egg slightly beaten
2 cups flour, sifted	¾ cup sugar
½ cup ice water	¼ cup cornstarch
½ pound almond paste	

Cut the butter into the all-purpose flour as for pastry. Add the water and mix. Refrigerate overnight or long enough to chill thoroughly. Roll out ¼ inch thick and in a rectangle about 4 by 12 inches. Crumble the almond paste (¾ cupful) and add the slightly beaten egg, sugar, and cornstarch, and blend together. Then shape the almond paste mixture into a roll about ¾ inch in diameter. Place this roll on the pastry, and roll the pastry around it. Close the seams tightly with the fingers dipped in water. Some women prefer to seal it with egg whites. It is important to do a good job so as to keep the filling from oozing out during the baking. Place on a greased baking sheet seam side down. Bake in a hot oven, 400°, for 30 minutes, then set the heat regulator at 325°. Bake 15 minutes longer. Slice the cooled roll with a sharp knife as desired.

People bestow many compliments on *oliebollen,* or Dutch fritters. *Fat balls,* as they commonly are called, are made by frying spoonfuls of a soft, light yeast dough like that used for doughnuts in deep fat. A food reporter notes that doughnuts in this territory, as in some homes of up-state New York, are known by their leavening. Those made with yeast dough are *doughnuts,* and the ones from a quick dough containing baking powder are *fried cakes.* Waffles, too, are extremely well liked by people of Dutch extraction and their neighbors.

Thrilling Suppers at the Lake

I tasted another food specialty of the Dutch and some people living in other communities, *hot pigs in the blanket,* in a supper at a lake cottage. Such jolly meals are a definition for good food and fun wrapped together. The menu was perfect for a cool summer evening. We dined on a porch overlooking water that mirrored the surrounding trees and the sunset colors of the sky.

LAKE SUPPER
Hot Pigs in the Blanket
Tart Potato Salad
Corn-on-the-Cob
Assorted Vegetable Relishes
Peaches and Cream
Orange-Chocolate Cookies

My hostess demonstrated how to make the pigs in the blanket, a delightful hot sandwich.

She mixed 1 pound of pork sausage, 3 crushed rusks, 1 egg, and 1 cup of milk, and seasoned the composition with a little salt and a few twirls of a pepper mill. She shaped it like frankfurts, or as she said, "Like fingers 1 inch in diameter." Then she cooked the meat slowly in a frying pan, not to brown, but to steam and thus remove some of the fat. After that she rolled light yeast dough thin, cut it in rectangles, and wrapped each little sausage in one, sealing the edges. She let the pigs rise a few minutes. Then she ran a baking sheet covered with them into a moderately hot oven, 375°, baked them, and served them hurried from the oven to the table. She said she substitutes biscuit dough for the yeast one on some occasions, and then pricks every pig's blanket several times with a fork before baking it. Also she sometimes makes the pigs of 1 pound of ground lean pork mixed with ¼ pound of ground beef.

Supper at the lake! That connotes Michigan and summertime. People eat their picnic meals by the side of the road, in the woods, on the shores, or in their dining rooms within view of the water. Many families have summer houses only a few miles from their town homes. As the week grows old they frequently invite some of their friends who do not have a place at the lake to drive out for a Saturday supper or for dinner on Sunday. And the guests, according to the traditional custom, usually take along food for a hostess present, such as a big chocolate cake — in some homes this means a layer yellow cake with chocolate frosting — or a batch of cookies.

On week-ends everyone travels on wheels, or at least

has an ambition to do so, for this is the land of motor car outings. Also it is the home of many, many lakes, such as those along its borders, Erie, St. Clair, Huron, Michigan, and Superior, and almost countless crystal clear inland ones. Delicious food and surprisingly cosmopolitan dishes characterize the cuisine. In the gaiety and number of food festivals it vies with its buddies, Wisconsin and Minnesota. That is logical. Only a delightful lake crossing separates Michigan from Badger territory, the neighborly state to the west.

Food Traditions Provide Pleasant Memories

Wisconsin is a hotbed of good cooks. They, like their friends in Michigan and Minnesota, turn out meals with an international flavor. Indeed, you may dine from one end of Europe to the other in the state. Most of the women who brought the blueprints for Old World cookery from overseas have gone, but their grandchildren relish many of the dishes on which they grew up. They cling to food traditions as the only connecting link with the native lands of their forefathers.

As a food reporter leisurely eats a fruit-topped *kolache,* the hostess regales her and other guests with colorful tales of a Czech grandmother's bustling kitchen. There she learned by affectionate guidance how to make the heavenly tasting yeast-leavened rolls. In other quarters sincere praise exalts thin Swedish pancakes and marble-sized meat balls in brown gravy, a galaxy of German tortes that wear hats of whipped cream, savory Welsh pasties spouting steam and fragrance when cut at the table, berry filled pies with Belgium-style crusts, *lefse* — a flat Norwegian potato bread — and many more heirloom treasures. These and other imported dishes fit into the state scene as harmoniously as the sleek black and white cows that dot the landscape. While some of the old-time recipes are followed faithfully, most of them have been altered by that magic called Americanization.

Anyone who appreciates the cultural background of Wisconsin is alert to the frequent talk, especially in the

East, about how the cuisines of all the central states are alike, and consist mainly of meat and potatoes. Through many such dissertations I have suffered to abide an opportunity to speak. In these minutes of painful waiting a standard rebuttal has evolved to meet the challenge. In it I climb out of the saddle in the short grass country of western Kansas and go off to school in Wisconsin. There, I explain, my eyes opened to the food differences among the Heart of America states — and there I took my first trip to Europe!

A School Girl's Diary

To recapture some of my early impressions of Wisconsin foods I resurrected my diary of college years. Tucked here and there between references to examinations, budget troubles, canoe trips, ice boating, and what he and she said and did are recorded a few gastronomic discoveries in the style of a home economics food major ambitious to do an acceptable job.

"Tortes usually are the dinner desserts when I visit the homes of my friends. They are of infinite variety. My favorite is called *schaum torte*. It is quite unlike anything we have in Kansas. The sweet, crisp meringue browns lightly during baking. Then it's split and filled to overflowing with whipped cream and fully ripe strawberries. Out of this world in taste!

"On the canoe trip we stopped at a lovely green spot along the shores of Lake Mendota. Jack cooked squaw corn. People here eat this hearty dish with dashes of ketchup or chili sauce.

"At Helen's and Bob's the dessert was a steamed cranberry pudding with a smooth, rich, sugar-and-cream sauce. Mrs. H. says this hot dessert is the Wisconsin Christmas pudding.

"Ate my first real German dinner. Heavy. Sauerbraten, potato dumplings, and cheese cake, with coffee.

"Macaroni and cheese surprises out-of-the-state students. As much cheese as macaroni gets into the dish. Excellent.

"Rutabagas are served much more than they are at home, and they taste sweeter.

"Soups are filling, almost a complete meal. Instead of being made with beef and vegetables in Kansas ranch style, often they're a thin rich with butter white sauce with a sieved cooked vegetable, or vegetables, added.

"Sauerkraut is cooked in all languages. Boy Scout troops like it with wieners for their suppers, as boys in the Sunflower State choose hamburgers in buns.

"Cheese soufflés are luncheon favorites. As a standard Saturday supper they never disappoint. I marvel at their height and wonder why they don't fall.

"Coffee cakes and sweet rolls tease you to eat. Some of them have a faint taste of cardamom. But no rolls on this planet earth surpass the *kolache*. I've sworn allegiance to both the apricot- and prune-topped ones for the rest of my life.

A Bratwurst Sandwich Hits the Spot

"In Milwaukee we stopped at a stand on the shore of Lake Michigan for a bratwurst sandwich. It resembles a hot dog, only the cooked sausage is larger than a wiener. It is browned on a grill, and plunked between a split long bun. Hits the spot if you're hungry.

"Enjoyed my first Cornish dinner at the Hopkins' home. (Dorothy says in her home near Fort Atkinson a pasty comes to the dinner table every Thursday. Salt and black pepper are the seasonings.) For dessert we had Devonshire or clotted cream with plum preserves, and a light fruit cake yellow with saffron. Neither Mr. H. nor I cared for the cake.

"Excellent whitefish finds the platter on many Fridays.

"You just don't have much pie without aged cheddar cheese — the Wisconsin kind.

"Wild red raspberry jam — there's a treat for you. I honestly concede it is as super delicious as the sand hill plum butter of Ford County, Kansas. That's quite a concession!"

These observations of a school girl suggest the outstanding characteristics of the cuisine. To a surprising extent they outline many of the present variations between the meals of the area and those in Kansas. About the only change is that some of the long-time Wisconsin favorites now are accepted by the Plains States. *Schaum torte* offers an example. It appears at parties and special occasion meals far from Lake Michigan's shores.

"Use Butter for Its Taste"

The cooks' chorus in this dairyland joyfully chants, "Flavor with butter." Scarcely a recipe is described without the caution, "Use butter for its taste" — a statement that speaks for a universal belief in the goodness of churned cream.

Tourists rarely complain that cheese is difficult to locate at mealtime, for almost all kinds enjoyed by Americans are produced and distributed in the state. Many varieties duplicate old-world types. Their English, French, Dutch, Italian, and Scandinavian names designate their origins.

Although the old custom of serving cheese slices in the main course still holds, uncounted mouth-watering dishes also feature this dairy food as an important ingredient. "Cheese soufflé," according to a Madison home economics friend who with her radio programs is in close contact with women all over the state, "symbolizes Wisconsin as batter bread connotes Virginia. In their respective locales each of these majestic dishes comes from the ovens as tall as a gentleman's silk hat. Thoughts of the traditional supper or luncheon that spotlights the soufflé makes all Badger hearts beat a little faster."

SATURDAY SUPPER
Cheese Soufflé
Buttered Peas
Hot Rolls   Pickles
Fruit Salad

Sometimes glasses of chilled tomato juice start the meal. The salad takes a duel role — both the salad and dessert ones. Broccoli, spinach, and other green vegetables substitute at times for the peas. Their selection depends primarily on the season. For a more substantial meal, or when there are guests, ribbons of bacon or slices of baked ham escort the soufflé.

"Why not call the macaroni and cheese *Wisconsin cheese and macaroni?*" a visitor asked. It is an appropriate question, for equal parts of the two foods are placed in the baking dish.

To a pound of each about 2 cups of milk are poured over. Favored seasonings to scatter between the layers include dry mustard, salt, melted butter, Worcestershire sauce, sliced pimento, sliced stuffed olives, cubes of canned corned beef, shreds of dried beef, diced celery, small oysters, bits of cooked or canned fish, and thin strips of salami.

The cook butters the baking dish, starts with the boiled macaroni, and adds it and alternate layers of cut-up cheddar cheese. The yellow cheese is on top. After she pours in the milk she crumbles on a few crackers. Then, true to the Wisconsin tradition, she adds dots of butter.

Two minutes before she takes the cheese and macaroni from the oven she scatters on shredded Swiss cheese for that final taste touch.

In the kitchen as she works and talks to a food reporter she emphasizes in no uncertain manner, "We never cook Swiss cheese. To us that is a punishable crime. We add it at the zero hour, 2 minutes before the hot food is served. Usually we scatter shreds of it on steaming soups just before we carry the bowls to the table. And when the hamburger is in the bun we tuck in thin strips of it for our classic *swissburger*."

Here Come the Cheese Sandwiches

Cheese sandwiches glorify everyday meals with about the same frequency hot biscuits glorify those of the South. Among the popular cold types is one that resembles a New York favorite. Badgers build their sandwich with slices of sweet onion, butter, rye bread, and Swiss cheese, while New Yorkers generally use a sharp cheddar cheese. A rule passed from person to person, often by men, is to soak the onion slices a half hour in cold, salted water, and then to drain them, before sandwich making starts. Only extremely thick slices of Swiss cheese qualify for sandwich making — "thick as the bread," some gentlemen say.

Juicy red apples and cheese unite in numerous dishes when autumn foliage spreads its glow over the countryside. An old-fashioned sandwich that remains popular is toasted in two ways, with word bouquets and by the oven. The hostess lifts pan-fried apple rings to crunchy slices of buttered toast. She places rather thin cheddar cheese slices on top. Then she runs these open-face creations into the oven long enough to melt the cheese. To complete the set-up for a perfect October evening she lists other requirements. Crisp hearts of celery, cups of hot cocoa or tea, and stacks of raisin-nut cookies do the honors for food. Then with six or eight congenial guests who like to talk, a lively crackling fire on the hearth, and a bright harvest moon gleaming through the window — what else is there to wish for?

Smooth, velvety cheese sauce lends its cheery color and zippy flavor to scalloped and creamed dishes. "Just use it in any creamed dish," a native cook suggests. "It is most diplomatic and gets along well with fish, meat, vegetables, breads, and fruits."

Salads Resemble Costume Jewels

Red and white stand for Wisconsin, as loyal Badgers know. For red and white on salad plates, tomato aspic and cheese satisfy. Some cooks push spoonfuls of the cooled cheese into the jelly just before it congeals. Others fold it in as the aspic starts to thicken. Either way, the trim often is mayonnaise dolled up with finely cut cucumber in summer, chopped cucumber pickle in winter.

Cheese rings are fancy enough for guest meals and buffet suppers, and tasty enough to start a flow of compliments. Generally colorful fruits — fresh, frozen, or canned — decorate the service. Hostesses heap them in the center of the ring which may contain one or several kinds of cheese. Cream cheese — a mixture of cream and blue cheeses — and cottage cheese most frequently win this glamorous role. Heated, salted crackers accompany the salad. Cole slaw and German potato salad also personify Wisconsin.

When men entertain, the Dutch lunch gets a break. They select sturdy fare like cold cuts. These are likely to include liver sausage, salami, thuringer and other smoked sausages, corned beef, and ham. Then there are potato chips, German potato salad, rye bread, and several kinds of cheeses. To sample them spread out on a table tastes like a cook's tour of Europe — Gouda, Swiss, blue, brick, one that contains caraway seeds, an Italian variety such as *Provalone* or *Asiago,* and *Nokkelost* — the Norwegian cheese flavored with cloves.

Large trays of sweet onion slices, after soaking half an hour in salted cold water, and drained, occupy an important place in the menu. Beer and coffee are the beverages.

Anyone traveling in the area soon realizes he is in the Heart of America gelatin belt, the region where jellied salads and desserts assume great prominence in the finest meals. Tomato aspic with cottage cheese has been described. Countless other successes quiver under the slightest touch of a fork, a testimony for their delicacy. Canned fruits assume leadership in all varieties of winter time salads and desserts. Cooks display a touch of genius in featuring the sirups drained from them to make the jelly. For example, *pear sirup,* pointed up with a few drops of lemon juice and gelatinized, holds diced oranges and seeded green grapes with distinction.

Canned Pear Halves Appear With Cheese

Canned pear halves, after the hollows are filled with a few drained canned red cherries, turn their cut sides down on greens as if to hide the prize. Their tops often carry tempting shreds of pimento or plain cheddar cheese or crumbled blue cheese decorations. Another treat features fresh or canned pear halves, cut side up, on greens; their cavities overflow with red cranberry relish or cranberry-orange relish. Spiced peach halves heaped with the crimson sauce long have dressed salad plates in a gay mood. Natives like this one best with chicken or pork. The color comes from berries which grow in the local marshes that blush in autumn with their harvest.

Cherry flavored gelatin, women say, is just right if made with pineapple juice as the liquid. They fold in the un cooked cranberry-orange relish as it starts to thicken. With fish, as with chicken and pork, they say it is not easily sur passed. Many cooks add pieces of pineapple to the salad. They also mold small chunks of pineapple and balls of cream cheese containing nuts in lemon flavored gelatin. And they gelatinize hot sweetened applesauce, and chill and mold it. Usually they subtly flavor the mayonnaise for it with nutmeg.

It is just one of the salads that unite so satisfactorily with toasted cheese sandwiches to make luncheon on a snowy day a heart-warming experience.

Every season boasts of topnotch salads. Apple cider salad comes with September as regularly as the feel of frost in the air and boisterous cheers from football stadiums. In it sweet cider and gelatin join forces and hold chopped red-skinned apples, nuts, and celery.

For spring, dainty cream cheese balls rolled in chopped nuts and red-ripe strawberries alternate in the ring mold. Raspberry or strawberry flavored gelatin immerses them. "A pretty dish, that is what it is," confided a hostess. "It has eye appeal, so important during the spring fever days. And it suggests the ladylike blossoms in the woods."

Throughout the year the salad bowls, like those in most of the United States, present the mixed green salad leaves glistening with French dressing. Wisconsin cooks venture even farther. They cannot resist tossing in a few slivers of yellow cheddar, crumbs of blue, or slivers of pale honey-colored Swiss cheese. And when the snow beats against the windows and the countryside turns a pure white, women open cans of their thinly sliced bread-and-butter pickles and distribute a few of them in the green salad. That gives a favored spicy touch.

The Chili Sauce Was Heated

Most families vote for pickles as the A-1 accessory food. The popularity of these appetizers goes back to pioneer days when women knew — as they do today — that an enjoyable relish can lift a plain meal above the commonplace. Cucumber pickles rank first, with *chunk* and *bread-and-butter types* the topnotchers. The latter are in such thin slices! Cooks explain why; they use vegetable slicers rather than knives in cutting the cucumbers. Mustard and dill pickles are other favorites.

Chili sauce also repeatedly rakes in medals in the relish class. And no wonder! The natives use it in so many ways.

At a guest dinner near Green Bay, roast pork assumed the position of honor on the platter. Like flowers surrounding it were tiny hot cooked and scooped out turnips buttered and filled with the red of heated chili sauce. Either chili sauce or ketchup, as mentioned, traditionally associates with squaw corn, the entree of the nothern woods, canoe trips, and of the luncheon on Saturday when the youngsters are home from school.

Squaw Corn Arrived Early

Squaw corn came to Wisconsin soon after the white men started to build houses — or before! Possibly someone carried it from New England, where it seems to have originated. Lumberjacks of the fabulous North Woods made it with dried corn and bacon until the convenient creamed style of canned corn came along. Then they switched to it. Sportsmen and school boys say it still is their favorite, although green corn cut from the cobs, frozen corn, and the canned whole kernels will do. Frequently both onion and green pepper are pan-fried in the bacon drippings before the corn is added. And in this region where sausages are so much in demand, mothers often brown slices of frankfurts in the frying pan before they dump in the corn.

Warm meat-vegetable casseroles put pep into daily winter meals. Lima beans and sausages pair off in one stand-by. Cole slaw goes with it. And what observing visitor fails to note that sauerkraut and wieners typify Wisconsin in much the same way chili con carne personifies New Mexico?

Every nationality group springs its own tricks with sauerkraut. It is amazing how all of them taste just right. Almost all cooks agree that a proverbial pinch of sugar is one touch of magic in all sauerkraut dishes. A trace of sugar also qualifies as a Wisconsin cook's idea of how to improve the taste of root vegetables such as rutabagas, carrots, and turnips. She adds it with the other seasonings. Winter squash ranks as a favorite throughout the state, too. (It is much the same story in all the North Country across the United States; the people there like and extensively use the root vegetables and winter squash.)

Broccoli, cauliflower, and cabbage illustrate beautifully the popularity of butter and cheese for seasoning. Cooks briefly boil these vegetables uncovered in salty water until they are just barely tender. They serve them with melted butter doused over and grated cheese — usually cheddar — sprinkled on. Women sometimes send a cruet of soy sauce or vinegar to the table with them. Red cabbage is extensively enjoyed. Natives add acid to protect the elusive color during the cooking and to give additional flavor. Vinegar or sliced sour apples most frequently team with the vegetable. German communities prefer the fruit.

The home chefs have an interesting habit of parboiling whole small onions until partly tender in salted water, after which they drain them. Then they immerse them in cheese sauce for the remainder of the gentle cooking. Peas grow on a commercial scale, and like the marvelous sweet corn they enjoy wide prestige. Usually both are cooked quickly in water and dressed with butter. Some families like the taste of cream, unthickened, in peas. A Polish custom used in serving cooked cauliflower, cabbage, green beans, and asparagus has been widely accepted. Cooks carefully brown soft bread crumbs in butter and pour the mixture over the hot vegetable.

For festive dinners a Wisconsin hostess adores presenting platters of cooked vegetables. They provide an exhibit of the beauty of many of the gifts from the state's gardens.

The Savory Soups Satisfy

Three words describe the soups — *tasty, hearty,* and *satisfying.* Step into a kitchen on a cold day and sniff the split pea soup — no wonder the people are happy to be alive. Take a few spoonfuls, taste the spicy bits of sausage in it, and then revel in the full-bodied flavor that comes from the steaming kettle. That is one Wisconsin soup story.

Perhaps the cream soups outstrip all others for distinctive

regional appeal. Their foundation consists of a thin, butter flavored, smooth white sauce paired off with a single cooked and sieved vegetable, or a medley of vegetables. Cream of tomato, pea, mushroom, spinach, corn, and asparagus win much approval. Shreds of yellow or Swiss cheese generally decorate these soups. At the men's residence halls of the University of Wisconsin the soup headliner features cooked tomatoes, potatoes, carrots, celery, and onions sieved into the piping hot white sauce. Sometimes this Cardinal vegetable soup is put together with white sauce made of equal parts of milk and beef stock and the mixture of vegetables.

Fish talk abounds, and gifts from the Great Lakes challenge the cooks. Naturally, in such an environment, the fish dishes usually reach a high plane of tastiness. Frequently they attain the peak of perfection. The lake food, and also that from rivers, probably awakens more enthusiasm in the cities than in rural homes. Most people revere whitefish, trout, and perch. Ardent fans also praise bass, wall-eyed pike, muskellunge, and pickerel. Whitefish livers are at a premium, and the canned eggs command high prestige as American caviar.

A trio of fastidious women — all alert, imaginative cooks — invited me into their kitchens to watch a play-by-play preparation of their favorite dishes. Their creations demonstrate fish cookery at its best.

Trout fresh from Lake Michigan answered in the Port Washington call. This is how it was prepared.

Place a fish that weighs 3 to 3½ pounds, split in halves, and with the bones removed, skin down, in a shallow, greased baking dish. Sprinkle salt, pepper, and ¼ cup of lemon juice over it, pour on a cup of heavy cream, and scatter ¼ pound, or about 1¼ cups, of shredded aged cheddar cheese over the cream. Bake 25 minutes in a very hot oven, 450°, and lo! an elegant dish comes forth to delight hungry people.

WISCONSIN FISH DINNER
Baked Trout, Port Washington
French Fried Potatoes
Cole Slaw
Cherry Pie

Fillets of whitefish, fresh out of Lake Superior's cold water at Ashland, carry the lead role in the second au gratin delicacy.

The cook makes the white sauce with 2½ cups of whole milk, 5 tablespoons each of butter and flour, and seasonings of salt and pepper. She measures ¾ cup of shredded aged cheddar cheese and fills a shallow baking dish with alternate layers of the sauce, cheese, and fillets (2 pounds) cut in cubes, starting and ending with the sauce. There are at least two layers of cheese and fish. She sprinkles the fish with salt and pepper, and dribbles on lemon juice. After it has been baked in a moderate oven, about 350°, about 40 minutes, the dish is something to rave about. (Connoisseurs pronounce whitefish fresh from the chilly depths of Lake Superior and promptly grilled a masterpiece of the region. Who would question their judgment?)

Barbecued fish are highly welcome in Milwaukee, and to some extent in many other cities and towns. Trout, whitefish, and bass are excellent selections. My Milwaukee hostess brought out a dressed fish weighing between 3 and 4 pounds. She placed it in a greased shallow pan and sprinkled on salt. Over it she poured the barbecue sauce. Then she baked it about 45 minutes in a moderate oven, 375°.

Barbecue sauces vary, but she quickly mixes her favorite.

She browns 2 tablespoons of finely chopped onions in a bit of fat, about a tablespoonful. To this she adds 1 cup of tomato ketchup, 2 tablespoons of vinegar, ¼ cup of lemon juice, 3 tablespoons of Worcestershire sauce, 2 tablespoons of brown sugar, ½ teaspoon of salt, and a dash of pepper. After the mixture simmers 5 minutes she pours it bubbling hot over the fish.

The regional fish dinner, as already indicated, presents potatoes of some kind — usually French fried, scalloped, or au gratin. Stewed tomatoes, luscious with the taste of butter and delicate with a subtle suggestion of basil, give cole slaw a run for a place in the menu. Cherry pie walks away with the dessert honors.

Meats, in Wisconsin Styles

Platters reflect the cooking artistry of all or almost all European nations and races. (How many nations? That is anyone's guess, but when the state of Wisconsin's birthday cake in 1948 had 100 candles the Wisconsin Home Economics Association published a collection of recipes for the favorite nationality foods. The treasures came from home kitchens. *Folkways in Foods* presents directions for making dishes of Belgian, Bohemian, Croatian, Danish, Dutch, English, Finnish, French, German, Italian, Jewish, Lithuanian, Norwegian, Polish, Scotch, Swedish, Swiss, and Welsh descents.)

Sauerbraten with gingersnap gravy, pork shanks with potatoes and sauerkraut, veal birds, Hungarian veal paprika, veal cooked with sour cream gravy, and veal balls in tomato sauce illustrate a few of the immortals. Upside-down ham-cranberry loaves deserve a mention. The meat mixture is pressed into a pan spread first with a sprinkling of brown sugar and then with thick cranberry sauce. When baked the showpiece is inverted to exhibit its colorful crown.

Ham rolls with cheese sauce offer an admirable example of how meat and cheese prosper in the hands of culinary artists. Women spread ground cooked ham, seasoned with mustard, on a sheet of biscuit dough, roll it like a jelly roll, and then slice and bake the pinwheels. They serve cheese sauce over the filled spirals, which indicates how the yellow sauce occupies the spotlight accorded gravy in some places.

To acquire a perspective on some intriguing sausages, a visit to Sheboygan, Green Bay, or Milwaukee is rewarding. In these and other urban centers the array of the varied German types interests everyone with a curiosity about what Americans like to eat. The *bratwurst* of Milwaukee contains veal with some pork, and is cooked. It is enjoyed broiled, in the home, and on outdoor grills. Due to its veal content, the sausage does not fry out like pork sausage. Then there is *bockwurst*, a highly specialized product. Markets carry it from about New Year's Day until Easter. It is composed of veal, eggs, and chives or parsley with seasonings. This sausage has a high moisture content, and is quite perishable. That explains why its season is brief.

Marie Antoinette is reported to have asked why men and

women rioting outside the palace at Versailles with cries for bread did not eat cake. Ask a native of the Badger State why he eats bread instead of cake and he is likely to reply, "Because it tastes so good." Some of the local breads justify the sincere praise. In variety they are about as numerous as the sailboats on any shimmering inland lake. Many of them qualify as worthy entries for state fair exhibits. Indeed, Wisconsin is in the center of what remains of the area famed for the superiority of home-baked yeast breads.

When a visitor from afar receives an invitation to a tea in Milwaukee or any of a number of other cities she frequently is surprised to find when she arrives at the party scene that only coffee streams from the gleaming silver spouts. And the trays display tempting, fancy breads instead of cakes. The bite-sized rolls are delicate, dainty, sugary, and sometimes spicy. They melt in the mouth.

The *Bohemian tart,* a party type of *kolache,* tempts at some of these gala occasions. Teaspoons of the light yeast dough yield wee tarts. The trick is to pat this soft dough — scarcely more than a heaping thimbleful of it — into an oblong shape. Then a scant teaspoon of the filling, identical with that used for a larger kolache, is placed on the center of the dough. Cooks splash it with finely chopped nuts. They punch a hole in each end of the oblong dough and lift up one end, twist it, and lay the opening over the luscious filling so it shows. The process is repeated with the other end. Then they crowd these fruit-topped baby rolls close together in a greased pan. After they are light the oven claims them. When women proudly take the exotic fragrance from the oven they dust on confectioners' sugar. The teatime dream has come true!

A kolache for family meals commonly measures from 4 to 5 inches in diameter. When the "cooky," or circle of yeast dough, is light, cooks press the center down with their fingers, and add the filling. A thin rim of dough surrounds and extends a little above it.

KOLACHE

1 cup butter or other shortening	2 cakes compressed yeast
½ cup sugar	2 cups milk
¼ teaspoon mace	1 teaspoon salt
4 egg yolks	Flour to make soft dough

Cream shortening, add sugar, and cream again. Add beaten egg yolks, the milk scalded and cooled until lukewarm, and yeast dissolved in a little of the tepid milk. Stir in flour to make a soft dough. Let it rise until double in bulk. Then roll it out like biscuit dough, 1 inch thick, and cut in circles with a cutter 2 inches in diameter. Make a dent in the center of each circle with a finger. Spread with fruit, jam, or other filling. Brush with melted shortening. Let the dough rise until the kolaches are double in size. Bake in a hot oven, 425°, about 20 minutes.

In the informal poll among the brigade of cooks I engaged in kolache talk, the fillings listed in the degree of popularity were poppy seed, cottage cheese, prune, apricot, and date-nut. Dried fruits, cooked until thick and sweetened, and subtly spiced, make the prune and apricot fillings.

People of Bohemian descent ardently support their preference for the poppy seed concoction. "Just taste," they say, as they pass the wonderous proof of their wisdom. To make it they grind poppy seed and stir 1 cup of it and ½ cup of sugar into ½ cup of heavy cream. They heat the mixture slowly and gently just long enough to melt the sugar.

Holiday Breads Crossed the Ocean

The North Central American descendants of many European nations brag about their excellent loaves of breads and coffee cakes. And why not? Their yeast-leavened creations deserve extravagant adjectives. The coffee cakes not only grace the breakfast table; they hold forth for mid-morning and mid-afternoon refreshment with coffee. They associate with fruit compotes in the dessert course at luncheon, dinner, and supper. One of my home economics friends, a native of Wausau and now a resident of Nebraska, says her idea of dessert luxury is cinnamon coffee cake like her mother makes when served with applesauce or other fruit and coffee.

Strudels, stollens, prune ladders, cardamom rings, Danish

kringles, and *houska* are but a few of the famous loaves. Most European nations prize historic breads, especially for the Christmas and Easter seasons. Because the United States, where wheat flour is abundant, has no traditional loaves for special occasions, Wisconsin families take their grandmothers' recipes — fondly carried across the Atlantic Ocean — and adapt them to the American scene, often with the aid of home economists. The light loaves usually are laden with fruits and tasty with spices. Among the choice Christmas breads described most glowingly are the *Norwegian Jule Kage,* the *Danish Soster Kage, stollen,* and a braided Bohemian loaf, *Vanocka.*

Recipes for these and other exotic North Central breads could easily and magnificently fill a chapter in a cook book. To select only one entitled to blue ribbons is about as easy for a roving food scout as to stand on a Wisconsin wind-kissed hill early in winter, while the clouds spit giant-sized snow-flakes, and attempt to decide which flakes deserve beauty awards. The common denominator of snowflakes is their pristine beauty. All the fancy breads, if analyzed, possess a common characteristic — it is a soft yeast dough, delicately flavored, faintly sweetened, and rich with eggs and butter.

Like the Crescent of a New Moon

I watched a cook turn out what she calls *Christmas crescents.* The dough carries a tinge of nutmeg and shredded lemon rind. She rolls it in the shape of a triangle, and about 1/3 inch thick. Then she spreads chopped dates, nuts, drained red and green maraschino cherries, and candied pineapple over its surface. She starts at the wide end and rolls the dough like a jelly roll. Then she shapes it on the greased baking sheet like the crescent of a new moon, bakes it, and then frosts the golden brown-crusted bread. Its fragrance! Words fail to express it!

Frostings for fancy breads are thin — just a light, sweet jacket. To make them women frequently stir 2 tablespoons of boiling water and a teaspoon of lemon juice into 1½ cups of confectioners' sugar. They also sprinkle some doughs with equal parts of coconut and sugar before baking, and in this way eliminate the frosting.

The fruited loaves do not overshadow Scandinavian and other types of rye breads and salted rolls so flavorful when served with cheese. White bread, made with milk as the liquid, hot from the oven, and sliced and spread with wild raspberry jam, provides unforgettable eating pleasure. Memories of how this homely snack tasted in warm kitchens after the trek home from school through the cold are what former Badgers high in The Loop skyscrapers of Chicago frequently talk about when they enchantingly speak to a food reporter of their childhood memories.

Quick breads, tasty with fruits, have their friends. Although they are comparatively lightweight competitors for the yeast-leavened loaves, their popularity is growing. *Cranberry-nut,* flavored with shredded orange peel; *date-nut,* and *banana-nut* breads spell sandwich success. Many households keep these home-baked, cooled, and wrapped loaves in freezers as an aid to on-the-spur-of-the-moment hospitality. All they require is quick slicing and spreading with butter or cream cheese.

Muffins of all kinds are stirred up confidently and quickly. Those containing cranberries, apples, and blueberries are universal favorites. Wisconsin also is a dumpling center. Some of the more noted numbers contain liver, other ground meats, parsley, and cheese. And who misses potato dumplings in jaunts about the state?

Every racial group prefers and makes its own style of doughnuts. Most of them are yeast-leavened. These tempting treats show up regularly on the region's tables.

Tortes Lead the Desserts

Whipped cream frosting distinguishes the cakes, which in other respects resemble those baked elsewhere. After it is sweetened and flavored, the fluffy cream is spread on the layers or loaves shortly before they are served. If added earlier the cake goes into the refrigerator for safe keeping. The cream carries many flavors, like that of shredded orange and lemon peels, burnt sugar sirup, coconut, crushed pineapple, and melted chocolate. Some homemakers mix 1 cup of powdered sugar, 6 tablespoons of cocoa, and 2 cups of whipping cream. They chill it for 3 hours and then whip it to spreading consistency. After that they flavor it with vanilla and frost the cake. Butter-rich frostings vie with the whipped cream ones for the state-wide championship.

Some women win their cooking spurs with what they call a *quick cream frosting*. This is how they make it.

Scald 2 cups of milk and add ⅓ cup each of sugar and all-purpose flour and ¼ teaspoon of salt, blended. Cook slowly, stirring constantly, until the mixture thickens and becomes smooth. Cool, chill, and keep covered in the refrigerator until ready for use. When it is time to frost the cake, cream 1 cup each of butter and powdered sugar together until very light and add 1 teaspoon of vanilla. Stir the two mixtures together and whip with the beater until the combination is light and fluffy. Spread the frosting between the layers and on the tops and sides of the cake. Sprinkle with toasted and salted nuts.

Between the ardent popularity of fancy yeast breads and tortes, both cakes and pies compete for recognition. The *torte,* especially along Lake Michigan's shores, leads all other desserts. Visitors consider it one of the distinctive food clues to the region — it is a sure sign of Wisconsin.

Schaum torte is the queen. Other charming, rich, and tasty members of this branch of the dessert family include almond-jelly, apricot-almond, butterscotch-nut, bread crumb-pineapple, baked cottage cheese, pineapple-cheese, chocolate-butter, cranberry-eggnog, jelly-sour cream, lemon, mocha, orange, pecan, pistachio-orange, poppy seed, rum, carrot, chocolate-potato, apple, maraschino cherry, and blitz tortes. While this list is by no means complete, it indicates something of the tremendous variety.

Pies really never lack for favorable attention especially if they carry cherry, lemon meringue, apple, pumpkin, mince, cranberry, cranberry-nut, cranberry-raisin, or red raspberry fillings. Cheese is married to all of them execpt the lemon meringue. Wedges of pie, triangles of nippy cheese, and coffee! Where is the loyal Badger who has not thrilled to such a dessert?

Pie à la mode and sundaes also end many meals. Visitors in Wisconsin almost always note the superior quality of much of the ice cream. Natives define a gallon of it and an assortment of sauces in the freezer as an aid to hospitality. They say, "Just let our friends come when they can. An easy-to-fix sundae will show up during the evening without kitchen commotion." A spring dessert dear to many a native's heart is vanilla ice cream on angel food cake slices with lemon sauce ladled over — plus tea.

Cookies Are Highly Popular

Although cooky baking flourishes throughout the year, the big campaign swings into full tilt as the Christmas season approaches. Many a homemaker during the Yuletide makes and keeps at least 5 to 10 kinds on hand. The Wisconsin Electric Power Company, the Milwaukee Gas Company, and other utility organizations throughout the state exhibit samples of many cookies. Recipes and directions for making them are provided for thousands of women who visit the home service departments of these organizations.

The active baking season starts around December first. Its volume increases every day for about two and one-half weeks. There are candy canes frosted with red and white stripes, Christmas trees, little men and women, camels, dolls, Santa Claus, stockings, animals, and toys represented by cookies. Some of them are molded with the hands. The cook manipulates the dough as an artist works with clay. Indeed, in a few homes children prepare for the cooky baking season by shaping make-believe cookies with clay. Thus they acquire skill to use when they work at their mothers' sides.

Fancy cookies frequently decorate Christmas trees. For example, bell-shaped ones frosted white carry a letter in red frosting. When hung on the branches they broadcast to all who look — "Merry Christmas" or "Season's Greetings."

Countless people in Wisconsin believe that to share cookies and coffee or wine with guests composes an intrinsic part of holiday hospitality.

There's Showmanship With Fruits

Many families bake apples in the traditional way. Others slice the cored, unpared fruit and arrange it in a shallow casserole. They sift sugar on top and pour on cream to supply the necessary moisture. The oven cooking proceeds as usual.

Two native small red fruits, cranberries and Door County cherries, brighten and flavor many meals. Their juices, canned, bloom like May flowers on the Christmas tables of the region, and set a proper atmosphere for the turkey that follows. As an appetizer, little glasses of chilled sparkling red cherry juice, with a touch of almond flavoring added, also give holiday meals a tasty send-off.

Over a fruit cocktail, such as a mixture of diced oranges and bananas and green grapes spooned into glasses, the hostess pours cranberry juice for a superb color and flavor combination.

Steamed cranberry pudding stars as the queen of the traditional desserts in Yuletide dinners. The peerless rich sauce that almost always crowns it is decreed by custom and beloved for its buttery taste. (Baked cranberry puddings intrigue, too.) For the holidays in countless homes as many as four or five of these puddings are steamed at a time for quick reheating when needed. Because this dessert personifies Wisconsin at the holly hanging, candle lighting season the recipe is presented as an insight into what is stirred into the mixing bowls before Santa Claus comes down the chimney.

CRANBERRY PUDDING

1½ cups sifted flour	½ cup chopped nuts
½ teaspoon salt	½ cup molasses
1 pint cranberries	2 tablespoons cold water
½ cup shredded citron	1½ teaspoons soda

Mix and sift flour and salt. Combine cranberries, cut in halves, citron, nuts, and molasses; add dry sifted ingredients.

Add water in which the soda has been dissolved and mix well. Pack into a well-greased 1½-quart mold, cover, and steam 4 hours. Serve with Wisconsin sauce.

WISCONSIN SAUCE

1 cup sugar
½ cup butter

½ cup cream

Melt butter, add sugar and cream. Bring to a boil, add vanilla, and serve on cranberry pudding. Half white and half brown sugar may be used. Some cooks mix the ingredients in the top of a double boiler and heat until well blended. This sauce also garnishes other puddings with remarkable success, especially the baked and spiced apple ones, like those that feature the full-flavored fruit from the Kickapoo orchards.

In this territory rice often glorifies the dessert course, where it is much more at home than as a base for gravy. Lightly sweetened, fluffy boiled kernels, with whipped cream folded in, elevate many a meal above the commonplace. Generally with this *heavenly rice,* as it sometimes is called, hostesses pass butterscotch sauce or heated maple sirup. The sap from which maple sirup is made runs from trees in the state. Near Martell, where the natives cook it down over open fires, they turn the occasion into a festival. Men, women, and children play games and sing as the sap boils.

Some baked fruit puddings, faintly warm, are adorned with ice cream. Among the more frequently praised ones are lemon, apple, sour cream, sour cream-raisin, and prune-nut puddings.

Pies with crumb crusts quite generally have been simplified into puddings. Women say it is a good plan to press the crumb mixture of crushed cookies or graham crackers and shortening into the bottom of a pan and top it with a fruit or other filling. When so prepared it easily may be cut into individual servings and lifted to dessert plates. They have experienced difficulty in removing triangles of crumb crust pies from pans. Cooks say the fragile rims have a habit of breaking.

Anyone who in spring or summer visits Door County, the spout of the Wisconsin tea kettle that protrudes into Lake

Michigan, remembers acres of perfumed white drifts — the blossoms — or a landscape brilliant with red fruit and green leaves. Both are supremely beautiful sights. This county and Michigan rank among the top cherry growing sections of the world. From these areas the fruit travels in all directions for conversion into those juicy pies Americans like to confront at mealtime.

Some of the quick cherry desserts are masterpieces. For one of them cooks spread a rich baking powder biscuit dough in the bottom of a buttered pan. Then they pour on drained, canned cherries. When baked the dough is on top and becomingly browned. The pudding is cut for serving. Usually it draws a slightly thickened cherry sauce as a companion. Natives polish up their pretty adjectives in the anticipation, enjoyment, and remembrance of cherry float.

CHERRY SURPRISE FLOAT

1 cup flour	½ cup sugar
2 teaspoons baking powder	1 egg
¼ teaspoon salt	¼ cup milk
¼ cup butter	

Sift the dry ingredients. Cream the butter, add the sugar, and cream again. Beat in the egg. Add the dry ingredients and milk alternately and pour into a buttered baking dish 8 or 9 inches in diameter and 2½ to 3 inches deep. Mix these ingredients: 1 No. 2 can of unsweetened pie cherries, juice and all; ½ cup of sugar, and ¼ teaspoon of salt. Pour this mixture into the baking dish, too.

Bake in a moderately hot oven, 375°, about 45 minutes. The cake portion comes to the top and browns beautifully, or as people in Wisconsin and Michigan say, "It floats on the cherries." Serve warm or cold with a thickened cherry sauce or whipped cream.

Near the cherry country is Brussels, settled by Belgians. Here great numbers of Belgian pies go into and come out of the home ovens. Instead of pastry a soft dough is pressed into the pans to make the crusts. It contains yeast, shortening, milk, eggs, sugar, mashed potatoes, and flour. The dough is allowed to rise before the filling is added. The apple, prune, and berry treats are simply scrumptious.

A Galaxy of Food Celebrations

In these neighborhoods Maypoles are wound in front of the homes on May 1. Other festivals also come along, such as the harvest feast of Kirmess, which still occupies a part of three days every week for six weeks. This North Country has a remarkable fondness for food celebrations. Its people have much in common, especially a keen appreciation of the earth's gifts. After a food reporter who has feasted on both northern scenic beauty and exotic food with her Badger friends crosses either the Mississippi River or the St. Croix River, she is in another land of laughing waters, Minnesota.

Sky-blue lakes continue to sparkle by the roadsides, and tall silos, like sentinels, watch over nearby dairy barns. Not until stark functional cylinders of concrete appear — the grain elevators that reach toward the clouds — does Minnesota tip her hand. She is both a milling empire and a top dairy-land. Farther west swelling wheat fields forget the Great Lakes and give promise of the approaching Great Plains.

Everywhere are signs of the people who developed today's cuisine. What eloquent proof they offer of how a melting pot of races makes America great! Every third year St. Paul puts on a Festival of Nations. During the week 30 nationalities celebrate. The various groups prepare their favorite dishes to display and sell to the public. Before the tide of European settlers gained momentum, Yankees dominated the state. Social and business life, like the cooking skills, reflect their poignant influences. Anyone with a good appetite and open eyes recognizes delightful touches of New England and foreign accents side by side in Minnesota's meals. The Scandinavian prestige especially shows.

And what about the colorful food festivals? No other area can hold a candle to the number of these celebrations in the tri-state region of Minnesota, Wisconsin, and Michigan. Jamborees honor everything from bread, cherries, cheese, and fish to onions, red raspberries, pancakes, and rutabagas. Always gay, and sometimes bordering on the burlesque, these occasions afford pleasure and camaraderie. They glorify agriculture. The people love queens. They crown their own. A traveler, by zig-zagging hundreds of miles across the countryside, repeatedly sees bright spotlights turned on locally abundant products. As one thoughtful Minnesota farm woman defined the phenomenon, "For some of us not too far away from our parents' and grandparents' stories of countries where food is not so plentiful as in the U.S.A., it is a form of flag waving and frolicking."

Townspeople Turn Out With Dipnets

Spring calls up the smelt festivals of Michigan and Wisconsin. Around March 20 to April 5, when the fish swim up the Menominee River to spawn, townspeople and tourists in Marinette, Wisconsin, for instance, turn out with dipnets and seines. They crowd the river banks with poles, machines to lift nets, and baskets filled with shining fish. As they move around in the darkness with flashlights, they resemble — from a distance — swarms of fireflies on a summer night. Bonfires blossom along the river's banks and send their incense toward the stars. Fireworks travel skyward at intervals, and men, women, and youths stand knee-deep in the river to bring in a catch with every drag of the seines. The activity builds up to a climax, the crowning of the Smelt Queen.

Minnesota pays homage to Bohemian rolls on Kolache Day, some time in September. Then people in Montgomery assemble to enjoy the wonderful fruit-topped bread and coffee. Hopkins promotes a red raspberry festival, Atwater a watermelon day, and Ortonville a big sweet corn dinner and a program of entertainment. Springfield features a sauerkraut jubilee, with jovial eating contests, dancing, and other amusements. Another food frolic comes off at Milan in August, the lefse fete in honor of Norwegian flatcakes. On the second day everyone eats his fill of lefse and coffee without cost.

Monroe, Wisconsin, crowns a Cheese Queen, and the assembled multitudes feast to their hearts' content on limburger and Swiss cheese. In the same state at Cumberland a Rutabaga King bows once a year to his neighbors; the "bagies" are honored by a parade of decorated floats, band concerts, and speech making. Michigan's food celebrations, to name a few, include cherry, peach, and grape festivals, apple shows, smelt, herring, trout, perch, and bass jamborees, lumberjack picnics, and onion, sugar beet, and pancake jamborees.

Ice cream, potatoes, strawberries, and other favored foods give the citizens of the three states an opportunity — or an excuse — for merrymaking. As already noted, the patterns for all these gala occasions follow the same general lines. A prized local product is singled out for recognition. Part of the pleasure derives from eating in some form. Also neighbors get together to visit, enter contests, and play games. Of course the continuity of these community gatherings means people like them.

Wild Rice — a Glorious Food

Wild rice, the glorious food of the wilderness, thrives to the north in Minnesota where the summer air carries that rare, winy quality. Indians, two in a canoe, paddle out in the morning sunshine to harvest luxuriant grain heads. On the shore at night the jingle of bells and the shuffle of feet to the rhythm of tom-toms sometimes may be heard. Observers see the flash of fur, feathers, and beads, and vivid paint over red skin as ceremonial dances progress.

Wherever about the countryside food talk springs up, the native water grass wins praise. Many people living elsewhere are amazed when they discover it is no kin to the rice grown commercially in Texas, Louisiana, Arkansas, and California. The Indians thresh the seed heads into their canoes with two sticks. On the shore the rice goes into large kettles over open fires; heat loosens the hulls, and enhances the flavors.

Workers pour the warm food into wide bark baskets and toss and shake them until the stalks and foreign substances blow away. Then they dump it into cement or wooden vats, and a boy or man wearing mocassins "jigs" it with a peculiar tramping step to separate the shells from the kernels. They toss the rice again, and guide it into bags for marketing.

How To Cook Wild Rice

Everyone in Minnesota considers his way of cooking wild rice the best in the nation! People agree on one step, though, a thorough washing of the grains — three or four washings in warm water. Thus they drain off the chaff. Some women and men (many Minnesota men know how to cook, and tens of thousands of them appreciate through experience the fruits of culinary artists when they taste sublime food) submerge wild rice to a depth of an inch in boiling water. They cover the bowl and set it aside several hours or overnight. The seeds absorb the water and swell. Then after they have been steamed from 30 to 45 minutes in a double boiler and seasoned with salt, pepper, and butter, the fluffy, plump, tender kernels earn their reputation as one of the nation's best tasting treats.

Other natives handle the rice quite differently. They do not cook it. Instead they pour boiling water over the washed grains and let them stand 20 minutes. They drain off the liquid and add more boiling water. This process is repeated three or four times more, or until the grains are swollen, fluffy, and tender. Then they drain and season them and put them in a hot oven to stay warm until served.

This regional delicacy locally rates as the perfect accompaniment for game and fish, and as an esteemed dressing to stuff into wild ducks and barnyard birds, like turkey. No competitor threatens its supremacy. Chopped, sautéed mushrooms frequently are mixed into the dressing. Some men say they always secretly hope, after a guest meal, that there will be leftover wild rice to reheat the next morning for breakfast. Serve it in a bowl with sugar and cream, they say.

This water grass once upon a time grew so densely in the northern sections of the nation that the early explorers, such as those who traveled along Wisconsin's Fox River, had to cut a passage for their canoes through it. (Wild rice still grows in northern Wisconsin, too. There in summer the Indians harvest it. Badgers enjoy it in their special occasion meals, as with game, fish, and poultry dinners.) In recent years the acreage has decreased astonishingly, while the demand for the rice by food connoisseurs across the United States has increased immensely. As a result the Indians' favorite now is a luxury item that strains and spoils many food budgets.

11,000 Lakes for Fishermen

Minnesota, a fisherman's paradise, also is the locale of enthusiastic fish eaters. Some 11,000 lakes in the state encourage sportsmen and the cooks. Most men and women living there consider their fish and game dinners the real McCoy, or the top ones of the world. Men say that as a setting for the most wonderous food experience, nothing else compares with the North Country where some of the lakes are surrounded with virgin forests. These fishermen explain that they sit on the boulders at the water's edge to eat the fish they catch in the cold water and cook immediately. They speak of the peace and solitude in the remnants of the wilderness that once covered much of their state, and of how the environment rejuvenates their spirits.

No doubt the Scandinavian touch also is reflected in the liking for fish. Wall-eyed pike, small-mouthed bass, lake trout, pike, and whitefish answer as general favorites. The smoking of fish has developed into a sizable industry on the scenic North Shore, that 400-mile stretch on Lake Superior. Smart hostesses — especially those in the environs of the Twin Cities, where an unusually gracious colony of them dwells — sometimes feature smoked fish in a lettuce salad along with fresh tomatoes and onions.

Sour milk takes the limelight in fish cookery. As an example of how it performs, pike fillets are soaked from 35 to 45 minutes in salted sour milk. After draining, and dredging the fish in flour, natives pan-fry the fillets in butter or other fat, such as bacon drippings, until they are brown and crispy.

Fish soups, chowders, and puddings appeal at mealtime on frosty days. The well-filled bowls, with their clouds of steam, conjure similar food pictures in Norway, Sweden,

Denmark, and New England. Creamed finnan haddie also pleases on a wide scale. Clever fingers flake the parboiled haddock into rather large pieces and fold them and a little diced onion into a creamy white sauce. Women simmer the union gently a few minutes to develop and blend flavors, but not long enough to destroy what good cooks hold desirable, the flavor and texture of raw onions.

Across the United States shrimp has more admirers than any other sea food; in Minnesota homes its pink beauty often shows atop creamed finnan haddie. Some families vouch for the tastiness of codfish balls, as did their New England forebears, and in other households a faint whisper of curry powder in them and creamed codfish is noted frequently enough by a wandering food scout to eliminate surprise.

To Minneapolis goes the distinction for being the largest lutfisk or lutefisk market outside the Scandinavian countries. This imported fish, a species of cod, is dried and salted across the Atlantic Ocean. Minnesota women or the people in their markets soak and cook it in water, a tedious process. When dressed for the table the hot fish is rich with melted butter or streams of white sauce flavored with mustard. Indeed, many fish dishes carry a vague but tantalizing flavor of mustard or dill. Boiled potatoes escort most of them.

A White Christmas Is Expected

Natives take a white Christmas for granted, as one of the blessings of the state. They frequently mention nature's guarantee of a snow-covered landscape at the Yuletide season. They speak happily of the glistening new flakes that often fall on Christmas Eve to blanket cities, towns, and farms alike. Then many families gather joyously around candle-lit tables to feast on the traditional Swedish Christmas Eve supper. It consists of lutfisk, boiled potatoes, melted butter, a baked rice pudding fruity with soft raisins, and coffee. I suspect there are cookies, too. And more than one cup of coffee per capita!

Hostesses vote for fish pies, in Americanized versions.

Cooks cram the flaky pastry crusts full of deftly seasoned creamed fish and bake the fat pies to an appealing brown. Artistic women often cut the pastry in fancy shapes. One pie I saw resembled a fish. Just imagine the sensation it was when set before the host with a special flourish as something worth showing off as well as tasting.

MINNESOTA FISH DINNER
Trout Pan-fried in Butter
Wild Rice
Cucumbers in Sour Cream
Hot Buttered Rolls
Berry Sherbet
Crisp Cookies
Coffee

In some kitchens creamed shrimp is spooned over the crisp-crusted pan-fried trout, although most people prefer the butter-browned fish with lemon quarters at its side. The universal treatment of cucumbers is to pare, slice thinly, and salt them, and then to soak them for a couple of hours in a vinegar-sugar marinade. About a tablespoon of sugar to a half cup of cider and tarragon vinegars, mixed, are favored proportions. When available, chopped green onions may be added to the cucumbers. Shortly before mealtime cooks drain the vegetables, fold them into thick sour cream, and sprinkle on chopped chives. Many natives inquire, "What other relish could taste so delicious with fish?"

One answer from hundreds of homes is, "Crushed pineapple, drained, and chilled, with chopped cucumber in lemon flavored gelatin." In the dessert picture a berry sherbet beautifully fills the frame. Sometimes sherbets made with a blend of fruit and berry juices win the spot of honor, like the all-time favorite, red raspberry-orange sherbet. Then there are Minnesota men who admit they prefer blueberry or apple pie to top off fish.

Tiny Meat Balls Disappear Quickly

The ladies' church groups — especially the Lutherans — prepare and serve colorful smörgasbord suppers, usually for fund raising. At these memorable meals many evidences are set out of Americanization in action on kitchen ranges and work counters. While considerable difference is observed between the relatively simple menus of Minnesota and the commonly more elaborate ones of Sweden (which often contain upwards of 50 dishes!), the local feasts deserve plaudits. And they get them! Winter snows drift high without dampening the spirit of fellowship and mirth at these suppers. People flock to them in mouth-watering anticipation, and go away pleased, well fed, and with a wish to return the next time.

Swedish meat balls always disappear like hotcakes from the smörgasbords. It is little wonder, for they possess a certain superb, undefinable quality that cooks of other than Scandinavian descent rarely can duplicate.

The formula for success, some women say, is first to mix half as much lean pork as beef, finely ground. To 1 pound of beef and ½ pound of pork they add about ½ cup of dry bread crumbs soaked in ½ cup of milk, 1 egg, 1 small minced onion, and seasonings. They knead the mixture to blend and distribute the ingredients; almost all cooks work a teaspoon each of sugar and salt and a bit of pepper into the 1½ pounds of meat. Traces of spices, such as ginger, nutmeg, and allspice, occasionally are included, but the experts warn, "Keep the spicy taste subdued — or subtle."

Several women demonstrated to me how they shape the meat mixture into tiny marbles and brown them in butter or other fat. The trick of the performance is to shake the frying pan almost continuously so the dancing balls will brown uniformly and retain their perfect shape. When a rich golden brown surrounds them, natives lift them to a hot platter. They make a medium thick gravy with the pan drippings, flour, and equal parts of milk and water, and drop the balls into the bubbling sauce to simmer lazily for a quarter of an hour.

Some households cook meat loaves slowly atop the range in heavy, covered utensils. They insist this Swedish method gives a supremely moist product, beautifully browned. Another characteristic of Minnesota women is their custom of referring to casserole combinations as "hot dishes."

The capable ladies who excel in putting on smörgasbords also line row after row of exquisite cookies on their baking sheets throughout the year, especially as Christmas approaches. It is customary for mothers and their married daughters, sisters, or two close friends to get together for the day once a year for a holiday cooky baking spree. They visit as they work, have lunch together, and then divide the spoils of their endeavors. The traditional S-shaped spritz — rich with butter and almond flavored, and often containing grated almonds — perhaps steals the show.

For parties, dainty sugar rusks also delight with coffee or tea, and always receive an ovation in a native's descriptions of taste treats. People point out that rusks deliver the fragrance and flavor of butter and crushed cardamom seeds to the mouth in a most pleasing manner.

Almost spellbound I watched one of my hostesses make these rusk treats. She formed the cooky dough into small balls with a diameter of a half dollar or less. She baked them on a baking sheet in a very hot oven, 450°, about 10 minutes. Then she startled her attentive observer by cutting through the hot spheres to divide them into halves; after that she arranged them in a shallow pan, and put them in a slow oven, 300°, to toast until golden brown. The enthusiasm of the guests who gobbled them up in a hurry suggests their appeal, and why they are called *sugar rusks*. Indeed, Minnesota's Scandinavian type cookies command the admiration of all women, even their neighbors of German extraction, who in their own right are cooky making artists.

Of course cooky baking extends around the calendar. Here is a state in which practically all homes with children, and many without youngsters, consider a cooky jar as important a bit of equipment as a frying pan. Mothers cannot figure out how little school boys and girls can grow up happily without cookies in the kitchen. They point out that a dessert served with them pleases a child and is easier to eat than cake without scattering crumbs about the premises. In some communities a child on his birthday carries a treat of home-made cookies to the pupils and the teacher in his room at school. Some mothers decorate these special occasion ones. Just about all kinds come to everyday home meals, but drop cookies are the most popular. They are easy and quick to bake.

Look in the gardens of some of the families of Czech ancestry and note how the poppies are growing. Later their tiny black seed appear in a variety of tasty cakes and breads. The *kolache,* crowned with poppy seed, cottage cheese, or fruit fillings, is much liked in Minnesota, as it is in the state to the east. In many Polish communities exotic wafers and cakes for religious festivals evolve in home kitchens.

Game Cookery Approaches Perfection

Men deserve and accept credit for helping women prepare local game dinners in which ducks, pheasants, and venison take leading roles. Indeed, many a husband-chef really shines when he tries his hand at game and fish cookery. Most gentlemen of the region not only know how to talk interestingly about food but also how to enjoy it.

MINNESOTA GAME DINNER
Ducks or Pheasants
Wild Rice
Braised Celery or Buttered Peas
Tossed Green Salad
Fruits
Coffee

Perhaps buttered peas (frozen) most frequently fill the vegetable dish in game dinners, although many clever hostesses prefer lengthwise cuts of celery simmered until tender in bouillon and then seasoned with butter, salt, pepper, and a dash of lemon juice. They also like peas and lima beans, cooked separately and buttered and then combined.

Green salads for these native feasts generally feature two or three kinds of leaves, cold and crisp, with lettuce the mainstay. Usually they are tossed with French dressing. Often poppy seed is scattered over the top of the greens for a distinctive regional touch. A salad some households tailor to glamorize the game menu consists of lettuce, tomato quarters, orange sections, and sweet onion rings, drenched with a piquant French dressing.

Not that cole slaw is out of style. Plates of it enliven many game and fish meals. A Minnesota version that tastes luscious flaunts a dressing of sour cream blended with vinegar and sugar; it is pointed up with chopped chives and lots of celery seeds. The cabbage shreds are so crisp they will snap between the fingers.

Women frequently vote for a fruit dessert to end the feast. Men candidly confess to a preference for fruit pies, or a berry sherbet plus sour cream cup cakes, frosted white and decorated with California walnuts. Ice cream with fresh or frozen strawberry or red raspberry sauce also vies for top billing in the dessert course. Minnesota people know something about ice cream! Their factories make vast amounts of it. Some of it sells to people living elsewhere. They consider it fine eating, especially when teamed with local berries.

The fruit desserts frequently have their start in cans. Many home chefs choose two or three contrasting kinds, like green gage plums and red-black cherries, plus fresh orange sections. A little fresh lemon or lime juice is trickled over the plums and cherries. In color this dessert resembles a pale green, deep red, and golden corsage.

Please Pass the Coffee!

Coffee meets no competition in the area for the top title in the beverage class. No doubt the Scandinavian and Germanic backgrounds of many of the people account for the custom of adults commonly drinking steaming hot java five times daily. Children are equally big-time drinkers — of milk.

Hot Rolls Command a Big Following

All the world's famed breads bake in the state's ovens. Here is a stronghold for the homemade yeast-leavened ones. Even a casual observer finds examples of perfection. Especially is this the case with the light, piping hot rolls that instantly melt the butter spread on them daily in thousands of homes. These are the delicate, dainty kind, and are not duplicated in all areas. Hot biscuits are relished, too, but they play second fiddle to their distant kin — hot yeast rolls.

Hostesses capitalize on the popularity of homemade bread and almost always serve some kind of it at parties and guest dinners. The rolls are trumps for such occasions, but loaves of homemade bread sliced as thin or thick as the cook wishes also fare well. Charming little thin bread and butter sandwiches grace buffet tables. Some families work celery seeds into the creamed butter and spread the mixture on slices of bread, tuck them into paper bags and heat them in a medium oven, 350°. They serve them piping hot!

Six queens rule the pies — apple, blueberry, cherry, lemon meringue, pumpkin, and mince, with the blueberry numbers regarded by many natives as the most regal and beautiful of all. A Minnesota blueberry pie is rather deep. The sugared berries are baked between two layers of flaky, tender, rich pastry soon after they have been plucked from the bushes. Natives insist that berries fresh from the blue coverlet which spreads over so many acres make the superlative pies. Seasoning these berries that taste of the outdoors requires only dots of the buttercup yellow of freshly churned butter, a few drops of lemon juice — but not enough to taste, and a touch of salt. Minnesota in summer — what is it? Well, one definition is that it connotes a lazy, all-day cruise on a clear lake or river with blueberry pie and coffee to fall back on when hunger arrives.

Cakes of countless descriptions figure prominently and with distinction in the area's dessert news. Many tall and stately angel foods wear a thin white frosting, a butter-confectioners' sugar one, with a faint scent of almond. That almond taste, almost always vague and indistinct, frequently pleases the tongue wherever in the state cakes, cookies, puddings, and other desserts are eaten. Pineapple sponge and chiffon sponge cakes, with a variety of flavors, have more than a toe hold in the cuisine. Remnants of them, when a cook is fortunate enough to have such dessert insurance, are sliced, sprinkled with confectioners' sugar, and toasted to escort fruit compotes.

Minnesota is pancake country of the first magnitude. While griddlecakes in vast numbers are hurried from the griddle to breakfast plates, they also capture lots of bouquets at parties, where they take the dessert role with dignity. I observed one hostess form a wreath of eight tiny pancakes, thin and hot, on every warmed dessert plate. In this case she spooned luscious thick red raspberry jam in the centers, although she said she often uses strawberry jam or lingonberry sauce. On the jam she dropped blobs of whipped cream.

Blue Cheese Ripens in Vast Caves

Minnesota cooks possess imaginative talent with cream desserts. As a homespun example, alternate layers of chilled rosy rhubarb sauce, brown sugar, and sour cream fill the bill. Slightly crushed fresh strawberries, red raspberries, sliced peaches, or the frozen berries or fruit frequently take the place of rhubarb.

In caves along the mighty Mississippi River near St. Paul commercial firms cure blue cheese on an impressive scale. A hostess stunt is to mash the cheese and mix it with thick cream. Home chefs freeze the blend in the refrigerator tray, slice it, and serve the dairy's gift with crisp, heated crackers, coffee, and on some occasions with fruit, such as choice apples or pears.

Blueberries with sugar and cream, and in pancakes, waffles, puddings, pies, and tarts connote Minnesota as truly as they do that faraway country Down East in Maine. Surprisingly, at least to many visitors in the state, are the blueberry soups at a meal's beginning. This Polish delicacy contains the berries, water, sugar, thin lemon slices, and the flavor of cinnamon. And just before my hostess announced dinner she stirred sour cream into its fruity depths. In Minnesota, too, I first met a blueberry topped coffee cake — which since has made many a Kansas morning coffee party a success!

Chilled rice puddings refuse to surrender their historic prestige, which is an attitude the natives applaud. One of the exotic kinds has whipped cream folded into the cooked, chilled, and fluffy rice, with enough gelatin dissolved in it to enable the snow to hold its shape when molded. Chopped, blanched almonds are concealed in the taste treat; there is a welding of sweet softness with crunchy accents. As a companion it draws a hot berry sauce as regularly as the water lilies bloom in August. Either fresh or frozen strawberries or red raspberries are heated with sugar and slightly thickened with cornstarch. Women advise, "Pour a little of the vivid fruity mixture over the rice, taste, and then count your blessings."

Homely Scandinavian type puddings of infinite variety make winter's long visit something to contemplate and enjoy. Many of them start out thriftily with dry bread put through a food chopper to make crumbs. The woman who loves to work with a spoon in her hand mixes sugar, spices, and melted butter with them, and alternates layers of the crumbs and fruit — whatever she has on hand, like applesauce, soft cooked prunes, or stewed dried apricots — in the baking dish, with the crumbs on top. After baking in a slow oven, 325°, the pudding is served warm or cooled, with a chilled vanilla or almond flavored soft custard, or with cream. Swedish style prune puddings sometimes skip the oven. Layers of crumbs, prunes, and whipped cream take their turns in a bowl, with the cream on the bottom and top. After chilling several hours or overnight the divinely delicious dish is ready to serve. Few desserts can match its luxurious taste.

Steaks Wear Butter Polka Dots

Beef is the favorite meat of the Minnesota populace. Thick, juicy steaks signify good eating! Some cooks like to spread broiled porterhouse steak with a paste of blue cheese mashed and mixed with cream and a bit of Worcestershire sauce. They run it back under the heat just long enough to melt the cheese. The men who eulogized the state's fare advised me to write down the cheese-cream proportions for use when I returned home, or ½ cup of cheese to 2 table-spoons of thick cream. Incidentally, all the cream that enters into food conversations is heavy. And all the plain broiled steaks described wear big polka dots of butter to the table, which melt their flavor and richness over the seared browned meat.

A Cool Climate Favors Gardens

Corn-on-the-cob, hot, smeared with butter, and sprinkled with salt and pepper, makes the summer meals something to tell the world about. The climate is ideal for the production of such crops as peas and corn; excellent varieties of both are grown commercially. It may not be Minnesota succotash, but regardless of its name many families adore corn, cut from the cob, peas, and green limas (fresh, frozen, or canned), separately cooked, seasoned, and then mixed. A little minced onion and cream lend flavors to this medley. Swedish brown beans are stocked by hundreds of grocery stores, where they sell steadily from one year to another.

Pan-fried tomatoes greet the people at mealtime when summer matures in Minnesota, and, like other foods, the crimson vegetable takes to cream. Cooks delicately brown the firm red slices in butter without flouring them, lift them to a hot dish, add cream to the pan drippings, and heat the sauce. They pour it piping hot over the tomatoes. Salt, pepper, and a trace of sugar supply the seasoning.

Both rutabagas and turnips taste unusually sweet and wonderful in the north states along the Great Lakes and in North Dakota. Of course the cool weather aids in putting superlative flavors into these root vegetables, but the cooks also help. After the vegetables are cooked tender, they drain, mash, season, and whip them until light. Then they fold in just enough whipped cream to provide flavor and airiness.

For the most noble summer dinner, fried chicken wins

the platter position. The young, disjointed birds, after being rolled in seasoned flour, are pan-fried. Wild rice or new potatoes and some of the best offerings of the gardens and berry patches are accompaniments.

MINNESOTA SUMMER DINNER

Fried Chicken   New Potatoes
Milk Gravy
Sweet Corn   Fried Tomatoes
Green Salad
Hot Buttered Rolls
Double-Decker Shortcake
Coffee

As already indicated, in some kitchens wild rice takes preference over new potatoes in the perfect summer dinner, and blueberry pie, berry sherbet, or ice cream may occupy the important dessert spot on the menu. But double-decker shortcake, made with red raspberries, connotes Minnesota to me, for there I first lifted a forkful of the ambrosial dessert to my lips. To sample it once provides assurances that one will forever feast on it when summer comes — if the berries are available.

My hostess, a home economist in business, kindly explained that the first step is to divide the soft biscuit dough (2 cups of flour with an egg yolk and 2 tablespoons of butter added) into two equal parts. She pats one of them into a 7- or 8-inch square pan, and spreads on about 2 cups of lush ripe red raspberries mixed with ½ to ⅔ cup of sugar. Then she pats or rolls out the cover to fit from the second half of the dough. The shortcake bakes in a hot oven, 400°, about ½ hour. Then comes that breathless moment of cutting it into six or eight squares — preferably six — and hurrying it to eager people at the table.

But first it draws a topping of chilled raspberry hard sauce. This is regular hard sauce, made with butter and sugar, with a few raspberries folded in for color and flavor. Another custom, and one worthy of recommendation, is to serve the hot shortcake with a chilled sauce.

To make it the cook starts out with ½ cup of butter. She melts it, adds 1 cup of sugar, and stirs in 1 cup of ripe raspberries, mashed. Then she adds 1 tablespoon of cornstarch dissolved in a little water and cooks the mixture a few minutes.

If cooled and chilled it tastes very good, and appears at its frothy best when the cook folds in an egg white, beaten stiff.

While the last bite of this marvelous dessert tastes as good as the first, it provokes a feeling akin to sadness. Thoughts of the brevity of the berry season are at the root of the momentary melancholia. Only a reminder of how delicious the same shortcake is when made with strawberries, blueberries, or mellow ripe peaches revives depressed spirits, and personifies an intelligent hostess's tact.

Memories of marvelous winter pudding bring additional comfort. They embrace the soufflés, floating islands, and the previously mentioned Scandinavian types with which so many Minnesota cooks have a special flair. Frequently they whip ice cream in their electric beaters at the last minute for a quick pudding sauce. They say it is smooth, cool, and sweet on the tongue.

Even a seasoned food reporter reluctantly leaves Minnesota for new fields. She remembers the smell of baking bread, cookies, and blueberry pies. She tastes in memory the fish from cold water hurried to the frying pan and then to the platter. And as she waves goodby to one of her favorite regions, she gives thanks for her many generous friends who live there.

The Farm Belt

Sometimes you can spot a woman from the Farm Belt in a metropolitan food market. She may have arrived on the scene by way of a San Francisco cable car, the New York subway, a Chicago trolley, or by bus or motor car in any one of a hundred and more other cities. Her appearance is no clue. It is what she says.

As she selects her groceries she is likely to comment to a friend, or possibly a salesman, "I have a meat-potato-gravy husband." This is a regional expression that often is misinterpreted. It refers to substantial meals, and in no sense implies a lack of variety. When she utters such a statement the shopper identifies herself as having roots in the land of corn kings and champion wheat growers.

At a social gathering, you frequently can recognize the guests who live or have lived among the open fields. The homing instinct crops out in their eagerness to depart. It developed in agricultural people through the generations as they made great efforts, regardless of the weather and other circumstances, to return to their farms in time to get the chores well under way before dark and supper. The country supper — ah! that is the magic. Like a magnet it draws the family and often a few friends around the table to share the fruits of home cooking. Natives prefer it — dishes lovingly prepared — to all other kinds.

Farmhouse meals do not confine their charms to rural places. They win bouquets in the cities and towns. Did not many of the business tycoons and top feminine executives there come off the farms? They carry, wherever they go, a liking and profound respect for the breakfasts, dinners, and suppers they left behind them. One of their dreams, which people sometimes call ambition, is to recapture or duplicate them in urban quarters.

A Farm Empire of Two Parts

From a strictly culinary standpoint this agricultural empire divides into two parts, the central farm states and North and South Dakota. The Nebraska cuisine is somewhat like that of both sections, but in the eastern counties it is more closely related to the one in Iowa. An atmosphere of the Mountain West permeates western Nebraska and western Kansas, and signs of the Southwest prevail, too, in parts of the Sunflower State. Ohio, Indiana, and Illinois enjoy a close kinship. To the south they share the Ohio River Valley, and to the north the Great Lakes. To them pioneers came by water to establish new homes. People from the South — especially Virginia and North Carolina, and to a smaller extent from South Carolina — poured into what now are the southern and central areas of the three states. In the 1840's and later the big German migration spilled across the countryside. Many cities, like Cincinnati, Indianapolis, and East St. Louis, Illinois, (and St. Louis!), and uncounted other nearby communities in the region still reflect its influence. The cookery became a harmony of southern and German dishes. That is what it is today.

To the north the early settlers arrived mainly through the Western Reserve. They were mostly New Englanders and upstate New Yorkers. In more recent times the expansion of the huge industrial centers, like Cleveland and Gary, has attracted new Americans from all European countries. Thus the cuisine has become an interesting blend of many nationalities. Nevertheless it features original dishes that set it apart from other sections of the United States.

These states are the stars in that branch of straightforward cookery known as the farmhouse style.

In the central states — Ohio, Indiana, Illinois, Iowa, Nebraska, and Kansas — meat-potato-gravy husbands, the good eaters, are the rule rather than the exception. Save in isolated cases the meat is beef or pork. It is not veal. And it is not lamb. The potatoes are the fluffy, snowy white, hot mashed ones piled high in a warm serving dish. Thick pats of butter melt on them and form tempting, yellow pools. Or they are honest baked or boiled potatoes, piping hot. Some meats, like steak, dictate that the spuds must be fried — raw slices cooked to a golden brown in fat.

The gravy boat is big and friendly. It invites second and third helpings. If roast beef or pork is on the platter the gravy is the brown kind made with the water in which the potatoes cooked, or with plain water. With pork chops, chicken fried steaks, sausage cakes, chicken, and other skillet treats it is milk gravy of a medium brown shade flecked with deeper brown crumbs scraped from the bottom of the pan. Hoosiers refer to these tasty morsels as "brownies."

When corn is in season, roasting ears almost too hot to touch are on the table, with plenty of butter, salt, and pepper.

People living in the Farm Belt are mighty particular about their corn. It must be field-fresh and just right. They like plump kernels that are firm enough to offer a little resistance to pressure. The husks must be a rich green, and the silks at the ends of the cobs moist. They insist the ears must be cooked as soon as possible after being pulled from the stalks, for then, they say, the sugar starts turning to starch.

Natives remove the husks at the last minute before they drop the ears into boiling water to cook briefly, or about 5 minutes. They bemoan the increasing market practice of offering only "undressed" corn. Frequently some of them say, "Just imagine anyone foolish enough to buy roasting ears (a name North Carolinians also use) that have been husked for hours or days!" Residents of the region prefer to have their own corn patch, but lacking it they gladly drive a few miles to buy the ears from a farmer. They also patronize the farmers' markets. After they return home on a July day the shoppers act as if the corn is butter. They hurriedly crowd it on top the milk bottles or in any other available place in the refrigerator. Coolness, they point out, helps to prevent a loss of moisture and thus aids in preserving eating quality.

In Iowa some excellent cooks roast the corn in the oven. They believe it tastes best when so handled. This is how a home-economics-trained food columnist in Des Moines says the job can be done successfully.

Cut off the stem end and the end silks down to the corn. Remove all but two layers of the husks. Place the corn on racks in the oven with at least an inch of space between the ears. Do not let them touch. Set the heat regulator at 400°. Every 10 minutes turn the corn, and after 15 minutes pull the husks back from the tip end. In from 20 to 25 minutes this top delicacy of the area usually is ready to eat, although the time depends on the size of the kernels and their freshness.

"Let everyone remove the husks from his helping," the natives say, and then add, "only make it helpings." This is a part of the ceremony. They almost always slip off easily and usually take the silks with them.

Vine-ripened Tomatoes Are Served

Vine-ripened tomatoes are in the meal, too, if the local gardens are bearing. Hostesses peel and present them in thick slices or in salads. It is something of a country habit to team them with lettuce and cucumbers. Almost everyone maintains that nothing except wilted garden lettuce can hold a candle to an uncooked vegetable relish as a genuine, old-fashioned treat. In Indiana I met one of the prime vegetable mixtures. It came out of the refrigerator directly to the family-style meal in a huge glass bowl which seemed to say, "Help yourself as many times as you like." My hostess explained how she made it.

"I use the same system my mother and grandmother followed," she confessed. "It's easy and we like it. Just alternate slices of peeled ripe tomatoes, cucumbers, and sweet onions in the bowl. Then pour over them a dressing composed of equal parts of cider vinegar and water, usually ½ cup of each. But first dissolve ¼ cup of sugar in it. Add salt and pepper to season. The important point is to chill thoroughly before serving to blend and develop the flavors."

Iowa people laud uncooked, chopped vegetable relishes with meats, especially barbecued ones. One Des Moines hostess serves frankfurts on cheese buns with the tastiness on top. The combination is her family's first choice for the backyard suppers of summertime.

To make about a quart of the salad substitute she grinds and drains 6 medium-sized peeled and cored tomatoes, 3 medium-sized sweet onions such as Bermudas, and 3 sweet green peppers minus the seeds. Into the medley she stirs 2 tablespoons of olive or salad oil and 1 tablespoon of cider vinegar. She seasons it to taste with salt and pepper and chills it a few hours before use.

Then there is that characteristic Indiana relish composed of ground mangoes and cabbage with celery seeds, vinegar, sugar, mustard, and salt for seasonings. Kansans and Nebraskans often settle for sliced cucumbers dressed with vinegar, salt, and black pepper.

A stranger in Ohio and Hoosier country learns that sweet

green peppers are *mangoes.* Usually in Illinois they are *pickles* — green peppers filled with a mixture of chopped vegetables. I met a gracious lady in Houston, Texas, who originally hailed from Indiana. While living in New Jersey she observed some first-of-the-season green peppers in the market where she was shopping. "I'd like a half dozen mangoes," she said. The salesman replied, "I'm sorry but we do not have them." Annoyed, but politely, she retorted, "Oh, yes you do. I see them." Somewhat confused, he answered, "Please show me where they are." After she pointed to them he looked at her rather sadly, as he picked up a paper bag, and said, "Madam, those are sweet green peppers."

Wilted Lettuce at Oak Hills

If it is spring in southern Ohio, central or southern Indiana and Illinois, or many other places throughout the Farm Belt, wilted lettuce — lush bowls of it — come from the kitchens as one of the most highly prized of all native dishes. Its preparation is a rite mothers demonstrate with care to their daughters. Strangers marvel that such a simple process zooms to its great importance — that the people make so much fuss over it. But the regional cooks stand pat on their belief that fine food, simply prepared and lightly seasoned, yields perfection.

This is how I learned to wilt lettuce from my husband's mother, a talented cook, who had for a time lived in the southern parts of Ohio and Indiana with her parents.

Wash the tender, young leaves of garden lettuce and place them in a large bowl. (*I observed the bowl at Oak Hills was extremely generous in size and that although always well filled at the meal's start it was empty before time for dessert!*) On the center top of the lettuce finely dice a few green onions, tops and all, and heap them in a little haystack. (Some Ohio cooks sprinkle the sugar on the onions instead of adding it to the vinegar.) Cut strips of bacon into cubes and pan-fry it until crisp and brown. Then lift it to a warm plate and add cider vinegar, diluted to taste with water, salt, pepper, and a little sugar, to the drippings. Heat the mixture to the boiling point and pour it bubbling hot over the onions. Toss the leaves to distribute the dressing and to wilt them slightly. Serve immediately with the bacon as a garnish or fold it through the salad. Perfect wilted lettuce is faintly warm and somewhat crisp.

One dark rainy autumn afternoon I sat at a beautifully appointed candlelit tea table and engaged in a fascinating conversation with a highly successful Indianapolis business woman — a woman who likes to cook. She spoke of the many wonderful, forthright dishes of her native area — the central Farm Belt. Affectionately she described the clouds of steaming mashed potatoes, and then the wilted lettuce. As she talked each of us had our dreams. In memory I smelled the mingled aroma of warm vinegar and baby green onions, and tasted the wilted, yet crisp lettuce in the southeastern Kansas farm home with the family gathered around the table for spring's favorite treat. . . . And then my hostess described her choicest spring and early summer luncheon and supper menus. Both speak for country cooking in a Maytime mood.

HOOSIER LUNCHEON
(Business Woman's Favorite)
Wilted Lettuce with Bacon
Hard-cooked Egg Slices
Hot Corn-meal Muffins
Iced Tea

EARLY SUMMER SUPPER
Puffy Omelet
Pan-fried Rice Cakes
Buttered Garden Peas
Wilted Lettuce
Strawberries and Cream
Hot Tea

The leaf lettuce that whispers so tenderly of spring wears many dressings. One favorite consists of sour or sweet cream — the heavy kind — vinegar, and seasonings of sugar and salt. To spy snappy, brittle, and tender leaves (often *Bibb lettuce,* a Kentucky original that grows so successfully in some spots, such as in South Indianapolis) on the table gives a native the same glad feeling as does a glimpse of daffodils growing by the front porch and the season's first birds from the south in the apple trees. And then there are the cooked

dressings in which eggs, sour cream, vinegar, sugar, and salt —
and often a bit of mustard — blend as they steam until thickened in the top of a double boiler. These *boiled dressings,* as
women call them, come out smooth as velvet when experienced hands stir and whip them.

The Cash Customers Wanted Chopped Cabbage

The cabbage salads of the Farm Belt frequently are
wonderous affairs. Country cooks vie with one another as to
who can cut the vegetable into the finest, thinnest shreds, although some Cornhuskers prefer cabbage chopped rather
than shredded. The home economist who manages the tea
room of a department store in Lincoln decided, for a change,
to serve shredded instead of chopped cabbage salad. An impressive wail of friendly protest arose from the clientele, who
begged to have the chopped version restored to the menu.
In Nebraska's Bohemian communities it is traditional to
add to the cole slaw a few tiny green peas, when they are in
season.

An Iowa custom, rarely observed elsewhere, is to crown
the cabbage salad with crumbled blue cheese. Considerable
research with this cheese has been conducted at the Iowa
State College. There the dairy department sells some of the
supply it makes, which the students, members of the faculty,
and visitors delight in buying for use in their homes and
to send as gifts to friends. Newton is another center for the
famed Iowa blue cheese.

Cottage cheese is another food people rally around with
enthusiasm. While some households occasionally use it as
an ingredient in pies and cakes, it is on the salad plates and
in the relish dishes that this old standby really shines. Everyone has his favorite seasonings; cream, salt, celery salt, and
chopped green onions and tomato are general favorites.

It Was a Molded Salad at the Ohio Ox Roast

No food scout jaunts around the region without noticing
the popularity of molded salads and desserts. One summer

evening I went to an Ohio Ox Roast given at Cleveland by the local home economists for members of the American Home Economics Association. As a Kansan, I was well versed in pit barbecuing, but I had a keen curiosity about the salad. I expected it to be a gelatinized one. And it was. Thousands of people throughout the Farm Belt adore cut-up fruits crowded into gelatin. They use the combination on lettuce with salad dressing for a salad, and in stemmed glasses with a topknot of whipped cream as dessert. Cake usually accompanies the latter service. One of the Iowa beauties shows off canned Bing cherries in ruby-colored cherry-flavored gelatin. Whipped cream is its crowning glory, angel food cake its escort.

At the Iowa covered dish luncheons of the rural women's clubs — Indiana people call their versions of them *pitch-ins* — it is not surprising to find half of the dishes gelatinized ones, both the vegetable and fruit editions. One of my most appreciated home economist friends, an Iowan fully recognized as an epicure, now lives in Florida. While she was in her childhood home she acquired a fondness for a gelatin triumph at the supper table — red flavored gelatin containing bananas and orange pieces. Now she likes it, with whole milk poured over, for breakfast. On its native soil this dish also traditionally contains black walnuts. There whipped cream associates with it.

Women Mold Green Salads, Too

Although the mixed green salad gets an all-American rating — is certainly is favored in the Farm Belt — some women in Iowa wonder if it is not overworked in their menus. They point with pride to their exhibits of trim, refreshing molded green ones. And they find them appealing to almost everyone. These clever cooks use at least two kinds of lettuce, primarily because they want contrasting shades of green. Favorites are head and garden leaf lettuce, or head and Bibb lettuce. They make a lemon flavored gelatin, and add such seasonings as salt, vinegar, and pepper.

Some of them shake in a little Worcestershire sauce. They prepare, mix, marinate, and chill in French dressing for about 15 minutes such vegetables as tiny sticks of green peppers, chopped green onions, thinly sliced radishes, and wee wedges of small, firm, red-ripe tomatoes. When the jelly starts to congeal they fold in the drained vegetables and the crisp but finely shredded lettuce. For a chef's salad or one that with hot buttered rolls will make the main course at luncheon, they add cheddar cheese and cooked ham and/or chicken. To provide interest they cut part of the yellow cheese and the meat in cubes and some of it in julienne strips.

They pour the mixture into a plain or fancy mold first brushed with a bland salad dressing. Then they chill it. Every woman has her pet ideas about how to garnish the salad when turned out, but general selections are perky lettuce leaves and mayonnaise thinned with French dressing or sour cream.

Kansas is farther to the south and west than the other states of the Farm Belt, and thus is nearer to the cuisine of the Southwest. Her cooks dash chili powder into dishes somewhat more freely than most other women of the area. One of their favorites is Waldorf salad molded in lemon flavored gelatin with the proverbial pinch of chili powder blended in for subtle seasoning. The entire region serves many chicken salads in the centers of gelatinized Bing cherry rings.

Many Ohio people vote for clear lemon jelly with cut-up fruits and cottage cheese suspended in it. In Buckeye kitchens a splash of pimento often is dropped in to contribute color. In some old Ohio and Indiana families clear lemon jelly is the traditional accompaniment to roast turkey. It is made with unflavored gelatin, sugar, and a generous quantity of fresh lemon juice. The tart delicacy stars in the main course of holiday and other special occasion meals. Everyone has his own stemmed dessert glass filled with it.

Indiana and Illinois households boast what they call *relish salads* — something that complements the meat. Applesauce nipped with horse-radish and gelatinized delightfully associates with pork. And there is that unforgettable gooseberry salad. I inveigled the recipe for it from a most gracious home economist, formerly on the extension staff at Purdue University and now married to a corn king. Every time the triumph appears in my home I am grateful to her.

GOOSEBERRY SALAD

1 pint canned gooseberries	1 cup crushed bananas
1 package lime-flavored gelatin	Water
1 cup sugar	

Drain the gooseberries, add the sugar, and set over low heat just to melt the sugar. Measure the gooseberry juice and add enough water to provide 2 cupfuls. Heat to the boiling point and make the gelatin with it. When the mixture starts to congeal fold in the gooseberries and bananas. Chill and serve thinly spread with mayonnaise and then with whipped cream.

This A-1 Salad Contains Marshmallows

Although Kansas and Nebraska hostesses seldom realize it, one of their A-1 fruit salads is gelatinized by the marshmallows it contains. They make this treat year in and year out for special occasions. It responds to two names, *overnight fruit salad and twenty-four hour salad*. Combinations of fruits in it vary, but one well liked consists of equal parts of pitted, canned white cherries or Royal Annes, canned pineapple pieces, and quartered marshmallows. When green grapes are seasonable they occasionally substitute for the cherries. Other culinary artists also add shredded blanched and toasted almonds. The dressings vary little. Women cook a mixture of eggs, lemon juice, and seasonings, and when it is cool they fold in whipped cream. They blend it with the fruits and marshmallows and set the salad in the refrigerator for from 12 to 24 hours. Some families like to chill it in a shallow pan, and then cut it in squares for serving. Instead of cutting it, other households prefer to break it up with two silver forks and heap it in lettuce cups. The universal garnishes are dabs of the fluffy salad dressing and maraschino cherries. It evolves into one of the elite frozen salads when poured into a refrigerator tray instead of into a pan.

Corsage salads, so named because of the appearance of the fruits and often melon balls in lettuce cups, blossom from one end of the area to the other. In both Iowa and Nebraska they frequently wear celery seed dressing. To make it, cooks first soak the celery seed in 2 tablespoons of cold water overnight. In the morning they heat vinegar with seasonings of sugar, salt, and paprika, cool it, and beat in chilled salad oil. Then they stir in the celery seed and the little water that surrounds them.

Black Walnuts for the Wellesley Cake

The farmhouse dessert can be depended on for luscious eating. It may be a chocolate cake, high and handsome, with frosting swirled on it. Ohio people commonly select *Wellesley fudge cake,* which they have adopted for a classical meal ending. Often it wears a white boiled frosting, although some families prefer a thick fudge one. One of my Dayton friends tints the portion of the frosting used for spreading between the layers a pale or pastel green. She adds a drop or two of peppermint flavoring, and then for a genuine regional touch folds in a few chopped black walnuts. (Unfortunately the supply of these native nuts has diminished greatly.) White frosting covers the top and sides of her cake. She usually keeps a cellophane-wrapped one in her home freezer to tempt her guests and to share with them.

Nebraska people are proud of their *poppy seed cake.* The white layers that hold the tiny black seed frequently are put together with a creamy yellow custard filling and are topped and surrounded by the rich brown of a chocolate-coffee or mocha frosting. If food can occasionally be breath-taking with its beauty, as some of the natives believe, this dessert fills the bill. The knife cuts through the dusky sweet frosting into the creamy-white cake dotted with black seeds and through the pale yellow filling. Everyone lets out his belt a little farther and rejoices that good cooking has not perished from the earth.

POPPY SEED CAKE
(Cornhusker Style)

½ cup poppy seed	1½ teaspoons baking powder
½ cup cold water	¼ teaspoon salt
¾ cup shortening	¾ cup milk
1½ cups sugar	4 egg whites, stiffly beaten
2 cups cake flour	

Soak the poppy seed overnight in the cold water. Sift the flour, baking powder, and salt together three times. Cream the shortening and sugar, and continue the creaming until the combination is fluffy. Add the poppy seed-water mixture. Then alternately add the dry ingredients and the milk. Carefully fold in the beaten egg whites. Bake in two 9-inch layer cake pans in a moderately hot oven, 375°, 18 to 20 minutes.

The Waitress Was an Apple Pie Fan

If strawberries are ripe, the dessert is strawberry short-cake. Cold, red, juicy berries, and piping hot, crusty baked layers of biscuit dough continue to make the dessert a memory builder. Cream is passed to pour over it. Or the dessert may be pie — almost any kind — like apple, cherry, pumpkin, lemon meringue, plum, gooseberry, rhubarb, rhubarb-custard, or maybe some of those red cherry tarts. It usually is fresh-cut pie still a little warm from the oven. Look closely and there may be tell-tale signs of sugary juices bubbling up through the vents from beneath. The apple filled one probably makes more meals red letter occasions than the others. For as the waitress in Brown County, Indiana, said, "This noon we have three kinds of pie, open-face apple, lattice apple, and covered-apple." A southern Illinois cook frequently fills the pastry lined pan with thin slices of sugared apples and then pours over them ½ cup of heavy sour or sweet cream. When baked — what a pie! Who would attempt to surpass it?

The three Ohio River states uphold the taste of their pumpkin pies with noble fervor. Many people living there derive pleasure from talk about their magnificent *pum'kin* pies as if the colloquial name makes them taste better. The tea room of a Columbus, Ohio, department store offers them on the menu the year around. Residents of the Buckeye State do not consider the dessert merely as a gift of the harvest season. "Not by a long shot," they say, "when we have canned pumpkin ready for the mixing bowls." If there is a favorite garnish — usually no trimming is used — it is whipped cream flavored with molasses or maple sirup. Northern Ohio has sizable maple sugar orchards. Her people are extremely fond of the maple flavor. Indeed, the number of favorite maple dishes equals that of Vermont and western New York. Maple Charlottes, cookies, apple dumplings, custard, and gingerbread represent a few of the most praised ones. One of my good friends, a Cleveland newspaper's food editor, told me that every spring her mailbox fills with inquiries about recipes that feature maple sugar and sirup. Indiana and Illinois have the sugar trees, too, but not enough to make more than a drop or two in the sirup pitchers there. In pioneer times there was just about enough sap to boil down for local use.

Germans Like Their Linzer Torte

At the Iowa State College's cafeteria the cherry pies disappear quickly from the counters, perhaps the most rapidly of all pies. The berry- and fruit-filled ones rarely wait long for acceptance. Indianapolis people speak not of cherry tarts, but of *red cherry tarts*. The filling for them is custard-with-cherries. It is baked in individual pastry shells. Then it is topped with a meringue, traditionally sprinkled with chopped black walnuts, and lightly browned. Fruit-custard pies have a never-ending popularity in the southern parts of Illinois, Indiana, and Ohio. Then there is *linzer torte* — a form of pie. One of its strongholds is in that classic German-American town, Belleville, Illinois, across the Father of Waters from St. Louis, Missouri.

When my hostess showed me how to prepare it, she first rolled the pastry as usual. Then she spread on softened butter, folded one side over the other, and rolled it again. Next she repeated the process. After she had fitted the rich pastry into the pie pan she sprinkled about 3 tablespoons of sugar over the bottom. Then she arranged halves of pitted damson plums over the surface to cover the pastry. She counted the plums — there were 25. Over them she scattered what she called a crumble topping. To make it she mixed ½ cup of sifted flour, ¾ cup of sugar, ¼ cup of butter (margarine may be used), and ½ teaspoon of cinnamon until the combination was crumbly. This treat, when baked, answers as the community's foremost dessert.

Also in the southern parts of Illinois, Indiana, and Ohio, another pie comes to the dinner table to the delight of everyone seated around it. The cook sweetens pitted plums and simmers them with a little water until they become tender. Then she slightly thickens the fruity mixture with a little cornstarch and stirs in butter for its flavor. This filling, dusted with traces of cinnamon, ends up as a lattice creation that makes the meal a momentous occasion. "You serve it fresh and still a little warm," a high school home economics student confided to me. "And when my mother makes the pie and puts a spoonful or two of vanilla ice cream on top, it — well, it's simply divine."

The southern sections of the Ohio River states, like Kentucky are famed, too, for their fresh fruit *kuchens*. Especially do the locally grown freestone peaches rise to new taste heights in these desserts. The natives like to have a freshly baked one for Saturday supper and enough left over to enjoy for Sunday breakfast with their coffee.

Hoosier Cooks Praised Cream Pie

Then there is that immortal Indiana cream pie, which also is made next door in Illinois. Perhaps the samples that may be tasted today are something like the last of the Mohicans — disappearing natives. I found the memorable, rich, and delicious dessert in the nationally known tea room of a large and hospitable Indianapolis department store, where for several days I was a welcomed guest. There I had the privilege of discussing Hoosier foods over luncheon tables with some of the state's best cooks, the home economists on the staff, and women from the city and other places. Always we wound up with talk of cream pie. And twice the tea room pastry cooks baked the dessert as a treat for us!

Today's home chefs who make the historic pie chill the pastry lined pan in the refrigerator. Most of them also chill the filling. It is composed of ½ cup each of brown and white sugars, 2 tablespoons of flour, and 2 cups of thin cream. A few clever cooks use the old-fashioned way of mixing the filling. After having my memory refreshed in Hoosier land I remembered that one of my mother's friends, a native of Illinois, used to follow it in her western Kansas home. At that time it seemed like a hocus pocus stunt to me, but the pie certainly was rewarding. Now I wonder how anyone is adept enough to do it. The authentic Hoosier way is to dump the sugars and flour into the pastry lined pan, pour on the cream, and with experienced fingers deftly mix the filling without tearing the rich pastry. Most women also sprinkle on a suggestion of nutmeg.

Salad Along the Banks of the Wabash

If the farmhouse dessert is not a gelatin one, or chocolate cake, poppy seed cake, or some other member of the large cake family, or pie, the chances are it is ice cream. In Ohio, and elsewhere for that matter, it may wear chocolate sauce and nuts. If the Iowa occasion warrants something of a splurge the dessert is likely to be cherry pie à la mode. Many a Hoosier hostess is a little embarrassed to present plain ice cream. She likes to pile the raspberry-pink of raspberry salad on ivory-colored vanilla ice cream for the contrasts of color and of flavor. A stranger along the banks of the Wabash is likely to inquire, "Is this a salad?" And then add, "It tastes like red raspberry sherbet to me." The Hoosier, who never has lost the charming friendliness of genuine country people, usually replies, "That's just what we call it." Indiana *raspberry salad* is red raspberry sherbet — poked full of crunchy salted pecans, and it tastes wonderful. Although most families buy the commercial products, a few women freeze it in their refrigerator trays. This is the way one superb cook explained how she does it.

> Rub the red raspberries through a sieve and measure out 1 cup of the pulp. To it add the juice of 1 lemon, 1 cup of sugar, and 1 cup of whole milk. Fold in 1 cup of cream, whipped but not overly stiff. Then fold in at least ½ cup of coarsely chopped salted pecans. Freeze in the refrigerator tray, stirring once.

Throughout the region milk sherbets have a great following — one that challenges the water ices. This is the area, too, where glasses of sherbet go to the best of dining tables with the main course, or as the women say, "To complement the meat, like cranberry or pineapple sherbet with turkey, chicken, or pork." Farmhouse cooks pamper the meats in their meals!

Indiana hostesses are skillful — a talent they share with their neighbors — in making sweet sauces to dress up frozen desserts. They like to glamorize the ice-cream balls available in many of their markets and to keep a supply on hand in their freezers. They roll them in chopped nuts before pouring on the sauce, usually a chocolate, butterscotch, or toffee one. A Hoosier has a weakness for nuts, the native hickory nuts and black walnuts, and for pecans and California walnuts. Young women sometimes confess to a food reporter that they "fix their own" as an aid to their budgets. By this expression they refer to the shelling.

This Business Man Uses an Electric Blender

In Nebraska dyed-in-the-wool Cornhuskers talk plaintively about *raw egg* ice cream. This is the local name for the homemade frozen uncooked custard type stirred up so generally in former years. "When the dasher comes out," they say, "it is soft, cool, fluffy — and heavenly tasting!" One of the business men of Lincoln, who likes to dabble in cooking for a pastime, spoke almost as if he had been successful in the quest for the Holy Grail. His wife has an electric blender, and he has discovered that he can make a dish of ice cream with it in a hurry. He adds a little — for measurements are not his forte! — chopped ice, powdered milk, cream, egg, a touch of vanilla, sugar, and a few grains of salt. "I just turn on the juice and let the ice cream blend," he beamed. "It tastes much like the 'raw egg' kind just after the dasher is pulled from its frozen depths. And that means GOOD."

Cornhuskers are almost as choosey about their ice creams as they are about roasting ears. This is one of the many culinary reasons why it is pleasant to visit them. Tall glasses almost overflow with what the people there know as *home style malted milk*. Nothing is to be gained by trying to drink or sip the tempter through a straw. It is so thick with vanilla ice cream and chocolate sauce that nearly everyone eats it with a spoon. *Mondae sundae* has three scoops of ice cream, all different, wearing three kinds of sauces — vanilla ice cream with chocolate sauce, chocolate ice cream with marshmallow sauce, and strawberry ice cream with strawberry sauce. Imagine how members of the high school and college crowds like to put this one away!

Natives of Nebraska have a special fondness for the chocolate-mint combination — which they call *Russian mint* in honor of a favorite local candy — in ice cream, sweet sauces, candy, and a variety of desserts. Jayhawkers share this liking. One of Topeka's good cooks makes a chocolate pie with a mint flavored meringue that wins the compliments of her hordes of friends. Chocolate angel food cakes with the taste of mint also bring neighborhood fame to their creators.

A Cornhusker refers to thick sweet sauces for ice cream and other desserts as "goupe." When he wishes to describe a thick sauce he says it is "goupey." This is a different treat from the Hoosier's *dip*. A dip is a clear, sweet sauce made with sugar, water, and cornstarch. It is flavored with generous amounts of lemon juice and butter, grated lemon peel, and often with a whiff of nutmeg. (Members of some households refer to vanilla sauce as a dip, but the majority of Hoosiers say that is a mistake, correctly speaking. A true dip has a special mission, that of redeeming second-day cake or leftover gingerbread, but it also enhances some other desserts.)

Gingerbread in Indiana is a bread on its first appearance. It is cut in squares, and each one is topped with a thick piece of yellow butter. And never, many natives emphasize, is it to be spoiled with whipped cream! In a few communities elsewhere, though, whipped cream is used on it, but mainly in Ohio, Indiana, Illinois, Iowa, and Nebraska, gingerbread is a bread, not a dessert. A Kansan occasionally kicks over the traces and serves it with vanilla ice cream, and sometimes with whipped cream. Ohio people are devoted to gingerbread and other *cup cakes* — their name for hot breads baked in muffin pans. Butter goes with them to the table. They are the richer muffins, usually known in other regions as cake-style muffins.

Feathery hot yeast rolls glisten with the butter spread on them and take the blue ribbons as the top bread for special meals. Some women occasionally prefer bacon drippings as the shortening in making them, for a taste they like with cooked vegetables and vegetable salads. In Kansas guest luncheons frequently call for small cinnamon rolls, too. But for the everyday meals, white bread, unheated, goes to the table. That is one custom of the Farm Belt that Southerners fail to appreciate! Nebraska has a perfect right to boast of its tall, round loaves of dark rye bread that contain caraway seeds and shredded orange peel.

Maple Hill Scotch Are Short Bread Experts

My Topeka cousin and her husband, a native of Scotland, find that some of the short bread in and nearby the village of Maple Hill, Kansas, cannot be surpassed overseas. Many people of Scotch descent live in that area. At Christmas time, in preference to recipes she acquired abroad, my cousin traditionally bakes the tea-time treat from a recipe given her by an old lady living in this Scotch-American community.

Lindsborg, Kansas, famed for its Swedish dishes, every week of the year can show rye as well as wheat bread that is worthy of medals. Different nationality groups throughout the region especially affect the bread baking activities. What better proof is needed of Nebraska's diverse population than the treats on the bread trays there? The Cornhusker-Bohemians excel with the exotic kolache — the fruit-topped rolls. Some bakeries in Lincoln and Omaha sell them. There many home kitchens make a good use of their poppy seed grinders on baking day. The household appliance counters of the department stores stock the device when it can be imported from Czechoslovakia. When one cannot be purchased a young homemaker either borrows a grinder from her mother or a neighbor or else she uses an old-fashioned coffee mill as a makeshift. She first runs bread through it to fill the cracks where the tiny precious seeds might get lost.

In most neighborhoods the biscuits are high, and their crusts are brown. When pulled apart gently their interiors show layer after layer of hot flakiness. Jayhawkers and Cornhuskers like to spread them with butter and sand hill plum or other jelly in much the same way as a native of Ohio uses butter and apple butter. Peach preserves are a favorite spread, too. In southern Illinois, where soft wheat grows, some of it is milled for an excellent quality of soft wheat flour — the kind the South prefers. Along the Ohio River and extending to the central sections of Indiana and Illinois the biscuits frequently are the small, thin, crusty kind Dixie adores. There, too, white corn meal is purchased by many households. Indeed, some of the finest cookery in the southern areas of the tri-states — Ohio, Indiana, and Illinois — suggests contact with Kentucky kitchens.

I once met a charming lady in the Blue Grass State who told me that the trouble with the cooks living to the north was that too many of them had been born "on the wrong side of the River!" One of my southern Ohio home economist friends described to me two of her favorite cookery tricks. One is to brown flour a light tan to supply its exquisite, delicate flavor when used to thicken sauces and especially gravy. She says the night before Thanksgiving, for instance, always suggests to her the kitchen fragrance of the browning flour, and the anticipation of turkey gravy to follow the next day. The other stunt is to make jam cake with yellow tomato preserves. Browned flour and the love for jam cakes speak the Kentucky language.

In other parts of the region yellow corn meal goes into the bowl to make the corn bread. About twice as much flour as meal is the universal proportion. Women say the addition of a tablespoonful or two of sugar and plenty of eggs aids in turning out a creditable product. The leavening depends on which kind of milk is employed, sweet or sour.

The fondness for salt rising bread lingers on from pioneer days. Especially do local bakeries along the Ohio River and northward to the central counties sell many loaves of it. The modern version answers as a reasonable facsimile of the old-time one. The main difference now comes from a wide use of bolted corn meal, which does not ferment so rapidly as the usually unavailable unbolted kind. Sweet rolls pair off with coffee everywhere, although most noticeably in areas near the Great Lakes, and in Iowa and Nebraska. A bite into one often reveals a sweet caramel top, and below it soft, chewy raisins and pecans or California walnuts.

Coffee wins the distinction as the foremost breakfast and dinner beverage of the region. Some households select hot tea for the supper drink, or milk. Indeed, the milk drinkers — both adults and children — are steadily becoming more numerous. The tall, tinkling glasses on the tables in summer contain iced tea.

"We Expect Peas To Taste Like June"

Usually the first observation visiting epicures from other areas to the central Farm Belt make concerns what they regard as the bland foods. These mid-Americans like what they refer to as the *natural flavors*. They say they put the season on the table whenever possible. Or as one woman said to me, "We depend on vegetables fresh from the garden row, an occasional squirt of fresh lemon juice, dewy-fresh berries, and the warm-from-the-oven charm in baked foods. We expect peas to be plump and taste like June, and apples ruddy and juicy with October on their breath. We rely on cranberry sauce and salads to color and flavor our winter feasts. The cook's challenge is to coax out and never to hide a food's taste."

Certainly the women who prepare the farmhouse meals require relatively few seasonings. "Just give us salt, pepper, vanilla, butter, sugar, cream, cider vinegar, lemon and almond extracts, and celery salt and we'll get along," one Iowa woman remarked. "Of course we like to have plenty of eggs and milk, too, for we think they improve many dishes. Sage, discreetly added, is important in bread dressings and sausage, and we have used touches of it, celery seed, and mint — especially peppermint — since the covered wagon days. Now we often add crushed red and white peppermint candy for flavoring. We like to have tomatoes, celery, onions, nuts, and raisins, too. I couldn't cook my best without them. Relishes, both the cooked and uncooked ones, also pep up our meals. Cherry olives give many dinners a lift. So also do all kinds of cucumber pickles and spiced peaches and rosy crabapples.

"Our hands are quite easy going with celery salt. We sprinkle it into many vegetable dishes, such as scalloped potatoes and tomatoes, and add it to tomato juice, avocado slices, cottage cheese, potato salad, and ham loaf. Many salad dressings carry a taste of it. And I can't imagine how buttered noodles could win friends without a few shakes of this seasoning.

"Celery seeds frequently contribute their taste. When we use them the flavored salt stays on the shelf. We soak the seeds in hot water a few minutes, or if including them in a dish that contains fat, like buttered noodles, we heat them in it. These tricks bring out their delicacy. Sometimes women buy crushed celery seeds for the same purpose."

In many homes the tomato ketchup bottle goes to the table three times a day along with the sugar bowl. Men and boys, and sometimes the fairer sex, shake it over their breakfast bacon and fried eggs, on sausage, and on fish, baked beans, hamburgers, and meat loaf — on almost anything that appeals to their fancy. They enthuse over chili sauce and mustard. And when a native sees the first crocus, and buds on the pussy willows, dreams start unwinding of the horse-radish and pork team.

Soldiers Believed Nutmeg Cured Malaria

Chili powder enters more homes every year, and garlic and chives are winning larger circles of friends. As for the other herbs, they are — to put it bluntly — distasteful to thousands of people. Yet they are slowly gaining ground. Nutmeg remains a favorite spice in the Ohio River Valley section. There its popularity extends back to the era following the War Between the States. Many a veteran returned from military service with malaria. Nutmeg then was the favored home remedy for the malady, and thus occupied a spot of honor in many cupboards. The cooks, having it on hand, learned that a restrained grating of the nut often enhanced a dish. This explains the unique Indiana custom of dusting cold sliced pork with a suggestion of the spice. Some Hoosiers greatly commend this platter treat.

Breakfast is a square meal, man's size. It starts with a chilled orange, tomato or grapefruit juice, half a grapefruit, applesauce, stewed prunes, or possibly some other fruit or combinations of fruits, and maybe cantaloupe during its season. Then in winter hot cereal follows, often with raisins or cut-up dates in it. Summer brings the crisp ready-to-serve cereals, frequently with sliced bananas, fresh peaches, or home grown berries on top. Brown and white sugars and cream make the round of the table. Next a hot platter appears with its warm offering, frequently bacon and eggs. And as previously mentioned, there is coffee! One of the best ways to start a lively food conversation along the countryside is to mention coffee brands. Everyone staunchly defends his pet one.

This is pancake territory of importance — the land of wheat cakes, thin or thick, large and small. Bread-crumb pancakes also fare well. Corn meal fans like to add from 1/3 to 1/2 cup of the meal for part of the flour in making the batter for the family's breakfast supply of wheat cakes. Some Cornhuskers favor hot griddlecakes spread with thick sour cream and sprinkled with brown sugar. People living in southern Illinois and southern Indiana frequently select sorghum or honey and butter as the accompaniments. But most of the residents elsewhere will settle for butter and sirup of some kind. If maple sirup is not available they make it with brown and white sugars, corn sirup, and water; the mixture is boiled about 5 minutes. Occasionally an Iowan will top a stack of buttered pancakes, two or three, with a fried egg.

Seedless Persimmons Fell Near the Rabbit Trap

By some, such meals are considered typically American. They may be. At least Mrs. Ohio (also Mrs. Indianapolis) is regarded in many commercial circles as Mrs. Uncle Sam. The Buckeye State long has been a test area, the place where manufacturers like to put their new food products on the market for a trial run. If the people there buy them, business men say the chances for a national acceptance are excellent. With this all-American atmosphere spreading from Ohio westward over the central Farm Belt like an autumn haze, a food scout's job of locating distinctive regional treats becomes an unrelenting coverage of the countryside. There abide most of the native culinary creations that exemplify the region's cooking at its best. Let's take persimmon pudding as the A-1 example.

Of course people in some other localities extol the virtues of this dish, too, and especially North Carolinians. Perhaps the Tar Heels sponsored it when they became Hoosiers, as so many of them did before the middle 1850's. Arkansas, Kentucky, and Illinois know its rich taste, but their citizens do not support it with the fervor of a native Hoosier. The dessert is lauded by almost everyone in the southern and central counties of Indiana, where the trees are native. They do not grow in the northern counties. In the tea room of an Indianapolis department store persimmon pudding is on the luncheon menu every day, to the gratification of many people of the state and visitors from other regions. It is made with the frozen fruit.

The native persimmon is small, it contains many seeds, and it is not edible until after autumn's first killing frost. The method of harvesting is to spread a bed of straw under the trees to soften the fall of the fruit. Every morning the fallen supply is gathered. The broken persimmons are quickly sieved and frozen. Women use food mills for the sieving. The device greatly simplifies their work. They add a little milk to the fruit to speed up the process.

Indiana has some trees that bear seedless persimmons, due to the vigilance of a young man about 25 years ago. He picked up a handful of choice fruit from the ground after setting a rabbit trap. Later, when he tasted one, he observed that it was flavorful and seedless. Then he discovered all the fruit was without seeds. So he decided to look for more of it on the next trip to the trap line. On that journey he again located the tree, and found that without exception its persimmons had no seeds. Root cuttings from it have developed into the seedless trees now growing. Some Hoosiers think there should be one or more of them in the backyard of every home in the southern and central counties of the state!

Persimmon puddings vary. Some are steamed. Others are baked. Then there is the newcomer, the uncooked kind that contains the sweetened pulp, graham cracker crumbs, cut-up marshmallows, and nuts. It ripens in the refrigerator several hours before appearing on the table. Most families prefer either the baked kind, which often is stirred several times as it cooks, or the steamed ones. They want them served while warm, and with a hard sauce, whipped cream, or possibly dip on top. One school of cooks votes for the unspiced pudding; a considerably smaller one favors a touch of spices.

The paw-paw rates as one of nature's interesting gifts in the Ohio River Valley. The natives especially vouch for its taste immediately following the first frost. They say it then is in its prime — and for only two or three days. As proof that the country in the boy does not leave him when he grows up, there are busy executives in the cities and towns who annually set aside a day or a half day to go to the country to eat their fill of paw-paws. Perhaps a further reason for the jaunt is the mellow sunshine of the season and the beauty of the countryside in its most brilliant dress.

Popped Corn Is a Popular Snack

When it comes to snacks, the Farm Belt generally will settle for popped corn. Iowa grows more of this corn than any other state. Her people are true to the fluffy, white, expanded kernels, salted and buttered. Popcorn vending machines and sidewalk stands are an authoritative trademark of central Farm Belt cities and towns. A traveler observes dignified men and women munching on the crisp kernels with an informal enthusism equal to that of the boys and girls. Tradition decrees it is proper.

Except in isolated instances fudge is the top-ranking candy. It is most highly praised when studded with black walnuts.

Black walnuts command a high prestige in all of the communities where they grow. Near the Missouri-Kansas line the Jayhawkers have borrowed the walnut pie of the Ozarks for a rich, satisfying meal ending. Hoosiers especially toast their hickory nut cake with praise. Indeed, they arise in food conversations to nominate it as the greatest of all their dishes! The white cake contains nuts, and the 7-minute frosting over it is sprinkled with them. The natives cover the cake tightly and let it stand to absorb the flavor of the nuts.

And what treasures from the kitchens do the regional mothers mail to their children far away at school or in homes of their own? These gifts most frequently are home baked treats like cookies and loaves of special breads. Big cans of popped corn and boxes of popcorn balls also travel these same routes.

Steak Dinners Awaken Slumbering Appetites

The mere mention of Chicago, Omaha, or Kansas City steak dinners awakens slumbering appetites all across the United States. They stand for the ultimate in good eating to millions of Americans. They signify top quality beef, corn-fed, and steaks that are hot and juicy. Most natives like the steak quite thick, in some instances as much as 2 inches. They broil it, often until slightly charred on the outside, and rare or medium-rare within. It comes to the table sputtering on a platter too hot to touch without hand protection. The individual plates on which it is served are warmed, too. People consider steak a meal in itself, although there are potatoes of some sort, like French-fried ones, alongside. There may be a lettuce salad with blue cheese dressing, or a lettuce, tomato, and cucumber one. Often the salad is dispensed with and a few slices of sweet onions and tomatoes do the honors. And there are hot rolls.

Some out-state Jayhawkers and Cornhuskers feature sun-flower potatoes in the steak dinner. The cook shreds the pared potatoes coarsely and drops little mounds of them in a frying pan containing hot fat. She browns them on one side, and then on the other. They are crisp outside, tender and soft within. Anyone who uses a little imagination notes that their appearance somewhat resembles the sunflowers that in summer turn the prairies into acres of gold. Omaha steak houses feature Italian spaghetti as well as French-fried potatoes in their meals. The seasonings everywhere are salt and pepper, pats of butter, and sometimes a few drops of lemon juice dribbled on the melting butter.

Ohio, Indiana, Illinois, Iowa, and Nebraska people boost more for pork than do Kansans. Not that the Jayhawkers do not relish it, but rather that they like beef better. They usually have had more cattle than hogs, and always more wheat than corn, and that makes a difference. Everyone in the central Farm Belt considers roast beef one of the most regal of all meats. It outclasses steak in some popularity polls. Perhaps my eldest brother's food talk typifies a masculine reaction. He says, "Why bother about menu planning? Just start with roast beef or steak and end with cherry pie. That's what we like on this ranch." But a population that grows up in a country where the feed lots fill with cattle for their final feast on grains and other concentrates is realistic enough to know that not all the beef carcass is steak, or roasts. Other great dishes have developed with the less demanded cuts.

Kansas runs up the banners for short ribs of beef. Her cooks like to flour and brown them, and then braise them with vegetables like onions, potatoes, carrots, and celery. And the swing to barbecued beef ribs has reached considerable momentum. The southeastern counties of the Sunflower State are becoming famous for them. The browned ribs are braised in a barbecue sauce instead of water. Iowa cooks excel with barbecued pork chops. They spread the meat with mustard and ketchup, sprinkle on celery seed, and bake two or more layers of the chops.

Barbecued sandwiches, both of beef and pork, have many fans. They commonly consist of the cooked and cut-up or shredded meat heated in a barbecue sauce. The mixture tops a toasted half of a bun. In Indiana the custom is to add an uncooked vegetable relish — its mango-cabbage mixture — before putting on the other toasted half of the bun. In the all-day Kansas beef tours, which Kansas cattlemen make to inspect the production and feeding methods of their ranch neighbors, the noon meal has become quite famous for its barbecued beef. In many instances these occasions are important politically as well as noteworthy fraternal gatherings.

While the barbecue is not strange to any part of the Farm Belt, Kansas and Nebraska — which touch the Mountain West — occasionally put on one that makes the Mountain Men and even the Southwesterners sit up and take notice. "What would we do without the barbecue?" a Cornhusker asked. "It is our way of handling big crowds, as when a dam is dedicated, there is political speech making, or celebrations are staged by large organizations." The Kansas-Nebraska barbecue — or the Farm Belt one — generally is the pit type. Men use pitchforks to lift the cheesecloth-burlap wrapped bundles of meat from the pit, where they have cooked slowly for about 12 hours. To feed 600 people an hour they use one cafeteria-style line, and for 2,500 people four lines. An expert meat carver is at the first table with two sandwich makers at his side. They put the meat in buns, commonly without buttering them. Depending on the order of the day, guests help themselves or are served the hot dish or dishes — generally scalloped potatoes and/or baked beans. Next is the salad, usually cole slaw, and then the dessert, often fruit and cookies.

The men who pour the coffee have few idle moments. At the big barbecues they serve it from pitchers. In Nebraska more pitchers of "white coffee," as the natives call that with cream added, normally are emptied than of black coffee. In some communities the proportion is 3 to 1. Milk in half-pint bottles and straws are provided for the children, or perhaps chocolate milk.

· Natives describe the perfect way to make the coffee for a crowd like this.

"Go to a creamery or some other place that has clean live steam. There fill a 10-gallon cream can about two-thirds full of water. Add 2 pounds of coffee tied loosely in a cheesecloth bag. Then turn in live steam to fill the can. Finally adjust the tight fitting lid. By the use of this method it is easy to transport wonderful tasting coffee to the barbecue scene. It stays hot a long time."

Barbecue chefs like to have reserve supplies on hand.

That is an outcropping of a trait common to all ranch people. They usually buy such canned items as baked beans and sweet potatoes, and dill pickles that can be sliced and substituted for salad. While some barbecues provide a hot, peppery sauce to ladle over the meat, the traditional, typical style is not to include one.

Farm Belt People Are Stingy With Chili?

Chili con carne has traveled north and east from the Southwest with a speed almost unparalleled by other regional dishes. People call it *chili,* and are inclined to think of anyone who says chili con carne as affected. It takes someone from the Southwest to observe the mild seasoning most natives use. My 12-year old nephew from Durango, Colorado, politely inquired of me about it. "Why do people in Kansas, Nebraska, and Iowa add such a stingy bit of chili powder?" he asked. "You can scarcely taste it."

The Farm Belt cooks make other changes, too, from the Santa Fe, New Mexico, methods. For instance, they almost always use kidney beans, usually the canned ones. They heat the beans in the sauce. Naturally, their dish tastes differently from one with the hot sauce served on the same plate with pinto or Mexican pink beans. Several years ago chili houses were quite the vogue in Indianapolis. Then everyone ordered chili two-way or chili three-way. Chili two-way consists of the meat-tomato-pepper sauce mixture spooned over heated kidney beans. Chili three-way starts out with the layer of beans, then one of spaghetti, and lastly the sauce. These names appear in some Hoosier conversations today. And throughout the state, especially in the capital city, good cooks commonly fold both kidney beans and spaghetti into chili con carne.

In Nebraska some women include cubed potatoes in this dish that speaks of the Southwest. "Don't add them too early," they warn, "or the spuds will become mushy. Barely allow time for them to become tender." I also encountered soy chili in Illinois and again in Ohio.

ILLINOIS SOY CHILI

1 pound ground beef or pork	1 teaspoon sugar
1 small onion, chopped	1 tablespoon chili powder
2 cups tomatoes or tomato purée	1 teaspoon salt
1 cup cooking water from the beans	3 cups cooked soy beans

Brown the meat and onion in the fat from the meat and add the other ingredients except the beans. Simmer gently ¾ hour. Then add the beans and thoroughly heat. Many families prefer less chili powder.

The dish calls for either beef or pork, as do so many recipes in Ohio, Indiana, Illinois, Iowa, and Nebraska. In Iowa, for example, the meat-tomato sauces for cooked spaghetti or macaroni frequently are made with ground pork. A farmhouse style cook, especially if she lives in town, also cuts pork in cubes and simmers them in a little water until tender. Then she uses them, seasoned with salt and pepper, along with cut-up celery in salads and to make an *à la king*. She also grinds this *mock chicken* for sandwiches. If she must use veal, which is none too well received, she cooks it with pork. She says that conceals the veal taste! Scrapple, regionally, is corn-meal mush with cooked ground pork or beef stirred through it.

Buckeye People Like the Celery Taste

Of all the methods of preparing beef and pork, no one is dearer to the natives' hearts than teaming the meat with bread dressing. It is the same type of dressing the cooks stuff into poultry. The seasonings are simple — salt, pepper, butter, and possibly a trace of sage, minced onion, and finely cut celery or tiny celery leaves. Many women first pan-fry the onion and celery gently to tenderize and very lightly color the onion — a yellow hue. People in Ohio have a rather heavy hand with celery. Sometimes the roast, like a loin of pork, shares space in the pan with the dresing. Pockets to accommodate the stuffing also are cut in some meats. Then there is the stunt of wrapping thin meat slices around the dressing and fastening them with twine or toothpicks.

One universal platter favorite starts out with thick pork

chops. They really are cut in pairs with a slit made between the two. After flouring and browning the openings are filled with dressing. The chops are crowded together in a pan and braised slowly, with a little water added, for from 1 to 1½ hours. Spareribs tied around dressing also bake in countless ovens in the wintertime.

IOWA SUNDAY DINNER
(For Company)
Tomato Juice
Baked Pork Chops   Dressing
Mashed Potatoes   Milk Gravy
Green Beans
Apple Sauce
Buttered Hot Rolls
Head Lettuce   Blue Cheese Dressing
Fruited Gelatin   Whipped Cream
Angel Food Cake

Some Jayhawkers rave about *beef birds* — small thin pieces of round steak wrapped around spoonfuls of dressing, fastened securely, floured, browned, and simmered gently in water until tender. Other country women wind a large thin round steak around the dressing — it resembles a jelly roll cake — and braise it like the *birds*. Both methods are designated as excellent gravy makers, a point that sets them on a pedestal and enhances their appeal.

Nebraska is an important dairy state, and many households cheer for *veal birds* prepared like the Kansas ones made of beef. But they have a neat trick. They add finely ground pork to the bread dressing. People living in Cincinnati and its environs — and indeed in all of Ohio — have a high regard for the taste of mushrooms. This liking shows up in their *ham birds.* They make a bread dressing that contains considerable celery and some onion and wrap thin cooked ham slices around spoonfuls of it. Then they secure the rolls with toothpicks or twine, add canned mushroom soup, cover the pan, and bake their favorite in a moderate oven, 350°, to heat and blend the flavors. They also scallop cabbage with mushrooms for a winning dish, and serve crisply coated pan-fried eggplant with creamed mushrooms.

Hoosiers favor their pork special. "What is it?" almost all visitors inquire. They learn it is the sliced eye of pork loin. Women flour or dip it in egg and crumbs, and pan-fry it to a crisp brown on the outside. It is tender and moist within. The center cuts of the loin also occasionally are sliced, flattened out, and sold as pork special. With this skillet treat meaty milk gravy and fluffs of mashed potatoes answer as worthy teammates.

Why Remove the Pork Rind?

An Indiana cook is likely to follow an old-time custom in seasoning. She lays one — no more and no less — bay leaf on top of every cut of pork that goes into the oven to roast. The Cornhuskers choose a different procedure. They substitute a few caraway seeds for the bay leaf. Many an Iowa woman sprinkles a very little crushed sage on the breaded or baked pork steaks or chops for the last 5 minutes of cookery. Hoosiers praise sliced fresh side pork — caught before it is converted into bacon — pan-fried. They also cheer for the milk gravy that follows it. The native cooks have a unique habit of not removing the rind. Instead they slash it at intervals so the slices will lie flat in the pan. When asked why they do not cut off the rind, they reply, "Why do it? What is gained? No one eats it. Anyhow our family always has left it on."

Iowa excels with pork sandwiches, where in some communities they lead hamburgers as a popular choice. They are floured and expertly pan-fried pork tenderloin slices tucked into buns. Cole slaw escorts them. A Kansas sandwich that wins something like the same acclaim traditionally is made with slices of hot roast beef — but more frequently in these modern days with beef pot roast! The cook lays the meat on a slice of white bread and ladles brown gravy, piping hot, over it. She drops fluffs of mashed potatoes at its side, and adds a slice of tomato, a cucumber pickle, or a little cole slaw, or possibly all three.

From one end of the area to the other the kitchens at all seasons frequently emit a tell-tale sound. Children welcome it with, "Goody, we're having Swiss steak for dinner." It is the rhythmical thump of a heavy saucer or a meat hammer as the cook pounds the flour into the meat. Natives prefer a cut of round steak about 2 inches thick for this treasure. Without much complaint, though, they will settle for one somewhat thinner, possibly from 1 to 1½ inches. They brown the meat deeply on both sides in a little fat, after first cooking 2 chopped onions in it. They save the onions until the beef is brown, and then scatter them on top. Around the meat they pour 2 cups of liquid, frequently 2 cups of cooked or canned tomatoes. They cover the heavy pan and simmer the beef until it is fork-tender. That means anyone can cut it with a fork without half trying. After the beautiful Swiss steak is lifted to the hot platter the cook reaches for the flour cannister and starts the gravy making. Natives toast this tomato flavored gravy with appetite-whetting compliments, especially when spooned over mashed potatoes.

Another regional platter treat is braised pork shoulder steaks plus milk gravy touched with black pepper and horse-radish. Mashed, boiled, or baked potatoes go with them to the dinner plates.

Lindsborg Fried Chicken Is Tops

Fried chicken à la Farm Belt! Natives believe it cannot be surpassed. What expert is wise enough to define on what its excellence depends? It is different from other fried chicken. No one questions that. But how and why? Commonly the young chickens are somewhat larger than those preferred in the South. The dressed weights ordinarily vary from 2½ to 3 pounds. Cooks refrigerate the disjointed pieces. Then they rub seasoned flour into them, or toss them in a paper bag containing it. They brown them in a heavy frying pan with fat about ½ inch deep. The fat is hot. Many women let a drop of water fall into it. If it sizzles they say, "Add the chicken."

Often the natives keep the pieces moving until they are browned on all sides. Then they reduce the heat. They cover the pan and cook the chicken gently until it is tender. That usually takes from 30 to 45 minutes. Most of them remove the lid for the last 10 minutes to encourage crispness. Perhaps the gentlemen of the feed lots have a part of the answer for the delicious taste. They say some of it comes from the poultry's feed — plenty of grain and lots of skimmed milk.

Of course there are other tricks. My capable assistant of twenty some years pins her faith on the addition of cream to chicken as it cooks. No one tasting her productions argues the point with her. She calls her method the *Lindsborg* (Kansas) *way* in honor of her native village.

First she browns the floured chicken in a little fat. Then she pours on cream, sweet or sour and thin or thick, to the depth of an inch. (She prefers sour cream — the heavy kind.) After that she reduces the heat and covers the pan. The chicken cooks very slowly until tender, usually about 45 minutes. She takes off the lid during the last quarter hour of cooking. Quail and pheasants — when the hunter brings them into the kitchen — veal chops, and chicken fried beefsteak also respond to her treatment. The gravy that eventually comes out of the frying pan is faultless. She believes that all it needs for distinguished table service is plenty of mashed potatoes!

SUNDAY DINNER
(Ohio Style)
Fried Chicken   Brown Gravy
Mashed Potatoes
Buttered Peas
Perfection Salad
Hot Rolls
Chocolate-Nut Sundae
Iced Tea

Frequently red-ripe tomatoes play the salad role. If the jellied perfection salad is used, it commonly is made in advance, and with tomato juice as part of the liquid.

Geese Are Served by the Bohemians

Ohio people consider chicken and celery combinations as something special. One dish I tasted in Cincinnati offered proof of their sound judgment. My hostess browned the floured disjointed chicken. She arranged the pieces in a shallow pan. Then she scattered chopped celery, including some of the tender leaves, over the top. After that she poured on a little water and tucked the pan in a slow oven, 325°, to cook until its contents were tender.

Of course the natives welcome baked chicken with wheat bread (white) dressing. Turkey is the first choice for Thanksgiving Day. Most families also prefer it for Christmas. The Bohemian communities of Nebraska get off the beam — or so they say. A family there usually selects a goose or ducks for the December holiday. Also there are thousands of Kansans who prefer a standing rib roast of beef for the occasion.

Most of the bright performers in farmhouse style cooking, women who really are acquainted with their kitchens, are experts in the preparation and serving of fricassee of chicken with dumplings or noodles. Some Kansans of the ranch country find that everyone hurries to the table a little faster if beef with dumplings or noodles appears. Ohio is a noodle center. Her cooks employ smart stunts to give them special appeal. Often they tint the broth a deeper yellow for a sunny effect. They butter the cooked, drained noodles, too. And they mix them with cheese sauce. Because these culinary experts are conscious of how texture contrasts improve a dish they also add crisp toppings. Perhaps the favorite is tiny bread cubes — *bread blocks,* they call them. They either toast the bread or pan-fry it in butter to make it crunchy. Another stunt is to pan-fry a few of the cooked noodles in butter until they are crisp and brown, and to give them the crowning role. Then there is the old-time favorite combination — noodles with a pot roast and brown gravy.

One of my New York home economist friends confesses she acquired an affection for noodles in her Harrison, Ohio, home. She presented me with one of her pet versions.

To the hot, drained, cooked noodles she added a lavish quantity of butter. Then she mixed in crushed poppy seeds and slivers of blanched, toasted almonds. As the final touch she grated the yellow of lemon peel and the green of lime peel on top. "It has the beautiful yellow and green Ohio-in-spring look," she declared as she ran it in a moderate oven to heat thoroughly.

The Food Star of Tippecanoe County

Indiana is proud of her topnotch chicken-noodle creation. That I met, too, through a friend, one of my university roommates. She is a native of Tippecanoe County in that state. Whenever after classes she was hungry she eulogized her mother's version of chicken and noodles. Thoughts of the dish were as sweet and haunting to her as the strains of a Viennese waltz. This old-time food number is as popular today as ever.

When the chicken, simmered gently in seasoned water, is tender, the Hoosier home chef removes it from the broth. She discards the bones and cuts the meat fine. In the meantime she cooks the finely cut noodles in the broth. When they are ready she adds the chicken. After being heated it is a great picnic dish — this shredded chicken and noodles. It travels to the outdoor meal in a large kettle. Many mothers feature it in backyard suppers when entertaining other families or groups of children. Another sure-to-be-present picnic dish is the Hoosier kidney bean salad. I learned of it from the same Tippecanoe County friend. And I have met it on the visits I have made to Hoosier territory. Here is the way the natives make it.

Mix the chilled canned beans with chopped cucumber pickles, cut-up celery, sliced hard-cooked eggs and chopped mangoes (or sweet peppers!). Add 1 unpared, cored, and diced apple. Then pour on vinegar to season and sprinkle with salt and pepper.

One of the revered Iowa farmhouse chicken specialties also comes from the fricassee kettles. The cook removes the meat and discards the bones. She spreads the cut-up chicken in a rather shallow pan. Then she tops it with a seasoned bread dressing which she pats on top. Over this she pours enough chicken broth to provide sufficient moisture. She bakes the entree to heat and brown. After that she serves it cut in squares with a molded cranberry salad alongside.

Baked beans are as much American as the Fourth of July. Every region has its ideas about how to prepare them. The

Boston baked ones are at home in the Farm Belt, but they do not rule the roost. Indiana, for instance, likes brown sugar in her beans, but prefers sorghum to molasses. And there are various other regional variations. But the characteristic baked beans, farmhouse style, contain tomatoes in some form — the canned vegetables, tomato juice, tomato ketchup, canned tomato soup, or chili sauce. About a half cup of tomatoes or a derivative of them to 2 cups of uncooked beans is the most common proportion. A bean pot is not regarded as necessary. Any heavy casserole of oven-proof glass or earthenware does the job satisfactorily. Illinois, an important producer of soy beans, knows how to bake these nutritive legumes so they taste good. Ohio cooks possess the same skill.

ILLINOIS BAKED BEANS

3 cups cooked soy beans	3 tablespoons molasses
½ teaspoon dry mustard	2 teaspoons Worcestershire sauce
1 teaspoon salt	½ cup boiling water
⅛ teaspoon pepper	½ cup chili sauce
¼ cup salt pork, diced	

Combine all the ingredients except the salt pork in a baking dish. Cook the pork in a frying pan until delicately browned. Add the drippings to the mixture. Arrange the pork on top. Bake 1 hour in a moderate oven, 350°.

Praise for Shell-outs and Hull-outs

Hoosiers and southern Ohio people speak kindly of many varieties of beans. They literally sing the praises of *shell-outs*. This is what they call cranberry beans. Indeed, many of the natives do not know that shell-outs in other states have another name. People in the southern counties also rate cornfield beans highly. These are the large green beans dear to Kentuckians. These Indiana and Illinois people share a fondness for them with their neighbors across the Ohio River. Some of the mature beans are shelled and cooked with the cut-up, younger pods. Hoosiers refer to them as *hull-outs*. The succotash of Ohio, Indiana, and Illinois usually contains corn and cut-up green beans. The seasonings are butter, salt, and pepper. When a cook wishes to go fancy she adds a third vegetable, green lima beans. Many northern Ohio homes prefer lima beans and corn teamed together for succotash.

Thick bean soups belong to the farmhouse. Usually they vary but little in these agricultural states. The vegetable generally cooks with a ham bone. Many women add an onion. Some Kansas and Nebraska people also like to include tomatoes. And almost everyone peps them up with horse-radish just before serving.

Indiana households consider the Hoosier bean soup, which is almost thick enough to classify as a stew, a fine supper main dish for Saturdays. Some women also feature it in dinners on exceptionally busy days. They say it requires little pot watching. "Use Great Northern beans, not the navy or pea kind," one of my hostesses advised. "We like the meaty ones for this dish. It is traditional to cook an onion with the beans or to have sliced onion with them. At our house we serve the raw sweet onion slices in vinegar. Salt and black pepper season them. We select either pork or ham for the meat. For a still heartier meal, I tuck a few potatoes in the kettle with the ham or pork and beans. I add them just in time to become tender."

SATURDAY SUPPER
(Hoosier Style)
Beans with Pork and Potatoes
Sliced Onions in Vinegar
Corn Bread
Wilted Lettuce or Cole Slaw
Baked Apples

Chicken-noodle soup is a classic throughout the area. Most Kansans consider a beef soup thick with vegetables as unbeatable. The spoon always finds onions, rice or potato cubes, celery, and tomatoes in it. And there are many tiny hunks of tender beef, too.

SATURDAY SUPPER
(Jayhawker Style)
Thick Beef-Vegetable Soup
Crackers
Molded Waldorf Salad
Applesauce Cake
Milk

The boiled dinner follows two patterns. In one ham or a ham-bone with whole potatoes and cabbage wedges takes the honors. The other one is more like a New England version, with fresh beef — frequently the brisket — substituted for corned beef. The vegetable medley traditionally does not include beets. The central Farm Belt — or at least many of its people — holds that beets are for pickling, not for the vegetable dish. Cornhuskers, by the way, like caraway seeds in their beet pickles. Neither turnips nor rutabagas have large circles of friends. Generally the people say they are willing to give their share of these vegetables to folks who live far away — to persons who like them! There are a few communities, especially in Ohio and Nebraska, where turnips are more popular. Summer squash is another vegetable with a doubtful acceptance in the area. The Des Moines or acorn squash, on the other hand, is relished.

Usually cooks cut them in halves. They scoop out the seeds and bake them inverted — cut sides down — in a pan containing a little water. Frequently they arrange them on a platter and fill their yellow cavities with a creamed food. Creamed chicken or creamed dried beef often win the distinction of converting the vegetable into a main dish. Many households like to bake sausage and also ham loaf, shaped in balls, in the squash.

Potatoes win hands down as the king of the vegetables. These are the white or Irish kind. Save in a small percentage of the homes sweet potatoes comparatively take a back seat. Scalloped spuds maintain an even keel of popularity throughout the year. In the winter thin pork chops or slices of ham frequently bake on their tops. Then they are an entree. In the summer women wrap the casserole filled with the spuds in newspapers; they go to picnics to support the fried chicken, and to barbecues to complement the beef.

Ohio enjoys cooked onions more than the other states. The women cream them. They also serve them in cheese sauce. Green beans, except in the Ohio River Valley region, must be young and succulent if they are to win compliments.

Cooked vegetables, creamed in white sauce, are losing their prestige. More and more families now choose either butter or butter and unthickened cream to dress them.

Macaroni and cheese compose a firmly entrenched supper main dish. The usual method of preparing the treat is with white sauce. But tomatoes sometimes get involved in it. In countless kitchens tomato sauce takes the white sauce role.

Tuna Recipes From the Mother-in-Law

By no stretch of the imagination can the people who live in the region classify as enthusiastic fish eaters. Canned salmon and tuna have earned an established foothold in the cuisine. Both are enjoyed. Most families prefer the salmon thoroughly chilled, with lemon or vinegar, and escorted by potatoes fried fresh. They also like salmon loaves with creamed peas. And they cream salmon and serve it on toast. Many women are tuna recipe hounds. They have files and files of them, which do not suffer from neglect. The tuna-noodle-mushroom soup casserole, often topped with crushed potato chips, takes the blue ribbons as the most dependable quick supper dish. The recipes for it are legion. Some women add cheese, others fold in green peas, sliced hard-cooked eggs, or a variety of other foods. Help with making this modern classic is about the first request a bride makes of her mother-in-law, for she finds that her new husband adores his mother's version of this special favorite of his boyhood. At kitchen showers for brides these recipes always show up.

FARM BELT FISH DINNER
(A Nebraska Special)
Tuna-Noodle Casserole
Buttered Asparagus
Carrot Sticks   Cherry Olives
Lemon Meringue Pie

Shrimp walks away with honors in the sea food class, although oysters please many people, especially when served in stews. Baked halibut has its sponsors. Good cooks like to bake a slice of it on a bed of bacon, chopped. Then they scatter on shredded cheese a few minutes before they take it from the oven.

There is a considerable gain year by year in the number of flood control projects, state lakes, and large farm ponds. In some instances the increasing local production of fish is quite gratifying. The bamboo fishing pole has not disappeared.

The advent of packaged frozen fillets has given an impetus to the sale of fish. As with meat, the natives team them with bread. They line a greased shallow pan with crumbs. Then they place the fish on top, and scatter on more of the bread. As a final touch they pour on melted butter, margarine, or bacon drippings. Or they make a barbecue sauce with the melted fat by adding vinegar or lemon juice, salt, pepper, and a touch of Worcestershire sauce. They dribble it over the fillets before they bake them in a hot oven. More frequently the cook rolls the fish in flour and pan-fries it in bacon fat.

The Aunt in Wichita Adores Apples

Then there are apples. A Farm Belt kitchen is not well stocked without them. Like potatoes they always have been an integral part of meals. Families like them "for a vegetable," as they say, in salads and desserts. Often women spread packaged frozen apples in a shallow pan, and dust on sugar and a few grains of salt. Then they distribute golden dots of butter over the surface. They call the fruit, after it has baked slowly for about 40 minutes, the perfect selection for "a vegetable" in the main course of a meal. Autumn brings pan-fried apples to the entire area, and especially to the Ohio River Valley. There on frosty evenings anyone walking down a street in the towns smells the fragrance of the apples turning to a delicate brown in the frying pans. Traces of brown sugar and salt answer for seasonings, bacon drippings for the fat.

Apple dumplings never surrender their prestige. The cook wraps the sugared, buttered, cored fruit in coats of rich biscuit dough and crowds it into a shallow pan. If she uses spice it generally is nutmeg, just a smattering. Then she adds ½ cup of hot water and runs the promise of a de luxe meal ending into a hot oven. She bastes the dessert several times with melted butter mixed with hot water. This she says yields steam that helps to produce the coveted crisp crusted, shiny, brown dumpling with a tender, fruity heart.

It frequently requires mental gymnastics for a native instantly to single out the taste triumphs of his area. That is the rule with people all across the United States with the exception of some persons in the South and especially New Orleans, and in California. When I was in Baton Rouge a member of the foods staff of the University of Louisiana asked me about Kansas foods. She said, "I suppose you will write about apple dishes when you present your native favorites." I was taken back, and explained that while Jayhawkers like apples, they make dishes with them which people in other places invented. Then she added, "But surely no state uses apples in so many different ways and as frequently as the Kansans. When I visit my aunt in Wichita we have apples in all kinds of dishes and every day for the two weeks I am with her." Then I explained again, possibly to gain time while thinking about her suggestion, "All states use apples freely." To which she rejoined with the final words, "Not Louisiana!"

In the Jayhawker supper menu presented earlier in this chapter apples show up in two ways, in molded Waldorf salad and somewhat disguised in the applesauce cake chockfull of raisins and California walnuts. An applesauce cake frequently substitutes, especially with the younger families, for a holiday fruit cake. (Fruit cakes in the farmhouse style of cooking are the dark loaves. The nut breads, on the other hand, are light in color.)

Other favored desserts include *berry cobblers*, sometimes with two crusts but perhaps more commonly with one, *biscuit-berry* shortcake, and in the Ohio River Valley the *floating island*. There a southern name for it was borrowed. The natives speak of *floats*. Often diced oranges, sliced bananas, and sliced peaches or other fruit occupy the bottom of a glass bowl or individual serving dishes. Next the cook adds the meringue. Then she pours on hot soft custard and presses the meringue into it. Some women use a flat wire whisk to combine the meringue and the custard and leave its decorative imprint on top. A few households brown the meringue lightly in a broiler.

Modern Farm Machinery Is a Kitchen Aid!

Perhaps no more radical change has come to the food picture in the Farm Belt than the almost complete disappearance of the tremendous meals once served to big groups of field workers. Mainly the crowds of harvesters have vanished. The extraordinary development and use of farm machines in recent years has wrought the miracle. In Iowa, for instance, only at silo filling time do very many men normally congregate on the same job. Usually then the neighbors help one another out. The rule is for everyone to eat breakfast and supper at home. (Corn shellers must be fed, too, but the groups are smaller.)

The wives go with their husbands for the day. A part of the festive, hearty dinner — the kind the meat-potato-gravy men like — is prepared in advance. The women take some foods from the freezer. They reheat the rolls, cakes, and pies, and quickly cook the different vegetables. The meal satisfies. It is delicious. Following it the dishes frequently are stacked in the electric dish washer. The occasion promotes neighborliness by bringing friends together. It is an event almost everyone looks forward to with pleasure — in contrast to the old days when women stayed awake nights worrying about the problem of feeding 20 men for three meals on several successive days. From personal knowledge and experience I know how that task appeared to women living in the wheat empire that extends through Ford County, Kansas.

One of the observations a roving food reporter always makes is the interest of men in good cooking. In Minneapolis I heard about the glories of Dakota kitchens. It was on a golden autumn afternoon just before I boarded a train to go west. No doubt my eyes were agog as I listened to an executive of a large milling company describe the Dakota pheasant dinners, farmhouse style. "I go out almost every year to visit our neighbors to the west and do a little shooting," he explained. "And I, while proud of our Minnesota cooking, am here to say that Dakota women also know much about the art. You may have dinner in a modest country home, but the linen is spotless white. The dishes, glassware, and silver gleam.

"The highlight, of course, is the platter heaped with rich brown pheasant. It is a colorful, not a pale-face meal. It matches the flaming gold and scarlet of the countryside. The Indian squash is mashed and whipped light. Its deep orange hue complements the gray of the wild rice at its side. Glasses of shimmering jelly, like choke cherry and high-bush cranberry, always are nearby. And then there are those crisp, homemade dill pickles! The gravy? It's brown and wonderful — it contains cream. The rolls are light and feathery — and also hot. They're just as good as those my Danish mother used to make. Perhaps by then you don't care much about the dessert, but who can refuse the maroon-hued baked apples and the thick, country cream lavished on them? Or the cookies? And, of course, the coffee is plentiful, hot, and wonderful."

In the subsequent days as I visited with good cooks in the Dakotas I told them of the advance notice I had received of their culinary artistry. They modestly smiled. Obviously they appreciated the tribute. But they all agreed that the hunters who come in the fall are active all day. The fresh air and exercise, they pointed out, promote ravenous appetites. "That helps," one country woman remarked, "to give our meals the enviable reputation they have achieved with many of our visitors."

Maybe so, I thought a hundred times at I traveled about the countryside. Certainly a keen appetite is a boon to the enjoyment of good food. But even if that is discounted it is quite apparent that the two states have their share of excellent cooks — and then some! In the first place, the Scandinavian influence dominates the kitchens. This partly explains the marvelous breads, cakes, and cookies. It also motivates a generosity in adding butter and cream as ingredients in dishes. And while the use of both is declining, due to the increasing prices of dairy products, they still appear right along on farm tables, and especially for anything like a special occasion. Cream, the women say, cannot be eliminated from the kitchen if the meal is to reach the highest pinnacle of delicious eating.

"There's Nothing to Cooking Pheasants!"

Pheasants are regarded by the natives about like beef in Kansas and pork in Iowa. Women have learned about preparing them from long experience.

"There's nothing to it," a farm woman in South Dakota assured me, "especially if you are of Scandinavian descent. You just cook them like chicken. Of course you must remember they aren't fat like well-fed barnyard fowls. That's because a pheasant always is walking, walking, walking. Sometimes he runs like the wind — that fast. Unless you supply fat the meat is dry. We choose cream. I venture the opinion that your Kansas friends in Lindsborg use it in cooking game and poultry, too.

"We flour the pieces of pheasant and brown them carefully in fat. Our preference is for butter, but we use other kinds, too. Then we place the pieces in a heavy pan and pour on cream to a depth of about an inch. We prefer thick, sour cream, but make the best of what we have. Then we cover the pan and run it in a slow oven, about 325°, to cook lazily for from 1½ to 2 hours, or possibly less — just until the pheasant is tender. It is a good idea to remove the lid for the last half hour. The drippings in the pan team with milk and flour to make a wonderful gravy. Salt and pepper are the only seasonings.

"If the occasion is super special we cook only the pheasant breasts for it. They are the choicest parts. The drumsticks are extremely muscular. Of course we like them, too. We cook them later the same way, only we allow more time."

The wild ducks of the Dakotas, in contrast to the pheasants, are fat. Natives say they are "fat enough to burst." In the grain fields there the birds feed for a time in preparation for the flight south. Women like to bake them. There is no one method of procedure. People who champion rare duck are in the minority. They run the unstuffed birds into a very hot oven, 450°, for about 20 minutes. But most families stuff them with whole onions, apples, or oranges and discard the vegetable or fruit after the roasting. They bake the game in a moderate oven, 350°, for from 2 to 2½ hours, or until it is well done. It is traditional to baste the birds frequently — as often as every 15 minutes — with orange juice. The one rule for the menu planner is to serve a tart jelly of some kind in the duck dinner.

No one doubts that the Dakotas belong to the Farm Belt. They are great wheat producers. Especially does their Durham wheat bring fame. This is the type used by manufacturers of macaroni and spaghetti products. Curiously, the people of the two states do not especially relish these foods in their meals.

The local cooks excel with crisp dill pickles of many varieties. They are experts in the kitchen with fish. Indeed, these people are the great fish eaters of the prairies. When lutfisk is in season it is extremely popular. It is dressed with melted butter and draws boiled potatoes as a companion. Also cream sauce flavored vaguely with mustard shows up on many tables.

Smörgasbords Have a Loyal Following

Of the meats, beef is the king. Pork ranks second, and veal third. Lamb is a slow fourth. Perhaps the favorable standing of veal comes, at least in part, from the sour cream gravy that escorts it. Jellied veal loaves also enjoy considerable prestige. Then there are the many dishes, like Swedish meat balls, in which beef, pork, and veal get together with tasty results. Creamed veal carries a tinge of nutmeg. Even some vegetables are seasoned deftly with this spice. Carrots and cabbage are two examples.

Cottage cheese is a mainstay in family meals. People

in the Dakotas like it with brown sugar and cream. They welcome many kinds of Norwegian and Swedish cheeses, especially for the smörgasbords. These meals are the money raisers for the church groups. They also are exhibits, equal to the pheasant dinners, of the products of the region's finest cookery. Indeed, the cuisine is reminiscent of that of Minnesota.

This is North Country. Geography politely sets it aside from the remainder of the Farm Belt. The natives like root vegetables. Turnips, rutabagas, and parsnips are especially esteemed. The varieties of all local vegetables grown necessarily are those adapted to a short but fast growing season. The Buttercup squash provides a splendid example.

Winter squash have a tremendous number of friends. All scalloped vegetables please. And then there are the potatoes! Who has not heard of those that grow in the Red River Valley?

It might be difficult to prove, but the mashed potatoes seem to be fluffier than the same dish in some other areas. That certainly ties them to the rest of the Farm Belt, where splendid mashed potatoes and gravy are the rule. When asked about the secrets with these two dishes, a North Dakota woman told me, "Cream in both cases. We add a little thick cream when mashing potatoes. That makes them whip up lighter and more deliciously. And we add cream to many of our best meat dishes as they cook. Thus the drippings, which flavor the gravy, are especially tasty." As in Minnesota, the mashed turnips and rutabagas depend to some degree on the small quantity of whipped cream folded in for their lightness and taste.

The salads are affected by the long winters. Many of the makings are shipped in from other regions. Tomato aspic easily reigns as the queen of the winter ones. Women cut the gay red jelly into tiny cubes. They combine them with many salad vegetables. Favorites include crisp, thin onion rings, fine shreds of lettuce and cabbage, chopped celery, and parsley. For Christmas salad plates in "the land of the

Dacotahs" the red cubes of tomato aspic and sprigs of parsley show off the season's colors on lettuce. Another delight consists of canned cranberry jelly, topped off with finely cut celery, and then with the dressing and slivers of salted almonds.

At the community meals, often smörgasbord style, the fruit salads in big bowls invite the guests to help themselves. The dressing stands by in another bowl. It is the cooked type, fluffy and delicious with whipped cream.

Here are two states where open-face sandwich making flourishes as an art. Many of them are small and beautiful as well as flavorful. For a spring treat, the small school boy said: Use peanut butter, with chopped green onion added, spread on rye bread. Coffee and milk are the two beverages. And what coffee drinkers the adults are!

All of the American Cakes Appear

The medals of honor go to the baked foods. Every luscious cake Americans like to bite into comes from the home ovens at one time or another. I kept track of a few of them that I encountered. The list is a memory chest of triumphs that personify the area. The angel foods include chocolate, orange, and mocha flavored ones. Then there is the *mocha cake* made with very strong coffee. On it sliced bananas and whipped cream substitute for the frosting. *Spring beauty* is a dainty, ladylike sponge cake. Its frosting is the 7-minute kind with sliced strawberries folded in.

A galaxy of orange and lemon cakes is made. All of them are worthy of prize awards. The occasional use of marshmallows in the frostings for them is a regional habit. (Marshmallow-chocolate pies represent the pie family with distinction, as do the sour cream-raisin and date pies, which always are chilled before serving.) *Nugget cake* is made with sour milk and brown sugar; it contains lots of chopped dates and California walnuts. And who has counted the kinds of chocolate cakes? Those made with sour cream have a popularity edge over the others. There also is that fabulous *whipped cream cake.* In it heavy cream, whipped, takes the shortening role. It truly melts in the mouth.

This is the layer cake women refer to with unlimited pride. "It's so moist and tender," they say. "And it is a change. We put whipped cream into the batter, rather than on top of the cake. But don't try to make it without heavy cream, or that with a butterfat content of from 35 to 38 per cent."

WHIPPED CREAM CAKE

1½ cups whipping cream	2 teaspoons baking powder
3 eggs, beaten thoroughly	½ teaspoon salt
2¼ cups cake flour	½ to 1 teaspoon almond flavoring
1½ cups sugar	

Whip the heavy cream until stiff and fold in the thoroughly beaten eggs. Sift together the flour, sugar, baking powder, and salt. Fold the mixture into the whipped cream and eggs. Blend in the almond extract. For most people ½ teaspoon suffices. Or use 1 teaspoon of vanilla instead. Pour into two greased and floured cake pans. Bake in a moderate oven, 350°, from 30 to 35 minutes. "Serve the cake plain," women advise. "Or put the layers together with a bright red jelly and dust confectioners' sugar on top. Or spread your favorite orange filling between the layers and cover the top and sides with white boiled frosting. To make this frosting answer for a filling and cake covering, too, just add, when it is ready to spread, ½ cup of cut-up strawberries or thoroughly drained crushed pineapple. And don't hesitate to serve this dessert to the most fastidious of guests."

The cookies are the delicate, rewarding Scandinavian ones. Christmas time is their gala season, but they appear during all the months. By tradition they contain butter. Many of them still do, but economic pressures are forcing women to adapt their recipes to the use of other less expensive shortenings. Good cooks are making the right-about-face a successful project. And as previously indicated, the trend also is toward a reduction in the kitchen use of whipped cream.

The Women Use Cream Skillfully

A Dakota woman has a certain philosophy in regard to the role of whipped cream in cooking. She holds that success depends on handling it, as an ingredient or a garnish, in a way so it will bring out the taste of a food, not mask it. The cream is flavored according to what it trims — to complement it. With gingerbread she likes the lemon taste in the garnish. With peach-apricot and cherry upside-down cakes she chooses a touch of almond extract. And she sees to it that on chocolate desserts the whipped cream decoration carries a little spice.

Three noble taste triumphs sampled on my food scouting in the Dakotas are *thimble cookies, cornets,* and thickened fruit juice desserts. My hostess made the thimble dainties by dipping little balls of cooky dough in beaten egg white and rolling them in coconut. She lined them up on the baking sheet. Then she washed her silver thimble, put it on a finger, and pressed it into each cooky ball to make what she called "a dent." After the baking she immediately used the thimble again to outline the cavities. She filled them with jelly or jam just before serving.

Cornets are thin wafers about the size of a small pancake. While they still were very hot, the hostess in the county seat town where I learned about them quickly rolled each one into a cone. She used a scrubbed carrot to facilitate the shaping — she rolled the cooky around the vegetable and then removed it. At serving time she filled them with whipped cream mixed with tart fruit preserves.

The fruit juice dessert, thickened with cornstarch, came to the table in a big glass bowl. My thoughtful hostess explained that she made it with grape juice pointed up with lemon juice and sweetened. It was very cold. And characteristic of the region, and the Swedish influence, the garnish was whipped cream.

Splendid Breads Personify the Dakotas

Breads — yeast breads — connote the two states. Talented cooks shine in making them. There are coffee cakes and rolls galore. Even the cinnamon rolls frequently display a native touch. When they are in the pan to rise the cook pours on a little white clover honey and thick sour cream. These rolls are what the natives refer to as "gooey;" a Pennsylvania cook would speak of them as sticky.

The rye breads are of the types the American-Scandinavian cooks know so well how to perfect. The yeast rolls are light, feathery, hot, and frequent visitors to the table. In some homes they appear daily. And then there is that standby in the bread box — the loaves of white bread that are many a regional cook's claim to fame.

Who could wish for a more enjoyable experience than the farewell one I had in the Dakotas? We sat down in the friendly, homey kitchen — this hospitable rural woman and I. It was in that delightful country on the westward slopes of prehistoric glacial Lake Agassiz that always has been so fascinating to geologists. She took the generous sized loaves of bread from the oven. The fragrance and sight of these masterpieces were almost too much to endure without exclamations. Then my hostess set out a plate of yellow butter she had churned a few hours earlier, and a glass of plum jelly. She cut off two crusty warm heels of the bread — one for her and one for me. After that she reached for the coffee pot. She poured the steaming amber liquid into our cups, and passed the sugar and cream. We sat almost purring with great contentment as we ate and supped. Out of the corners of our eyes we watched one of those vivid sunset displays for which the Great Plains cannot be surpassed. Thus a native daughter's food tour of the Farm Belt came to an end.

The Mountain West

No MATTER how you look at the Mountain West it is
beautiful. From an airplane, your automobile, a
streamlined continental train, and the tiny coaches of cog
and narrow gauge railroads that climb on mountain sides
above rainbows into the clouds, your views are thrilling. On
the ski runs and saddle trails they enchant. You feel near
the country. After you eat in the chuck lines a few days you
begin to figure how you can stretch your schedule to stay
longer.

You like the purebred western food, the universal

cordiality of ranch people, and the flow of talk about the table at headquarters. You experience sweater weather in summer that makes a cup of hot tea more inviting than an iced drink. Women discuss their baking problems in this country that spreads out at the top of the world. They explain how high altitudes force them to modify recipes their sisters on the plains follow successfully. Trout, elk, bears, and whitefaces enter the conversation. You try to listen to every word, to translate the jargon of the cowboys, and to show roast beef and hot biscuits the proper respect, all at the same time. No three-ring circus was ever more exciting.

Salt Lake City is different. There a cosmopolitan cuisine shows up in many homes. In the main it stems from influences of the Church of Jesus Christ of Latter-day Saints, generally known as the Mormon Church. Missionaries return from many nations and climes with a fondness for exotic meals experienced while away. Back home they offer renditions of choice menus to their families and friends. Converts in foreign lands who emigrate to the United States to establish homes near the stately Mormon Temple prepare their food masterpieces and invite their neighbors to try them. Recipe exchanges follow.

Boise knows the taste of Basque dishes; it is home to the largest colony of Basques in all North America. Signs of frontier tables appear throughout the region, as in the typical game and fish dinners, tasty sourdough breads, and Dutch oven treats. Garden vegetables and orchard fruits attain superb succulence in cool mountain spots where they grow.

Let's Round Up the States

Anyone who attempts to round up the states in the Mountain West, meets some questions. No one will protest making fence around Colorado, Wyoming, Utah, Montana, Idaho, and Nevada. In thoughts of the vast ranch empire I hesitate to cut out Texas even though no jagged, shining, snow clad peaks jut its expansive sky line.

Perhaps some of the tall, lean and lanky cow men in the mountains help put the Lone Star State into the heart. When asked if they always have lived in glorious Montana, Colorado or Nevada a surprising number replied, "I'm from Texas," or "I was a cowpoke on the trail north from Texas." One erect, dignified ranchman of 80 years who entertained at his home 60 miles from the nearest town said, "I grew up among the bluebonnets, but I've lived in Wyoming and loved it for more than half a century."

Isolation Earmarks Ranch Kitchens

Life in ranch kitchens varies somewhat with their locations, as between New Mexico and Montana, or Arizona and Wyoming. Yet a characteristic isolation produces a likeness of activities, although distances continue to shorten like magic. Some ranchers fly their own planes. Almost all of them travel over improved roads in passenger cars, station wagons, and trucks. Every year foodstuffs become more convenient.

Frozen foods, freezer locker plants, home freezers, refrigerators, pressure saucepans and cookers, groceries better packaged and distributed, and a wider variety of canned foods stimulate menu changes. But there are no corner stores and delicatessens to fall back on in an emergency. A cowbelle (wife or daughter of a cattleman) cannot send junior on his bicycle to the drugstore for a carton of ice cream at the last minute when unexpected company drives into the yard. She must be ready for emergencies. Necessity encourages her to think ahead, to plan, and trade intelligently when she goes to town. (Mountain people refer to shopping as *trading.*) Perhaps the trip comes off once a week or once a month, and occasionally even less frequently when deep snows fill the roads. Kitchen preparedness yields rich dividends in self-reliance and independence.

In the ranch kitchen's motto, *"Make do with what you have,"* the cook finds strength and solace. She uses what she has at the moment to turn out an acceptable meal. This philosophy fosters resourcefulness. She learns the art of substituting one food for another when supplies are low. "Why worry about a shortage of granulated sugar?" the mountain woman asks. "You certainly have brown sugar, molasses, honey, table sirup, and jellies and jams to tide you through until the trip to town is in the cards."

Neither do mothers commonly waste time, effort and patience in coaxing people to eat. The pampered child of the city with anxious parents who beg and bribe him to swallow the food on his plate has no counterpart on cattle spreads, as ranches are called. And garnishes receive little or no attention. Cooks figure the standing rib roast of beef needs no parsley to win acceptance at the table. They hold that potato salad will suffice without radish roses to decorate the top. The major concern is to provide plenty of delicious, sustaining grub — a cowboy's name for food — to please and appease the hungry people who eat in their chuck lines, or the places where meals are served on ranches. Activity in the invigorating air takes care of the appetite!

White Tops Out of History's Pages

What is the food fare of the Mountain West?

Rainbow trout from cold, snow-fed, transparent water, quickly dressed, rolled in flour and corn meal, and hurried to the frying pan to brown in butter or bacon fat give one answer.

Thick steaks and enormous standing rib roasts of beef, cooked rare — or as cowpunchers say, "So you can hear the calves bawl" — call only for salt, pepper, and an invitation to dinner.

Chicken fried steaks, the thin slices rolled in seasoned flour and browned in beef fat, and rich brown sop or gravy to dress accompanying hot biscuits also speak for the region.

Chocolate potato cakes — spiced, walnut-studded loaves, frosted with fudge or penuchi — send men away from the table smacking their lips.

A hostess stacks six or eight large, thin pancakes with

butter and jelly between them, surrounds the shortcake so made with a fluffy meringue, scatters on broken nut meats, and runs it into a quick oven to brown delicately. She carries the delectable showpiece to the table with the gusto of the chief steward on an ocean liner delivering baked alaska to the captain's table.

On rare occasions you meet sourdough bread. I have watched past masters of the art, usually old cow or sheep men, take a piece of the soft dough and with a certain apt twist and toss of the hand shape the biscuits. They let them rise until light and then bake them in Dutch ovens for part of the refreshments at a shindig, or square dance. You can almost see the white tops of covered wagons on the old California trail come out of the pages of history when you view the colorful western dance costumes and eat the old-fashioned hot bread.

Lamb roasts with blistering hot gravy, and wild currant jelly on the side, rate as topnotch fare.

Halves of Rocky Ford cantaloupes, filled with vanilla ice cream and sprinkled with salted pecans, provide a perfect dessert when the weather is warm enough.

Colorado people drink sparkling red cherry cider, and talk about the deliciousness of pitted, sweetened cherries as sauce or baked in pies.

At Utah tea parties I met the most refreshing and exotic hot fruit punches served this side of heaven, and luscious candies the like of which you rarely encounter on this planet.

Nevada votes for lamb or mutton stew flavored with garlic and with dumplings on top, while Montana sticks by her Mulligan stew of beef and vegetables simmered to remarkable tastiness.

Denver sandwiches pick up spirits and conquer appetites after regional sporting events such as a rodeo (here pronounced *ro'-dee-o*), skiing, hunting, or fishing.

After day is done, Westerners often get in their cars with their families and friends, relax, leave the world behind, and drive many miles for a picnic supper.

The Cowbelle Goes to Town

When a cowbelle arrives in town to replenish the grocery supply, her trading list contains at least some of the basic items. She buys staples in large quantities, and rarely purchases all of them at one time. Also she selects a few of the more perishable foods, such as citrus fruits and bananas, and other seasonal items, like cranberries in autumn. Here is a list of the standard supplies I saw written on a blackboard in a kitchen 37 miles from the nearest town. The cook says she keeps a record from day to day of what to buy on the next trip to the markets.

A Ranch Trading List

baking powder	java (coffee)
bacon	ketchup
salt pork	lick (table sirup)
canned cow (evaporated milk)	molasses
canned fruits	potatoes
canned vegetables	pepper
corn meal	skunk eggs (onions)
dried fruits	sugar
flour	rice
gelatin	vinegar

Most ranchers stock pantries that intrigue city cooks who live in cramped quarters. I well recall one such Mother Lode of good things to eat. The lady of the house designed the space to meet her requirements. Trips to town, 70 miles away, frequently are months apart in cold weather. At one side of the basement in her home, and partitioned off from it, is a closet which was excavated from the earth and lined with cement. Cross ventilators — tunnels dug several feet through the soil to openings — provide constant air change. To my astonishment I found they are not closed until the mercury in the thermometer outside dips to 12° below zero! Down to that point the temperatures in the closet remain safely above freezing. The room, with shelves on three sides, resembles a miniature food market.

Practically all ordinary kinds of canned fruits and vegetables line the shelves in neat rows. At their sides stand gallon-sized tins and bottles of table sirup. Vinegar, molasses, and glasses of jams, jellies, and preserves — made with wild and mountain grown berries and fruits — also await the cook's pleasure. Root vegetables and potatoes in bins represent the garden. Citrus fruits, which remain in excellent condition for several weeks, flaunt their yellow and orange colorings. At the shelf-less side of the pantry hangs a bunch of bananas which remind you of the village grocery stores of your childhood.

After glancing over the contents of such a pantry you wonder what is left for the freezers to claim. If you look in several of them in ranch country you note three foods commonly monopolize the space — ice cream, bread, and meat. In the cold weather much of the meat and game hangs in nature's storage plant, the outdoors, generally on the north side of the house. Usually a few dressed chickens, and trout frozen in blocks of ice are kept in the home freezer. Vegetables and fruits rarely make much of a showing. There simply is not room for them. Lockers in freezing plants at the nearest town supplement the home storage of frozen foods.

Cowboys Like Hearty Breakfasts

The number of meals daily dealt out (in cowboy vernacular deal means *serve*) depends primarily on the size of the ranch and the work at hand. Breakfast commonly comes off at dawn, or before it, as at 4 a.m. Dinner is set on the table whenever the cow hands arrive back at headquarters, any time from 11 o'clock in the morning until 4 o'clock in the afternoon. On some large properties two giant-sized meals suffice, but generally the ranch cook also provides supper. Usually leftovers from dinner have their inning in the evening. In describing the day's last meal, a cowboy in Wyoming may have engaged in wishful thinking when he said, "We have something light, such as small steaks or hamburgers."

RANCH BREAKFAST
Tomato or Fruit Juice
Oatmeal or Other Cereal
Chicken Fried Steak
Hot Biscuits　　Brown Gravy
Fried Eggs (optional)
Cow Salve (butter)　　Lick (sirup)
Java (coffee)

Two Big "B's" — Beef and Biscuits

Beef and biscuits are the foundations of most ranch meals. Anyone who believes mammoth beef roasts and thick, juicy steaks go at dining tables daily confronts real disappointment. Of course cattlemen and buckaroos, as cowboys also are known, do not refuse either of the favorites; to them these beef cuts, if cooked rare, typify the ultimate in fine eating.

"When an animal is slaughtered," a cow man lamented in a talk with me, "we have some cuts that are less tender than the prime steaks and roasts. That's the way God builds critters (cattle). We cannot afford to discard this meat. The business of our spread is to produce and sell cattle at a profit. It's strictly a commercial venture, and we are always aware of the value of beef."

Many ranch people do not enjoy bottled meat sauces. Some of them say, "Sauces dilute the beef taste." Others like tomato ketchup on almost everything, including beef and biscuits.

Cowbelles Accept the Cooking Challenge

Cowbelles face problems involved in preparing the less desirable cuts of meat as a chore to master. In this respect they follow the pattern of men who cook at cow camps. *Son-of-a-gun* stew, described in the chapter on the Southwest, carefully salvages meat sundries. The regional delicacy known as *mountain oysters* likewise indicates a cook's thrifty hand. Oysters or calves' fries are the testicles removed from bull calves to convert them into steers. After cleaning and flouring, the oysters are pan-fried to a golden brown. Ranchers consider the dish as a delicious rival of sweetbreads.

Recipe files in the Mountain West contain directions for preparing countless tempting dishes made with brains, liver, sweetbreads, kidneys, heart, and tongue. This unusual cooking ability with the meat sundries also is found in the cities. In Denver one elite hostess served me Kidney Newburg (she used lamb kidneys instead of a Yankee cook's lobster in the dish). Another fashionable lady in the same city passed crisp, brown coated calves' brains heaped on toast and topped with mushroom sauce. She explained that she parboils the brains, dips them in egg and crumbs, and browns them in butter. To dress them she adds cut-up sautéed mushrooms to cream sauce.

Whitefaces Frequently Detain the Cow Hands

Ranch women also excel with substantial dishes that feature the less tender cuts of beef. Stews probably scoop up the most medals of merit, with pot roasts a close runner-up. Soup, meat balls, meat loaves, and barbecued treats gather in the chosen field, too. Hamburgers fully maintain their all-American prestige. A western cook frequently gives them different interpretations. For example, she browns the patties, tops them with onion slices, and then bakes the meat cakes in a peppery barbecue sauce. Whitefaces or Hereford cattle have a habit of detaining cow hands on the ranges. That is why dishes which will hold up in good condition for late meals always are at a premium. Barbecued hamburgers are good at waiting, as are meat loaves cooked in a barbecue sauce or with canned tomato soup poured over them.

Chicken fried steak, previously mentioned, comes as the fulfillment of a Westerner's desire for beef at breakfast, dinner, and supper! The cook pounds the thin round or chuck steak, dredges it with seasoned flour, and slowly pan-fries it in melted beef suet. Some cooks pour in a touch of water after the meat is browned, to aid in the tenderizing. Not the least of the steak's charm is its smooth, rich, brown gravy, the perfect complement to potatoes and biscuits.

Mountain cooks certainly know how to salvage leftover meat. In many instances they prefer to combine it with drifts of hot mashed potatoes whipped to a froth of flavor. Usually they cut the meat into small pieces, and add remnants of gravy, scraped onion, and whatever seasonings are desired. Then they layer the potatoes and meat mixture alternately in a baking dish, with the spuds on the bottom and top. Dots of butter encourage quick browning in a moderate oven.

Both bacon and ham are popular. Salt pork is essential for seasoning beans. Even so, pork occupies a back seat in a majority of regional menus. Beef, mutton or lamb, fish, and game take turns in the driver's seat. Much of the land reaches altitudes too high for corn to thrive; early frosts cut off the growing season abruptly. In many places attempts at hog production spell financial loss.

Please Pass the Pinch-Offs

If you were to receive a *buck,* as the Westerner often refers to a dollar, for every pan of biscuits baked in a week throughout the region you would be on easy street for quite some time. Biscuits are the staff of life, the beginning and ending of many meals. Like the cowboy biscuits of the Southwest, they are tall, tender, hot, and more like bread than pastry. Usually they measure about 3 inches in diameter. Commonly the cook crowds them into a shallow pan in which a little fat has been melted. She first individually dips the tops of the circles of dough into the fat. The biscuits bake in a very hot oven, 450°, about 12 minutes. Their tops and bottoms become brown, but the crust does not cover their sides.

At the table cowboys break open the flaky hot biscuit, and spread on cow salve — butter — or margarine, or spoon gravy over it. They pour *lick,* the preferred name for maple flavored or other table sirup, over the last two or three buttered biscuits to round out the meal. I have yet to hear a cowboy complain when no dessert appears after he has downed a few biscuits swimming in sirup.

Popular in many quarters, although not considered a substitute for lick, are the fruity spreads. They include jellies, jams, and butters from native berries and homegrown fruits, plus honey. Both Utah and Colorado are famed honey producing states. Red raspberries, strawberries, huckleberries, red and black currants, plums, cherries, peaches, and apricots have a kinship to the Mountain West. Indeed, they are favored food children of the area.

How To Bake Biscuits in a Cow Camp

Biscuits appear regularly in practically all meals cooked away from ranch headquarters, as during a roundup, and in most home prepared breakfasts and dinners. For roundups the chuck wagon hauls the supplies and cooking utensils. If a lone cowpuncher goes on a mission, as to drift fence (or check and repair it), to be gone for several meals, he carries his food, utensils, and bed roll on his horse. He commonly measures the flour, salt, and baking powder needed for the biscuits before he starts, then ties the muslin sack containing the mix on his saddle. To men of his profession — the lads with the 10-gallon hats — goes the credit for creating the forerunners of the commercial packaged mixes.

When the cowboy decides it is about the hour to hit the hay, he builds a campfire. After the embers glow he cooks his bacon. The drippings assume the shortening role in the biscuits, with water for the liquid. If the skillet is his only utensil, other than a pail for coffee making, he "makes do" with it. He bakes drop biscuits in the covered frying pan set over the embers. Larger crews take Dutch ovens on their expeditions. In them are baked the unsurpassable "hot rocks," as biscuits sometimes are called.

Perhaps the most accomplished trick of the cow camp cook is the way he eliminates the mixing bowl. He opens his bag of flour, baking powder, and salt mix, digs a hollow in it with his hand, and then works in the shortening and water to make a soft dough that does not stick to his fingers. He shapes it in a roll as for refrigerator cookies, and pinches off pieces; this custom indicates why biscuits often are called *pinch-offs*. He dips the dabs of dough in a pan containing a bit of melted fat, lines them up in rows in it, and then bakes them.

Those Irrepressible Pumpkin Rollers

How he knows the amount of flour to incorporate in the dough to maintain the correct proportion to the other ingredients he cannot explain. He says he uses $1\frac{1}{2}$ teaspoons of baking powder and ½ teaspoon of salt to 1 cup of flour, but he measures with his eyes rather than with cups and spoons. He thinks a generous quarter cup of shortening is about right for 1 cup of water. That is his master recipe. He states nonchalantly that he knows by the feel of the dough how deep to reach for the flour, or how much flour to work into the dough.

Two gratifying results of his performance make the sketchy recipe pardonable. Superb biscuits and the appearance of the flour in his improvised mixing bowl justify his inability to standardize his directions for other cooks to follow. I have observed men so skillful and precise that I doubt if a microscope would suggest that biscuits had been mixed in the bag of flour. And no definition fills the bill better to describe *deliciousness* than do most cow camp pinch-offs.

A biscuit shooter (the cook) of considerable genius used to deal out chuck at my father's cattle spread. On those red letter occasions when my father took my mother, my two elder brothers, and me to camp for a day's outing, I stood entranced at his side as he made the biscuits. I remember particularly how he added water to the dough instead of milk, and his explanation, "It makes them tender." Never could I understand how his big biscuits — truly out of this world — could be called by the same name as my mother's smaller buttermilk or sour cream biscuits — also heavenly tasting — which she baked at home. Questions about which kind I liked better, asked by teasing pumpkin rollers (the amateur cowboys) I always put in the same category as the favorite query of the hired girls in that era, "Who do you like best, your father or mother?"

Related to biscuits are other darlings of chuck lines. Dumplings generally lend appeal to the less tender cuts of meat. Hot pancakes, generously buttered and doused with sweet sirup, start many days pleasantly. And fruit cobblers, made with spoonfuls of soft biscuit dough baked on heated and sweetened fruits and berries, deserve a special eulogy.

How could a dessert be superior in looks and taste to a cherry, apricot, peach, or red raspberry cobbler?

Meet the Popular Dutch Oven

The heavy utensil known as the Dutch oven required no introduction a couple of generations ago. Even earlier it helped solve the baking problems of California's forty-niners. In it pioneers on the western trek and cowpunchers on the range cooked their meals over the glowing embers of camp-fires. Today the esteem for the kettle still rides high in the Mountain West, at picnics in the backyards and open spaces, and for special occasions on ranches.

This oven, made of cast iron, distributes heat evenly and holds it efficiently. The kettle has three legs about 2½ inches long, and a vertical edge 1½ inches wide around the top. A concave lid that holds the embers heaped on it fits snugly. Thus the heat bakes the food within from the top and bottom. To provide the correct amount of heat requires seasoned judgment; of course, it is controlled by the coals under and on top of the oven. Western cooks know how to do the job. To a humble food explorer's way of thinking, the opportunity to eat fried chicken and biscuits or sour-dough bread cooked in a Dutch oven is worth a trip across the continent any time.

Sourdough Bread Is Disappearing

Sorrowfully to everyone who delights in the characteristic taste of sourdough bread comes the realization that this treat is disappearing from the American scene. For the most part, as has been mentioned previously, only a few of the older people in the Mountain West possess the technique with this historic staff of life. A sympathetic home econo-mist with the extension service of the University of Wyoming explains the decline in the baking of this favorite bread. She says no one has been able to standardize recipes for the starter. The varying and unpredictable sourness looms up as a stumbling block to inexperienced cooks.

To distinguish sourdough bread from the usual run of biscuits you need only consider the leavenings. In sourdough bread a starter of active yeast is used, and in biscuits it is baking powder. The temperamental yeast must be treated with the respect accorded a prima donna. It is capable of turning out a masterpiece, or of giving a disappointing performance. Its behavior is partly controlled by keeping it in a warm room to step up activity, or in a cool one, 40° to 50°, to quiet it down.

A gifted sourdough cook always leaves at least a quarter cup of the starter in a crock when baking. To the remainder of it he adds soda, salt, sugar, liquid, and flour to make a perfect dough. By some form of mysticism he seems to determine just how much. Frequently he tosses in baking powder, as if for good measure. He tells you the dough is pliable. An observer notes it also is soft. He kneads it briefly to mix the ingredients, then pinches off the biscuits and shapes them with that indescribable toss and twist of his hand. He smears them with the small amount of fat melted in the pan, lets them rise until double in bulk, and bakes them like other biscuits. Sometimes he bakes the dough in small loaves.

The Sheepman Borrows Some Starter

To make delicious pancakes the cook adds milk, sugar, and beaten eggs along with the flour, salt, soda, and starter. He whips the mixture just barely enough to give it a fair degree of smoothness, and then bakes spoonfuls of it on a hot griddle. When you eat either the biscuits or pancakes, dripping with melting butter, you decide they must have been featured in the Olympic feasts where someone invented the "food for the gods" expression.

To the small quantity of unused starter the cook gives affectionate attention. He mixes in about 1½ cupfuls of lukewarm water and stirs in enough flour to make a paste. Then he covers the crock and sets it aside in the environment he deems favorable, or as nearly the perfect temperature as he can provide. Within a few hours the yeast ordinarily multiplies enough to leaven bread.

For best results sourdough should be used daily. That is why it is a natural in the sheep jockey's (sheepherder's) wagon. Daily baking controls or holds down the sourness. Also the experienced sourdough artists know how to sweeten the starter with soda, unless it is too sour for redemption. Their granddaughters are baffled by it, and their guesses on the amount of soda to stir in frequently involve them in trouble.

I talked with a sheepman who confessed, "Sometimes when I think of sourdough bread I get so hungry that I can't shake the longing for it. Then I tell my wife I must go see how our bands of sheep are doing and check up on the camp jack, the man who services our sheep camps. I drive almost a hundred miles and borrow some of the starter a jockey has in his crock, and return home happy. There must be a gleam in my eyes or else my wife is a mind reader. Before I have time to say anything she suggests, 'Honey, let's have sourdough biscuits for dinner.' Then I'm in paradise for a few hours, as I anticipate, eat, and then recollect one of the best foods man ever invented."

Corn Bread Provides a Welcome Touch

Hot corn bread, never on a par with biscuits in the Mountain West, nevertheless ushers an occasional welcome touch of variety into ranch meals. Yellow meal is the first choice of cooks. In this area, where pancakes enter almost all conversations about superior foods, many a cowbelle stirs a little meal into the batter for that corn taste Americans like to get hot off the griddle. She uses less baking powder in the higher altitudes than is specified in the recipes followed by her friends who live at lower altitudes.

I met an Idaho cook who favors her guests with light-as-a-feather potato pancakes. When hungry, to remember the taste of these hot cakes is to be eternally haunted by their deliciousness. The recipe for them illustrates how mountain cooks feature potatoes, mashed and beaten light, as a staple ingredient in many supreme dishes.

IDAHO PANCAKES

¾ cup mashed potatoes
¾ cup flour
1 teaspoon salt
4 beaten egg yolks

½ cup evaporated milk
¾ cup potato water
4 stiffly beaten egg whites

Mix the potatoes, flour, and salt, and add the egg yolks, evaporated milk, and potato water. Then fold in the egg whites. Bake spoonfuls of the lightness on a hot griddle for the browned cakes that resemble delicate soufflés.

Red Beans Are at Home on the Range

Bean compositions of countless descriptions go to ranch tables most frequently in homes equipped with pressure cookers, which shorten the cooking time. The pinto beans of the Southwest enjoy considerable prestige in the area, and kidney beans rise to the occasion and assume many stellar menu roles. Some mountain cooks open commercially canned baked beans, add individual touches, and rebake them in a moderate oven, 350°, for about an hour.

Coloradoans frequently insert a couple of whole cloves in a small onion or in onion slices to bury in the beans slated for rebaking. (Curiously enough, one sometimes detects a vague taste of cloves in chili con carne in Colorado.)

Many cooks add tomato ketchup and molasses, and chopped pimento, green pepper, and onion to canned beans and bake the mixture an hour. Kidney beans occupy an important spot in the winter months, where they brighten meals; all eyes focus on them at many autumn picnics. A favorite quick ranch specialty, red beans, borrows a few neat tricks, such as vinegar, sugar, and spices, from the Swedish cuisine.

RANCH RED BEANS

1 No. 2 can kidney beans
2 tablespoons sugar
¼ to ½ teaspoon cinnamon

¼ cup vinegar
¼ cup margarine

Mix all the ingredients and simmer the mixture from 20 to 30 minutes. To convert the vegetable dish into a sturdy entree, wreath the beans around meat or game balls, cooked in simmering water or bouillon, and then browned in fat.

Java Fills the Cup That Cheers

Coffee, or *java* in ranch jargon, bows to no competitor in the beverage group. The infusion is strong. A large percentage of the ranch population likes it black and unsweetened, although some cow hands touch it up with canned *cow* (evaporated milk) or even cream. A few of them have been known to stir in sugar. As has been noted, when a buckaroo rides away on a ranch chore to be gone overnight he carries coffee and a pail on his saddle so that in some favorable location he can fill the cup that cheers.

Gay Red Gelatin Appeals to Cow Men

Cowbelles achieve considerable success with the salads they put together. Of course some ranchmen remark, "I'll take my grass in beef." They pointedly declare they prefer "platter salads," or beef that grass has helped produce. Yet almost never do these cow men resist a gay red gelatin salad filled with diced bananas, green grapes, and whatever other fresh or canned fruits the cook includes. They also feast quite avidly on red gelatin that molds apples, walnuts, celery, and chopped raw cranberries or cranberry-orange relish.

Cowbelles say that a merit of molded salads is that, if kept in a cold place, they hold up in splendid condition even though dinner is delayed.

Like women in other cold countries, cowbelles lean heavily on canned fruits for winter salad plates. One of the regional favorites consists of orange flavored gelatin to which has been added canned fruit cocktail (drained), a diced banana, the sections of an orange pulled apart or shredded, and a scant teaspoonful of grated orange rind.

Cole slaw, carrot-cabbage slaw, and sliced tomatoes almost always win the approval of ranchmen. Tossed green salads are in the ascendancy, especially in the parts of Colorado and Utah where wonderful mountain lettuce grows. Green salads demand a French dressing; cowbelles frequently add tomato ketchup or Worcestershire sauce to it. For fruit salads the homemade cooked dressings without oil reign supreme.

An unforgettable salad I sampled in ranch country goes by the inviting name of *Snow on the Mountain*. On a long table — spread with an old-fashioned linen damask cloth dyed crimson and with pine branches and nuts as the center-piece — dark green plates displayed the salad's whiteness to advantage. To make this tempter, my hostess explained, she cuts marshmallows, blanched almonds, and canned pineapple into small pieces and chills the mixture. Just before meal-time she folds it into crisp, fine shreds of cabbage and heaps it in peaks on the plates. Then she crowns them with snow dressing, commonly referred to as *Snow Sauce*.

SNOW SAUCE

½ cup sugar	¼ cup vinegar
1 tablespoon flour	juice of 3 lemons
½ teaspoon salt	4 egg whites, stiffly beaten
3 tablespoons boiling water	

Mix the sugar, flour, and salt, and add the boiling water, then the vinegar, lemon juice, and beaten egg whites. This mixture is cooked over water until thick and smooth, and then chilled. For an elegant touch fold in a small drift of whipped cream.

A Chuck Wagon Is the Pie-Box

Among the desserts, pie basks in the spotlight. One indication of its position appears in a cowboy's conversation when he speaks of the chuck wagon, dear to his heart, as the *pie-box*. The favorites are many: apple, cherry, raisin, sour cream-raisin, dried apple, dried apricot, prune, cranberry, and mincemeat. Mincemeat pie often is made with venison or elk meat. Occasionally green tomato pie appears. The tomatoes are cut in thin slices plus vinegar, sugar, and spices. And even more of a sensation than the pie is green tomato cobbler. Normally pie fillings in the Mountain West lead a dual life, in pies and in cobblers.

Ranch women have their men enthusiastically eating the cakes that come from their ovens. On old-time ranches the biscuit shooter seldom bothered to bake cakes. He figured pies and cobblers, bolstered by hot biscuits and sirup, were adequate. And almost everyone agreed. Nowadays cowbelles on cattle ranches consistently reap top honors with their loaf cakes much as southern belles in their plantation kitchens capture the ribbons with layer cakes. For variety some of the western batters, originated for loaf pans, occasionally are baked in layers.

The loaf cakes are wonderful to behold, and even more marvelous to taste. They enjoy an enviable reputation as good keepers. In that lies the paradox! Only rarely do they have a chance to exhibit their ability to retain moist freshness for several days. Everyone who sniffs the cake as it bakes is likely to hang around until it comes from the oven, and then wistfully watch the cook spread frosting over it. When she obligingly punctures the loaf with a knife she releases its spicy breath. Such fragrance teases the nose and stimulates the palate. The onlookers are in suspense until they taste, and when they do take a bite they experience the acme of culinary excellence. The prettiest adjectives slip out without effort. And before the cook knows what has happened, only a few crumbs remain.

This region definitely has a corner on potato cakes, the kind with which the Pennsylvania Dutch territory also excels. If you think the plebeian name creates an impression the loaf is ordinary, "Partner," as the cowboys say, "you are due for a revelation." The flavor is so celestial I resolved to bake potato cakes the rest of my life. While mountain cooks cherish their pet recipes, which vary in some details, the cake universally contains cocoa or chocolate and California walnuts, and often spices and raisins. Its name comes from the mashed potatoes that help form the batter.

I lost my heart to a fudge potato loaf, faintly flavored with lemon and chock-full of toasted almonds. Another that captivated me consisted of two chocolate layers put together with a date-walnut filling; it was frosted white. Commonly the icings are cooked, with fudge and penuche types universal favorites. Cooks add nuts, or sprinkle them lavishly on the freshly frosted cake.

Rocky Mountain frosting frequently contributes a characteristic regional crown. It is a boiled frosting with marshmallows not entirely melted, and these are the "rocks." The marshmallows are cut in eighths with scissors, and added to the beaten egg white into which is whipped the stream of hot sirup. Almond and vanilla flavorings in equal parts enhance the traditional frosting.

Other loaf cakes ranchers boast about in food conversations are prune, date, applesauce, pumpkin, and all kinds of nut cakes. Indeed, any chocolate cake containing nuts appeals to them. Slices of these good cakes are perfect with stewed, canned, fresh, or frozen fruits in the dessert role.

A Kitchen With Various Altitudes!

In many parts of the Mountain West high altitudes affect kitchen procedures. Even a cook new to the area catches on in a couple of days to the fact that it takes longer to cook foods to tenderness than in the lower altitudes from which she has migrated. The difference in time is due to the decreased air pressure. Because high altitudes spread like a blanket over the region, pressure cookers and saucepans are standard kitchen equipment.

Cake recipes require adjustments at elevations of 5,000 feet and more above sea level. About one-third of the United States, so far as square miles go, lies in the lofty belt, but for the most part this country is sparsely populated. Formerly mountain women learned to bake the hard way. By trial and error they found out which recipes worked in their kitchens. They cherished the successful ones like precious jewels. To aid new cooks in avoiding the disappointments of failures and the waste of ingredients, considerable research on high altitude cooking has been conducted by the home economics staffs of the regional land-grant colleges. The Colorado Experiment Station was one pioneer in the search for improvements in cake baking in the high country.

Attached to the home economics building at the Colorado College of Agriculture and Mechanic Arts at Fort Collins is a unique structure, which has some resemblance to a silo. It is built of steel. Within it you see a kitchen in which the various atmospheric pressures at altitudes of from 5,000 to 10,000 feet above sea level are duplicated.

In this laboratory standard cake formulas were baked under the different conditions, and the necessary corrections made. These improved recipes were sent to homemakers in the high places, who used them in their kitchens. From the joining of hands and pooling of results, the scientists and practical home cooks provided adequate information for a small cookbook on baking cakes at high altitudes. This bulletin not only aids many cake bakers in the mountainous areas of the West, but also travels to grateful people in various high spots elsewhere throughout the world.

Bands of Sheep Dot the Landscape

If you visit this area you discover soon that you are in sheep as well as cattle country. Occasionally you see acres of pens sprawled on the range, or perhaps on the desert. From afar they appear as tiny corrals built by a child with sticks. If you drive about in autumn to admire the lemon colored aspen leaves and other color splashed on the mountains you frequently meet bands of sheep on their way to the feed lots or shipping points. Sometimes the bands are remarkably large, perhaps many thousand head. In the spring you encounter the reverse movement, bleating sheep on their way to the range. Their movements resemble wooly waves rippled by the wind.

Although northern Colorado, in the Fort Collins district, rates as a mammoth lamb feeding center, most people who live there admit they do not care to eat the meat. They say, "We'll settle for beef." An opposite reaction comes from other parts of the Mountain West. Residents of Wyoming, Utah, and Nevada, and the territory stretching westward from there to the Pacific Ocean, generally bill lamb and mutton as top eating. Discriminating hostesses proudly offer it to guests.

Men who own bands of sheep regret that only a few of their countrymen appreciate how superior in flavor mutton is to lamb. "I do not refer to a *biddy,* or even a *spreader* (aged ewes)," one tall, handsome sheepman told me, "but rather to those superb animals that have just graduated from lambhood. They are what we select for our table. No lamb is allowed in our kitchen. We find the same difference between good quality mutton and lamb as between beef and veal. Of course many people think they are eating lamb when what they have on their plates is excellent mutton. After all, 'What's in a name?' I should not complain so long as they buy and enjoy the meat we produce."

For special occasions, roasted leg of lamb goes glamorous on western platters. Smart hostesses often select an escort of onions, a vegetable that holds its own in the menu. For a dinner party they sometimes have the leg bones removed and a strip of pork tenderloin inserted. After the roast is rolled and tied, the cook cuts little slits over its surface and inserts slivers of garlic. She rubs lemon juice and Worcestershire sauce over the surface. Then she bakes the pièce de résistance uncovered in a slow oven, 325°, until thoroughly cooked.

Utah People Like Mint Sauce

Another tricky way women handle lamb roast is to slice it about a half hour before mealtime. They spread a well-seasoned onion purée between the meat slices and on top, and scatter, over all, buttered bread crumbs. Then they brown the roast in a warmer oven, at about 400°, for 30 minutes. These attractive platters simplify carving for the host.

More frequently the cook chooses not to have the leg of lamb boned. She roasts it to perfection and sends it to the table escorted by a bowl of luscious gravy made with water or potato water for liquid, or possibly with half water and half milk.

Wild gooseberry jam or red currant jelly frequently carries off the relish honor when lamb is on the menu. (They also are served with game, although many Idaho people prefer a sauce made from the small black fruit of swamp currants.) Mint sauce maintains an ardent following in Utah. There the herb grows profusely along the banks of irrigation ditches, and may be had for the gathering. When you look in the Beehive State's "fridges," the colloquial name for refrigerators, you see an amazing number of "bottles" (as glass fruit jars are called) of homemade mint sauce.

WYOMING GUEST DINNER
Roasted Leg of Lamb
Browned Potatoes
Creamed Baby Onions
Tossed Green Salad
Brown Gravy   Gooseberry Jam
Apple Cobbler
Coffee

Frequent substitutions include baked for browned potatoes, and hot biscuits for the cobbler, with a dessert of any fresh fruit.

Trout From Clear, Cold Water

In the Mountain West many homes every week enjoy trout from clear, cold water, or from blocks of ice. Native cooks know better than to attempt to pretty up this regional delicacy with sauces. They strive to develop the natural flavors rather than hide them. They roll the fish in corn meal or flour, or both, and once in a blue moon in fine bread crumbs.

"Mother is particular," my niece in Colorado reports, "not to get the flour or corn meal into the body of the fish. She says it forms an untasty, doughy mass. She browns trout in butter or bacon drippings, and serves it with lemon quarters. That goes for our rainbow, steelhead, cutthroat, and speckled varieties. They all are wonderful 'to smell up the pan,' as the fellows say."

MONTANA TROUT DINNER
Rainbow Trout
Fried Raw Potatoes and Onions
Buttered Peas
Hot Biscuits   Currant Jelly
Fruit Compote
Coffee

Trout dinners during the Yuletide season appear in some households with the regularity that green branches gathered in the mountains bedeck their premises. Then, as through-out the winter, the fish come to the kitchens in blocks of ice, or at least frozen. When they are frozen in water soon after being taken from the stream or lake and dressed, not one person in a hundred detects a difference in taste from trout eaten in summer soon after they are caught. In these winter dinners proud anglers wear the same beaming expression as they do in summertime when their fork pricks the golden brown, crispy crusted fish — if my Colorado brother's expression is typical. At the sight of the platter his face lights up like it does when he sees the gleam of trout rising to the fly.

At Wyoming Picnics in the Snowy Range

Mountain men regard their home territory as a happy hunting ground. They like to shoot game fowl, and eat them. Pheasants and ducks often rocket before you in the West.

If you talk with food specialists on the extension staffs of the land-grant colleges you realize anew the importance of game in the region's meals. For instance, about a third of Wyoming's annual meat supply consists of it. Major social events for summer students and their families at the University of Wyoming include picnics at the Science Camp in the nearby Snowy Range. They accommodate as many as 2,000 guests at a time! Always the position of honor in the menus goes to game supplied by the State Game Commission.

The Agricultural Extension Service of the College of Agriculture of the University conducts demonstrations on the dressing out and cooking of game. As an aid in stretching locker space, boning techniques are emphasized. How to cook game takes the spotlight for the women. The evening ends with everyone tasting different dishes, with guessing contests about the kinds of meat sampled.

Popular game of the region and their average dressed weights are: elk, 350 pounds; deer, 165 pounds; antelope, 85 pounds; moose, 500 to 600 pounds; and mountain sheep, 250 pounds. Most persons nominate elk as their first choice. To praise it they say, "It is the most like beef."

How To Cook Game

Deerburgers and *elkburgers* are as much at home in the area as hamburgers and lamburgers. The less tender cuts of game generally make their bow in meat loaves, balls, patties, and mincemeat. Cooks also braise them. Dried elk, when cured in the manner of dried beef, creamed, and served on split hot biscuits makes a visitor rejoice that he is in the Mountain West.

Antelope à la Stroganoff appears as a hostess number. To make this dish a western cook uses mushroom soup instead of mushrooms. She says it furnishes the desired flavor economically and conveniently, and that it also helps to keep the sour cream from separating in the cooking.

One glorious September day I drove north from Rawlins, Wyoming, with the enthusiastic, co-operative home demonstration agent, for dinner and a visit on a ranch. It was the season for antelope, and that partly explains the menu.

RANCH GAME DINNER
Tenderloin of Antelope
Fried Raw Potatoes
Green Beans   Sliced Tomatoes
Hot Biscuits
Currant Jelly   Gooseberry Jam
Sliced Peaches and Cream
Coffee

The tenderloin slices, dredged in seasoned flour and pan-fried in bacon fat, were something easy and pleasant to enjoy. So was the brown gravy that came with them. Delicious as the food was, I most treasure memories of chatting with the lady of the house, an expert game cook. Her pointers on how to handle this culinary chore developed like this.

"I never begrudge men and women, if they can shoot accurately, the thrill that comes when they see proud antlers outlined against the sky. My hope is that the hunter will take care of the animal he gets if he expects women to cook it. You can't make tasty dishes of meat that has not been treated correctly before it reaches the kitchen.

"The first step is to realize you are to cook game, not beef or mutton. Game is different. The meat is darker, leaner, and inclined to be dry.

"For the sake of good flavor you have to remove all the fat and skin from the meat before cooking it. Then you replace the fat. I like to use beef suet. Bacon drippings also are fine.

"Before you put the meat on to cook you must decide whether you wish to retain the characteristic gamy flavor, or to submerge it. Then you are ready to act.

"If you like the gamy taste you prepare the meat, once the skin and fat are removed, as if it were beef or mutton. You can lard a roast of venison or elk or lay strips of bacon over it.

"In case you wish to mask the gamy flavor that so many people praise and relish, you can choose from various western kitchen tricks. You will want to cook the meat well done. If there are any strange odors they disappear in the longer cooking. You can brush on a barbecue sauce as the meat cooks, a real peppery one."

Don't Forget the Seasoning Shelf!

"Chicken fried steaks or strips of game coated with egg and crumbs and pan-fried in bacon drippings retain little of the wild taste if they acquire a crisp, brown crust. You can spread mustard on a roast before it goes into the oven. And that reminds me, don't be misled by the dark color of elk and deer meat and think the roasts are cooked prematurely. They require from 25 to 30 minutes per pound in an oven with a temperature of 300° to 325°. If you like a seared, brown taste you increase the temperature to 450° for the last half hour.

"Pot roasts are no trouble. You can cook them in barbecue sauce, tomato paste or sauce, tomatoes with chopped green peppers and onion added, or sour cream. Or you can take a tip from the Germans and make sauerbraten. Most cookbooks contain a recipe for it. You soak the meat a couple of days before cooking it in a mixture of water, vinegar, onion, lemon slices, salt, pepper, and spices. You turn it occasionally to help distribute the sauce.

"Curried game can be wonderful. And curry powder takes care of any strong flavor. Elk curry is heavenly on rice. Venison and elk make extra fine mincemeat and acceptable chili con carne.

"I almost forgot about the seasoning shelf. It is the magic wand of the kitchen. Smart cooks stock it with tomato paste and sauce, tomato ketchup, Worcestershire sauce, garlic, curry powder, chili powder, and black pepper. Game calls for lots of pepper. And above all, do serve the meat hot. Whatever fat it contains congeals quickly as it cools, and the taste is better before it hardens.

"Frugality, or the practice of thrift, becomes a ranch woman's second nature. Always you aim to be self-reliant, to help the spread make profits. You avoid waste like the plague. I save the scraps of fat trimmed from game and make soap with them — only it's 'no go' with venison fat. That's because a deer has no gall bladder. I prefer bear fat for soap making."

When we drove back to town that cool evening we traveled over the old Oregon Trail for a stretch. The fresh Wyoming wind touched our faces, and the blue-white of newly fallen snow glistened like a million diamonds in the mountains ahead. As the black night gradually crept around us I continued to repeat to myself, as I thought of the day at the ranch, "All this, too, is America, a most refreshing part of it."

The City Food Is Colorful, Too

While ranch cooks write one of the more romantic chapters in the Mountain West's cuisine, the cities and towns also contribute color to it. As has been indicated, the Mormon Church influences the meals of Utah. That the missionaries bring food ideas home from foreign lands cannot be doubted by a visitor to the state. One gracious gentleman described his favorite company meal as he presided over the Dutch ovens at a canyon supper staged below a colorful aspen grove. You need not be a sleuth to detect that he served his church in Italy.

UTAH DINNER
Meat Balls with Spaghetti
French Fried Artichoke Hearts
Tossed Green Salad
Hard Rolls
Fresh Fruit

As previously mentioned, some converts to the church in the Scandinavian countries, England, and other faraway places go to Utah to live. Of course they prepare their favorite dishes, and show the new neighbors how to make them. For a century this broadening of the cuisine has been under way.

One priceless morning in Salt Lake City, when the sunshine was golden, the sky blue, the air dry and clear, and the mountain views perfect, I went to the home of a journalist friend for a late breakfast. A recollection of the menu brings thoughts of good things to eat, warm friendliness, and lively food talk. On that occasion I met pancake balls (*ableskivers*) for the first time, a true gastronomical discovery.

UTAH GUEST BREAKFAST
Fruit Cup
Broiled Ham Slices
Ableskivers
Sirup   Jelly
Milk

Utah, like Colorado, grows magnificent sun-ripened fruits. Although large quantities of them travel by truck and train to other areas, the people at home are prolific fruit eaters. Fruit cups of many kinds offer the most marvelous preview to a meal imaginable. In them many splendid kinds lend their mellow, ripe fragrance and flavors to celestial blends.

As I glowed inwardly and with words over the meal starter, I made two observations. *Ableskivers* definitely are unusual in the United States. And no coffee was served.

These hot pancake balls came from the kitchen puffy, light, browned, and tempting. We pulled them apart, and added butter and jelly for a taste sensation so pleasant that I asked, "Where can you buy a griddle with wells with which to make ableskivers?" "In Salt Lake City," my hostess replied. Danish emigrants brought the breakfast specialty to the area long ago. Its deliciousness caught on at once.

The Word of Wisdom of the Church contains stern prohibitions against the use of alcohol, tea, coffee, and tobacco, and all foods, beverages, and habits Mormons believe impair human efficiency. Naturally this affects the cuisine. For instance, the people are great milk drinkers.

I was a guest one afternoon at a fascinating tea party. The

table appeared like a stunning color photograph, for it displayed dainty sandwiches, tiny cakes, and unusual candy. No tea was poured. In place of the proverbial pot a sparkling glass punch bowl, wafting delicate steam clouds above, caught my eyes. The aroma of the hot spiced punch teased the appetite. Then I took a sip and recognized instantly that the fruity elixir fell short only of what the angels drink.

Hostesses in the Beehive State excel with their hot fruit beverages. The iced ones have merits, too, but give a cook fruit juices, spices, sugar, and hot water and she demonstrates she is a culinary artist and craftsman.

When friends drop in for an informal visit many Americans in other areas traditionally offer, as a token of hospitality, a cup of tea or coffee with cookies, crackers, and cheese, sandwiches, or whatever else is at hand. The Mormon custom is to pass candy or punch, or both.

And such candies as they pass! Perhaps the queens of the candy ball are the *brunettes,* or chocolate-coated creams. One bite and they are irresistable. The puffed mints simply melt instantaneously in your mouth. Chocolate covered orange sticks also are a delight.

Ice Cream, and Garden Blossoms

Home candy making flourishes throughout the year. As the Christmas season approaches, kitchens step up the production of sweets. They emit the fragrance of chocolate and vanilla, and glow with the colors of candied red and green cherries and the pale yellow of crystallized pineapple. Little pyramids of nut meats supply a festive note. Some women drive to commercial candy kitchens to buy the chocolate used in dipping their cream centers. The centers are made by cooking thick cream, sugar, and corn sirup, and flavoring with vanilla. More cooks make their own chocolate coating. The creamy centers go gay with chopped crystallized fruits and nuts. Those intended for mailing often end up in a roll, covered with semi-sweet chocolate. The lucky recipient slices off the sweetness as she chooses.

Just as the cooks know how to make fine candy, they also reach a peak of perfection with ice creams. The old-fashioned freezer with the dasher remains useful in many quarters. Some of the younger families stage ice cream socials. The boys take turns at the crank while the girls cut the cakes they have baked. Other groups also enjoy the virtues of home-made ice cream. As one woman of middle age remarked, "I like to have a freezer of ice cream on Sunday afternoons when my garden is at its best. Then many friends stop by to see the blossoms. With ice cream and cake to serve them, it's easy and fun to be hospitable."

In the younger households, which rarely have a dining room nowadays, the hostess frequently arranges a *Utah smörgasbord*. She sets up a buffet on the kitchen counter, and provides such treats as meat balls, buttered hot home-made rolls, and a selection of molded salads in fancy shapes. The guests help themselves and return to the living room to sit around the dining table.

Hamburger suppers also appeal to younger married couples. The menu is a three-piece affair, with hamburgers, a tossed green salad, and a luscious dessert.

Ice cream sodas furnish much luncheon pleasure. Chocolate, caramel, and pineapple tie for first rating.

A dark fruit cake, frosted white, answers as the traditional wedding cake. Weddings in the Temple take place in the morning; they are followed by a breakfast at the bridegroom's home. The bride's parents give the reception later in the day.

All kinds of mouth watering cakes evolve from Utah kitchens, but possibly the chocolate cakes studded with California walnuts or pecans take the prizes. *Caramel sundae cake* ever is in demand. The white layers carry caramel filling, and a cooked marshmallow frosting converts the creation into a picture in white. Then the cook pours on a thin confectioners' sugar frosting, tinted and flavored with caramel. The luscious brown sweet trickles invitingly over the cake's top and down its sides.

Like the pies of all the Mountain West, those of Utah

often are gorgeous. The famous quartet — apple, cherry, boysenberry, and blue plum — start a chorus of compliments regardless of whether they are made with fresh, frozen, or canned fruits. In the seasons for gooseberries and peaches, pies filled with them steal the dessert show.

Mountain Fruits and Berries Win Fame

Colorado basks in the fame of her red raspberries, as well as cherries, apricots, peaches, pears, and melons. Red raspberry ice cream frequently ends company and Sunday dinners when the berries are in season. Cooked cherry sauce is a favorite with baked ham or lamb. One of the unusual pies contains a mixtue of cherries and raspberries. These mountain people also like cherries — sugared, pitted, and chilled — as a compote, with either cake or cookies as the escort. Perhaps to them the peak of cherry enjoyment is to eat the fruit from the stems. If it is inclined to be tart they dunk it in mounds of sugar. Some hostesses present sweet cherries on their stems after they have been dipped in a thick sirup made of port wine and sugar and chilled. They chill them in a compartment beneath the freezer in the refrigerator.

As previously indicated, mountain grown vegetables reach a succulence rarely duplicated elsewhere. Colorado produces marvelous pascal celery, two crops a year. The state's more than a thousand commercial growers win special recognition for the summer supply. Cooks have a habit of cutting the crisp stems, which they refer to as *ribs,* quite fine and adding them to all kinds of salads and casserole dishes. Colorado tables also win distinction for stuffed celery.

Utah's green celery likewise is famous. One of the state's topnotch dishes is *celery au gratin.* Her tomato-onion creations are legion. Just name the vegetable, and if it grows in the temperate zone you are likely to find it at one time or another in the lush gardens of these two mountain states.

Many vegetables end up in pickles of various descriptions. Likewise some of the fruits and berries spark the region's meals with jellies, jams, and preserves. Traditional in some homes are sunshine preserves — sour cherry, apricot, and strawberry. In preparing them the heat of the sun actually does part of the cooking. This trio of spreads appears in many homes for breakfast on Christmas Day.

Picnics Are Highly Popular

Some Utah families like best of all to cook and eat their meals on the beach of Great Salt Lake. Almost all of them enthuse over canyon suppers. Between majestic mountains many exquisite narrow canyons invite natives to bring food prepared at home, or else to cook it in the open over glowing coals. One of my fond recollections is of food served at a chickaree in a Utah canyon. The chicken fried in a Dutch oven was something to write home about.

In the Mountain West you observe a trend toward the preparation of hot picnic meals in home kitchens. It perhaps is more noticeable in Colorado than elsewhere. There the altitudes are high and the air is cool all summer. Cooking in water is a tedious task on campfires. Patience sometimes wears thin before the eating starts, especially among children. Coffee commonly is the only liquid prepared on the spot. However, pan-frying works out satisfactorily; griddlecakes that warm the body and soul present no cooking problem.

Restrictions on where fires can be built are becoming more stringent, in an attempt to reduce the deplorable number of forest fires. Especially is this true in Colorado, for within her borders lie more national parks than in any other state. The cooked-at-home picnic meals constantly win more and more favor.

PICNIC IN THE ROCKIES
Hot Soup
Meat Loaf Sandwiches
Baked Beans
Potato Salad
Assorted Crisp Vegetable Relishes
Cherry Upside-down Cake
Campfire Coffee

Veteran picnickers store in baskets many kinds of canned soups ready for opening and quick reheating on the spur of the moment. Often people mix two or three kinds. Some cooks add less than an equal amount of water to produce a thick soup. Everyone treasures her individual touches.

The soup heats on the kitchen range and is then poured into a vacuum bottle. The ideal situation is to provide a small vacuum bottle of soup for every picnicker. If it is thin straws are tucked in through which to sip the hot, refreshing meal starter. It is easy to hand everyone his own bottle of soup. There is no pouring and dividing to claim attention, and no worry about spilling. Serving cups are unnecessary.

The meat loaf that is baked at home is delivered covered and well wrapped with newspapers or a blanket. Then it is carved quickly at the picnic spot, and the warm slices are slipped between buttered buns or in bread and butter sandwiches. Mountain women say it is easier than pan-broiling hamburgers over a campfire.

The beans generally are commercially canned ones. The cook seasons them as she likes, pours them into a pot, and heats them in the home oven. Then she transports them, pot and all, wrapped like the meat loaf.

Many cooks put the potato salad together a day early; that is, they mix the dressing into the hot spuds and set the dish in the refrigerator to ripen. Crisp vegetable relishes, like lots of tiny celery strips, minced onion, chopped cucumber, and bits of green pepper are folded in just before the picnickers leave home.

A bountiful assortment of uncooked vegetables goes to mountain picnics — cauliflower florets, cucumber and carrot sticks, radishes, lettuce wedges, rings of sweet peppers, celery, and tomatoes. They are carried from home in a dampened muslin bag, such as a sugar sack, surrounded by waxed paper.

For dessert, upside-down cake rings the bell. Cherry, apricot, and pineapple are top numbers. Upside-down cake provides the craved sweetness and the desired tang of fruit. It is cut in triangles, the cake canopied with fruit, and eaten from the fingers. No dishes, forks, or spoons put in an appearance. Sticks of candy and semi-sweet chocolate bars are doled out to the mountain climbers.

By the time such a feast is well under way, the coffee — which is set over the coals soon after reaching the picnic grounds — is ready.

Some families consistently choose pie instead of upside-down cake. They have pie carriers among their picnic paraphernalia. These devices are made of plywood, with two or three shelves. There is a door at one side, and a handle on top. They deliver their treasures from the kitchen to the picnic in prime condition.

Let the Men Cook!

In Wyoming, Montana, and many communities elsewhere throughout the Mountain West some of the old ranch traditions survive. One is that men should do the cooking over campfires, and the women take over in home kitchens. The custom stems from the early days when men cooked on the ranches. Many of them display a pride in their skill in preparing food. They are artists with Dutch ovens. No wonder their wives say to sisters from afar, "Please don't spoil our men! They like to cook at picnics. They are good at it. We don't want women to help them, and make them dependent."

Here is a typical menu for meals eaten in the open where men display their culinary skills.

WESTERN PICNIC
Mutton Stew with Vegetables
Hot Biscuits   Jelly
Tossed Green Salad
Finger Fruits
Fudge
Coffee

The women take charge of preliminary preparations, like making the fudge and salad dressing, washing the salad greens, and preparing the meat and vegetables for cooking. At that point their labors cease. The chief cook braises the mutton in a Dutch oven, and adds potatoes, onions, carrots, and often turnips. At the right moment the biscuits go into another Dutch oven to bake. When they start to take on the last golden brown flush, the snappy, chilled salad leaves are tossed with the dressing. Then the coffee is made.

Favorite dessert fruits include sweet cherries with stems, bunches of grapes, pears, or apples to eat from the hand. Many kinds of candy make the final rounds, although a pan of fudge with nuts embedded in it scores as the finalist in all popularity contests.

While nibbling on the sweets, the guests — warmed and mellowed by companionship and food — often become expansive and declare they are so near heaven in the mountains that they have escaped from the world of care. Then they sing, *When It's Springtime in the Rockies* and *Why, Oh Why Did I Ever Leave Wyoming?* and countless other sentimental and plaintive western songs. When the hour grows late, some wise gentleman — perhaps with thoughts of a cattle or sheep deal coming up — glances at the moon and stars, and then at his watch to confirm his appraisal of the hour. He announces, "It's time to go."

As a tribute to a way of American life they adore, the picnickers often sing the parting number that takes the place of *Home Sweet Home* at cowboy balls. The men and women, who have eaten well around the campfire, stand and sing, *Goodby, Old Paint, I'm a-leavin Cheyenne.*

The Pacific Northwest

LADY LUCK beamed on us the summer morning we drove north into Oregon. Billowy white clouds tossed in a blue sky as if to complement the ocean and its foamy spray. Mammoth logs securely chained on trucks flashed by on the run to lumber mills. Soon noon came with a stop for lunch. Posters advertising salmon derbies gave evidence of where we were, as did the giant and gorgeous editions of *Crab Louis* everyone ordered, and then concentrated on in reverent silence. On again to the north and west. Occasionally black-berry thickets darkened the green at the roadsides with blue-black fruit. Hours passed and dinner time arrived, with the choice between baked salmon or fried razor clams a weighty problem. Up bright and early the next morning, we headed for the City of Roses — Portland — and a week later for Seattle and the Puget Sound area, undisputed urban centers for fabulous food markets.

Visiting these northwestern markets for the first time tests the veracity of the eyes. The exhibits appear too good to be true. You expect to awaken any second to find the myriads of fresh berries, fruits, vegetables, fish, and sea food a fantasy. When the tourist realizes the glamorous displays are spread on counters to tempt the palate and pocketbook he laments a temporary home in a hotel room without a kitchen, if such a stopping place is his lot. Almost everyone in such a predicament takes a mental note of what to order for future meals, and buys a few fruits to snack on. Or if visiting with friends, he rejoices at their thoughtfulness as they adhere to the accepted custom and ask which native treats he wishes to try first.

Salmon Gives Color to Markets

Salmon is the word that slips most eagerly and easily from the tongue. And why not? Is not the excellence of the fish from streams that flow into the Pacific Ocean from northern California to Alaska recognized from coast to coast? Anyone who browses around the Northwest a few days learns that the Columbia River and Puget Sound areas enjoy an exuberant prestige for the delicacy of their catch and man's culinary skill in barbecuing it.

What the markets offer depends on the season, but they make a rewarding showing the year around. All the vegetables of the temperate zone grow in the two states. Among the locally produced berries and fruits are blackberries, blueberries, gooseberries, huckleberries, cranberries, dewberries, loganberries, "phenomenal" berries, nectar berries, youngberries, boysenberries, strawberries, red and black raspberries, red currants, sweet cherries (dark and light), freestone peaches, prunes, apricots, pears, and apples.

Fish and sea food abound. Oysters, razor clams, crabs, Alaska shrimp, halibut, Alaska black cod, sole, Pacific perch, and salmon are general pets. Cheese making flourishes about the countryside, along with other expressions of dairying on a grand scale. Poultry raising is a major industry, with the turkey herds exceptionally large. Filberts and walnuts with light colored shells rank as important crops. In the eastern sections just before harvest, tremendous wheat fields form a golden sea that makes a wandering Kansan feel at home. Peas stretch their green over countless acres in the wheat country. Cattle ranches of the Mountain West, stocked with white faces and black Angus, cover vast areas. On the ranges bands of sheep graze. In this mecca for sportsmen outdoors cookery ranks as an art, with many sourdough experts around the campfires. Old men reminisce about the Klondike, where many times food was as valuable as the gold. They recall how before the rush north began they tossed a piece of the dough back in the flour sack to rest until the evening before the next batch of biscuits or pancakes was started. That was in their ranching days in eastern Oregon and Washington.

In such a picturesque environment a food reporter's thoughts naturally pivot around one question. How do the good cooks excel with nature's bounty? Presently one cue develops, for much food talk winds up in an eulogy of huckleberry pie. Seeing the berries, which are different from their relatives of the same name farther east, and understanding the extent of their widespread growth explains why dishes including them became immortal in the cuisine of Oregon Territory. Tasting them suggests the reason why more recent triumphs have not forced them to relinquish their honored position.

Many huckleberries that grow from the redwood districts of northern California throughout much of Oregon, Washington, and western Idaho are large. While some of them show the characteristic deep blue color, others are a dark, rich red, or a surprising azure blue. Natives hold that the larger and darker the berry the better its flavor. Those of the coastal areas are red and smaller than the ones that grow in the mountains. The latter ripen in September. Their season is brief. Hundreds of families take an annual weekend outing to the fields to gather a supply to use fresh and to can and freeze. The Indians rely on the mountain crop for generous eating while fresh and to dry for winter meals.

In taste, northwestern huckleberries are sweeter than their eastern relatives; they contain fewer seeds. The bushes on which they grow are so handsome that many people include them in their gardens with other ornamental shrubs. Florists gather truck loads of them and the sword fern for decorative purposes.

The fresh berries are found in many markets from late July almost until Christmas. Then the frozen supply makes its appearance. Indeed, huckleberry pies, muffins, and griddlecakes in many households rate as traditional treats during the holiday season.

Wild blackberries prosper by the highways near the ocean and elsewhere. From August until October they bear fat, juicy berries, mostly of Himalaya types that have escaped from cultivation. In the homes their sharp-sweet flavor, which natives refer to as *zippy-sweet,* gives pies, cobblers, jellies, and jams a new claim to fame. The somewhat sweeter dewberry — native trailing blackberry — also thrives in the two states, and obligingly ripens early in summer. Much of its glory is reflected by its illustrious cousins, like the tart, purplish-red loganberry and its milder flavored hybrid, the "phenomenal" berry; the large, juice filled, purple-black youngberry; and the even larger boysenberries. Eastern style blueberries are cultivated in many communities, and the plantings continue to multiply.

A universal kitchen practice is to substitute one kind of berries for another in recipes. Cooks also mix two or more varieties in dishes, as equal parts of loganberries and youngberries. They say the blend brings out the best flavors of both.

Berry pies are a favorite dessert from the Canadian border to California. Their most striking quality, other than superb flavor, is unusual depth. Between the two flaky pastry crusts lies a thicker layer of berries than in most of Uncle Sam's pies. Berry chiffon and cream pies are legion. In the latter the creamy filling and lightly sugared berries alternate in the baked pastry shell. Frozen, canned, and fresh berries take lead roles in the region's pies, with the calendar determining the selection.

Berry Desserts, Cold and Hot

The Christmas ambrosia of sliced oranges and shredded coconut welcomes the color and flavor of frozen berries, especially strawberries, tossed in to mix. Berry desserts, as numerous as the majestic mountain peaks of the area, convert many a dinner's last course into a refreshing, fragrantly-flavorful success. They embrace the berry shortcakes, bavarians, milk sherbets, steamed puddings, and ice creams, and a rich number I never have met elsewhere, the *frango*. This is a substantial dish, and it is appreciated especially at the close of an otherwise light meal. Its texture is flaky, its richness a rare eating pleasure.

RASPBERRY FRANGO

1 cup sugar	1 cup crushed red raspberries
1 cup hot milk	1 tablespoon lemon juice
4 egg yolks	2 cups whipping cream

Stir the sugar into the hot milk and pour over the well-beaten egg yolks; return to the double boiler and cook over water, stirring continuously, until the mixture thickens slightly. Cool, chill, add the crushed and lightly sweetened berries, and fold in the whipped cream. Freeze quickly in a refrigerator tray and serve garnished with a few perfect berries.

The Seattle home economist who introduced the dessert to me explained that you never go wrong on strawberry or maple frango, thus tactfully giving me the pleasure of expressing an emphatic ditto for one featuring red raspberries.

A homey dish of grandmother's vintage much enjoyed today consists of small cubes of unfrosted cake in individual serving dishes, crowned with berries and sweetened whipped cream. Some households prefer to substitute a soft vanilla ice cream for the whipped cream. This softer than regular ice cream won favor first in the Pacific Northwest.

Berry and fruit crisps carry the banners for appealing baked desserts throughout the year. *Rhubarb crisp* maintains an ardent following from one January to another. This rosy herb, universally called a fruit and used like one, comes to markets after the first of the year, with Sumner, Washington, a noted center of production.

The dessert includes a fruit such as sliced apples or diced rhubarb or berries, with a mixture of sugar or flour added, placed in the bottom of a baking dish, or indvidual baking dishes. The crumbs are pressed on top. They consist of ½ cup of butter or margarine, 1 cup of sugar, ¾ cup of flour, and a few grains of salt, often with a dash of spice added, rubbed together until crumbly. Women bake it in a hot oven, 425°. The crusty top calls for a crown of whipped cream or soft ice cream.

Apple, apricot, and peach *betties* also score regional dessert honors. For them the cook arranges and bakes alternate layers, at least two, of both prepared fruit and sweetened and spiced bread crumbs, with the crumbs on top. For a crunchy, tasty regional touch she scatters on a few walnut meats before running the betty into the oven to bake. Peach, pear, and berry cobblers are universal favorites. Most cooks sweeten the pears with brown sugar and spice them with ginger.

British Columbia Influences the Meals

A food scout observes a quiet Canadian or English undertone in some of the meals. One splendid example is the fruit or berry *duff*, which becomes "boiled" dumplings in the U.S.A. Another sign of the friendly kitchens across the border to the north is the very deep fruit or berry pies, often baked in a casserole, with one crust, a top one. Then there are the little chess pies or tarts, abundant in British Columbia, that also show up in Washington and Oregon and startle a visiting food reporter. Instinctively she looks out of the window to note whether the magnolias are in bloom. To her *chess pies* always have spelled the South.

It is in menu planning that the hot berry and cherry puddings show a unique sectional habit. Women speak of serving them as the one warm note in an otherwise cold meal, such as one with a hearty fish salad as the main dish.

The Fruit Basket Overflows

Washington apples and Oregon pears represent the area's fruit basket with a poise born of the assurance and experience of wide acceptance throughout the United States and abroad. Their superior quality wins friends wherever exported. The fruits grow in the orchards of both states, but the apples that start their trek to extensive markets in September speak for Washington, and the pears for Oregon. Jonathans, Red and Golden Delicious, Winesaps, Yellow Newtowns, and Rome Beauties are some of the apple varieties. Northwesterners also adore their local summer apples, even if less famed nationally, for they supply the much appreciated sweet-tart sauce.

From the not infrequent bumper crops the portion of the fruit kept at home ends up in about all the apple dishes known to man. In a region where fruit compositions dominate the salad scene, it is not amazing to discover apple salads quite the ticket. *Waldorf salad,* that apple, celery, nut composition which originated on New York's Fifth Avenue, has been adopted on the Pacific shores. Indeed, northwestern cooks give their own interpretations to the classic. One of them is to mold the ingredients in lemon flavored gelatin made with canned apple juice or sweet cider as part of the liquid. Likewise apple juice spiced with a little sirup drained from sweet pickles assumes the liquid role and enhances the cabbage flavor in another old-timer, *perfection salad.* To taste is to praise, and to swear always to have apple juice and sweet pickles on the cupboard shelves when perfection salad is the order of the day.

Plump and juicy apple pies, with a touch of cinnamon or nutmeg, nobly personify the Northwest. And baked apples, like baked pears, know the thrill of whole hearted approval. Sometimes they flaunt hats of pretty cranberry, mint, or orange sherbet or vanilla ice cream for a union of fine flavors. Almost every household upholds a special method of baking apples, but one, which has the approval of members of the foods staff of the University of Washington, follows. Pare the upper third of cored apples and bake them pared ends down in a pan containing a little sugar sirup. When just tender remove the apples from the oven, invert them in the pan, and baste several times with the sirup as they cool.

Before baking, cavities in the cored fruit often are stuffed with goodies such as nut meats, honey, dates, bits of candied ginger, and raisins. To dress up the servings some hostesses pile meringue over and around each apple to cover it. Then they stick the airy cover in porcupine fashion with slivers of Oregon filberts. One of the advantages of these homegrown nuts to the imported ones is that they may be sliced without crumbling. Their flavor also is more buttery. Pleasing to the eyes and palate are the meringue jacketed apples, baked in a slow oven, 325°, for 10 minutes, or until the tips of the fluffiness are lightly browned.

Before taking off for home, most tourists who jaunt around the scenic Northwest tuck a few packages of the unusual local apple and apricot candies in their bags to present to their friends. One of my hostesses gave me the recipe she follows in making the confection.

APPLE CANDY

2 cups sieved apples	6 tablespoons cold water
2 cups sugar	1 cup chopped walnuts
A few grains of salt	4 teaspoons lemon juice
2 tablespoons unflavored gelatin	Powdered sugar

Cook the washed unpeeled apples, cut into small pieces, in just enough water to prevent them from sticking to the pan. When soft, put them through a sieve and measure. Add the sugar and salt, and cook the mixture until it becomes thick, stirring constantly to prevent scorching. In the meantime soak the gelatin in the cold water to soften it. Add it to the hot apples and stir to dissolve. Then remove from the heat, add to the nuts and lemon juice, and pour into a shallow pan. Cool, and refrigerate. When set, cut into small squares and roll in powdered sugar. Apricot candy is made the same way with the fresh or dried fruit.

Pears Are Served Throughout the Year

Pears are an around-the-year fruit in the Northwest. Summer brings the juicy Bartletts. Indeed, people commonly refer to them as *summer pears.* Almost everyone likes them pared and sliced with sugar and cream. Chilled, pared, cored, and quartered ripe ones topped with mint sherbet or vanilla ice cream are a standard regional dessert. For a sundae, all that is needed is chocolate sauce. If crowned with creamy cottage cheese to which bits of candied ginger have been added, they become a much praised salad. Usually lettuce lines the plates.

Of the autumn and winter varieties, the Bosc, pronounced *bosk,* comes first. It is the russet fruit with a long neck, and is at its best from September to January. The Anjou (*an-jo*), green or creamy yellow when ripe, follows in October and lasts until April. The Comice (*comeese*) wears a deep pink to red blush. It is available from October to February. The Nelis (*nell-iss*) makes its bow in January, and tastes wonderful until June. All of these varieties are excellent. When ripened properly they are brimful of juice and flavor, and are sweet.

Northwesterners know how to treat fruits successfully. They stress the wisdom of picking pears from the trees at the first hint of ripeness, or when the stems show a tendency to separate from the spurs if they lift the fruit slightly. They point out that pears ripened on the tree may become gritty. Their technique is simple and exacting. They pick the fruit and wrap it singly in paper and then refrigerate it. When ready to use their home supply they let the desired quantity stand at room temperature a few days, still wrapped in paper, and daily apply the touch test for ripeness. When the fruit becomes slightly soft at the stem end it is ready to chill and to enjoy.

Hostesses Favor Pears in Shells

Many people prefer to eat chilled pears from the hand. On some occasions hostesses serve both the unpared Anjou and Comise divided into lengthwise halves with the cores removed. They are eaten from the shells with a spoon, like a cantaloupe. Pears also accompany cheese and crackers for dessert.

Northwesterners like to broil the cored halves, brushed with melted butter and sprinkled with brown sugar, long enough to glaze their tops. They add dots of bright jelly to the center of each one and serve them on the platter with the meat.

Anjou and Bosc pears are autumn and winter favorites for baking.

One of the widely accepted methods of preparation is to first place the cored lengthwise halves cut-side down in just enough water to cover the bottom of the baking dish. Most cooks add the juice of half a lemon to the water. They bake them covered in a moderately hot oven, 375°, until almost cooked — 20 to 25 minutes. Then they turn them cut-side up and add 1 to 2 teaspoons of sugar to each half and complete the baking, uncovered. It takes from 10 to 15 minutes longer to glaze the fruit. Sometimes the hostess puts a chocolate mint of silver dollar size on top of each pear half just as the fruit comes from the oven. The candy melts into a creamy chocolate sauce. Short-cut cooks insert 3 or 4 whole cloves in the pear halves during the last part of the baking. She serves this quickly spiced fruit hot with meat.

Another highly recommended procedure is to stand the whole washed pears upright in a deep casserole, pour on a sugar sirup composed of equal parts of sugar and water boiled together for a few minutes, cover the dish, and run it in a slow oven, 325°, for 1½ hours. Many exceptional cooks choose brown sugar for sweetening pears regardless of how they are prepared. Especially do they prefer it to white sugar when making pie.

For a breakfast dish de luxe, Northwesterners first pare and core pears and leave them whole. They sprinkle on lemon juice and add a generous teaspoon of brown sugar to the center of each one. Then they stuff the cavities with pork sausage first cooked until crumbly in a heavy frying pan and drained. They bake the fruit upright in a deep dish, with a little water poured around it, in a moderate oven, 350°, until tender.

Pears — pared, cut in diamond shapes or cubes, and dressed with lime or lemon juice — take the lead as A-1 escorts to the curries, a family of foods that has increased in popularity regionally since World War II. Diced pears often substitute for all or part of the apples in Waldorf salad. And pared, cored pear halves, dipped in lemon juice, form a favored base for crab, shrimp, and other sea food salads, as well as chicken salad. One of the more handsome and appealing numbers consists first of pared and cored fresh pear halves dipped in orange juice, or drained canned ones, placed cut side down on greens. The rounded or upper side is coated with cream cheese that has been moistened with orange juice and whipped until smooth and light; it is studded with vivid homegrown red currants or bits of bright jelly. Canned pears tinted red, yellow, pink, and green also grace many regional salad plates. The rule is to add the coloring to the sirup, and to bring the fruit to a boil in it. Some cooks flavor the red sirup with cinnamon, the yellow with orange slices, the pink with wintergreen, and the green with mint. They chill the gay colored pears before draining them for the salad plate.

Peaches Grow on Volcanic Ash Soil

The Northwest's freestone peaches need no introduction nationally. They, like the apples and pears, have skyrocketed up the success ladder wherever marketed. They are honored at home. Here is the way one Washington home economist — a splendid cook in her own right — describes them.

"Our peaches are superb — juicy, flavorful, tender — the kind the juice drips from. Big crops of them grow in the volcanic ash soil of the Yakima and Wenatchee valleys of our state. They could not be finer. We like them pared and sliced with sugar and cream. Then we dice them fine, add sugar to sweeten, and refrigerate them to start the juices. That's how we make one of the most delightful sundae sauces for vanilla ice cream. For a refreshing salad we mold the yellow-ripe slices and blueberries or huckleberries in cherry flavored gelatin pointed up with lemon juice. We serve the jewel on crisp greens with creamy cottage cheese, the kind the Northwest likes.

"Many of us can a supply of these peaches for winter use. My favorite peach dish? Well, I have to admit it is the old-fashioned peach pie or cobbler, sugary and cinnamon spiced."

Women Believe in Salad Preparedness

While the Northwest is acquainted with and fond of the standard salad dressings, her cooks have invented a few of their own for pouring over fruits. In one, ¼ cup of lemon juice and ½ cup each of powdered sugar and salad oil, with a pinch of salt, are whipped with a rotary beater to mix. Cooked berry dressings are even more unique and cheery in color. In them tart berry and lemon juices are cooked over water with sugar and eggs, and later chilled. Whipped cream is folded in before serving. And then there is *cranberry dressing*, an especially fortunate choice for lettuce in a baked salmon dinner, on turkey and chicken salads, and on any fruit salad that contains apples or segments of grapefruit or oranges. To make it natives blend equal parts of cranberry sauce and salad oil and include lemon juice, salt, and sugar as seasonings.

Women in widely scattered neighborhoods enthuse equally over their definition of *salad preparedness,* a jar of uncooked cranberry relish in the refrigerator.

To make it they grind 1 pound or 4 cups of cranberries in the food chopper, and stir in 2 cups of sugar. They permit the mixture to ripen at least a day or two before using it. Many of them grind the pulp and yellow portion of half an orange with the cranberries, while others substitute a pared apple, cored, for the orange.

Often they freeze the relish in the refrigerator tray, cut it in squares, and serve it on greens as a frozen salad to accompany chicken, turkey, or any hot meat. More frequently they moisten the relish with French dressing and scatter it over fruit salads of all descriptions. Many superior cooks vouch enthusiastically for the way the cranberry-orange mixture over pears elevates the salad. When scattered on the chilled, juicy white of the fruit with crisp greenery in the background, the ruby relish, blended with piquant French dressing, produces a vibrant treat that enlivens almost any meal. With chopped unpared apple and half as much celery added, the relish often is molded in gelatin for one of those priceless made-ready-in-advance salads, tart enough to satisfy and gay enough to spark up a meal. Apple sauce, frozen and sliced, accompanies pork with real success.

Grandmother Liked Cranberries, Too

Cranberries, native to the marshes of the Northwest and now cultivated extensively and successfully, are firmly entrenched in the affections of the people. And in the region's cuisine! In Portland I chatted one afternoon with a successful business home economist who led me in her conversation to her pioneer grandmother's kitchen, in showing that the origins of many of today's favorite dishes trace back to old-time favorites.

"Grandmother tenderly simmered the home cured ham for Christmas in crimson, tart, cranberry sauce," she said. "I shall always remember how the horseshoe slices tasted and my thrill when it was my turn to be served from the platter. From this early day custom evolved a regional liking for meat and cranberry combinations.

"Grandmother considered cranberry and gooseberry pies perfect endings for fish dinners. No one has discovered better food teams than baked salmon and trimmings topped off with a lattice cranberry pie, or boiled halibut followed by a two-crust gooseberry pie. Other pies that evolved with the little red berries are those in which equal measures of cranberries and pared, cored, and sliced apples or pears compose the filling.

"And have you heard of our *ice water cake?* Grandmother told me, as I watched her bake the tender white layers and frost them with old-fashioned boiled frosting, how the 'receipt,' as she called it, was invented by a rural woman who had an icy mountain stream near her kitchen door. The water was easier to get than milk.

"Then there was the spectacular 6-layer white cake, put together at serving time with whipped cream and sliced bananas, or in advance with rich, melt-in-the-mouth chocolate frosting. Grandmother baked it in three layers, and split each one with a knife that had a long, thin, sharp blade, to make two layers. At church socials and country school parties it was the talk of the evening, and mighty good eating, too."

Prunes enter kitchen chatter nowadays as of old. And by *prunes* the natives refer to Italian or date plums, which are enjoyed fresh as well as dried. Many other varieties of plums also grow in the fruit wonderland of the Pacific Northwest. The men single out fresh prune pie for compliments, as their sweethearts, wives, and mothers inform a food reporter that they add a smattering of cinnamon and clove to the filling. Usually someone in every group refers to *dried prune pies* and the familiar pioneer trick of sprinkling the filling, before adjusting the top crust in position, with a few drops of cider vinegar. Dried prunes steamed until soft enough for the pits to be removed bulge on salad plates with innumerable luscious fillings, like nuts, cheddar or cottage cheese, finely chopped Waldorf salad, apple chutney, thin slices of apples or pears, and candied fruits. And *prune cakes,* carefully spiced and crowded with nuts, suggest the many delightfully homespun kitchens of the area. Members of the family scent them on their return home. "What smells so good?" they inquire.

Let's Also Eat the Lettuce

Fruit salads divide into two distinct kinds, those arranged on plates, and the gently tossed kind. Both occupy the spotlight on the buffet, and in sit-down meals, too, for guests and home folks alike. One noticeable characteristic of many plate salads is reflected by the habit clever cooks have of scattering French dressing on the bed of lettuce before adding fruit. A mother explained it like this, "Not many people eat lettuce unless dressing is poured over it, yet almost everyone seems to prefer the fruit without dressing. At least they wish to add a smidgeon of it themselves in their own way.

From my home economics instructor at the University of Washington I learned this stunt of giving the lettuce enough appeal so it will be eaten, and then passing additional dressing for the fruit to please the people who wish to use it."

Quarters of chilled bright red cinnamon apples, and mounds of coarsely grated raw apples, with a touch of lemon juice folded in, may be strangers to salad plates in some parts of America, but certainly not in the Northwest. And hostesses in few areas, other than in California and Florida, present such a luxuriant variety of fruits. A northwestern cook selects fresh, canned, or frozen ones, whatever she has in her kitchen. She rarely places them on lettuce without a tasty touch of something — of "this or that," as she says, to accentuate flavors.

Pear halves she sprinkles with orange or lime juice or with white wine, while the salvaged maraschino cherry juices are brought out to douse over yellow peach halves. Apricots, cut in two, receive a baptism of sweetened orange juice, or are first chilled in a simple sugar sirup with shredded orange peel added, and then drained. Cherries, the plump, red-black beauties, sweet and plentiful enough to furnish an excuse for Americans elsewhere to swear allegiance to the region, surrender their pits; some women then chill them in a simple sugar sirup into which a little sherry wine has been stirred. The gorgeous berries come to the plates as they are, except perhaps the strawberries, which often need sweetening. For appearances sake, most women jauntily dip the berry tips in the snow of powdered sugar. Grapes, cut in halves and christened with berry juice; melon balls splashed with lime juice, and sprigs of mint, as plentiful as the sunflowers in Kansas, complete the set-up for a fruit plate in the Pacific Northwest.

With tossed fruit salad, the dressing is added and tenderly distributed; then spoonfuls of quivering, bright colored jelly — often cranberry, red currant, or crabapple — or scoops of vanilla or fruit ice cream are dropped on top.

Berry, apricot, and peach ice creams vie in the cook's dreams for this decorative role; she judiciously gives all of them their big moments, each in turn.

Even western cole slaw goes merry with fruit. Into the salad of crisp, fine cabbage shreds, moistened with a thick cream and cider vinegar dressing, the cook stirs cut-up cherries, plums, peaches, or apples, or mixtures of fruits. Likewise the big hearted cole slaw opens its doors to vegetables, when fruited salad does not fit into the menu. Cooked peas, finely cut celery, thinly sliced florets of cauliflower, and red-rimmed radish circles join with fluffs of parsley to transform the plebeian dish into one of the wonder, even if humble, salads of the Northwest.

They Call It "Louie"

Crab Louis occupies the spotlight from one generation to another as the royal fish salad of the Pacific Northwest. It is hearty enough for the entree or indeed the meal; the classic appears on the mealtime scene both to please the palate and the eyes and to appease the appetite. Some families like clam broth or steamed littleneck clams with clam broth as the prelude to the *louie,* their affectionate and everyday name for the dish. Shredded lettuce on a dinner plate is the foundation for the noble creation. On it at the center is arranged a mound of cooked body crab meat, with the legs around the outside. Between the two, slices of hard-cooked eggs, uncooked tomatoes, carrots, and cucumbers, and often cooked asparagus tips and green beans — marinated in French dressing and chilled — form a colorful circle. The dressing is doused over all — Thousand Island or mayonnaise, tinted and seasoned with ketchup, chili sauce, and pimentos, and frequently French dressing as well. Parsley or water cress provide the garnish.

Man is blessed by the variety of food he finds on this planet, but he who has not tasted the Northwest's *Dungeness crab* has been cheated of one of the nation's gustatory joys. People who relish sea food generously praise its flavor. While it is dug on the beaches throughout the region, it is most abundant at Dungeness, Washington, where the cold waters of the Pacific Ocean meet those of Puget Sound. First time visitors to the region who are accustomed to the also wonderful blue crabs of the Atlantic and Gulf of Mexico coasts are amazed at the larger size of the northwestern ones. They are pleased to discover that the meat picked from the shells is sweet and delicious. Crab Louis is merely one of the many fascinating dishes in which it stars. *Crab à la king* might be called the bride's choice. That is because it eliminates the traditional chicken à la king from so many of the area's wedding breakfasts.

Barbecued crab answers as a regional specialty, and brings memories to me of good eating and fun around a Portland supper table. My hostess, a clever and gracious newspaper woman, after piloting me about a food market and answering a barrage of questions, prepared the treat in my honor. She explained her cooking technique as she worked.

First she broke the bodies of the cleaned hard-shell crabs into 2 to 4 pieces and cracked the legs. Then she placed them in a large baking dish, poured on barbecue sauce to cover, and heated them thoroughly in a really hot oven, 375°, or about 20 minutes by the clock. She basted the sea food several times while it heated with the barbecue sauce she stirred up in a jiffy with bouillon, ketchup, garlic, and soy and Worcestershire sauces. The feast was presented in individual soup plates, with a scarlet claw centered in each, and a slice of ripe tomato inserted in the claw. An olive, she said, sometimes substitutes for the tomato. After providing snowy white dish towels to everyone for bibs and plenty of paper napkins, she joined in the enthusiasm of the guests around the table.

As an epicure and an excellent cook, she named crabs and salmon the blue ribbon numbers in the region's barbecue class, although she has a high regard for barbecued halibut and other fish. Cracked crabs, in her estimation, rate as a de luxe delicacy almost unparalleled.

Also she singles out *fried crab legs* as a sublime treat. In preparing them the first step is to remove the meat from the cooked legs carefully in an effort to keep it whole. Then it often is dipped in beaten egg with a little milk added and after that in fine cracker crumbs; it is tenderly pan-fried, or fried in deep fat until golden brown. Of course there are other methods. Speedy cooks usually follow a quicker route; they omit the breading and gently pan-fry the body and leg meat in butter just to heat and lightly brown it.

Northwesterners substitute fried crab legs for oysters in the famed peacemaker or oyster loaf of New Orleans. This is how they do it.

They scoop out a loaf of bread (or large soft rolls), leaving a shell. They lightly spread melted butter and a tart mayonnaise on the inside surface. After toasting it in a moderate oven, 350°, until piping hot, they fill the loaf or rolls with the fried crab legs and garnish them with lemon quarters and parsley. Natives vouch for the creation, which they say not only makes for peace but also for happiness and contentment.

Take Your Pick of the Clams

Thoughts of how good clams taste spur children and adults to dig them when on the beaches. Most food conversations glow with compliments for razor clams. Their name derives from their sharp edges and their shape, which resembles a razor hone. They almost always are available in the markets the year around. One clam often is enough for a serving. Razor clams are so tender that natives bake and fry them successfully, and make a chowder with them without skinning their necks. (Curiously, many families insist that the casserole of macaroni and cheese fails to please unless minced clams are included.)

Butter clams, small, tender, and rich in flavor, answer as chowder favorites. While the *big horse clams* are plentiful and end in many chowder kettles, natives consider them inferior to the *razor* and *butter* varieties. Coos Bay, Oregon, is home to the enormous *Empire* clams, which individually weigh from 4 to 5 pounds. They have large necks from which the skin is scraped with a knife before the necks are split and cut into steaks. When the flesh is pounded, dipped in seasoned corn meal, and pan-fried until crispy and tender, the treat wins praise. The more tender body flesh, cut in strips, is either pan-fried or fried in deep fat.

Another fabulous member of the northwestern clam family is the *geoduck,* pronounced *goo-y-duck.* It dwells all the way from British Columbia to San Diego, but especially prospers on the wide, silty beaches of Puget Sound. Many people consider this place its habitat. The geoduck frequently weighs 6 pounds, and, like the Empire type, one clam often makes a family meal. Its picturesque name derives from its resemblance to a headless, legless duck, with the shells forming its wings and the wrinkled neck skin the down. The creamy meat, cut into steaks, commonly is fried like razor clams, only more slowly for it is less tender. Some women pound it before cooking. The neck meat, after being put through a food chopper, is utilized in chowders. And as everyone advises a visiting food reporter, a geoduck is not just a curiosity, but a fine clam with a tasty, rich flavor of its own.

Hard-shell clams or *quahogs* also abound on the beaches, and are favored when steamed and when converted into broth or chowder. Soft-shell clams are dug, too, for chowders and soups. Edible cockles exist quite widely. They are relatives of the clams, and wear interesting heart shaped shells. Their main use also is in soup kettles and bowls. Campers and picnickers along the beaches prize purple clams, which, although not available in commercial quantities, are excellent when cooked.

Oysters Small, Oysters Big

The Northwest's oyster story divides into two parts, that of the *Olympias,* and of the *Pacific* oysters. The former are tiny, often 100 to the pint, and the latter are too large to swallow whole. The Olympias make wonderful stews; the Pacifics are ideal for frying, creaming, and as an ingredient in countless dishes. The region's oysters are either too small or too large for serving on the half shell, but the cocktails — Olympias heaped in tiny chilled glasses and with a peppy sauce poured over them — achieve acclaim from almost everyone who samples them. One distinctive dish owes its success to the oyster and crab combination. The cook surrounds a few small oysters or pieces of large oysters with flaked, cooked crab meat that has been mixed with baking powder and cracker crumbs, and shapes the mixture so it appears like a good sized eastern oyster. She dips it in beaten egg and then in crumbs and pan-fries it, or fries it in deep fat.

Late winter and early spring bring small smelt in such multitudinous numbers that they blacken the rivers of the Northwest on their return from the ocean to spawn. Tributaries of the lower Columbia River experience such terrific runs that the people turn out to scoop up the wiggly fish in whatever nets they have — and in hats, shirts, baskets, and bird cages! The family eats its fill of the fish and then prepares a supply for future use by freezing, canning, smoking, and pickling.

These smelt or *eulachon* differ from eastern varieties. In length they average about 8 inches; their flesh is soft, rather fat, and pleasing in flavor. Many households prefer to bake or broil them, although some cooks like to pan-broil them in a heavy pan lightly brushed with fat. Other culinary artists follow a rule of handling them like mountain trout. They roll the fish in seasoned corn meal and pan-broil them about 3 minutes on each side, or broil them on one side only $1\frac{1}{2}$ inches from the heat, or bake the larger ones, often in milk, from 12 to 15 minutes in a hot oven, 425°.

An old lumberman gave me his recipe for preparing smelt, which he explained is real he-man's fare.

He heats 2 tablespoons of bacon fat in a pan and lightly browns a little minced onion, garlic, and green pepper in it. Then he adds a can of tomato sauce and simmers the mixture gently about 5 minutes. Next he stirs in $\frac{1}{2}$ cup of cider vinegar and cooks the sauce 2 minutes longer. In the meantime he pan-fries the fish briefly until their exteriors are brown and crispy. He lifts them to a hot platter and pours on the bubbly red sauce, and then serves them immediately to keep the fish from losing their crustiness.

Rainbow Trout Flash in Cold Streams

Cutthroat and *rainbow* trout flash in cold streams and call the sportsmen — who need no coaxing — as also do *eastern brook* and *Dolly Varden* trout. Then there is the king of game fish, the *steelhead*. These delicately flavored specimens are cooked by Northwesterners simply and briefly. They operate on the theory that their responsibility is not to develop or impart new flavors but merely to preserve the fragile and magic ones that already exist.

Northern halibut, caught along the Oregon, Washington, and Alaskan coasts from July to December, unquestionably is one of the West Coast's best food gifts. It is the largest of the flat fishes. Often it attains a length of 6 feet, and a weight of 60 pounds. The markets offer it in chunks and slices. This is a fat fish, and cooks invariably wish to broil or bake it. They broil slices about 1½ inches thick without turning them. Cheese sauce frequently complements both the broiled and baked kinds. Some households feature a molded rhubarb sauce with halibut and other fish. Versions of it are many, but in one the cherry flavored gelatin is dissolved in hot rhubarb sauce, zipped up with a few shakes of tabasco sauce and vinegar. When the cardinal mixture thickens, chopped celery and green onions are folded in, tops and all. A watchword of most of the regional women in making molded salads and desserts is to incorporate at least one crisp food in them.

Crayfish, or fresh water lobsters, are so abundant in many lakes, parts of Puget Sound, and along some streams that they, too, figure in the area's cuisine. The common treatment is to cook them about 20 minutes, or until their shells turn a bright red. Some persons add pickling spices and white wine to the water. Gourmets, with napkins tucked under their chins, tear the tail from the fish, tip it to the mouth, and suck out the meat. They scrape the greenish fat from the top of the body and spread it on a cracker to eat with the claw meat. Some households remove the cooked meat from the shells and utilize it instead of crab meat in Crab Louis. Other times they dip it in a mixture of beaten egg perked up with lemon juice and Worcestershire sauce, roll it in crumbs, and then brown it beautifully in butter. Salad made of the tail meat enjoys an enviable reputation in some quarters.

Salmon Outshines All Other Fish

In these two states of magnificent marine food, where fishing is everyone's sport, facial expressions change when salmon talk evolves. Everyone takes the supremacy of this fish for granted, in the way they greet one month as it arrives and bid good-by to the other as it departs. Indeed, Northwesterners believe that their baked salmon dinners, the aftermath of successful fishing expeditions, or of trips to markets, afford one of the pure epicurean experiences of the nation. Most other Americans agree with them. The expansion of canning and freezing facilities has given the Northwest's fish to people from coast to coast, and promoted it to a top position among the national favorites. The region boasts of two varieties. The *King* or *Chinook* often is quite large; it weighs from 10 to 50 pounds. The *Silver* salmon is smaller, perhaps with a weight of 3 or 4 pounds, and occasionally as high as 15 pounds. The period from May to September usually brings the greatest supply of these fish.

Every kitchen treasures and uses its own brand of cookery secrets with them. Almost universally people prefer thick chunks to steaks or slices because they retain more moisture in cooking. Traditionally some kind of sauce accompanies the pièce de résistance, like egg, tomato, lemon, chive, wine, or tartar sauce. Frequently salmon is stuffed with a well-seasoned bread dressing for baking. Some of the dressings taste of finely chopped dill pickle, which betrays a Scandinavian influence. The lumber and fishing industries through the years have drawn many Scandinavian settlers. The skillful cookery of the Norsemen has made its imprint on the regional cuisine.

The usual procedure in baking salmon is to run it into a hot oven, 425°, and allow 10 to 15 minutes per pound, depending on the thickness of the fish. When preparing salmon for a crowd some natives prefer to wrap it in what they refer to as "butcher's paper," or heavy wrapping paper. They salt and pepper a 10- to 20-pound salmon inside and out, wrap it in six layers of paper, and bake it in a slow oven, 275°, 3 to 4 hours. Before serving the treat they split open the paper on one side of the fish with a sharp knife. They generally pull the paper back to remove the salmon's skin with it.

Smaller portions commonly are baked with sour or sweet cream poured over them. The cook sprinkles a 2-pound piece of salmon with salt and pepper, pours on 1½ cups of cream, and bakes it in a moderate oven, 350°, about 50 minutes, or until no raw color shows when she pierces the flesh with a knife. Citizens of Scandinavian descent enthusiastically approve of the cream-fish cookery, which was established before their arrival. The pioneers who came to the Northwest from various parts of the nation thought cream made fish taste better.

Salmon is simmered in water, too, or "boiled," as people speak of it, and also is pan-fried, and broiled. Leftovers are in demand for salmon à la king, loaves, casserole combinations, sandwiches, salads, and many other dishes to which the flavor and color of the fish lend appeal.

All Aboard for the Barbecue

Salmon bakes and barbecues personify the Northwest, as the clambake speaks for New England. My Corvallis hostess, a member of the foods staff at the Oregon State College, described the salmon bake which she and her friends enjoy in this way:

"Obtain two clean pine boards about 1 foot wide and 2 feet long for every fish you wish to plank. Soak the boards in cold water for at least an hour before use as a safeguard against scorching.

"Split the fish, after the backbone has been removed, in

two lengthwise halves, and nail each half skin down on a plank. Drape strips of bacon over the nails.

"Support the planked fish with stones at the edge of a medium sized fire burned to coals. The trick is to broil the fish without loss of juices, and to brown its surface lightly. When it is half cooked reverse the plank — place its upper half nearest the ground.

"A fish from 1 to 1½ inches thick cooks in about an hour. Remove it from the board with a wide spatula and leave the skin on the plank. In the meantime cook potatoes in their jackets to serve with it. Place the spuds in a pail, add a little water, adjust the lid, and set the pail near the coals. Potatoes so cooked are an appetizing cross between boiled and baked ones. Now pass the butter."

Salmon Barbecuing à la Seattle

In the Puget Sound area, and indeed all along Washington's coast, salmon barbecues serve as the traditional form of beach entertaining for large groups of people. The way to put on one of these gala affairs is described by an up and coming business home economist of Seattle.

"We favor a salmon barbecue for entertaining a large crowd. Such a gathering provides many people to admire the cookery art, and to become eloquent about the fragrance of the salmon as it broils, and to thrill over the moist tenderness and heavenly taste as they eat it.

"The salmon must be fresh and fat. Open it through the back, leaving the belly uncut and the fins on. Thus the skin is unbroken, and will retain the tasty fat. Opening the salmon through the back also gives a uniform thickness of flesh when the fish is spread out for cooking. Remove the head, and scale the fish or not as you wish. Many old-timers skip what they consider an unnecessary process. Sprinkle on salt with a generous hand.

"Start the fire well in advance of the party, or about 2½ hours before the barbecue, to give it time to burn to coals. Alder, apple, and maple woods are the best selections for fuel in this area. Secure the salmon skin side down on a large plank, with mesh wire stretched across to hold it in place. Lean the plank against an improvised railing beside the fire or sharpen one end and drive it into the ground. Judge the distance from the fire with precision, for on the decision hangs perfection. The fish must not be overcooked. The distance should be such as to provide slow cookery. From 1½ to 2½ hours are required to broil salmon, depending on its thickness and the intensity of the heat.

"Cook only on one side. Some barbecue experts brush a lively sauce over their prize as it broils, others prefer melted butter. The traditional menu is simple."

SEATTLE SALMON BARBECUE
Barbecued Salmon
Potato Salad (optional)
Tossed Green Salad
Buttered French Bread
Apple Pie à la Mode
Coffee

Barbecue fans, and their name is legion, design and build ingenious contrivances to simplify the cooking and to safeguard their results. One Seattle gentleman has made a rectangular grill of pipe, with handles on both sides, on which to lay the fish. This enables him to turn it, and thus cook it on both sides. He secures it in place with mesh wire. Just before serving his showpiece he dramatically tosses a few pieces of green alder on the coals to produce a dense smoke, which imparts that coveted smoky flavor so highly favored in fish by northwestern people.

Kippered Salmon Makes Fine Sandwiches

The vivid color and eye appeal of smoked and kippered salmon in the food markets make an unforgettable picture. Despite the splendid canneries and freezers of the region, salt salmon also continues as a favorite. Indeed, the pioneer custom of putting salmon bellies down in salt, as pork sometimes is cured in the Farm Belt, has not disappeared from the area. (Salt cod also is popular. Much of the supply for the national market is produced in Alaska and Washington.) Both jerked and kippered salmon are given a light cure before smoking. The kippered fish also is steamed before it is smoked. Thus it contains a higher proportion of water than the jerked product, and is more perishable. In the markets it appears red, due to the practice of dipping it in a bath of vegetable coloring. The dip is decorative; it does not insure longer keeping.

Kippered salmon, sliced thin, makes elegant sandwiches. Some families like it warmed in the oven and served with melted butter and lemon juice poured over it, while others prefer it heated in thin cream, seasoned with black pepper, and served with boiled or baked potatoes. The *jerked* fish, sliced, is layered in scalloped potatoes for a hearty dish of marvelous flavor. It also appears in sandwiches, salads, and in a rich cream sauce ladled over toast. One of my hostesses broiled smoked salmon to prove how good it can be. She rolled the half-inch slices in salad oil before cooking them. Quarters of lemon, pats of melting butter, and parsley decorated the platter.

Other smoked and kippered fish also find a genuine welcome in the area. *Smoked smelt* are eaten like sardines, and often are covered with tomato sauce and baked slowly until most of the sauce is absorbed. One of the delicacies of Northwesterners is kippered Alaska black cod. The cooks remove its skin and pour on milk to cover. They bring it to a boil, allow it to stand about 10 minutes, and then heat it again to the boiling point just before serving.

British Columbia provides ample quantities of *finnan haddie,* which people in the area like to boil, bake in milk or cream, and serve with boiled potatoes. Fish and chips show up in meals, too; frequently halibut, cut in pieces about 1 by 1½ inches, is the fish. North of the Washington-Canadian border French style fried potatoes supply the accompaniment — while south of it potato chips often fill the bill.

No one chapter devoted to the culinary triumphs of the Pacific Northwest can be designed that will do full justice to the variety of sea food, the vegetables and fruits, and other locally grown products and the dishes featuring them.

Pansies in Front, Asparagus at the Rear

The Northwest grows a high percentage of the canned and frozen peas produced in the United States, and large amounts of the asparagus. And as my Portland guide informed me, it is traditional to have a pansy bed in the front yard and a bed of asparagus at the rear of the house. Many backyards also provide room for a few hills of pole beans and at least a half dozen tomato plants. Usually the good cooks prepare and season the succulent vegetables simply. The trend is to a wider use of the herbs in all three Pacific Coast States. Cheese frequently teams with garden products. For instance, a cook almost instinctively lays thin slices of aged cheddar cheese on the toast before pouring on creamed asparagus. The Oregon *giant* or *Yount* bean with pods 8 to 12 inches long almost never is seen in markets outside of the Northwest; it is cooked like green beans. One rather unusual bean dish is the sweet-sour one with a sauce similar to that used in New England for Harvard beets.

Just as parsley gets mixed up with all kinds of California foods, fresh mint repeatedly shows up in the seasoning role throughout the Northwest. It grows wild and frequently is available in bountiful amounts. Instead of parslied carrots and potatoes, the minted vegetables answer to the dinner roll call, and minted, buttered beets are traditional. A lack of sunshine in autumn gives the area bumper crops of green tomatoes to pan-fry and utilize in other ways. Baked potatoes, as in Idaho to the east, often are scooped out, mashed, and seasoned, and piled back in their shells for reheating at meal-time. A regional culinary stunt is to season these stuffed potatoes to flatter the platter's treat. With fish, for example, prepared mustard and chopped dill pickle are folded into the spuds. Also the humble vegetable occasionally becomes the entree by a slight-of-hand performance, such as adding grated cheese, minced cooked meat, or flaked cooked fish. Another vegetable dish that tastes wonderful and suggests the North Country as authoritatively as the Northern Lights contains cooked, mashed, and seasoned rutabagas or turnips beaten light, with cooked, sieved, unsweetened apples added.

Natives Like the Taste of Cheese

Northwesterners are cheese makers, eaters, and enthusiasts. They serve their marvelous aged cheddar and creamy cottage cheeses at the least excuse — no doubt to some extent for their remarkable food values but primarily because they like that cheese *taste*. As already indicated, the best regional cooks say cheese sauce is a natural with fish. They sprinkle muffin tops before baking with shredded cheese, and turn out cheese waffles and biscuits to team with their jellies and jams. Cottage cheese is at home on both fruit and vegetable salad plates, and when stirred into the French dressing used on salads. Ice cream enjoys a fabulous prestige, and as mentioned, some of it is of a softer consistency than ice cream in other regions. When you are in the area watch for it on salads and desserts, where its coolness and tastiness provide the perfect crown, and a wonderful climax to the meal.

The Fruit Closets Are Full

Take a look into a few northwestern fruit closets, freezers, and freezer lockers and the reason why the fruits and berries of summer are so much in evidence throughout the year becomes apparent. Certainly no other area can boast of a higher per capita supply of jams, jellies, preserves, and canned or frozen fruits and vegetables. In making the jellies, jams, and other sweet, fruity spreads, native cooks like to combine different fruits and berries. Frequently they mix the deep red, plump cherries — such as the Bings and Lamberts — with loganberries or blackberries. Usually they first grind or else cook the pitted cherries in a little water to insure tenderness. Equal measures of quince, cranberry, and apple juices compose the famous and beautiful *paradise jelly*. It is as popular here as in New England. Pear honey, ripe apricot jam, and the old-fashioned fruit butters also deserve honorable mention, and generous applause.

While most of the fruity spreads are eaten on hot puffy yeast rolls, toast, muffins, griddlecakes, hot biscuits, and waffles, they also appear in the hearts of muffins and countless other dishes. Cake jelly rolls filled with apricot or spiced jam transform the simple coffee hour into a festive occasion. Equal parts of red currant jelly and prepared mustard compose a handsome red and yellow accompaniment to ham.

Deep in the hearts of women who like to cook, regardless

of where they live, exists the desire to perfect a few delicious *show-off dishes* with which to amaze neighbors, other friends, and strangers alike. One northwestern custom illustrates the fruition of this longing. People call it *heavenly hash*. One charming lady who excels in evolving the tutti-frutti delight described her technique.

"You start the campaign early in the spring by sterilizing several pint jars. Then you make preserves with the different home grown berries and fruits as they ripen. I usually make the first plunge with rhubarb. For the preserves I mix a scant cup of sugar into every cup of prepared fruit and allow the mixture to stand until the juice forms; then I bring it to a boil. Later, after it has been standing a few hours, I gently boil it until it is quite thick. I pour a layer into each sterilized jar, cover them with sterilized lids, and set them aside in a cool, dry place. Gooseberries commonly make a second layer; I tint the preserves made with them a soft green. Then come strawberries, apricots, red raspberries, boysenberries, peaches, pears, purple plums, and quinces. When the jars are filled I set them aside for the ultra special occasions. In serving heavenly hash I dip into the jar with a large spoon and carefully take out the contents so the layers will not be disturbed. To dramatize the rainbow hued delicacy, I select a shallow dish in which to display it, one that is plain."

Hot Breads Win Applause

The people of the Northwest like all kinds of yeast breads, coffee cakes, and rolls — the melt-in-the-mouth kinds Scandinavians know so well how to make. Many of the traditional European Christmas and Easter breads have been integrated into the region's cuisine. Bake shops almost always feature sticky yeast rolls called *walnut caramel rolls*. They are made with Oregon grown walnuts, the ones that wear light colored shells. The tastes of cardamom and poppy seeds can be detected in many superior coffee breads.

Muffins, griddlecakes, and waffles command considerable prestige. Those made from huckleberries already have been mentioned. For dessert large griddlecakes with coarsely chopped nuts added to the batter sometimes are baked, spread with butter and jam, and stacked four or five layers high on a large plate. For serving they are cut in wedges. Bits of dried fruits also occasionally are stirred into the batter for griddlecakes. Frequently butter and a colorful berry sirup, heated, dress the hot-off-the-griddle treat.

Oregon raises two important nut crops, the walnuts marketed mainly by a California association of growers, and filberts, which resemble hazelnuts, but are larger. Oregonians like to substitute sliced filberts for almonds in lemon-butter sauce served on fish, broccoli, and other foods. Filbert pies climax meals with the success pecan pies encounter in Louisiana and Texas. Most people hold that filbert and banana flavors have an affinity for each other. Who would not agree after tasting sandwiches made of banana-filbert bread and butter? Nut and fruit quick breads, perfect companions to salads, tea, and coffee, are area favorites, as they also are in California. Filbert sundaes cover themselves and the hostess with glory in the dessert course. They consist of vanilla ice cream topped with crunchy roasted filberts and maple flavored sirup. Penuche with filberts is regarded as an ace in candy circles. Both salted and glacé filberts and walnuts are present in holiday and other special occasion meals, at parties, and on the coffee table to please snackers.

Raw Apple and Pear Cakes Have Friends

It is neither surprising nor disappointing to discover that northwestern women possess a talent for mixing nuts into doughs and batters, and into their frostings. Nor is it unusual to find that some of the old families of Oregon still use the pioneer way of spicing walnuts. They now treat filberts in the same manner. One home economist describes her grandmother's technique as follows.

"Stir an egg white with a fork and break it apart, but do not beat it. Dip the walnuts or filberts into it, lift them out with a slotted spoon, and roll them in a sugar-cinnamon mixture as for making cinnamon toast. Spread the nuts in a shallow pan and run them in a very slow oven, 250°, for 15 minutes, or until their exteriors are crusty."

All of the cakes Americans adore are baked in the Northwest. A few unique kinds also are encountered. *Sauce cakes,* as natives refer to applesauce cakes, are old-timers which appear with and without frosting. Women recommend them for their excellent flavor and splendid keeping qualities. Raw apple, pear, and peach cakes belong to the region. They, too, may wear an appealing frosting, although they fare well without one. When unfrosted, many local people like to spread the slices with a soft, nippy cheese. Broken nut meats and unpared apples or pears, or peeled peaches are added to the cake batter. The fruit first is put through a food chopper. In some kitchens the pear cake is spiced lightly with ginger, and the peach number with cinnamon.

English and Canadian cakes classify as favorites. *Pound cake* serves as one example. North of the Washington-British Columbia border tea accompanies it, while to the south coffee is the escort. *Caraway seed cakes* are another importation from the north, as also is *MacDonald cake.* Canadians like the latter unfrosted with cups of tea. Northwestern cooks Americanize it with a luscious chocolate frosting. The *angel food cakes* deserve ovations for their tenderness, height, and delicate flavor. After they are sliced and topped first with vanilla ice cream and then with berries, no one doubts that the Northwest is the place to visit at dessert time.

Maid of Honors, Canadian tea party sweets, are tasted in the Northwest on special occasions. A home economist made them before my eyes to teach me all the secrets.

She pressed cooky dough into wee muffin pans to line the bottoms and sides. Then she dropped a dab of jam and a few chopped walnuts into each one and baked the tarts. At serving time she added dots of whipped cream to each one to decorate them and to heighten the flavor. Whipped cream is the area's definition of an elaborate garnish. A cook seasons it according to the dish it is to embellish, as with salt for soups, sugar and spices for gingerbread and pumpkin pie, and berries and nuts for sponge and angel food cakes.

The Northwest Is a Land of Beef Eaters

Beef ranks as the topnotch meat. Almost everyone watches for a chance to speak a good word for Oregon beef, and to express a hope he soon will face it on his plate. Lamb is popular, too, but pork — with the exception of ham and bacon — receives less attention in the kitchens than in most other areas. A Washington dish known as *corn and pork cake* or *corn-meal mush,* has bits of cooked ham interspersed in it. Women usually mold it in a loaf pan, and then slice and pan-fry it to brown on both sides, as with Pennsylvania Dutch scrapple. They serve it on a bed of fairly thick gravy. Milk gravies are the rule in this region, where they are used on potatoes, bread, and biscuits, but almost never on rice. The South praises red-eye gravy with fervor — Oregonians refer to the same product, made by adding water to the pan in which the ham is pan-broiled, as *brindle gravy.* The name originated on the ranches from the way split biscuits appear when dunked in it.

Mincemeat has been made with venison for so many generations that hundreds of women in the Northwest believe it is essential, or at least highly desirable, for their holiday pie fillings. Wild ducks qualify as favorites in these two states, where every autumn the countryside blooms with men wearing red caps and shirts. After their hunting adventures end, sociable friends gather around countless numbers of tables for game dinners.

Roast turkey generally puts on more than a once-a-year appearance. Poultry raising flourishes in the region, and turkey on Thanksgiving and Christmas is a custom in a high proportion of the families. A home economist connected with the University of Washington lauds an addition to the dressing that smacks of the Chinese. She adds sliced crunchy canned water chestnuts to it before stuffing the regal bird. Most Oregonians prefer crisp roasted filberts instead of chestnuts in the dressing. Fried turkey is not seasonal. For ultra special occasions young turkey, boned and fried, competes with cracked crab for selection. Eggs, too, are a mainstay; omelets rise to the occasion — often high enough to take the entree role.

The Pacific Northwest enchants visitors every month in the year with the promise of Christmas. The holly and evergreen trees set the stage for holiday thoughts. When the gala season is in the offing the youngsters and many of their elders drive to the mountains to skim down the snowy sides like lightning on skis. In the car they carry along sandwiches and vacuum jugs of hot tomato juice, chocolate, or soup for refreshment on the way home. Usually the sandwiches are double. They contain two fillings, like bologna and cheese, bacon and lamb, and bacon and egg salad with tomato slices.

During the Yuletide the homes are resplendent with greens garnered from the woods and the white chrysanthemums that usually still are in bloom. Holly wreaths, their centers heaped with choice apples and pears, and walnuts and filberts, form table centerpieces. Even the casseroles on the buffet tables sometimes wear wreaths especially made for them. Choice apples, polished highly enough to delight a teacher, are scooped out, filled with fruit salads, and decorated with tiny candles in holders. They are lighted to flicker their charms at the proper moment. From the minute you step into the house as a guest at a buffet supper, often a smörgasbord, until you drink the last drop of coffee and eat the last *spritz* — the ever-present Swedish *S*-shaped cooky — you feel that you are in an enchanted Christmas land.

California

CALIFORNIA to you may mean home, a vacation spot, acres of fruit trees in bloom, mammoth vegetable gardens, vineyards dreaming in the sun, or miles of twinkling lights viewed at night from the San Francisco or Hollywood hills. Maybe it suggests stately walnut trees and ancient redwood groves, ships sailing through the Golden Gate into romantic mists, sun-bathing on Carmel's white sands, or a casual way of living. All of these interpretations and many others are authentic. To a food reporter the Golden State denotes friendly women who improvise as they work in their kitchens. And how they can cook!

It is the place where a hostess plans supper parties for the days when the Oriental cherry trees outside her dining room windows froth with pink and white blossoms. She stocks her cupboards with an assortment of dishes — often pottery — in the right colors and large enough to display the foods commonly served on them. Showmanship is her watchword, and glamorous meals her goal.

She gives the impression that she gets dinner easily. Usually she does. Her attitude encourages guests to relax in thoughts of not making extra work, although their common horse sense explains that expert planning and kitchen craftsmanship turn the trick. When company is delayed she accepts their tardiness with composure. Has she not on occasions been held up by traffic or stopped too long in a friend's garden to admire a new rose or tuberous begonia? She is a past master in cooking in advance to avoid the last minute flurry. She also knows how to plan meals that seem to improve as they wait.

Women throw open the kitchen doors to new short cuts, labor saving products and devices, and easy, attractive recipes. They believe nutritive value, taste, and beauty in meals, and the size of grocery bills are what count. They begrudge unnecessary time spent over the range.

Many everyday dinners appear dramatic enough to face the camera when color spreads for national magazines are photographed. Big wooden or pottery salad bowls emit the scent of garlic or oregano. They show off crisp greens of many kinds tossed with salad oil, wine vinegar, and seasonings. Just about every household has pet seasonings, often secret. These distinctive trademarks are a family's pride and joy.

Caesar Salad Traveled Fast

Americans, wherever they live, look to California for salad inspiration. Almost never are they disappointed. Soon after *Caesar salad* became the vogue on the West Coast its popularity spread like a prairie fire across the country. The original plus its many variations caught on quickly. This is the one in which salad oil and grated dry cheese — often Parmesan, and sometimes with crumbled blue cheese — are added to a bowlful of mixed greens with salt and pepper to taste. Then a one-minute egg or a raw one is broken on top. The home chef squeezes on the juice of two lemons and tosses the leaves to coat them and to blend the ingredients. Just before serving the creation he mixes in *croutons,* or crunchy toasted French bread cubes, first dribbled with a little oil in which a crushed garlic clove has been steeped.

One noticeable characteristic of California green salads shows in the way natives mix them in bowls large enough to prevent spilling and to permit giant-size servings. Frequently they carry them directly to the table where everyone with pomp and ceremony helps himself. What a delight the medley of greens is! Not only are the brittle, snappy leaves from the familiar tight heads of lettuce included. There also are those from loose ones with pretty bronze edges and from that dainty cut-leaf type. Natives call the latter one *oakleaf lettuce.* Strangers think it resembles dandelion greens. Chicory, endive, escarole, romaine, and water cress also ably represent the salad greens grown and enjoyed in the state.

A Californian tears the crisp leaves of the multi-shades of green apart in rather large bite-sized pieces and usually drops them into a wooden or pottery bowl first rubbed with garlic. She generally selects French dressing. Often she makes it with salad or olive oil and wine vinegar, which may or may not be herb flavored.

Freehand cooks — the group divides about equally between men and women — exhibit their seasoning talent in the bowls. Some of the pet additions include chopped chives and other herbs, freshly ground black pepper, chopped green onions, cooked or canned artichoke hearts, slivers of green peppers, cut-up cooked vegetables, celery seed, bean sprouts, and toasted bread cubes tumbled in at the last minute. Shrimp, crab meat, and flaked tuna; strips of chicken, cold meats, and cheese; crumbled blue cheese, and chopped or sliced hard-cooked eggs or combinations of them convert the bowl of greens into a main dish for luncheon. Some handsome renditions wear a collar of ripe tomato slices around the rim. These ripe-red vegetable wheels occasionally display chartreuse fluffs of mashed and seasoned avocado.

Culinary artists often make the dressing on the greens with everyone around the table looking on. They drop the chilled oil on first and toss the leaves to coat them. Then they judiciously add the seasonings, the personal favorites. Next they scatter on wine vinegar and continue the tossing and tasting. The sampling, they declare, enables them to achieve the exact effect on the palate desired.

California initiated the small or medium salad as a meal opener. The custom was copied in many homes across the United States. Mothers commended it because most members of the family enjoyed the health-giving greens more before they filled up on other foods. Then something happened — the general evaporation of domestic help of all kinds. Now Californians, like other Americans, commonly serve two-course dinners with the salad a companion to the entree. Some women, as if to bolster up their spirits, say a salad complements the fish or meat it escorts. And then they add, "Giving up an appetizer salad means eliminating a course. It certainly saves steps."

Before he dines many days in the Pacific Coast country a visitor encounters that fabulous *green goddess salad dressing*. It has wandered from San Francisco's historic Palace Hotel to homes throughout the Golden State. Natives label it as one of the finest additions to mixed green salads. If they wish a more substantial dish they toss crab meat, shrimp, or chicken with the greens.

GREEN GODDESS DRESSING

1 ¾-ounce can anchovy fillets
1 garlic clove
1 small onion
1 cup mayonnaise
⅔ cup heavy cream or undiluted evaporated milk
2 tablespoons lemon juice
¼ cup wine vinegar, tarragon flavored
¼ cup minced parsley
¼ teaspoon black pepper, freshly ground
Salt to taste

Rub the anchovy fillets, garlic, and onion through the food chopper or chop them extremely fine. Combine with the other ingredients and mix thoroughly. Chill in the refrigerator several hours to blend the flavors. Pour them over the greens and toss them to coat every leaf.

Many Gorgeous Fruit Plates Appear

Stunning fruit salads, like the great variety of topnotch vegetable ones, also speak for the Golden State. Both are regional institutions. And so are the gorgeous fruit luncheon plates. Many a hostess pins her faith and culinary reputation on them. Let's look into her kitchen as she assembles the color pictures on the chilled plates. She sets four or five lettuce cups, cold and brittle, on each one. Then she fills them with whatever fruits, berries, and melons (balls or rings cut from them) are available, to provide color and flavor contrasts. In the center of each she unmolds a gay gelatin salad crowded with fruits, or with fruits and vegetables. Or is it that favorite California rainbow hued tutti-frutti one composed of thin layers of gelatin of different flavors and colors?

Somewhere down the street or road another woman is preparing a salad luncheon. On the chilled plates are three large lettuce nests. Each holds its prize: mixed fruits; fish or sea food like shrimp, crab, or tuna; and a vegetable salad. Sometimes one of the three is molded, for as California women say, "You can get that kind ready in advance and thus avoid the last minute rush."

Inviting paper cups often nestle among the fruits and lettuce on many of the plates. They hold pineapple or other frozen fruit ices for a refreshing touch.

French dressing frequently accompanies the fruit assortments. Most cooks substitute lemon juice for vinegar when fixing it. Cooked dressings made with eggs, vinegar, sugar, and fruit juices also have friends. They are the fluffy kinds that when cool usually call for the smooth richness of whipped cream. Regardless of whatever one is selected, it is passed for individual serving. In calorie-conscious California many women refuse all kinds and take lemon juice instead — at least during the weeks when they are "dieting."

Hot yeast rolls often supply a warm note in the meal. Or they share the role with tea or coffee. Typically Californian are Parker House rolls with orange sections baked in their folds or grated orange peel mixed into the dough. Both wear orange frosting. Sometimes this topping adorns cinnamon rolls. Then the cook splashes them with a whiff of cinnamon. When hot bread and a sugary frosting meet, stickiness results. The natives relish them together, much as a Philadelphian likes his sticky cinnamon buns. Indeed, almost everyone raves about the orange crown on rolls.

To make it first cream 3 tablespoons of butter and 1½ cups of sifted confectioners' sugar. Whip in 3 tablespoons of orange juice, 2 tablespoons of lemon juice, 1¼ teaspoons of grated orange peel, and a few grains of salt. Beat the mixture until smooth and fluffy before the fragrant rolls come from the oven. Then spread it on them.

A Galaxy of Fruits Is Available

Among the wide variety of locally grown fruits that appear on luncheon plates are the citrus favorites like oranges, grapefruit, tangerines, and kumquats. Perhaps strawberries, red raspberries, and boysenberries win the most laurels for the berries. Prunes and dates generally answer for the dried fruits. Usually the former are steamed until just soft with care not to overcook; then they are pitted and stuffed with California walnuts. The dates frequently are the large ones; they, too, appear fat with nuts.

Summer brings the melons. Some fruit plates feature balls of them, others show the peeled rings or slices filled with mixed fruits. Summer also ushers to the scene the handsome cherries, nectarines, peaches, pears, and apricots. (Large supplies of them are canned for use all across the United States.) Apricot halves, both the fresh and canned ones, frequently are cream cheese filled and almond garnished. Plump plums give their blush and sweet-tart piquancy when in season, and soft ripe figs add their distinctive, mild taste. Hawaiian pineapple, fresh, frozen, and canned, occupies the spotlight in many California fruit combinations. Banana chunks coated with mayonnaise and rolled in chopped California walnuts rarely are passed by. And then there are the grapes with tight fitting skins. Wee bunches or single specimens of them decorate the plates as well as provide tastiness. For examples, there are the small lovely green, seedless Thompsons, the firm-fleshed Tokays and the red-skinned Flame Tokays, the large yellow-green Malagas, the flavorful Muscats, the long, greenish Ladyfingers, the dull purple Emperors, and the large black Ribiers. (Many of the Thompson Seedless and Muscat grapes end up as raisins.)

Hostesses Make Spoon Salads, Too

As an accompaniment to the fruit plate or salad, a protein rich food of some kind is an established rule in many households. A mound of cottage cheese frequently fills the bill. Hostesses like to stud it with nuts or strips of ripe olives. They also heap tiny mounds of salted California walnuts and almonds on the plates. And they tuck cheese-stuffed celery and raw vegetable relishes here and there near the lettuce. Hot rolls sometimes yield to tiny turkey, chicken, ham, or tuna sandwiches, or to cheese biscuits. One of the more popular biscuits has a dab of soft pimento cheese baked on its top.

Avocado trees grow in the state and often produce generous crops. It is no surprise to find yellow-green slices of them in fruit salads. Often avocado on the half shell appears on lettuce garnished with lemon slices. Natives call it a *spoon salad.* They squeeze the citrus juice over the avocado, sprinkle on salt, and "fall to." Some families prefer to fill the fruit's cavity with a piquant French dressing or a peppery cocktail sauce. Others choose mixed fruits, usually with pineapple predominating. Celery and shrimp salad heaped in avocado halves compose a hearty pink and green luncheon dish that tastes as good as it looks.

Perhaps the A-1 California fruit salad is the very pleasing

one that is easy to make. Sections of grapefruit and slices of peeled avocado of about the same size alternate on greens. French dressing goes over them. In autumn rosy-orange slices of cultivated Japanese persimmons (of Chinese origin!) enter this salad. This delicious and beautiful number has become traditional for the Thanksgiving dinner. At Christmas time many women scatter colorful pomegranate seeds over the grapefruit-avocado combination.

Broiled Fruits Bring Out Food Flavors

Fruit relishes, Californians say, possess a remarkable ability to bring out the best flavors of foods with which they associate. That hints why they broil fruits to escort meat and fish. Fewer women in the area shun the use of their broiling ovens than elsewhere. "Why," they exclaim, "broiling is one of the easiest and quickest ways to cook. And it does wonders for foods."

Grapefruit halves are the most frequently broiled fruit. They do not classify as a platter companion because frequently they start the meals in cool weather, including breakfast, brunch, and dinner. Most cooks make no addition to them. They slowly broil the fruit to heat it. Others add such things as sherry wine, maraschino cherry juice, or brown sugar and butter. Hot grapefruit juice starts the day for one of my favorite Los Angeles home economists, a television star. She pours boiling water into the freshly extracted juice.

Some women pour honey or maple flavored sirup into the golden centers of drained canned cling peach halves and dot them with butter. They broil them until heated throughout and freckled on top with brown patches of sugar and butter. Then they send them to the table on the platter with little pig sausages or country sausage. These same peach halves filled with mincemeat or cranberry sauce and grilled often add character to the chicken dinners.

Broiled canned pears with dots of butter and bits of mint jelly at their hearts glorify lamb. Then there are the *ketchup apples* introduced to me by a friend from Georgia who has adopted California as her home. She considers them the perfect relish to serve with ham and all other pork dishes. And she recommends them with baked beans. People who taste them almost always consider her judgment excellent. This is how she makes them.

Place cored, unpared crosswise halves of apples cut-side up in a shallow baking pan, and top each one with 1 tablespoon each of brown sugar and tomato ketchup plus a dab of butter. Pour a little water around them and bake them until tender, or about ½ hour, in a moderate oven, 350°. Invert them in the pan to aid in their absorption of the juices. Serve warm or cold.

Baked orange halves personify California, although opinions about them vary. Not about the way they taste. Everyone seems to vote for their excellent flavor. But some women believe they take too long to bake, others think they still are worth the effort. Anyhow they go to the table with ham, pork, veal, lamb, duck, and chicken. They appear both cold and warm. I tasted them first at a memorable buffet supper on Russian Hill in San Francisco. There my two clever hostesses, natives of Iowa, presented them with baked ham. They were so superbly delicious that to this day I associate thoughts of baked orange halves with the city where I met them and my hospitable friends.

How To Bake Oranges

First the Californian cooks the whole oranges in water to cover for about half an hour. Then she drains and cools them. Next she cuts them in halves, spreads them out in a pan, and pours on sirup. This she makes by briefly boiling 2 cups of sugar with the same quantity of water and ¾ cup of corn sirup. After that she covers the pan and bakes the orange halves in a moderate oven, 350°, about 1½ hours.

For one of the salads to write home about, women arrange the chilled baked orange halves with fluffs of water cress on plates. Seasoned cream cheese, whipped light as a cloud, is the garnish. Anyone who meets this delicacy may rest assured that he either is in California or else his hostess has succumbed to the magic of that state's home kitchens.

Oranges and Cranberries Join Forces

Cranberries do not grow in California, but they arrive from the Pacific Northwest to team with oranges in the uncooked relish. One of my hostesses heaped generous spoonfuls of it atop thick slices of navel orange slices. She arranged them like flowers on the platter around the Christmas turkey.

The California method of preparing the relish is to put 1 pound of the berries and 1 orange through the coarse blade of the food chopper. Then the cook mixes in the juice and the grated peel of another orange and 2 cups of granulated sugar. She sets the mixture, covered, in the refrigerator to ripen a few days before use.

A cousin of this relish embellishes many food conversations and meals. Cooks make it by grinding 1 pound of cranberries with 2 lemons, seeds discarded. Then they mix in 2 cups of orange marmalade. They chill the mixture a day or two and serve it with turkey, chicken, or tuna dishes. And as one of my friends in the Golden State said, "If there is a hot buttered roll handy, just spread some of the fruity mélange on it. It's the kind of a good thing the gods chant praises about."

In California a food reporter observes endless short cuts the women make without sacrificing results. For example, one hostess in a jiffy stirred up a cranberry sherbet in my honor.

She blended 1 cup of sweetened canned grapefruit juice into 2 cups of cooked cranberry sauce, added a drop of mint flavoring, and froze the ruby, sweet-tart fruity mixture in her refrigerator.

It accompanied fish, but she says she also uses it with equal success when meats or poultry are on the menu.

One of her favorite jams starts out with thick cranberry sauce, 2 cups of it. She adds ½ cup of crushed pineapple, canned, and cooks the mixture until it thickens. Then she stirs in 2 or 3 tablespoons of port wine. Often she cooks a teaspoon of grated yellow lemon peel with the cranberries and pineapple. That, she thinks, enhances the taste.

Fruit Ends Many Meals

Fruit desserts, often a definition for simplicity itself, are legion. Showmanship in service multiplies their charms. Many a hostess presents fresh-from-the-orchard ones with crackers and cheese. Often soft Monterey Jack cream cheese is her first choice. Others arrange them along with mounds of berries and melon balls on giant plates. At buffet suppers guests easily can help themselves to whatever kinds they prefer. Cream cheese, softened with a little water and whipped light, is in readiness if anyone wishes to spoon it over the fruit. A crushed berry sauce also awaits for the same purpose. Usually it consists of crushed and sugared ripe strawberries or red raspberries. Gelatinized cheese rings bordered by fruits and often filled with them answer as another acceptable dessert.

Natives like sun-ripened apricots for breakfast and in lunch boxes, picnic baskets, pies, and cobblers. For ices and sherbets, punch, and jams, people say they cannot be matched. One of the summer's delights is the pared and crushed luscious ripe fruit, touched up with sugar, on vanilla ice cream. *Apricot sundae,* Californians call it.

There are families who speak with superlatives about jam from the fully ripened fruit, soft, mellow, and golden. They announce that they "cook" it in sunshine. This is how they go about it.

They mix the cut-up fruit with sugar and the chopped blanched kernels from some of the pits that they crack. Then they bring the mixture to a boil and heat it just long enough to dissolve the sugar. After that they pour it into a pan and set it in the sunshine to "cook," or evaporate, to the right thickness. Once a day they stir it. The spread that gives even the best of buttery, tawny toast a lift is sealed in sterile glasses.

Dried or dehydrated apriocts have sponsors in their home territory. A newspaper woman of Los Angeles, a cook of distinction, presents *apricot bavarian* made with the cooked, sweetened, and mashed dried fruit. (She says the fresh and canned ones also may be used.) Her sense of the dramatic shows in the background she selects for this tasty lightness. She hollows out a daffodil cake, a yellow and white marble loaf. Then she heaps the apricot mixture in it. Jaunty little wisps of whipped cream provide the trim. Always it is the food hit of the evening.

Prune Whips Team With Walnuts

Prune whips exhibit crunchy crests of California walnuts. A bite of them also often reveals a vague, intriguing suggestion of orange and lemon flavors. Some households freeze this pudding.

Fruit and nut breads contribute richly to the state's sandwich lore. These loaves include many versions of such prime ones as prune, date, banana, orange, and raisin numbers.

Women describe how they prepare stewed prunes in the refrigerator. They soak them in apricot nectar, pineapple juice, or water to cover for a couple of days. First they wash the fruit and put it in a glass jar. Then they pour on the fruit juice or water, adjust the lid, and set it in the refrigerator.

For a confection, prunes steamed until barely soft are pitted. Women then stuff them with sweetness and crunchiness. Often the filling contains California walnuts with fondant or pieces of marshmallows rolled in coconut. Some families like peanut butter mixed with grated orange peel. The cook rolls the bulging prunes in granulated sugar. She stores them in a tightly covered container lined with waxed paper for at least two weeks. Then the treasured Christmas sweetmeats are ready for eating.

The home-grown dates, like the dried prunes, play a part on salad plates and in fruit cups many months of the year. They are baked in pies, cookies, and cakes. *Date pie,* although delicious, is rich and filling. Its place is in a very light meal or at a dessert party when coffee is its companion. For one of the favorites, cooks soak the cut-up fresh fruit in thin cream several hours, often overnight. Then they add egg yolks and one egg white and bake the mixture in a pastry-lined pan. It draws a meringue topping.

Cooked fruits frequently are superb. Baked apples and pears decorated with orange sauce, and subtly spiced, baked peaches and nectarines with cream or ice cream deserve the recognition menu planners give them. Some women bake pears in port wine. Indeed, the union of fruit and wine in desserts classifies as a traditional custom. That is not surprising for this important industry — California produces about 90 per cent of the American wines — dates back to pre-Revolutionary War days. It had its start in 1769 in the planting of a vineyard at Mission San Diego. Today Californians use wines extensively as the beverage of hospitality and as an adjunct in good cooking. They like the flavor and bouquet it imparts to their food.

Corsages of Fruit Decorate Tables

Tempting compotes resemble nosegays in crystal dishes. They are beautiful combinations of fruits simmered separately in a simple sugar sirup, chilled, and then ladled into serving dishes with as much regard for color arrangement as in a bouquet. In another type one fruit is cooked, the second one is not. A classic example starts with whole ripe peaches pared and tenderly poached in sugar sirup until barely tender. Then the native drains and chills them. She pours the peach sirup over red raspberries but does not cook them. When cool they crown the peaches. My husband and daughter acquired a deep affection for this dessert during the happy summers our family spent in Carmel. They set it apart as one of California's best gifts to good eating.

Sliced fresh peaches bathed in a cooked cherry sauce make another dessert cheerful to face — and to eat. Women cook the pitted sweet cherries, add a little sugar, and chill them before topping the yellow-ripe slices.

Fruits and berries, mixed and sweetened, also pleasantly end meals. Pared, sliced, and sugared peaches and figs, peaches and pitted sweet cherries, and strawberries and cantaloupe balls merit the blue ribbons bestowed on them. Some families pour port wine over the berries and melon. Honeydew melon balls topped first with chilled and drained canned fruit cocktail and then with mint sherbet tastily illustrate the state's habit of presenting upside-down sundaes.

Like Jewels in a Showcase

A Michigan-born friend who lives in San Francisco overlooking the Bay delights her guests with a spectacular view and also with her custard-fruit dessert. Although simple, the creation qualifies as the ultimate in delectability. She bakes the perfect custard, chills it thoroughly, and at mealtime unmolds the delicacy on a great plate. Around it she wreaths the choicest fruits and berries, like jewels. She serves it at the table. If her guests are not calorie conscious she passes lightly sweetened whipped cream.

This friend also relies on canned fruits for easy to prepare and eat desserts. As an example, she drains chilled canned peaches and apricots and places them in a large glass bowl. Into them she folds an equal measurement of fresh fruit or berries and pours on a little sherry wine. Among her favorite fresh fruit selections are strawberries, red raspberries, pitted sweet cherries, sliced ripe figs, and orange sections. She matches the fresh fruit or berries with preserves, like those made of strawberries, red raspberries, cherries, and figs. With oranges she uses orange marmalade. She stirs the sweet into the mixture. While it does not show, it is the touch of mystery that keeps everyone guessing.

Almost all visitors to California remark about the splendid muskmelons. Among the famous members of this family that grow there are the cantaloupes, Honeydews, Honey Balls, Casabas, Persians, and Crenshaws. The Persian melon may be stored a long time, often until Christmas. That is why some people call it the *Santa Claus melon*. The Crenshaw is large. On the outside it resembles the Casaba. Its flesh is like that of the Persian variety but it has a taste of its own. Watermelons also are produced.

Probably the Southerners who have moved to the West Coast saw to it that their Christmas dessert *ambrosia,* composed of sliced oranges and shredded coconut, became a star in their new home. At any rate it comes out at the holiday season as regularly as the poinsettias bloom in the gardens. For it the native cooks usually cut peeled navel oranges in irregular sized pieces instead of presenting them in sections.

All the great American pies from apple to youngberry filled ones represent the Golden State. Prune, apricot, and date pies have been mentioned. Then there are the raisin ones of such great variety and marvelous taste. Often they are faintly flavored with orange and lemon and sometimes with cider. Many of them contain California walnuts. New England's *sour cream* and Dixie's *buttermilk raisin* pies also come from western ovens.

Lemon meringue pie, a national topnotcher, boasts of admirers on the West Coast that reach into the hundreds of thousands. Many women step from their kitchens to a nearby tree with glossy green leaves to gather the yellow citrus fruit used in making it. Sportsmen say it is an A-1 dessert in fish dinners. Men also take off their hats to boysenberry pie à la mode. To them it is as miraculous as manna from the sky.

Tender, Yet Crisp Vegetables

Products of California's gardens, like those of her orchards, spark up meals throughout the nation — in green, frozen, and canned forms. The state's cooks chalk up honors in preparing the succulent vegetables. Indeed, they set the pace that many women living in other places try to follow. First of all, most vegetables are not overcooked. While they come off the range tender, they retain a certain crispness. No doubt this achievement is due mainly to Oriental influences. The citizens of Chinese descent strive not to destroy the texture of a vegetable in preparing it. Perhaps the Westerners' universal fondness for crunchy green salads also inspires a respect for the garden gifts that are not flabby when cooked. Two members of the extremely large vegetable family enjoyed more locally than in most other regions are globe or Paris artichokes and summer squash. The artichoke is the flower bud of a large thistle. Most women boil it in salted water until the bottom is tender enough so a fork will pierce it. Among the common additions to the cooking water are onion slices, a garlic clove, and thin lemon slices. Many people also pour in 2 or 3 tablespoons of salad oil. It provides glossiness as well as flavor. Each whole artichoke goes to the table on a salad plate escorted by a small bowl of melted butter if the vegetable is hot, mayonnaise if it is cold. Many hostesses serve the butter or mayonnaise, in which the leaves are dunked, in tiny Chinese bowls or in nut cups. For informal occasions wee paper cups fill the role. When artichokes are served on plates with other vegetables the cook cuts them in two, and gives each person one lengthwise half. The number of artichoke dishes in the cuisine is expanding. The vegetable is stuffed, used in casserole combinations, and incorporated in appetizers and salads.

Squash Is Seasoned With Ketchup

Food shoppers pick the small, firm, and young summer squash, the kind that have very tender skins and practically no seeds. As one home economist pointed out to me, "They are so easy to prepare. All you have to do is to wash them. You don't even have to slice them unless you wish to. Just simmer them in a little salted water until tender. Then add butter. Or if you wish, mash them before adding the butter." It is something of a California custom to season buttered squash extravagantly with tomato ketchup. And natives also cut the tender cooked, unseasoned squash in strips, dip them in egg and crumbs, and fry them.

Zucchini, the slender dark green vegetable with lengthwise stripes of white, in shape resembles a cucumber. Often people call it the *Italian squash.* Californians like to catch it when tiny and young, too. They cut it in crosswise slices without paring it, and then pan-fry it with a touch of sliced onion in salad oil. When it is tender they sometimes spread the white circles with green rims on an ovenproof platter or plate, sprinkle on grated Parmesan or other hard cheese, and broil them just long enough to melt the cheese.

Some families like ¼-inch thick long slices of zucchini, dipped in egg and cracker crumbs, first pan-fried and then baked in tomato sauce with the cheese on top. Others prefer the long slices seasoned with salt and pepper and then lightly dredged in flour. Then cooks sprinkle them lightly with oil and bake them in a very hot oven, 450°, about 20 minutes, or until tender. One of my hostesses at this stage runs them under the broiler a few seconds to brown still more. Another of her prized stunts is to rub the baking sheet with a cut clove of garlic before arranging the zucchini strips on it to bake. Orange-hued carrots and green-white zucchini are paired in countless menus for their flavor and color contrasts.

Broccoli Appears in Sandwiches

The tiny *summer squash,* like the *patty pans* and *crook-necks,* when cooked sometimes are scooped out and stuffed with various seasoned mixtures. Then they are baked to heat. Another neat trick I learned when a dinner guest in Los Angeles is that of simmering together until tender, tiny whole yellow crooknecks, pale greenish-white patty pans, and coin-like slices of zucchini. The medley tasted good, and it was attractive, too.

Asparagus is an extremely popular vegetable. In California one pound of it scarcely is considered ample for serving two persons. While it generally is liked best when hot, many families enjoy the cooked spears chilled and served as a salad.

Broccoli certainly qualifies as an important favorite. Commonly the green buds and tender stalks come from the kitchen piping hot and dressed with butter and toasted, chopped almonds or a Parmesan style cheese. It teams with chicken in casseroles, and the sandwich in which it tops chicken or turkey slices on bread or toast is a classic. Cheese sauce goes over it and then the sandwich is broiled until the sauce is flecked with brown.

Carrots brighten meals from one end of California to the other. One of the top salads in the opinion of children, as well as their elders, features shredded or ground ones, mixed with dressing and raisins and often with unpared apple and orange sections. Carrots invariably are cooked with a touch of onion, either dry onion cut very fine or snips of the green plants. "The onion," women say, "gives either carrot circles or the shredded vegetable a magic flavor."

Fava beans are gaining rapidly in favor. They are similar to limas, only larger, and are cooked in the same ways. Some people call them *horse beans*.

Raw relish vegetables personify California. They replace the salad in some meals and are the darlings of the young hostess. At parties she arranges them near bowls of *dips,* as the mixtures for dunking them and potato and corn chips are called. Some of these gala set-ups — such as clouds of ivory colored and seasoned cream cheese and mashed and seasoned soft green avocado pulp, with chop plates of crisp, colorful vegetable slices — bring that garden-fresh look to the table regardless of the season.

These same uncooked vegetable relishes garnish meats and salad and sandwich plates. And on the buffet, often with ripe olives, they snuggle among ice cubes or in large flaring bowls filled with crushed ice. At outdoor meals a wooden bucket sometimes holds them in the ice. Among the favorites are the old-time standbys, carrot sticks, celery, and radishes; then there also are tiny red and yellow tomatoes and raw broccoli and cauliflower buds.

Californians Are Cheese Eaters

A roving food scout notices the way Californians dote on cheese! Frequently they select a hard one like Parmesan to grate and use in cooking. Generally they make sauces with cheddar cheese. For dessert with crackers and fruit, Monterey Jack cream cheese vigorously challenges all other contenders. Natives insist it is a *must* for their best tasting Mexican dishes.

Cheese and vegetables unite in appealing combinations. Winning ones pop up almost every place, such as the following:

Globe artichokes, cooked, split in lengthwise halves (the choke is removed), stuffed with a cheese-bread crumb dressing, and baked to heat.

Cooked buttered asparagus spread on an ovenproof platter, sprinkled with shredded cheese, and broiled.

Green beans served in cheese sauce.

Cabbage, carrots, and cauliflower au gratin.

Creamed celery sprinkled with cheese and shredded, toasted almonds.

Halves of cooked chayotes, pronounced *chä-yó-tays* (the squash with one seed, or vegetable pears that natives of New Orleans call *mirlitons*), with cheese on top and run in the oven to heat.

Corn and cheese in casserole combinations.

Eggplant slices, broiled, with cheese scattered on, and also slices baked in cheese sauce.

Onions dressed with cheese in many styles.

Potato dishes featuring cheese without end.

Winter squash, cut in pieces of individual serving size, baked as usual, and then stripped with thin cheese slices and run back in the oven briefly to melt the cheese.

Tomato halves brushed with mayonnaise, sprinkled with seasonings and generously with shredded cheese, and broiled.

Countless cheese and green pepper combinations.

Mexico Contributes Rich Colors

In the Golden State more cheese-pepper dishes are eaten than elsewhere north of the Mexican border. A cook is likely to boast that she makes quick work of peeling the chili pepper pods. First she washes them. Then she spreads them in a shallow pan and broils them until their skins blister. After that she dumps them in a paper bag, twists the end to close it, and sets the package aside for a quarter of an hour. Next she turns on the cold water and washes off the loosened skins under the faucet.

Pepper-cheese custard pleases many gourmets with its exotic yellow and green complexion and authoritative flavor. For it strips of peeled green chili peppers and cubes of American cheese are layered in a greased casserole. Over the mixture cooks pour seasoned milk and eggs, 1 cup of milk to 3 beaten eggs. They bake it in a slow oven, 300°, and remove it when its center is set or is firm. Another of the classics consists of peeled green chili pepper pods, with the seeds and stems removed, filled with Monterey Jack or mild cheddar cheese. Women pin the pods shut with toothpicks, dip them in beaten eggs and flour, and fry them in deep fat, 380°, to brown. These stuffed peppers call for a well-seasoned tomato sauce as an accompaniment.

Buttered steamed vegetables, as women proudly refer to them, speak the California language. Beets and carrots so treated produce handsome, rewarding examples of the system's merits. Cooks shred the vivid red or orange roots into a heavy pan or casserole, add salt, pepper, and butter, adjust the lid, and run the utensil in a moderate oven, 350°. They leave it to its own devices about a half hour; the food steams into delectablity with a mingling of buttery-vegetable succulence.

While few people designate the state as a bean eating region, it is a wonder, for visitors connect with a multiplicity of dried bean dishes such as those containing lima, kidney, navy, cranberry, or pink and red Mexican beans, to name a few. Especially do they taste a variety of lusty Mexican inspired compositions, often labeled as *barbecue, chili,* or *Spanish* style beans. In many of them the red, pink, or kidney beans cook with onions, green peppers, and tomato sauce, along with seasonings of salt, garlic, freshly ground black pepper, chili powder, and salad oil or drippings. For additional satisfaction some of them include cubes of salt pork or beef cut up as for stewing, or ground. Some households freeze a supply of these prepared bean dishes for quick meals. Or as one friend in Los Angeles said, "To please guests from the East who like them as well as we do."

Rice Grows in California, Too

Most of the rice produced in the state has short, round grains. Natives steam them in the same manner as the long, thin Oriental and more plump southern varieties are handled. Many women vouch for their special brands of cookery. And how varied these methods are! Some families choose fried rice Chinese style.

To make it the cook for 5 minutes slowly pan-fries chopped onion, celery, and green pepper in salad oil—often peanut oil. Then she adds strips of chopped cooked meat, usually fresh pork or ham. After a gentle pan-frying for 10 minutes she stirs in the steamed rice and soy sauce. When it is thoroughly heated she serves the tempter on a hot platter and garnishes it with minced parsley.

Another dish that appeals widely is *Spanish rice,* which was borrowed from people South of the Border. The state is filled with recipes for it. Usually the uncooked rice is pan-fried until a golden brown before the tomatoes, onion, and green pepper are added. Some versions include small meat balls made with ground beef. Natives pan-fry the meat balls, chopped onion, and green pepper with the browned rice about 5 minutes. Then they add canned tomatoes, water, and whatever seasonings they like. Covered, they simmer the combination until the rice absorbs the liquid and is tender and fluffy.

Green rice gets its name from the minced parsley folded into it. Most households use as much as $\frac{1}{2}$ to 1 cupful of the greenery to 2 cups of the hot steamed cereal. Some of them like to toss the parsley, butter, a bit of minced onion, and chopped almonds into the hot rice at the last minute. They serve it promptly with chicken, turkey, or meat.

Californians have a habit of toasting their rice in a heavy skillet before steaming it. They use low heat and stir the kernels until lightly browned. The important precaution, women warn, is not to scorch it. In other instances they toast the rice in a fairly hot oven, 375°. They use a shallow pan to contain the cereal, and bake it, stirring occasionally, until the kernels turn a golden brown. Toasted rice when steamed tastes different, or as natives say, "It has a parched flavor unlike white rice prepared in the ordinary way. We think it is delightful."

Parsley knows its way around in California kitchens. One of the most revered hamburgers contains 1 cup of the minced green leaves to a pound of ground beef. Also the herb enters salad bowls, and when chopped it contributes a decoration of green to cooked vegetables like mashed carrots and sweet potatoes, and cauliflower. On soups the minced leaves team with finely chopped chives. And some loaves of piping hot garlic bread show the flecks of bright green.

The State Votes for Garlic Bread

A cook's discretion with garlic frequently determines her culinary reputation. Natives stress that a clever woman adds neither too little nor too much garlic, yet she never omits it from a dish it improves. An old homely saying warns: *When in doubt use less than you think is needed rather than more.* As previously indicated, the tossed green salad carries its aroma. And garlic bread represents the Golden State as hot biscuits typify the South.

Traditionally it consists of a long loaf of sour French bread enriched with garlic butter and warmed in a friendly oven. To prepare it slice a clove or two of garlic into ¼ pound of butter or margarine; after it has been standing for from ½ to 1 hour remove the herb, which by that time has imparted some of its pungency to the fat.

Some people like to cut the loaf in lengthwise halves, smooth the garlic butter or margarine over the cut surface with a spatula, and set it aside for an hour or longer to let the flavor permeate. Occasionally they scatter on grated Parmesan cheese and minced parsley before putting the two halves together to form a loaf to tuck into a paper bag. They heat the neat package in a moderately hot oven, 375°, from 10 to 15 minutes.

Other home chefs prefer to slash the bread diagonally to make pieces of the desired thickness, but they do not cut quite through the loaf; that is, they do not sever the slices from it. Then they distribute the butter or margarine on the cut surfaces, and often grated hard cheese as well. Next they heat the bread in a paper bag, as described, and in serving let everyone break off the portion he desires.

Many men in the region dabble in cooking as a creative hobby. One such gentleman took me into the culinary work-shop of his Marin County home to demonstrate how he prepares parsley for garlic bread and other cooked dishes. He lays the leaves on a board and chops them very fine with a knife. Then he wraps them in cheesecloth and squeezes out the juices. Parsley so treated becomes fluffy and retains its vivid green when heated. This practice illustrates the value Californians place on color in foods and the pains they take to protect it.

Medium hard rolls, split in lengthwise halves, occasionally substitute for big loaves of bread. After covering their cut surface with garlic or plain butter or margarine, most people arrange them on a rack in a pan. They broil them cut side up. Often they also generously sprinkle the tops of the buttered rolls with a grated hard cheese before heating them.

Californians hold that bread hot to the touch supplies an essential note in informal meals; especially do they like it with salads. Frequently they butter slices of bakery bread (not the French type), put them together in the shape of a loaf, and tie them, or place them in a loaf pan so as to hold them in position. They brush the tops with melted butter, dust on paprika, and heat them in a very hot oven, 450°, about 10 minutes. The slices come out crunchy and toasted on the outside, and buttery, soft, and fragrant within. Another custom is to heat an unsliced loaf of bread from the bakery, after brushing the crust with butter, for that heavenly fragrance and a fresh-from-the-oven taste. Raisin bread, toasted or converted into French toast, also represents the Golden State.

Olive trees with their silvery gray foliage decorate the landscape, and remind a visitor of the early Spanish padres who initiated the industry. Ripe olives, canned, call California home, while the pickled green fruit comes mainly from Mediterranean countries. *Garlic olives* boast of ardent friends.

To prepare them mix about a cup of juice drained from the ripe fruit with ¼ cup of olive or salad oil, and add 2 sliced garlic cloves and the olives. There should be enough liquid to cover the fruit. A few hours later remove the garlic; then the relish is ready to serve when desired.

Other herb flavored olives also enhance many meals. For them add an individual choice of herbs, like a bit of bay leaf, a few rosemary leaves, a hot chili pepper, celery leaves, and maybe garlic to salad or olive oil, and let it stand in the refrigerator for a time, perhaps 3 days or more. Good cooks say they shake it several times every day. Then they pour it over the drained canned fruit. After a few days a distinctive accessory food is ready to serve.

Cooks cut pieces of ripe olives from their pits as if by second nature, and some of them use the canned ripe slices or rings. They stir them into many dishes, such as spaghetti combinations, macaroni and cheese, chicken pies, sandwiches, gravy, escalloped corn, rarebit, and white and cheese sauces for dressing such vegetables as carrots and cauliflower. *Tamale pie* rich with them announces to a traveler that he is in California or the Southwest. The versions are legion. They are splendid examples of the multitudinous hearty, tempting casserole dishes of the state, which with a tossed salad, a crunchy hot bread, a fruit dessert, and a beverage — frequently a table wine — compose a characteristic meal pattern.

The mere mention of a filled casserole suggests the many substantial spaghetti dishes so popular in the Golden State. Home economics teachers appraise them as the first choice of the teen-age crowd. Look at the school lunch menus. Spaghetti in some form almost always occupies the spotlight. "It ranks with mashed potatoes as something good to eat," high school boys often remark.

Most of the spaghetti dishes have a noticeable Italian background. For feeding a crowd many a hostess rates them as an unparalleled choice. Another California entree of importance, *polenta,* also has been popularized by people of Italian ancestry who live on the West Coast. When a woman tries to decide what to have for a Sunday guest supper she is likely to waver between spaghetti with a meat sauce and polenta. If it is the latter, she alternates yellow corn-meal mush, slices of soft Monterey Jack cheese, and flavorful tomato sauce in the baking dish, and sprinkles grated American or cheddar cheese on top. She bakes the dish until its top is golden. Chicken and beef sauces also enhance polenta. Usually her menu is simple.

CALIFORNIA SUPPER PARTY
Polenta
Mixed Green Salad
Garlic French Bread
Red Table Wine
Coffee

The walnuts that star in meals and food conversations proudly carry the name of the state in which they grow in larger amounts than in any foreign nation. Natives insist people in other localities make a mistake when they talk of English walnuts, for these trees are of Persian origin. Sugared California walnuts appear not only on Thanksgiving and Christmas dinner tables but also on other special occasions, as for Sunday company dinners and buffet suppers.

While directions for preparing the confection vary from one household to another, most of them start out with a sirup made by boiling 1½ cups of sugar with ½ cup of liquid, like water, orange juice, or sherry wine, to the soft ball stage, 240°. Cooks quickly stir in vanilla, if desired, and 3 cups of walnut halves, and pour the mixture onto waxed paper and separate the nuts immediately. When orange juice plays the liquid role its flavor is reinforced by the addition of 1 teaspoon of the grated peel. Some women drop a touch of spice into the sirup. *Penuche,* a favorite Mexican type of brown sugar candy, sometimes substitutes for the sugar sirup.

Roasted walnuts with cheese, crackers, and fruit answer for dessert; they are presented warm or cold, as the hostess prefers. To roast them she simply spreads the unshelled nuts in a shallow pan and heats them in a very hot oven, 450°, about 15 minutes. Natives explain that it is a good idea to stir them several times as they heat.

February Brings Pink Almond Blossoms

Almonds, introduced centuries ago to the region around the Spanish missions, continue to flourish. Just as many natives of New England and Virginia are captivated by apple blossoms, Californians go into ecstasy over the clouds of soft pink flowers on almond trees that arrive in February as one of the first trees to bloom. Perhaps a Chinese influence contributes to the delightful almond-chicken dishes of the region. As already indicated, the nuts make a pleasing addition to green rice, especially if it is presented with poultry. Almonds finely chopped and mixed with butter or margarine and sirup or honey and spread over slices of cooked sweet potatoes illustrate a Westerner's conception of candied sweets. To taste is to admit they are worthy to vie with the best southern editions of the dish.

In autumn mashed sweet potatoes, flavored with orange juice and grated peel, are standard fare. Most families serve them in casseroles. For parties, especially those staged buffet style, the baking dish may be replaced by hollowed out orange shells. They compose a symphony in yellow and orange when spread in their piping hot, colorful loveliness on a big platter or chop plate.

Perhaps the most common way to blanch almonds is first to cover the shelled nuts with cold water and heat them to the boiling point. Then women drain and plunge them into cold water. The skins slip off readily. Many cooks dispense with the blanching as a waste of effort. (Less time in the kitchen is their motto!) They chop the nuts, sauté them in a little oil or butter, and use them on cooked fish or vegetables, and other foods. Both toasted almonds and California walnuts yield their crunchy texture and rich flavors to chicken salads.

To fix them pour oil and nuts, with 1 tablespoon of olive or other salad oil for each cup of nuts, into a shallow pan. Toast them in a moderate oven, 375°, stirring occasionally, until they turn a light brown. Then drain them on paper towels. Usually salt is sprinkled on. When cool, store them in airtight containers in the refrigerator.

Cream soups in the Golden State frequently wear minced parsley with either toasted almonds, sliced, or grated Parmesan cheese as a garnish, as do many chicken soups.

While the dishes in which these two popular California nuts appear are almost as endless as the state's cheerful yellow poppies, all nibblers refer to at least two candies in which they assume stellar roles. Everyone kindly contributes to a food scout her pet recipes for *rocky road* and *almond roca* candies, both of which personify and glorify the Far West.

ROCKY ROAD CANDY

1 pound milk chocolate	1 cup California walnuts
½ pound marshmallows	

Sprinkle the marshmallows, after they have been cut into small pieces with kitchen scissors moistened frequently in cold water, and the broken nut meats over the bottom of a buttered 8- by 8-inch pan. Melt the chocolate over *lukewarm* water, as in a double boiler. This process takes a full hour, for if the chocolate is hurried by heating over warmer water the candy will turn out an unattractive white. Pour the melted chocolate over the marshmallows and nuts. When cool, mark in squares and cut with a knife. The size of the pan is important, as the sweet is at its best if quite thick. '

Other kinds of rocky road candies also are authentic regional confections. In one of them penuche is poured over the marshmallows and nuts.

ALMOND ROCA CANDY

1 pound butter	1 cup cut-up almonds
2 cups sugar	

Cook the ingredients, mixed, over low heat. Stir constantly until the mixture becomes a medium brown, but use care not to scorch it. Turn into a buttered pan, and while hot sprinkle on a few additional almonds chopped extremely fine. For further adornment press pieces of milk chocolate candy bars on top the hot candy and as they melt spread them over it for a thin frosting.

To Californians almond roca candy connotes home as do peanut brittles to people living in the southern coastal states.

Abalone Is King at Monterey

Californians classify as fish eaters. Some of the Pacific Coast specialties they praise and feature have been described in the preceding chapter, but there are a few that belong primarily to the Golden State. *Abalone* is one of them. A relative of the oyster, this large mollusk wears one great shell, rough and brown outside, and mother-of-pearl within. Its habitat is the Pacific Coast — especially in the Monterey area, where on a balmy, moonlit winter night I first succumbed to its delicacy in chowder.

The flesh of abalone is solid, and requires pounding to soften before cooking. In many markets it has been prepared for the frying pan. Crosswise slices are called *abalone steaks*. Cooks dip them in beaten egg and fine cracker crumbs and pan-fry them quickly in oil or butter to brown on both sides, allowing no more than 2 minutes on each side. Overcooking produces toughness.

Kitchens in the Monterey-Carmel district and other scattered spots excel with *abalone chowder*. For it the cook does not pound the meat; instead she simmers it in water until tender and then grinds it. When a Yankee sips it, thoughts of New England and clams mingle with those of California and abalone. Both clam and abalone chowder may be defined as milk-potato-onion and bacon or salt pork compositions. Some western coastal families glamorize their service by substituting generous sized abalone shells for bowls; first they polish them until the bowls shine, then they close the holes with cement.

No visitor hangs around southern California long without encountering praise for the *albacore,* the prize of many a deep sea fishing expedition. This fish also is known as the *long-fin tuna*. It usually is about 3 feet long and frequently weighs from 15 to 20 pounds. Natives like it best when baked, but they also enjoy it when broiled. It is a fat fish, and most abundant from January to August. It is excellent in flavor.

Perhaps the *barracuda* rates as the most popular of southern California fish. Its habitat extends from Santa Barbara southward. The flesh is white and remarkably free of bones. It is best baked, culinary experts say — either whole if small or sliced in fillets when large. Fishermen catch this one every month of the year.

Another fish topic in the Los Angeles and San Diego areas is the beautifully colored *California yellowtail*. It, like the barracuda, is taken from the waters around Santa Barbara and on south. The flesh is of a fine flavor somewhat suggestive of the albacore. This is a large fish; it is marketed in chunks for baking, and various other kitchen sizes, as it also is a favorite for broiling and pan-frying.

Sand Dabs Are Praised Highly

Sand dabs belong exclusively to northern California waters. They are small, flat fish with firm, white flesh, and a superb flavor. Most people praise them highly. They are at their best when pan-fried, but also are tasty when broiled.

California shrimp come from the San Francisco and San Pablo Bays. They are tiny and lack the brilliant coloring of the much larger Seattle and Alaska shrimp. They taste good and are a welcome, delicious garnish on broiled fish. That is where I first met them. My second contact with the novelty (to me) was when one of my hostesses served them creamed over a super salmon loaf. Expert cooks also include them in scalloped oysters and add them to salads. On some of the beaches a food reporter's eyes open wide when she observes people buying paper bags filled with the freshly cooked little brown shrimp. They eat them deftly, after first cracking and removing the shells.

If any part of the nation prizes more distinctive crab

dishes than those of California its kitchens must literally be buried under recipe files. The *Dungeness crab,* described in the chapter on the Pacific Northwest, scores much success at mealtime. Equal parts of grapefruit segments and crab meat in cocktail sauce compose one applauded appetizer. The sweet, steamed meat also teams with artichoke hearts in salads. And like other fish appetizers it appears in green pepper cups. Many cooks cream it with artichoke hearts and with asparagus. They make curries with it, and know how to turn out deviled crab. Then there is *crab cioppino.*

Cioppino — pronounced *cho-peen-o,* with accent on the second syllable — is that original specialty of Fisherman's Wharf in San Francisco which visitors and natives alike enjoy eating. I have tasted two versions of it. In one crab starred. In the other the chef said crabs, shrimp, sea bass, halibut, and rock cod shared honors. The fish are cut in about 2-inch pieces. They simmer in a tomato sauce seasoned with onion, parsley, and oil — and also basilica. This is sweet basil. The Italians use it not only in sea food stews, but also in green salads, and their Minestrone or soup. Cioppino is messy to eat, but with a bib and plenty of paper napkins the rite is something of a lark. When shared with good comrades it is fun.

Pismo clams are most plentiful at the California beach by that name. They are large, often weighing as much as 1½ pounds. And they make excellent chowder, as many Americans know, for these clams are canned to help fill the chowder kettles across the nation.

Swordfish are taken from southern California waters, and their steaks especially delight the epicures. Some of the other fish caught along the southern coast are black sea bass (also known as jewfish), white sea bass, California halibut (a flounder), kingfish, mackerel, mullet, and rock bass. Tuna is canned in the region, and California cooks regard it and a can opener as true friends. Superior tuna recipes would fill a book. Sardines also are canned from San Diego north to Monterey, where to watch the fishing fleet go out at night is a picturesque sight. The boats sail away in darkness, for then they can locate the schools of *pilchards* (the sardines of the Pacific Coast in contrast to the herrings of Maine) by their trails of phosphorescent light, which the fishermen cannot see in bright moonlight.

Please Pass the Lamb

Lamb is California's favorite meat. Regional cooks achieve distinction in seasoning it. They almost always rub the roast, before putting it in the oven, with a cut garlic clove, or fill tiny pockets cut over the surface with slivers of garlic. Many of them baste it with red or white table wine mixed with a little salad oil. Another accepted practice is to marinate lamb in a barbecue sauce or French dressing before cooking it. Artichoke hearts are a classic and traditional addition to lamb stew. Then there are the lamb and lima bean stews that cannot be outclassed anywhere. Stews in California are well seasoned; frequently they contain faint whispers of herbs, and wine as part of the water. Pork ranks below lamb and beef in favor, although sweet-sour spareribs win epicurean honors, not only in the shadows of the cities' Chinatowns but also elsewhere across the state. Often the natives soak spareribs in orange juice and herbs before broiling or barbecuing them. The use of herbs in cooking increases every year, with marjoram, basilica, oregano, and chives competing for championship ratings. In many instances they are home grown. "It sometimes seems that the number of our herb gardens is increasing faster than the cooks who know how to use them," a Los Angeles home economist remarked to me.

Turkey, roasted to a turn, dominates the Thanksgiving and Christmas dinners, but seasons do not bar it from the table on other gala occasions. Fried turkey enjoys prestige. Many markets sell the parts for the convenience of customers who wish to select a few special cuts for frying instead of buying a whole bird. Fried turkey with spoon bread compose a regional treat. Fried chicken lacks the popularity it rates in the South and the central Farm Belt, but broiled or barbecued chicken never lacks for approval.

Californians appreciate seasonings — not as a substitute for good cooking, which they consider basic, but to give a dish distinction. For instance, they borrow from the centuries of experience of Chinese epicures and keep soy sauce on the kitchen shelf. With it they baste chicken, turkey, lamb, pork, and veal during roasting; they say it encourages beautiful, rich browning and oozes fine, subtle flavor. Often, too, they soak veal, lamb, and pork cups in the Oriental magic, usually with garlic and oil added; then they prepare the meat in the customary way.

Flavor-wise cooks also borrow inspiration from the Far East when preparing their delightful egg dishes, which usually mysteriously and faintly taste of soy. They mix generous shakes of it with butter to dress cooked vegetables like peas, cauliflower, lima beans, broccoli, celery, and Brussels sprouts. Another specialty features cut celery, onion quarters, bean sprouts, and strips of green pepper simmered in a bit of salted water until tender-crisp, and then dressed with butter and soy sauce. Mixed green salads including bean sprouts claim a French dressing daintily touched with soy. Heated, the sauce frequently dots the baked or fried fish on the platter, a custom reminiscent of the New Orleans Creole habit of sprinkling a smidgeon of tarragon or pepper vinegar over such treats.

The Belgian hare industry thrives in many communities. Rabbit de luxe dishes please thrifty-minded, flavor-conscious households. Curried rabbit, like curried fish, turkey, chicken, eggs, and lamb, highlights many meals.

A hint of curry powder also may be detected in some gravies and in the mayonnaise that complements the sweet, delicate crab meat on the salad plate.

Oregano seasons vegetable and avocado salads, meat concoctions, and other foods, especially those of Mexican origin. Californians also seek the smoky flavor that pinch hits for the tantalizing tang of smoke developed in cookery over an open wood fire. Suppose we take a bite of hamburger, pork chops, baked beans, a baked sea food, potatoes scalloped in cheese sauce, a corn concoction, or one of countless other old-time friends. What is the different taste? Usually it is of hickory smoke flavored salt or liquid smoke. These commercial products, hostesses advise, provide an easy, quick, and satisfying answer when the family hankers for that barbecue flavor at the supper table.

Barbecues Are Great Fun

The Golden State excels in outdoor cooking and dining. Its climate encourages eating in the sunshine by day, under the stars at night. Visitors sometimes find that the references to barbecues are confusing until they learn that the natives speak of the fireplace, stove, or other cooking device, as well as the social gathering, as a *barbecue*.

After a food reporter makes a few inspection trips and participates in several barbecues she decides there are as many different arrangements for outdoor cookery as enthusiasts for the foods prepared on them! Many of these contrivances are a far cry from the pioneer's hole in the ground lined with stones in which a fire was built and burned to embers for cookery purposes, but the ideal aimed at is the same . . . robust food to conquer gnawing appetites. What is there to expect, look for, and find? First and foremost, a visitor hopes to enjoy that breath-taking, mouth-watering aroma of sizzling steaks over coals. It blends with the fragrance of sparkling-clear coffee brewing nearby, the merriment of hospitable people, and the interplay of lively conversation.

Books have been written on how to construct and put on a barbecue. Many families build their own. Wherever the location is, there, too, is an important part of the home. Usually it is a favored sheltered situation in the garden or patio, although some kitchens contain a grill as well as an up-to-date range. Sometimes it is in the game room. Many types of stationary and portable barbecues are used. Occasionally the grill is mounted on an easy-to-push wheel-barrow, or perhaps the host pulls it out on a little play wagon, the kind children adore.

Barbecue accessories or gadgets are numerous, but wise mothers of children merely list long-handled toasting forks, spatulas or flippers, and spiked grills for buns, frankfurts, and hamburgers as *musts*. Once the paraphernalia is acquired and the art of building a proper fire is mastered, Californians face that eternal question of mankind: what shall we have to eat?

And Now, What Shall We Cook?

What to cook may be the million dollar question; at least it seems to evoke that many answers. Most families confide that they have one standard menu; it works out successfully with their facilities, and pleases their palates. They repeat it over and over, but introduce variety with different vegetables, relishes, and desserts. The master menu for these privately prized meals is a grilled meat of excellence teamed with a frosty-cold mixed green salad in a giant bowl, a long loaf of crunchy, crusted French bread, and endless cups of piping hot coffee.

For seasoning the bill-of-fare, people select vegetables from *a* to *z* — *asparagus* to *zucchini* — and to win enviable reputations as casual hosts and hostesses they assemble them in advance and carry them to the barbecue's table at the right moment. The oft-used, faithful scalloped potatoes put in frequent appearances, as do green peas, green beans, summer squash, Spanish, chili, or Mexican beans, and dozens of other pleasantries that had their beginnings and their established roots in a garden.

Among the meats favored are steaks, chops, hamburgers, split frankfurts, spareribs, lamb riblets, ham slices, and bacon. Grilled chicken, turkey, wild duck, and fish are relished. To simplify the description of their preparation, natives say: cook them on the barbecue's grill rather than in the range's broiling oven. Swab or paint them or not, as you wish, with a stinging or mild sauce as they cook. Some families prefer to serve the barbecue sauce in individual bowls and let everyone dunk or not dunk his meat or chicken, according to his wishes.

Chefs favor all sorts of contrivances for applying the zest, but the common one consists of a white cloth tied to one end of a stick. One of my hosts gathered herbs from his garden and made a little broom of them to use in spreading it over the cooking meat. When the tempting goodness was off the grill and everyone eagerly sat around to partake of it he tossed the bouquet of herbs on the coals to perfume the evening air. As we dined, our hostess — the chef's wife — gave a step by step account of how she makes Christmas gifts for her friends, the kind that convey "from our house to yours" greetings. She forms the coarser herbs from the garden into cunning little wreaths of greenery, and braids fat bunches of garlic cloves on stalks to accompany them.

Kabobs Have Champions, Too

Some brothers and sisters of the skillet specialize in *kabobs,* 3-inch squares of beef steak or lamb threaded on green sticks, such as those from bay trees. They wash the small branches and whittle a point at one end. When impaling the meat on them they leave an inch between each piece to aid in thorough cooking. Many experts hold the kabobs above the coals, while others prop them over heat. Trout fresh from cold water, dressed, wrapped in bacon, and grilled, exemplify fine and historic California eating. Bacon for barbecue cookery is sliced somewhat thicker than for breakfast appearances.

Lamb riblets and chicken legs on many garden tables draw small bowls of heated, peppery barbecue sauce as an escort. Guests may ladle some of the sauce over the food, or as previously mentioned, they can dunk it, perhaps with the fervor of a Pennsylvania Dutchman when doughnuts and coffee come his way.

Some vegetables respond beautifully when grilled alongside the meat. Take tomato halves, quarter inch slices of eggplant, and wedges of zucchini, swathed first in seasoned salad oil. What could taste better than this, hot off the griddle? Canned fruits, like cling peach halves and pineapple rings, and bananas in their skins broiled to perfection also rate the superlatives lavished on them.

Baked potatoes often whet the appetite and then help to appease it. Some families set a portable one-burner sheet iron oven on one corner of the barbecue to cook them, and there is a variety of other arrangements for handling the assignment. For example, countless barbecues contain ovens. One custom is to pass bowls of sour cream and chopped chives or green onions with the potatoes. Indeed, one of the distinctive culinary habits of the state is to dress cooked and raw vegetables with seasoned sour cream.

An ice-cold, clean-tasting, tangy green salad withstands all major competition in its field, although some barbecues show trays, iced bowls, or buckets of crisp relishes. For anyone who collects food pictures for enjoyment in retrospect — a normal, mature amusement — the large wooden bowls heaped with black ripe olives and rings of red Italian onions, called *torpedo onions,* are not to be overlooked.

As already noted, long, brown loaves of French bread are heated and buttered. One procedure is to split them in lengthwise halves and lay the cut surfaces on the grill, and then dip the toasted areas in a shallow pan containing melted butter. Etiquette dictates it is proper to break off little snippets of this bread to take up all the buttery or peppery sauces from the plate. Not to take advantage of the opportunity is almost a sacrilege.

Chefs Disagree About Corn-on-the-Cob

When available, corn-on-the-cob glorifies barbecue menus. Everyone defends, both with eloquence and proof-of-the-pudding evidence, his private system of roasting the ears. There are many methods. Some noble chefs strip them down to the last four husks, soak them in iced water from 1/2 to 1 hour, drain, and place them on the hot grill for at least 5 to 10 minutes. They turn them several times for even cookery. Wrapping the ears in aluminum foil and then roasting them 10 minutes in the coals is a fairly recent innovation.

Some gentlemen who are clever over a barbecue with a bed of thick, glowing coals pull back the husks, remove the silks, and spread on garlic flavored butter; then they draw the husks back in place to conceal the kernels and tie them with fine wire. They roast the ears so dressed for from 15 to 20 minutes on the grill, turning them five or six times to repeatedly expose all surfaces to the heat. Of course they put on gloves when they cut off the wire and pull off the husks, but that presents no problem. Many a man has several pairs of these fancy heat-protecting mitts. Indeed, if all Californians wearing them in their gardens on a Saturday evening waved their hands at the same minute, the state from the air would suggest the flags of all nations fluttering happily side by side in the Pacific breezes!

Because sweet peppers and tomatoes cooked together to perfection show up at many barbecues, where they take to meat as a duck takes to water, they qualify as a regional food escort. One of my hostesses demonstrated how she puts the dish together. She soaks the sweet bell peppers in iced water for an hour or so, and then drains and dices them, discarding the seeds and coarse membranes. Then she slowly pan-fries the peppers until they are just soft and lightly browned. Next she drains off the oil and folds in an equal quantity of peeled and chopped tomatoes. After that she adds salt, black pepper, and a few gratings of onion and sets the heavy frying pan on the back of the grill to bubble and sputter softly. She says it takes at least 30 minutes of leisurely simmering to develop the rich flavors.

Gentlemen Chefs Like Zesty Smoke

Opinions vary on the right choice of fuel for barbecues. Favorite woods include oak, hickory, madrone, manzanita, and hard maple. Some men say they rely on compressed sawdust logs — which grocers sell in bundles — when other wood is difficult or costly to get. Charcoal for grates that accommodate it solves fuel problems for thousands of families. Some gentlemen chefs swear by the merits of the zesty smoke they obtain with small branches of myrtle, bay, or alder thrown on the coals, while others settle only for what they call *unadulterated oak smoke.* There also are charcoal users who lay a few apple wood twigs near the coals for the flavor-fragrance they supply. Pet practices of this nature blossom about the gardens of the area as profusely as the flowers.

Desserts vary greatly, but barbecue fans point out that they have one common feature — they are ready for service and may be offered with next to nothing of effort when the gala moment arrives. They are planned for and prepared in advance. Among the more fortunate selections, the experts say, are fresh fruit with crackers and cheese, fruit or berry pies, cobblers, cakes, cookies with fruit, melons, and hollowed out watermelon shells filled with fruits and melon balls. Hot coffee, an impressive never-ending fountain of it, flanks the sweet meal ending, and contributes to the jovial contentment of the crowd.

California assumes leadership of a national calibre not only with barbecues but also with original dishes and meals. Inspiration from many nations aids in stirring the contents of its kettles. Mexican cookery is extremely popular, and it becomes more so every year. Indeed, from San Francisco on south the Golden State belongs to the Southwest. The Mountain West and its food traditions claim its ranch country. Striking Chinese, Italian, French, and Armenian influences reach the home tables in many areas. And there are tasty signs at dinnertime of most of the other nations around the world and the states across the United States. Cosmopolitan, colorful, creative, casual, and cheering are compliments that fit the California cuisine.

The Hawaiian Islands

A FOOD SCOUT'S PENCIL works overtime in Hawaii. I had scarcely stepped off the plane onto the palm-fringed shore before I started jotting down delicious observations. I marveled at the spontaneous hospitality in the Paradise of the Pacific, and how parties spring up on the spur of the moment — at the drop of a coconut hat! I exhausted my vocabulary of adjectives on the beautiful flowers before the sun dipped into the sea the first evening. When I reluctantly turned in for the night, with the sound of the surf in my ears, I reveled in a well-fed, glad-to-be-alive feeling.

At this Crossroads of the Pacific you are ever conscious of the Stars and Stripes flying high against the blue of tropical skies. More Americans of Oriental ancestry appear every-place you go than on the Mainland. As you would expect, this harmonious mingling of the races affects the cuisine. Cooks of high calibre in all groups lend imagination and skill. Local deep-hued fruits — handsome like your favorite costume jewels — strange green vegetables, and exotic fish brighten meals. The distinctive dishes of the sun-drenched Islands are gems in Uncle Sam's culinary crown.

While Palm Trees Glistened

After roaming around Hawaii I sat down one perfect evening with my genial traveling companion, a Mainland home economist, on the lanai of our cottage beside the beach at Waikiki. The *lanai* is the Hawaiian porch-like living room designed to bring the weather indoors. I had rounded up the characteristic foods and recorded descriptions of them. The hour for appraisal had arrived. At that moment new-made friends appeared to inquire about my search for the food treats of the Islands. In true Hawaiian fashion they slipped a feathery, fragrant ginger lei around my shoulders, and gave me a gorgeous fresh coconut cake, the equal of which I had never seen or tasted. After the presentation they settled down in comfortable chairs to share and to soften my concern about how authentic my epicurean discoveries were. Everyone joined in spirited food talk as we looked out at palm trees that glistened like cellophane in the moonlight, and the evening slipped by with magical speed. Our farewells included promises to meet later at a *luau*.

A Luau for Home Economists

This original celebration feast of the Polynesians was offered in a spirit of Thanksgiving to their gods. It has been modernized in some respects and has lost its religious sig-nificance, but it remains the eloquent expression of Hawaiian hospitality.

Excitement ran high in our bungalow on the beach the day the telephone brought a cordial invitation from the Hawaiian Pineapple Company. A luau in honor of visiting home economists was coming up!

Among the guests at that memorable gathering the following week were many *kamaainas* (old-time residents of the Islands) to whom luaus are no innovation. They ranked this party as the superlative in native feasts.

Women, both hostesses and guests, wore gay native dress — muumuus or holokus — and their costumes and the men's bright aloha shirts stirred color into the festive scene. Everyone joyfully accepted and wore a lei of fragrant flowers, the symbol of friendship. Hawaiian musicians strummed their ukuleles and sang the plaintive, nostalgic love songs of their people. Girls in grass skirts floated into the graceful hula, the famous dance of the South Pacific.

The tables were set under the stars — stars so low flying that they appeared almost within grasp. Ti leaves — pronounced *tee* — and lacy ferns formed table covers; there were rectangles of the leaves for individual place mats. Everyone was charmed by the decorations — blossoms, mangoes, bananas, fresh pineapple prepared in luau style, and watermelons cut down until they resembled partly opened flowers. (Ti leaves are used to wrap foods for cooking, in flower arrangements, to cover tables, and to make grass skirts.)

Many guests stood around the *imu* (underground oven) to watch the removal of the cooked pig and its food accompaniments. Some of us found our thoughts drifting to the shores of Cape Cod, where in quite a different setting we had observed with the same eagerness the uncovering of clams and lobsters at a bake.

A few hours before the guests arrived the thoroughly cleaned and dressed pig had been rubbed inside and out with salt. Smooth porous rocks, heated in the imu, were added to its body cavity. Well-supported in a basket made of wire mesh, it was deposited on a thick bed of banana leaves spread over heated rocks in the underground oven. More banana leaves and stalks were arranged over the pig after it was lowered into the pit. Around it were placed laulaus (pork, fish, and taro leaves wrapped in ti leaves and tied) and bananas and sweet potatoes in their scrubbed jackets. The food was covered with wet burlap, ti leaves, and earth. The cooking had continued for between 3½ and 4 hours.

The pork was carved before it was carried to the table. Everyone unwrapped the laulau at his plate, and welcomed the bananas and sweet potatoes served with meat from the imu. Among other Hawaiian foods to put in an appearance was poi (explained later). It was escorted by tasty lomi salmon, a dish that may be likened to a frappé, a concoction composed of tiny bits of ice, and almost a paste of salted salmon, fresh tomatoes, and both green and dry onions. (Hawaiians do not season pork highly; they serve it with condiments. One of their favorite combinations consists of a mona — gourd — filled with onions and small fresh, hot chili peppers.)

Among other characteristic tempting foods at every plate were chicken and luau (taro leaves) cooked with coconut milk; mullet baked in ti leaves; dried squid; sticks of fresh sugar cane; and haupia, a coconut pudding. Marvelous coconut cake and fresh fruits were passed at the meal's end.

Food and Happiness Are Shared

This festive scene made us feel we were far away on another planet rather then in a part of the United States. The blend of friendliness, tasty food, flowers that perfumed the air, the shining tropical moon rising above the mountains, haunting native music, and beautiful hula dancers made me wonder why the people of Hawaii are so generous and kindly.

Almost at this very instant, as if he were a mind reader, the President of the Hawaiian Pineapple Company arose to express his pleasure in sharing the luau experience with guests from the Mainland. Then he explained, "Whatever graciousness exists in Hawaii today is a gift of the Hawaiians.

These cheerful, joy-loving people have for centuries delighted in sharing their happiness and food with guests. By practicing hospitality they taught later arrivals something of the art." That bestowed credit for the wonderful aloha spirit of the Islands to the Polynesians, who have lived for centuries in the Paradise of the Pacific. (*Aloha* in Hawaii means love, cherrio, good-by, here's how, greetings, and anything pleasant.)

One of Hawaii's Finest Pineapples

That the spotlight plays frequently on pineapples in Hawaiian food conversations is no mystery. The production of the fruit and of sugar, and caring for a steady flow of tourists comprise the three main commercial enterprises of the region.

Although pineapples are native to South America, they have been grown in the Islands for many years. Perhaps the first plantings were made by Spanish explorers. Not until after the Smooth Cayenne variety was introduced in 1866 and the fruit was canned commercially in 1892 did its culture assume economic importance. Now it is shipped in such large quantities all over the world that to many persons pineapples connote Hawaii.

Residents fully appreciate that the fruit ceases to ripen once it is severed from the plant. This characteristic explains why ripe pineapples in the Islands taste sweeter and superior to those we obtain on the Mainland, which necessarily must be shipped in a less mature state. Indeed, the heavenly juice almost spurts out as your knife pierces the pulp.

My daughter treasures a childhood memory of a gorgeous pineapple (it was grown in a highly favorable location and selected by a crop expert) given to our family by a plantation manager on our first trip to the Islands. We wished personally, as a lark, to cut the juicy fruit in our hotel quarters. My husband dressed in his swimming trunks, climbed into the bathtub and sliced the pineapple. Quantities of surplus juice fell into the tub rather than on the carpet. Our family, leaning over the tub, ate the pieces in watermelon fashion, literally up to our ears in delicious juice. No pineapple ever tasted better!

Due to the convenience of canned pineapple, local cooks use it as enthusiastically as do women on the Mainland. But they can and do buy fresh fruit in the markets throughout the year, although the supply is more plentiful and the flavor more delectable during the summer.

Then Comes the Thump Test

When a Hawaiian shopper selects a pineapple she places no confidence in color or leaf pulling as guides to ripeness. She observes the crown (the top leaves), and if it is small and compact she concludes the fruit at least is well developed. Then she applies the *thump* test with a thumb and finger. A dull, solid sound, in contrast to a hollow one, indicates ripeness and plenty of juice. It is like testing a watermelon.

Practically all the world's pineapple dishes enter the food picture here, and some of the fruity treats rarely show up elsewhere. Tall glasses of tea clink with ice and display long juicy spikes of honey-colored pineapple to eat from the fingers. Cubes of fresh pineapple, canned litchi, and preserved kumquats are impaled on toothpicks and stuck in a bed of crushed ice for the colorful dessert in a Chinese dinner. Canned pineapple rings topped with cheese sauce often accompany fish salad on Friday, broiled bacon on other days. And hot pineapple muffins are married to chicken salad. Spiced or pickled pineapple, gay with color, enjoys popularity comparable to that of peach pickle in the South, and of red beet or pickled eggs in Pennsylvania Dutch country. It usually is tinted red or green.

Pineapple pies, of the cream, coconut cream, and chiffon types, are well acquainted with dessert plates. I discovered a unique kind with two crusts — the peeled, diced fruit is mixed with flour, egg, sugar, and lemon juice (as are some rhubarb fillings) and dotted with butter before the pastry top goes on.

Among the praised conserves are those in which peeled pineapple is run through a food chopper and cooked with orange juice and sugar until thickened. Chopped, candied orange peel and nuts are added. Pineapple-papaya jam has a faint taste of ginger.

Fresh pineapple generally shows up at mealtime in lengthwise slices. The two popular ways to cut it are known as the *luau* and *family* styles. In the luau style the pineapple is not peeled. The cook cuts crosswise slices about 1½ inches thick from the top and bottom and reserves them. With a long, slender knife she cuts around the fruit ½ inch inside the rind. Then she pushes out the loosened portion in one piece. She slices it in halves lengthwise, removes the core, cuts the pineapple in finger-like pieces, and arranges them in the shell. She replaces the top and bottom, and sets the fruit on a small plate; it appears never to have been touched by a knife after it was separated from the plant. To serve the kingly treat, the hostess lifts off the top and takes out the juicy spears with a fork.

For the family style of service she cuts off and discards the pointed green leaves and a ¾-inch slice from both the top and bottom of the fruit. She holds the pineapple upright on a cutting board and with a sharp knife pares off the rind in strips from top to bottom. Then she cuts diagonal grooves around the fruit to eliminate the eyes. She divides it into crosswise or lengthwise slices, whichever she prefers, and removes the fibrous core. Guests need not be coaxed to help themselves!

Pineapple boats made from the shells or rinds contribute interest to the menu when they hold mixed fruits, fruit salads, sherbets, or curry sauce, as they often do. To prepare them natives cut the pineapple and its green top leaves in two lengthwise pieces — or into quarters if the fruit is large. They trim the leaves for a neat appearance, and then with precision cut the fruit away from the rind so the walls, ½ inch thick, retain their shape.

Coco palms along the shores, that lean seaward and

proudly toss their leafy plumes in the breezes, yield a favored fruit. Fresh coconut contributes brilliantly to countless dishes, but its appearance in daily meals is restricted somewhat by the time and effort required for preparation.

This kitchen ritual has been simplified by the wide acceptance of the Hawaiian grater. The convenience consists of a strip of steel 7 inches long, $1\frac{1}{2}$ inches wide, and $\frac{1}{4}$ inch thick. It curves upward at one end, which has a saw-tooth edge, with each tooth about $\frac{1}{8}$ inch deep. The other end of the metal strip is screwed firmly into a heavy piece of wood, 14 inches square and $1\frac{1}{4}$ inches thick, or to the wooden seat on which the operator sits as she holds half of a coconut in both hands.

She scrapes the interior of the fruit over the metal teeth. The meat drops into a pan set below. That first snowy white coconut, free from brown specks, is reserved for garnishing. Islanders decrease the fall of brown fiber into the grated coconut by wrapping a damp cloth around the outside of the shell.

To a Kansan unfamiliar with coconut kitchen chores, the people of Hawaii appear agile in husking the fruit, piercing holes in its eyes, draining out the liquid (and reserving it on some occasions for cookery purposes), and breaking the nuts open. The technique for the latter task is to brush off the loose fibers from the shell, then tap the coconut with a hammer around the center halfway between the two ends. It splits in two quickly.

How To Milk a Coconut

While Island women consider the production of coconut milk a task, it does not rate as an unsurmountable one to anyone who has lived on a Wisconsin dairy farm. They pour 2 cups of boiling water over 4 cups of grated fresh coconut and let the mixture stand about 20 minutes. Then they strain it through a poi cloth or a double thickness of cheesecloth, pressing to extract all the liquid.

When the milk is not used immediately, Hawaiians store

it in the refrigerator like cow's milk. The cardinal rule in cooking with it is to use low heat, and never to boil it. The milk can be gradually brought to the boiling point without curdling if it is stirred constantly. Four cups of grated coconut yield 2 cups of milk.

For coconut cream the milk is refrigerated a few hours. A thick substance rises to the top. When this is skimmed off, lo! you have a cream that will whip when cold. Six cups of grated coconut produce about 2 cups of the cream. I tasted the elegant dessert topping of the tropics with baked bananas. My hostess explained that she dipped the peeled fruit into honey mixed with lemon juice, dotted the bananas with butter, and baked them until soft. The bananas were served warm, with a crown of the unusual whipped cream garnished generously with shredded coconut. The dessert is one to write home about, if you refrain from referring to the calories hidden in it.

Countless wonderful coconut dishes evolve in Hawaiian kitchens. One of the popular stunts is to make coconut chips or strips; you find them in Mainland markets sealed in airtight cans. In Hawaii they assume many of the roles ordinarily played elsewhere by nuts. Cooks sprinkle them over fruit salads and frosted cakes, and on cookies, puddings, ice cream, and other desserts for crunchy texture and pleasing flavor.

A Treat for the Parties

In several homes I visited, coconut strips are prepared at intervals. Husked coconuts with the water drained out are heated about an hour in a slow oven, 300°, to loosen the meat. After a nut is cool it is split open with a hammer in the conventional manner, and the meat is taken out in as large pieces as possible. Without removing the outer brown skin, it is sliced as thin as is practicable. Many women employ potato slicers for this purpose.

The thin slices are spread in a shallow pan or on a baking sheet and toasted in a very slow oven, 200°, for 2 hours. Then the heat is reduced to 150°, and the slow baking continues 2 hours longer, or until the strips brown lightly around the edges. Throughout the cooking the coconut must be stirred frequently to encourage even browning. When cool, the tasty strips are salted and kept in readiness for the parties that habitually pop up, and to enjoy in daily meals.

To attempt to describe all the exotic coconut creations of the Islands would be an almost endless assignment. A few of the specialties are so distinctive and characteristic of this part of Uncle Sam's domain that they cannot be omitted from a consideration of the nation's superlative dishes. As an instance, the marvelous coconut layer cakes are unforgettable.

They frequently consist of three thin white layers, made with coconut milk as the liquid. Sheet and two-layer cakes also take honors. Lemon or pineapple fillings often are spread between them. Cooked white frosting, which the fresh coconut softens somewhat, covers the top and sides of the cake. Freshly grated coconut is scattered on with an extravagant hand. In some households pineapple juice substitutes for water as the liquid in the frosting.

Coconut ice cream wins compliments whenever it appears. A 10-year-old Kansas girl, who discovered it while vacationing in the Islands with her parents, promptly decided that the dessert and swimming with a surfboard provide adequate inducement to return at the first opportunity.

Then there are coconut cream and coconut custard pies, frequently with pineapple added. *Haupia,* the traditional coconut pudding, usually greets guests at luaus. Cut in squares, it shows up on ti leaves. It is eaten from the fingers.

HAUPIA

2½ tablespoons cornstarch	⅛ teaspoon salt
3 tablespoons sugar	2 cups coconut milk

Make a smooth paste of the dry ingredients and ½ cup of coconut milk. Stir in the remaining milk after it has been scalded, but not boiled, over *low* heat. Cook gently until clear and thick enough to coat a spoon. Pour into a shallow pan, and set in a cool place to become firm. For a more delicate pudding, but one that will not hold a perfect shape when cut, use only 2 tablespoons of cornstarch.

Melt-in-the-mouth coconut cream candies definitely rate among the top sweet thrills of the Islands. Perhaps the easiest one to turn out is made by melting ½ pound of marshmallows over very low heat and stirring in 4 cups of freshly grated coconut. The mixture is dropped from a spoon onto waxed paper. For additional appeal the candy frequently is tinted a delicate pink or green before being dipped up with a spoon.

More typical of the Islands is cooked candy like that which contributed a decorative note to the festive table of the home economics department of the University of Hawaii. The confection was gay in white, red, and green. A simple recipe for this creamy confection was given to me by a charming hostess, and I regard it as one of my Hawaiian finds.

COCONUT CREAM CANDY

1½ cups sugar	2 teaspoons light corn sirup
½ cup water	1½ cups freshly grated coconut

Combine the sugar, water, and corn sirup, and boil the mixture until it spins a thread 2 inches long, 248°. Wipe the crystals from the sides of the pan, take the candy from the heat, stir in the coconut, and boil the mixture until it is very thick, 226°. Then remove it from the heat and beat the sweetness until it becomes creamy and of the proper consistency to drop from a spoon onto waxed paper. For a characteristic touch, stir ¼ cup of canned crushed pineapple, drained, into the candy, along with the coconut.

Perhaps few Mainlanders share the effervescent enthusiasm of one *malihini* — stranger — for chicken and luau. I wish I might frequently meet this stalwart dish. To prepare it, the cook cuts the chicken in small pieces and simmers it gently in water until tender. She serves it in some of the broth with a crown of cooked, finely cut taro leaves (luau) heated in coconut milk.

Spoon coconuts are another taste adventure. Hawaiians saw the tops from immature nuts, then chill them. They serve them with straws — through which guests sip the nectar or liquid — and spoons are provided for eating the meat. The shells are saved, sawed in halves, and filled with fruit combinations — either salads or cocktails — ice cream, or sherbet.

Banana Treats Are Legion

On my many drives in Hawaii I admired the decorative clumps of banana trees shading houses with their gigantic leaves that contrast so strikingly with the bunches of pale yellow fruit. In food talk you soon learn about superlative banana dishes. The cooked fruit especially wins praise. With baked ham, for example, guava jelly and baked bananas, shiny and brown, are the traditional companions.

Three varieties enter constantly into these conversations. *Bluefields* for eating raw, and *Chinese* or *Cavendish* and *Apple bananas* for cooking top the list.

Hawaiian women run the fruit into the oven with the nonchalance that their Mainland sisters put potatoes in to bake. Frequently they do not skin the bananas. They wash and spread them in a shallow pan with no water, or just enough to cover the bottom of the baking dish. They cook them in a moderate oven, 350°, from 30 to 45 minutes, or until the bananas become soft and the skins start to burst. At the table, guests push them open and insert butter, salt, pepper, and a squeeze or two of lemon or lime juice. As they taste and sniff the fragrance they rejoice that they are in the Paradise of the Pacific.

Sometimes cooks peel bananas, cut them in lengthwise halves, and top them with butter, lemon juice, and sugar; butter, passion fruit juice, and sugar; butter, guava jelly, and sugar; or similar and equally appetizing combinations. Then they bake them.

I carry the banner high for pan-fried bananas. You select firm Apple or under-ripe Bluefield bananas and peel them. Apple bananas generally are cooked whole, while Bluefields are cut in lengthwise halves. You slowly heat them in butter, using a heavy frying pan. When the fruit shows a delicate light brown, add a large spoonful of guava jelly and let it bubble up. Then pour in from $1/3$ to $1/2$ cup of sherry wine. In the simmering that ensues, a sauce — thick as heavy cream or corn sirup — develops around the softened bananas. With pork, chicken, or ham, Hawaiians ask, what could be better? I have heard men exclaim that one bite of the concoction gives the ocean a deeper blue, prompts the stars to come nearer, and makes Island life more enchanting.

For satisfying refreshment on a summer day, banana sherbet holds its venerated place in the sun. Some hostesses prefer to serve a scoop of it and one of mint sherbet in the same glass, as a perfect ending to almost any dinner.

The recipe most popular can boast of a host of ardent followers. Some women call it *1-2-3 sherbet*. To make it they mix the juices of 1 lemon and 2 oranges into 3 mashed bananas. Then they boil 1 cup each of sugar and water together about 5 minutes to make a sirup, cool it, and then fold the sweetening into the bananas. They place the mixture in a refrigerator tray and forget about it, for as Island people joyfully announce, the dessert requires no stirring during freezing because the bananas insure smoothness.

Perhaps the most famous tall glass drink, typical of the region, consists of a ripe banana mashed and whipped into a cup of pineapple juice. Chill it and then one sip introduces a de luxe thirst quencher.

Take Your Pick of Cakes

If anyone were brave enough to try to select the blue ribbon banana cake, he would face problems. There are so many superb versions! Almost everyone has more than one kind deserving praise. About the only similarity they possess is that mashed banana is mixed into the batter.

I am inclined to nominate *banana devil's food* as the queen. It definitely captivates chocolate lovers, of which there are many. Generally it is all dressed up with a white cooked frosting in which marshmallows have been melted. But when I recall the delicacy of a sour cream banana cake studded with English walnuts, I simply cannot demote it to red ribbons and second place. It wears an orange flavored frosting to complement its sweet, banana-nut flavored layers.

A tie for top position is the best way out for a food reporter-judge.

One of my gracious hostesses described her favorite winter dinner for guests. In the menu banana cake assumes responsibility for sending people away from the table in a happy frame of mind. She says it always rises to the occasion.

WINTER DINNER
Papaya Cocktail
Pork Loin Roast
Baked Squash   Luau
Guava Jelly
Stuffed Tomato Salad
Pineapple Sherbet
Banana Devil's Food Cake
Coffee

Banana-cream, banana-coconut cream, banana-coconut custard, and banana-chiffon pies reap extravagant compliments. Here is a two-crust banana pie I discovered in Honolulu.

BANANA PIE

4 cups sliced bananas	1 teaspoon cinnamon
½ cup pineapple juice	1 tablespoon butter
½ cup sugar	Pastry for 2 crusts

The dainty Chinese-American girl who demonstrated how to make the pie soaked the sliced ripe, firm fruit in the pineapple juice about a half hour. Then she drained the bananas and arranged them in a 9-inch pan lined with pastry. She sprinkled on the sugar and cinnamon, mixed, poured on the pineapple juice in which the fruit soaked, dotted the butter on top, and added the pastry cover. She baked the pie in a hot oven, 400°, about 35 minutes. While people of Chinese ancestry especially relish this dessert, almost everyone who samples it nods in approval of its goodness.

More Hawaiian Fruits

Hawaii grows an astonishing number of attractive fruits. Markets glow with their bright colors, and countless dishes reflect their ambrosial flavors. Avocados tempt almost everyone in summer, autumn, and winter. While they appear on salad plates universally, it is the curried dish and the sherbet featuring the green food that seem to belong only to the Islands.

For the curry, cooks preheat the peeled and diced avocado in the top of a double boiler, or add it directly to the hot white sauce. Women learned long ago that prolonged heat brings out a bitter flavor. This, home economists say, comes from the tannin that avocados contain. The sauce for curried avocados is made with coconut milk.

In the smooth green sherbet, which coconut cake loves to escort, the flavors of lemon, orange, and pineapple juices are detected. In appearance it resembles pistachio ice cream.

Peeled and diced avocados also go into soups, scrambled eggs, omelets, and other warm dishes — but just a minute before the dish is served. For a surprise and treat, *guava-avocado ketchup* fills the bill.

When avocado on the half shell is set before Mainlanders, they reach for salt and quartered lemon or lime but some of the natives choose the sugar bowl instead. Dusting on a touch of sweetening is a custom borrowed from the Chinese.

A Tame Fruit Goes Wild

Guavas were introduced into Hawaii about a century ago. They flourished and have gone wild. Now they grow profusely along the roadsides. For the sake of convenience many households keep a few trees in their gardens. The fruit is used in an enviable variety of superior dishes. Guava jelly unites with peanut butter for a children's favorite sandwich. For party fare many a hostess pins her chances for success to *guava mousse* served with coconut-crested sponge cake. (The top of the baked cake is spread with brown sugar, butter, and grated fresh coconut, and broiled briefly to a tempting brown.) It would take a library of cook books to record all the guava recipes.

Mangoes, with their pleasing peach-pineapple flavor, inspire cooks to outdo themselves in concocting elegant dishes. They grow on dome-shaped trees blessed by many persons for the shade they afford. When partly ripe, the fruit glorifies tables in the manner of tart summer apples. Sweet-tart sauce, mango sauce cake, brown betty, pie, and a long array of other good things to eat are prepared with mangoes.

The fruit is a clever diplomat. It gets along well with citrus fruits, pineapples, and papayas in salads and cocktails. In shortcakes and frozen desserts it is delicious, and jams and marmalades made of it deserve the bouquets tossed in their direction. Unfortunately the supply of mangoes, especially of the fine quality *Pirie* and *Hayden* varieties, does not meet the market demands. The *Hayden* is the same variety as the one spelled *Haden* by some people in Florida and Hawaii.

Mango chutney has no rival as an accompaniment for the many Hawaiian curried entrees. The chutney and guava jelly share the distinction of being the two most popular home preserved foods. I rarely talked with women who like to cook without hearing a reference to a special mango chutney recipe they consider tops.

Whenever anyone speaks of mangoes, I experience a tingle of excitement. Again I am in Hilo, the guest of the supervisor of home economics. First I look through the front windows of her comfortable living room to a wide expanse of the Pacific Ocean. Then I walk across the room to gaze into a garden filled with out-of-this-world orchids. I relive the remarkable supper party and recall fond memories of the mango pie. My hostess explained how she made it.

She cooked the sliced, partially ripe mangoes with thin lemon slices, sugar, and a whiff of cloves, and thickened the mixture with a touch of cornstarch. When thoroughly chilled, she added it to the crisp, baked pastry shell, and for a crowning touch spread on whipped cream.

As she served triangles of the mango pie I realized that forever I would remember that evening, gay with exotic food, fine conversation, many kinds of orchids, and the surf's song as it splashed softly against the sands.

Papayas sometimes are described as melons that grow on trees. You need not be in Hawaii long to learn they start

breakfasts. When served chilled on the half shell like cantaloupe, and with lemon or lime juice, almost everyone enjoys
them. Those who do not like the first taste usually succumb
within a few days to their appeal, and become boosters for
their delightful flavors.

Slices of papayas show up on salad and dessert plates.
That old tradition of serving mixtures of cut fruits in papaya
halves, either as salads or cocktails, lingers through the
years. The small papayas — those with a diameter of 3 to 5
inches — are called *solo papayas* and enjoy great prestige.

With the fruit abundant throughout the year, no Hawaiian need worry about getting an adequate supply of
vitamin C. Research at the University of Hawaii indicates
papayas contain more of this vitamin than oranges.

One of the characteristic regional sweet spreads features
papayas and pineapple. Many women who gave me samples
of the sweet also provided the recipe.

They peel both fruits and put them through a food chopper.
Then they simmer 2 cups of pineapple pulp and 3 cups of
papaya pulp, with a teaspoon of fresh ginger juice stirred in,
about a half hour. They measure the fruit and add an equal
quantity of sugar. For another 30 minutes the simmering continues; due to the thickening, they stir the bubbling mixture
frequently.

The newly made jam is a treat on taro biscuits. (Hot
taro biscuits are a Hawaiian delicacy. The mashed, cooked
root is used for part of the flour.)

Fresh *litchis* surprise almost everyone who tastes them
the first time. Their pleasing flavor bears almost no resemblance to the dried fruit known as litchi nuts, which many
Mainlanders meet in the Chinese quarters of their larger
cities. When you remember that raisins carry little of the
fresh grape taste your wondering ceases.

Litchis for the Salads

To peel the red-coated litchi, to remove the seed from its
white heart, and to taste the fruit — well, that thrills a food

scout. After this experience I constantly looked, wherever I went in Hawaii during June and July, for fresh litchis in salads. The quest on my part was fruitful at least once. A graceful, pretty Japanese-American waitress set a fruit salad before me. I scarcely could believe my eyes, for on the crisp greens were litchi halves filled with cottage cheese, with chopped preserved ginger added. The canned fruit, imported from the Orient, neatly lines grocery shelves 365 days of the year, but the crop of local fresh litchis never is large enough.

Then there is *poha jam*. I met it at breakfast one morning at Waikiki. On crunchy buttered toast, its flavor reaches new heights. With black coffee, I drank a toast to it right then and there much to the curiosity of the waiters, but not to my associates who were versed in the ways of food explorers.

A native of Brazil, the *poha* is a member of the ground cherry family that grows at fairly high altitudes, as on Maui and Hawaii Islands. Later I tasted a somewhat thinner poha jam served over vanilla ice cream. As I raved about the perfect sundae, my hostess tantalized me by relating how marvelous fruit salads in papaya halves are, when the same kind of poha jam serves as the dressing.

Breadfruit Is Baked, Now

Someone removed breadfruit from Island trees and ate it long before a *haole* — pronounced *howly* and meaning a member of the Caucasian race — ever set foot on the Island. Nowadays almost everyone bakes the fruit, which always is cooked before you eat it. Malihinis — strangers — frequently experience difficulty with breadfruit recipes. Natives say the trouble almost always stems from their failure to select fruit in the proper state of maturity. Green breadfruit, although full size, is hard. When steamed, it serves as a starchy vegetable. Ripe breadfruit is soft and beginning to turn yellow. Very ripe breadfruit is soft and mushy, with streaks of brown and speckles of fruit sugar. When baked and served with butter and a suspicion of cinnamon, guests are glad to help themselves when it is passed in their direction.

Soursop! What a name for the heart-shaped fruit with such an agreeable acid flavor. Its taste blends beautifully with bananas, oranges, and pineapples. Its juice, extracted by pressing the pulp through a ricer, puts something special into gelatin dishes, frozen desserts, and cold drinks composed of a medley of fruit juices. This is a large fruit; it frequently weighs as much as 5 pounds.

Other favorites that grow in Hawaii include carissa or natal plums, ketambilla, mountain apples, roselle; yellow, hard-shelled water lemons or passion fruit; star apples or carambola, Surinam cherries, and tamarind. The bright red mountain apples flourish in the deep mountain valleys of all the Islands; they are for sale at roadside fruit stands. Almost everyone eats them from the hand — the little apples are delectable.

A few of the women with whom I chatted recommended the calyxes of the roselle as a possible substitute for cranberries. They warned that they must be cooked and sweetened thoroughly.

When figs are ripe, though they rarely are abundant, anyone in the Islands usually meets up with one or two peeled and crushed ones on top of coconut pudding. Be thankful if you are served such a treat, for figs and coconut have an affinity for each other, at least in Hawaii.

Taro Is the No. 1 Vegetable

Chinese cabbage, edible pod peas, and taro compose the flavored vegetable trio. The cabbage with elongated heads, a description that distinguishes it from the vegetable with round heads, gets involved both in salads and cooked dishes. Both are grown extensively.

Expert cooks prepare pod peas like English peas, but they break only the tips from the pods and remove the strings. Shelling is eliminated. They cook neither the peas nor cabbage long. Oriental influences extend to vegetable cookery. Most garden products are taken from kettles before they lose all their crispness.

Taro definitely ranks as the greatest of all vegetables. For hundreds of years it has performed its lead role in Hawaiian meals. *Poi* is made from the corm, or underground root. As an indication of the high regard for the plant's leaves, you need only to read the name assigned to them, which is *luau*. That, too, designates the native feast.

Because the corm frequently irritates the hands if peeled before it is cooked, the usual procedure runs like this. Wash the taro and cook it in boiling water about 1½ hours or until tender. Then peel, cube, and slice or mash it — and serve the vegetable hot with butter, pan-fried, creamed, scalloped, or made into a vast variety of other dishes.

You Can Buy Poi

Poi-making is no cinch. That is why much of it nowadays is purchased in cans, plastic bags, or thick, moist cotton sacks. Wherever I went in the markets I saw quantities of this former staff of life.

Preparation of poi, either in the home kitchen or a factory, has no short cuts. It is necessary to pound and knead the cooked, peeled, cubed taro root. Then it is put through a poi bag of stout porous cloth. Incidentally, this old-time method of sieving foods continues through the years in many homes.

When people first sample poi they often are amazed that it is so tasteless. It appears as a thick, gray paste. The cook adds water to produce the desired consistency. *One-finger poi* is thick; a mouthful of it clings to the forefinger twirled gracefully in the mass. *Two-finger poi* is somewhat thinner; it takes two fingers to deliver it from the bowl to the mouth. *Three-finger poi* is thinnest of all. Three fingers must be held tightly together and cupped for successful eating. While dining without a knife, fork, and spoon formerly was proper in the region, now only at luaus do fingers supplant silverware.

Most malihinis (newcomers) fail miserably to appreciate the merits of the sticky poi. They complain that it lacks flavor. When permitted to ferment for a few days, which is not an uncommon practice, it acquires an acid taste akin to that of buttermilk. To enjoy it plain or fermented, the natives insist you need a salty accompaniment, like lomi salmon.

Many residents of the Islands are fond of poi. Children especially like to see it in their breakfast cereal bowls. Visitors are presented poi cocktails, a token of hospitality, in many places. All of them have a milk base. Regardless of what anyone's reactions to the dish are, no one can laugh off its accomplishments in helping to build a magnificent race. Who can accuse the Polynesians in Hawaii of being a puny people? Their remarkable physical development gives the nutritionist something to think about.

Taro leaves with their stems, or with stems removed and neatly rolled, lend their green hue to practically all markets. When cooked like spinach they are delicious and entirely lacking in the bitter flavor sometimes noticed in cooked leaves. Taro leaves require a rather long cookery, about 45 minutes. Taro biscuits and taro cakes (similar to potato cakes) are two examples of superb food. They would be welcome at mealtime on many occasions far away from this sun-drenched land.

Certainly no one on Hawaii's shores disputes the right *laulaus* have to the title of a distinctive creation. As the malihini learns by experience, it is something of an art to unwrap the hot bundles gracefully.

Laulaus can be bought ready for steaming, or you can make your own. They consist of pieces of pork and salted butterfish or salmon wrapped in luau (taro) leaves and then in a covering of ti leaves to form pulolos, or flat bundles. Each one is tied firmly with the fibrous part of ti leaves, or with string. They are steamed from 4 to 6 hours, often in an electric roaster or in the well cookers of modern ranges. Originally they were prepared in the imu, and still are for the luau (feast) .

Food scouts from the Mainland consider the wide employment of *shoyu* (Japanese) or *soya* (Chinese) sauce and fresh ginger root the most colorful custom in meat cookery. The sauce retails in gallon glass jugs. Ginger grows profusely in the Islands, and the root seasons countless dishes. Ginger root does not come from the same plant that yields fragrant blooms for many a gorgeous lei.

The cook bastes meat roasts with soy sauce to aid in obtaining its flavor and as a help in deep browning. She rubs the leg of lamb with crushed ginger root before putting it in the oven. Meat sauces generally feature soy or ginger or both.

Teriyaki steaks please almost everyone who tastes them. Commonly sirloin or cubed steaks are featured in this appealing platter offering although other cuts also are used.

TERIYAKI STEAK

3 pounds beef	1 clove garlic
½ cup soy sauce	1 small piece of ginger root, crushed
2 tablespoons sugar	

Pound the meat, score it by slashing against the grain, and then cut it in pieces 4 inches long, 3 inches wide, and ½ inch thick. Or cut it in thin slices across the grain. Mix the other ingredients. More garlic and ginger may be added. Soak the meat in the sauce at least a half hour, then drain it and save the liquid to baste hamburgers, roasts, and spareribs on subsequent days. Place the beef on a rack and broil it over charcoal or in the range's broiler. When it is brown on one side turn it and complete the browning. Serve it in buns for the favored picnic food of the Islands.

For the fabled "meat on sticks" that visitors enthuse over when they spy them on the buffet, the strips of beef are cut extremely thin — about ⅛ inch — and in 1- to 1½-inch squares. They are soaked in the sauce as for Teriyaki steak and then impaled on bamboo sticks about ⅛ inch in diameter. Usually from 4 to 6 pieces are put on every stick. During the broiling the bamboo does not burn readily like some woods.

While many Oriental style meat dishes maintain a well-established toe hold in meals, sweet-sour spareribs win the most applause. Considerable pork is consumed in both Oriental and American type dishes.

Hamburgers in buns frequently are topped with crunchy onions and bean sprouts. And small hamburgers stacked in big wooden bowls attract lei-bedecked guests at buffet suppers throughout the islands.

Fish Names Are Tongue Twisters

For centuries Islanders have relied on native fish for the backbone of their meals. A trip to the market in Honolulu to inspect the different kinds introduces new names to visitors. For tongue exercise people try to pronounce some of the fish adapted to baking, such as *awa, moi, mullet, weke, kumu, red snapper, opakapaka, uku,* and *uhu.* For more of a tryout they consider the best selections for frying: *ahi, ono, mahimahi, hapuupuu, uhu, opakapaka, puala, weke,* and *uu.* To complete the talk fun, for steaming and boiling there are *mullet, moi, awa, kumu, uu, ahu, ono, opelu,* and *aholehole.*

Women the world over like to escape dishwashing. The Hawaiians are no exception. They line the pans for cooking fish with ti leaves, which resemble large corn leaves. Of course this coating facilitates the removal of cooked food to the platter.

Flowers Walk In, Too

Frequently smart cooks wrap ti leaves around fish before baking or broiling them. They also have a habit of filling the body cavities with strips of bacon or salt pork before covering them with the green. Every package is tied with split ti leaves. It takes about 1½ hours to bake these fish bundles in a moderate oven, 350°.

One of my favorite memories of the Islands concerns mullet baked and served in ti leaf boats, out-of-this-world coconut cake for dessert, and spirited, congenial company. We were on the lanai of my cousins' home in Honolulu, seated in comfortable chairs and on the hikiee, a broad couch, the most distinctive piece of Hawaiian furniture. That porch-like living room warrants its reputation for bringing the outdoors within, and it also permits flowers from the garden to walk in, too. At least they seem to be at your side.

Among tasty fish treats cooked outdoors over an open fire, nothing surpasses mullet or mio, at least in my experience and estimation. The dressed fish are split and the body cavities filled with the liquid from coconuts. Then the fish are wrapped individually in ti leaves. The green packages are broiled on glowing coals and guests impatiently wait for the time to pitch in with gusto.

Fish chowder, New England style, is not uncommon. Driving around over the Islands one frequently sees plain white wooden churches with tall steeples (not on village greens but in semi-tropical settings), and occasionally one talks with Hawaiians who speak with a Boston accent. And why not? Many early settlers (*haoles*) in this Paradise of the Pacific were New England missionaries who left their imprints on the life of these flowery areas. When I tasted baked beans ladled from an earthen pot, and sampled steamed Indian pudding, I speculated about the cooks who first experimentally added a touch of fresh ginger root to the Yankee favorites.

Macadamia Nuts Have Many Friends

No consideration of Hawaii's good foods wisely overlooks Macadamia nuts, an importation from Australia. Many local groves bear bountiful crops. The rich, unroasted nuts are stirred into cakes, cookies, and other baked dishes. Buffet tables present roasted and salted versions, along with candied and minted ones. Perhaps the most exquisite confection of the region consists of clusters of the nuts, chocolate coated. The twosome — chocolate covered Macadamias and creamy coconut candy — challenges all other sweets for the gold medal.

Along the beauteous Kona Coast of the Big Island, Hawaii, coffee plantations extend down the steep mountain slopes to the ocean. The amiable home demonstration agent driving me along the spectacular highway smiled when I observed, "The cherries are almost ripe." This was before she had a chance to explain that the trees bear coffee berries. Then she related how she parks her car at the side of the highway and literally walks up and down the plantations to carry the gospel of better homemaking and nutrition to people who live by coffee production.

People sip Kona coffee in some quarters. Coffee and mocha flavor desserts. A confection many women prepare for guests features Macadamia nuts candied in coffee flavored sirup. To make it they boil brewed coffee and sugar together, add a suspicion of cinnamon, and coat the nuts with the sweetness.

Hostess Tricks With Foods

If I had to describe the aloha spirit of Hawaii with one word in a brilliant neon sign, *Hospitality* would outstrip all competitors. That explains why the Islands are a storehouse of magnificent hostess dishes. The invitation to share a family meal frequently is issued at the last minute in an eager, spontaneous fashion. Such natural friendliness impresses guests. But even the planned parties carry a casualness that prompts people to forget the world's problems, at least for a few hours. Due to the scarcity of domestic help, buffet meals continue to gain prestige. They also have the advantage of imparting the desired informal atmosphere.

Almost every famous hostess with whom I chatted assigned the curry supper to first place for the guest meal. Then, almost before I could say Jack Robinson, these charming ladies ushered me to their china cupboards to look at the dishes on which they serve curries. Wooden plates and Cantonese china, often of the coin, rose, or cabbage patterns, were lifted from the shelves most frequently. Relish trays invariably were colorful and abloom with Oriental decorations, or they were made of glass. Every woman confessed one advantage of the menu is that the curry may be prepared in advance, refrigerated, and quickly reheated at mealtime. The menu has been standardized.

CURRY SUPPER
Curried Chicken, Turkey, or Shrimp
Rice   Condiments
Green Salad
Fresh Pineapple

Among the favored condiments almost always present on the table are mango chutney, grated fresh coconut, chopped peanuts, and other nuts. Other selections are quartered limes or lemons, pineapple pickle, fried onions, chopped crisp bacon, chopped hard-cooked eggs, orange marmalade, ripe olives, raisins, and grated cheese.

Coconut milk, rich and flavorful, universally contributes to the exotic, wonderful taste of curry sauce. Evaporated milk, quick and easy to use, substitutes for it when time is short. The sauce is prepared early and refrigerated.

Chicken, turkey, and shrimp curries lead in popularity, although curried lamb maintains a faithful following. Many households treasure and use heirlom recipes, but in most of them the chicken or turkey — gently simmered tender — is cut in 2-inch pieces. The cook browns it lightly in a little fat along with bits of onion, garlic, and fresh ginger root. Then she makes the sauce for it.

Chicken curry with crushed pineapple stirred in is known in many areas of our globe as *Hawaiian curry*. On gala evenings it comes to the table in shells of half pineapples with some of the green top leaves attached. On other equally gay occasions it is encircled by a rim of fluffy rice. Some cooks mold the rice in small cups, turn it out, and splatter the whiteness with minced parsley. Other women broil canned pineapple chunks until slightly browned and use them to garnish the plate of curried chicken, turkey, or shrimp, and rice.

Tossed green salads make themselves at home in the many meals featuring curry. Following them comes a fruit dessert like pineapple sherbet, or pieces of fresh pineapple soaked several hours in Madeira wine. The cook heaps the fruit in a pineapple shell, if the curry is not served in one, and decorates it with puffs of sweetened whipped cream.

Chicken pie graces many guest tables. It is similar to Mainland versions, except for a faint suggestion of fresh ginger in its depths.

Island cooks depend on the touch of ginger for elusive flavoring. Many of them peel the root, and slice or crush it, and then soak it in a little water or wine. The liquid, rather than the ginger goes into the pie or other dish. When in a hurry women finely shred the peeled root and add it without the preliminary soaking.

GUEST SUPPER
Chicken Pie
Buttered Pod Peas
Baked Bananas
Fruits
Candied Macadamia Nuts
Coconut Chips
Coffee

While Beef à la Stroganoff does not command as many supporters as curried dishes and chicken pie, it plays the guest dish role with considerable success.

COMPANY SUPPER
Beef à la Stroganoff
Broccoli
Jellied Guavas
Coconut Sponge Cake
Coffee

Hawaiian barbecues and beach picnics bear a pronounced likeness to those of California. The sauces for basting meats as they broil reveal one difference. They contain more soy sauce and frequently a seasoning of curry powder.

Dinner in a Nutshell

For a picturesque Hawaiian hostess menu, *Dinner in a Nutshell* fills the bill. The hospitable director of the cafeteria at the University of Hawaii invited a group of home economists from the Mainland to such a supper party in her apartment. She gave her appreciative guests a play-by-play account of how she prepares the entree. In her words, this is the procedure.

"You simmer the chicken until tender, remove it from the bones, which you discard. Then to the meat with some of the broth you add all the good things: diced ripe tomatoes, chopped fresh onions, green peppers, and ginger; cubes of pan-fried bacon; well-seasoned whole kernel corn (fresh, frozen, or canned) ; grated fresh coconut, seasonings, and sherry.

"You select coconuts of medium size, one for each person to be served. After the husks are removed you saw the tops off about one-fourth the way down. You pour out the liquid and remove about half the white meat with an Hawaiian grater. For every chicken used you add 2 cups of grated coconut to the chicken-vegetable mixture. You almost fill the coconut shells with the heated mixture and then seal on the lids with a flour and water paste. For 1½ to 2 hours you steam the coconuts in a tightly covered pan containing an inch of water, either in a moderate oven, 350°, or on top of the range over low heat. During the cookery you baste the coconuts three times with water."

At the table everyone removes the top from his coconut. The heavenly aroma whets the appetite, and a few bites of the luscious food elevate the evening to delicious, memorable hours. With this main dish we enjoyed pan-fried bananas and for dessert lengthwise slices of juicy fresh pineapple, and coffee.

Exotic Blossoms Spell Hawaii

Visitors to Hawaii enthuse daily over the charming table flower arrangements. "One precaution we heed," the kamaaina says, "is to call on the heavens to give us restraint. Exotic blosoms are so profuse that it takes courage and will power not to overdo the decorations."

When you analyze the centerpieces you conclude that part of the appeal is in their simplicity. I recall the festive table at a tea party given by the home economics department of the University of Hawaii, a picture cherished by the guests. Two low coconut branches, each with a cluster of their shiny yellow blossoms that resembled carved ivory, were centered on the polished wood. Over them was draped a lei of flower petals in different shades of yellow.

Leis frequently decorate the ends of dining tables. Those composed of tiny blossoms, like crown flowers, sometimes entwine the candlesticks or the stem of a compote that holds a single pineapple resplendent with its leaves.

Hostesses impale blossoms on coconut sticks, the center vein of coconut leaves, and stick them into bright colored fruits, flower arrangers, and snowy white coral. They scatter hibiscus flowers on table tops for colorful effects. Sometimes their background consists of ti leaves and dainty ferns rather than fabric. The beauties among local fruits frequently compose the centerpieces as a change from petals.

At parties — formal and informal — men, women, and children wear leis, the necklaces of flowers. They are made from such plants as orchids, Chinese violets, ilima (royal flower of Hawaii), ginger lilies, pikaki (a member of the jasmine family), tuberoses, crown flowers, ice plant, plumaria, gardenias, carnations, lehuas (one of the loveliest), and a hundred other blossoms.

If you leave Hawaii on a white steamship, with leis around your shoulders, you will wish to cast a wreath on the water after you are well out, possibly off Waikiki Beach or Diamond Head. When it floats ashore you have a portent and promise of a return to the Paradise of the Pacific. I believe in the omen, for it brought me back on a delightful pilgrimage, an appropriate *aloha* to a gustatory tour of the United States.

Bibliography of Cookbooks

American Regional Cookery, Sheila Hibben (Little, Brown).

Coast to Coast Cookery, Recipes from America's Newspaper Food Editors, Introduced and Selected by Marian Tracy (Indiana University Press).

The Ford Treasury of Favorite Recipes from Famous Eating Places (Simon & Schuster).

The New Connecticut Cookbook, Woman's Club of Westport (Harper).

The Yankee Cook Book, Edited by Imogene Wolcott (Coward-McCann).

Mrs. Appleyard's Kitchen, (Boston), Louise Andrews Kent (Houghton Mifflin).

New England Cook Book, Kay Morrow (Culinary Arts).

Out of Vermont Kitchens, Compiled by Trinity Mission of Trinity Church in Rutland and the Women's Service League of Burlington (Watts).

Secrets of New England Cooking, Ella Shannon Bowles and Dorothy S. Towle (Barrows).

Stillmeadow Kitchen, Gladys Taber (Macrae-Smith).

Toll House Tried and True Recipes, Ruth Wakefield (Barrows).

What's Cookin' — in New Hampshire, Edited by Sybil Hogan (Workshop Cards).

Mennonite Community Cook Book, Mary Emma Showalter (Winston).

Pennsylvania Dutch and Their Cookery, J. George Frederick (Business Bourse).

Pennsylvania Dutch Cook Book, Compiled from tested recipes handed down by the early Dutch settlers in Pennsylvania (Culinary Arts).

Pennsylvania Dutch Cookery, Ann Hark and Preston A. Barba (Schlechter's, Allentown, Pennsylvania).

The Pennsylvania Dutch Cook Book, Ruth Hutchinson (Harper).

Coahoma Cooking, Coahoma Women's Club, Coahoma, Mississippi.

Cross Creek Cookery, Marjorie Kinnan Rawlings (Scribner).

Culinary Gems From the Kitchens of Old Virginia, Irene Lawrence King (Dodd-Mead).

Dixie Dishes, Marion W. Flexner (Hale).

From My Ozark Cupboard, Cora Pinkley-Call (Allan).

How I Cook It, Virginia McDonald (Glenn).

Out of Kentucky Kitchens, Marion W. Flexner (Watts).

Recipes from Old Virginia, The Virginia Federation of Home Demonstration Clubs (Dietz).

Secrets of Southern Cooking, Ethel Farmer Hunter (Prentice).

Some Favorite Southern Recipes, Duchess of Windsor (Scribner).

The Southern Cook Book, Marion Brown (University of North Carolina Press).

Williamsburg Art of Cookery, Helen Bullock (Dietz).

A Cook's Tour of the Eastern Shore of Maryland, Edited by the Junior Auxiliary of Memorial Hospital, Easton, Maryland, (Farrar, Straus).

Charleston Receipts, Compiled by the Junior League of Charleston, South Carolina.

Coastal Cookery, Cassina Garden Club of St. Simon's Island, Georgia.

Conch Cooking, Luise Putcamp and Virginia Z. Goulet (Luise of Key West).

Eat, Drink and Be Merry in Maryland, Frederick Philip Stieff (Putnam).

Long Island Seafood Cook Book, J. George Frederick and Jean Joyce (Business Bourse).

Main Line Cook Book (Philadelphia), Ethel W. Stokes and Mary H. Huber (Abelard).

Maryland Cookery, Compiled by the Maryland Home Economics Association.

New York Cookbook, Maria Lo Pinto (Wynn).

The Key West Cook Book, The Woman's Club of Key West (Farrar, Straus).

200 Years of Charleston Cooking, Rhett, Gay and Woodward (Random).

De Bonnes Choses à Manger, St. Matthews Guild, Houma, Louisiana.

Gourmet's Guide to New Orleans, Natalie Scott and Caroline Merirck Jones (Scott and Jones).

Mme. Bégué's Recipes, (Harmanson).

New Orleans Cook Book, Lena Richard (Houghton Mifflin).

Picayune Creole Cook Book, (New Orleans Times-Picayune).

The Creole Kitchen Cook Book, Virginia Cooper (Naylor).

A Taste of Texas, Jane Trahey (Random).

Elena's Famous Mexican and Spanish Recipes, Elena Zelayeta, 650 Victoria Street, San Francisco, 27.

Elena's Fiesta Recipes, Elena Zelayeta, Ward Ritchie Press, Los Angles, 27.

Historic Cookery, Mrs. Fabiola C. de Baca Gilbert, New Mexico College of Agriculture and Mechanic Arts, State College, New Mexico.

Mexican Cookbook, Erna Fergusson (Rydal).

Recipe Roundup, St. Margaret's Guild, Albuquerque, New Mexico.

Roundup Recipes, Bonnie and Ed Peplow (World).

The Texas Cook Book, Arthur and Bobbie Coleman (Wynn).

What's Cooking in South Texas, Compiled by the Chemcel Woman's Club of Kingsville and Bishop, Texas.

Folkways with Foods, Compiled by the Wisconsin Home Economics Association.

Food of My Friends, Virginia Safford (University of Minnesota Press).

Old World Foods in New World Families, Lelia McGuire of the Merrill Palmer School (Wayne University Press).

The Real Dutch Treat Cook Book, Rie Ykema Steenberger (Wm. B. Eerrman's).

Amana Recipes, Recipes of the Amana Society of East Central Iowa, Compiled by the Ladies' Auxiliary of the Homestead Welfare Club. (Homestead Welfare Club, Homestead, Iowa).

Cook Book, The First Lutheran Ladies' Aid, Fargo, North Dakota.

The Best from Midwest Kitchens, Ada B. Lothe and Berta L. Griem (M. S. Mill).

Angie Earl's Treasured Lion House Recipes, (Bookcraft, Salt Lake City).

Everyday Recipes for Home and School, Compiled by Nell Strowig, Supervisor of Homemaking in the Public Schools, Salt Lake City.

High Altitude Recipes, as Tested in the Denver Solitaire Kitchen, Lillian S. Kennedy (Morey Mercantile Company).

Phi Upsilon Omicron High Altitude Cook Book, University of Wyoming, Laramie.

Pioneer Recipes, Deseret News, Salt Lake City.

Mary Cullen's Northwest Cook Book, Cathrine C. Laughton (Binfords and Mort, Portland).

Brown Derby Cookbook (Doubleday).

Sunset All-Western Cook Book, Edited by Genevieve Callahan (Lane).

Sunset Barbecue Book (Lane).

Sunset Cook Book of Western Recipes, Edited by Emily Chase (Lane).

The California Cook Book, Genevieve Callahan (Barrows).

The West Coast Cook Book, Helen Brown (Little, Brown).

Western Cook Book, Kay Morrow (Culinary Arts).

Fruits of Hawaii, Carey D. Miller and Katherine Bazore (University of Hawaii Agricultural Experiment Station).

Hawaiian and Pacific Foods, Katherine Bazore (Barrows).

The Hilo Woman's Club Cook Book, (Hilo, Hawaii, Tribune-Herald).

Ways to Use Vegetables in Hawaii, Lind, Bartow and Miller (University of Hawaii Agricultural Experiment Station).

Index

Index 547

The Author

Nell Nichols is a trained home economist who just never has wanted to stop learning more and more interesting facts about foods. She holds her bachelor's degree in home economics from Kansas State College, and her master's degree in this field from the University of Wisconsin.

Beyond this background, she has been observing the trends and interests in food with the "home folks eye" and the professional workers' eye since the early 1930's. As a member of the editorial staff of Woman's Home Companion, *she has been given the green light for her first love and as food field reporter has been assigned to find out homey secrets of cooking successes.*

Her "Food Calendar," "Good Food" and other features in the Companion *have expressed her wish to share these personal observations and inspirations with everyone interested in American foods. Now* Good Home Cooking Across the U.S.A. *captures in book form the highlights of an extensive three-year tour of the cooking centers and byroads' kitchens in all 48 states and Hawaii.*

*Composed in Linotype Baskerville by The
Iowa State College Press.
Chapter headings and running heads in Ludlow
Garamond Bold Italic.
Paper stock: 60-pound Warren's Cumberland English Finish.
Cover cloth: Bancroft's Arrestox No. 4175.*

SOUFFLE SALAD
(Basic Recipe)

Dissolve

1 pkg. lemon or lime flavorings in
1 cup of boiling water

Add

½ cup cold water
2 tablespoons vinegar or lemon juice
¼ cup mayonnaise
1/8 teaspoon salt

Blend well with a rotary beater. Pour into freezing tray. Quick chill in the freezing unit (without changing control) 15 to 20 minutes. The mixture will still be soft in the center. Turn into a mixing bowl and beat until smooth. Fold in 1 to 2½ cups of vegetables, fruits, fish, poultry, meat, cheese, hard cooked eggs. Pour into 1 quart mold or individual molds. Chill until firm about 30 minutes. Serve on salad greens.

Variation - Vegetable Tuna Souffle Salad

Make basic souffle salad using lime-flavored gelatin. After you have beaten the gelatin mixture, fold in 1 cup grated carrots, 1 cup shredded cabbage, ½ cup diced cucumber, 1 tablespoon finely chopped onion. Mold in ring mold and fill center with tuna fish.